UNITED NATIONS COMMISSION ON INTERNATIONAL TRADE LAW

UNCITRAL
2012 Digest of Case Law on the Model Law on International Commercial Arbitration

UNITED NATIONS
New York, 2012

NOTE

Symbols of United Nations documents are composed of capital letters combined with figures. Mention of such a symbol indicates a reference to a United Nations document.

UNITED NATIONS PUBLICATION
Sales No. E.12.V.9
ISBN 978-92-1-133793-8

This publication has not been formally edited.

Publishing production: English, Publishing and Library Section, United Nations Office at Vienna.

Contents

Part two—List of cases

INTRODUCTION TO THE UNCITRAL 2012 DIGEST OF CASE LAW ON THE MODEL LAW ON INTERNATIONAL COMMERCIAL ARBITRATION (1985, WITH AMENDMENTS AS ADOPTED IN 2006)

THE UNCITRAL MODEL LAW ON INTERNATIONAL COMMERCIAL ARBITRATION

1. The UNCITRAL Model Law on International Commercial Arbitration[1] ("the Model Law") was adopted by the United Nations Commission on International Trade Law (UNCITRAL) on 21 June 1985, at the end of the eighteenth session of the Commission. The General Assembly, in its resolution 40/72 of 11 December 1985, recommended "that all States give due consideration to the Model Law on International Commercial Arbitration, in view of the desirability of uniformity of the law of arbitral procedures and the specific needs of international commercial arbitration practice". The Model Law was amended by UNCITRAL on 7 July 2006,[2] at the thirty-ninth session of the Commission (see below in this section, para. 4). The General Assembly, in its resolution 61/33 of 4 December 2006, recommended "that all States give favourable consideration to the enactment of the revised articles of the Model Law, or the revised Model Law (…), when they enact or revise their laws (…)".

2. The Model Law was developed to address considerable disparities in national laws on arbitration. The need for improvement and harmonization was based on findings that national laws were often particularly inappropriate for international cases. The Model Law constitutes a sound basis for the desired harmonization and improvement of national laws. It covers all stages of the arbitral process from the arbitration agreement to the recognition and enforcement of the arbitral award and reflects a worldwide consensus on the principles and important issues of international arbitration practice. It is acceptable to States of all regions and the different legal or economic systems of the world. Since its adoption by UNCITRAL, the Model Law has come to represent the accepted international legislative standard for a modern arbitration law and a significant number of jurisdictions have enacted arbitration legislation based on the Model Law.

3. The form of a model law was chosen as the vehicle for harmonization and modernization in view of the flexibility it provides to States in preparing new arbitration laws. Notwithstanding that flexibility, and in order to increase the likelihood of achieving a satisfactory degree of harmonization, States are encouraged to make as few changes as possible when incorporating the Model Law into their legal systems. Efforts to minimize variation from the text adopted by UNCITRAL are also expected to increase the visibility of harmonization, thus enhancing the confidence of foreign parties, as the primary users of international arbitration, in the reliability of arbitration law in the enacting State (see below in this section, para. 13).

4. The revision of the Model Law adopted in 2006 includes article 2 A, which is designed to facilitate interpretation by reference to internationally accepted principles and is aimed at promoting a uniform understanding of the Model Law. Other substantive amendments to the Model Law relate to the form of the arbitration agreement and to interim measures. The original 1985 version of the provision on the form of the arbitration agreement (article 7) was modelled on the language used in article II (2) of the Convention on the Recognition and Enforcement of Foreign Arbitral Awards (New York, 1958)[3] ("the 1958 New York Convention"). The revision of article 7 is intended to address evolving practice in international trade and technological developments. The extensive revision of article 17 on interim measures was considered necessary in light of the fact that such measures are increasingly relied upon in the practice of international commercial arbitration. The revision also includes an enforcement regime for such measures in recognition of the fact that the effectiveness of arbitration frequently depends upon the possibility of enforcing interim measures. The new provisions on interim measures and preliminary orders are contained in chapter IV A of the Model Law.

5. Legislation based on the Model Law has been enacted, at the date of the *Digest*, in around ninety jurisdictions which come from all legal traditions, and have very different economies, and levels of development.[4] The number of academic works dedicated to the Model Law grows

[1] *Official Records of the General Assembly, Fortieth Session, Supplement No. 17* (A/40/17), annex I; United Nations publication, Sales No. E.95.V.18.

[2] *Official Records of the General Assembly, Sixty-first Session, Supplement No. 17* (A/61/17), annex I; United Nations publication, Sales No. E.08.V.4.

[3] United Nations, *Treaty Series*, vol. 330, No. 4739, p. 38.

[4] Information on jurisdictions having enacted legislation based on the Model Law is provided on UNCITRAL's website at http://www.uncitral.org.

constantly,[5] as does the amount of related case law available from various sources. Its contribution to the goal of unification of international trade law is definitely significant.

PROMOTING UNIFORM INTERPRETATION OF UNCITRAL INSTRUMENTS: CLOUT AND DIGESTS

6. UNCITRAL, in accordance with its mandate,[6] has undertaken the preparation of the tools necessary for a thorough understanding of the instruments it develops and for their uniform interpretation.

7. UNCITRAL has established a reporting system for case law on UNCITRAL texts (CLOUT).[7] CLOUT was established in order to assist judges, arbitrators, lawyers, and parties to business transactions, by making available decisions of courts and arbitral tribunals interpreting UNCITRAL texts; and in so doing, to further the uniform interpretation and application of those texts. CLOUT covers case law related to conventions and model laws prepared by UNCITRAL, although the majority of its cases refers to the United Nations Convention on Contracts for the International Sale of Goods (Vienna, 1980),[8] and to the Model Law.

8. A network of national correspondents, appointed by the Governments of States that are party to at least one of the UNCITRAL conventions or have enacted at least one of the UNCITRAL model laws, monitors the relevant judicial decisions in the respective countries and reports them to the UNCITRAL Secretariat in the form of an abstract. Voluntary contributors can also prepare abstracts for the attention of the Secretariat, which may publish them in agreement with the national correspondents. The Secretariat edits and indexes all of the abstracts received and publishes them in the CLOUT series. The network of national correspondents ensures coverage of a large number of domestic jurisdictions. The availability of CLOUT in the six official languages of the United Nations greatly enhances the dissemination of the information. These two elements are essential to promote uniformity of interpretation on the widest possible scale.

9. In light of the large number of cases collected in CLOUT on the Model Law, the Commission requested a tool specifically designed to present selected information on the interpretation of the Model Law in a clear, concise and objective manner. This request originated the *Digest* of case law on the Model Law.[9]

10. The goal of harmonized interpretation of the Model Law has greatly benefited from CLOUT, and it is expected that the *Digest* will further support it. As highlighted by article 2A of the Model Law, in the interpretation of the Model Law, "regard is to be had to its international origin", and the *Digest* aims at promoting uniformity in its application by encouraging judges to consider how the Model Law has been applied by courts in jurisdictions where the Model Law has been enacted.

11. The *Digest* presents the information in a format based on chapters corresponding to chapters of the Model Law. Each chapter contains a synopsis of the relevant case law for each article, highlighting common views and reporting any divergent approach. The *Digest* is meant to reflect the evolution of case law and, therefore, updates will be periodically released. While the CLOUT system reports cases in the form of abstracts, the present Digest makes reference also to the full text of a decision whenever this is useful to illustrate the point. This *Digest* was prepared using the full text of the decisions cited in the CLOUT abstracts and other citations listed in the footnotes. The abstracts are intended to serve only as summaries of the underlying decisions and may not reflect all the points made in this *Digest.* Readers are advised to consult the full text of the listed court and arbitral decisions rather than relying solely on the CLOUT abstracts.

12. The *Digest* does not constitute an independent authority indicating the interpretation to be given to individual provisions but rather serves as a reference tool summarizing and pointing to the decisions that had been included in the *Digest*. The purpose of the *Digest* is to assist in the dissemination of information on the Model Law and further promote its adoption as well as its uniform interpretation. In addition, the *Digest* is meant to help judges, arbitrators,

[5] UNCITRAL prepares yearly a *Bibliography of recent writings related to the work of UNCITRAL*, available on UNCITRAL's website at http://www.uncitral.org.

[6] UNCITRAL should be active, inter alia, in "[...] promoting ways and means of ensuring a uniform interpretation and application of international conventions and uniform laws in the field of the law of international trade [and] collecting and disseminating information on national legislation and modern legal developments, including case law, in the field of the law of international trade; [...]": General Assembly resolution 2205 (XXI) of 17 December 1966, available on UNCITRAL's website at http://www.uncitral.org. For details concerning the mandate for the progressive development of the law of international trade, see also the report of the Secretary-General contained in document A/6396 (*Official Records of the General Assembly, Twenty-first Session*, Annexes, agenda item 88, document A/6396, reproduced in UNCITRAL Yearbook, vol. I: 1968-1970, part one, chap. II, sect. B); the report of the Fifth Committee of the General Assembly at its twenty-first session on the relevant agenda item (*Official Records of the General Assembly, Twenty-first Session*, Annexes, agenda item 88, document A/6594, reproduced in UNCITRAL Yearbook, vol. I: 1968-1970, part one, chap. II, sect. D); and the relevant summary records of the proceedings of the Sixth Committee, which are contained in the *Official Records of the General Assembly, Twenty-first Session*, Sixth Committee, 947th-955th meetings and of which excerpts are reproduced in the UNCITRAL Yearbook, vol. I: 1968-1970, part one, chap. II, sect. C.

[7] *Official Records of the General Assembly, Forty-third Session, Supplement No. 17* (A/43/17), paras. 98-109. CLOUT reports are published as United Nations documents A/CN.9/SER.C/ABSTRACTS/1 to A/CN.9/SER.C/ABSTRACTS/xx. The CLOUT reports are also available on UNCITRAL's website at http://www.uncitral.org.

[8] United Nations *Treaty Series*, vol. 1498, No.25567, p. 3 (see FN 57).

[9] *Official Records of the General Assembly, Fifty-sixth Session, Supplement No. 17* (A/56/17), para. 390.

[10] *Official Records of the General Assembly, Fifty-ninth Session, Supplement No. 17* (A/59/17), paras. 87-91.

practitioners, academics and Government officials use more efficiently the case law relating to the Model Law.[10]

13. States, when enacting the Model Law, have in certain instances made modifications to certain provisions, despite recommendation to make as few changes as possible when incorporating the text into their legal system (see above in this section, para. 3). The *Digest* indicates, to the extent possible, where a diverging interpretation of a specific provision originates from a modification made to the Model Law provision when enacted in the domestic legislation.

ACKNOWLEDGEMENT OF CONTRIBUTIONS

14. The *Digest* is the result of the cooperation between the national correspondents and the UNCITRAL Secretariat. Its first draft, prepared in 2012, greatly benefited from the contributions of Frédéric Bachand, Lawrence Boo and Stephan Kröll. Before being published in the current format, the *Digest* was further edited by the UNCITRAL Secretariat.

For questions or comments on the *Digest*,
please contact the Secretariat of UNCITRAL

(International Trade Law Division,
Office of Legal Affairs,
United Nations,
Vienna International Centre
P.O. Box 500,
1400 Vienna, Austria,
uncitral@uncitral.org).

Part one

DIGEST OF CASE LAW

CHAPTER I. GENERAL PROVISIONS

Article 1. Scope of application*

*(1) This Law applies to international commercial** arbitration, subject to any agreement in force between this State and any other State or States.*

(2) The provisions of this Law, except articles 8, 9, 17 H, 17 I, 17 J, 35 and 36, apply only if the place of arbitration is in the territory of this State. (Article 1 (2) has been amended by the Commission at its thirty-ninth session, in 2006)[11]

(3) An arbitration is international if:

(a) the parties to an arbitration agreement have, at the time of the conclusion of that agreement, their places of business in different States; or

(b) one of the following places is situated outside the State in which the parties have their places of business:

(i) the place of arbitration if determined in, or pursuant to, the arbitration agreement;

(ii) any place where a substantial part of the obligations of the commercial relationship is to be performed or the place with which the subject matter of the dispute is most closely connected; or

(c) the parties have expressly agreed that the subject matter of the arbitration agreement relates to more than one country.

(4) For the purposes of paragraph (3) of this article:

(a) if a party has more than one place of business, the place of business is that which has the closest relationship to the arbitration agreement;

(b) if a party does not have a place of business, reference is to be made to his habitual residence.

(5) This Law shall not affect any other law of this State by virtue of which certain disputes may not be submitted to arbitration or may be submitted to arbitration only according to provisions other than those of this Law.

**Article headings are for reference purposes only and are not to be used for purposes of interpretation.*

***The term "commercial" should be given a wide interpretation so as to cover matters arising from all relationships of a commercial nature, whether contractual or not. Relationships of a commercial nature include, but are not limited to, the following transactions: any trade transaction for the supply or exchange of goods or services; distribution agreement; commercial representation or agency; factoring; leasing; construction of works; consulting; engineering; licensing; investment; financing; banking; insurance; exploitation agreement or concession; joint venture and other forms of industrial or business cooperation; carriage of goods or passengers by air, sea, rail or road.*

---

[11] Article 1 (2) of the Model Law as adopted in 1985 reads as follows: "The provisions of this Law, except articles 8, 9, 35 and 36, apply only if the place of arbitration is in the territory of this State."

TRAVAUX PRÉPARATOIRES

The *travaux préparatoires* on article 1 as adopted in 1985 are contained in the following documents:

1. Report of the United Nations Commission on International Trade Law on the work of its eighteenth session (*Official Records of the General Assembly, Fortieth Session, Supplement No. 17* (A/40/17)), paras. 11-333.
2. Reports of the Working Group: A/CN.9/216; A/CN.9/232; A/CN.9/233; A/CN.9/245; A/CN.9/246, annex; A/CN.9/263 and Add. 1-2; A/CN.9/264. Relevant working papers are referred to in the reports.
3. Summary records of the 306th, 307th, 319th, 330th and 332nd UNCITRAL meetings.

The *travaux préparatoires* on article 1, paragraph 2, as amended in 2006, are contained in the following documents:

1. Report of the United Nations Commission on International Trade Law on the work of its thirty-ninth session (*Official records of the General Assembly, Sixty-First session, Supplement No. 17* (A/61/17), paras. 87-181 and annex).
2. Reports of Working Group II (Arbitration) on the work of its forty-third session (A/CN.9/589, paras. 101-103); and forty-fourth session (A/CN.9/592, paras. 44 and 45). Relevant working papers, considered by Working Group II (Arbitration), are referred to in the reports of the sessions of the Working Group.

(Available on the Internet at www.uncitral.org).

INTRODUCTION

1. Article 1 defines the scope of application of the Model Law by reference to the notion of "international commercial arbitration", and provides for a broad definition of the terms "international" and "commercial" (see below, section on article 1, paras. 3-8). Article 1 recognizes extensively the freedom of the parties to submit a dispute to the legal regime established pursuant to the Model Law.[12]

2. Another aspect of applicability is the territorial scope of application (see below, section on article 1, paras. 9-11). The territorial criterion governing most of the provisions of the Model Law was adopted for the sake of certainty and in view of the following facts. In most legal systems, the place of arbitration is the exclusive criterion for determining the applicability of national law. Where the national law allows parties to choose the procedural law of a State other than that where the arbitration takes place, parties rarely make use of that possibility. The enactment of the Model Law also obviates any need for the parties to choose a "foreign" law, since the Model Law grants to the parties a wide freedom in shaping the rules of the arbitral proceedings. In addition to designating the law governing the arbitral procedure, the territorial criterion is of considerable practical importance in respect of articles 11 (*Appointment of arbitrators*), 13 (*Challenge procedure*), 14 (*Failure or impossibility to act*), 16 (*Competence of arbitral tribunal to rule on its jurisdiction*), 27 (*Court assistance in taking evidence*) and 34 (*Application for setting aside as exclusive recourse against arbitral award*), which entrust State courts at the place of arbitration with functions of supervision and assistance to arbitration. It should be noted that the territorial criterion legally triggered by the parties' choice regarding the place of arbitration does not limit the arbitral tribunal's ability to meet at any place it considers appropriate for the conduct of the proceedings, as provided by article 20 (2) (*Place of arbitration*), (see below, section on article 20, paras. 8 and 9).

CASE LAW ON ARTICLE 1

Substantive field of application—"international commercial arbitration"—paragraphs (1), (3) and (4)

"International"—paragraphs (3) and (4)

Places of business in different States—paragraphs (3)(a) *and (4)*

3. Article 1 (3) *(a)* defines arbitration as international if "the parties to an arbitration agreement have, at the time of the conclusion of that agreement, their places of business in different States". Article 1 (4) provides for guidance in situations where "a party has more than one place of business" or where "a party does not have a place of business". The vast majority of situations commonly regarded as international will meet the criterion referred to in article 1 (3) *(a)*.[13] The term "place of business" has been considered in some courts to include any location from which a party participates in economic activities in an independent manner.[14] It should thus include activities such as the establishment of

[12] Some States (for instance, Australia, Singapore) have extended the application of the legislation enacting the Model Law to cases where parties have agreed that that legislation applies ("opt-in" basis) even if a case would otherwise not be "international" under the definition in article 1. Such "opting in" may also be achieved by adopting rules which specifically state that the legislation enacting the Model Law applies—(*Electra Air Conditioning B.V. Appellant v. Seeley International Pty. Ltd.*, Federal Court, Australia, 8 October 2008, [2008] FCAFC 169).

[13] CLOUT case No. 101 [*Private Company "Triple V" Inc. Ltd. v. Star (Universal) Co. Ltd. and Sky Jade Enterprises Group Ltd.*, High Court—Court of First Instance, Hong Kong, 27 January 1995], [1995] HKCFI 368, available on the Internet at: http://www.hklii.hk/eng/hk/cases/hkcfi/1995/368.html; CLOUT case No. 77 [*Vibroflotation A.G. v. Express Builders Co. Ltd.*, High Court—Court of First Instance, Hong Kong, 15 August 1994], [1994] HKCFI 205, also available on the Internet at http://www.hklii.hk/eng/hk/cases/hkcfi/1994/205.html; CLOUT case No. 786 [Cairo Regional Center for International Commercial Arbitration, No. 1/1994, Egypt, 31 October 1995].

[14] CLOUT case No. 106 [Supreme Court, Austria, 2 Ob 547/93, 10 November 1994], where the term "place of business" is interpreted in the context of article 1 of the United Nations Convention on Contracts for the International Sale of Goods (Vienna, 1980).

a production plant, sales/marketing base,[15] distribution, transport, or the place where the financial and administrative functions of the business are carried out. Ascertaining the place of business may be difficult if a respondent refuses to disclose its own identity or its place of business.[16]

Place where a substantial part of the obligations is to be performed—paragraph (3)(b)*(ii)*

4. Article 1 (3)*(b)* and (3)*(c)* broadens the notion of internationality. Paragraph (3)*(b)*(ii) refers to the "place where a substantial part of the obligations of the commercial relationship is to be performed". In interpreting that phrase, a Hong Kong court clarified that the place where the breach of obligations occurred was not a relevant consideration.[17]

5. Courts have held that, in cases concerning agreements for the sale of goods, the place of delivery and acceptance of goods[18] or of transfer of risks and loading operations[19] should be considered as the place where a substantial part of the obligations was performed. In cases involving agreements between parties having their place of business in the same jurisdiction, the arbitration was considered international because goods were to be transported between ports, and it was considered that the place where a substantial part of the obligations was undertaken was situated outside the jurisdiction.[20] While the courts in the cases referred to in this paragraph appeared to have generally interpreted the term "a substantial part" of the obligations to mean "most of" the obligations, one court took a different approach and considered that so long as some substantial activities were performed outside the place of business of one of the parties, the arbitration could be considered as international. [21]

Place with closest nexus to the subject-matter of the dispute—paragraph (3)(b)*(ii)*

6. It has been held that even where both parties had their places of business in the same State and the agreement was governed by the law of that State, if the place of substantial performance of the contract and the place with which the subject matter of the dispute was most closely connected were in different States, the arbitration agreement would still fall within the meaning of "international" under paragraph (3)*(b)*(ii).[22] In an agreement for the design of a project, a court concluded that, even though the parties' places of business were in the same State, the arbitration was still international because the agreement provided that the overall supervision and development of the project was to be carried out in another State and, therefore, was most closely connected with that State.[23]

"Commercial"—footnote to paragraph (1)

7. The Model Law does not provide a strict definition of the term "commercial". The footnote to article 1 (1) calls for "a wide interpretation" and offers an illustrative and open-ended list of relationships that might be described as commercial in nature, "whether contractual or not".[24] The purpose of the footnote is to circumvent any technical difficulty that may arise, for example, in determining which transactions should be governed by a specific body of "commercial law" that may exist in some legal systems. Several decisions have indeed adopted this approach by providing that the term "commercial" should be construed broadly having regard to manifold activities which form an integral part of

[15] *McDowell Valley Vineyards, Inc. v. Sabaté USA Inc.*, District Court, California, United States of America, 2 November 2005, [2005] WL 2893848 (N.D. Cal. 2005), where the term "place of business" is interpreted in the context of article 1 of the United Nations Convention on Contracts for the International Sale of Goods (Vienna, 1980).

[16] CLOUT case No. 601 [*China Ocean Shipping Co., Owners of the M/V. Fu Ning Hai v. Whistler International Ltd., Charters of the M/V. Fu Ning Hai*, High Court—Court of First Instance, Hong Kong Special Administrative Region of China, 24 May 1999], [1999] HKCFI 693, also available on the Internet at http://www.hklii.hk/eng/hk/cases/hkcfi/1999/655.html.

[17] CLOUT case No. 20 [*Fung Sang Trading Limited v. Kai Sun Sea Products and Food Company Limited*, High Court—Court of First Instance, Hong Kong, 29 October 1991], [1991] HKCFI 190, also available on the Internet at http://www.hklii.hk/eng/hk/cases/hkcfi/1991/190.html.

[18] CLOUT case No. 20 [*Fung Sang Trading Limited v. Kai Sun Sea Products and Food Company Limited*, High Court—Court of First Instance, Hong Kong, 29 October 1991], [1991] HKCFI 190, also available on the Internet at http://www.hklii.hk/eng/hk/cases/hkcfi/1991/190.html; CLOUT case No. 58 [*Ananda Non-Ferrous Metals Ltd. v. China Resources Metal and Minerals Co. Ltd.*, High Court—Court of First Instance, Hong Kong, 12 July 1993], [1993] HKCFI 136, also available on the Internet at: http://www.hklii.hk/eng/hk/cases/hkcfi/1993/136.html; CLOUT case No. 75 [*China Resources Metal and Minerals Co. Ltd. v. Ananda Non-Ferrous Metals Ltd.*, High Court—Court of First Instance, Hong Kong, 7 July 1994], [1994] HKCFI 198], also available on the Internet at http://www.hklii.hk/eng/hk/cases/hkcfi/1994/198.html.

[19] CLOUT case No. 208 [*Vanol Far East Marketing Pte. Ltd. v. Hin Leong Trading Pte. Ltd.*, High Court, Singapore, 27 May 1996].

[20] CLOUT case No. 39 [*Katran Shipping Co. Ltd. v. Kenven Transportation Ltd.*, High Court—Court of First Instance, Hong Kong, 29 June 1992], [1992] HKCFI 173, also available on the Internet at http://www.hklii.hk/eng/hk/cases/hkcfi/1992/173.html; CLOUT case No. 706 [*Fustar Chemicals Ltd. v. Sinochem Liaoning Hong Kong Ltd.*, High Court—Court of First Instance, Hong Kong, 5 June 1996], [1996] 2 HKC 407.

[21] *Mitsui Engineering and Shipbuilding Co. Ltd. v. PSA Corp, Keppel Engineering Pte. Ltd.*, High Court, Singapore, [(2003) 1 SLR 446].

[22] CLOUT case No. 208 [*Vanol Far East Marketing Pte. Ltd. v. Hin Leong Trading Pte. Ltd.*, High Court, Singapore, 27 May 1996].

[23] CLOUT case No. 108 [*D. Heung & Associates, Architects & Engineers v. Pacific Enterprises (Holdings) Company Limited,* High Court—Court of First Instance, Hong Kong, 4 May 1995].

[24] A/CN.9/264, Analytical commentary on draft text of a model law on international commercial arbitration, under article 1, paras. 16-21, available on the UNCITRAL website at http://www.uncitral.org/uncitral/en/commission/sessions/18th.html.

international trade.[25] The Indian Supreme Court referred to the term "commercial" as used in the Model Law and interpreted it to include all "commercial relationships" in contradistinction to relationships of a matrimonial, family, cultural, social or political nature. In that case, the court took the view that a contract for consultancy services fell within the meaning of "commercial".[26] The same court held in another case that the relationship between a company and a director, who had also entered into a contract with the company, had a "commercial" element and, therefore, the arbitration clause in the contract should apply.[27] A Canadian court held that the commercial nature of a relationship was not dependent upon the qualification of the parties as merchants or commercial persons.[28] For example, the sale of a residential property was considered as involving a commercial relationship, particularly where the sale was transacted in a business-like manner, with the assistance of professional realtors, and within a legal framework appropriate for a transaction involving a large sum of money.[29] Furthermore, an arbitration case pursuant to the North American Free Trade Agreement (NAFTA) between a private investor and a State party to the NAFTA was said to be a commercial arbitration for the purposes of the Model Law as the primary relationship between the investor and the host State related to investment.[30]

8. However, not all relations related to business would be "commercial".[31] Where the relation was that of employer/employee as opposed to one of professional services by an independent contractor, the same was considered as non-commercial within the meaning of the Model Law.[32] On the other hand, a Canadian court had held that "liability in tort was an arbitrable matter, provided that the relation that created that liability was of a "commercial nature".[33] Nonetheless, a claim for wrongful dismissal and the tort of negligent misrepresentation was later held not to satisfy the "commercial" requirement.[34]

Territorial scope of application—paragraph (2)

9. The principle embodied in article 1 (2) is that the Model Law as enacted in a given State applies only if the place of arbitration is in the territory of that State. However, article 1 (2) also contains important exceptions to that principle, to the effect that certain articles apply, irrespective of whether the place of arbitration is in the enacting State or elsewhere (or, as the case may be, even before the place of arbitration is determined). These articles are the following: articles 8 (1) and 9, which deal with the recognition of arbitration agreements, including their compatibility with interim measures ordered by a court, article 17 J on court-ordered interim measures, articles 17 H and 17 I on the recognition and enforcement of interim measures ordered by an arbitral tribunal, and articles 35 and 36 on the recognition and enforcement of arbitral awards. Courts have issued decisions applying the principle that the provisions of the Model Law apply only if the place of arbitration is in the territory of the enacting State.[35]

---

[25] CLOUT case No. 390 [*Re Carter et al. and McLaughlin et al*, Ontario Court, Canada, 1 February 1996], also available on the Internet at http://canlii.ca/t/1vtr3; CLOUT case No. 502 [*The United Mexican States v. Metalclad Corp.*, Supreme Court of British Columbia, Canada, 2 May 2001], also available on the Internet at http://canlii.ca/t/4xfw.

[26] *R.M. Investment and Trading Co. v. Boeing Co.*, Supreme Court, India, 10 February 1994, [A.I.R. 1994 S.C. 1136]. Although the Court was interpreting a provision not forming part of the Model Law, it made specific mention (at para. 14) that it was aided by reference to the use of the term "commercial" in the Model Law. The court took the view that promoting the sale of an aircraft was a provision of "commercial and managerial assistance and information which may be helpful to [the company]'s sales efforts with customers" making the relationship between them a commercial one.

[27] *Comed Chemicals Limited v. C N Ramchand*, Supreme Court, India, 6 November 2008, [A.I.R. 2009 S.C. 494], also available on the Internet at http://www.indiankanoon.org/doc/55003.

[28] CLOUT case No. 390 [*Re Carter et al. and McLaughlin et al,* Ontario Court, Canada, 1 February 1996], also available on the Internet at http://canlii.ca/t/1vtr3.

[29] Ibid.

[30] CLOUT case No. 502 [*The United Mexican States v. Metalclad Corp.*, Supreme Court of British Columbia, Canada, 2 May 2001], also available on the Internet at http://canlii.ca/t/4xfw. Mexico had argued that, despite the wide meaning to be given to the term "commercial", the relationship between Mexico and the investor was not commercial in nature as it was a regulatory relationship in that the dispute had arisen due to the exercise of a regulatory function by the Mexican municipality. This argument was rejected by the Court, which took the view that arbitration did not arise under an agreement between the Municipality and the investor in connection with regulatory matters but pursuant to NAFTA, which was an agreement dealing with the treatment of investors.

[31] A/CN.9/264, Analytical commentary on draft text of a model law on international commercial arbitration, under article 1, para. 18, which states that "Not covered are, for example, labour or employment disputes and ordinary consumer claims, despite their relation to business", available on the UNCITRAL website at http://www.uncitral.org/uncitral/en/commission/sessions/18th.html.

[32] CLOUT case No. 111 [*Borowski v. Heinrich Fiedler Perforiertechnik GmbH,* Alberta Court of Queen's Bench, Canada, 12 August 1994]; CLOUT case No. 505 [*Ross v. Christian and Timbers, Inc.*, Ontario Superior Court of Justice, Canada, 30 April 2002], also available on the Internet at http://canlii.ca/t/1wc57. In deciding whether to refer the parties to arbitration, the court held that the applicable statute was not the International Commercial Arbitration Act that implements the Model Law in Ontario but rather the Arbitration Act which contained different though generally compatible rules.

[33] CLOUT case No. 586 [*Kaverit Steel and Crane Ltd. v. Kone Corp.*, Alberta Court of Appeal, Canada, 16 January 1992], [1992] ABCA 7 (CanLII), also available on the Internet at http://canlii.ca/t/1p6kc.

[34] CLOUT case No. 1048 [*Patel v. Kanbay International Inc.*, Ontario Court of Appeal, Canada, 23 December 2008], [2008] ONCA 867, also available on the Internet at http://canlii.ca/t/220b1.

[35] CLOUT case No. 13 (also reproduced under CLOUT case No. 383) [*Deco Automotive Inc. v. G.P.A. Gesellschaft für Pressenautomation mbH*, Ontario District Court, Canada, 27 October 1989]; CLOUT case No. 383 [*Deco Automotive Inc. v. G.P.A. Gesellschaft für Pressenautomation mbH,* Ontario District Court, Canada, 27 October 1989].

10. The omission of the word "only" in the enactment of the Model Law in one State has given rise to some controversy.[36] In two decisions, the Indian Supreme Court held that such omission makes the provision merely inclusive and "clarificatory" and would not prevent the court from assuming jurisdiction over arbitrations held or pending outside the State.[37] In another case, the same court held that, even though the word "only" has been omitted, the law will not apply to arbitrations outside the State.[38] (See also below, section on article 34, para. 12).

11. Although the place of arbitration was not located in the enacting State and thus pursuant to article 1 (2) only articles 8, 9, 17 H, 17 I, 17 J, 35 and 36 applied, a court referred to the definition contained under article 1 (3) to determine whether an arbitration was international within the meaning of the Model Law, based on the reasoning that the Act enacting the Model Law permitted reference to the definitions of the Model Law, without affecting the scope of application of the provision referred to in article 1 (2).[39]

Mandatory law, arbitrability—paragraph (5)

12. The Model Law does not determine which matters may or not be subject to arbitration. The existence of legislation providing that certain matters must be dealt with in or by a specific court action or by a certain prescribed procedure would not render, according to some court decisions, the Model Law inapplicable, or an otherwise valid arbitration agreement invalid or inoperable.[40] Issues arising from copyright, despite existence of a specified statutory regime for resolution, were held to be arbitrable by the Canadian Supreme Court.[41]

13. Some cases have arisen against companies involved in insolvency proceedings. Courts have generally held the view that steps taken in insolvency including petitions for liquidation in court were not matters subject to an arbitration agreement but were matters within the company law or insolvency law.[42] In one case involving a liquidation petition filed by a respondent in an arbitration, the court granted an injunction against the winding-up proceedings until after the disputes between the parties had been decided in arbitration.[43]

---

[36] India, The Arbitration and Conciliation Act, 1996.

[37] *Bhatia International v. Bulk Trading S. A. & Anr.*, Supreme Court, India, [(2002) 4 SCC 105]; *Venture Global Engineering v. Satyam Computer Services Ltd.*, Supreme Court, India, 10 January 2008, [(2008) 4 SCC 190: A.I.R. 2008 SC 1061], also available on the Internet at http://indiankanoon.org/doc/75785. In the earlier decision, the Court used that reasoning to grant interim measure in aid of an arbitration pending in Paris. In the latter case, *Venture Global,* however, the Indian Supreme Court assumed jurisdiction over an award rendered in an arbitration under the rules of the London Court of International Arbitration (LCIA) made outside India and ruled that it was competent to consider an application to set aside the foreign award. The court stated that the Indian legislature "is also not providing that Part I will "*only*" apply where the place of arbitration is in India (emphasis in original). Thus, the legislature has not provided that Part I is not to apply to arbitrations which take place outside India."

[38] *Shreejee Traco (I) Pvt. Ltd. v. Paper Line International,* Supreme Court, India, [(2003) 9 SCC 79].

[39] CLOUT case No. 28 [*BWV Investments Ltd. v. Saskferco Products Inc., UHDE-GmbH, et al.,* Saskatchewan Court of Queen's Bench, Canada, 19 March 1993].

[40] CLOUT case No. 116 [*BWV Investments Ltd. v. Saskferco Products Inc. et. al. and UHDE GmbH*, Saskatchewan Court of Appeal, Canada, 25 November 1994], [1994] CanLII 4557 (SK CA), also available on the Internet at http://canlii.ca/t/1nqlf, (this case revised CLOUT case No. 28 [*BWV Investments Ltd. v. Saskferco Products Inc., UHDE-GmbH, et al.,* Saskatchewan Court of Queen's Bench, Canada, 19 March 1993]); CLOUT case No. 526 [*Union Charm Development Ltd. v. B+B Construction Co., Ltd.*, High Court—Court of First Instance, Hong Kong Special Administrative Region of China, 12 June 2001], [2001] HKCFI 779, also available on the Internet at: http://www.hklii.hk/eng/hk/cases/hkcfi/2001/779.html, where the claimant applied for an order that it may proceed with arbitration instead of proceeding with proof of debt, notwithstanding the fact that the defendant was in liquidation, and the court, exercising its discretion, ordered the parties to proceed with arbitration. Some States (for instance, New Zealand, Singapore, Malaysia) that have enacted the Model Law have made this position clear by adding wording to the effect that "The fact that any written law confers jurisdiction in respect of any matter on any court of law but does not refer to the determination of that matter by arbitration shall not, of itself, indicate that a dispute about that matter is not capable of determination by arbitration."

[41] *Desputeaux v. Éditions Chouette (1987) inc.*, Supreme Court, Canada, [2003] 1 S.C.R. 178, 2003 SCC 17, available on the Internet at http://canlii.ca/t/1g2jh, where the fact that a statutory provision assigns an exclusive jurisdiction to a particular judicial system does not prohibit or exclude arbitration. The court in the case examined the objectives of the statutory provision governing questions of copyright and held that the provision is not intended to exclude arbitration.

[42] *Re Sanpete Builders* (*S*) Pte. *Ltd.,* High Court, Singapore, [1989] SLR 164; CLOUT case No. 707 [*In the Matter of Mech-Power Hong Kong—China Limited,* High Court—Court of First Instance, Hong Kong, 4 June 1996], [1996] HKCFI 307, also available on the Internet at: http://www.hklii.hk/eng/hk/cases/hkcfi/1996/307.html.

[43] *Metalform Asia Pte. Ltd. v. Holland Leedon Pte. Ltd.,* Court of Appeal, Singapore, [2007] 2 SLR 268.

Article 2. Definitions and rules of interpretation

For the purposes of this Law:

(a) "arbitration" means any arbitration whether or not administered by a permanent arbitral institution;

(b) "arbitral tribunal" means a sole arbitrator or a panel of arbitrators;

(c) "court" means a body or organ of the judicial system of a State;

(d) where a provision of this Law, except article 28, leaves the parties free to determine a certain issue, such freedom includes the right of the parties to authorize a third party, including an institution, to make that determination;

(e) where a provision of this Law refers to the fact that the parties have agreed or that they may agree or in any other way refers to an agreement of the parties, such agreement includes any arbitration rules referred to in that agreement;

(f) where a provision of this Law, other than in articles 25(a) *and 32 (2)*(a), *refers to a claim, it also applies to a counter-claim, and where it refers to a defence, it also applies to a defence to such counter-claim.*

TRAVAUX PRÉPARATOIRES

The *travaux préparatoires* on article 2 as adopted in 1985 are contained in the following documents:

1. Report of the United Nations Commission on International Trade Law on the work of its eighteenth session (*Official Records of the General Assembly, Fortieth Session, Supplement No. 17* (A/40/17)), paras. 11-333.
2. Reports of the Working Group: A/CN.9/233; A/CN.9/245; A/CN.9/246, annex; A/CN.9/263 and Add.1-2; A/CN.9/264. Relevant working papers are referred to in the reports.
3. Summary records of 307th, 308th, 319th, 330th, 332nd and 333rd meetings.

Article 2 was not amended in 2006.

(Available on the Internet at www.uncitral.org).

CASE LAW ON ARTICLE 2

Definitions—paragraphs *(a)-(c)*

"Arbitration"—paragraph (a)

1. Courts have consistently adopted the view that the process of arbitration requires as essential ingredients the existence of a dispute or the potential of a dispute requiring resolution between the parties, an agreement to refer such disputes to a third person as arbitrator and whose decision is to be final and binding upon the parties.[44]

2. In a case, it was questioned whether pre-arbitral dispute resolution processes agreed to by the parties would negate the intention to arbitrate. In that case, the parties had agreed, as an initial step, to submit their disputes to an expert for a non-binding opinion before allowing the initiation of arbitral proceedings. The court held that the inclusion of such a preliminary step did not vitiate the parties'

[44] CLOUT case No. 690 [*Mayers v. Dlugash*, High Court—Court of First Instance, Hong Kong, 10 June 1994]; CLOUT case No. 627 [*Sport Maska Inc. v. Zittrer and others*, Supreme Court, Canada, 24 March 1988], also available on the Internet at http://canlii.ca/t/1ftfs.

intention to arbitrate. Such procedure was considered not to be, in any way, inconsistent with the concept or definition of "arbitration".[45]

3. The German Federal Court of Justice decided that an internal jurisdiction established by the statutes of an association did not fulfil the criterion of arbitration because the impartiality and independence of the arbitral tribunal was not assured.[46] In another German case, the statutes of an association provided for a compulsory dispute resolution procedure to solve disputes between the association and its members, and provided that the decisions rendered could subsequently be challenged in courts. It was decided that such a possibility of recourse to court was inconsistent with the notion of arbitration.[47]

"Arbitral tribunal"—paragraph (b)

4. The role of expert appraisers and auditors has been distinguished from the office of arbitrators. In an application to terminate the mandate of an "arbitrator" in a dispute involving two business partners who appointed an accountant to determine how their business assets would be distributed, a court held that the accountant was an expert and not an arbitrator.[48] In doing so, the court observed that the expert was given an investigative as opposed to a judicial function. In a Canadian Supreme Court decision, the agreement for sale of assets of an insolvent company provided for a "final and binding" valuation of the company's auditors valuation for sale. The auditor's role was held to be one of evaluation rather than arbitration.[49]

5. The Singapore Court of Appeal held that even if a document was titled "award", made pursuant to a mandate to "determine all issues of procedure for the assessment which shall be final," and provided that "decision and findings on all issues of procedure, liability and quantum were to be final", such a document was not an arbitral award if it was not made by an arbitrator.[50] In that case, the court examined the distinction between the role of an arbitrator and that of an expert undertaking a valuation exercise. The court took the view that the paramount distinction between the obligations of an arbitrator and those of an expert was that an expert did not act solely on the evidence before him and had the discretion to adopt inquisitorial processes and use his personal knowledge and experience to determine the matter without the obligation to seek the parties' views or consult them. An expert was also freed from procedural and evidential intricacies or niceties that might attach to an arbitral process, with no obligation to make a decision on the basis of the evidence presented to him, but could act on his subjective opinion. The "single most significant distinction between expert determination and litigation/arbitration", in the view of another court was that, while an arbitrator was required to hear the parties on all the issues that were to be determined, an expert did not need to do so.[51]

Parties' autonomy—paragraphs *(d)* and *(e)*

Non-mandatory provisions—paragraph (d)

6. Party's autonomy is an important principle of the Model Law, illustrated by the high number of provisions in the Model Law referring to the agreement of the parties.[52] Autonomy of the parties in determining the rules of procedure is of special importance in international cases since it allows the parties to select or tailor the rules according to their specific wishes and needs, unimpeded by traditional and possibly conflicting domestic concepts, thus obviating the risk of frustration or surprise. Courts may have adopted differing approaches in the determination of the non-mandatory character of certain provisions of the

---

[45] *Westco Airconditioning Ltd. v. Sui Chong Construction & Engineering Co. Ltd.*, High Court—Court of First Instance, Hong Kong, [1998] HKCFI 946, available on the Internet at http://www.hklii.hk/eng/hk/cases/hkcfi/1998/946.html.

[46] Bundesgerichtshof, Germany, III ZB 53/03, 27 May 2004, available on the Internet at http://www.dis-arb.de/en/47/datenbanken/rspr/bgh-case-no-iii-zb-53-03-date-2004-05-27-id281.

[47] Oberlandesgericht Naumburg, Germany, 10 Sch 01/00, 17 April 2000, available on the Internet at http://www.dis-arb.de/de/47/datenbanken/rspr/olg-naumburg-az-10-sch-01-00-1-datum-2000-04-17-id57.

[48] CLOUT case No. 690 [*Mayers v. Dlugash,* High Court—Court of First Instance, Hong Kong, 10 June 1994].

[49] CLOUT case No. 627 [*Sport Maska Inc. v. Zittrer and others*, Supreme Court, Canada, 24 March 1988], also available on the Internet at http://canlii.ca/t/1ftfs.

[50] *Evergreat Construction Co. Pte. Ltd. v. Presscrete Engineering Pte. Ltd.*, Court of Appeal, Singapore, [2006] 1 SLR 634.

[51] *Metalform Asia Pte. Ltd. v. Holland Leedon Pte. Ltd.,* Court of Appeal, Singapore, [2007] 2 SLR 268.

[52] As an illustration, the following terms are used in the Model Law regarding parties' autonomy: "unless otherwise agreed by the parties" (in articles 3, 11 (1), 17 (1), 17 B (1), 20 (2), 21, 23 (2), 25, 26, 29, 33 (3)); "unless the parties have agreed" (in articles 24 (1), 31 (2)); "the parties are free to agree" (in articles 11 (2), 13 (1), 19 (1), 20 (1), 22); "failing such agreement" (in articles 11 (3), 13 (2), 19 (2)); "unless the agreement on the appointment procedure provides other means" (in article 11 (4)); and "subject to any contrary agreement by the parties" (in article 24 (1)).

Model Law. For instance, a court in Canada[53] held that article 34 (*Application for setting aside as exclusive recourse against arbitral award*) is a non-mandatory provision while a court in New Zealand[54] took a contrary view (see below, section on article 34, paras. 5-8).

Reference to arbitration rules—paragraph (e)

7. Article 2 *(e)* clarifies that the non-mandatory provisions of the Model Law may be supplemented or varied by parties' agreement and that such agreement may be effected through the adoption of arbitration rules. Arbitration rules may be amended from time to time. Where the incorporating words in the arbitration agreement provide for the adoption of arbitration rules "for the time being in force", the same have been held to mean, in a case, the rules applicable at the time the arbitration commences.[55] The reference to arbitration rules may also be made through parties' naming of an institution in the arbitration clause. By naming an arbitral institution, courts have held that the parties have adopted its institutional rules of arbitration unless the clause provides for the application of another set of rules.[56] (See also below, section on article 8, paras. 22-24).

[53] *Noble China Inc. v. Lei Kat Cheong*, Ontario Court of Justice, Canada, 4 November 1998, [1998] CanLII 14708 (ON SC), published in (1998) 42 O.R. (3d) 69, available on the Internet at http://canlii.ca/t/1vvkr.

[54] *Methanex Motunui Ltd. v. Spellman*, Court of Appeal, Wellington, New Zealand, 17 June 2004, [2004] 3 NZLR 454.

[55] *Navigator Investment Services Ltd. v. Acclaim Insurance Brokers Pte. Ltd.,* Court of Appeal, Singapore, [2010] 1 SLR 25; *Black & Veatch Singapore Pte. Ltd. v. Jurong Engineering Ltd.,* Court of Appeal, Singapore, [2004] 4 SLR(R) 19; *Car & Cars Pte. Ltd. v. Volkswagen AG,* High Court, Singapore, [2010] 1 SLR 625.

[56] See for instance: *Insigma Technology. Co. v. Alstom Technology Ltd.*, Court of Appeal, Singapore, 2 June 2009, [2009] SGCA 24, [2009] 3 SLR(R) 936, where the arbitration clause provided for arbitration to be submitted before the Singapore International Arbitration Centre (SIAC), and to be conducted in accordance with the Rules of Arbitration of the International Arbitration Court of the International Chamber of Commerce (ICC). The respondent in the arbitration unsuccessfully challenged the arbitral tribunal's decision upholding jurisdiction.

Article 2 A. International origin and general principles

(As adopted by the Commission at its thirty-ninth session, in 2006)

(1) In the interpretation of this Law, regard is to be had to its international origin and to the need to promote uniformity in its application and the observance of good faith.

(2) Questions concerning matters governed by this Law which are not expressly settled in it are to be settled in conformity with the general principles on which this Law is based.

TRAVAUX PRÉPARATOIRES

Article 2 A was adopted in 2006.

The *travaux préparatoires* on article 2 A as adopted in 2006 are contained in the following documents:

1. Report of the United Nations Commission on International Trade Law on the work of its thirty-ninth session (*Official records of the General Assembly, Sixty-first session, Supplement No. 17* (A/61/17), paras. 87-181 and annex 1).

2. Relevant working papers, considered by Working Group II (Arbitration), are referred to in the reports of the sessions of the Working Group.

(Available on the Internet at www.uncitral.org).

INTRODUCTION

1. When adopting amendments to the Model Law, in 2006, UNCITRAL considered whether the Model Law should include a provision along the lines of article 7 of the United Nations Convention on Contracts for the International Sale of Goods (Vienna 1980),[57] which was designed to facilitate interpretation by reference to internationally accepted principles. Similar provisions are also included in other model laws prepared by UNCITRAL, including article 3 of the UNCITRAL Model Law on Electronic Commerce (1996).[58] UNCITRAL agreed that the inclusion of such a provision would be useful and desirable because it would promote a more uniform understanding of the Model Law.[59]

CASE LAW ON ARTICLE 2 A

2. Even prior to the adoption of article 2 A, the international origin of the Model Law had provided a basis for a court in Hong Kong to be more liberal in adopting a broader interpretation of article 7 of the Model Law than it would otherwise have been under its domestic law. In that case, the court ruled that an arbitration clause contained in another document could be incorporated without specific incorporating words, departing from an earlier decision of the superior court.[60]

---

[57] United Nations, *Treaty Series*, vol. 1498, No. 25567, p. 3. Article 7 of the Convention reads as follows: "(1) In the interpretation of this Convention, regard is to be had to its international character and to the need to promote uniformity in its application and the observance of good faith in international trade. (2) Questions concerning matters governed by this Convention which are not expressly settled in it are to be settled in conformity with the general principles on which it is based or, in the absence of such principles, in conformity with the law applicable by virtue of the rules of private international law."

[58] *Official Records of the General Assembly, Fifty-first Session, Supplement No. 17* (A/51/17), annex I; United Nations publication, Sales No. E.99.V.4.

[59] On the interpretation by courts of a similar provision in the United Nations Convention on Contracts for the International Sale of Goods (1980), see UNCITRAL Digest of Case Law on the United Nations Convention on the International Sale of Goods, United Nations Publication, Sales No. E.08.V.15, part one, sphere of application and general provisions, article 7.

[60] CLOUT case No. 78 [*Astel-Peiniger Joint Venture v. Argos Engineering & Heavy Industries Co. Ltd.*, High Court—Court of First Instance, Hong Kong, 18 August 1994], [1994] HKCFI 276, also available on the Internet at http://www.hklii.hk/eng/hk/cases/hkcfi/1994/276.html.

Article 3. Receipt of written communications

(1) Unless otherwise agreed by the parties:

(a) any written communication is deemed to have been received if it is delivered to the addressee personally or if it is delivered at his place of business, habitual residence or mailing address; if none of these can be found after making a reasonable inquiry, a written communication is deemed to have been received if it is sent to the addressee's last-known place of business, habitual residence or mailing address by registered letter or any other means which provides a record of the attempt to deliver it;

(b) the communication is deemed to have been received on the day it is so delivered.

(2) The provisions of this article do not apply to communications in court proceedings.

TRAVAUX PRÉPARATOIRES

The *travaux préparatoires* on article 3 as adopted in 1985 are contained in the following documents:

1. Report of the United Nations Commission on International Trade Law on the work of its eighteenth session (*Official Records of the General Assembly, Fortieth Session, Supplement No. 17* (A/40/17)), paras. 11-333.

2. Reports of the Working Group: A/CN.9/246, annex; A/CN.9/263 and Add.1-2; A/CN.9/264. Relevant working papers are referred to in the reports.

3. Summary records of the 332nd UNCITRAL meeting.

Article 3 was not amended in 2006.

(Available on the Internet at www.uncitral.org).

INTRODUCTION

1. Article 3 sets out the conditions under which a written communication is considered to have been received by the addressee. The requirements for delivering documents and communicating notices are provided for in the Model Law under a number of articles, including article 13 (*Challenge procedure*), article 16 (3) (*Competence of arbitral tribunal to rule on its jurisdiction*), article 17 C (1) (*Specific regime for preliminary orders*), article 21 (*Commencement of arbitral proceedings*), article 24 (*Hearings and written proceedings*), article 25 (*Default of a party*), article 31 (*Form and contents of award*) and article 34 (3) (*Application for setting aside as exclusive recourse against arbitral award*).

CASE LAW ON ARTICLE 3

Receipt of written communications—paragraph (1)

Written communications to which paragraph (1) is applicable

2. Courts have considered paragraph (1) to be applicable to written communications by a party to the other party (ies), such as the notice of request for arbitration,[61] as well as to written communications by the arbitral tribunal to the parties, including the delivery of the arbitral award under

[61] CLOUT case No. 384 [*Skorimpex Foreign Trade Co. v. Lelovic Co.,* Ontario Court of Justice, Canada, 26 April 1991]; CLOUT case No. 20 [*Fung Sang Trading Limited v. Kai Sun Sea Products and Food Company Limited,* High Court—Court of First Instance, Hong Kong, 29 October 1991], [1991] HKCFI 190, also available on the Internet at http://www.hklii.hk/eng/hk/cases/hkcfi/1991/190.html. Note: the use of terms such as "filed" may have a different meaning to that of "delivered" or "received" in the context of commencement of arbitration (see: *Bell Canada v. The Plan Group,* Court of Appeal for Ontario, Canada, 7 July 2009, [2009] ONCA 548, available on the Internet at http://canlii.ca/t/24brq.

article 31 (4).[62] (See also below, section on article 21, para. 3 and section on article 31, para. 12).

Actual receipt of written communications

3. A notice sent by courier to the respondent's place of business and signed for upon receipt by a representative of the respondent was held to be received in accordance with article 3 (1)*(a)*.[63] Conflicting decisions have been rendered as to whether the mere acknowledgement of receipt of a letter constitutes evidence of knowledge of its content, as the document may be delivered to a person who is not the addressee and who has no obligation to ensure that the document reach the addressee.[64]

4. In a case before a German court, the respondent resisted enforcement of an award, arguing that it had neither received the request for arbitration nor the award, because these communications were sent to the address for service indicated in the agreement, without further checking the actual location of the respondent. The court rejected the challenge, ruling that the arbitral tribunal had no duty to investigate whether the address indicated in the agreement was accurate.[65] Similarly, in a situation where a communication was addressed to a party and delivered to the party's mailing address and not returned by the post or courier company, an Australian court held that it could be assumed that someone associated with the party had signed for, and received, it.[66]

Deemed receipt of written communications

5. In a case where the address of the party to be notified could not be found, a court held that all reasonable steps should be made by a party to inquire into the location of the recipient and communications should be addressed to all the recipient's known addresses. Such inquiries have been held to include searches in available registers to determine the recipient's current address.[67]

6. The existence of local regulations deeming dispatch of documents as sufficient proof of delivery does not necessarily override the requirement set out in article 3. An award made in Russia against a German corporation was refused enforcement in Germany when it was shown that the claimant had not made inquiries to ascertain the respondent's current address.[68]

---

[62] CLOUT case No. 29 [*Kanto Yakin Kogyo Kabushiki-Kaisha v. Can-Eng Manufacturing Ltd.*, Ontario Court of Justice, Canada, 30 January 1992].

[63] Ibid.

[64] CLOUT case No. 967 [Madrid Provincial High Court, Spain, Section 19, Case No. 225/2006, 12 September 2006]; CLOUT case No. 969 [Madrid Provincial High Court, Spain, Section 21, Case No. 208/2006, 18 April 2006]; CLOUT case No. 971 [Constitutional Court, Spain, Case No. 2771/2005, 5 July 2005].

[65] CLOUT case No. 870 [Oberlandesgericht Dresden, Germany, 11 Sch 19/05, 15 March 2005], also available on the Internet at http://www.dis-arb.de/en/47/datenbanken/rspr/olg-dresden-case-no-11-sch-19-05-date-2005-03-15-id531. It should be noted that under German law, there is no requirement of "reasonable inquiry" concerning the address stipulated in an agreement.

[66] *Uganda Telecom Limited v. Hi-Tech Telecom Pty. Ltd.,* Federal Court, Australia, 22 February 2011, [2011] FCA 131, available on the Internet at http://www.austlii.edu.au/au/cases/cth/FCA/2011/131.html.

[67] CLOUT case No. 384 [*Skorimpex Foreign Trade Co. v. Lelovic Co.,* Ontario Court of Justice, Canada, 26 April 1991].

[68] CLOUT case No. 402 [Bayerisches Oberstes Landesgericht, Germany, 4 Z Sch 50/99, 16 March 2000], also available on the Internet at http://www.dis-arb.de/en/47/datenbanken/rspr/bayoblg-case-no-4-z-sch-50-99-date-2000-03-16-id13, where the request for arbitration, though deemed properly delivered under the International Arbitration Law of Russia was held to violate the respondent's right to be notified. It may be noted that the law in some jurisdictions provide that service of documents on corporations incorporated or carrying on business within the jurisdiction would be deemed delivered if sent to the corporation's registered office address. Such registered office addresses do not need to be the actual place of business of the corporation.

Article 4. Waiver of right to object

A party who knows that any provision of this Law from which the parties may derogate or any requirement under the arbitration agreement has not been complied with and yet proceeds with the arbitration without stating his objection to such non-compliance without undue delay or, if a time-limit is provided therefor, within such period of time, shall be deemed to have waived his right to object.

TRAVAUX PRÉPARATOIRES

The *travaux préparatoires* on article 4 as adopted in 1985 are contained in the following documents:

1. Report of the United Nations Commission on International Trade Law on the work of its eighteenth session (*Official Records of the General Assembly, Fortieth Session, Supplement No. 17* (A/40/17)), paras. 11-333.

2. Reports of the Working Group: A/CN.9/233; A/CN.9/245; A/CN.9/246, annex; A/CN.9/263 and Add.1-2; A/CN.9/264. Relevant working papers are referred to in the reports.

3. Summary records of the 308th and 332nd UNCITRAL meetings.

Article 4 was not amended in 2006.

(Available on the Internet at www.uncitral.org).

INTRODUCTION

1. Article 4 operates to prevent one who is aware of a procedural defect in the arbitral process from raising it subsequently to resist the continuation of the arbitration or the enforcement of an adverse award made against it. This provision relates to non-compliance of those provisions of the Model Law which are of a non-mandatory nature as well as to all contractual requirements set out in the arbitration agreement.

CASE LAW ON ARTICLE 4

Conditions of the waiver

2. The term "without undue delay" has been interpreted by a German court to mean that a party must state its objection either at the next scheduled oral hearing or, if no such hearing is scheduled, in an immediate written submission.[69] In that case, the claimant had requested an oral hearing but the arbitrator ruled that he would consider the matter on the basis of documents only. As the respondent did not serve any submission in defence, the arbitrator proceeded to make the award. The respondent's application for refusal of enforcement failed for the reason, inter alia, that the objection against the absence of oral hearing was not raised by the defendant without undue delay. Another German court stated that an objection to an infringement of due process must be raised without undue delay, i.e., at the latest with the closing plea.[70]

3. An arbitral tribunal ruled in one case that, if the objection was raised "within a reasonable period", it would operate to negate the waiver. In that case, the arbitral tribunal also stated that the waiver of the right to arbitrate under an arbitration clause should not be presumed. It has to be

[69] CLOUT case No. 659 [Oberlandesgericht Naumburg, Germany, 10 Sch 08/01, 21 February 2002], also available on the Internet at http://www.dis-arb.de/de/47/datenbanken/rspr/olg-naumburg-az-10-sch-08-01-datum-2002-02-21-id166.

[70] Oberlandesgericht Stuttgart, Germany, 1 Sch 08/02, 16 July 2002, available on the Internet at http://www.dis-arb.de/de/47/datenbanken/rspr/olg-stuttgart-az-1-sch-08-02-datum-2002-07-16-id187.

clear and unequivocal in expressing the party's intention to waive its contractual right to have the dispute settled by arbitration.[71]

4. The issue of whether or not there has been a waiver was held by a Hong Kong court as one that has to be decided by the arbitral tribunal and not by the court. In that case, a party had applied to the court for security for costs instead of applying to the arbitrator. The applicant insisted that the court had jurisdiction as the defendant had waived its right to object to the non-compliance by not serving a written objection within 28 days after it knew of such non-compliance. The court held that it had no jurisdiction to decide on the waiver as that was a matter to be decided by the arbitral tribunal.[72]

Effect of the waiver

5. Where, by virtue of article 4, a party was deemed to have waived its right to object, a German court held that that party would be precluded from raising the objection during the subsequent phases of the arbitral proceedings. After the award has been issued, such a party may not invoke non-compliance with the arbitration procedure or agreement as a ground for setting aside the award[73] or as a reason for refusing its recognition and enforcement.[74] It should be pointed out that a waiver has this latter effect only in cases where the applicable legislation enacting the Model Law includes a provision similar to that of article 4.[75] (See below, section on article 34, paras. 42 and 45)

---

[71] CLOUT case No. 780 [Cairo Regional Center for International Commercial Arbitration, No. 312/200, Egypt, 28 November 2004].

[72] CLOUT case No. 676 [*Attorney-General v. Vianini Lavori Spa*, High Court—Court of First Instance, Hong Kong, 11 February 1991], [1991] HKCFI 221, available on the Internet at http://www.hklii.hk/eng/hk/cases/hkcfi/1991/221.html.

[73] Oberlandesgericht Stuttgart, Germany, 1 Sch 08/02, 16 July 2002, available on the Internet at http://www.dis-arb.de/de/47/datenbanken/rspr/olg-stuttgart-az-1-sch-08-02-datum-2002-07-16-id187; see also CLOUT case No. 637 [Presidium of the Supreme Court, Russian Federation, 24 November 1999].

[74] CLOUT case No. 659 [Oberlandesgericht Naumburg, Germany, 10 Sch 08/01, 21 February 2002], also available on the Internet at http://www.dis-arb.de/de/47/datenbanken/rspr/olg-naumburg-az-10-sch-08-01-datum-2002-02-21-id166.

[75] Ibid.

Article 5. Extent of court intervention

In matters governed by this Law, no court shall intervene except where so provided in this Law.

TRAVAUX PRÉPARATOIRES

The *travaux préparatoires* on article 5 as adopted in 1985 are contained in the following documents:

1. Report of the United Nations Commission on International Trade Law on the work of its eighteenth session (*Official Records of the General Assembly, Fortieth Session, Supplement No. 17* (A/40/17)), paras. 11-333.

2. Reports of the Working Group: A/CN.9/233; A/CN.9/245; A/CN.9/246, annex; A/CN.9/263 and Add.1-2; A/CN.9/264. Relevant working papers are referred to in the reports.

3. Summary records of the 309th and 332nd meetings.

Article 5 was not amended in 2006.

(Available on the Internet at www.uncitral.org).

INTRODUCTION

1. Article 5 is a key provision of the Model Law. It emphasizes that the role of courts to intervene in arbitrations conducted under the Model Law is limited strictly to such matters as are specifically provided in this Law. The Model Law envisages court involvement in the following instances. A first group comprises issues of appointment, challenge and termination of the mandate of an arbitrator (articles 11, 13 and 14), jurisdiction of the arbitral tribunal (article 16) and setting aside of the arbitral award (article 34). These instances are listed in article 6 as functions that should be entrusted, for the sake of centralization, specialization and efficiency, to a specially designated court or, with respect to articles 11, 13 and 14, possibly to another authority (for example, an arbitral institution or a chamber of commerce). A second group comprises issues of court assistance in taking evidence (article 27), recognition of the arbitration agreement, including its compatibility with court-ordered interim measures (articles 8, 9 and 17 J), and recognition and enforcement of interim measures (articles 17 H and 17 I) and of arbitral awards (articles 35 and 36).

2. Beyond the instances in these two groups, "no court shall intervene," "in matters governed by this Law". Article 5 by itself does not take a stand on what is the appropriate role of the courts but guarantees that all instances of possible court intervention are defined in this Law, except for matters not regulated by it (for instance, consolidation of arbitral proceedings, contractual relationship between arbitrators and parties or arbitral institutions, or fixing of costs and fees, including deposits).

CASE LAW ON ARTICLE 5

Intervention by courts in arbitration limited to specific matters

3. Courts have consistently upheld article 5 (or enactments thereof) as a mandatory provision of the Model Law,[76] confirming that it is the basic rule for determining whether court intervention was permissible under the Model Law in a particular case.[77] Article 5 is interpreted by courts to illustrate the emphasis of the Model Law in favour of arbitration as article 5 may be invoked to exclude court involvement in any general or residual matters not expressly listed in the Model Law.[78] Courts have echoed that, in all matters governed by the Model Law, court intervention would be appropriate only to the extent such inter-

[76] *Noble China Inc. v. Lei Kat Cheong*, Ontario Court of Justice, Canada, 4 November 1998, [1998] CanLII 14708 (ON SC), published in (1998) 42 O.R. (3d) 69, available on the Internet at http://canlii.ca/t/1vvkr.

[77] CLOUT case No. 77 [*Vibroflotation A.G. v. Express Builders Co. Ltd.*, High Court—Court of First Instance, Hong Kong, 15 August 1994], [1994] HKCFI 205, also available on the Internet at http://www.hklii.hk/eng/hk/cases/hkcfi/1994/205.html.

[78] CLOUT case No. 18 [*Rio Algom Limited v. Sammi Steel Co.,* Ontario Court of Justice, Canada, 1 March 1991]; CLOUT case No. 116 [*BWV Investments Ltd. v. Saskferco Products Inc. et. al. and UHDE GmbH*, Saskatchewan Court of Appeal, Canada, 25 November 1994], [1994] CanLII 4557 (SK CA), also available on the Internet at http://canlii.ca/t/1nqlf.

vention was expressly sanctioned by the Model Law itself.[79] First instance courts have interpreted article 5 as necessarily subject to the territorial limitations contained in article 1 (2) and have considered that article 5 would therefore not apply to cases where the place of arbitration is outside of the State applying the Model Law[80] or where the arbitration has been terminated.[81] Further, a court ruled that article 5 does not prevent a court from intervening in matters outside the scope of the law.[82]

4. Similarly, in matters not governed by the Model Law, even if such matters relate directly to arbitration, courts have considered that they are not limited to exercise their powers. In this regard, the Canadian Supreme Court held that article 5 does not prevent a court, when approached to enforce a foreign arbitral award, from taking into account the operation of statutory time limitation. In that case, an award made in the Russian Federation in September 2002 was sought to be enforced in the jurisdiction of Alberta in January 2006, more than three years after the award was made. One of the grounds for resisting enforcement was that the enforcement was sought after the two year time limitation under Alberta law. The argument that article 5 operates to limit a court from applying the statutory limitation was rejected.[83]

Judicial support

5. Courts have interpreted article 5 (or enactments thereof) to limit courts' intervention but not to limit the support that courts can provide to arbitral tribunals. An application for stay of the arbitration or to prevent an arbitrator from continuing the proceedings pending a court review of his earlier decision was held to constitute requests for court intervention barred by article 5.[84] Also, an application for a mandatory injunction to order a party to deliver goods pending the arbitration has also been rejected on a similar ground, with the court reasoning that it would constitute an abuse of process.[85] In a Hong Kong case where it was shown that a party had refused to disclose its place of business to avoid posting security for costs of the arbitration and where the arbitral tribunal lacked the power to grant such orders, the court assisted the tribunal by making appropriate orders. In the court's view, article 5 did not prevent the court from doing so as the issue of security for costs was not a matter governed by the Model Law. [86]

6. The power of the court to provide judicial assistance could be abused if the party seeking such assistance did so in contravention of the agreed procedure or the directions of the arbitral tribunal. In a Singapore case, a party applied for issuance of a subpoena to compel the person named to disclose documents or answer questions on documents, whereas the arbitral tribunal had earlier rejected such a request. The court application was rejected and the applicant was considered as having abused process.[87] (See below, section on article 27, para. 5).

---

[79] CLOUT case No. 16 [*Quintette Coal Limited v. Nippon Steel Corp. et al.*, Court of Appeal for British Columbia, Canada, 24 October 1990], [1990] B.C.J. No. 2241; CLOUT case No. 182 [*International Civil Aviation Organization (ICAO) v. Tripal Systems Pty. Ltd.*, Superior Court of Quebec, Canada, 9 September 1994], also in [1994] JQ No. 2692; CLOUT case No. 391 [*Re Corporación Transnacional de Inversiones, S.A. de C.V. et al. v. STET International, S.p.A. et al.*, Superior Court of Justice, Canada, 22 September 1999], [1999] CanLII 14819 (ON SC), also available on the Internet at http://canlii.ca/t/1vvn5; CLOUT case No. 392 [*Compagnie Nationale Air France v. Libyan Arab Airlines,* Superior Court of Quebec, Canada, 15 February 2000]; CLOUT case No. 513 [*Western Oil Sands Inc. v. Allianz Insurance Co. et al.*, Alberta Court of Queen's Bench, Canada, 2 February 2004], 2004 ABQB 79 (CanLII), also available on the Internet at http://canlii.ca/t/1gc7m; CLOUT case No. 516 [*Microtec Sécuri-T Inc. v. Centre d'Arbitrage Commercial National et International du Québec (CACNIQ),* Superior Court of Quebec, Canada, 14 March and 2 June 2003]; *Mitsui Engineering & Shipbuilding Co. Ltd. v. Easton Graham Rush and another,* Supreme Court, Singapore, 16 February 2004, [2004] 2 SLR(R) 14; [2004] SGHC 26; *NCC International AB v. Alliance Concrete Singapore Pte. Ltd.*, Court of Appeal, Singapore, 26 February 2008, [2008] SGCA 5, [2008] 2 SLR(R) 565; *Sunway Damansara Sdn Bhd v. Malaysia National Insurance Bhd & Anor,* Court of Appeal, Malaysia, [2008] 3 MLJ 872; *Compagnie Nationale Air France v. Mbaye*, Court of Appeal of Quebec, Canada, 31 March 2003, [2003] CanLII 35834 (QC CA), available on the Internet at http://canlii.ca/t/284nd.

[80] CLOUT case No. 383 [*Deco Automotive Inc. v. G.P.A. Gesellschaft für Pressenautomation mbH,* Ontario District Court, Canada, 27 October 1989].

[81] *Indian Oil Corporation v. Atv Projects India Ltd. & Anor WP* (C), Delhi High Court, India, 9 July 2004, 4967/2003, available on the Internet at http://indiankanoon.org/doc/1944087/.

[82] *Sundra Rajoo v. Mohamed Abd Majed,* High Court, Malaysia, 23 March 2011, (D24-NCC(ARB) 13-2010).

[83] CLOUT case No. 1009 [*Yugraneft Corp. v. Rexx. Management Corp.,* Supreme Court, Canada, 20 May 2010], 2010 SCC 19, [2010] 1 S.C.R. 649, also available on the Internet at http://canlii.ca/t/29sh0.

[84] *Mitsui Engineering & Shipbuilding Co. Ltd. v. Easton Graham Rush and another,* Supreme Court, Singapore, 16 February 2004, [2004] 2 SLR(R) 14; [2004] SGHC 26. The party in that case failed in its challenge under article 13 before the arbitral tribunal and applied to court for a review under article 13 (3). The court noted the report of UNCITRAL on the work of its eighteenth session *(Official records of the General Assembly, Fortieth Session, Supplement No. 17* (A/40/17), paras. 122 to 125); it further noted that the arbitral tribunal should be allowed to decide whether to continue the arbitration or await the decision of the court on challenge and that the court should not have control over that decision.

[85] *NCC International AB v. Alliance Concrete Singapore Pte. Ltd.*, Court of Appeal, Singapore, 26 February 2008, [2008] SGCA 5, [2008] 2 SLR(R) 565.

[86] CLOUT case No. 601 [*China Ocean Shipping Co., Owners of the M/V. Fu Ning Hai v. Whistler International Ltd., Charters of the M/V. Fu Ning Hai*, High Court—Court of First Instance, Hong Kong Special Administrative Region of China, 24 May 1999], [1999] HKCFI 693, also available on the Internet at http://www.hklii.hk/eng/hk/cases/hkcfi/1999/655.html.

[87] *ALC v. ALF,* High Court, Singapore, [2010] SGHC 231.

Article 6. Court or other authority for certain functions of arbitration assistance and supervision

The functions referred to in articles 11 (3), 11 (4), 13 (3), 14, 16 (3) and 34 (2) shall be performed by ... [Each State enacting this model law specifies the court, courts or, where referred to therein, other authority competent to perform these functions.]

TRAVAUX PRÉPARATOIRES

The *travaux préparatoires* on article 6 as adopted in 1985 are contained in the following documents:

1. Report of the United Nations Commission on International Trade Law on the work of its eighteenth session (*Official Records of the General Assembly, Fortieth Session, Supplement No. 17* (A/40/17)), paras. 11-333.

2. Reports of the Working Group: A/CN.9/232; A/CN.9/233; A/CN.9/245; A/CN.9/246, annex; A/CN.9/263 and Add.1-2; A/CN.9/264. Relevant working papers are referred to in the reports.

3. Summary records of the 309th, 310th, 311th and 332nd UNCITRAL meetings.

Article 6 was not amended in 2006.

(Available on the Internet at www.uncitral.org).

INTRODUCTION

1. Article 6 enables States enacting the Model Law to designate the court or authority to perform the functions under articles 11 (3), 11 (4) and 14; to decide on the challenge of an arbitrator under article 13 (3) and on a preliminary issue of jurisdiction under article 16 (3); and to deal with applications to set aside an award under article 34 (2).

2. It may be noted that some States designate one single court or level of courts or authority to perform all these functions,[88] while others designate a competent authority to perform administrative functions and courts to perform the adjudicative functions of dealing with challenges and review of arbitral decisions.[89]

CASE LAW ON ARTICLE 6

3. There is no case law reported on article 6.

[88] Most States name State courts for the purposes of article 6 of the Model Law, such as Australia (International Arbitration Act 1974, section 18 as amended in 2010), Bermuda (Bermuda International Arbitration Act 1993, section 25), Denmark (Act 553 of 2005, Section 5), Germany (Arbitration Law 1998, section 1025(3)), Japan (Law 138 of 2003, article 5), India (Arbitration and Conciliation Act, 1996, Section 11). Some States name non-court institutions as the authority, such as the Philippines (Republic Act 9285, Alternative Dispute Resolution Act 2004, section 26 names the "National President of the Integrated Bar of the Philippines (IBP) or his duly authorized representative" as the authority to perform the functions under Arts 11(3), 11(4), 13(3) and 14(1) in ad hoc arbitration").

[89] For instance, Singapore (International Arbitration Act Cap 143A, section 8 names the Chairman of the Singapore International Arbitration Centre or "any person" the Chief Justice appoints, to perform the functions under article 11 (3) and (4) of the Model Law while the High Court is designated to perform all other functions required under the law); Malaysia (Arbitration Act 2005, sect 13 names the "Director of the Kuala Lumpur Regional Centre for Arbitration" for appointing arbitrators but in Section 15, the High Court is designated to deal with challenges against arbitrators), Hong Kong Special Administrative Region of China (Arbitration Ordinance, section 13, names the Hong Kong International Arbitration Centre as the competent authority to perform the functions under articles 11 (3) and (4) and the Court of First Instance is the competent court to perform the functions referred to in articles 13 (3), 14, 16 (3) and 34 (2) of the Model Law).

CHAPTER II. ARBITRATION AGREEMENT

Article 7. Definition and form of arbitration agreement

[As adopted in 1985]

(1) "Arbitration agreement" is an agreement by the parties to submit to arbitration all or certain disputes which have arisen or which may arise between them in respect of a defined legal relationship, whether contractual or not. An arbitration agreement may be in the form of an arbitration clause in a contract or in the form of a separate agreement.

(2) The arbitration agreement shall be in writing. An agreement is in writing if it is contained in a document signed by the parties or in an exchange of letters, telex, telegrams or other means of telecommunication which provide a record of the agreement, or in an exchange of statements of claim and defence in which the existence of an agreement is alleged by one party and not denied by another. The reference in a contract to a document containing an arbitration clause constitutes an arbitration agreement provided that the contract is in writing and the reference is such as to make that clause part of the contract.

TRAVAUX PRÉPARATOIRES

The *travaux préparatoires* on article 7 as adopted in 1985 are contained in the following documents:

1. Report of the United Nations Commission on International Trade Law on the work of its eighteenth session (*Official Records of the General Assembly, Fortieth Session, Supplement No. 17* (A/40/17)), paras. 11-333.

2. Reports of the Working Group: A/CN.9/216; A/CN.9/232; A/CN.9/233; A/CN.9/245; A/CN.9/246, annex; A/CN.9/263 and Add.1-2; A/CN.9/264. Relevant working papers are referred to in the reports.

3. Summary records of the 311th, 320th and 332nd UNCITRAL meetings.

(Available on the Internet at www.uncitral.org).

[*As amended in 2006*]

Option I—Article 7. Definition and form of arbitration agreement

(As adopted by the Commission at its thirty-ninth session, in 2006)

(1) "Arbitration agreement" is an agreement by the parties to submit to arbitration all or certain disputes which have arisen or which may arise between them in respect of a defined legal relationship, whether contractual or not. An arbitration agreement may be in the form of an arbitration clause in a contract or in the form of a separate agreement.

(2) The arbitration agreement shall be in writing.

(3) An arbitration agreement is in writing if its content is recorded in any form, whether or not the arbitration agreement or contract has been concluded orally, by conduct, or by other means.

(4) The requirement that an arbitration agreement be in writing is met by an electronic communication if the information contained therein is accessible so as to be useable for subsequent reference; "electronic communication" means any communication that the parties make by means of data messages; "data message" means information generated, sent, received or stored by electronic, magnetic, optical or similar means, including, but not limited to, electronic data interchange (EDI), electronic mail, telegram, telex or telecopy.

(5) Furthermore, an arbitration agreement is in writing if it is contained in an exchange of statements of claim and defence in which the existence of an agreement is alleged by one party and not denied by the other.

(6) The reference in a contract to any document containing an arbitration clause constitutes an arbitration agreement in writing, provided that the reference is such as to make that clause part of the contract.

Option II—Article 7. Definition of arbitration agreement

(As adopted by the Commission at its thirty-ninth session, in 2006)

"Arbitration agreement" is an agreement by the parties to submit to arbitration all or certain disputes which have arisen or which may arise between them in respect of a defined legal relationship, whether contractual or not.

TRAVAUX PRÉPARATOIRES

The *travaux préparatoires* on article 7 as amended in 2006 are contained in the following documents:

1. Reports of the United Nations Commission on International Trade Law on the work of its thirty-second session (*Official Records of the General Assembly, Fifty-fourth Session, Supplement No. 17* (A/54/17)); thirty-third session (*Official Records of the General Assembly, Fifty-fifth Session, Supplement No. 17* (A/55/17)); thirty-fourth session (*Official Records of the General Assembly, Fifty-sixth Session, Supplement No. 17* (A/56/17)); thirty-fifth session (*Official Records of the General Assembly, Fifty-seventh Session, Supplement No. 17* (A/57/17)); thirty-sixth session (*Official Records of the General Assembly, Fifty-eighth Session, Supplement No. 17* (A/58/17)); thirty-seventh session (*Official Records of the General Assembly, Fifty-ninth Session, Supplement No. 17* (A/59/17)); thirty-eighth session (*Official Records of the General Assembly, Sixtieth Session, Supplement No. 17* (A/60/17)); thirty-ninth session (*Official records of the General Assembly, Sixty-First session, Supplement No. 17* (A/61/17), paras. 87-181 and annex).

2. Reports of Working Group II (Arbitration) on the work of its thirty-second session (A/CN.9/468, paras. 88-106); thirty-third session (A/CN.9/485, paras. 23-77); thirty-fourth session (A/CN.9/487, paras. 22-63); thirty-sixth session (A/CN.9/508, paras. 18-50); forty-third session (A/CN.9/589, paras. 108-112); and forty-fourth session (A/CN.9/592, paras. 46-80).

3. Relevant working papers, considered by Working Group II (Arbitration), are referred to in the reports of the sessions of the Working Group, including:

A/CN.9/WG.II/WP.108 and Add.1; A/CN.9/WG.II/WP.110; A/CN.9/WG.II/WP.111; A/CN.9/WG.II/WP.113 and Add. 1; A/CN.9/WG.II/WP.118; A/CN.9/WG.II/WP.136; A/CN.9/WG.II/WP.137 and Add. 1.

(Available on the Internet at www.uncitral.org).

INTRODUCTION

1. Modelled to a large extent after article II (1)[90] of the 1958 New York Convention, the 1985 version of article 7 (1) sets out the conditions under which an agreement will be characterized as an arbitration agreement to which the Model Law applies. The second paragraph of the 1985 version of article 7, which is modelled after article II (2)[91] of the 1958 New York Convention, deals with formal requirements of validity: one—the writing requirement—is of general application, while the other concerns situation where, instead of including an arbitration clause in their contract, the parties include a reference to a document containing an arbitration clause. Whether the parties' intention to submit to arbitration ought to be unequivocally expressed is not explicitly addressed in article 7 (2), but the issue has nevertheless arisen in some cases (see below, section on article 7, paras. 21 and 22).

2. Article 7 was amended in 2006 in order to respond to concerns voiced by an increasing number of scholars, practitioners and judges, who were of the view that the formal requirements set out in the original version of article 7 should be amended to better conform to international contract practices.[92] If the parties have agreed to arbitrate, but have entered into the arbitration agreement in a manner that does not meet the formal requirement, any party may have grounds to object to the jurisdiction of the arbitral tribunal (see below, section on article 7, paras. 13-22, and section on article 8, para. 15). It was pointed out by practitioners that, in a number of situations, the drafting of a written document was impossible or impractical. In such cases, where the intention of the parties to arbitrate was not in question, the validity of the arbitration agreement ought to be recognized. In amending article 7, UNCITRAL adopted two options, which reflect two different approaches on the question of definition and form of arbitration agreements. The first approach follows the detailed structure of the original 1985 text. It confirms the validity and effect of a commitment by the parties to submit to arbitration an existing dispute ("*compromis*") or a future dispute ("*clause compromissoire*"). It follows the 1958 New York Convention in requiring the written form of the arbitration agreement but recognizes a record of the "contents" of the agreement "in any form" as equivalent to traditional "writing". The agreement to arbitrate may be entered into in any form (e.g. including orally) as long as the content of the agreement is recorded. This new rule is significant in that it no longer requires signatures of the parties or an exchange of messages between the parties. It modernizes the language referring to the use of electronic commerce by adopting wording inspired from the 1996 UNCITRAL Model Law on Electronic Commerce[93] and the 2005 United Nations Convention on the Use of Electronic Communications in International Contracts.[94] It covers the situation of "an exchange of statements of claim and defence in which the existence of an agreement is alleged by one party and not denied by another". It also states that "the reference in a contract to any document" (for example, general conditions) "containing an arbitration clause constitutes an arbitration agreement in writing provided that the reference is such as to make that clause part of the contract". It thus clarifies that applicable contract law remains available to determine the level of consent necessary for a party to become bound by an arbitration agreement allegedly made "by reference". The second approach defines the arbitration

[90] Article II (1) of the 1958 New York Convention reads as follows: "Each Contracting State shall recognize an agreement in writing under which the parties undertake to submit to arbitration all or any differences which have arisen or which may arise between them in respect of a defined legal relationship, whether contractual or not, concerning a subject matter capable of settlement by arbitration."

[91] Article II (2) of the 1958 New York Convention reads as follows: "The term 'agreement in writing' shall include an arbitral clause in a contract or an arbitration agreement, signed by the parties or contained in an exchange of letters or telegrams."

[92] Explanatory Note by the UNCITRAL Secretariat on the Model Law on International Commercial Arbitration, in UNCITRAL Model Law on International Commercial Arbitration 1985, with amendments as adopted in 2006, United Nations publication, Sales No. E.08.V.4 (available on the Internet at http://www.uncitral.org/pdf/english/texts/arbitration/ml-arb/07-86998_Ebook.pdf), Part Two, para. 19.

[93] *Official Records of the General Assembly, Fifty-first Session, Supplement No. 17* (A/51/17), annex I; United Nations publication, Sales No. E.99.V.4b; UNCITRAL Yearbook, vol. XXVII: 1996, part three, annex I.

[94] General Assembly resolution 60/21, annex; United Nations publication, Sales No. E.07.V.2.

agreement in a manner that omits any formal requirement. No preference was expressed by the Commission in favour of either option I or II, both of which are offered for enacting States to consider, depending on their particular needs, and by reference to the legal context in which the Model Law is enacted, including the general contract law of the enacting State.[95] Both options are intended to preserve the enforceability of arbitration agreements under the 1958 New York Convention.[96]

CASE LAW ON ARTICLE 7

Scope of application of article 7

3. As article 7 is not among the provisions listed in article 1 (2), it does not apply if the place of arbitration is either undetermined or located in a foreign jurisdiction. Nevertheless, courts have occasionally applied article 7 while considering agreements which purported to provide for arbitration in a foreign jurisdiction.[97]

Definition of "arbitration agreement"—paragraph (1)

4. The definition of an "arbitration agreement" contained in the first sentence of the 1985 version of article 7 (1) has not been amended in 2006.

5. In addition to setting out the constituent elements of an arbitration agreement (see below in this section, paras. 6-10), paragraph (1) seeks to provide greater clarity by identifying factors which are to have no bearing on the characterization process (see below in this section, paras. 11 and 12).

One of the constituent elements of an arbitration agreement: existence of a binding commitment by the parties to refer to arbitration

6. Pursuant to paragraph (1), some elements are essential to any arbitration agreement. One of the requirements relates to the existence of a binding commitment by the parties to refer to arbitration. That requirement has given rise to difficulties in cases involving agreements that depart from the commonly-found language pursuant to which the parties agree that any dispute arising out of, or in connection with, their contract shall be referred to final and binding arbitration.[98]

7. In some cases, the issue was whether the parties' dispute resolution agreement was too unclear or contradictory to support a finding that they had undertaken to resort to arbitration. One example is a German decision involving a contract which contained both a forum selection clause and an arbitration clause. The court in that case ultimately rejected an argument to the effect that the forum selection

---

[95] Explanatory Note by the UNCITRAL Secretariat on the Model Law on International Commercial Arbitration, in UNCITRAL Model Law on International Commercial Arbitration 1985, with amendments as adopted in 2006, United Nations publication, Sales No. E.08.V.4 (available on the Internet at http://www.uncitral.org/pdf/english/texts/arbitration/ml-arb/07-86998_Ebook.pdf), Part Two, para. 19.

[96] In that respect, the Commission also adopted, at its thirty-ninth session in 2006, a "Recommendation regarding the interpretation of article II, paragraph 2, and article VII, paragraph 1, of the Convention on the Recognition and Enforcement of Foreign Arbitral Awards, done in New York, 10 June 1958" (A/61/17, Annex 2). The Recommendation was drafted in recognition of the widening use of electronic commerce and enactments of domestic legislation as well as case law, which are more favourable than the 1958 New York Convention in respect of the formal requirement governing arbitration agreements, arbitration proceedings, and the enforcement of arbitral awards. The Recommendation encourages States to apply article II (2) of the 1958 New York Convention "recognizing that the circumstances described therein are not exhaustive". In addition, the Recommendation encourages States to adopt the revised article 7 of the Model Law. Both options of the revised article 7 establish a more favourable regime for the recognition and enforcement of arbitral awards than that provided under the 1958 New York Convention. By virtue of the "more favourable law provision" contained in article VII (1) of the 1958 New York Convention, the Recommendation clarifies that "any interested party" should be allowed "to avail itself of rights it may have, under the law or treaties of the country where an arbitration agreement is sought to be relied upon, to seek recognition of the validity of such an arbitration agreement".

[97] *Thyssen Canada Ltd. v. Mariana (The),* Federal Court—Court of Appeal, Canada, 22 March 2000, [2000] CanLII 17113 (FCA), [2000] 3 FC 398, available on the Internet at http://canlii.ca/t/4l97; CLOUT case No. 70 [*Nanisivik Mines Ltd. and Zinc Corporation of America v. Canarctic Shipping Co. Ltd.,* Federal Court—Court of Appeal, Canada, 10 February 1994], [1994] 2 FC 662, also available on the Internet at http://canlii.ca/t/4nkm; CLOUT case No. 365 [*Schiff Food Products Inc. v. Naber Seed & Grain Co. Ltd.,* Saskatchewan Court of Queen's Bench, Canada, 1 October 1996], 1996 CanLII 7144 (SK QB), also available on the Internet at http://canlii.ca/t/1nsm0; *Ferguson Bros. of St. Thomas v. Manyan Inc.,* Ontario Superior Court of Justice, Canada, 27 May 1999, [1999] OJ No. 1887; *Dongnam Oil & Fats Co. v. Chemex Ltd.,* Federal Court—Trial Division, Canada, 10 December 2004, [2004] FC 1732 (CanLII), available on the Internet at http://canlii.ca/t/1jh5v.

[98] *Jagdish Chander v. Ramesh Chander & Ors*, Supreme Court, India, 26 April 2007, available on the Internet at http://www.indiankanoon.org/doc/1913246/, where the Court stated that: "[T]he words used should disclose a determination and obligation to go to arbitration and not merely contemplate the possibility of going for arbitration. Where there is merely a possibility of the parties agreeing to arbitration in future, as contrasted from an obligation to refer disputes to arbitration, there is no valid and binding arbitration agreement."

clause entailed that the parties could not be said to have undertaken to submit to arbitration, and interpreted the forum selection clause as applying only to situations where the courts' intervention was sought in connection with the arbitration.[99] In another case, a clause providing that "[t]he arbitration power of this contract belongs to the court(s) of the place where the seller is situated" was held to be too uncertain to be enforceable.[100] The Hong Kong Court of Appeal reached a similar conclusion in a case involving a dispute resolution clause alluding to mediation.[101]

8. In other cases, parties contended that multi-step dispute resolution agreements providing for arbitration, but only after attempts had been made to resolve the dispute through other extrajudicial processes, were not arbitration agreements within the meaning of article 7 (1). This argument has generally been rejected, as is illustrated by a 2008 decision of the Hong Kong District Court. The court considered that the parties had concluded an arbitration agreement, emphasizing that resort to arbitration, although conditional, was mandatory in that nothing could be interpreted as giving the parties a choice between arbitration and litigation.[102]

9. A third category of cases involves situations where the parties were alleged not to have undertaken to submit to arbitration within the meaning of article 7 (1) on the ground that their dispute resolution agreement offered a choice between arbitration and litigation. In a number of cases, the argument rested on clauses providing that either party "may" require that the dispute be resolved by arbitration. Such was the case in a Hong Kong Court of Appeal decision, where the argument was dismissed on the ground that once a party had elected to resort to arbitration that choice becomes binding on the other party.[103] However, courts have also ruled that similar language entailed that the parties had not undertaken to resort to arbitration.[104] Other cases involved clauses explicitly granting to the claimant the option of either resorting to arbitration or

---

[99] Bundesgerichtshof, Germany, VII ZR 105/06, 25 January 2007, available on the Internet at http://www.dis-arb.de/en/47/datenbanken/rspr/bgh-case-no-vii-zr-105-06-date-2007-01-25-id653; see also: Bundesgerichtshof, Germany, III ZR 214/05, 12 January 2006, available on the Internet at http://www.dis-arb.de/en/47/datenbanken/rspr/bgh-case-no-iii-zr-214-05-date-2006-01-12-id524; *Arta Properties Limited v. Li Fu Yat Tso et al.*, High Court—Court of First Instance, Hong Kong, 2 June 1998, [1998] HKCU 721; *P. T. Tri-M.G. Intra Asia Airlines v. Norse Air Charter Limited*, High Court, Singapore, 12 January 2009, [2009] SGHC 13; *Pccw Global Ltd. V. Interactive Communications Service Ltd.*, High Court—Court of Appeal, Hong Kong Special Administrative Region of China, 16 November 2006, [2006] HKCA 434, available on the Internet at http://www.hklii.hk/eng/hk/cases/hkca/2006/434.html, where apparently inconsistent forum selection and arbitration clauses were reconciled; *Rampton v. Eyre*, Ontario Court of Appeal, Canada, 2 May 2007, [2007] ONCA 331, available on the Internet at http://canlii.ca/t/1rb0d.

[100] *Tai-Ao Aluminium (Taishan) Co. Ltd. v. Maze Aluminium Engineering Co. Ltd. & Another,* High Court—Court of First Instance, Hong Kong Special Administrative Region of China, 17 February 2006, [2006] HKCFI 220, available on the Internet at http://www.hklii.hk/eng/hk/cases/hkcfi/2006/220.html.

[101] *Kenon Engineering Ltd. v. Nippon Kokan Koji Kabushiki Kaisha*, High Court—Court of Appeal, Hong Kong Special Administrative Region of China, 7 May 2004, [2004] HKCA 101, available on the Internet at http://www.hklii.hk/eng/hk/cases/hkca/2004/101.html.

[102] *Ho Fat Sing t/a Famous Design Engineering Co. v. Hop Tai Construction Co. Ltd.*, District Court, Hong Kong Special Administrative Region of China, 23 December 2008, [2008] HKDC 339, available on the Internet at http://www.hklii.hk/eng/hk/cases/hkdc/2008/339.html; see also, to the same effect: *Westco Airconditioning Ltd. v. Sui Chong Construction & Engineering Co. Ltd.*, High Court—Court of First Instance, Hong Kong, 3 February 1998, [1998] HKCFI 946, available on the Internet at http://www.hklii.hk/eng/hk/cases/hkcfi/1998/946.html. For another decision giving effect to multi-tier dispute resolution clauses, see: *Grandeur Electrical Co. Ltd. v. Cheung Kee Fung Cheung Construction Co. Ltd.*, High Court—Court of Appeal, Hong Kong Special Administrative Region of China, 25 July 2006, [2006] HKCA 305, available on the Internet at http://www.hklii.hk/eng/hk/cases/hkca/2006/305.html.

[103] *Grandeur Electrical Co. Ltd. v. Cheung Kee Fung Cheung Construction Co. Ltd.*, High Court—Court of Appeal, Hong Kong Special Administrative Region of China, 25 July 2006, [2006] HKCA 305, available on the Internet at http://www.hklii.hk/eng/hk/cases/hkca/2006/305.html, where the court added in that case that "in the light of the emphasis given to party autonomy in relation to dispute resolution by arbitration, a clause in a contract providing for disputes to be settled by arbitration should not readily be construed as giving a choice between arbitration and litigation unless that is specifically and clearly spelt out." See also, reaching a similar conclusion: *Pccw Global Ltd. v. Interactive Communications Service Ltd.*, High Court—Court of Appeal, Hong Kong Special Administrative Region of China, 16 November 2006, [2006] HKCA 434, available on the Internet at http://www.hklii.hk/eng/hk/cases/hkca/2006/434.html; CLOUT case No. 389 [*Canadian National Railway Company v. Lovat Tunnel Equipment Inc.*, Ontario Court of Appeal, Canada, 8 July 1999], 1999 CanLII 3751 (ON CA), also available on the Internet at http://canlii.ca/t/1f9mg; CLOUT case No. 813 [*Tianjin Medicine & Health Products Import & Export Corporation v. J. A. Moeller (Hong Kong) Limited*, High Court—Court of First Instance, Hong Kong, 27 January 1994], [1994] HKCFI 351, also available on the Internet at http://www.hklii.hk/eng/hk/cases/hkcfi/1994/351.html, CLOUT case No. 38 [*China State Construction Engineering Corporation, Guangdong Branch v. Madiford Limited*, High Court—Court of First Instance, Hong Kong, 2 March 1992], [1992] HKCFI 160, also available on the Internet at http://www.hklii.hk/eng/hk/cases/hkcfi/1992/160.html; CLOUT case No. 368 [*Campbell et al. v. Murphy*, Ontario Court—General Division, Canada, 9 August 1993], [1993] CanLII 5460 (ON SC), also available on the Internet at http://canlii.ca/t/1vskk; *WSG Nimbus Pte. Ltd. v. Board of Control for Cricket in Sri Lanka,* High Court, Singapore, 13 May 2002, [2002] SGHC 104.

[104] *C.C.I.C. Consultech International v. Silverman*, Court of Appeal of Quebec, Canada, 24 May 1991, 1991 CanLII 2868 (QC CA), available on the Internet at http://canlii.ca/t/1pfsx; *Librati v. Barka Co. Ltd.*, Superior Court of Quebec, Canada, 5 December 2007, [2007] QCCS 5724, available on the Internet at http://www.jugements.qc.ca/php/decision.php?liste=53365293&doc=E4DA59C7A17BF2492B07BCA86534262FE0F1219570C7F13782CA6067823146F6&page=1; *Jagdish Chander v. Ramesh Chander & Ors*, Supreme Court, India, 26 April 2007, available on the Internet at http://www.indiankanoon.org/doc/1913246/.

commencing an action before the courts of a designated jurisdiction. While one court has found such a clause to constitute an arbitration agreement on the ground that the claimant's choice of arbitration was binding on the defendant,[105] other courts have ruled that it did not amount to an undertaking to submit to arbitration within the meaning of the Model Law.[106] Furthermore, courts have refused to interpret clauses providing that arbitration had to be commenced within a specified time limit as granting to the claimant the option of commencing a court action in the event that it chose not to resort to arbitration within that timeframe.[107] Finally, in one Indian case, the court found that a clause providing that disputes between the parties "shall be referred to arbitration *if the parties so determine*"[108] was "not an arbitration agreement but a provision which enables arbitration only if the parties mutually decide after due consideration as to whether the disputes should be referred to arbitration or not."[109]

10. The constituent elements of an arbitration agreement are listed exhaustively in article 7 (1). There is no requirement that the agreement also address issues such as the place of arbitration, the applicable rules of procedure, the language of the arbitration or the number of arbitrators and the method pursuant to which they are to be appointed. This point was emphasized by the Supreme Court of India, in a case where the validity of the arbitration agreement was challenged on the ground that it contained provisions concerning the number of arbitrators which contravened applicable mandatory rules. After noting that nothing in article 7 (1) suggests that the number of arbitrators is a constituent element of an arbitration agreement, the court found that the "validity of an arbitration agreement does not depend on the number of arbitrators specified therein."[110]

Factors irrelevant to the characterization process

11. In addition to containing provisions setting out the constituent elements of an arbitration clause, article 7 (1) lists several factors which are to be treated as irrelevant while determining whether an agreement deserves to be characterized as an arbitration agreement for the purposes of the Model Law.

12. The first factor concerns the scope of the agreement: parties may refer to arbitration "all or certain disputes which have arisen or which may arise between them." The overwhelming majority of cases concern arbitration agreements which apply only to one or several categories of disputes. While determining whether a particular dispute falls within the ambit of the agreement is occasionally problematic (see below, section on article 8, para. 28), it is widely accepted that such restrictions have no bearing on the characterization of the agreement. The second factor concerns the nature of the disputes that the parties intend to submit to arbitration. Article 7 (1) makes clear that the notion of arbitration agreement is not restricted to an agreement relating to the resolution of contractual disputes. An arbitration agreement may relate to disputes concerning a "defined legal relationship, *whether contractual or not*,"[111] and the *travaux préparatoires* indicate that this expression "should be given a wide interpretation so as to cover all non-contractual commercial cases occurring in practice (e.g. third party interfering with contractual relations; infringement of trademark or other unfair competition)."[112] Finally, the last sentence of article 7 (1) states that an arbitration agreement may be in the form of an arbitration clause inserted in a contract or in the form of a separate agreement, also a widely-accepted proposition that has not created difficulties.

---

[105] CLOUT case No. 44 [*William Company v. Chu Kong Agency Co. Ltd. and Guangzhou Ocean Shipping Company*, High Court—Court of First Instance, Hong Kong, 17 February 1993], [1993] HKCFI 215, also available on the Internet at http://www.hklii.hk/eng/hk/cases/hkcfi/1993/215.html.

[106] *Empressa de Turismo Nacional & Internacional v. Vacances sans frontière ltée*, Court of Appeal of Quebec, Canada, 9 October 1992, 1992 CanLII 3546 (QC CA), available on the Internet at http://canlii.ca/t/1pdxq; *Importations Cimel Ltée v. Pier Augé Produits de Beauté*, Court of Appeal of Quebec, Canada, 27 October 1987, 1987 CanLII 1165 (QC CA), available on the Internet at http://canlii.ca/t/1stlg.

[107] CLOUT case No. 449 [*China Merchant Heavy Industry Co. Ltd. v. JGC Corp.*, High Court—Court of Appeal, Hong Kong Special Administrative Region of China, 4 July 2001], [2001] HKCA 248, also available on the Internet at http://www.hklii.hk/eng/hk/cases/hkca/2001/248.html; *Tommy C.P. Sze. & Co. v. Li & Fung (trading) Ltd. & Others,* High Court—Court of First Instance, Hong Kong Special Administrative Region of China, 28 October 2002, [2002] HKCFI 682, available on the Internet at http://www.hklii.hk/eng/hk/cases/hkcfi/2002/682.html.

[108] Emphasis added.

[109] *Jagdish Chander v. Ramesh Chander & Ors*, Supreme Court, India, 26 April 2007, available on the Internet at http://www.indiankanoon.org/doc/1913246/.

[110] CLOUT case No. 177 [*M.M.T.C. Limited v. Sterlite Industries (India) Ltd.*, Supreme Court, India, 18 November 1996], also available on the Internet at http://www.indiankanoon.org/doc/1229987/.

[111] Emphasis added.

[112] A/CN.9/264, Analytical commentary on draft text of a model law on international commercial arbitration, under article 7, para. 4, available on the UNCITRAL website at http://www.uncitral.org/uncitral/en/commission/sessions/18th.html.

Formal requirements (1985 version of article 7 (2))

The writing requirement

13. The requirement that an arbitration agreement be in writing ("writing requirement") under article 7 (2), as adopted in 1985, seeks "to ensure that parties do not get forced into arbitration unless it is clear beyond doubt that they have agreed to it."[113] When the Model Law was adopted in 1985, it had been decided that an arbitration agreement had to be in writing even though oral arbitration agreements were, at the time, not unknown in practice and even recognized by some national laws.[114] Yet, it is not required under article 7 (2) that arbitration agreements be signed by all parties.[115] An agreement is also to be considered in writing if it is contained "in an exchange of letters, telex, telegrams or other means of telecommunication which provide a record of the agreement,"[116] and this exchange need not be between the parties.[117] Further broadening the notion of writing, article 7 (2) provides that an agreement would also be in writing where the parties have exchanged "statements of claim and defence in which the existence of an [arbitration] agreement [was] alleged by one party and not denied by the other." The Supreme Court of India has ruled that, in light of the principle of party autonomy and the "need to minimize the supervisory role of courts in the arbitral process," courts should refrain from adding formal requirements of validity of arbitration agreements that are not enumerated in article 7 (2).[118]

14. A key question arising in connection with the writing requirement is whether consent not expressed in writing may suffice where the content of the agreement is recorded in a document, or whether consent must always be expressed in a writing—albeit not necessarily in a writing containing the parties' signature. This question is of significant practical importance in cases where the parties engaged in a contractual relationship further to a written contractual offer containing an arbitration clause that was never responded to in writing. In one case, the court refused to find that the writing requirement had been met, pointing out that article 7 "cannot be complied with unless there is a record whereby the [party against whom the agreement is invoked] has *in writing* assented to the agreement to arbitrate."[119] However, other courts have interpreted the requirement less strictly and found, on similar facts, that because "in this age of electronic international business transactions, (…) a liberal interpretation should be given" to article 7 (2), tacit consent to an arbitration agreement set out in writing is sufficient.[120]

15. Another controversial question is whether documents which are not contemporaneous with the agreement to arbitrate may be considered records of the agreement within the meaning of article 7 (2). One court ruled that they could not, on the ground that "[a]rticle 7 (2) precludes the adoption of memoranda in writing being relied upon which post-date the agreement to arbitrate."[121] However, that finding was subsequently criticized in decisions pointing out, inter

---

[113] CLOUT case No. 44 [*William Company v. Chu Kong Agency Co. Ltd. and Guangzhou Ocean Shipping Company*, High Court—Court of First Instance, Hong Kong, 17 February 1993], [1993] HKCFI 215, also available on the Internet at http://www.hklii.hk/eng/hk/cases/hkcfi/1993/215.html.

[114] A/CN.9/264, Analytical commentary on draft text of a model law on international commercial arbitration, under article 7, para. 6, available on the UNCITRAL website at http://www.uncitral.org/uncitral/en/commission/sessions/18th.html.

[115] See for instance: CLOUT case No. 365 [*Schiff Food Products Inc. v. Naber Seed & Grain Co. Ltd.*, Court of Queen's Bench, Saskatchewan, Canada, 1 October 1996], 1996 CanLII 7144 (SK QB), also available on the Internet at http://canlii.ca/t/1nsm0.

[116] For examples of cases involving an arbitration agreement concluded by fax and which was held to meet the requirements of article 7 (2), see: CLOUT case No. 62 [*Oonc Lines Limited v. Sino-American Trade Advancement Co. Ltd.*, High Court—Court of First Instance, Hong Kong, 2 February 1994], [1994] HKCFI 193, also available on the Internet at http://www.hklii.hk/eng/hk/cases/hkcfi/1994/193.html; *Great Offshore Ltd. v. Iranian Offshore Engineering & Construction Company*, Supreme Court of India, India, 25 August 2008, available on the Internet at http://www.indiankanoon.org/doc/394001/; see also: CLOUT case No. 87 [*Gay Constructions Pty. Ltd. and Spaceframe Buildings (North Asia) Ltd. v. Caledonian Techmore (Building) Limited & Hanison Construction Co. Ltd. (as a third party)*, High Court—Court of First Instance, Hong Kong, 17 November 1994], [1994] HKCFI 171, also available on the Internet at http://www.hklii.hk/eng/hk/cases/hkcfi/1994/171.html, where the court held that a document setting out a contractual claim to which was attached the arbitration clause at issue amounted to a letter providing a record of the author's agreement to arbitrate within the meaning of article 7 (2); and *Ferguson Bros. of St. Thomas v. Manyan Inc.*, Ontario Superior Court of Justice, Canada, 27 May 1999, [1999] OJ No. 1887, where the court held that a cheque referring to an invoice amounted to a record of the issuer's consent to an arbitration clause inserted in a contractual offer to which the issuer had heretofore not replied in writing.

[117] *Jiangxi Provincial Metal and Minerals Import and Export Corporation v. Sulanser Co. Ltd.*, High Court—Court of First Instance, Hong Kong, 6 April 1995, [1995] HKCFI 449, available on the Internet at http://www.hklii.hk/eng/hk/cases/hkcfi/1995/449.html.

[118] *Great Offshore Ltd. v. Iranian Offshore Engineering & Construction Company*, Supreme Court, India, 25 August 2008, available on the Internet at http://www.indiankanoon.org/doc/394001/.

[119] CLOUT case No. 64 [*H. Small Limited v. Goldroyce Garment Limited*, High Court—Court of First Instance, Hong Kong, 13 May 1994], [1994] HKCFI 203, also available on the Internet at http://www.hklii.hk/eng/hk/cases/hkcfi/1994/203.html (emphasis added).

[120] See for instance: CLOUT case No. 365 [*Schiff Food Products Inc. v. Naber Seed & Grain Co. Ltd.*, Court of Queen's Bench, Saskatchewan, Canada, 1 October 1996], 1996 CanLII 7144 (SK QB), also available on the Internet at http://canlii.ca/t/1nsm0; *Achilles (USA) v. Plastics Dura Plastics (1977) ltée/Ltd.*, Court of Appeal of Quebec, Canada, 23 November 2006, [2006] QCCA 1523, available on the Internet at http://canlii.ca/t/1qf7d.

[121] CLOUT case No. 43 [*Hissan Trading Co. Ltd. v. Orkin Shipping Corporation*, High Court—Court of First Instance, Hong Kong, 8 September 1992], [1992] HKCFI 286, also available on the Internet at http://www.hklii.hk/eng/hk/cases/hkcfi/1992/286.html.

alia, that oral arbitration agreements later evidenced through writings emanating from the parties did comply with the writing requirement set out in article 7 (2).[122]

16. Finally, courts have tended to interpret broadly the words "statements of claim and defence," concluding that they included not only formal submissions to an arbitral tribunal or a court, but also claims asserted between the parties outside of the litigation or arbitration context.[123]

Incorporation by reference to a document containing an arbitration clause

17. The last sentence of article 7 (2) addresses the situation where the parties, instead of including an arbitration clause in their contract, include a reference to a document containing an arbitration agreement. Article 7 (2) confirms that an arbitration agreement may be formed in that manner provided, firstly, that the contract in which the reference is found meets the writing requirement discussed above and, secondly, that "the reference is such as to make that clause part of the contract." The document referred to need not to be signed by or to emanate from the parties to the contract.[124]

18. One question that arises in connection with the last sentence of article 7 (2) is whether the arbitration agreement contained in the document must be explicitly referred to in the reference. The *travaux préparatoires* confirm that this should not be the case: "the text clearly states [that] the reference need only be to the document; thus, no explicit reference to the arbitration clause contained therein is required."[125] While a similar conclusion has been reached by several courts,[126] other courts have found that an explicit mention of the arbitration agreement was needed in order for the reference to be operative.[127]

---

[122] CLOUT case No. 44 [*William Company v. Chu Kong Agency Co. Ltd. and Guangzhou Ocean Shipping Company*, High Court—Court of First Instance, Hong Kong, 17 February 1993], [1993] HKCFI 215, also available on the Internet at http://www.hklii.hk/eng/hk/cases/hkcfi/1993/215.html; *P.T. Wearwel International v. Vf Asia Ltd.*, High Court—Court of First Instance, Hong Kong, 19 August 1994, [1994] 3 HKC 344; *Indowind Energy Ltd. v. Wescare (I) Ltd. & Anr.*, Supreme Court, India, 27 April 2010, available on the Internet at http://www.indiankanoon.org/doc/997909/.

[123] CLOUT case No. 87 [*Gay Constructions Pty. Ltd. and Spaceframe Buildings (North Asia) Ltd. v. Caledonian Techmore (Building) Limited & Hanison Construction Co. Ltd. (as a third party)*, High Court—Court of First Instance, Hong Kong, 17 November 1994], [1994] HKCFI 171 also available on the Internet at http://www.hklii.hk/eng/hk/cases/hkcfi/1994/171.html.

[124] CLOUT case No. 78 [*Astel-Peiniger Joint Venture v. Argos Engineering & Heavy Industries Co. Ltd.*, High Court—Court of First Instance, Hong Kong, 18 August 1994], [1994] HKCFI 276, also available on the Internet at http://www.hklii.hk/eng/hk/cases/hkcfi/1994/276.html; *Thyssen Canada Ltd. v. Mariana (The)*, Federal Court—Court of Appeal, Canada, 22 March 2000, [2000] CanLII 17113 (FCA), [2000] 3 FC 398, available on the Internet at http://canlii.ca/t/4197; CLOUT case No. 460 [*Hercules Data Comm Co. Ltd. v. Koywa Communications Ltd.*, High Court—Court of First Instance, Hong Kong Special Administrative Region of China, 23 October 2000], [2001] HKCFI 71, also available on the Internet at http://www.hklii.hk/eng/hk/cases/hkcfi/2000/71.html; *Fai Tak Engineering Co. Ltd. v. Sui Chong Construction & Engineering Co. Ltd.*, District Court, Hong Kong Special Administrative Region of China, 22 June 2009, [2009] HKDC 141, available on the Internet at http://www.hklii.hk/eng/hk/cases/hkdc/2009/141.html.

[125] A/CN.9/264, Analytical commentary on draft text of a model law on international commercial arbitration, under article 7, para. 8, available on the UNCITRAL website at http://www.uncitral.org/uncitral/en/commission/sessions/18th.html.

[126] See for instance: CLOUT case No. 127 [*Skandia International Insurance Company and Mercantile & General Reinsurance Company and various others*, Supreme Court, Bermuda, 21 January 1994], also in [1994] Bda LR 30; CLOUT case No. 70 [*Nanisivik Mines Ltd. and Zinc Corporation of America v. Canarctic Shipping Co. Ltd.*, Federal Court—Court of Appeal, Canada, 10 February 1994], [1994] 2 FC 662, also available on the Internet at http://canlii.ca/t/4nkm; CLOUT case No. 391 [*Re Corporación Transnacional de Inversiones, S.A. de C.V. et al. v. STET International, S.p.A. et al.*, Superior Court of Justice, Canada, 22 September 1999], [1999] CanLII 14819 (ON SC), also available on the Internet at http://canlii.ca/t/1vvn5, confirmed in *Corporación Transnacional de Inversiones v. Stet International*, Ontario Court of Appeal, Canada, 15 September 2000, [2000] CanLII 16840 (ON CA), available on the Internet at http://canlii.ca/t/1cvn9; CLOUT case No. 78 [*Astel-Peiniger Joint Venture v. Argos Engineering & Heavy Industries Co. Ltd.*, High Court—Court of First Instance, Hong Kong, 18 August 1994], [1994] HKCFI 276, also available on the Internet at http://www.hklii.hk/eng/hk/cases/hkcfi/1994/276.html; CLOUT case No. 87 [*Gay Constructions Pty. Ltd. and Spaceframe Buildings (North Asia) Ltd. v. Caledonian Techmore (Building) Limited & Hanison Construction Co. Ltd. (as a third party)*, High Court—Court of First Instance, Hong Kong, 17 November 1994], [1994] HKCFI 171, also available on the Internet at http://www.hklii.hk/eng/hk/cases/hkcfi/1994/171.html; *Ferguson Bros. of St. Thomas v. Manyan Inc.*, Ontario Superior Court of Justice, Canada, 27 May 1999, [1999] OJ No. 1887; *Lief Investments Pty. Limited v. Conagra International Fertiliser Company*, Supreme Court of New South Wales—Court of Appeal, Australia, 16 July 1998, [1998] NSWSC 481, available on the Internet at http://www.austlii.edu.au/au/cases/nsw/NSWSC/1998/481.html; *Fai Tak Engineering Co. Ltd. v. Sui Chong Construction & Engineering Co. Ltd.*, District Court, Hong Kong Special Administrative Region of China, 22 June 2009, [2009] HKDC 141, available on the Internet at http://www.hklii.hk/eng/hk/cases/hkdc/2009/141.html; *Ho Fat Sing t/a Famous Design Engineering Co. v. Hop Tai Construction Co. Ltd.*, District Court, Hong Kong Special Administrative Region of China, 23 December 2008, [2008] HKDC 339, available on the Internet at http://www.hklii.hk/eng/hk/cases/hkdc/2008/339.html; *Tsang Yuk Ching t/a Tsang Ching Kee Eng. Co. v. Fu Shing Rush Door Joint Venture Co. Ltd.*, High Court—Court of First Instance, Hong Kong Special Administrative Region of China, 5 September 2003, [2003] HKCFI 680, available on the Internet at http://www.hklii.hk/eng/hk/cases/hkcfi/2003/680.html; *P.T. Wearwel International v. Vf Asia Ltd.*, High Court—Court of First Instance, Hong Kong, 19 August 1994, [1994] 3 HKC 344; *Pueblo Film Distribution Hungary K.F.T. (Hungary) v. Laurenfilm S.A.*, Tribunal Supremo, Spain, 31 May 2005, rec. 743/2003, 28079110012005201465 (Id cendoj), available on the Internet at http://www.poderjudicial.es/search/indexAN.jsp; *Concordia Agritrading Pte. Ltd. v. Cornelder Hoogewerff*, High Court, Singapore, 13 October 1999, [1999] SGHC 269, [1999] 3 SLR(R) 618.

[127] *Concordia Agritrading Pte. Ltd. v. Cornelder Hoogewerff*, High Court, Singapore, 13 October 1999, [1999] SGHC 269, [1999] 3 SLR(R) 618; CLOUT case No. 34 [*Miramichi Pulp and Paper Inc. v. Canadian Pacific Bulk Ship Services Ltd.*, Federal Court—Trial Division, Canada, 9 October 1992], ("It appears to be an accepted rule of construction that in order to incorporate into the bill of lading an arbitration clause, clear and precise language such as 'including the arbitration clause' is necessary. General wording such as 'incorporating the general terms and conditions of a charterparty' is insufficient.")

19. The requirement that the reference be "such as to make th[e] clause part of the contract," can raise some difficulties in practice, as is illustrated in a Canadian case in which the parties to a bill of lading had incorporated all the terms set out in the charter party under which it had been issued. The charter party contained an arbitration clause, but that clause was limited to disputes arising under the charter party. The court, relying on English cases, found that because the reference made no explicit mention of the arbitration clause, and because the arbitration clause made no reference to disputes relating to any bill of lading issued under the charter party, the parties could not be said to have intended to incorporate the arbitration clause so as to make it applicable to disputes relating to the bill of lading. The court stated that its conclusion would have been different if the arbitration clause had expressly provided that it applied to disputes relating to bills of lading issued under the charter party, or if the reference in the parties' contract had explicitly mentioned the arbitration clause.[128] This case is to be contrasted with a Hong Kong case dealing with a similar situation. The parties to a sub-sub-contract had incorporated the terms set out in a sub-contract, but without explicitly mentioning the arbitration clause inserted therein. Furthermore, the terms of the arbitration clause limited its scope to disputes between the contractor and the sub-contractor arising in relation to the sub-contract. Nevertheless, the court found that the parties to the sub-contract had sufficiently intended to incorporate the arbitration clause, with the modifications required to make it operative in the context of their sub-sub-contract.[129]

20. Whether an arbitration clause ought to be viewed as set out in an external document, rather than being part of the parties' contract, raises intricate questions in the context of web-based electronic commerce. The Supreme Court of Canada held that an arbitration clause found in terms and conditions easily accessible by clicking on a hyperlink appearing at the bottom of pages visited by the customer was not an external clause. To the court, only "a clause that requires operations of such complexity that its text is not reasonably accessible," or a clause contained in separate web pages and for which no hyperlink is provided, deserve to be characterized as an external clause.[130]

Must the parties' intention to submit to arbitration be unequivocally expressed?

21. A final question that arises under article 7 is whether the parties' intention to submit to a process that is arbitral in nature must be unequivocally expressed. Despite that article 7 makes no mention of such a requirement, some Canadian courts have considered it essential to the validity of any arbitration agreement that it explicitly state the parties' obligation to resort to arbitration as well as the final and binding nature of awards issued by the arbitral tribunal.[131] More recent cases, however, have given effect to arbitration agreements that did not mention that awards would be final and binding.[132] Furthermore, the earlier cases are arguably inconsistent with a decision of the Quebec Court of Appeal holding that consent to arbitration is not subject to special or distinctive formal requirements.[133]

---

[128] CLOUT case No. 70 [*Nanisivik Mines Ltd. and Zinc Corporation of America v. Canarctic Shipping Co. Ltd.*, Federal Court—Court of Appeal, Canada, 10 February 1994], [1994] 2 FC 662, also available on the Internet at http://canlii.ca/t/4nkm; see also: *Thyssen Canada Ltd. v. Mariana (The)*, Federal Court—Court of Appeal, Canada, 22 March 2000, [2000] CanLII 17113 (FCA), [2000] 3 FC 398, available on the Internet at http://canlii.ca/t/4l97; *Dongnam Oil & Fats Co. v. Chemex Ltd.*, Federal Court—Trial Division, Canada, 10 December 2004, [2004] FC 1732 (CanLII), available on the Internet at http://canlii.ca/t/1jh5v,; CLOUT case No. 178 [*Siderurgica Mendes Junior S.A. v. "Icepearl" (The)*, Supreme Court of British Columbia, Canada, 31 January 1996], [1996] CanLII 2746 (BC SC), also available on the Internet at http://canlii.ca/t/1f1n1. See also: *Concordia Agritrading Pte. Ltd. v. Cornelder Hoogewerff*, High Court, Singapore, 13 October 1999, [1999] SGHC 269, [1999] 3 SLR(R) 618. For other cases where courts dismissed arguments to the effect that the parties had agreed to incorporate an arbitration clause set out in a distinct document, see: CLOUT case No. 673 [*Trans-medica Pharma-Handelsgesellschaft mbH v Ananda Pharmaceuticals & Chemicals Ltd.*, Court of Appeal, Hong Kong, 22 June 1990], [1990] HKCA 332, also available on the Internet at http://www.hklii.hk/eng/hk/cases/hkca/1990/332.html; CLOUT case No. 43 [*Hissan Trading Co. Ltd. v. Orkin Shipping Corporation*, High Court—Court of First Instance, Hong Kong, 8 September 1992], [1992] HKCFI 286, also available on the Internet at http://www.hklii.hk/eng/hk/cases/hkcfi/1992/286.html; *Newmark Capital Corporation Ltd. and Others v. Coffee Partners Ltd. and Another*, High Court—Court of First Instance, Hong Kong Special Administrative Region of China, 8 February 2007, [2007] HKCFI 113, available on the Internet at http://www.hklii.hk/eng/hk/cases/hkcfi/2007/113.html.

[129] CLOUT case No. 78 [*Astel-Peiniger Joint Venture v. Argos Engineering & Heavy Industries Co. Ltd.*, High Court—Court of First Instance, Hong Kong, 18 August 1994], [1994] HKCFI 276, also available on the Internet at http://www.hklii.hk/eng/hk/cases/hkcfi/1994/276.html.

[130] *Dell Computer Corp. v. Union des Consommateurs,* Supreme Court, Canada, 13 July 2007, [2007] SCC 34, [2007] 2 SCR 801, available on the Internet at http://canlii.ca/t/1s2f2.

[131] *2961-8667 Québec Inc. v. Fafard,* Court of Appeal of Quebec, Canada, 31 March 2004, [2004] QJ No. 4085, REJB 2004-60643.

[132] *Investissement Charlevoix Inc. v. Gestion Pierre Gingras Inc.*, Court of Appeal of Quebec, Canada, 21 June 2010, [2010] QCCA 1229 (CanLII), available on the Internet at http://canlii.ca/t/2bcbk.

[133] *Achilles (USA) v. Plastics Dura Plastics (1977) ltée/Ltd.*, Court of Appeal of Quebec, Canada, 23 November 2006, [2006] QCCA 1523 (CanLII), available on the Internet at http://canlii.ca/t/1qf7d.

22. Courts in other jurisdictions have occasionally held that the parties' undertaking to resort to arbitration must be unambiguously expressed.[134] However, the majority of cases dealing with ambiguous arbitration clauses are inconsistent with this proposition. Examples of that latter trend can be found in two decisions of the German Federal Court of Justice relating to contracts in which were inserted seemingly contradictory dispute resolution clauses, one providing for arbitration and the other providing for the exclusive jurisdiction of the courts of a designated jurisdiction. Rather than concluding that the parties had not validly undertaken to resort to arbitration—which would be the logical conclusion in a jurisdiction requiring an unequivocal expression of the parties' intention[135]—, the court interpreted the clauses with a view to reconciling them and giving effect to both, and ultimately concluded that the forum selection clause was only intended to operate in connection with requests for court's intervention in relation to the arbitral process.[136]

Formal requirements (option I—article 7 (2) to (4) as adopted in 2006)

23. There is no case law reported on article 7 (2) to (4) (option I) as adopted in 2006.

Formal requirements (option II—article 7 as adopted in 2006)

24. There is no case law reported on article 7 (option II) as adopted in 2006.

[134] *D. Andrés v. Díez Carrillo S.L.*, Audiencia Provincial de Palma de Mallorca (sección 5ª), Spain, 5 October 2006, rec. apel. 399/2006, available on the Internet at http://www.poderjudicial.es/search/indexAN.jsp.

[135] See, by analogy, *Empressa de Turismo Nacional & Internacional v. Vacances sans frontière ltée*, Court of Appeal of Quebec, Canada, 9 October 1992, 1992 CanLII 3546 (QC CA), available on the Internet at http://canlii.ca/t/1pdxq; *Importations Cimel Ltée v. Pier Augé Produits de Beauté*, Court of Appeal of Quebec, Canada, 27 October 1987, 1987 CanLII 1165 (QC CA), available on the Internet at http://canlii.ca/t/1stlg, where courts refused to refer the parties to arbitration on the basis of a clause giving the claimant the option of either resorting to arbitration or commencing an action before the courts of a designated jurisdiction.

[136] Bundesgerichtshof, Germany, VII ZR 105/06, 25 January 2007, available on the Internet at http://www.dis-arb.de/en/47/datenbanken/rspr/bgh-case-no-vii-zr-105-06-date-2007-01-25-id653; Bundesgerichtshof, Germany, III ZR 214/05, 12 January 2006, available on the Internet at http://www.dis-arb.de/en/47/datenbanken/rspr/bgh-case-no-iii-zr-214-05-date-2006-01-12-id524.

Article 8. Arbitration agreement and substantive claim before court

(1) A court before which an action is brought in a matter which is the subject of an arbitration agreement shall, if a party so requests not later than when submitting his first statement on the substance of the dispute, refer the parties to arbitration unless it finds that the agreement is null and void, inoperative or incapable of being performed.

(2) Where an action referred to in paragraph (1) of this article has been brought, arbitral proceedings may nevertheless be commenced or continued, and an award may be made, while the issue is pending before the court.

TRAVAUX PRÉPARATOIRES

The *travaux préparatoires* on article 8 as adopted in 1985 are contained in the following documents:

1. Report of the United Nations Commission on International Trade Law on the work of its eighteenth session (*Official Records of the General Assembly, Fortieth Session, Supplement No. 17* (A/40/17)), paras. 11-333.

2. Reports of the Working Group: A/CN.9/216; A/CN.9/232; A/CN.9/233; A/CN.9/245; A/CN.9/246, annex; A/CN.9/263 and Add.1-2; A/CN.9/264. Relevant working papers are referred to in the reports.

3. Summary records of the 312th, 330th and 332nd UNCITRAL meetings.

Article 8 was not amended in 2006.

(Available on the Internet at www.uncitral.org).

INTRODUCTION

1. Similar in purpose and content to article II (3) of the 1958 New York Convention,[137] article 8 (1) relates to the so-called "negative" effect of the arbitration agreement, which prevents the parties from commencing court actions in relation to matters falling within the scope of the agreement. Article 8 (1) compels courts to refer an action to arbitration under certain conditions. A first condition, which is substantive in nature, requires that the subject-matter of the dispute fall within an arbitration agreement which is neither null and void, inoperative nor incapable of being performed. A second condition, which is procedural, requires that the referral to arbitration be sought no later than when the party requesting it submits its first statement on the substance of the dispute. Some cases further suggest that article 8 also requires that there exist a dispute between the parties (see below, section on article 8, para. 43). The referral of an action to arbitration entails that it cannot be further continued before domestic courts.[138]

2. Article 8 (2) allows arbitration proceedings to be commenced or continued even where an application to refer a case to arbitration ("referral application") is pending. The practical effect of this provision is to delegate to the arbitral tribunal, rather than the court, the decision as to whether the arbitration should proceed while a referral application is pending.

CASE LAW ON ARTICLE 8

Scope of application of article 8

3. Pursuant to article 1 (2) of the Model Law, the fact that the place of arbitration is located in a foreign jurisdiction has no bearing on the applicability of article 8.

[137] Article II (3) of the 1958 New York Convention reads as follows: "The court of a Contracting State, when seized of an action in a matter in respect of which the parties have made an agreement within the meaning of this article, shall, at the request of one of the parties, refer the parties to arbitration, unless it finds that the said agreement is null and void, inoperative or incapable of being performed."

[138] *Comtec Components Ltd. v. Interquip Ltd.*, High Court—Court of First Instance, Hong Kong Special Administrative Region of China, 3 December 1998, [1998] HKCFI 803, available on the Internet at http://www.hklii.hk/eng/hk/cases/hkcfi/1998/803.html.

Similarly, the law chosen by the parties to govern the contract in which the arbitration clause is inserted has no impact on the conditions under which a referral application will be granted.[139] Such conditions are therefore always governed by the law of the jurisdiction in which the court operates.

4. Article 8 states that it applies where a court is seized of an "action." If the court is not seized of an action, article 8 is not applicable and no referral order may be obtained.[140] Courts have occasionally held article 8 to be inapplicable in cases involving proceedings other than ordinary contractual or extra-contractual actions, and that therefore did not constitute "actions" within the meaning of that provision. For example, one court found that the existence of an arbitration agreement did not prevent it from ruling on a pre-action application seeking to obtain documents from a prospective defendant.[141] Furthermore, applications seeking the liquidation of a company have been found not to be "actions" for the purposes of article 8.[142] However, a court found that article 8 could operate in a case involving an application to set aside a default judgment on the merits of an action: as the underlying dispute fell within the scope of a valid arbitration agreement, the court held that article 8 required it to disregard a requirement, normally applicable under local law, that the applicant's defence has a real prospect of success.[143] Also, the German Federal Court of Justice held that article 8 was applicable not only to ordinary actions, but also to summary documents-only proceedings known as *Urkundenprozess*.[144] Finally, it is clear from article 9 that article 8 is inapplicable where the court is seized of applications seeking interim measures of protection (see below, section on article 9, para. 1).

5. One Canadian court has found that the concept of "action" referred to in article 8 includes an application for an order striking a notice of arbitration. The court was of the view that "the purpose of article 8 (1) [...] is to grant parties limited access to the courts to resolve jurisdictional disputes of a legal nature due to the court's expertise compared with that of the arbitrator, the desire to avoid multiple legal disputes over the jurisdiction of the arbitral tribunal, and the interest of finality." According to that decision, article 8 (1) may thus be used to seek a court ruling on the arbitral tribunal's jurisdiction.[145] However, other Canadian courts seized of very similar cases have concluded that article 8 (1) did not allow for such judicial intervention on jurisdictional issues, as this provision only comes into play when the court is seized of an action dealing with the merits of the dispute.[146]

The public policy favouring the enforcement of arbitration agreements

6. Courts have emphasized the importance, while applying the Model Law, of taking into consideration that party autonomy is one of its philosophical cornerstones. For example, several decisions, including one unanimous decision of the Supreme Court of Canada, have explicitly relied on the "very strong public policy" that the intention of parties who have agreed to resort to arbitration ought to be

---

[139] See for instance: *Francis Travel Marketing Pty. Limited v. Virgin Atlantic Airways Limited*, Supreme Court of New South Wales—Court of Appeal, Australia, 7 May 1996, [1996] NSWSC 104, available on the Internet at http://www.austlii.edu.au/au/cases/nsw/NSWSC/1996/104.html; CLOUT case No. 352 [*Nutrasweet Kelco Co. v. Royal-Sweet International Technologies Ltd. Partnership*, Court of Appeal for British Columbia, Canada, 23 February 1998], [1998] CanLII 5734 (BC CA), also available on the Internet at http://canlii.ca/t/1d73p.

[140] CLOUT case No. 386 [*ATM Compute GmbH v. DY 4 Systems, Inc.*, Ontario Court of Justice, Canada, 8 June 1995].

[141] *Timoney Technology Limited & Anor. v. ADI Limited*, Supreme Court of Victoria (Commercial and Equity Division), Australia, 17 October 2007, [2007] VSC 402, available on the Internet at http://www.austlii.edu.au/au/cases/vic/VSC/2007/402.html.

[142] *Liu Man Wai and Another v. Chevalier (Hong Kong) Ltd.*, High Court—Court of First Instance, Hong Kong Special Administrative Region of China, 29 January 2002, [2002] HKCFI 399, available on the Internet at http://www.hklii.hk/eng/hk/cases/hkcfi/2002/399.html; *Hoo Cheong Building Construction Co. Ltd. v. Jade Union Investment Ltd.*, High Court—Court of First Instance, Hong Kong Special Administrative Region of China, 5 March 2004, [2004] HKCFI 21, available on the Internet at http://www.hklii.hk/eng/hk/cases/hkcfi/2004/21.html; *Re Southern Materials Holding (H.K.) Co. Ltd.*, High Court—Court of First Instance, Hong Kong Special Administrative Region of China, 13 February 2008, [2008] HKCFI 98, available on the Internet at http://www.hklii.hk/eng/hk/cases/hkcfi/2008/98.html.

[143] *Dah Chong Hong (Engineering) Ltd. v. Boldwin Construction Co. Ltd.*, High Court—Court of First Instance, Hong Kong Special Administrative Region of China, 4 October 2002, [2002] HKCU 1180, available on the Internet at http://www.hklii.hk/eng/hk/cases/hkcfi/2002/242.html.

[144] Bundesgerichtshof, Germany, III ZR 214/05, 12 January 2006, available on the Internet at http://www.dis-arb.de/en/47/datenbanken/rspr/bgh-case-no-iii-zr-214-05-date-2006-01-12-id524; Bundesgerichtshof, Germany, III ZR 22/06, 31 May 2007, available on the Internet at http://www.dis-arb.de/en/47/datenbanken/rspr/bgh-case-no-iii-zr-22-06-date-2007-05-31-id668.

[145] CLOUT case No. 1044 [*Jean Estate v. Wires Jolley LLP*, Ontario Court of Appeal, Canada, 29 April 2009], [2009] ONCA 339 (CanLII), also available on the Internet at http://canlii.ca/t/23bpn.

[146] CLOUT case No. 1016 [*Dens Tech-Dens, k.g. v. Netdent-Technologies Inc.*, Court of Appeal of Quebec, Canada, 26 June 2008], [2008] QCCA 1245, also available on the Internet at http://canlii.ca/t/1z6lw; *El Nino Ventures Inc. v. GCP Group Ltd.*, Supreme Court of British Columbia, Canada, 24 December 2010, [2010] BCSC 1859, available on the Internet at http://canlii.ca/t/2f4bs.

fully given effect to.[147] Another line of cases has affirmed that "predictability in the enforcement of dispute resolution provisions is an indispensable precondition to any international business transaction and facilitates and encourages the pursuit of freer trade on an international scale."[148] The importance of the right to arbitrate has also been highlighted: one court has characterized it as a "fundamental right",[149] and it was stated by the German Federal Court of Justice to derive from the constitutional rights to personal freedom and private autonomy.[150] Further illustration of this pro-party autonomy approach can be found in Ugandan and Kenyan cases explicitly alluding to the courts' duty to actively encourage resort to arbitration and other means of extrajudicial dispute resolution.[151]

[147] *Burlington Northern Railroad Co. v. Canadian National Railway Co.*, Supreme Court, Canada, 21 January 1997, [1997] 1 SCR 5, 1997 CanLII 395 (SCC), available on the Internet at http://canlii.ca/t/1fr5f, adopting the dissenting judge's reasoning in *Burlington Northern Railroad Co. v. Canadian National Railway Co.*, Court of Appeal for British Columbia, Canada, 18 May 1995, [1995] CanLII 1802 (BC CA), available on the Internet at http://canlii.ca/t/1ddcq; see also, CLOUT case No. 619 [*Boart Sweden Ab and others v. NYA Strommes AB and others*, Ontario Supreme Court—High Court of Justice, Canada, 21 December 1988]; CLOUT case No. 74 [*Automatic Systems Inc. v. E.S. Fox Ltd. and Chrysler Canada Ltd.*, Ontario Court of Appeal, Canada, 25 April 1994], [1994] CanLII 1857 (ON CA), also available on the Internet at http://canlii.ca/t/6jzq; CLOUT case No. 116 [*BWV Investments Ltd. v. Saskferco Products Inc. et. al. and UHDE GmbH*, Saskatchewan Court of Appeal, Canada, 25 November 1994], [1994] CanLII 4557 (SK CA), also available on the Internet at http://canlii.ca/t/1nqlf; CLOUT case No. 179 [*The City of Prince George v. A.L. Sims & Sons Ltd.*, Court of Appeal for British Columbia, Canada, 4 July 1995], [1995] CanLII 2487 (BC CA), also available on the Internet at http://canlii.ca/t/1dd92; *Chung Siu Hong Celment and Others v. Primequine Corporation Ltd. And Others*, High Court—Court of First Instance, Hong Kong Special Administrative Region of China, 28 September 1999, [1999] HKCFI 1472, available on the Internet at http://www.hklii.hk/eng/hk/cases/hkcfi/1999/1472.html.

[148] CLOUT case No. 586 [*Kaverit Steel and Crane Ltd. v. Kone Corp.*, Alberta Court of Appeal, Canada, 16 January 1992], [1992] ABCA 7 (CanLII), also available on the Internet at http://canlii.ca/t/1p6kc; CLOUT case No. 74 [*Automatic Systems Inc. v. E.S. Fox Ltd. and Chrysler Canada Ltd.*, Ontario Court of Appeal, Canada, 25 April 1994], [1994] CanLII 1857 (ON CA), also available on the Internet at http://canlii.ca/t/6jzq; *Corporación Transnacional de Inversiones v. Stet International*, Ontario Court of Appeal, Canada, 15 September 2000, [2000] CanLII 16840 (ON CA), available on the internet at http://canlii.ca/t/1cvn9, confirming CLOUT case No. 391 [*Re Corporación Transnacional de Inversiones, S.A. de C.V. et al. v. STET International, S.p.A. et al.*, Ontario Superior Court of Justice, Canada, 22 September 1999], [1999] CanLII 14819 (ON SC), also available on the Internet at http://canlii.ca/t/1vvn5; *Canada (Attorney General) v. S.D. Myers Inc.*, Federal Court—Trial Division, Canada, 13 January 2004, [2004] 3 FCR 368, available on the Internet at http://canlii.ca/t/1g7jc; CLOUT case No. 1014 [*Bayview Irrigation District #11 v. United Mexican States*, Ontario Superior Court of Justice, Canada, 5 May 2008], [2008] CanLII 22120 (ON SC), also available on the Internet at http://canlii.ca/t/1wwtf; CLOUT case No. 116 [*BWV Investments Ltd. v. Saskferco Products Inc. et. al. and UHDE GmbH*, Saskatchewan Court of Appeal, Canada, 25 November 1994], [1994] CanLII 4557 (SK CA), also available on the Internet at http://canlii.ca/t/1nqlf; CLOUT case No. 119 [*ABN Amro Bank Canada v. Krupp Mak Maschinenbau GmbH*, Ontario Court of Justice—General Division, Canada, 23 December 1994], also in [1994] CanLII 7355 (ON SC), also available on the Internet at also available on the Internet at http://canlii.ca/t/1vtn8.; CLOUT case No. 501 [*Grow Biz International, Inc. v. D.L.T. Holdings Inc.,* Prince Edward Island Supreme Court—Trial Division, Canada, 23 March 2001], [2001] PESCTD 27, also available on the Internet at http://canlii.ca/t/4tjr; *Cangene Corp. v. Octapharma AG*, Court of Queen's Bench of Manitoba, Canada, 30 June 2000, [2000] MBQB 111 (CanLII), available on the Internet at http://canlii.ca/t/4vtk; *Ace Bermuda Insurance Ltd. v. Allianz Insurance Company of Canada*, Court of Queen's Bench of Alberta, Canada, 21 December 2005, [2005] ABQB 975 (CanLII), available on the Internet at http://canlii.ca/t/1m8vm; CLOUT case No. 1049 [*Louis Dreyfus S.A.S. v. Holding Tusculum B.V.*, Superior Court of Quebec, Canada, 8 December 2008], [2008] QCCS 5903 (CanLII), also available on the Internet at http://canlii.ca/t/21v03; CLOUT case No. 70 [*Nanisivik Mines Ltd. and Zinc Corporation of America v. Canarctic Shipping Co. Ltd.,* Federal Court—Court of Appeal, Canada, 10 February 1994], [1994] 2 FC 662, also available on the Internet at http://canlii.ca/t/4nkm; *GPEC International Ltd. v. Canada (Canadian Commercial Corporation)*, Federal Court—Trial Division, Canada, 2 April 2008, [2008] FC 414 (CanLII) available on the Internet at http://canlii.ca/t/1wgpt; *Comandate Marine Corp. v. Pan Australia Shipping Pty. Ltd.*, Federal Court, Australia, 20 December 2006, [2006] FCAFC 192 at paras. 191ff, available on the Internet at http://www.austlii.edu.au/au/cases/cth/FCAFC/2006/192.html; High Court—Court of First Instance, Hong Kong Special Administrative Region of China, *Chung Siu Hong Celment and Others v. Primequine Corporation Ltd. And Others*, 28 September 1999, [1999] HKCFI 1472, available on the Internet at http://www.hklii.hk/eng/hk/cases/hkcfi/1999/1472.html.

[149] *Laurentienne-vie, Cie d'assurances Inc. v. Empire, Cie d'assurance-vie*, Court of Appeal of Quebec, Canada, 12 June 2000, [2000] CanLII 9001 (QC CA), available on the Internet at http://canlii.ca/t/1f8mt.

[150] CLOUT case No. 406 [Bundesgerichtshof, Germany, II ZR 373/98, 3 April 2000], also available on the Internet at http://www.dis-arb.de/en/47/datenbanken/rspr/bgh-case-no-ii-zr-373-98-date-2000-04-03-id6.

[151] *East African Development Bank v. Ziwa Horticultural Exporters Limited*, High Court at Kampala, Uganda, 20 October 2000, [2000] UGCommC 8; *Alfred Wekesa Sambu & 4 others v. Mohammed Hatimy & 12 others,* High Court at Nairobi, Kenya, 16 May 2007, Civil Suit 1281 of 2006; *Livingstone Kamadi Obuga v. Uhuru Kenyatta & 3 others*, High Court at Nairobi (Nairobi Law Courts), Kenya, 18 December 2006, Civil Suit 1159 of 2006.

Courts may not refer an action to arbitration on their own motion

7. Article 8 only mentions cases where referral to arbitration is requested by a party to the action. It does not explicitly state whether a court can refer an action to arbitration on its own motion. However, it is clear from the *travaux préparatoires* that article 8 implicitly prevents a court from doing so,[152] and courts have confirmed that they may only refer an action to arbitration if a request to that effect has been made by a party.[153]

Mandatory nature of referral to arbitration where the conditions set out in article 8 are met

8. Parties resisting referral applications sometimes contend that courts enjoy a residual discretionary power allowing them to dismiss such applications despite that the conditions set out in article 8 have been met. Typically, such parties will argue that proceeding to arbitration would—in the circumstances of the case—prove inefficient, inconvenient, too expensive or unfair. However, most cases addressing this question have found article 8 to be

---

[152] A/CN.9/264, Analytical commentary on draft text of a model law on international commercial arbitration, under article 8, para. 3 available on the UNCITRAL website at http://www.uncitral.org/uncitral/en/commission/sessions/18th.html.

[153] CLOUT case No. 1072 [High Commercial Court, Croatia, 29 April 2001], VTS RH, Pž-5168/01; CLOUT case No. 1071 [*Hrvatsko Mirovinsko Osiguranje d.o.o. v. EDIS d.o.o.*, High Commercial Court, Croatia, 17 April 2007], XLVII Pž-6756/04-3; *D. Andrés v. Díez Carrillo S.L.*, Audiencia Provincial de Palma de Mallorca (sección 5ª), Spain, 5 October 2006, rec. apel. 399/2006; *Kolinker Industrial Equipment Ltd. v. Longhill Industries Ltd. & Another*, District Court, Hong Kong Special Administrative Region of China, 3 June 2004, [2004] HKDC 65, available on the Internet at http://www.hklii.hk/eng/hk/cases/hkdc/2004/65.html; CLOUT case No. 508 [*United Laboratories, Inc. v. Abraham*, Ontario Superior Court of Justice, Canada, 8 October 2002], [2002] CanLII 17847 (ON SC), also available on the Internet at http://canlii.ca/t/1cl2h.

mandatory, meaning that where the conditions set out therein are met, courts have no other option than to refer the action to arbitration. A leading example is a Supreme Court of Canada decision[154] which followed a series of Canadian decisions to the same effect.[155] Several decisions rendered in other Model Law jurisdictions also stand for the proposition that article 8 is mandatory.[156]

9. Cases which hold otherwise are far less usual. Examples include two Canadian decisions which predate the Supreme Court of Canada decision referred to in paragraph 8 above,[157] as well as a Kenyan decision stating that courts enjoy a discretionary power to rule on the merits of an action even where the conditions set out in article 8 are met.[158]

The substantive condition: an action falling within an arbitration agreement that is neither null and void, inoperative nor incapable of being performed

The object of the courts' enquiry

10. The object of the substantive enquiry to be performed by the court under article 8 is twofold: a court must be satisfied that the arbitration agreement is, firstly, neither null and void, inoperative nor incapable of being performed and, secondly, applicable to the dispute to which the action relates. As article 8 merely seeks to delineate the grounds upon which referral to arbitration may be denied, it does

---

[154] *GreCon Dimter Inc. v. J. R. Normand Inc.*, Supreme Court, Canada, 22 July 2005, [2005] SCC 46 (CanLII), available on the Internet at http://canlii.ca/t/1l6wn.

[155] CLOUT case No. 586 [*Kaverit Steel and Crane Ltd. v. Kone Corp.*, Alberta Court of Appeal, Canada, 16 January 1992], [1992] ABCA 7 (CanLII), also available on the Internet at http://canlii.ca/t/1p6kc; CLOUT case No. 31 [*Gulf Canada Resources Ltd. v. Arochem International Ltd.*, Court of Appeal for British Columbia, Canada, 10 March 1992], [1992] CanLII 4033 (BC CA), also available on the Internet at http://canlii.ca/t/1q096; CLOUT case No. 112 [*Kvaerner Enviropower Inc. v. Tanar Industries Ltd.*, Court of Queen's Bench of Alberta, Canada, 13 July 1994], [1994] CanLII 9242 (AB QB), also available on the Internet at http://canlii.ca/t/2brch, confirmed in *Tanar Industries Ltd. v. Kvaerner Enviropower Inc.*, Alberta Court of Appeal, Canada, 25 October 1994, [1994] ABCA 346 (CanLII), available on the Internet at http://canlii.ca/t/2dbkn; CLOUT case No. 74 [*Automatic Systems Inc. v. E.S. Fox Ltd. and Chrysler Canada Ltd.*, Ontario Court of Appeal, Canada, 25 April 1994], [1994] CanLII 1857 (ON CA), also available on the Internet at http://canlii.ca/t/6jzq; CLOUT case No. 381 [*Fibreco Pulp Inc. v. Star Shipping A/S*, Federal Court—Court of Appeal, Canada, 24 May 2000], [2000] CanLII 15323 (FCA), also available on the Internet at http://canlii.ca/t/4l31. Other cases: CLOUT case No. 70 [*Nanisivik Mines Ltd. and Zinc Corporation of America v. Canarctic Shipping Co. Ltd.*, Federal Court—Court of Appeal, Canada, 10 February 1994], [1994] 2 FC 662, also available on the Internet at http://canlii.ca/t/4nkm; CLOUT case No. 1015 [*Sport Hawk USA Inc. v. New York Islanders Hockey Club*, Ontario Superior Court of Justice, Canada, 5 May 2008], [2008] CanLII 20338 (ON SC), also available on the Internet at http://canlii.ca/t/1wsr8; CLOUT case No. 619 [*Boart Sweden AB and others v. NYA Strommes AB and others*, Ontario Supreme Court—High Court of Justice, Canada, 21 December 1988]; CLOUT case No. 9 [*Coopers and Lybrand Limited (Trustee) for BC Navigation S.A. (Bankrupt),* Federal Court—Trial Divison, Canada, 2 November 1987]; *Dongnam Oil & Fats Co. v. Chemex Ltd.*, Federal Court—Trial Division, Canada, 10 December 2004, [2004] FC 1732 (CanLII), available on the Internet at http://canlii.ca/t/1jh5v; *Arbella S.A. v. Aghia Markella (The)*, Federal Court—Trial Division, Canada, 28 April 1995, [1995] FCJ No. 723; *Cangene Corp. v. Octapharma AG*, Court of Queen's Bench of Manitoba, Canada, 30 June 2000, [2000] MBQB 111 (CanLII), available on the Internet at http://canlii.ca/t/4vtk; CLOUT case No. 34 [*Miramichi Pulp and Paper Inc. v. Canadian Pacific Bulk Ship Services Ltd.*, Federal Court—Trial Division, Canada, 9 October 1992].

[156] *Rondabosh International Ltd. v. China Ping an Insurance (Hong Kong) Co. Ltd.*, High Court—Court of First Instance, Hong Kong Special Administrative Region of China, 29 December 2009, [2009] HKCFI 1198, available on the Internet at http://www.hklii.hk/eng/hk/cases/hkcfi/2009/1198.html, at para. 5; *Ocean Park Corporation v. Proud Sky Co. Ltd.*, High Court—Court of First Instance, Hong Kong Special Administrative Region of China, 28 November 2007, [2007] HKCFI 1221, available on the Internet at http://www.hklii.hk/eng/hk/cases/hkcfi/2007/1221.html; *Good Year Professional Service Co. v. Penta-Ocean Construction Co. Ltd.*, High Court—Court of First Instance, Hong Kong Special Administrative Region of China, 5 November 2002, [2002] HKCFI 786, available on the Internet at http://www.hklii.hk/eng/hk/cases/hkcfi/2002/786.html; CLOUT case No. 521 [*F & D Building Services Engineering Co. Ltd. v. Chevalier (E & M Contracting),* High Court—Court of First Instance, Hong Kong Special Administrative Region of China, 23 February 2001], [2001] 3 HKCFI 824, also available on the Internet at http://www.hklii.hk/eng/hk/cases/hkcfi/2001/824.html; CLOUT case No. 604 [*Glencore International A.G. v. Bright China International Ltd. & Others*, High Court—Court of First Instance, Hong Kong, 24 April 1998], [1998] HKCFI 878, also available on the Internet at http://www.hklii.hk/eng/hk/cases/hkcfi/1998/878.html; *Orienmet Minerals Co. Ltd. v. Winner Desire Ltd.*, High Court—Court of First Instance, Hong Kong, 7 April 1997, [1997] HKCFI 299, available on the Internet at http://www.hklii.hk/eng/hk/cases/hkcfi/1997/299.html; CLOUT case No. 688 [*China National Electronic Import & Export Shenzhen Company v. Choi Chuk Ming (trading as ERWO Enterprises Company)*, High Court—Court of First Instance, Hong Kong, 9 March 1993], [1993] HKCFI 100, also available on the Internet at http://www.hklii.hk/eng/hk/cases/hkcfi/1993/100.html; *Mugoya Construction & Engineering Ltd. v. National Social Security Fund Board of Trustees & another*, High Court, Nairobi (Commercial Division Milimani Courts), Kenya, 27 July 2005, Civil Suit 59 of 2005, available on the Internet at http://kenyalaw.org; CLOUT case No. 128 [*Tai Hing Cotton Mill Limited v. Glencore Grain Rotterdam B. V. and another*, Court of Appeal, Hong Kong, 24 November 1995], [1995] HKCA 626, also available on the Internet at http://www.hklii.hk/eng/hk/cases/hkca/1995/626.html, CLOUT case No. 44 [*William Company v. Chu Kong Agency Co. Ltd. and Guangzhou Ocean Shipping Company*, High Court—Court of First Instance, Hong Kong, 17 February 1993], [1993] HKCFI 215, also available on the Internet at http://www.hklii.hk/eng/hk/cases/hkcfi/1993/215.html; *Pathak v. Tourism Transport Ltd.*, High Court, Auckland, New Zealand, 20 August 2002, [2002] 3 NZLR 681.

[157] *Zeldin v. Goldis*, Ontario Superior Court of Justice, Canada, 9 August 2000, [2000] O.J. No. 3001; *Simmonds Capital Limited v. Eurocom International Limited*, Federal Court –Trial Division, Canada, 15 January 1998, [1998] CanLII 7229 (FC), available on the Internet at http://canlii.ca/t/4cvg.

[158] *Governors Balloon Safaris Ltd. v. Skyship Company Ltd. County Council of Trans Mara,* High Court at Nairobi (Milimani Commercial Courts), Kenya, 11 September 2008, Civil Case 461 of 2008, available on the Internet at http://kenyalaw.org.

not purport to create material rules governing the validity, operativeness, performability and interpretation of arbitration agreements. Such material rules are not found in the rest of the Model Law either: only the definition of an arbitration agreement (article 7 (1)), the writing requirement (article 7 (2)) and the separability of the arbitration clause (article 16 (1)) are addressed in the Model Law. Unlike articles 34 and 36,[159] article 8 does not indicate under which law questions of validity, operativeness, performability and interpretation of the arbitration agreement are to be assessed.

(i) An arbitration agreement that is neither null and void, inoperative nor incapable of being performed

11. The cases illustrate the variety of circumstances under which the arbitration agreement invoked by the party seeking a referral order may be found to be non-existent, null and void, inoperative or incapable of being performed.

(1) No consent or no valid consent to the alleged arbitration agreement

12. Referral to arbitration may be denied on the ground that the respondent to the referral application never undertook, or never validly undertook, to resort to arbitration as alleged by the party seeking a referral order. The issue has arisen in a number of different scenarios.

13. At times the problem relates to whether, as a matter of fact, the respondent to the referral application ever consented to the alleged arbitration agreement. In some cases the respondent simply denies having expressed the intention to enter into any arbitration agreement.[160] In other cases the respondent does not deny having undertaken to resort to arbitration, but contends that it did so with parties other than the party seeking a referral order, who is thus alleged not to be a party to the arbitration agreement it invoked.[161] Other times the issue rather relates to whether, as a matter of law, the consent to the arbitration agreement expressed by the respondent was valid and effective, such as where consent is said to have been vitiated by deceit or fraud.[162] The issue of consent arises differently in a third group of cases concerning allegedly unclear or pathological dispute resolution clauses. Here, the problem relates not to the existence or validity of the respondent's consent to contractual terms, but rather to whether those terms express an intention to resort to final and binding arbitration.[163]

[159] See articles 34(2)*(a)*(i), 34(2)*(b)*(i), 36(1)*(a)*(i) and 36(1)*(b)*(i).

[160] *Mariana Maritime S.A. v. Stella Jones Inc.*, Federal Court—Court of Appeal, Canada, 24 May 2002, [2002] FCA 215 (CanLII), available on the Internet at http://canlii.ca/t/4j2c; CLOUT case No. 1011 [*H & H Marine Engine Service Ltd. v. Volvo Penta of the Americas Inc.*, Supreme Court of British Columbia, Canada, 9 October 2009], [2009] BCSC 1389, also available on the Internet at http://canlii.ca/t/262c8; *Achilles (USA) v. Plastics Dura Plastics (1977) ltée/Ltd.*, Court of Appeal of Quebec, Canada, 23 November 2006, [2006] QCCA 1523, available on the Internet at http://canlii.ca/t/1qf7d; *Newmark Capital Corporation Ltd. and Others v. Coffee Partners Ltd. and Another*, High Court—Court of First Instance, Hong Kong Special Administrative Region of China, 8 February 2007, [2007] HKCFI 113, available on the Internet at http://www.hklii.hk/eng/hk/cases/hkcfi/2007/113.html; *Pacific Crown Engineering Ltd. v. Hyundai Engineering & Construction Co. Ltd.*, High Court—Court of First Instance, Hong Kong Special Administrative Region of China, 23 April 2003, [2003] HKCFI 924, available on the Internet at http://www.hklii.hk/eng/hk/cases/hkcfi/2003/924.html; *Cathay Pacific Airways Ltd. v. Hong Kong Air Cargo Terminals Ltd.*, High Court—Court of First Instance, Hong Kong Special Administrative Region of China, 7 March 2002, [2002] HKCFI 9, available on the Internet at http://www.hklii.hk/eng/hk/cases/hkcfi/2002/9.html; *Seca Africa Ltd. v. Kirloskar Kenya Ltd. & 3 others,* High Court at Nairobi, Kenya, 28 January 2005, Civil Suit 307 of 1999, available on the Internet at http://kenyalaw.org; *Shell Hong Kong Ltd. v. Esa Consulting Engineers Ltd. and Another*, High Court—Court of First Instance, Hong Kong Special Administrative Region of China, 25 November 1998, [1998] HKCFI 1003, available on the Internet at http://www.hklii.hk/eng/hk/cases/hkcfi/1998/1003.html; CLOUT case No. 586 [*Kaverit Steel and Crane Ltd. v. Kone Corp.*, Alberta Court of Appeal, Canada, 16 January 1992], [1992] ABCA 7 (CanLII), also available on the Internet at http://canlii.ca/t/1p6kc; *APC Logistics Pty. Ltd. v. C.J. Nutracon Pty. Ltd.*, Federal Court, Australia, 16 February 2007, [2007] FCA 136, available on the Internet at http://www.austlii.edu.au/au/cases/cth/federal_ct/2007/136.html; CLOUT case No. 671 [*Landale Development Limited v. Zhum Heng Development Limited,* District Court, Hong Kong, 12 January 1990], [1990] HKDC 1, also available on the Internet at http://www.hklii.hk/eng/hk/cases/hkdc/1990/1.html; *Ocean Park Corporation v. Proud Sky Co. Ltd.*, High Court—Court of First Instance, Hong Kong Special Administrative Region of China, 28 November 2007, [2007] HKCFI 1221, available on the Internet at http://www.hklii.hk/eng/hk/cases/hkcfi/2007/1221.html.

[161] *Eastern and Southern African Trade & Anor. v. Hassan Basajjabalaba & Anor.*, High Court at Kampala, Uganda, 13 April 2007, [2007] UGCommC 30; *Mehta Electrical Limited & 4 others v. N. K. Brothers Limited & another*, High Court, Nairobi (Milimani Commercial Division), Kenya, 16 August 2005, Civil Suit 37 of 2005, available on the Internet at http://kenyalaw.org/.

[162] CLOUT case No. 504 [*D.G. Jewelry Inc. et al. v. Cyberdiam Canada Ltd. et al.*, Ontario Superior Court of Justice, Canada, 17 April 2002].

[163] Bundesgerichtshof, Germany, VII ZR 105/06, 25 January 2007, available on the Internet at http://www.dis-arb.de/en/47/datenbanken/rspr/bgh-case-no-vii-zr-105-06-date-2007-01-25-id653; *Pccw Global Ltd. v. Interactive Communications Service Ltd.*, High Court—Court of Appeal, Hong Kong Special Administrative Region of China, 16 November 2006, [2006] HKCA 434, available on the Internet at http://www.hklii.hk/eng/hk/cases/hkca/2006/434.html; *Tai-Ao Aluminium (Taishan) Co. Ltd. v. Maze Aluminium Engineering Co. Ltd. & Another*, High Court—Court of First Instance, Hong Kong Special Administrative Region of China, 17 February 2006, [2006] HKCFI 220, available on the Internet at http://www.hklii.hk/eng/hk/cases/hkcfi/2006/220.html; *Tommy C.P. Sze. & Co. v. Li & Fung (trading) Ltd. & Others,* High Court—Court of First Instance, Hong Kong Special Administrative Region of China, 28 October 2002, [2002] HKCFI 682, available on the Internet at http://www.hklii.hk/eng/hk/cases/hkcfi/2002/682.html; *Arta Properties Limited v. Li Fu Yat Tso et al.*, High Court—Court of First Instance, Hong Kong, 2 June 1998, [1998] HKCU 721; CLOUT case No. 44 [*William Company v. Chu Kong Agency Co. Ltd. and Guangzhou Ocean Shipping Company*, High Court—Court of First Instance, Hong Kong, 17 February 1993], [1993] HKCFI 215, also available on the Internet at http://www.hklii.hk/eng/hk/cases/hkcfi/1993/215.html.

(2) Arbitration agreement not validly transferred to the party making the referral application or to the party responding thereto

14. Another relatively common scenario involves situations where a party to the action was originally not a party to the arbitration agreement but is alleged to have later become a party thereto through assignment, subrogation or a similar occurrence. Several cases confirm that a referral application may be resisted on the ground that the obligation to arbitrate arising out of the original agreement has not transferred to the respondent to the referral application,[164] or that the party seeking a referral order has not acquired the right to compel the respondent to resort to arbitration.[165]

(3) Formal requirements not met

15. Courts seized of referral applications have also allowed the validity of the alleged arbitration agreement to be challenged on the ground that, even though from a factual standpoint there may have been a meeting of the minds between the parties, applicable formal requirements were not met. For example, in several cases courts have considered a contention that a reference to external contractual terms could only validly incorporate an arbitration clause contained therein if the reference was explicitly mentioned in the arbitration clause.[166] In other cases, the debate focused on whether the writing requirement set out in article 7 (2) had been met (see above, section on article 7, paras. 13-22).[167]

(4) Condition precedent to the arbitration agreement taking effect not fulfilled

16. Several cases stand for the proposition that the substantive requirement set out in article 8 will not be met if the parties' undertaking to arbitrate is subject to a condition that has not been fulfilled. For example, in one case the court considered an argument asserting that the arbitration agreement would only become binding after the setting up of an arbitral tribunal by the applicant football association, which had not yet occurred.[168] In another case the court considered an objection asserting that, since a condition to the entry into force of a licence agreement had not yet been fulfilled, the arbitration clause contained therein had no effect.[169]

[164] Bundesgerichtshof, Germany, VII ZR 105/06, 25 January 2007, available on the Internet at http://www.dis-arb.de/en/47/datenbanken/rspr/bgh-case-no-vii-zr-105-06-date-2007-01-25-id653; CLOUT case No. 561 [Bundesgerichtshof, Germany, XII ZR 42/98, 3 May 2000], also available on the Internet at http://www.dis-arb.de/en/47/datenbanken/rspr/bgh-case-no-xii-zr-42-98-date-2000-05-03-id5; CLOUT case No. 1046 [*PS Here, L.L.C. v. Fortalis Anstalt*, Court of Appeal of Quebec, Canada, 19 March 2009], [2009] QCCA 538, also available on the Internet at http://canlii.ca/t/22ts1; *EDF (Services) Limited v. Appleton & Associates*, Ontario Superior Court of Justice, Canada, 4 September 2007, [2007] CanLII 36078 (ON SC), available on the Internet at http://canlii.ca/t/1sr48; *ABN Amro Bank Canada v. Krupp MaK Maschinenbau GmbH,* Ontario Court of Justice—General Division, Canada, 7 June 1995, [1995] CanLII 7081 (ON SC), available on the Internet at http://canlii.ca/t/1vt6l; *The Incorporated Owners of Sincere House v. Sincere Co. Ltd.*, Lands Tribunal, Hong Kong Special Administrative Region of China, 18 May 2005, [2005] HKLT 30, available on the Internet at http://www.hklii.hk/eng/hk/cases/hklt/2005/30.html.

[165] *Pacific Erosion v. Western Quality Seeds*, Supreme Court of British Columbia, Canada, 9 September 2003, [2003] BCSC 1743 (CanLII), available on the Internet at http://canlii.ca/t/1rs.

[166] CLOUT case No. 34 [*Miramichi Pulp and Paper Inc. v. Canadian Pacific Bulk Ship Services Ltd.*, Federal Court—Trial Division, Canada, 9 October 1992]; *Thyssen Canada Ltd. v. Mariana (The)*, Federal Court—Court of Appeal, Canada, 22 March 2000, [2000] CanLII 17113 (FCA), [2000] 3 FC 398, available on the Internet at http://canlii.ca/t/4l97; *Dongnam Oil & Fats Co. v. Chemex Ltd.*, Federal Court—Trial Division, Canada, 10 December 2004, [2004] FC 1732 (CanLII), available on the Internet at http://canlii.ca/t/1jh5v; *9110-9595 Québec inc. v. Bergeron*, Court of Appeal of Quebec, Canada, 12 October 2007, [2007] QCCA 1393, available on the Internet at http://canlii.ca/t/1tb5l.

[167] CLOUT case No. 44 [*William Company v. Chu Kong Agency Co. Ltd. and Guangzhou Ocean Shipping Company*, High Court—Court of First Instance, Hong Kong, 17 February 1993], [1993] HKCFI 215, also available on the Internet at http://www.hklii.hk/eng/hk/cases/hkcfi/1993/215.html; CLOUT case No. 688 [*China National Electronic Import & Export Shenzhen Company v. Choi Chuk Ming (trading as ERWO Enterprises Company)*, High Court—Court of First Instance, Hong Kong, 9 March 1993], [1993] HKCFI 100, also available on the Internet at http://www.hklii.hk/eng/hk/cases/hkcfi/1993/100.html; *P.T. Wearwel International v. Vf Asia Ltd.*, High Court—Court of First Instance, Hong Kong, 19 August 1994, [1994] 3 HKC 344; *Ferguson Bros. of St. Thomas v. Manyan Inc.*, Ontario Superior Court of Justice, Canada, 27 May 1999, also in [1999] OJ No. 1887; CLOUT case No. 78 [*Astel-Peiniger Joint Venture v. Argos Engineering & Heavy Industries Co. Ltd.*, High Court—Court of First Instance, Hong Kong, 18 August 1994], [1994] HKCFI 276, also available on the Internet at http://www.hklii.hk/eng/hk/cases/hkcfi/1994/276.html; *Achilles (USA) v. Plastics Dura Plastics (1977) ltée/Ltd.*, Court of Appeal of Quebec, Canada, 23 November 2006, [2006] QCCA 1523, available on the Internet at http://canlii.ca/t/1qf7d; *ABN Amro Bank Canada v. Krupp MaK Maschinenbau GmbH,* Ontario Court of Justice—General Division, Canada, 7 June 1995, [1995] CanLII 7081 (ON SC) available on the Internet at http://canlii.ca/t/1vt6l; *APC Logistics Pty. Ltd. v. C.J. Nutracon Pty. Ltd.*, Federal Court, Australia, 16 February 2007, [2007] FCA 136, available on the Internet at http://www.austlii.edu.au/au/cases/cth/federal_ct/2007/136.html.

[168] *Wong King Chuen and Another v. The Hong Kong Football Association Ltd.*, High Court—Court of First Instance, Hong Kong Special Administrative Region of China, 15 August 2007, [2007] HKCFI 854, available on the Internet at http://www.hklii.hk/eng/hk/cases/hkcfi/2007/854.html.

[169] *Cecrop Co. v. Kinetic Sciences Inc.*, Supreme Court of British Columbia, Canada, 9 April 2001, [2001] BCSC 532 (CanLII), available on the Internet at http://canlii.ca/t/4xl1; see also: CLOUT case No. 19 [*Krutov. v. Vancouver Hockey Club Limited*, Supreme Court of British Columbia, Canada, 22 November 1991], [1991] CanLII 2077 (BC SC), also available on the Internet at http://canlii.ca/t/1cr44; *Thorn Security (Hong Kong) Ltd. v. Cheung Kee Fung Cheung Construction Co. Ltd.*, High Court—Court of Appeal, Hong Kong Special Administrative Region of China, 30 July 2004, [2004] HKCA 217, available on the Internet at: http://www.hklii.hk/eng/hk/cases/hkca/2004/217.html.

17. A related question is whether failure to proceed to mediation or another non-adjudicative process as required under a multi-step dispute resolution agreement can affect the binding nature of an arbitration clause and render it inoperative or incapable of being performed. A Ugandan decision found that it did not,[170] as had a previous decision rendered by a court in Hong Kong.[171]

(5) Arbitration agreement no longer in effect

18. Clearly, and as numerous cases illustrate, the respondent to the referral application may object on the ground that a once-existing arbitration agreement has ceased to be binding on grounds of termination, rescission, abandonment, repudiation, waiver and the like.[172] An illustration can be found in a decision of the Hong Kong Court of Final Appeal, finding that the arbitration clause inserted in an employment contract had been superseded by a subsequently-concluded employment contract containing no arbitration clause.[173]

(6) Arbitration agreement invalid because the dispute is not arbitrable

19. A number of cases further confirm that courts will refuse to refer a dispute to arbitration, when the dispute is inarbitrable pursuant to mandatory, public policy-based rules which prohibit enforcement of arbitration agreements

---

[170] *Fulgensius Mungereza v. Africa Central,* Supreme Court at Mengo, Uganda, 16 January 2004, [2004] UGSC 9.

[171] *Westco Airconditioning Ltd. v. Sui Chong Construction & Engineering Co. Ltd.*, High Court—Court of First Instance, Hong Kong, Hong Kong, 3 February 1998, [1998] HKCFI 946, available on the Internet at http://www.hklii.hk/eng/hk/cases/hkcfi/1998/946.html.

[172] See for instance: CLOUT case No. 382 [*Methanex New Zealand Ltd. v. Fontaine Navigation S.A., Tokyo Marine Co. Ltd., The Owners and all Others*, Federal Court—Trial Division, Canada, 9 January 1998], [1998] 2 FC 583 at paras 22 ff., also available on the Internet at http://canlii.ca/t/4cn6; CLOUT case No. 1042 [*Bombardier Transportation v. SMC Pneumatics (UK) Ltd.*, Court of Appeal of Quebec, Canada, 4 May 2009], [2009] QCCA 861, also available on the Internet at http://canlii.ca/t/23fzp; CLOUT case No. 512 [*Instrumenttitehdas Kytola Oy v. Esko Industries Ltd.*, Court of Appeal for British Columbia, Canada, 15 January 2004], [2004] BCCA 25 (CanLII), also available on the Internet at http://canlii.ca/t/1g9sw; CLOUT case No. 65 [*ODC Exhibit Systems Ltd. v. Lee, Expand International et al.*, Supreme Court of British Columbia, Canada, 28 November 1988], 1988 CanLII 3297 (BC SC), also available on the Internet at http://canlii.ca/t/22ksn; *Cecrop Co. v. Kinetic Sciences Inc.*, Supreme Court of British Columbia, Canada, 9 April 2001, [2001] BCSC 532 (CanLII), available on the Internet at http://canlii.ca/t/4xl1; *Comandate Marine Corp. v. Pan Australia Shipping Pty. Ltd.*, Federal Court, Australia, 20 December 2006, [2006] FCAFC 192, available on the Internet at http://www.austlii.edu.au/au/cases/cth/FCAFC/2006/192.html; *Aggressive Construction Company Limited v. Data-Form Engineering Limited*, High Court—Court of First Instance, Hong Kong Special Administrative Region of China, 13 October 2009, [2009] HKCU 1533, available on the Internet at http://www.hklii.hk/eng/hk/cases/hkcfi/2009/952.html; CLOUT case No. 522 [*Paladin Agricultural Ltd. & Others v. Excelsior Hotel (Hong Kong) Ltd.*, High Court—Court of First Instance, Hong Kong Special Administrative Region of China, 6 March 2001], [2001] HKCFI 1271, also available on the Internet at http://www.hklii.hk/eng/hk/cases/hkcfi/2001/1271.html; *P & O Nedlloyd Limited v. Wah Hing Seafreight (China) Co. Ltd.*, High Court—Court of First Instance, Hong Kong Special Administrative Region of China, 25 November 1999, [1999] HKCU 1412, available on the Internet at http://www.hklii.hk/eng/hk/cases/hkcfi/1999/90.html; *Comtec Components Ltd. v. Interquip Ltd.*, High Court—Court of First Instance, Hong Kong Special Administrative Region of China, 3 December 1998, [1998] HKCFI 803, available on the Internet at http://www.hklii.hk/eng/hk/cases/hkcfi/1998/803.html; CLOUT case No. 706 [*Fustar Chemicals Ltd. v. Sinochem Liaoning Hong Kong Ltd.*, High Court—Court of First Instance, Hong Kong, 5 June 1996], [1996] 2 HKC 407; *Tommy C.P. Sze. & Co. v. Li & Fung (trading) Ltd. & Others,* High Court—Court of First Instance, Hong Kong Special Administrative Region of China, *28 October 2002, [2002] HKCFI 682*, available on the Internet at http://www.hklii.hk/eng/hk/cases/hkcfi/2002/682.html.

[173] *Paquito Lima Buton v. Rainbow Joy Shipping Ltd. Inc.*, Court of Final Appeal, Hong Kong Special Administrative Region of China, 28 April 2008, [2008] HKCFA 30, available on the Internet at http://www.hklii.hk/eng/hk/cases/hkcfa/2008/30.html.

in certain areas. Issues of arbitrability have arisen, in the context of referral applications, in cases involving consumer contracts,[174] competition,[175] corporate affairs,[176] construction liens,[177] fraud,[178] work-related injuries[179] and tortious liability.[180]

(7) Arbitration agreement invalid because it is abusive or unconscionable

20. Another situation where the arbitration agreement will be deemed "null and void, inoperative or incapable of being performed" is where it is shown to be so unfair or one-sided as to be non-binding under the rules of contract applicable to the case. Illustrations can be found in cases involving arbitration clauses inserted in consumer contracts: courts seized of applications based on article 8 have considered challenges to the arbitration clause relying on contract law-based defences to the enforceability of clauses that are unconscionable, abusive or unfair.[181]

(8) Arbitration agreement invalid because of the invalidity of non-severable provisions thereof

21. An arbitration agreement will also be null and void, inoperative or incapable of being performed if non-severable provisions thereof are found to be invalid. In one case, a court dismissed a referral application on the ground that the provisions of the arbitration agreement relating to the constitution of the arbitral tribunal were contrary to public policy and therefore null.[182] In another case, the court refused to refer the action to arbitration on the ground that the provisions designating the applicable arbitration rules did not comply with mandatory provisions relating to the validity of external clauses contained in standard form contracts (adhesion contracts).[183]

(9) Arbitration agreement designating an arbitral institution or appointing authority that is either non-existing or uncooperative

22. The Model Law affords parties extensive freedom with respect to the conduct of the arbitral procedure (article 19), a freedom that entails that they may choose to arbitrate under the aegis of an arbitral institution. Similarly, the Model Law emphasises party autonomy in the constitution of the arbitral tribunal (article 11 (2)), and explicitly provides for the possibility of delegating to an institution the power to appoint arbitrators (article 2 *(d)*). Difficulties often arise in practice when the arbitration agreement's provisions designating an institution or an appointing authority

[174] *Dell Computer Corp. v. Union des Consommateurs,* Supreme Court, Canada, 13 July 2007, [2007] SCC 34, [2007] 2 SCR 801, available on the Internet at http://canlii.ca/t/1s2f2.

[175] *Comandate Marine Corp. v. Pan Australia Shipping Pty. Ltd.*, Federal Court, Australia, 20 December 2006, [2006] FCAFC 192, available on the Internet at http://www.austlii.edu.au/au/cases/cth/FCAFC/2006/192.html.

[176] *Canada (Attorney General) v. Reliance Insurance Company*, Ontario Superior Court of Justice, Canada, 5 October 2007, [2007] CanLII 41899 (ON SC) (winding-up), available on the Internet at http://canlii.ca/t/1t514; Bundesgerichtshof, Germany, II ZR 65/03, 19 July 2004, available on the Internet at http://www.dis-arb.de/en/47/datenbanken/rspr/bgh-case-no-ii-zr-65-03-date-2004-07-19-id312; *Clínica Columbia S.A. v. RMN San Antonio S.L.*, Juzgado de Primera Instancia, Bilbao, Spain, 2 November 2005; *Acier Leroux Inc. v. Tremblay*, Court of Appeal of Quebec, Canada, 11 March 2004, [2004] CanLII 28564 (QC CA), available on the Internet at http://canlii.ca/t/1gnmj; *Investissement Charlevoix Inc. v. Gestion Pierre Gingras Inc.*, Court of Appeal of Quebec, Canada, 21 June 2010, [2010] QCCA 1229, available on the Internet at http://canlii.ca/t/2bcbk.

[177] CLOUT case No. 116 [*BWV Investments Ltd. v. Saskferco Products Inc. et. al. and UHDE GmbH*, Saskatchewan Court of Appeal, Canada, 25 November 1994], [1994] CanLII 4557 (SK CA), also available on the Internet at http://canlii.ca/t/1nqlf; CLOUT case No. 183 [*Automatic Systems Inc. v. Bracknell Corp.*, Ontario Court of Appeal, Canada, 25 April 1994], [1994] CanLII 1871 (ON CA), also available on the Internet at http://canlii.ca/t/6jzp.

[178] *Agrawest & AWI v. BMA*, Prince Edward Island Supreme Court—Trial Division, Canada, 23 June 2005, [2005] PESCTD 36 (CanLII), available on the Internet at http://canlii.ca/t/1l40z.

[179] *Paquito Lima Buton v. Rainbow Joy Shipping Ltd. Inc.*, Court of Final Appeal, Hong Kong Special Administrative Region of China, 28 April 2008, [2008] HKCFA 30 at paras. 46 ff., available on the Internet at http://www.hklii.hk/eng/hk/cases/hkcfa/2008/30.html.

[180] CLOUT case No. 586 [*Kaverit Steel and Crane Ltd. v. Kone Corp.*, Alberta Court of Appeal, Canada, 16 January 1992], [1992] ABCA 7 (CanLII), also available on the Internet at http://canlii.ca/t/1p6kc; CLOUT case No. 35 [*Canada Packers Inc. et al. v. Terra Nova Tankers Inc. et al.*, Ontario Court of Justice—General Division, Canada, 1 October 1992]; *Stephen Okero Oyugi v. Law Society of Kenya & Another*, High Court, Nairobi (Nairobi Law Courts), Kenya, 15 April 2005, Civil Suit 482 of 2004, available on the Internet at http://kenyalaw.org (referral denied on the ground that tort claims are inarbitrable under Kenyan law).

[181] *Dell Computer Corp. v. Union des Consommateurs,* Supreme Court, Canada, 13 July 2007, [2007] SCC 34, [2007] 2 SCR 801, available on the Internet at http://canlii.ca/t/1s2f2; Bundesgerichtshof, Germany, III ZR 265/03, 13 January 2005, available on the Internet at http://www.dis-arb.de/en/47/datenbanken/rspr/bgh-case-no-iii-zr-265-03-date-2005-01-13-id305; Bundesgerichtshof, Germany, III ZR 164/06, 1 March 2007, available on the Internet at http://www.dis-arb.de/en/47/datenbanken/rspr/bgh-case-no-iii-zr-164-06-date-2007-03-01-id661.

[182] *Desbois v. Industries A.C. Davie Inc.*, Court of Appeal of Quebec, Canada, 26 April 1990, [1990] CanLII 3619 (QC CA), available on the Internet at http://canlii.ca/t/1pjlg.

[183] *9110-9595 Québec inc. v. Bergeron*, Court of Appeal of Quebec, Canada, 12 October 2007, [2007] QCCA 1393, available on the Internet at http://canlii.ca/t/1tb5l.

are unclear, when they designate a non-existing institution or appointing authority, or when the designated institution or appointing authority refuses to cooperate as expected by the parties. Under such circumstances, a claiming party who is reluctant to proceed to arbitration may commence an action in court and object to its opponent's attempt to refer the dispute to arbitration on the ground that the problem at hand has rendered the arbitration agreement inoperative or incapable of being performed. (See below, section on article 36, para. 21).

23. In one Canadian case, the arbitral institution chosen by the parties had ceased to exist, and the parties disagreed as to whether another institution created subsequently was the legal successor of the first. The court ruled that it was, but its decision implicitly stands for the proposition that had this not been the case, the arbitration clause would have been invalid and incapable of enforcement.[184] An earlier Hong Kong decision, dealing with an almost identical question, is to the same effect.[185] In another case suggesting that problems with the designated arbitral institution or appointing authority may justify dismissing a referral application, the court found the arbitration agreement incapable of being performed on the ground that the arbitral institution designated therein—which had become practically inactive—was unwilling to administer the arbitration.[186]

24. However, other cases point in the opposite direction. For example, one court found that the fact that the arbitral institution designated by the parties had refused to appoint an arbitrator on the ground that, on a *prima facie* (or preliminary) assessment, the parties had not validly concluded an arbitration agreement, did not in itself justify the dismissal of a referral application.[187] In another decision, the court found that the fact that the parties had designated a non-existing arbitral institution did not entail that the arbitration agreement was inoperative or incapable of being performed.[188]

(10) Failure to commence arbitration within the deadline provided for in the arbitration agreement

25. Agreements sometimes provide that arbitration must be commenced within a given period following certain predetermined occurrences. The question then is whether, after a deadline expires, a party that commences an action in court may resist a referral application on the ground that the arbitration agreement has become inoperative. Several cases stand for the proposition that the fact that the right to commence arbitration is contractually time-barred does not justify the dismissal of a referral application brought under article 8.[189]

(11) Other circumstances

26. In several cases, parties have unsuccessfully sought to extend the scope of the phrase "null and void, inoperative or incapable of being performed." The Supreme Court of Canada found that an arbitration agreement was not rendered inoperative by the fact that the party seeking the referral of the action to arbitration had not yet taken steps to set the arbitration in motion.[190] Another court concluded that the parties' disagreement as to the location of the place of arbitration did not render their arbitration agreement inoperative.[191] The fact that an arbitration agreement did not set out the applicable rules of procedure was found to

[184] CLOUT case No. 509 [*Dalimpex Ltd. v. Janicki*, Ontario Court of Appeal, Canada, 30 May 2003], [2003] CanLII 34234 (ON CA), also available on the Internet at http://canlii.ca/t/6wwf.

[185] *Chung Siu Hong Celment and Others v. Primequine Corporation Ltd. And Others*, High Court—Court of First Instance, Hong Kong Special Administrative Region of China, 28 September 1999, [1999] HKCFI 1472, available on the Internet at http://www.hklii.hk/eng/hk/cases/hkcfi/1999/1472.html.

[186] *Ferguson Bros. of St. Thomas v. Manyan Inc.*, Ontario Superior Court of Justice, Canada, 27 May 1999, [1999] OJ No. 1887. See also: *Mugoya Construction & Engineering Ltd. v. National Social Security Fund Board of Trustees & another*, High Court, Nairobi (Commercial Division Milimani Courts), Kenya, 27 July 2005, Civil Suit 59 of 2005, available on the Internet at http://kenyalaw.org/; CLOUT case No. 557 [Bayerisches Oberstes Landesgericht, Germany, 4 Z SchH 13/99, 28 February 2000], also available on the Internet at http://www.dis-arb.de/en/47/datenbanken/rspr/bayoblg-case-no-4-z-schh-13-99-date-2000-02-28-id14.

[187] *Comtec Components Ltd. v. Interquip Ltd.*, High Court—Court of First Instance, Hong Kong Special Administrative Region of China, 3 December 1998, [1998] HKCFI 803, available on the Internet at http://www.hklii.hk/eng/hk/cases/hkcfi/1998/803.html.

[188] CLOUT case No. 57 [*Lucky-Goldstar International (H.K.) Limited v. Ng Moo Kee Engineering Limited*, High Court—Court of First Instance, Hong Kong, 5 May 1993], [1993] HKCFI 14, also available on the Internet at http://www.hklii.hk/eng/hk/cases/hkcfi/1993/14.html.

[189] CLOUT case No. 9 [*Coopers and Lybrand Limited (Trustee) for BC Navigation S.A. (Bankrupt),* Federal Court—Trial Divison, Canada, 2 November 1987]; CLOUT case No. 449 [*China Merchant Heavy Industry Co. Ltd. v. JGC Corp.*, High Court—Court of Appeal, Hong Kong Special Administrative Region of China, 4 July 2001], [2001] HKCA 248, also available on the Internet at http://www.hklii.hk/eng/hk/cases/hkca/2001/248.html; *Tommy C.P. Sze. & Co. v. Li & Fung (trading) Ltd. & Others,* High Court—Court of First Instance, Hong Kong Special Administrative Region of China, 28 October 2002, [2002] HKCFI 682, available on the Internet at http://www.hklii.hk/eng/hk/cases/hkcfi/2002/682.html; *Grandeur Electrical Co. Ltd. v. Cheung Kee Fung Cheung Construction Co. Ltd.*, High Court—Court of Appeal, Hong Kong Special Administrative Region of China, 25 July 2006, [2006] HKCA 305, available on the Internet at http://www.hklii.hk/eng/hk/cases/hkca/2006/305.html.

[190] *Burlington Northern Railroad Co. v. Canadian National Railway Co.*, Supreme Court of Canada, 21 January 1997, [1997] 1 SCR 5, 1997 CanLII 395 (SCC), available on the Internet at http://canlii.ca/t/1fr5f.

[191] *Abitibi-Price Sales Corp. v. C.V. Scheepv.Ondernemineg "Sambeek"*, Federal Court—Trial Division, Canada, 12 November 1998, [1998] CanLII 8706 (FC), available on the Internet at http://canlii.ca/t/498m.

have no bearing on its effectiveness.[192] And in a case where the arbitration agreement provided for the appointment of an arbitrator from a specific pre-constituted panel of arbitrators, a Kenyan court found that the fact that such panel had not yet been constituted did not render the agreement inoperative or incapable of being performed.[193]

27. Other cases show the willingness of some courts to adopt a more expansive view of the phrase "null and void, inoperative or incapable of being performed." One example is a decision of the German Federal Court of Justice holding that an arbitration agreement was incapable of being performed where the party against whom it was invoked did not have the financial resources needed to proceed to arbitration.[194] Another example is a Canadian decision in which the court dismissed a referral application on the ground that the party seeking a referral order had brought the dispute before a different arbitral institution than the one agreed to by the parties.[195] In a third case, the claimant had firstly sought to commence arbitration before the arbitral institution designated in the parties' agreement. However, after the defendant's refusal to pay its share of the advance on costs set by the institution, the claimant decided to commence an action in court, which the defendant subsequently sought to be referred to arbitration. The court dismissed the referral application on the ground that the arbitration agreement had become inoperative because of the defendant's refusal to participate in the arbitration, and this despite that the claimant could have chosen to pay the defendant's share of the advance on costs.[196]

(ii) Applicability of the arbitration agreement to the action's subject-matter

28. Before referring an action to arbitration under article 8, a court must not only find that the arbitration agreement is neither null and void, inoperative or incapable of being performed, but also that it is applicable to the dispute to which the action relates. The respondent can resist a referral application on the ground that the dispute does not fall within the ambit of the arbitration agreement. This issue has arisen in a number of cases, and courts have often dismissed referral application on this basis (see above, section on article 7, para. 12).[197]

---

[192] *Rampton v. Eyre*, Ontario Court of Appeal, Canada, 2 May 2007, [2007] ONCA 331, available on the Internet at http://canlii.ca/t/1rb0d.

[193] *M. M. Galgalo & 3 others v. Musikali Kombo & another*, High Court at Nairobi (Nairobi Law Courts), Kenya, 29 September 2006, Civil Case 382 of 2006, available on the Internet at http://kenyalaw.org/CaseSearch/view_preview1.php?link=98541151738508986403908.

[194] CLOUT case No. 404 [Bundesgerichtshof, Germany, III ZR 33/00, 14 September 2000], also available on the Internet at http://www.dis-arb.de/en/47/datenbanken/rspr/bgh-case-no-iii-zr-33-00-date-2000-09-14-id3; it should be noted that the court relied in its decision on a fundamental right of access to courts guaranteed by the German Constitution. Faced with a similar argument, a Ugandan court concluded that the respondent's impecuniosity could only justify the dismissal of a referral application if it had been caused by the applicant: *Fulgensius Mungereza v. Africa Central*, Supreme Court of Uganda at Mengo, Uganda, 16 January 2004, [2004] UGSC 9.

[195] *OEMSDF Inc. v. Europe Israel Ltd.*, Ontario Superior Court of Justice, Canada, 22 September 1999, [1999] O.J. No. 3594.

[196] *Resin Systems Inc. v. Industrial Service & Machine Inc.*, Alberta Court of Appeal, Canada, 13 March 2008, [2008] ABCA 104 (CanLII), available on the Internet at http://canlii.ca/t/1w296.

[197] See for instance: CLOUT case No. 1048 [*Patel v. Kanbay International Inc.*, Ontario Court of Appeal, Canada, 23 December 2008], [2008] ONCA 867, also available on the Internet at http://canlii.ca/t/220b1; *Pandora Select Partners, LP v. Strategy Real Estate Investments Ltd.*, Ontario Superior Court of Justice, Canada, 20 March 2007, [2007] CanLII 8026 (ON SC), available on the Internet at http://canlii.ca/t/1qw2b; CLOUT case No. 388 [*Temiskaming Hospital v. Integrated Medical Networks, Inc.*, Ontario Court of Justice—General Division, Canada, 31 March 1998]; CLOUT case No. 113 [*T1T2 Limited Partnership v. Canada*, Ontario Court of Justice—General Division, Canada, 10 November 1994]; CLOUT case No. 13 (also reproduced under CLOUT case No. 383) [*Deco Automotive Inc. v. G.P.A. Gesellschaft für Pressenautomation mbH*, Ontario District Court, Canada, 27 October 1989]; *Ocean Fisheries Ltd. v. Pacific Coast Fishermen's Mutual Marine Insurance Co. (C.A.)*, Federal Court—Court of Appeal, Canada, 30 October 1997, [1998] 1 FC 586, [1997] CanLII 6367 (FCA), available on the Internet at http://canlii.ca/t/4mzf; *Sumitomo Canada v. Saga Forest Carriers et al.*, Provincial Court of British Columbia, Canada, 22 November 2007, [2007] BCPC 373, available on the Internet at http://canlii.ca/t/1v1fj; Bundesgerichtshof, Germany, III ZR 281/00, 4 October 2001, available on the Internet at http://www.dis-arb.de/en/47/datenbanken/rspr/bgh-case-no-iii-zr-281-00-date-2001-10-04-id174; *Newmark Capital Corporation Ltd. and Others v. Coffee Partners Ltd. and Another*, High Court—Court of First Instance, Hong Kong Special Administrative Region of China, 8 February 2007, [2007] HKCFI 113, available on the Internet at http://www.hklii.hk/eng/hk/cases/hkcfi/2007/113.html; *Liu Man Wai and Another v. Chevalier (Hong Kong) Ltd.*, High Court—Court of Appeal, Hong Kong Special Administrative Region of China, 26 June 2002, [2002] HKCA 280, available on the Internet at http://www.hklii.hk/eng/hk/cases/hkca/2002/280.html; CLOUT case No. 89 [*York Airconditioning & Refrigeration Inc. v. Lam Kwai Hung Trading as North Sea A/C Elect. Eng. Co.*, High Court—Court of First Instance, Hong Kong, 16 December 1994], [1995] 1 HKCFI 166, also available on the Internet at http://www.hklii.hk/eng/hk/cases/hkcfi/1994/166.html; *Virginia E. Wambui O Tieno-Mbugua v. Africa Air Rescue Health Services (K) Ltd.*, High Court, Nairobi (Nairobi Law Courts), Kenya, 12 September 2006, Civil Case 563 of 2006, available on the Internet at http://kenyalaw.org/CaseSearch/view_preview1.php?link=73164421238255772063970; CLOUT case No. 1070 [*Berica v. Grupa Gava*, High Commercial Court, Croatia, 21 May 2007], XXVI Pž-8147/04-5.

The applicable standard of review: full review or prima facie?

29. Whether courts seized of referral applications should review the validity, operativeness, performability and applicability of the arbitration agreement fully or merely on a *prima facie* standard is a question that has not been answered in a consistent manner.

30. In several jurisdictions, including Croatia,[198] Spain,[199] Mexico,[200] Australia,[201] Uganda[202] and Kenya,[203] the cases show that courts have either not considered this issue or not considered it in detail, and have adopted the view that a full review would be required. Issues of validity, operativeness, performability and applicability would thus be analysed fully, and decisions relating thereto should be final.[204] In Ireland, a court that analysed the issue in detail said to be inclined to favour that standard.[205]

31. However, courts in other jurisdictions have preferred to apply a *prima facie* standard on the ground that, as arbitrators are empowered to rule on their own jurisdiction

---

[198] CLOUT case No. 1070 [*Berica v. Grupa Gava*, High Commercial Court, Croatia, 21 May 2007], XXVI Pž-8147/04-5.

[199] See for instance: *D. Andrés v. Díez Carrillo S.L.*, Audiencia Provincial de Palma de Mallorca (sección 5ª), Spain, 5 October 2006, rec. apel. 399/2006; *Clínica Columbia S.A. v. RMN San Antonio S.L.*, Juzgado de Primera Instancia, Bilbao, Spain, 2 November 2005.

[200] *Constructora Aboumrad Amodio Berho, S.A. de C.V. v. Cinemex Universidad, S.A. de C.V.*, Tercer Tribunal Colegiado en Materia Civil, Primer Circuito, Mexico, 8 March 2001, D.C. 1303/2001; *Desarrollos Empresariales S.A. de C.V. et al. v. Grupo Radio Centro S.A. de C.V.*, Décimo Segundo Tribunal Colegiado en Materia Civil, Primer Circuito, Mexico, 1 July 2004, R.C. 222/2004; *Servicios Administrativos de Emergencia S.A. de C.V. v. A.D.T. Security Services S.A. de C.V.*, Tercer Tribunal Colegiado en Materia Civil, Primer Circuito, Mexico, 19 May 2005, R.C. 14/2005; Suprema Corte de Justicia de la Nación (Primera Sala), Mexico, 11 January 2006.

[201] *Electra Air Conditioning B.V. v. Seeley International Pty. Ltd.*, Federal Court, Australia, 8 October 2008, [2008] FCAFC 169, available on the Internet at http://www.austlii.edu.au/au/cases/cth/FCAFC/2008/169.html; *Paharpur Cooling Towers Ltd. v. Paramount (Wa) Ltd.*, Supreme Court of Western Australia – Court of Appeal, Australia, 13 May 2008, [2008] WASCA 110, available on the Internet at http://www.austlii.edu.au/au/cases/wa/WASCA/2008/110.html; *Hi-Fert Pty. Ltd. & Anor v. Kiukiang Maritime Carriers Inc. & Anor*, Federal Court, Australia, 24 November 1998, [1998] FCA 1485, available on the Internet at http://www.austlii.edu.au/au/cases/cth/FCA/1998/1485.html; *Francis Travel Marketing Pty. Limited v. Virgin Atlantic Airways Limited,* Supreme Court of New South Wales—Court of Appeal, Australia, 7 May 1996, [1996] NSWSC 104, available on the Internet at http://www.austlii.edu.au/au/cases/nsw/NSWSC/1996/104.html; *Wes Trac Pty. Ltd. v. Eastcoast OTR Tyres Pty. Ltd.*, Supreme Court of New South Wales (Equity Division), Australia, 29 August 2008, [2008] NSWSC 894, available on the Internet at http://www.austlii.edu.au/au/cases/nsw/NSWSC/2008/894.html; *APC Logistics Pty. Ltd. v. C.J. Nutracon Pty. Ltd.*, Federal Court, Australia, 16 February 2007, [2007] FCA 136, available on the Internet at http://www.austlii.edu.au/au/cases/cth/federal_ct/2007/136.html.

[202] *Fulgensius Mungereza v. Africa Central,* Supreme Court of Uganda at Mengo, Uganda, 16 January 2004, [2004] UGSC 9; *Eastern and Southern African Trade & Anor. v. Hassan Basajjabalaba & Anor.*, High Court at Kampala, Uganda, 13 April 2007, [2007] UGCommC 30.

[203] *Very Rev. Peter Karanja & another v. Alice Wahito Ndegwa*, High Court, Nairobi (Nairobi Law Courts), Kenya, 8 March 2007, Civil Case 908 of 2006, available on the Internet at http://kenyalaw.org/CaseSearch/view_preview1.php?link=15223756450428451861332; High Court, Nairobi (Nairobi Law Courts), Kenya, 18 December 2006, Civil Case 1159 of 2006, available on the Internet at http://kenyalaw.org/CaseSearch/view_preview1.php?link=39586347845587159182714; *M. M. Galgalo & 3 others v. Musikali Kombo & another*, High Court, Nairobi (Nairobi Law Courts), Kenya, 29 September 2006, Civil Case 382 of 2006, available on the Internet at http://kenyalaw.org/CaseSearch/view_preview1.php?link=98541151738508986403908; *Virginia E. Wambui O Tieno-Mbugua v. Africa Air Rescue Health Services (K) Ltd.*, High Court, Nairobi (Nairobi Law Courts), Kenya, 12 September 2006, Civil Case 563 of 2006, available on the Internet at http://kenyalaw.org/CaseSearch/view_preview1.php?link=73164421238255772063970; *Velji Shamji Constructions Ltd. v. Westmall Supermarket Ltd.*, High Court, Mombasa, Kenya, 8 September 2005, Civil Suit 254 of 2004, available on the Internet at http://kenyalaw.org; *Mehta Electrical Limited & 4 others v. N. K. Brothers Limited & another*, High Court, Nairobi (Milimani Commercial Division), Kenya, 16 August 2005, Civil Suit 37 of 2005, available on the Internet at http://kenyalaw.org; *Stephen Okero Oyugi v. Law Society of Kenya & Another*, High Court, Nairobi (Nairobi Law Courts), Kenya, 15 April 2005, Civil Suit 482 of 2004, available on the Internet at http://kenyalaw.org; *Seca Africa Ltd. v. Kirloskar Kenya Ltd. & 3 others,* High Court, Nairobi, Kenya, 28 January 2005, Civil Suit 307 of 1999, available on the Internet at http://kenyalaw.org.

[204] This approach is also adopted in Germany (see for instance: Bundesgerichtshof, Germany, III ZR 214/05, 12 January 2006, available on the Internet at http://www.dis-arb.de/en/47/datenbanken/rspr/bgh-case-no-iii-zr-214-05-date-2006-01-12-id524; Bundesgerichtshof, Germany, III ZR 22/06, 31 May 2007, available on the Internet at http://www.dis-arb.de/en/47/datenbanken/rspr/bgh-case-no-iii-zr-22-06-date-2007-05-31-id668; Bundesgerichtshof, Germany, XI ZR 66/08, 13 January 2009, available on the Internet at http://www.dis-arb.de/en/47/datenbanken/rspr/bgh-case-no-xi-zr-66-08-date-2009-01-13-id905; Bundesgerichtshof, Germany, VII ZR 105/06, 25 January 2007, available on the Internet at http://www.dis-arb.de/en/47/datenbanken/rspr/bgh-case-no-vii-zr-105-06-date-2007-01-25-id653; Bundesgerichtshof, Germany, II ZR 65/03, 19 July 2004, available on the Internet at http://www.dis-arb.de/en/47/datenbanken/rspr/bgh-case-no-ii-zr-65-03-date-2004-07-19-id312; Bundesgerichtshof, Germany, III ZR 281/00, 4 October 2001, available on the Internet at http://www.dis-arb.de/en/47/datenbanken/rspr/bgh-case-no-iii-zr-281-00-date-2001-10-04-id174; CLOUT case No. 404 [Bundesgerichtshof, Germany, III ZR 33/00, 14 September 2000], also available on the Internet at http://www.dis-arb.de/en/47/datenbanken/rspr/bgh-case-no-iii-zr-33-00-date-2000-09-14-id3; Bundesgerichtshof, Germany, III ZR 164/06, 1 March 2007, available on the Internet at http://www.dis-arb.de/en/47/datenbanken/rspr/bgh-case-no-iii-zr-164-06-date-2007-03-01-id661). However, those cases have to be considered in light of the fact that the German arbitration law departs from the Model Law by providing, in article 1032(2), that prior to the constitution of the arbitral tribunal, a party may apply to the court for a decision on the effectiveness of a disputed arbitration agreement. This makes clear that, under German law, courts are expected to resolve as soon as possible—and fully—disagreements concerning the validity, operativeness, performability and applicability of arbitration agreements.

[205] *Barnmore Demolition and Civil Engineering Ltd. v. Alandale Logistics Ltd., Pynest Ltd., Dublin Airport Authority Plc and Barry Donohue (as liquidator of Pynest)*, High Court (Commercial), Ireland, 11 November 2010, [2010] No. 5910P, available on the Internet at http://arbitration.practicallaw.com/7-504-2765.

(article 16 (1)), they normally ought to rule first on issues of validity, operativeness, performability and applicability, subject to subsequent review by courts (see below, section on article 16, para. 3). For example, Hong Kong courts seized of referral applications have in most cases adopted the *prima facie* approach,[206] but they have also occasionally assumed that they were empowered to deal fully with issues of validity, operativeness, performability and applicability.[207] The *prima facie* approach was also adopted by the Supreme Court of India.[208]

32. The Canadian position was clarified in a Supreme Court decision adopting the *prima facie* approach, although with several caveats. The court held that where the objection to the referral of the case to arbitration only raises questions of law, those questions ought to be resolved immediately, and in a final manner, by the court. Where the objection raises disputed questions of fact, the court should normally refer the case to arbitration and let the arbitral tribunal make the first ruling on that objection. Where the objection raises mixed questions of fact and law, the case should normally be referred to arbitration unless the questions of fact require only superficial consideration of the documents submitted by the parties.[209] While this approach has frequently been followed by lower Canadian courts,[210] they have also occasionally continued to apply

[206] See for instance: *Pccw Global Ltd. v. Interactive Communications Service Ltd.*, High Court—Court of Appeal, Hong Kong Special Administrative Region of China, 16 November 2006, [2006] HKCA 434, available on the Internet at http://www.hklii.hk/eng/hk/cases/hkca/2006/434.html; *Fai Tak Engineering Co. Ltd. v. Sui Chong Construction & Engineering Co. Ltd.*, District Court, Hong Kong Special Administrative Region of China, 22 June 2009, [2009] HKDC 141, available on the Internet at http://www.hklii.hk/eng/hk/cases/hkdc/2009/141.html; *Ocean Park Corporation v. Proud Sky Co. Ltd.*, High Court—Court of First Instance, Hong Kong Special Administrative Region of China, 28 November 2007, [2007] HKCFI 1221, available on the Internet at http://www.hklii.hk/eng/hk/cases/hkcfi/2007/1221.html; *Newmark Capital Corporation Ltd. and Others v. Coffee Partners Ltd. and Another*, High Court—Court of First Instance, Hong Kong Special Administrative Region of China, 8 February 2007, [2007] HKCFI 113, available on the Internet at http://www.hklii.hk/eng/hk/cases/hkcfi/2007/113.html; *The Incorporated Owners of Sincere House v. Sincere Co. Ltd.*, Lands Tribunal, Hong Kong Special Administrative Region of China, 18 May 2005, [2005] HKCU 625, available on the Internet at http://www.hklii.hk/eng/hk/cases/hklt/2005/30.html; *New Sound Industries Ltd. v. Meliga (HK) Ltd.*, High Court—Court of Appeal, Hong Kong Special Administrative Region of China, 11 January 2005, [2005] HKCU 66, available on the Internet at http://www.hklii.hk/eng/hk/cases/hkca/2005/7.html; *Pacific Crown Engineering Ltd. v. Hyundai Engineering & Construction Co. Ltd.*, High Court—Court of First Instance, Hong Kong Special Administrative Region of China, 23 April 2003, [2003] HKCFI 924, available on the Internet at http://www.hklii.hk/eng/hk/cases/hkcfi/2003/924.html; CLOUT case No. 522 [*Paladin Agricultural Ltd. & Others v. Excelsior Hotel (Hong Kong) Ltd.*, High Court—Court of First Instance, Hong Kong Special Administrative Region of China, 6 March 2001], [2001] HKCFI 1271, also available on the Internet at http://www.hklii.hk/eng/hk/cases/hkcfi/2001/1271.html; *Nahai West Shipping Co. v. Hong Kong United Dockyards Ltd.*, High Court—Court of First Instance, Hong Kong, 5 February 1996, [1996] 2 HKC 639; *Liu Man Wai and Another v. Chevalier (Hong Kong) Ltd.*, High Court—Court of Appeal, Hong Kong Special Administrative Region of China, 26 June 2002, [2002] HKCA 280, available on the Internet at http://www.hklii.hk/eng/hk/cases/hkca/2002/280.html; *Cathay Pacific Airways Ltd. v. Hong Kong Air Cargo Terminals Ltd.*, High Court—Court of First Instance, Hong Kong Special Administrative Region of China, 7 March 2002, [2002] HKCFI 9, available on the Internet at http://www.hklii.hk/eng/hk/cases/hkcfi/2002/9.html; *Sun Fook Kong (Civil) Ltd. v. Wellead Construction & Engineering Co. Ltd. and another*, High Court—Court of First Instance, Hong Kong Special Administrative Region of China, 7 May 1999, [1999] HKCFI 233, available on the Internet at http://www.hklii.hk/eng/hk/cases/hkcfi/1999/233.html.

[207] See for instance: *Paquito Lima Buton v. Rainbow Joy Shipping Ltd. Inc.*, Court of Final Appeal, Hong Kong Special Administrative Region of China, 28 April 2008, [2008] HKCFA 30, available on the Internet at http://www.hklii.hk/eng/hk/cases/hkcfa/2008/30.html; *Rondabosh International Ltd. v. China Ping an Insurance (Hong Kong) Co. Ltd.*, High Court—Court of First Instance, Hong Kong Special Administrative Region of China, 29 December 2009, [2009] HKCFI 1198, available on the Internet at http://www.hklii.hk/eng/hk/cases/hkcfi/2009/1198.html; *Aggressive Construction Company Limited v. Data-Form Engineering Limited*, High Court—Court of First Instance, Hong Kong Special Administrative Region of China, 13 October 2009, [2009] HKCU 1533, available on the Internet at: http://www.hklii.hk/eng/hk/cases/hkcfi/2009/952.html; *Ho Fat Sing t/a Famous Design Engineering Co. v. Hop Tai Construction Co. Ltd.*, District Court, Hong Kong Special Administrative Region of China, 23 December 2008, [2008] HKDC 339, available on the Internet at http://www.hklii.hk/eng/hk/cases/hkdc/2008/339.html.

[208] *Shin-Etsu Chemical Co. Ltd. v. M/S. Aksh Optifibre Ltd. & Anr,* Supreme Court, India, 12 August 2005, available on the Internet at http://www.indiankanoon.org/doc/847271/.

[209] *Dell Computer Corp. v. Union des Consommateurs,* Supreme Court, Canada, 13 July 2007, [2007] SCC 34, [2007] 2 SCR 801, available on the Internet at http://canlii.ca/t/1s2f2.

[210] See for instance: CLOUT case No. 1042 [*Bombardier Transportation v. SMC Pneumatics (UK) Ltd.*, Court of Appeal of Quebec, Canada, 4 May 2009], [2009] QCCA 861, also available on the Internet at http://canlii.ca/t/23fzp; CLOUT case No. 1047 [*Dancap Productions Inc. v. Key Brand Entertainment Inc.*, Ontario Court of Appeal, Ontario, Canada, 13 February 2009], [2009] ONCA 135, also available on the Internet at http://canlii.ca/t/22h4f; CLOUT case No. 1048 [*Patel v. Kanbay International Inc.*, Ontario Court of Appeal, Ontario, Canada, 23 December 2008], [2008] ONCA 867, also available on the Internet at http://canlii.ca/t/220b1; *EDF (Services) Limited v. Appleton & Associates*, Ontario Superior Court of Justice, Canada, 4 September 2007, [2007] CanLII 36078 (ON SC), available on the Internet at http://canlii.ca/t/1sr48.

the full review standard.[211] Furthermore, in one case, the court refused to apply the *prima facie* approach on the ground that no evidence had been adduced as to whether the arbitration rules designated in the alleged arbitration agreement granted to arbitral tribunals the power to rule on their own jurisdiction.[212] Finally, while in one early case it was held that, as article 16 (1) is not applicable when the place of arbitration is located abroad, there was no reason to let the arbitral tribunal, in such circumstances, make a first ruling on issues of validity, operativeness, performability and applicability,[213] Canadian courts have since frequently adopted the *prima facie* approach in connection with arbitration agreements providing for a foreign place of arbitration (see below, section on article 16, para. 3).[214]

The procedural condition: the timeliness of the referral application

33. The cases address several issues relating to the requirement in article 8 that a referral to arbitration be requested no later than when the party seeking a referral order submits its first statement on the dispute. [215]

Strict or permissive application of the requirement?

34. A number of decisions have emphasized the need to apply this procedural requirement strictly. One example is an early Canadian case where the party seeking a referral order argued that, while its application had been filed after its first statement on the substance of the dispute, it had previously expressed extra-judicially to the respondent its intention to invoke the arbitration agreement. The court held that a request to arbitrate made extra-judicially was of no relevance, and—relying on the *travaux préparatoires* of the Model Law—highlighted the importance that the conditions under which actions will be referred to arbitration be objective and predictable.[216] In another case, the party seeking a referral order argued that its application was not untimely because, although it had previously filed a statement of defence, it had done so for the sole reason of avoiding being judged in default. The court held that these circumstances were irrelevant under article 8 on the ground that the timeliness requirement set out therein had to be applied strictly, but it nevertheless stayed the action and referred the parties to arbitration on the basis of local procedural rules.[217]

---

[211] See for instance: *Canada (Attorney General) v. Reliance Insurance Company*, Ontario Superior Court of Justice, Canada, 5 October 2007, [2007] CanLII 41899 (ON SC) (winding-up), available on the Internet at http://canlii.ca/t/1t514; CLOUT case No. 1046 [*PS Here, L.L.C. v. Fortalis Anstalt*, Court of Appeal of Quebec, Canada, 19 March 2009], [2009] QCCA 538, also available on the Internet at http://canlii.ca/t/22ts1.

[212] CLOUT case No. 1011 [*H & H Marine Engine Service Ltd. v. Volvo Penta of the Americas Inc.*, Supreme Court of British Columbia, Canada, 9 October 2009], [2009] BCSC 1389, also available on the Internet at http://canlii.ca/t/262c8.

[213] CLOUT case No. 13 (also reproduced under CLOUT case No. 383) [*Deco Automotive Inc. v. G.P.A. Gesellschaft für Pressenautomation mbH*, Ontario District Court, Canada, 27 October 1989].

[214] See for instance: CLOUT case No. 1047 [*Dancap Productions Inc. v. Key Brand Entertainment Inc.*, Ontario Court of Appeal, Canada, 13 February 2009], [2009] ONCA 135, also available on the Internet at http://canlii.ca/t/22h4f; CLOUT case No. 509 [*Dalimpex Ltd. v. Janicki*, Ontario Court of Appeal, Canada, 30 May 2003], [2003] CanLII 34234 (ON CA), also available on the Internet at http://canlii.ca/t/6wwf; *EDF (Services) Limited v. Appleton & Associates*, Ontario Superior Court of Justice, Canada, 4 September 2007, [2007] CanLII 36078 (ON SC), available on the Internet at http://canlii.ca/t/1sr48; CLOUT case No. 504 [*D.G. Jewelry Inc. et al. v. Cyberdiam Canada Ltd. et al.*, Ontario Superior Court of Justice, Canada, 17 April 2002], also in [2002] OJ No. 1465.

[215] In two cases, courts have held that, to comply with article 8, a referral application had to be made prior to the filing of any pleading on the substance of the dispute: CLOUT case No. 119 [*ABN Amro Bank Canada v. Krupp Mak Maschinenbau GmbH*, Ontario Supreme Court of Justice—General Division, Canada, 23 December 1994], [1994] CanLII 7355 (ON SC), also available on the Internet at http://canlii.ca/t/1vtn8 and *Megdev. Construction Limited v. Pioneer General Assurance Society Limited*, High Court, Nairobi, Kenya, 14 June 2005, Civil Suit 291 of 2001, available on the Internet at http://kenyalaw.org. However, the correctness of such reasoning was subsequently questioned, on the ground that it seemed clearly inconsistent with article 8: *ABN Amro Bank Canada v. Krupp MaK Maschinenbau GmbH,* Ontario Court of Justice—General Division, Canada, 7 June 1995, [1995] CanLII 7081 (ON SC), available on the Internet at http://canlii.ca/t/1vt6l.

[216] CLOUT case No. 33 [*Ruhrkohle Handel Inter GMBH and National Steel Corp. et al. v. Fednav. Ltd. and Federal Pacific,* Federal Court—Court of Appeal, Canada, 29 May 1992]; see also: CLOUT case No. 178 [*Siderurgica Mendes Junior S.A. v. "Icepearl" (The),* Supreme Court of British Columbia, Canada, 31 January 1996], [1996] CanLII 2746 (BC SC), also available on the Internet at http://canlii.ca/t/1f1n1; CLOUT case No. 355 [*Restore International Corp. v. K.I.P. Kuester International Products Corp.*, Supreme Court of British Columbia, Canada, 15 January 1999], [1999] CanLII 6297 (BC SC), also available on the Internet at http://canlii.ca/t/1d214; *Coldmatic Refrigeration of Canada Ltd. v. P.U.M.A. s.r.*, Ontario Court of Justice – General Division, Canada, 24 April 1998, [1998] OJ No. 1697. On the need to take the timeliness requirement literally and apply it uniformly in all legal systems, see, *ABN Amro Bank Canada v. Krupp MaK Maschinenbau GmbH,* Ontario Court of Justice—General Division, Canada, 7 June 1995, [1995] CanLII 7081 (ON SC), available on the Internet at http://canlii.ca/t/1vt6l.

[217] CLOUT case No. 15 [*Navionics Inc. v. Flota Maritima Mexicana S.A. et al.*, Federal Court—Trial Division, Canada, 17 January 1989].

35. In other cases, courts have adopted a more permissive approach and granted referral applications based on article 8 even though the timeliness provisions had not been strictly complied with. In one case, the party seeking a referral order had not sought to invoke the arbitration clause until well after filing its statement of defence, but the court ruled that this did not impact the admissibility of its application, because the possibility of seeking a referral order had been raised and discussed early on in the proceedings.[218] Another example is a 2002 decision where the court expressly held that the timeliness requirement under article 8 ought not to be applied strictly, and treated as admissible a referral application filed months after the party seeking a referral order had filed its statement of defence. To the court, the fact that the party seeking a referral order had expressed in its statement of defence its intention to invoke the arbitration agreement sufficed.[219]

Referral requested by the claimant

36. Whereas typically referral to arbitration is requested by the defendant in the court action, in a number of cases courts were seized of referral applications filed by the claimant. A question then arises as to whether, by commencing a court action, the claimant has taken a step that bars it from subsequently invoking the arbitration agreement.

37. Some cases involve claimants seeking to refer their own action to arbitration, and they have generally not been successful. One court was of the view that a referral application made in that context was inadmissible, because by filing a statement of claim, the applicant had necessarily submitted its first statement on the dispute.[220] Other courts have ruled in a similar manner.[221]

38. Also noteworthy is another group of cases where courts granted referral applications by claimants who had commenced court proceedings for the sole purpose of obtaining interim measures of protection.[222] A parallel can be drawn between those cases and article 9, which provides that requesting that a court issue interim measures of protection is not incompatible with an arbitration agreement (see below, section on article 9, paras. 1, 5 and 10).

What constitutes a "statement on the substance of the dispute"?

39. It is clear from the text of article 8 that a party will not necessarily be barred from seeking a referral of the action to arbitration if it takes a step in the judicial proceedings without invoking the arbitration agreement. It is only where that step amounts to a submission of a statement on the substance of the dispute that the procedural requirement of article 8 will be engaged.[223] For example, a referral application was deemed admissible even though the party seeking a referral order had, prior to filing its referral application, issued a demand for discovery of documents, requested copies of documents and sought particulars of the claimant's statement of claim.[224]

40. Relying on the pro-arbitration philosophy that underlies the Model Law, courts have tended to interpret the concept of a "statement on the substance of the dispute" narrowly.[225] In a case, a court found the fact that the party seeking a referral order had filed a statement of claim

[218] CLOUT case No. 356 [*Seine River Resources Inc. v. Pensa Inc.*, Supreme Court of British Columbia, Canada, 15 June 1999], [1999] CanLII 6579 (BC SC), also available on the Internet at http://canlii.ca/t/1d250.

[219] *Canada (Attorney General) v. Marineserve.MG Inc.*, Supreme Court of Nova Scotia, Canada, 24 May 2002, [2002] NSSC 147, available on the Internet at http://canlii.ca/t/5k7t.

[220] CLOUT case No. 33 [*Ruhrkohle Handel Inter GMBH and National Steel Corp. et al. v. Fednav. Ltd. and Federal Pacific*, Federal Court—Court of Appeal, Canada, 29 May 1992].

[221] *Pamela Akora Imenje v. Akora ITC International Ltd. & another*, High Court, Nairobi (Milimani Commercial Courts), Kenya, 17 August 2007, Civil Case 368 of 2005, available on the Internet at http://kenyalaw.org/CaseSearch/view_preview1.php?link=95900834646140632908983; *Chok Yick Interior Design & Engineering Co. Ltd. v. Fortune World Enterprises Ltd. and another*, High Court—Court of First Instance, Hong Kong Special Administrative Region of China, 29 January 2010, [2010] HKCFI 84, available on the Internet at http://www.hklii.hk/eng/hk/cases/hkcfi/2010/84.html; CLOUT case No. 1072 [High Commercial Court, Croatia, 29 April 2001], VTS RH, Pž-5168/01.

[222] *Hanjin Shipping Co. Ltd. v. Grand King Shipping Ltd.*, High Court—Court of First Instance, Hong Kong Special Administrative Region of China, 20 November 1998, [1999] HKCFI 403, available on the Internet at http://www.hklii.hk/eng/hk/cases/hkcfi/1998/403.html; High Court at Nairobi, Kenya, *Don-Woods Company Ltd. v. Kenya Pipeline Company Ltd.*, High Court at Nairobi, Kenya, 7 October 2005, Civil Suit 1041 of 2004, available on the Internet at http://kenyalaw.org/.

[223] See for instance: *Gilgandra Marketing Co-Operative Limited v. Australian Commodities & Marketing Pty. Ltd. & Anor*, Supreme Court of New South Wales, Australia, 22 October 2010, [2010] NSWSC 1209, available on the Internet at http://www.austlii.edu.au/au/cases/nsw/NSWSC/2010/1209.html.

[224] CLOUT case No. 178 [*Siderurgica Mendes Junior S.A. v. "Icepearl" (The)*, Supreme Court of British Columbia, Canada, 31 January 1996], [1996] CanLII 2746 (BC SC), also available on the Internet at http://canlii.ca/t/1f1n1.

[225] See for instance: *Marconi Communications Inc. v. Vidar-SMS Co. Ltd.*, United States District Court, Northern District of Texas, United States of America, 22 August 2001, Civil No. CV-1293-L (2001), where the court, applying what it characterized as a "strong presumption against waiver in arbitration-related matters," concluded that the party seeking a referral order had not submitted a statement on the substance of the dispute by filing a special appearance aimed at challenging the court's jurisdiction, filing a general denial of the claimant's claim, and pleading an affirmative defence raising independent grounds as to why the claimant could not succeed. Similarly, in CLOUT case No. 710 [*Louis Dreyfus Trading Ltd. v. Bonarich International (Group) Ltd.*, Supreme Court—High Court (Commercial List), Hong Kong, 24 March 1997], [1997] HKCFI 312, also available on the Internet at http://www.hklii.hk/eng/hk/cases/hkcfi/1997/312.html, the court held that a general denial of liability made in support of a motion for security for costs did not amount to a statement on the substance of the dispute.

against the claimant in a different—yet related—action to be of no consequence on the admissibility of its referral application.[226]

41. Some courts have interpreted more broadly the concept of a "statement on the substance of the dispute." One example is a New Zealand decision which held that a response to an application seeking an interim injunction constituted such a statement.[227]

Effect of a failure to invoke article 8 in a timely manner on separate, but related, actions

42. In one case involving two related actions raising similar issues and involving the same parties, a court concluded that the failure by the party seeking a referral order to invoke article 8 in a timely manner in one action prevented it from seeking the referral of the other action to arbitration, as the arbitration agreement had become inoperative as to the disputed issues.[228]

May referral to arbitration be denied on the ground that there is no dispute between the parties?

43. Several cases stand for the proposition that a referral application may further be dismissed on the ground that there exists no dispute between the parties.[229] This requirement is generally interpreted narrowly, as courts tend to require proof that the party seeking a referral order has unequivocally admitted the claim; a demonstration that no

[226] CLOUT case No. 522 [*Paladin Agricultural Ltd. & Others v. Excelsior Hotel (Hong Kong) Ltd.*, High Court—Court of First Instance, Hong Kong Special Administrative Region of China, 6 March 2001], [2001] HKCFI 1271, also available on the Internet at http://www.hklii.hk/eng/hk/cases/hkcfi/2001/1271.html.

[227] *The Property People Ltd. v. Housing NZ Ltd.*, High Court, Auckland, New Zealand, 7 December 1999, (1999) 14 PRNZ 66.

[228] *Charles Njogu Lofty v. Bedouin Enterprises Ltd.*, Court of Appeal at Nairobi, Kenya, 16 September 2005, Civil Appeal No. 253 of 2003, available on the Internet at http://kenyalaw.org.

[229] See for instance: CLOUT case No. 382 [*Methanex New Zealand Ltd. v. Fontaine Navigation S.A., Tokyo Marine Co. Ltd., The Owners and all Others*, Federal Court—Trial Division, Canada, 9 January 1998], [1998] 2 FC 583, also available on the Internet at http://canlii.ca/t/4cn6; *Mitsui et al. v. Egon Oldendorff et al.*, Supreme Court of British Columbia, Canada, 30 September 2003, [2003] BCSC 1478, available on the Internet at http://canlii.ca/t/1pwxv; *Fai Tak Engineering Co. Ltd. v. Sui Chong Construction & Engineering Co. Ltd.*, District Court, Hong Kong Special Administrative Region of China, 22 June 2009, [2009] HKDC 141, available on the Internet at http://www.hklii.hk/eng/hk/cases/hkdc/2009/141.html; CLOUT case No. 128 [*Tai Hing Cotton Mill Limited v. Glencore Grain Rotterdam B. V. and another*, Court of Appeal, Hong Kong, 24 November 1995], [1995] HKCA 626, also available on the Internet at http://www.hklii.hk/eng/hk/cases/hkca/1995/626.html; CLOUT case No. 521 [*F & D Building Services Engineering Co.Ltd. v. Chevalier (E & M Contracting)*, High Court—Court of First Instance, Hong Kong Special Administrative Region of China, 23 February 2001], [2001] 3 HKCFI 824, also available on the Internet at http://www.hklii.hk/eng/hk/cases/hkcfi/2001/824.html; *Tai-Ao Aluminium (Taishan) Co. Ltd. v. Maze Aluminium Engineering Co. Ltd. & Another*, High Court—Court of First Instance, Hong Kong Special Administrative Region of China, 17 February 2006, [2006] HKCFI 220, available on the Internet at http://www.hklii.hk/eng/hk/cases/hkcfi/2006/220.html; *Tommy C.P. Sze. & Co. v. Li & Fung (trading) Ltd. & Others,* High Court—Court of First Instance, Hong Kong Special Administrative Region of China, 28 October 2002, [2002] HKCFI 682, available on the Internet at http://www.hklii.hk/eng/hk/cases/hkcfi/2002/682.html; *Mitsui Oil (Asia) Pte. Ltd. v. Chun Yeung Industrial (HK) Ltd.*, High Court—Court of First Instance, Hong Kong Special Administrative Region of China, 24 September 1999, [1999] HKCFI 846, available on the Internet at http://www.hklii.hk/eng/hk/cases/hkcfi/1999/846.html; CLOUT case No. 710 [*Louis Dreyfus Trading Ltd. v. Bonarich International (Group) Ltd.*, Supreme Court—High Court (Commercial List), Hong Kong, 24 March 1997], [1997] HKCFI 312, also available on the Internet at http://www.hklii.hk/eng/hk/cases/hkcfi/1997/312.html; *P & O Nedlloyd Limited v. Wah Hing Seafreight (China) Co. Ltd.*, High Court—Court of First Instance, Hong Kong Special Administrative Region of China, 25 November 1999, [1999] HKCU 1412, available on the Internet at http://www.hklii.hk/eng/hk/cases/hkcfi/1999/90.html; *The Incorporated Owners of Sincere House v. Sincere Co. Ltd.*, Lands Tribunal, Hong Kong Special Administrative Region of China, 18 May 2005, [2005] HKCU 625, available on the Internet at http://www.hklii.hk/eng/hk/cases/hklt/2005/30.html; *Getwick Engineers Ltd. v. Pilecon Engineering Ltd.*, High Court—Court of First Instance, Hong Kong Special Administrative Region of China, 28 August 2002, [2002] HKCFI 189, available on the Internet at http://www.hklii.hk/eng/hk/cases/hkcfi/2002/189.html; *Leung Kwok Tim t/a Tim Yip Engineering Co. v. Builders Federal (Hong Kong) Ltd.*, High Court—Court of First Instance, Hong Kong Special Administrative Region of China, 17 March 2001, [2001] HKCFI 823, available on the Internet at http://www.hklii.hk/eng/hk/cases/hkcfi/2001/823.html; CLOUT case No. 460 [*Hercules Data Comm Co. Ltd. v. Koywa Communications Ltd.*, High Court—Court of First Instance, Hong Kong Special Administrative Region of China, 23 October 2000], [2000] HKCFI 71, also available on the Internet at http://www.hklii.hk/eng/hk/cases/hkcfi/2000/71.html; CLOUT case No. 460 [*Hercules Data Comm Co. Ltd. v. Koywa Communications Ltd.,* High Court—Court of First Instance, Hong Kong Special Administrative Region of China, 23 October 2000], [2000] HKCFI 71, also available on the Internet at http://www.hklii.hk/eng/hk/cases/hkcfi/2000/71.html; *Nassetti Ettore Spa v. Lawton Development Limited*, High Court—Court of First Instance, Hong Kong, 19 April 1996, [1996] HKCU 290.

substantial or arguable defence to the claim has been put forward will not suffice.[230]

Operation of article 8 in a multiparty context

44. Court proceedings frequently involve either multiple claimants, multiple defendants, or both multiple claimants and multiple defendants, and several issues relating to the application of article 8 in such contexts have arisen.

45. One concerns the applicability of article 8 to claims asserted by the defendant in a main action against a third party which the defendant seeks to hold liable in the event that the main action was granted. In several cases the defendant argued that, since the main action was not covered by an arbitration agreement, and since it would be desirable that all aspects of the dispute be dealt with in a single forum, the claim asserted against the third party should not be referred to arbitration despite that it falls within a valid and operative arbitration agreement. While in some cases courts accepted this argument and refused to apply article 8 to such third-party proceedings,[231] most cases—including a decision of the Supreme Court of Canada[232]—stand for the proposition that article 8 does apply in such a context even though the main action is to be decided by the court.[233]

46. A related question is whether the fact that only some of the parties to the action are bound by the arbitration agreement provides justification for dismissing a referral application. Here as well, the issue highlights a tension between the principle of party autonomy and a desire to avoid related disputes being dealt with in different forums. Most cases evidence the courts' commitment to party autonomy, as objections to referral applications based on

[230] See for instance: CLOUT case No. 521 [*F & D Building Services Engineering Co. Ltd. v. Chevalier (E & M Contracting)*, High Court—Court of First Instance, Hong Kong Special Administrative Region of ChinaHong Kong, 23 February 2001], [2001] 3 HKCFI 824, also available on the Internet at http://www.hklii.hk/eng/hk/cases/hkcfi/2001/824.html; *Fai Tak Engineering Co. Ltd. v. Sui Chong Construction & Engineering Co. Ltd.*, District Court, Hong Kong Special Administrative Region of China, 22 June 2009, [2009] HKDC 141, available on the Internet at http://www.hklii.hk/eng/hk/cases/hkdc/2009/141.html; CLOUT case No. 128 [*Tai Hing Cotton Mill Limited v. Glencore Grain Rotterdam B. V. and another*, Court of Appeal, Hong Kong, 24 November 1995], [1995] HKCA 626, also available on the Internet at http://www.hklii.hk/eng/hk/cases/hkca/1995/626.html; *Mitsui Oil (Asia) Pte. Ltd. v. Chun Yeung Industrial (HK) Ltd.*, High Court—Court of First Instance, Hong Kong Special Administrative Region of China, 24 September 1999, [1999] HKCFI 846, available on the Internet at http://www.hklii.hk/eng/hk/cases/hkcfi/1999/846.html; CLOUT case No. 710 [*Louis Dreyfus Trading Ltd. v. Bonarich International (Group) Ltd.*, Supreme Court—High Court (Commercial List), Hong Kong, 24 March 1997], [1997] HKCFI 312, also available on the Internet at http://www.hklii.hk/eng/hk/cases/hkcfi/1997/312.html; *P & O Nedlloyd Limited v. Wah Hing Seafreight (China) Co. Ltd.*, High Court—Court of First Instance, Hong Kong Special Administrative Region of China, 25 November 1999, [1999] HKCU 1412, available on the Internet at http://www.hklii.hk/eng/hk/cases/hkcfi/1999/90.html; *The Incorporated Owners of Sincere House v. Sincere Co. Ltd.*, Lands Tribunal, Hong Kong Special Administrative Region of China, 18 May 2005, [2005] HKCU 625, available on the Internet at http://www.hklii.hk/eng/hk/cases/hklt/2005/30.html; *Getwick Engineers Ltd. v. Pilecon Engineering Ltd.*, High Court—Court of First Instance, Hong Kong Special Administrative Region of China, 28 August 2002, [2002] HKCFI 189, available on the Internet at http://www.hklii.hk/eng/hk/cases/hkcfi/2002/189.html; *Leung Kwok Tim t/a Tim Yip Engineering Co. v. Builders Federal (Hong Kong) Ltd.*, High Court—Court of First Instance, Hong Kong Special Administrative Region of China, 17 March 2001, [2001] HKCFI 823, available on the Internet at http://www.hklii.hk/eng/hk/cases/hkcfi/2001/823.html; CLOUT case No. 460 [*Hercules Data Comm Co. Ltd. v. Koywa Communications Ltd.*, High Court—Court of First Instance, Hong Kong Special Administrative Region of China, 23 October 2000], [2000] HKCFI 71; CLOUT case No. 460 [*Hercules Data Comm Co. Ltd. v. Koywa Communications Ltd.*, High Court—Court of First Instance, Hong Kong Special Administrative Region of China, 23 October 2000], [2000] HKCFI 71, also available on the Internet at http://www.hklii.hk/eng/hk/cases/hkcfi/2000/71.html.

[231] *Guns N'Roses Missouri Storm Inc. v. Productions musicales Donald K. Donald Inc.*, Court of Appeal of Quebec, 18 May 1994, 63 Q.A.C. 54, available on the Internet at http://www.canlii.org/en/qc/qcca/doc/1994/1994canlii5694/1994canlii5694.html; *Ferguson Bros. of St. Thomas v. Manyan Inc.*, Ontario Superior Court of Justice, Canada, 27 May 1999, [1999] OJ No. 1887.

[232] *GreCon Dimter Inc. v. J. R. Normand Inc.*, Supreme Court, Canada, 22 July 2005, [2005] SCC 46 (CanLII), available on the Internet at http://canlii.ca/t/1l6wn.

[233] *Mitsui et al. v. Egon Oldendorff et al.*, Supreme Court of British Columbia, Canada, 30 September 2003, [2003] BCSC 1478, available on the Internet at http://canlii.ca/t/1pwxv; *Abitibi-Price Sales Corp. v. C.V. Scheepv.Ondernemineg "Sambeek"*, Federal Court—Trial Division, Canada, 12 November 1998, [1998] CanLII 8706 (FC), available on the Internet at http://canlii.ca/t/498m; *Turnbridge v. Cansel Survey Equipment (Canada) Ltd.*, Supreme Court of British Columbia, Canada, 17 February 2000, [2000] BCSC 287, available on the Internet at http://canlii.ca/t/53v2; *Shipowners' Mutual Protection and Indemnity Assoc (Luxembourg) v. Hodgetts & Anor*, Supreme Court of Queensland—Court of Appeal, Australia, 6 May 1998, [1998] QCA 88, available on the Internet at http://www.austlii.edu.au/au/cases/qld/QCA/1998/88.html; *Wes Trac Pty. Ltd. v. Eastcoast OTR Tyres Pty. Ltd.*, Supreme Court of New South Wales (Equity Division), Australia, 29 August 2008, [2008] NSWSC 894, available on the Internet at http://www.austlii.edu.au/au/cases/nsw/NSWSC/2008/894.html; *Ocean Park Corporation v. Proud Sky Co. Ltd.*, High Court—Court of First Instance, Hong Kong Special Administrative Region of China, 28 November 2007, [2007] HKCFI 1221, available on the Internet at http://www.hklii.hk/eng/hk/cases/hkcfi/2007/1221.html.

the involvement of parties who are not bound by the arbitration agreement have been rejected in most cases.[234] However, a line of Quebec cases stands for the proposition that, where the action involves parties who are not bound by the arbitration clause, courts enjoy a discretionary power designed to ensure that all claims will be resolved in a single forum and may either refer all parties to arbitration or dismiss the referral application if it appears preferable that all claims be resolved in court.[235]

47. Finally, in a case where only one of the defendants had sought a referral order on the basis of article 8, the court held that the defendant in question was only entitled to a referral order regarding the action commenced against it, and not those commenced against the other defendants.[236]

May courts impose conditions to orders referring the dispute to arbitration?

48. Although article 8 is silent about the possibility of imposing conditions on referrals ordered under that provision, courts have done so in several cases. For example, in two cases, courts have ordered the parties to complete the arbitration swiftly.[237] Courts have also occasionally referred actions to arbitration on the condition that the defendant undertook not to raise a defence of prescription in the arbitration proceeding.[238] In another case, the court referred the case to a religious tribunal selected by the parties in their arbitration agreement, but on the condition that it either proceed with the arbitration on a fixed timetable or clearly indicate its refusal to resolve the dispute.[239]

---

[234] CLOUT case No. 586 [*Kaverit Steel and Crane Ltd. v. Kone Corp.*, Alberta Court of Appeal, Canada, 16 January 1992], [1992] ABCA 7 (CanLII), also available on the Internet at http://canlii.ca/t/1p6kc; CLOUT case No. 619 [*Boart Sweden AB and others v. NYA Strommes AB and others*, Ontario Supreme Court—High Court of Justice, Canada, 21 December 1988]; *Canada (Attorney General) v. Marineserve.MG Inc.*, Supreme Court of Nova Scotia, Canada, 24 May 2002, [2002] NSSC 147, available on the Internet at http://canlii.ca/t/5k7t; CLOUT case No. 116 [*BWV Investments Ltd. v. Saskferco Products Inc. et. al. and UHDE GmbH*, Saskatchewan Court of Appeal, Canada, 25 November 1994], [1994] CanLII 4557 (SK CA), also available on the Internet at http://canlii.ca/t/1nqlf; CLOUT case No. 179 [*The City of Prince George v. A.L. Sims & Sons Ltd.*, Court of Appeal for British Columbia, Canada, 4 July 1995], [1995] CanLII 2487 (BC CA), also available on the Internet at http://canlii.ca/t/1dd92; CLOUT case No. 381 [*Fibreco Pulp Inc. v. Star Shipping A/S*, Federal Court—Court of Appeal, Canada, 24 May 2000], [2000] CanLII 15323 (FCA), also available on the Internet at http://canlii.ca/t/4l31. See *contra*: *Governors Balloon Sararis Ltd. v. Skyship Company Ltd. County Council of Trans,* High Court, Nairobi (Milimani Commercial Courts), Kenya, 11 September 2008, Civil Case 461 of 2008, available on the Internet at http://kenyalaw.org/. In *Paharpur Cooling Towers Ltd. v. Paramount (Wa) Ltd.*, Supreme Court of Western Australia – Court of Appeal, Australia, 13 May 2008, [2008] WASCA 110, available on the Internet at http://www.austlii.edu.au/au/cases/wa/WASCA/2008/110.html, the court dismissed the referral application, not because it considered that the presence of parties who were not bound by the arbitration agreement justified the dismissal of the application, but rather because it found that the parties were likely not to have intended the arbitration agreement to be applicable under such circumstances.

[235] *Décarel Inc. et al. v. Concordia Project Management Ltd.*, Court of Appeal of Quebec, Canada, 30 July 1996, 500-09-000596-957, available on the Internet at http://www.jugements.qc.ca; *Société de Cogénération de St-Félicien, Société en Commandite/St-Felicien Cogeneration Limited Partnership v. Industries Falmec Inc.*, Court of Appeal of Quebec, Canada, 25 April 2005, [2005] QCCA 441 (CanLII), available on the Internet at http://canlii.ca/t/1k8zj; Superior Court of Quebec, Canada, *Cogismaq International Inc. v. Lafontaine*, 20 March 2007, [2007] QCSC 1214, available on the Internet at http://canlii.ca/t/1r033; *Société Asbestos Limitée v. Charles Lacroix et al.*, Court of Appeal of Quebec, Canada, 7 September 2004, [2004] CanLII 21635 (QC CA), available on the Internet at http://canlii.ca/t/1hqvq; *Société du Port Ferroviaire de Baie-Comeau—Hauterive v. Jean Fournier Inc.*, Court of Appeal of Quebec, Canada, 26 November 2010, [2010] QCCA 2161, available on the Internet at http://canlii.ca/t/2dl92; *Location Imafa, s.e.c. v. Fedex Ground Package System Ltd.,* Superior Court of Quebec, Canada, 8 June 2010, [2010] QCCS 2829 (CanLII), available on the Internet at http://canlii.ca/t/2bdgk; *Distnet inc. v. Andritz Hydro ltée*, Superior Court of Quebec, Canada, 28 April 2010, [2010] QCCS 1921, available on the Internet at http://canlii.ca/t/29rg2.

[236] CLOUT case No. 17 [*Stancroft Trust Limited, Berry and Klausner v. Can-Asia Capital Company, Limited, Mandarin Capital Corporation and Asiamerica Capital Limited*, Court of Appeal for British Columbia, Canada, 26 February 1990], [1990] CanLII 1060 (BC CA), also available on the Internet at http://canlii.ca/t/1d7jd.

[237] *Fuller Austin Insulation Inc. v. Wellington Insurance Co.*, Saskatchewan Court of Queen's Bench, Canada, 15 September 1995, [1995] CanLII 5752 (SK QB), also available on the Internet at http://canlii.ca/t/1nrkb; *East African Development Bank v. Ziwa Horticultural Exporters Limited*, High Court, Kampala, Uganda, 20 October 2000, [2000] UGCommC 8.

[238] CLOUT case No. 72 [*Continental Resources Inc. v. East Asiatic Co. (Canada) et al.*, Federal Court—Trial Division, Canada, 22 March 1994]; CLOUT case No. 14 [*Iberfreight S.A. et al. v. Ocean Star Container Line AG and J.W. Lunstedt KG*, Federal Court—Court of Appeal, Canada, 2 June 1989].

[239] *Popack v. Lipszyc*, Ontario Court of Appeal, Canada, 30 April 2009, [2009] ONCA 365, available on the Internet at http://canlii.ca/t/23dl8, confirming *Popack v. Lipszyc*, Ontario Superior Court of Justice, 2 September 2008, [2008] CanLII 43593 (ON SC), available on the Internet at http://canlii.ca/t/20k54.

Possibility of relying on local procedural rules to stay the action or refer the parties to arbitration where the requirements of article 8 are not met

49. Several cases confirm that where the requirements of article 8 are not met, courts may nevertheless stay an action—or part thereof—on the basis of local procedural rules.[240] Courts have thus recognized the possibility of relying on local rules to stay part of an action not falling within the arbitration agreement while the rest of the claim was being arbitrated.[241] They have also agreed to stay an action despite that the party seeking a referral order had invoked the arbitration agreement after having submitted its first statement on the substance of the dispute. This occurred, for example, in one case where the defendant had filed a statement of defence under protest and for the sole purpose of avoiding being noted in default.[242] A similar approach was adopted in a case where the claimant had, a few days after instituting the action, amended its pleadings and indicated its intention to rely on the arbitration agreement. Assuming that the claimant's initial pleadings constituted a statement on the substance of the dispute, and that the claimant's referral application had therefore not been made in a timely manner, the court held that a stay of the action could and should be ordered on the basis of general powers recognized by local procedural rules.[243]

50. Another noteworthy group of cases involves multi-party situations where, after having referred claims involving some of the parties to arbitration, it was decided that courts—in order to avoid related claims being initiated simultaneously in different forums—could stay the actions involving parties who were not bound by the arbitration agreement and who could therefore not be referred to arbitration on the basis of article 8.[244]

---

[240] In addition to the cases discussed in this section, see: CLOUT case No. 113 [*T1T2 Limited Partnership v. Canada*, Ontario Court of Justice—General Division, Canada, 10 November 1994].

[241] See for instance: CLOUT case No. 72 [*Continental Resources Inc. v. East Asiatic Co. (Canada) et al.*, Federal Court—Trial Division, Canada, 22 March 1994].

[242] CLOUT case No. 15 [*Navionics Inc. v. Flota Maritima Mexicana S.A. et al.*, Federal Court—Trial Division, Canada, 17 January 1989], [1989] FCJ No. 13.

[243] *Bab Systems Inc. v. McLurg*, Ontario Court of Appeal, Canada, 11 May 1995, [1995] CanLII 1099 (ON CA), available on the Internet at http://canlii.ca/t/6jj1, where the court orders referral even if the application is untimely, but it does so not on the basis on article 8, but rather on the basis of domestic rules of procedure. In another case where the arbitration agreement was not invoked within the time limit set forth in article 8, the court refused to stay the action on the ground that domestic procedural rules invoked by the applicants did not allow it to do so: CLOUT case No. 17 [*Stancroft Trust Limited, Berry and Klausner v. Can-Asia Capital Company, Limited, Mandarin Capital Corporation and Asiamerica Capital Limited*, Court of Appeal for British Columbia, Canada, 26 February 1990], [1990] CanLII 1060 (BC CA), also available on the Internet at http://canlii.ca/t/1d7jd.

[244] See for instance: CLOUT case No. 619 [*Boart Sweden AB and others v. NYA Strommes AB and others*, Ontario Supreme Court—High Court of Justice, Canada, 21 December 1988]; *Agrawest & AWI v. BMA*, Prince Edward Island Supreme Court—Trial Division, Canada, 23 June 2005, [2005] PESCTD 36 (CanLII), available on the Internet at http://canlii.ca/t/1l40z; CLOUT case No. 112 [*Kvaerner Enviropower Inc. v. Tanar Industries Ltd.*, Court of Queen's Bench of Alberta, Canada, 13 July 1994], 1994 CanLII 9242 (AB QB), also available on the Internet at http://canlii.ca/t/2brch; CLOUT case No. 586 [*Kaverit Steel and Crane Ltd. v. Kone Corp.*, Alberta Court of Appeal, Canada, 16 January 1992], [1992] ABCA 7 (CanLII), also available on the Internet at http://canlii.ca/t/1p6kc.

Article 9. Arbitration agreement and interim measures by court

It is not incompatible with an arbitration agreement for a party to request, before or during arbitral proceedings, from a court an interim measure of protection and for a court to grant such measure.

TRAVAUX PRÉPARATOIRES

The *travaux préparatoires* on article 9 as adopted in 1985 are contained in the following documents:

1. Report of the United Nations Commission on International Trade Law on the work of its eighteenth session (*Official Records of the General Assembly, Fortieth Session, Supplement No. 17* (A/40/17)), paras. 11-333.

2. Reports of the Working Group: A/CN.9/216; A/CN.9/232; A/CN.9/233; A/CN.9/245; A/CN.9/246, annex; A/CN.9/263 and Add.1-2; A/CN.9/264. Relevant working papers are referred to in the reports.

3. Summary records of the 312th and 332nd UNCITRAL meetings.

Article 9 was not amended in 2006.

(Available on the Internet at www.uncitral.org).

INTRODUCTION

1. Article 9 expresses the principle that any interim measures of protection that may be obtained from courts under their procedural law are compatible with an arbitration agreement. That provision is ultimately addressed to the courts of any State, insofar as it establishes the compatibility between interim measures possibly issued by any court and an arbitration agreement, irrespective of the place of arbitration. Wherever a request for interim measures may be made to a court, it may not be relied upon, under the Model Law, as a waiver or an objection against the existence or effect of the arbitration agreement.[245]

CASE LAW ON ARTICLE 9

2. Article 9 only addresses the effect of an arbitration agreement by providing that it is not incompatible with such an agreement for a party to request or for a court to grant an interim measure of protection. Therefore, and as is clear from the *travaux préparatoires*,[246] article 9 does not in itself confer on courts the power to issue interim measures of protection in support of international commercial arbitral proceedings. This point was emphasized in a decision of the Singapore Court of Appeal concerning the courts' power to issue an order preventing the defendant from disposing or dealing with its assets in Singapore and relating to a dispute falling within the scope of an agreement providing for arbitration in London.[247]

3. The rules governing the power to grant interim measures, the types of measures available, the conditions under which they may be granted, and the relationship between the courts' power to issue such measures and that of the arbitrators are thus to be found elsewhere than in article 9. The fact that none of these issues was addressed in the 1985 version of the Model Law entails that they were, at that time, intended to be governed by domestic law. The situation is slightly different under the Model Law, as amended in 2006: article 17 J expressly confers on courts the power of issuing interim measures of protection, but local law continues to play an important role, firstly,

[245] Explanatory Note by the UNCITRAL Secretariat on the Model Law on International Commercial Arbitration, in UNCITRAL Model Law on International Commercial Arbitration 1985, with amendments as adopted in 2006, United Nations publication, Sales No. E.08.V.4 (available on the Internet at http://www.uncitral.org/pdf/english/texts/arbitration/ml-arb/07-86998_Ebook.pdf), Part Two, at para. 22.

[246] *Official records of the General Assembly, Fortieth Session, Supplement No. 17* (A/40/17), Annex I, para. 96 ("It was understood that article 9 itself did not regulate which interim measures of protection were available to a party. It merely expressed the principle that a request for any court measure available under a given legal system and the granting of such measure by a court of 'this State' was compatible with the fact that the parties had agreed to settle their dispute by arbitration").

[247] CLOUT case No. 741 [*Swift-Fortune Ltd. v. Magnifica Marine SA*, Court of Appeal, Singapore, 1 December 2006], also in [2006] SGCA 42, [2007] 1 SLR(R) 629, where the Court stated: "Article 9 was not intended to confer jurisdiction but to declare the compatibility between resolving a dispute through arbitration and at the same time seeking assistance from the court for interim protection orders". "Article 9 can have no bearing on the meaning and effect of a domestic law providing for interim measures".

because the power conferred on courts in relation to international commercial arbitral proceedings is the same power as they have in relation to proceedings in courts, and secondly because that power is to be exercised in accordance with local rules, albeit "in consideration of the specific features of international arbitration."[248] (See below, section on article 17 J, paras. 1-4).

Scope of application of article 9

4. Pursuant to article 1 (2), article 9 is excepted from the general rule according to which the Model Law applies only if the place of arbitration is located in the territory of the enacting State. Therefore—and as several cases illustrate—, article 9 also applies if the place of arbitration is either undetermined or located in a foreign jurisdiction.[249]

Rationale of article 9

5. The rationale for article 9 is that the granting of interim measures is sometimes essential to ensure the effectiveness of the arbitral tribunal's power to dispose of the merits of the case fully and in an effective manner. Also, the arbitral tribunal is sometimes unable to respond effectively to a party's need for interim measures of protection. Examples include situations where a measure is needed prior to the constitution of the arbitral tribunal, or where a measure needs to be granted against a third party over which the arbitral tribunal has no jurisdiction. As was held in several cases quoting from a leading decision of the English House of Lords, "[t]he purpose of interim measures of protection [...] is not to encroach on the procedural powers of the arbitrators but to reinforce them, and to render more effective the decision at which the arbitrators will ultimately arrive on the substance of the dispute."[250]

What constitutes an interim measure of protection?

6. The concept of an interim measure of protection is not defined in the 1985 version of the Model Law. However the *travaux préparatoires* show that the "range of measures covered by the provision [is] a wide one"[251] and includes pre-award attachments,[252] measures relating to the protection of trade secrets and proprietary information,[253] measures relating to the protection of the subject-matter of the dispute[254] and measures intended to secure evidence.[255] The Model Law, as amended in 2006, includes in article 17 (2) a detailed and comprehensive definition of an interim measure, but that provision relates to measures adopted by arbitral tribunals (and not to measures adopted by courts) (see below, section on article 17, paras. 3-5).

---

[248] The last sentence of article 17 J reads as follows: "The court shall exercise such power in accordance with its own procedures in consideration of the specific features of international arbitration."

[249] See for instance: *Front Carriers Ltd. v. Atlantic & Orient Shipping Corp.*, High Court, Singapore, 19 July 2006, [2006] SGHC 127, [2006] 3 SLR(R) 854; *Econ Corp. International Ltd. v. Ballast-Nedam International B.V.*, High Court, Singapore, 10 December 2002, [2002] SGHC 293, [2003] 2 SLR(R) 15; *Amican Navigation Inc. v. Densan Shipping Co.*, Federal Court—Trial Division, Canada, 21 October 1997, [1997] CanLII 6263 (CF), available on the Internet at http://canlii.ca/t/4cx9; CLOUT case No. 393 [*Frontier International Shipping Corp. v. Tavros (The)*, Federal Court—Trial Division, Canada, 23 December 1999], [2000] 2 FC 445, also available on the Internet at http://canlii.ca/t/45mh; CLOUT case No. 68 [*Delphi Petroleum Inc. v. Derin Shipping and Training Ltd.*, Federal Court—Trial Division, Canada, 3 December 1993]; CLOUT case No. 353 [*TLC Multimedia Inc. v. Core Curriculum Technologies Inc.*, Supreme Court of British Columbia, Canada, 6 July 1998], [1998] CanLII 3901 (BC SC), also available on the Internet at http://canlii.ca/t/1f6x9; CLOUT case No. 71 [*Trade Fortune Inc. v. Amalgamated Mill Supplies Ltd.*, Supreme Court of British Columbia, Canada, 25 February 1994], [1994] CanLII 845 (BC SC), also available on the Internet at http://canlii.ca/t/1dlj3.

[250] *NCC International AB v. Alliance Concrete Singapore Pte. Ltd.*, Court of Appeal, Singapore, 26 February 2008, [2008] SGCA 5, [2008] 2 SLR(R) 565, quoting from *Channel Tunnel Group Ltd. v. Balfour Beatty Construction Ltd.*, House of Lords, England, 17 February 1993, [1993] AC 334; *Front Carriers Ltd. v. Atlantic & Orient Shipping Corp.*, High Court, Singapore, 19 July 2006, [2006] SGHC 127, [2006] 3 SLR(R) 854; *Pathak v. Tourism Transport Ltd.*, High Court, Auckland, New Zealand, 20 August 2002, [2002] 3 NZLR 681; CLOUT case No. 692 [*The Owners of the Ship or vessel "Lady Muriel" v. Transorient Shipping Limited*, Court of Appeal, Hong Kong, 3 May 1995], [1995] HKCA 615, also available on the Internet at http://www.hklii.hk/eng/hk/cases/hkca/1995/615.html; see also A/CN.9/264, Analytical commentary on draft text of a model law on international commercial arbitration, under article 9, para. 2, available on the UNCITRAL website at http://www.uncitral.org/uncitral/en/commission/sessions/18th.html.

[251] *Official records of the General Assembly, Fortieth Session, Supplement No. 17* (A/40/17), Annex I, para. 96. See also CLOUT case No. 39 [*Katran Shipping Co. Ltd. v. Kenven Transportation Ltd.*, High Court—Court of First Instance, Hong Kong, 29 June 1992], [1992] HKCFI 173, also available on the Internet at http://www.hklii.hk/eng/hk/cases/hkcfi/1992/173.html.

[252] *Official records of the General Assembly, Fortieth Session, Supplement No. 17* (A/40/17), Annex I, para. 96.

[253] Ibid.

[254] A/CN.9/264, Analytical commentary on draft text of a model law on international commercial arbitration, under article 9, para. 4, available on the UNCITRAL website at http://www.uncitral.org/uncitral/en/commission/sessions/18th.html.

[255] Ibid.

7. Cases from jurisdictions that have adopted article 9 reveal that courts have also favoured a broad view of the types of interim measures that should be deemed not to be incompatible with an arbitration agreement. These measures include orders designed to prevent the defendant from disposing of assets against which an award favourable to the claimant could eventually be executed—such as an order authorizing a seizure before judgment, a *Mareva* injunction or an order for the arrest of a ship[256]—, orders authorizing the inspection of a property with a view to preserving evidence,[257] interlocutory injunctions,[258] orders to access premises in order to retrieve property,[259] as well as orders to sell perishable goods which are in dispute or as to which any question arises and which may otherwise become of no value while the dispute is pending.[260]

8. Further guidance on the concept of an interim measure of protection may be found in cases where the courts refused to hold that certain orders belonged in that category. One example is a Canadian case involving an order granting to the defendant to an action that had been referred to arbitration the costs of that action. The reviewing court subsequently discharged the order on the ground that, being a final cost order, it was neither interim nor protective within the meaning of article 9. The court added that "interim protection is 'interim' in that it is something done pending final determination of the issues on the merits."[261] Another court dismissed an application which purported to seek an interlocutory injunction as the circumstances of the case revealed that the applicant was in reality seeking to have the merits of its claim adjudicated immediately.[262]

9. One area of controversy concerns whether evidentiary orders that do not seek to preserve or conserve evidence that may become unavailable at the substantive hearing, but that rather merely seek to ensure that evidence not within the control of a party be produced, fall within the ambit of article 9. In a leading case decided in 1994, the Hong Kong High Court found that a subpoena was not an interim measure of protection. The court further held that a party seeking the court's assistance in such a context needed to proceed pursuant to article 27, and thus with the arbitral tribunal's authorization.[263] The decision is to be contrasted with a Canadian decision in a case involving a request to examine on discovery a third party to the arbitration. The court, referring to a statement in the *travaux préparatoires* of the Model Law to the effect that the concept of interim measures of protection includes measures to "secure evidence," concluded that the requested measure fell within the ambit of article 9 and suggested that a party seeking a court's assistance in evidentiary matters has the option of invoking either article 27 (where the request has been approved by the arbitral tribunal) or article 9 (in which case the arbitral tribunal's authorization is not necessary).[264] (See below, section on article 27, para. 6).

---

[256] CLOUT case No. 354 [*Silver Standard Resources Inc. v. Joint Stock Company Geolog, Cominco Ltd. and Open Type Stock Company Dukat GOK*, Court of Appeal for British Columbia, Canada, 11 December 1998], [1998] CanLII 6468 (BC CA), also available on the Internet at http://canlii.ca/t/1f0vk; CLOUT case No. 71 [*Trade Fortune Inc. v. Amagalmated Mill Supplies Ltd.*, Supreme Court of British Columbia, Canada, 25 February 1994], [1994] CanLII 845 (BC SC), also available on the Internet at http://canlii.ca/t/1dlj3; *Amican Navigation Inc. c. Densan Shipping Co.*, Federal Court—Trial Division, Canada, 21 October 1997, [1997] CanLII 6263 (CF), available on the Internet at http://canlii.ca/t/4cx9.

[257] CLOUT case No. 692 [*Transorient Shipping Limited v. The Owners of the Ship or vessel "Lady Muriel" v. Transorient Shipping Limited*, Court of Appeal, Hong Kong, 3 May 1995], [1995] HKCA 615, also available on the Internet at http://www.hklii.hk/eng/hk/cases/hkca/1995/615.html.

[258] *Osmond Ireland On Farm Business v. Mc Farland*, High Court, Ireland, 30 June 2010, [2010] IEHC 295, available on the Internet at http://www.bailii.org/ie/cases/IEHC/2010/H295.html; CLOUT case No. 353 [*TLC Multimedia Inc. v. Core Curriculum Technologies Inc.*, Supreme Court of British Columbia, Canada, 6 July 1998], [1998] CanLII 3901 (BC SC), also available on the Internet at http://canlii.ca/t/1f6x9; *Navi-Mont Inc. v. Rigel Shipping Canada Inc.*, Federal Court—Trial Division, Canada, 28 May 1997, [1997], CanLII 5130 (FC), available on the Internet at http://canlii.ca/t/4fln; *Pan Afric Impex (U) Ltd. v. Bank PLC and Another*, High Court at Kampala (Commercial Court Division), Uganda, 13 February 2008, [2008] UGCommC 18; *Blue Limited v. Jaribu Credit Traders Limited*, High Court at Nairobi (Milimani Commercial Courts), Kenya, 25 September 2008, Civil Suit 157 of 2008, available on the Internet at http://kenyalaw.org/CaseSearch; *Wellness Health & Fitness Centre Ltd. v. Shamsher Kenya Ltd.*, High Court at Nairobi (Milimani Commercial Courts), Kenya, 8 April 2008, Civil Suit 30 of 2008, available on the Internet at http://kenyalaw.org/CaseSearch/view_preview1.php?link=66135068947847118285177; *Santack Enterprises Limited v. Kenya Building Society Limited*, High Court at Nairobi (Nairobi Law Courts), Kenya, 5 March 2008, Civil Suit 298 of 2007, available on the Internet at http://kenyalaw.org/CaseSearch/view_preview1.php?link=83385438444435819008657; *Communications Carrier Ltd. & Another v. Telkom Kenya Limited*, High Court at Nairobi (Milimani Commercial Courts), Kenya, 14 November 2005, Civil Case 249 of 2007, available on the Internet at http://kenyalaw.org/CaseSearch/view_preview1.php?link=80881325820268507241760; *Ordina Shipmanagement Ltd. v. Unispeed Group Inc.*, Federal Court—Trial Division, Canada, 20 November 1998, [1998] CanLII 8785 (FC), available on the Internet at http://canlii.ca/t/494v.

[259] *Roko Construction Ltd. v. Aya Bakery (U) Ltd.*, High Court at Kampala (Civil Division), Uganda, 3 October 2007, [2007] UGHC 31.

[260] *Taxfield Shipping Ltd. v. Asiana Marine Inc. and others*, High Court—Court of First Instance (Construction and Arbitration Proceedings), Hong Kong Special Administrative Region of China, 7 March 2006, [2006] HKCFI 271, available on the Internet at http://www.hklii.hk/eng/hk/cases/hkcfi/2006/271.html.

[261] CLOUT case No. 393 [*Frontier International Shipping Corp. v. Tavros (The)*, Federal Court—Trial Division, Canada, 23 December 1999], [2000] 2 FC 445, also available on the Internet at http://canlii.ca/t/45mh.

[262] CLOUT case No. 11 [*Relais Nordik v. Secunda Marine Services Limited*, Federal Court—Trial Division, Canada, 19 February 1988].

[263] CLOUT case No. 77 [*Vibroflotation A.G. v. Express Builders Co. Ltd.*, High Court—Court of First Instance, Hong Kong, 15 August 1994], [1994] HKCFI 205, also available on the Internet at http://www.hklii.hk/eng/hk/cases/hkcfi/1994/205.html.

[264] CLOUT case No. 68 [*Delphi Petroleum Inc. v. Derin Shipping and Training Ltd.*, Federal Court—Trial Division, Canada, 3 December 1993].

10. Finally, one Singapore court has ruled that an injunction seeking to restrain a party from continuing an action commenced before a foreign court and brought in breach of an arbitration agreement is an interim measure of protection that is therefore not incompatible with that agreement.[265]

Possibility of contracting out of article 9

11. Article 9 does not indicate whether parties to an arbitration agreement governed by law enacting the Model Law may contract out of article 9. According to the *travaux préparatoires*, article 9 should neither "be read as precluding such exclusion agreements, [nor] be read as positively giving effect to any such exclusion."[266] In other words, article 9 is to be read as not taking any stance on this issue. Article 9 is not addressed to the parties, but to courts of a given State, and only expresses the principle that any interim measures of protection that may be obtained from courts under their procedural law are compatible with an arbitration agreement

12. In an Indian case, the court concluded that by agreeing to resort to arbitration in Singapore and, for subsidiary matters, conferring on the Singaporean courts jurisdiction to resolve disputes arising out of their agreement, the parties had validly excluded the power that Indian courts would otherwise have had to grant interim measures of protection in aid of a foreign arbitration.[267]

[265] *WSG Nimbus Pte. Ltd. v. Board of Control for Cricket in Sri Lanka*, High Court, Singapore, 13 May 2002, [2002] SGHC 104.

[266] *Official records of the General Assembly, Fortieth Session Supplement No. 17* (A/40/17), para. 97.

[267] *Max India Limited v. General Binding Corporation*, Delhi High Court, India, 16 July 2009, available on the Internet at http://www.indiankanoon.org/doc/317564/.

CHAPTER III. COMPOSITION OF ARBITRAL TRIBUNAL

Article 10. Number of arbitrators

(1) The parties are free to determine the number of arbitrators.

(2) Failing such determination, the number of arbitrators shall be three.

TRAVAUX PRÉPARATOIRES

The *travaux préparatoires* on article 10 as adopted in 1985 are contained in the following documents:

1. Report of the United Nations Commission on International Trade Law on the work of its eighteenth session (*Official Records of the General Assembly, Fortieth Session, Supplement No. 17* (A/40/17)), paras. 11-333.

2. Reports of the Working Group: A/CN.9/216; A/CN.9/232; A/CN.9/233; A/CN.9/245; A/CN.9/246, annex; A/CN.9/263 and Add.1-2; A/CN.9/264. Relevant working papers are referred to in the reports.

3. Summary records of the 312th and 332nd UNCITRAL meetings.

Article 10 was not amended in 2006.

(Available on the Internet at www.uncitral.org).

CASE LAW ON ARTICLE 10

1. Article 10 provides further evidence of the importance given to party autonomy in the Model Law. It grants to the parties complete freedom regarding the number of arbitrators.[268] One court ruled that an agreement between the parties to appoint an even number of arbitrators was within the scope of the parties' freedom under paragraph (1), and that the validity of the arbitration agreement did not depend on the number of arbitrators.[269] This holding is in line with the *travaux préparatoires*.[270]

2. A court does not have the power to modify the default rule of three arbitrators on grounds of cost-effectiveness or proportionality.[271]

[268] See for instance: *Electra Air Conditioning B.V. v. Seeley International Pty. Ltd.*, Federal Court, Australia, 8 October 2008, [2008] FCAFC 169, available on the Internet at http://www.austlii.edu.au/au/cases/cth/FCAFC/2008/169.html; *Gordian Runoff Ltd. (formerly Gio Insurance Ltd.) v. The Underwriting Members of Lloyd's Syndicates*, Supreme Court of New South Wales (Equity Division), Australia, 19 December 2002 (revised 5 February 2003), [2002] NSWSC 1260, available on the Internet at http://www.austlii.edu.au/au/cases/nsw/NSWSC/2002/1260.html.

[269] CLOUT case No. 177 [*MMTC v. Sterlite Industries (India) Ltd.*, Supreme Court, India, 18 November 1996], also available on the Internet at http://www.indiankanoon.org/doc/1229987/.

[270] A/CN.9/264, Analytical commentary on draft text of a model law on international commercial arbitration, under article 10, para. 2 available on the UNCITRAL website at http://www.uncitral.org/uncitral/en/commission/sessions/18th.html.

[271] *Thésaurus Inc. v. Xpub Média Inc.*, Court of Quebec, Canada, 20 August 2007, [2007] QCCQ 10436 (CanLII), available on the Internet at. http://canlii.ca/t/1t0f3.

Article 11. Appointment of arbitrators

(1) No person shall be precluded by reason of his nationality from acting as an arbitrator, unless otherwise agreed by the parties.

(2) The parties are free to agree on a procedure of appointing the arbitrator or arbitrators, subject to the provisions of paragraphs (4) and (5) of this article.

(3) Failing such agreement,

> *a) in an arbitration with three arbitrators, each party shall appoint one arbitrator, and the two arbitrators thus appointed shall appoint the third arbitrator; if a party fails to appoint the arbitrator within thirty days of receipt of a request to do so from the other party, or if the two arbitrators fail to agree on the third arbitrator within thirty days of their appointment, the appointment shall be made, upon request of a party, by the court or other authority specified in article 6;*
>
> *b) in an arbitration with a sole arbitrator, if the parties are unable to agree on the arbitrator, he shall be appointed, upon request of a party, by the court or other authority specified in article 6.*

(4) Where, under an appointment procedure agreed upon by the parties,

> *(a) a party fails to act as required under such procedure, or*
>
> *(b) the parties, or two arbitrators, are unable to reach an agreement expected of them under such procedure, or*
>
> *(c) a third party, including an institution, fails to perform any function entrusted to it under such procedure,*

any party may request the court or other authority specified in article 6 to take the necessary measure, unless the agreement on the appointment procedure provides other means for securing the appointment.

5) A decision on a matter entrusted by paragraph (3) or (4) of this article to the court or other authority specified in article 6 shall be subject to no appeal. The court or other authority, in appointing an arbitrator, shall have due regard to any qualifications required of the arbitrator by the agreement of the parties and to such considerations as are likely to secure the appointment of an independent and impartial arbitrator and, in the case of sole or third arbitrator, shall take into account as well the advisability of appointing an arbitrator of a nationality other than those of the parties.

TRAVAUX PRÉPARATOIRES

The *travaux préparatoires* on article 11 as adopted in 1985 are contained in the following documents:

1. Report of the United Nations Commission on International Trade Law on the work of its eighteenth session (*Official Records of the General Assembly, Fortieth Session, Supplement No. 17* (A/40/17)), paras. 11-333.
2. Reports of the Working Group: A/CN.9/216; A/CN.9/232; A/CN.9/233; A/CN.9/245; A/CN.9/246, annex; A/CN.9/263 and Add.1-2; A/CN.9/264. Relevant working papers are referred to in the reports.
3. Summary records of the 312th and 332nd UNCITRAL meetings.

Article 11 was not amended in 2006.

(Available on the Internet at www.uncitral.org).

INTRODUCTION

Party autonomy and default procedure

1. Article 11 addresses the constitution of the arbitral tribunal, a question of a significant practical importance. First and foremost, it grants parties extensive freedom with respect to who may be appointed as an arbitrator as well as to how arbitrators are to be appointed. Secondly, article 11 sets out several rules which are applicable unless otherwise agreed to by the parties: one prohibits discrimination based on nationality, while the others establish default appointment procedures that provide guidance when the parties have remained silent on the method of appointment of the arbitrator—or the arbitrators, in the case of a three-member arbitral tribunal. Thirdly, article 11 allows the court or the competent authority designated in article 6 to intervene in order to resolve deadlocks in the appointment procedure.

Scope of application of article 11

2. Article 11 is not among the provisions listed in article 1 (2) and thus does not apply where the seat of arbitration is either undetermined or located in a foreign jurisdiction. While the *travaux préparatoires* show that consideration has been given to the possibility of making article 11 applicable before the place of arbitration had been determined, the prevailing view was that the Model Law should not deal with court intervention relating to the composition of arbitral tribunal prior to the determination of the place of arbitration.[272]

CASE LAW ON ARTICLE 11

Party autonomy—paragraph (2)

3. As is clear from the text of article 11, the governing principle with respect to the constitution of the arbitral tribunal is party autonomy. The parties may choose the arbitrators directly, either before or after the dispute has arisen. The parties are also free to delegate to an appointing authority certain tasks in relation to the constitution of the arbitral tribunal.

4. In one decision, a German court confirmed that the agreement on the appointment of arbitrators referred to in paragraph (2) might be achieved by reference to arbitration rules.[273] Another German court further held that the parties may agree that one of them will choose which of two appointing authorities mentioned in their agreement would appoint the arbitrator.[274]

5. In one Spanish case suggesting that the parties' freedom is such that they are not limited to appointing individuals as arbitrators, the court upheld an award based on an arbitration agreement appointing a legal person as arbitrator.[275]

6. The *travaux préparatoires* indicate that the principle of party autonomy is not without limits. Parties could not exclude the assistance of the court or authority designated in article 6 in overcoming deadlocks in the appointment process. Parties could not derogate from the rule that decisions made pursuant to article 11 by the court or authority designated in article 6 are final.[276]

7. The Supreme Court of India has held that the provisions of the arbitration agreement setting out an appointment procedure could be disregarded in exceptional circumstances in order to ensure the expeditiousness and effectiveness of the arbitral proceedings; in that case the appointment procedure was disregarded after several attempts to constitute a functioning arbitral tribunal pursuant to its terms had proven unsuccessful.[277] That same court has also found that where the arbitration agreement names the person who shall act as arbitrator, that choice may be disregarded if justifiable doubts as to that person's impartiality or independence exist, or if other circumstances warrant the appointment of a different arbitrator.[278]

Court or other competent authority intervention in relation to the constitution of the arbitral tribunal—paragraphs (3) and (4)

8. Article 11 allows the court or other competent authority designated in article 6 to intervene to ensure that deadlocks in the appointment procedure will not prevent the arbitration from going forward. Court or other authority intervention can first occur under the default appointment procedure set out in paragraph (3): if the parties fail to appoint the arbitrators—individually or, in the case of a three-member

---

[272] *Official Records of the General Assembly, Fortieth Session, Supplement No. 17* (A/40/17), paras. 79-80 and 107-111.

[273] Oberlandesgericht Dresden, Germany, 11 Sch 01/01, 28 February 2001, available on the Internet at http://www.dis-arb.de/de/47/datenbanken/rspr/olg-dresden-az-11-sch-01-01-datum-2001-02-28-id1264.

[274] Oberlandesgericht Koblenz, Germany, 2 Sch 04/03 (2), 19 February 2004, available on the Internet at http://www.dis-arb.de/de/47/datenbanken/rspr/olg-koblenz-az-2-sch-04-03-2-datum-2004-02-19-id1278.

[275] *Sogecable S.A. v. Auna Telecomunicaciones S.A.*, Audiencia Provincial de Madrid (sección 14ª), Spain, 29 July 2005, res. 585/2005, 28079370142005100459 (Id cendoj).

[276] A/CN.9/264, Analytical commentary on draft text of a model law on international commercial arbitration, under article 11, para. 3, available on the UNCITRAL website at http://www.uncitral.org/uncitral/en/commission/sessions/18th.html.

[277] *Union Of India v. M/S. Singh Builders Syndicate*, Supreme Court, India, 26 February 2009, available on the Internet at http://www.indiankanoon.org/doc/276364/.

[278] *Indian Oil Corp. Ltd. & Ors. v. M/S Raja Transport(P) Ltd.,* Supreme Court, India, 24 August 2009, available on the Internet at http://www.indiankanoon.org/doc/2073/.

arbitral tribunal, collectively—, or if the party-appointed arbitrators in a three-member arbitral tribunal fail to agree on the third arbitrator, the court or competent authority is authorized to make the necessary appointments. The court or competent authority may also intervene where a deadlock occurs in an appointment procedure agreed to by the parties (a party fails to act as required under such procedure, the parties or the arbitrators are unable to reach an agreement expected of them under such procedure, or a third party fails to perform a function entrusted to it under such procedure). Here, the court or the institution's powers are broader, as paragraph (4) empowers them to "take the necessary measure" in light of the circumstances in which the deadlock occurred.

9. In a leading case on article 11, a Bermudan court held that the primary duty of a court asked to intervene pursuant to that provision is to ensure that the parties can resolve their dispute before an independent and impartial arbitral tribunal without delay.[279] It has also been pointed out that when an application is made pursuant to article 11, the parties ought to make suggestions to the court regarding persons they consider to be suitable candidates, because it is not the court's function to decide who should be appointed.[280]

10. In one case, the Ugandan institution designated pursuant to article 6 of the Model Law has stated that parties are under a mutual obligation to participate in the constitution of the arbitral tribunal, and that this obligation subsists even though one party may be of the view that no dispute exists between the parties.[281]

Existence of deadlock justifying the court's or the institution's intervention

11. Disagreements sometimes arise as to whether a deadlock actually exists in the applicable appointment procedure. In one Bermudan case, a court dismissed an argument to the effect that the procedure set out in the parties' arbitration agreement had not broken down, and that the court had thus no power to intervene pursuant to paragraph (4). The court added that, as a general rule, a court should refuse to intervene pursuant to article 11 only where it is clear that no deadlock of any sort truly exist.[282]

12. In relation to paragraph (4)*(c)*, it was found in one decision that the court should not appoint an arbitrator where the parties have delegated that task to an appointing authority that can be expected to perform its obligations.[283] However, where such appointing authority has declined or otherwise cannot be expected to perform its obligations, the court should take the necessary measures in accordance with paragraph (4)*(c)*.[284]

13. In another case, an arbitration clause contained in a standard construction agreement and normally used only in domestic transactions referred to the president of the "*Landesgericht*" (a German regional court) at the ordering party's place of business as appointing authority. The court competent to hear applications under paragraph (4) found that it had the power to make the appointment, as the fact that the ordering party's place of business was outside Germany rendered the clause inoperative. The court rejected the respondent's argument that the president of the equivalent court at the ordering party's place of business could act as appointing authority since, in the opinion of the court, by choosing a standard agreement normally used in German relationships and referring to a "*Landesgericht*", the parties had intended that appointments be made by a German authority.[285]

14. In a case where the parties had designated, in the arbitration agreement, a sole arbitrator who subsequently declined to serve as arbitrator, the court decided to appoint another arbitrator on the ground that the arbitrator initially designated had failed to perform its function under the procedure agreed to by the parties.[286] Also, where a dispute resolution clause provided that, before resorting to arbitration, the parties were to appoint a trusted third party to suggest a settlement of the dispute—a procedure that the parties had failed to follow—, the court ruled that it had the power to appoint an arbitrator where all previous attempts by the parties to reach a settlement had been unsuccessful.[287]

---

[279] *Montpelier Reinsurance Ltd. v. Manufacturers Property & Casualty Limited*, Supreme Court, Bermuda, 24 April 2008, [2008] Bda LR 24.

[280] *Henry Muriithi Mvungu & another v. Bruno Rosiello*, High Court, Nairobi (Milimani Commercial Courts), Kenya, 18 July 2006, Miscellaneous Civil Application 264 of 2006, available on the Internet at http://kenyalaw.org/CaseSearch/view_preview1.php?link=45490335730361202257126.

[281] *Uganda Post Ltd. v. R.4 International Ltd.*, Centre for Arbitration and Dispute Resolution, Uganda, 1 September 2009, [2009] UGCADER 5.

[282] *Montpelier Reinsurance Ltd. v. Manufacturers Property & Casualty Limited*, Supreme Court, Bermuda, 24 April 2008, [2008] Bda LR 24.

[283] Bayerisches Oberstes Landesgericht, Germany, 4 Z SchH 04/02, 13 May 2002, available on the Internet at http://www.dis-arb.de/de/47/datenbanken/rspr/bayoblg-az-4-z-schh-04-02-datum-2002-05-13-id181.

[284] Bayerisches Oberstes Landesgericht, Germany, 4 Z SchH 12/99, 20 June 2000, available on the Internet at http://www.dis-arb.de/de/47/datenbanken/rspr/bayoblg-az-4-z-schh-12-99-datum-2000-06-20-id10.

[285] CLOUT case No. 439 [Brandenburgisches Oberlandesgericht, Germany, 8 SchH 01/00 (1), 26 June 2000], also available on the Internet at http://www.dis-arb.de/de/47/datenbanken/rspr/brandenburgisches-olg-az-8-schh-01-00-1-datum-2000-06-26-id36.

[286] Bayerisches Oberstes Landesgericht, Germany, 4 Z SchH 02/98, 16 September 1998, available on the Internet at http://www.dis-arb.de/de/47/datenbanken/rspr/bayoblg-az-4-z-schh-02-98-datum-1998-09-16-id27.

[287] Hanseatisches Oberlandesgericht Hamburg, Germany, 14 Sch 02/98, 22 July 1998, available on the Internet at http://www.dis-arb.de/de/47/datenbanken/rspr/hanseat-olg-hamburg-az-14-sch-02-98-14-u-112-98-datum-1998-07-22-id80.

Admissibility of objection to arbitral jurisdiction

15. An important and controversial question is whether an application made pursuant to article 11 may be resisted on the ground that the arbitration agreement invoked by the applicant is non-existent, invalid or inapplicable to the dispute at hand. On the one hand, several cases either explicitly or implicitly stand for the proposition that a court intervening pursuant to article 11 may fully review all—or least some types of—objections to arbitral jurisdiction raised by the respondent.[288] However in other cases, courts have rather ruled that the arbitral tribunals' power to decide on their jurisdiction (article 16 (1)) entailed that objections to arbitral jurisdiction should either not be considered[289] or only lead to the dismissal of the application where they appear to be clearly well founded upon a *prima facie* review of relevant evidence.[290]

16. In one Ugandan case, it was held that the court or authority intervening on the basis of article 11 does not have the power to issue orders purporting to limit the tribunal's jurisdiction.[291] In one Kenyan case, the court dismissed the application to appoint an arbitrator on the ground that the time limit to render an award provided for in the arbitration agreement had expired and that the arbitral tribunal would therefore not be in a position to render a valid award.[292] Similarly, in another case, an application made pursuant to article 11 was dismissed on the ground that the applicant had also commenced a court action in relation to the same dispute.[293]

17. Finally, a Kenyan court held that, because the issue of the validity of the arbitration agreement had been previously decided by a court in the context of an application for interim measures of protection, it could not subsequently be re-argued in the context of an application based on article 11.[294]

Time limits

18. Where the parties have agreed on a procedure for the appointment of arbitrators, but have failed to determine the time limit for such appointment, a court decided that the thirty-day limit set out in paragraph (3) applied. Thus, if the defaulting party had not fulfilled its obligations under the appointment procedure agreed to by the parties within such time, the court should make the appointment on behalf

---

[288] *Alva Aluminium Ltd. Bangkok v. Gabriel India Limited*, Supreme Court, India, 16 November 2010, available on the Internet at http://www.indiankanoon.org/doc/1580383/; *National Insurance Co. Ltd. v. Boghara Polyfab (P) Ltd.,* Supreme Court, India, 18 September 2008, (2009) 1 SCC 267 (India SC), available on the Internet at http://www.indiankanoon.org/doc/1482268/; *M/S S.B.P. & Co. v. M/S Patel Engineering Ltd. & Anr.*, Supreme Court of India, India, 26 October 2005, (2005) 8 SCC 618, (India SC), available on the Internet at http://www.indiankanoon.org/doc/1820512/; *Visa International Ltd. v. Continental Resources (Usa) Ltd.*, Supreme Court, India, 2 December 2008, available on the Internet at http://www.indiankanoon.org/doc/1765502/; *M/S. Everest Holding Ltd. v. Shyam Kumar Shrivastava & Ors.*, Supreme Court, India, 24 October 2008, available on the Internet at http://indiankanoon.org/doc/847144/; *Rampton v. Eyre,* Ontario Court of Appeal, Canada, 2 May 2007, [2007] ONCA 331, available on the Internet at http://canlii.ca/t/1rb0d; *William Oluande v. American Life Insurance Company (K) Limited*, High Court at Nairobi (Nairobi Law Courts), Kenya, 10 February 2006, Miscellaneous Application Number 721 of 2004, available on the Internet at http://kenyalaw.org/CaseSearch/view_preview1.php?link=67250266121452379246971; *St-Jean v. Poirier*, Court of Quebec, Canada, 2 September 2010, [2010] QCCQ 7681 (CanLII), available on the Internet at http://canlii.ca/t/2cljv; *Villeneuve v. Pelletier*, Superior Court of Quebec, Canada, 27 January 2010, [2010] QCCS 320 (CanLII), available on the Internet at http://canlii.ca/t/27vzs; CLOUT case No. 438 [Bayerisches Oberstes Landesgericht, Germany, 4 Z SchH 01/99, 4 June 1999], also available on the Internet at http://www.dis-arb.de/de/47/datenbanken/rspr/bayoblg-az-4-z-schh-01-99-datum-1999-06-04-id21; Bayerisches Oberstes Landesgericht, Germany, 4 Z SchH 01/01, 23 February 2001, available on the Internet at http://www.dis-arb.de/de/47/datenbanken/rspr/bayoblg-az-4-z-schh-01-01-datum-2001-02-23-id79; *Ogunwale v. Syrian Arab Republic*, Court of Appeal—Lagos Division, Nigeria, 6 December 2001, [2002] 9 NWLR (Part 771) 127; *Bendex Eng. v. Efficient Pet. (Nig.)*, Court of Appeal—Enugu Division, Nigeria, 13 December 2000, [2001] 8 NWLR (Part 715) 333; *Banque Nationale du Canada v. Premdev. Inc.*, Court of Appeal of Quebec, Canada, 10 March 1997, [1997] CanLII 10830 (QC CA), available on the Internet at http://canlii.ca/t/1nf52; *Robitaille v. Centre Rail-Control Inc.*, Superior Court of Quebec, Canada, 17 May 2001, J.E. 2001-1153; *Lamothe v. Lamothe*, Superior Court of Quebec, Canada, 2 April 2001; *Voynaud v. Éditions La Pensée Inc.*, Superior Court of Quebec, Canada, 2 April 1998.

[289] See for instance: CLOUT case No. 506 [*Masterfile Corp. v. Graphic Images Ltd.*, Ontario Superior Court of Justice, Ontario, Canada, 26 June 2002]; CLOUT case No. 20 [*Fung Sang Trading Limited v. Kai Sun Sea Products and Food Company Limited*, High Court—Court of First Instance, Hong Kong, 29 October 1991], [1991] HKCFI 190, also available on the Internet at http://www.hklii.hk/eng/hk/cases/hkcfi/1991/190.html; CLOUT case No. 62 [*Oonc Lines Limited v. Sino-American Trade Advancement Co. Ltd.*, High Court—Court of First Instance, Hong Kong, 2 February 1994], [1994] HKCFI 193, also available on the Internet at http://www.hklii.hk/eng/hk/cases/hkcfi/1994/193.html.

[290] CLOUT case No. 109 [*Private Company "Triple V" Inc. v. Star (Universal) Co. Ltd. and Sky Jade Enterprises Group Ltd.*, Court of Appeal, Hong Kong, 7 July 1995], [1995] 3 HKCA 617, also available on the Internet at http://www.hklii.hk/eng/hk/cases/hkca/1995/617.html; CLOUT case No. 40 [*Pacific International Lines (PTE) Ltd. & Another v. Tsinlien Metals and Minerals Co. Ltd.*, High Court—Court of First Instance, Hong Kong, 30 July 1992], [1992] HKCFI 225, also available on the Internet at http://www.hklii.hk/eng/hk/cases/hkcfi/1992/225.html.

[291] *Uganda Post Ltd. v. R.4 International Ltd.*, Centre for Arbitration and Dispute Resolution, Uganda, 1 September 2009, [2009] UGCADER 5.

[292] *M-Link Communications Company Ltd. v. Communication Commission of Kenya & another*, High Court, Nairobi (Milimani Commercial Courts), Kenya, 23 November 2005, Civil Suit 2071 of 2000.

[293] *Henry Muriithi Mvungu & another v. Bruno Rosiello*, High Court, Nairobi (Milimani Commercial Courts), Kenya, 18 July 2006, available on the Internet at http://kenyalaw.org/CaseSearch/view_preview1.php?link=45490335730361202257126.

[294] *Pan African Builders & Contractors Ltd. v. National Social Security Fund Board of Trustees*, High Court, Nairobi (Milimani Commercial Courts), Kenya, 27 March 2006, Civil Case 701 of 2005.

of the defaulting party in accordance with paragraph (4).[295] It was also decided that parties were free to agree on shorter time limits for the appointment of arbitrators than those set out in paragraph (3). Thus, if a party or other person failed to perform its obligations under the appointment procedure agreed to by the parties within such time limit, the court would be competent to make the appointment in accordance with paragraph (4).[296]

19. A court seized of a request to appoint an arbitrator after a party had failed to comply with time limits provided for in the arbitration agreement held that it could extend such time limits in order to afford that party another opportunity to participate in the constitution of the tribunal.[297]

Exercise of the court's or the competent authority's discretion

20. Securing an independent and impartial tribunal was said in one case to be the major objective that ought to be pursued by the court or competent authority intervening on the basis of article 11,[298] while in another case it was said to be the paramount consideration.[299] It has also been explicitly identified as an important consideration in several other cases.[300]

21. While appointing an arbitrator, the court or the competent authority must abide by the parties' agreement regarding the arbitrators' qualifications. Therefore, a lawyer cannot be appointed if the agreement provides that the arbitrator has to be a physician.[301] When the parties' agreement is silent on qualifications, the court or competent authority will strive to appoint the most suitable candidate, not only in light of the need to secure an independent and impartial arbitral tribunal, but also in light of circumstances such as the law governing the merits,[302] the nature of the dispute[303] and the proposed arbitrators' availability.[304]

22. In one Ugandan case, the competent authority pointed out that the parties had to act in a diligent and prudent manner, and that objections to proposed candidates had to be substantiated.[305]

23. Despite that article 11 (5) provides that it is advisable to appoint an arbitrator of a nationality other than those of the parties, in one case an arbitrator of the same nationality than that of one the parties was appointed because the court was of the view that it would have been "both inconvenient and unfair to the parties and to the arbitrator to expect anyone of international repute to spend the length of time this case will require away from his home and his other interests."[306] In another case relating to a dispute involving American and Quebec parties, a Quebec court ruled that, because the arbitration agreement provided that the arbitration would be governed by the Quebec *Code of Civil Procedure*, the arbitrators to be appointed had to be from Quebec.[307]

24. In order to limit the risks that further applications will have to be filed, the Ugandan competent authority has developed a practice of appointing three additional arbitrators to whom the parties will be able to turn in the event that the chosen arbitrator happens to be unable to act.[308]

---

[295] Bayerisches Oberstes Landesgericht, Germany, 4 Z SchH 09/01, 16 January 2002, available on the Internet at http://www.dis-arb.de/de/47/datenbanken/rspr/bayoblg-az-4-z-schh-09-01-datum-2002-01-16-id173.

[296] Kammergericht Berlin, Germany, 23/29 Sch 16/01, 26 June 2002, available on the Internet at http://www.dis-arb.de/de/47/datenbanken/rspr/kg-berlin-az-23-29-sch-16-01-datum-2002-06-26-id221.

[297] *Gestion Christian Veilleux v. Chabot*, Superior Court of Quebec, Canada, 7 September 2006, [2006] QCCS 6071, available on the Internet at http://canlii.ca/t/1qhdb.

[298] CLOUT case No. 899 [Centre for Arbitration and Dispute Resolution, Uganda, 26 November 2004], cause No. 09/04.

[299] *Canadian Reinsurance Co. v. Lloyd's Syndicate PUM 91*, Ontario Court of Justice—General Division, Canada, 27 January 1995, 1995 CarswellOnt 2356, 17 CCLI (3d) 165, 6 BLR (3d) 102.

[300] See for instance: *Montpelier Reinsurance Ltd. v. Manufacturers Property & Casualty Limited*, Supreme Court, Bermuda, 24 April 2008, [2008] Bda LR 24; CLOUT case No. 895 [Centre for Arbitration and Dispute Resolution, Uganda, 17 March 2006], cause No. 01/06; CLOUT case No. 900 [Centre for Arbitration and Dispute Resolution, Uganda, 15 July 2004], cause No. 10/04; CLOUT case No. 897 [Centre for Arbitration and Dispute Resolution, Uganda, 30 September 2005], cause No. 03/05; *Denel (Proprietary Limited) v. Bharat Electronics Ltd. & Amp.*, Supreme Court, India, 10 May 2010, available on the Internet at http://www.indiankanoon.org/doc/432441/.

[301] Oberlandesgericht München, Germany, 34 SchH 11/09, 29 January 2010, available on the Internet at http://www.dis-arb.de/de/47/datenbanken/rspr/olg-münchen-az-34-schh-11-09-datum-2010-01-29-id1061.

[302] *Montpelier Reinsurance Ltd. v. Manufacturers Property & Casualty Limited*, Supreme Court, Bermuda, 24 April 2008, [2008] Bda LR 24.

[303] CLOUT case No. 895 [Centre for Arbitration and Dispute Resolution, Uganda, 17 March 2006], cause No. 01/06; CLOUT case No. 896 [Centre for Arbitration and Dispute Resolution, Uganda, 30 January 2006], No. 07/05; CLOUT case No. 897 [Centre for Arbitration and Dispute Resolution, Uganda, 30 September 2005], cause No. 03/05; *Canadian Reinsurance Co. v. Lloyd's Syndicate PUM 91*, Ontario Court of Justice—General Division, Canada, 27 January 1995, 1995 CarswellOnt 2356, 17 CCLI (3d) 165, 6 BLR (3d) 102; *Lavergne v. Pure Tech International Inc.*, Superior Court of Quebec, Canada, 9 July 1998, [1998] QJ No. 2308 (SC).

[304] CLOUT case No. 896 [Centre for Arbitration and Dispute Resolution, Uganda, 30 January 2006], cause No. 07/05.

[305] CLOUT case No. 897 [Centre for Arbitration and Dispute Resolution, Uganda, 30 September 2005], cause No. 03/05.

[306] *Quintette Coal Ltd. v. Nippon Steel Corp.*, Supreme Court of British Columbia, Canada, 24 March 1988, [1988] BCJ No. 492.

[307] *I-D Foods Corporation v. Hain-Celestial Group Inc.*, Superior Court of Quebec, Canada, 6 July 2006, [2006] QCCS 3889, available on the Internet at http://www.jugements.qc.ca/.

[308] See for instance: CLOUT case No. 897 [Centre for Arbitration and Dispute Resolution, Uganda, 30 September 2005], cause No. 03/05.

"Necessary measure[s]" that can be taken pursuant to paragraph (4)

25. A court intervening on the basis of paragraph (4) has no power to directly or indirectly compel an appointing authority chosen by the parties to appoint an arbitrator. The fact that a decision made pursuant to paragraph (4) is not subject to appeal supports the view that court intervention based on article 11 is intended to delay to the minimum extent the progress of the arbitral proceedings, and that the powers given to courts or appointing authorities in paragraph (4) are to be construed narrowly.[309]

26. The Supreme Court of India has held that the word "necessary" relates to "things which are reasonably required to be done or legally ancillary to the accomplishment of the intended act," and that "necessary measures" can thus be "stated to be the reasonable steps required to be taken."[310]

Court's power to dismiss the application to prevent an abuse of process

27. It has been held that, where it is clear that a party acting in bad faith has caused the contractually agreed appointment procedure to break down so as to gain some perceived advantage through a court appointment made under article 11 (4), a court application based on article 11 may be refused on discretionary grounds.[311]

No appeal—paragraph (5)

28. Decisions rendered pursuant to paragraphs (3) or (4) are not subject to appeal.[312] However, several decisions stand for the proposition that this rule only applies where the grounds of appeal directly relate to one of the appointment procedures set out in paragraphs (3) and (4), as opposed to matters that are peripheral to these procedures.[313] These decisions have held that paragraph (5) is not applicable where the appeal concerns whether the parties' dispute should be resolved by arbitration,[314] and, in one of those cases, the court pointed out that paragraph (5) will apply where, for example, the issue in appeal is whether the parties actually agreed on an appointment procedure.[315] However, in other cases, courts have held that paragraph (5) prohibits an appeal concerning whether the dispute falls within the arbitration agreement invoked by the party who sought the court's intervention.[316]

---

[309] *Montpelier Reinsurance Ltd. v. Manufacturers Property & Casualty Limited*, Supreme Court of Bermuda, Bermuda, 24 April 2008, [2008] Bda LR 24.

[310] *Ministry Of Railway, New Delhi v. Patel Engineering Company Ltd.*, Supreme Court of India, India, 18 August 2008, available on the Internet at http://www.indiankanoon.org/doc/1118593/.

[311] *Montpelier Reinsurance Ltd. v. Manufacturers Property & Casualty Limited*, Supreme Court, Bermuda, 24 April 2008, [2008] Bda LR 24.

[312] See for instance: *A.H. Turistica Peninsular S.L. v. DIRECCIONooo C.B.*, Audiencia Provincial de Zaragoza (sección 2ª), Spain, 6 February 2007, res. 52/07; Supreme Court, Jordan, 21 November 2006, No. 2006/1682; Supreme Court, Jordan, 18 December 2006, No. 2006/2598; Supreme Court, Jordan, 10 December 2003, No. 2003/3094; Supreme Court, Jordan, 9 March 2005, No. 2004/3820; Supreme Court, Jordan, 29 June 2006, No. 2005/4449.

[313] *Bendex Eng. v. Efficient Pet. (Nig.)*, Court of Appeal—Enugu Division, Nigeria, 13 December 2000, [2001] 8 NWLR (Part 715) 333.

[314] CLOUT case No. 109 [*Private Company "Triple V" Inc. v. Star (Universal) Co. Ltd. and Sky Jade Enterprises Group Ltd.*, Court of Appeal, Hong Kong, 7 July 1995], [1995] 3 HKCA 617, also available on the Internet at http://www.hklii.hk/eng/hk/cases/hkca/1995/617.html; *Bendex Eng. v. Efficient Pet. (Nig.)*, Court of Appeal—Enugu Division, Nigeria, 13 December 2000, [2001] 8 NWLR (Part 715) 333; *Ogunwale v. Syrian Arab Republic*, Court of Appeal—Lagos Division, Nigeria, 6 December 2001, [2002] 9 NWLR (Part 771) 127.

[315] CLOUT case No. 109 [*Private Company "Triple V" Inc. v. Star (Universal) Co. Ltd. and Sky Jade Enterprises Group Ltd.*, Court of Appeal, Hong Kong, 7 July 1995], [1995] 3 HKCA 617, also available on the Internet at http://www.hklii.hk/eng/hk/cases/hkca/1995/617.html.

[316] *Ms. Cristina-Victoria Utrilla Utrilla (Spain) v. Explotaciones Mineras Justiniano Muñoz S.L.*, Juzgado de lo Mercantil número 1 de Madrid, Spain, 5 July 2006, arbitrator appointment No. 15/06.

Article 12. Grounds for challenge

(1) When a person is approached in connection with his possible appointment as an arbitrator, he shall disclose any circumstances likely to give rise to justifiable doubts as to his impartiality or independence. An arbitrator, from the time of his appointment and throughout the arbitral proceedings, shall without delay disclose any such circumstances to the parties unless they have already been informed of them by him.

(2) An arbitrator may be challenged only if circumstances exist that give rise to justifiable doubts as to his impartiality or independence, or if he does not possess qualifications agreed to by the parties. A party may challenge an arbitrator appointed by him, or in whose appointment he has participated, only for reasons of which he becomes aware after the appointment has been made.

TRAVAUX PRÉPARATOIRES

The *travaux préparatoires* on article 12 as adopted in 1985 are contained in the following documents:

1. Report of the United Nations Commission on International Trade Law on the work of its eighteenth session (*Official Records of the General Assembly, Fortieth Session, Supplement No. 17* (A/40/17)), paras. 11-333.

2. Reports of the Working Group: A/CN.9/216; A/CN.9/232; A/CN.9/233; A/CN.9/245; A/CN.9/246, annex; A/CN.9/263 and Add.1-2; A/CN.9/264. Relevant working papers are referred to in the reports.

3. Summary records of the 313th, 330th and 332nd UNCITRAL meetings.

Article 12 was not amended in 2006.

(Available on the Internet at www.uncitral.org).

INTRODUCTION

1. Article 12 primarily addresses the important question of arbitrators' ethics. It does so firstly by imposing on each arbitrator a continuing duty to disclose to the parties circumstances likely to give rise to justifiable doubts as to his or her impartiality or independence. Secondly, article 12 states that an arbitrator may be challenged on the basis of circumstances that give rise to such doubts.[317]

2. Article 12 pursues two further objectives. The first is to reinforce party autonomy in the choice of arbitrators by providing that an arbitrator may be challenged if he or she does not possess qualifications required by the parties. The second, similar to the objective pursued by article 4, is to prevent parties from abusing the trust of their opponents by engaging in contradictory behaviour. That objective is achieved by forbidding a party from challenging an arbitrator appointed by it or in whose appointment it has participated—for instance pursuant to a procedure similar to that set out in article 6 (3) of the 1976 UNCITRAL Arbitration Rules[318] or 8 (2) of the 2010 revision of those Rules—on the basis of circumstance known to that party at the time of the appointment.

3. The use of the word "only" in the first sentence of paragraph (2) was intended to make clear that arbitrators cannot be challenged for other reasons than those mentioned in that sentence. The *travaux préparatoires* show that proposals were made to delete the word "only," but it was considered preferable to retain that word to clearly emphasize that possible additional grounds for challenge provided for in domestic law should not apply in the context of international commercial arbitrations.[319]

4. The procedure applicable to challenges to arbitrators is addressed in article 13.

[317] It should be noted that issues of independence and impartiality may also arise in the context of setting aside (article 34) or recognition and enforcement (articles 35-36) proceedings. Decisions rendered in that context may be relevant to the impartiality and independence requirements found in article 12. (See below, section on article 34, paras. 102-103.)

[318] A/CN.9/264, Analytical commentary on draft text of a model law on international commercial arbitration, under article 12, para. 6, available on the UNCITRAL website at http://www.uncitral.org/uncitral/en/commission/sessions/18th.html.

[319] *Official Records of the General Assembly, Fortieth Session, Supplement No. 17* (A/40/17), paras. 116-119.

CASE LAW ON ARTICLE 12

Mandatory nature of impartiality and independence requirements

5. The importance of the requirements of impartiality and independence under article 12 were highlighted in a decision of the Court of Appeal of Quebec. The case involved a dispute relating to a shipbuilding contract. As the Quebec government had subsidized the shipbuilder, a minister of the Quebec government signed the contract to guarantee the performance of the shipbuilder's obligation. The contract also contained a clause providing that disputes would be resolved by arbitration and that the minister would act as arbitrator. After having stated that the impartiality and independence of the tribunal were fundamental features of arbitration, the court held that a clause providing that disputes relating to a contract will be arbitrated by a party to that contract is inconsistent with the requirements of impartiality and independence, and is therefore null as contrary to public policy.[320]

Arbitrators' duty to disclose

6. The arbitrators' duty to disclose was analysed by the Hong Kong Court of First Instance. The court held that there was a difference between the circumstances on the basis of which an arbitrator may be challenged and the circumstances which fall within the arbitrators' duty of disclosure. The facts to be disclosed are not confined to those warranting or perceiving to be warranting disqualification but those that might found or warrant a *bona fide* challenge. Nevertheless, in that case, the court dismissed an argument to the effect that the challenged arbitrator had failed to sufficiently disclose a pre-existing relationship with a solicitor who had acted on behalf of one of the parties in the arbitration. Also noteworthy is the statement that an arbitrator's failure to comply with the disclosure requirement may, in itself, give rise to justifiable doubts as to that arbitrator's impartiality and independence.[321]

7. In another case, a court found that despite the fact that article 12 does not explicitly require an arbitrator to investigate whether he or she has questionable relationships or interests, the disclosure requirement imposed in paragraph (1) implies such a duty. An arbitrator is thus "obligated to conduct a conflicts check to see if he must disclose any circumstances that might cause his impartiality to be questioned."[322]

8. A German court has held that the disclosure duty only extends to facts that, on the basis of an objective assessment, can raise doubts as to the arbitrator's impartiality or independence. Applying that standard, the court found that an arbitrator had not breached its disclosure duty by not revealing that he and the respondent's managing partner were both members of the board of a German legal institute, that he was a limited partner in a company set up by the respondent's managing director, that he and that managing director were both engaged as arbitrators and experts in arbitral proceedings, and that he had failed to disclose his business relationships with the respondent's managing director.[323]

9. In another case, it was held that a lawyer appointed as arbitrator does not have to disclose that he or she has previously acted on behalf of a party where such activities were isolated instances, were unrelated to the dispute and had been terminated for some years.[324]

Justifiable doubts as to an arbitrator's impartiality or independence

The standard explained

10. One German court has held that an arbitrator could be challenged where the circumstances invoked gave rise to reasonable grounds for objectively suspecting its impartiality, and that proof that the arbitrator actually lacked impartiality was not required.[325] Similarly, after also stating that proof of actual partiality was not required, another German court ruled that a challenge would be successful where objective circumstances gave rise to justifiable doubts as to the impartiality or independence of the arbitrator.[326] A further German court has held that the "justifiable doubts as to his impartiality or independence" test set out in paragraph (2) generally corresponds to the test applicable to the disqualification of judges under local law.[327]

---

[320] *Desbois v. Industries A.C. Davie Inc.*, Court of Appeal of Quebec, Canada, 26 April 1990, [1990] CanLII 3619 (QC CA), available on the Internet at http://canlii.ca/t/1pjlg.

[321] *Jung Science Information Technology Co. Ltd. v. Zte. Corporation*, High Court—Court of First Instance, Hong Kong Special Administrative Region of China, 22 July 2008, [2008] HKCFI 606, available on the Internet at http://www.hklii.hk/eng/hk/cases/hkcfi/2008/606.html.

[322] *HSMV. Corp. v. ADI Ltd.,* Central District Court for California, United States of America, 8 November 1999, 72 F. Supp. 2d 1122 (C.D. Cal. 1999).

[323] CLOUT case No. 665 [Oberlandesgericht Naumburg, Germany, 10 SchH 03/01, 19 December 2001], also available on the Internet at http://www.dis-arb.de/de/47/datenbanken/rspr/olg-naumburg-az-10-schh-03-01-datum-2001-12-19-id165.

[324] Hanseatisches Oberlandesgericht Hamburg, Germany, 9 SchH 01/05, 12 July 2005, available on the Internet at http://www.dis-arb.de/de/47/datenbanken/rspr/hanseat-olg-hamburg-az-9-schh-01-05-datum-2005-07-12-id1170.

[325] Kammergericht Berlin, Germany, 28 Sch 24/99, 22 March 2000, available on the Internet at http://www.dis-arb.de/de/47/datenbanken/rspr/kg-berlin-az-28-sch-24-99-datum-2000-03-22-id118.

[326] CLOUT case No. 665 [Oberlandesgericht Naumburg, Germany, 10 SchH 03/01, 19 December 2001], also available on the Internet at http://www.dis-arb.de/de/47/datenbanken/rspr/olg-naumburg-az-10-schh-03-01-datum-2001-12-19-id165.

[327] CLOUT case No. 1062 [Oberlandesgericht Köln, Germany, 9 Sch (H) 22/03, 2 April 2004], also available on the Internet at http://www.dis-arb.de/de/47/datenbanken/rspr/olg-köln-az-9-sch-h-22-03-datum-2004-04-02-id291.

However, another German court added that in applying that test, consideration had to be given to the distinctive features of arbitration, including the parties' interest in appointing as arbitrator a person who they trust, which entailed that only very sensitive relationships between an arbitrator and the appointing party were problematic.[328]

11. Hong Kong courts have found that the "justifiable doubts as to his impartiality or independence" test set out in paragraph (2) is identical to the common law test applicable to judges, and it amounts to considering whether, on the basis of the circumstances invoked by the party bringing the challenge—including the relevant legal traditions and cultures—, there exists a real possibility that the arbitral tribunal was biased. The test is not whether the particular litigant thinks or feels that the arbitrator has been or may be biased. What rather matters is the viewpoint of the hypothetical fair-minded and informed observer, who would consider not whether it would be better for another arbitrator to hear the matter, but whether the challenged arbitrator might not bring an impartial and unprejudiced mind to the resolution of the dispute.[329]

Application of the standard in specific circumstances

12. The Court of Appeal of Quebec has held that justifiable doubts as to an arbitrator's impartiality or independence arise when the arbitrator is a government minister and the dispute relates to a contract to which the minister is a party.[330] That decision is to be contrasted with a Supreme Court of India decision relying on several earlier decisions and holding that arbitration clauses in government contracts providing that an employee of the governmental department at issue will act as arbitrator are neither void nor unenforceable, as it can be assumed that when senior officers of government, statutory corporations or public sector undertakings are appointed as arbitrators, they will function independently and impartially. The court pointed out, however, that a justifiable apprehension as to the impartiality and independence of the arbitrator could arise where he or she was involved in the contract at issue. Furthermore, the court held that this reasoning may not be applicable where the arbitrator is related to a company, an individual or a body other than the State or its instrumentalities.[331]

13. Several German cases have considered what constitute justifiable doubts as to an arbitrator's impartiality and independence. In one case, the court dismissed a challenge based on the fact that the impugned arbitrator's goddaughter was employed by the law firm who represented the other party. A key consideration in the court's reasoning was that that person had had no significant involvement in the case.[332]

14. A business relationship between one of the parties and the sole arbitrator was found not to give rise to justifiable doubts as to the impartiality or independence of the arbitrator, irrespective of whether the business relationship consisted of a single or repeated contacts.[333] Furthermore, it was found that the fact that a sole arbitrator, at one point in time, held an ownership interest in a limited partnership whose managing partner, at the time of the arbitration, was the managing director of one of the parties, did not give rise to justifiable doubts as to the impartiality or independence of the arbitrator.[334] According to another court decision, although the standard as to the impartiality of arbitrators was set at a high level, the mere fact that an arbitrator had participated as counsel in other proceedings involving a party to the arbitration did not justify a challenge.[335] Also, in what the court characterized as a borderline case, the challenge of an arbitrator based on criticism expressed by that same arbitrator in related arbitral proceedings and directed at the applicant was dismissed as ill-founded.[336]

15. An example of a case where a court allowed a challenge is provided in a 2006 German decision where the arbitrator appointed by one of the parties had previously acted as a court-appointed expert in independent proceedings for the taking of evidence between the same parties and relating to the very construction project that gave rise to the arbitration.[337] Other examples include a case where the arbitrator had published an article expressing his opin-

[328] Oberlandesgericht München, Germany, 34 SchH 05/06, 5 July 2006, available on the Internet at http://www.dis-arb.de/de/47/datenbanken/rspr/olg-münchen-az-34-schh-05-06-datum-2006-07-05-id557.

[329] *Jung Science Information Technology Co. Ltd. v. Zte. Corporation*, High Court—Court of First Instance, Hong Kong Special Administrative Region of China, 22 July 2008, [2008] HKCFI 606, available on the Internet at http://www.hklii.hk/eng/hk/cases/hkcfi/2008/606.html.

[330] *Desbois v. Industries A.C. Davie Inc.*, Court of Appeal of Quebec, Canada, 26 April 1990, [1990] CanLII 3619 (QC CA), available on the Internet at http://canlii.ca/t/1pjlg.

[331] *Indian Oil Corp. Ltd. & Ors. v. M/S Raja Transport(P) Ltd.*, Supreme Court, India, 24 August 2009, available on the Internet at http://www.indiankanoon.org/doc/2073/.

[332] Oberlandesgericht München, Germany, 34 SchH 05/06, 5 July 2006, available on the Internet at http://www.dis-arb.de/de/47/datenbanken/rspr/olg-münchen-az-34-schh-05-06-datum-2006-07-05-id557.

[333] Oberlandesgericht Hamm, Germany, 17 SchH 13/01, 22 July 2002, available on the Internet at http://www.dis-arb.de/de/47/datenbanken/rspr/olg-hamm-az-17-schh-13-01-datum-2002-07-22-id238.

[334] CLOUT case No. 665 [Oberlandesgericht Naumburg, Germany, 10 SchH 03/01, 19 December 2001], also available on the Internet at http://www.dis-arb.de/de/47/datenbanken/rspr/olg-naumburg-az-10-schh-03-01-datum-2001-12-19-id165.

[335] Hanseatisches Oberlandesgericht Hamburg, Germany, 6 SchH 03/02, 11 March 2003, available on the Internet at http://www.dis-arb.de/de/47/datenbanken/rspr/hanseat-olg-hamburg-az-6-schh-03-02-datum-2003-03-11-id216.

[336] CLOUT case No. 1062 [Oberlandesgericht Köln, Germany, 9 Sch (H) 22/03, 2 April 2004], also available on the Internet at http://www.dis-arb.de/de/47/datenbanken/rspr/olg-köln-az-9-sch-h-22-03-datum-2004-04-02-id291.

[337] Oberlandesgericht Karlsruhe, Germany, 10 Sch 02/06, 4 July 2006, available on the Internet at http://www.dis-arb.de/de/47/datenbanken/rspr/olg-karlsruhe-az-10-sch-02-06-datum-2006-07-04-id1294.

ion on the dispute at issue in the arbitration,[338] as well as a case where the arbitrator had previously provided to one of the parties an expert opinion dealing specifically with some of the issues that arose in the arbitration.[339]

16. In Hong Kong, the fact that one of the parties happens to be represented in the opening stages of the arbitration by a solicitor with whom the challenged arbitrator has had a social and professional relationship in arbitration-related matters has been found not to raise justifiable doubts as to that arbitrator's impartiality and independence.[340] In another case, the court dismissed a challenge focusing on the impugned arbitrators' refusal to disclose the details of non-substantive discussions concerning the possible candidates for the third arbitrator he had had with the party who had appointed him.[341]

17. Finally, in a decision in which it refused to appoint the arbitrator suggested by the applicant, a Ugandan arbitral institution designated as competent authority pursuant to article 6 pointed out that the proposed arbitrator was a director of that competent authority, and suggested that that fact raised justifiable doubts as to that person's impartiality.[342]

---

[338] CLOUT case No. 902 [Landgericht München II, Germany, 2 OH 1728/01, 27 June 2002], also available on the Internet at http://www.dis-arb.de/de/47/datenbanken/rspr/lg-münchen-ii-az-2-oh-1728-01-datum-2002-06-27-id508.

[339] Hanseatisches Oberlandesgericht Hamburg, Germany, 11 SchH 01/04, 28 June 2004, available on the Internet at http://www.dis-arb.de/de/47/datenbanken/rspr/hanseat-olg-hamburg-az-11-schh-01-04-datum-2004-06-28-id284.

[340] *Jung Science Information Technology Co. Ltd. v. Zte. Corporation*, High Court—Court of First Instance, Hong Kong Special Administrative Region of China, 22 July 2008, [2008] HKCFI 606, available on the Internet at http://www.hklii.hk/eng/hk/cases/hkcfi/2008/606.html.

[341] *Pacific China Holdings Ltd. v. Grand Pacific Holdings Ltd.*, High Court—Court of First Instance, Hong Kong Special Administrative Region of China, 18 July 2007, [2007] HKCFI 715, available on the Internet at http://www.hklii.hk/eng/hk/cases/hkcfi/2007/715.html.

[342] CLOUT case No. 900 [Centre for Arbitration and Dispute Resolution, Uganda, 15 July 2004], cause No. 10/04.

Article 13. Challenge procedure

(1) The parties are free to agree on a procedure for challenging an arbitrator, subject to the provisions of paragraph (3) of this article.

(2) Failing such agreement, a party who intends to challenge an arbitrator shall, within fifteen days after becoming aware of the constitution of the arbitral tribunal or after becoming aware of any circumstance referred to in article 12 (2), send a written statement of the reasons for the challenge to the arbitral tribunal. Unless the challenged arbitrator withdraws from his office or the other party agrees to the challenge, the arbitral tribunal shall decide on the challenge.

(3) If a challenge under any procedure agreed upon by the parties or under the procedure of paragraph (2) of this article is not successful, the challenging party may request, within thirty days after having received notice of the decision rejecting the challenge, the court or other authority specified in article 6 to decide on the challenge, which decision shall be subject to no appeal; while such a request is pending, the arbitral tribunal, including the challenged arbitrator, may continue the arbitral proceedings and make an award.

TRAVAUX PRÉPARATOIRES

The *travaux préparatoires* on article 13 as adopted in 1985 are contained in the following documents:

1. Report of the United Nations Commission on International Trade Law on the work of its eighteenth session (*Official Records of the General Assembly, Fortieth Session, Supplement No. 17* (A/40/17)), paras. 11-333.

2. Reports of the Working Group: A/CN.9/216; A/CN.9/232; A/CN.9/233; A/CN.9/245; A/CN.9/246, annex; A/CN.9/263 and Add. 1-2; A/CN.9/264. Relevant working papers are referred to in the reports.

3. Summary records of the 314th, 315th and 332nd UNCITRAL meetings.

Article 13 was not amended in 2006.

(available on the Internet at www.uncitral.org).

INTRODUCTION

1. Article 13 sets out a twofold procedure governing challenges to arbitrators. In a preliminary phase, challenges are handled within the arbitral proceeding, according to either a procedure agreed to by the parties or the default procedure set out in paragraph (2). Challenges that have not been successful at that preliminary phase may subsequently be brought to a court or competent authority, whose decision on the matter is final.

CASE LAW ON ARTICLE 13

2. In order to prevent challenges from being used as dilatory measures, the last sentence of paragraph (3) gives to the arbitral tribunal the option of pursuing the arbitration while a court application is pending.[343] It would be inconsistent with that sentence for a court to grant an injunction preventing the arbitral tribunal from pursuing the proceedings while a challenge to an arbitrator is pending.[344]

Scope of application of article 13

3. Article 13 is not among the provisions listed in article 1 (2) and therefore does not apply where the seat of arbitration is either undetermined or located in a foreign jurisdiction. While the *travaux préparatoires* show that it was considered to make article 13 applicable before the place of arbitration had been determined, the prevailing

[343] *Nikiforos v. Petropoulos*, Superior Court of Quebec, Canada, 21 June 2007, [2007] QCCS 3144, available on the Internet at http://canlii.ca/t/1s00b; *Groupe de Charles Lacroix v. Syndicat des Travailleurs Horaires de l'Amiante C.S.N. Inc.*, Superior Court of Quebec, Canada, 27 September 2002, [2002] CanLII 30068 (QC CS) available on the Internet at http://canlii.ca/t/1cm0x; *Monkland 5765 Plus v. 9101-8309 Québec Inc.*, Superior Court of Quebec, Canada, 30 January 2008, [2008] QCCS 253, available on the Internet at http://canlii.ca/t/1vlg3.

[344] *Mitsui Engineering & Shipbuilding Co. Ltd. v. Easton Graham Rush and another*, High Court, Singapore, 16 February 2004, [2004] SGHC 26, [2004] 2 SLR(R) 14.

view was that the Model Law should not deal with court intervention relating to the arbitral tribunal prior to the determination of the place of arbitration.[345]

Party autonomy—paragraph 1

4. While the parties are free to agree on a challenge procedure applicable in the arbitral proceeding, it is clear from paragraph (1) that court intervention pursuant to paragraph (3) is mandatory. The *travaux préparatoires* show that a suggestion made was to exclude the intervention of courts or other competent authorities relating to challenges on the ground that it could open the door to dilatory tactics; however, it was ultimately decided that such intervention was necessary to avoid unnecessary waste of time and delay.[346]

5. The parties' agreement on the challenge procedure applicable initially may involve incorporating by reference a procedure set out in arbitration rules.[347] According to one German court, the parties may go so far as to waive paragraph (2) altogether and exclude any challenge procedure within the arbitral proceeding.[348] Where the parties agree on a specific procedure for the challenge of arbitrators, neither the time limit for raising a challenge, nor the provision stating that the arbitral tribunal should rule first on such a challenge in paragraph (2) is applicable.[349]

The preliminary procedure—paragraph (2)

6. One court held that the expression "after becoming aware of" in paragraph (2) meant that the time limit for challenging an arbitrator starts running only from the point in time at which the challenging party acquired actual knowledge of the ground for challenge. Mere negligent ignorance of the ground for challenge, even to such a degree as to constitute constructive knowledge, has not been found sufficient to trigger the time limit.[350]

7. A party who could have challenged an arbitrator while the arbitral proceedings were ongoing but who failed to do so was found not to be barred from subsequently challenging the legality of the award on the basis of a reasonable apprehension of bias.[351]

Court intervention—paragraph (3)

8. A court intervening pursuant to paragraph (3) does not merely review the previous decision of the arbitral tribunal or institution on the challenge, it also reviews the challenge fully and makes an independent decision as to whether it should be allowed. It is therefore irrelevant to the court that the challenge may have been initially decided without the participation of the impugned arbitrator.[352]

9. In view of the urgency of matters relating to the composition of the arbitral tribunal or its ability to function, and in order to reduce the risk and effect of any dilatory tactics, short time-periods are set. However, one court has found that the thirty-day time limit provided for in article 13 (3) is not mandatory and may therefore be extended by the court.[353]

10. It has been held that a party who chooses not to request a court's intervention pursuant article 13 (3) cannot subsequently challenge the validity of the award on grounds similar to those on which it based its initial challenge.[354] (See also below, section on article 34, paras. 102-103).

---

[345] *Official Records of the General Assembly, Fortieth Session, Supplement No. 17* (A/40/17), paras. 79-80 and 133-134.

[346] Ibid, paras. 79-80 and 121-124.

[347] Oberlandesgericht Dresden, Germany, 11 Sch 01/01, 28 February 2001, available on the Internet at http://www.dis-arb.de/de/47/datenbanken/rspr/olg-dresden-az-11-sch-01-01-datum-2001-02-28-id1264.

[348] Hanseatisches Oberlandesgericht Hamburg, Germany, 9 SchH 01/05, 12 July 2005, available on the Internet at http://www.dis-arb.de/de/47/datenbanken/rspr/hanseat-olg-hamburg-az-9-schh-01-05-datum-2005-07-12-id1170.

[349] CLOUT case No. 442 [Oberlandesgericht Köln, Germany, 9 SchH 30/00, 14 September 2000], also available on the Internet at http://www.dis-arb.de/de/47/datenbanken/rspr/olg-köln-az-9-schh-30-00-datum-2000-09-14-id131.

[350] Kammergericht Berlin, Germany, 28 Sch 24/99, 22 March 2000, available on the Internet at http://www.dis-arb.de/de/47/datenbanken/rspr/kg-berlin-az-28-sch-24-99-datum-2000-03-22-id118.

[351] *Oiknine v. Rosenberg-Solny*, Superior Court of Quebec, Canada, 29 October 2009, [2009] QCCS 5106, available on the Internet at http://canlii.ca/t/26l5p.

[352] Oberlandesgericht München, Germany, 34 SchH 10/05, 6 February 2006, available on the Internet at http://www.dis-arb.de/de/47/datenbanken/rspr/olg-münchen-az-34-schh-10-05-datum-2006-02-06-id755. See also *Pacific China Holdings Ltd. v. Grand Pacific Holdings Ltd.*, High Court—Court of First Instance, Hong Kong Special Administrative Region of China, 18 July 2007, [2007] HKCFI 715, available on the Internet at http://www.hklii.hk/eng/hk/cases/hkcfi/2007/715.html.

[353] *Groupe de Charles Lacroix v. Syndicat des Travailleurs Horaires de l'Amiante C.S.N. Inc.*, Superior Court of Quebec, Canada, 25 August 2003, [2003] CanLII 35698 (QC CS), available on the Internet at http://canlii.ca/t/5z01.

[354] *Habitations d'Angoulème Inc. v. Létourneau*, Court of Quebec, Canada, 22 April 2005, [2005] CanLII 12888 (QC CQ), available on the Internet at http://canlii.ca/t/1k73x.

Article 14—Failure or impossibility to act

(1) If an arbitrator becomes de jure or de facto unable to perform his functions or for other reasons fails to act without undue delay, his mandate terminates if he withdraws from his office or if the parties agree on the termination. Otherwise, if a controversy remains concerning any of these grounds, any party may request the court or other authority specified in article 6 to decide on the termination of the mandate, which decision shall be subject to no appeal.

(2) If, under this article or article 13 (2), an arbitrator withdraws from his office or a party agrees to the termination of the mandate of an arbitrator, this does not imply acceptance of the validity of any ground referred to in this article or article 12 (2).

TRAVAUX PRÉPARATOIRES

The *travaux préparatoires* on article 14 as adopted in 1985 are contained in the following documents:

1. Report of the United Nations Commission on International Trade Law on the work of its eighteenth session (*Official Records of the General Assembly, Fortieth Session, Supplement No. 17* (A/40/17)), paras. 11-333.
2. Reports of the Working Group: A/CN.9/216; A/CN.9/232; A/CN.9/233; A/CN.9/245; A/CN.9/246, annex; A/CN.9/263 and Add.1-2; A/CN.9/264. Relevant working papers are referred to in the reports.
3. Summary records of the 314th, 319th, 320th and 332nd UNCITRAL meetings.

Article 14 was not amended in 2006.

(Available on the Internet at www.uncitral.org).

INTRODUCTION

Situations covered

1. Drawing from article 13 (2) of the 1976 UNCITRAL Arbitration Rules,[355] article 14 addresses situations where an arbitrator becomes unable—for reasons of fact or law—to perform his functions, or otherwise fails to do so without undue delay. In such instances, the termination of the arbitrator's mandate can first occur pursuant to the arbitrator's voluntary withdrawal from the proceedings or pursuant to an agreement of all parties involved in the arbitration. Where the arbitrator does not voluntarily withdraw and the parties do not agree to terminate the arbitrator's mandate, a party may seek from a court or competent authority designated in article 6 an order terminating the arbitrator's mandate.

2. Article 14 thus covers different grounds than articles 12 and 13, which address situations where an arbitrator's appointment is being questioned on the basis of doubts as to his impartiality or independence, or on the basis of an alleged failure to meet qualifications required by the parties. The difference between those provisions was highlighted in two Indian decisions where courts refused to terminate an arbitrator's mandate on the basis of an alleged apprehension of bias on the ground that such circumstances did not amount to an impossibility to act within the meaning of article 14.[356] Furthermore, unlike challenges made under article 13, an application seeking the termination of an arbitrator's mandate is not subject to any time limit.

3. As for article 14 (2), it is intended to prevent lengthy controversies by facilitating voluntary withdrawals from arbitrators in the situations alluded to in articles 13 (2) and 14 (1).[357]

---

[355] A/CN.9/264, Analytical commentary on draft text of a model law on international commercial arbitration, under article 14, para. 3, available on the UNCITRAL website at http://www.uncitral.org/uncitral/en/commission/sessions/18th.html.

[356] *Mr. Hasmukhlal H. Doshi & Another v. Mr. Justice M.L. Pendse & Others*, Bombay High Court, India, 17 April 2000, 2000 (3) BomCR 672, (2000) 2 BOMLR 684, 2000 (3) MhLj 690, available on the Internet at http://www.indiankanoon.org/doc/279232/; *Ahluwalia Contracts (India) Ltd. v. Housing And Urban Development*, Delhi High Court, India, 30 November 2007, 2007 (4) ARBLR 539, available on the Internet at http://www.indiankanoon.org/doc/406601/.

[357] A/CN.9/264, Analytical commentary on draft text of a model law on international commercial arbitration, under article 14bis, para. 1, available on the UNCITRAL website at http://www.uncitral.org/uncitral/en/commission/sessions/18th.html.

Scope of application of article 14

4. As article 14 is not among the provisions listed in article 1 (2), it does not apply if the place of arbitration is either undetermined or located in a foreign jurisdiction. While the *travaux préparatoires* show that it had been considered to render article 14 applicable before the place of arbitration had been determined, the prevailing view was that the Model Law should not deal with court intervention relating to the arbitral tribunal prior to the determination of the place of arbitration.[358]

CASE LAW ON ARTICLE 14

5. One Indian court pointed out that article 14 should not be interpreted as allowing courts to address issues relating to the arbitral tribunal's jurisdiction. The court emphasized that judicial review of jurisdictional issues may only occur pursuant to applications based on article 16 or article 34.[359]

De facto or *de jure* inability to perform functions as arbitrator

6. In one case providing an illustration of an arbitrator having become unable to perform his functions, the court terminated the mandate of an arbitrator who had been arrested and was detained in a foreign jurisdiction.[360] In another case, an Australian court pointed out that when an arbitrator resigns after having become unavailable on dates originally set for a hearing, such resignation did not occur for reasons provided for in article 14 (1), but rather for "[an]other reason" within the meaning of article 15.[361] An arbitrator's illness was held in one German case to cause an inability to perform within the meaning of article 14 (1).[362] Finally, in another German case where a judge had been wrongly granted a special administrative permission to serve as arbitrator required under the administrative regulations applicable to judges in the jurisdiction in question, the court found that that would not make the judge *de jure* unable to perform his functions as arbitrator, but made the granting of his special administrative permission challengeable. As the challenge was time barred, the court treated the appointment of the judge as granted with the special permission.[363]

Failure to act without undue delay

7. The *travaux préparatoires* indicated that, in determining whether an arbitrator had complied with the obligation to act without undue delay, courts should take into consideration the following factors: what action was expected or required of the arbitrator in light of the arbitration agreement and the specific procedural situation; if the arbitrator has not done anything in this regard, whether the delay has been so inordinate as to be unacceptable in light of the circumstances, including technical difficulties and the complexity of the case; if the arbitrator has done something and acted in a certain way, whether his conduct clearly falls below the standard of what could reasonably be expected. The *travaux préparatoires* also mentioned that "[a]mongst the factors influencing the level of expectations are the ability to function efficiently and expeditiously and any special competence or other qualifications required of the arbitrator by agreement of the parties."[364]

8. In one Ugandan case, the institution designated pursuant to article 6 terminated the mandate of an arbitrator who had failed to render an award one year after the commencement of the arbitration despite that the applicable rules of arbitration required the award to be rendered within two months. The court further held that it is not right for an arbitrator to withdraw from arbitral proceedings on the sole basis of an application made pursuant to article 14, and that it is inappropriate for an arbitrator to provide written reasons in response to an application based on article 14, as that provision does not give the arbitrator the right to be heard on such an application.[365]

---

[358] *Official Records of the General Assembly, Fortieth Session, Supplement No. 17* (A/40/17), paras. 79-80.

[359] *Shri Pinaki Das Gupta v. Publicis (India) Communications*, Delhi High Court, India, 7 October 2004, 115 (2004) DLT 345, (2005) 139 PLR 26, available on the Internet at http://www.indiankanoon.org/doc/1210300/.

[360] *Noble Resources Pte. Ltd. v. China Sea Grains and Oils Industry Co. Ltd.*, High Court—Court of First Instance, Hong Kong Special Administrative Region of China, 29 March 2006, [2006] HKCFI 334, available on the Internet at http://www.hklii.hk/eng/hk/cases/hkcfi/2006/334.html.

[361] *Gordian Runoff Ltd. (formerly Gio Insurance Ltd.) v. The Underwriting Members of Lloyd's Syndicates*, Supreme Court of New South Wales (Equity Division), Australia, 19 December 2002 (revised 5 February 2003), [2002] NSWSC 1260, available on the Internet at http://www.austlii.edu.au/au/cases/nsw/NSWSC/2002/1260.html.

[362] Oberlandesgericht Köln, Germany, 9 SchH 27/02, 11 April 2003, available on the Internet at http://www.dis-arb.de/de/47/datenbanken/rspr/olg-köln-az-9-schh-27-02-datum-2003-04-11-id323.

[363] Oberlandesgericht Hamm, Germany, 17 SchH 07/03, 18 September 2003, available on the Internet at http://www.dis-arb.de/de/47/datenbanken/rspr/olg-hamm-az-17-schh-07-03-datum-2003-09-18-id237.

[364] A/CN.9/264, Analytical commentary on draft text of a model law on international commercial arbitration, under article 14, para. 4, available on the UNCITRAL website at http://www.uncitral.org/uncitral/en/commission/sessions/18th.html.

[365] *Roko Construction Ltd. v. Aya Bakery (U) Ltd.*, Center for Arbitration and Dispute Resolution, Uganda, 22 August 2008, [2008] UGCADER 1.

9. Several cases stand for the proposition that an arbitrator's mandate may be terminated pursuant to article 14 where the arbitrator failed to render an award within the time limit agreed by the parties.[366]

Consequences of termination of an arbitrator's mandate

10. The termination of an arbitrator's mandate does not end the arbitral proceedings. Article 15 rather provides for the appointment of a substitute arbitrator. In one Indian case, the court pointed out that despite the termination of an arbitrator's mandate, interim measures of protection previously granted by a court continued to be operative.[367]

Possibility of contracting out of article 14

11. Article 14 is silent as to whether it may be excluded by agreement of the parties. The question is of particular practical importance in the context of institutional arbitration, as institutional arbitration rules usually provide that disputes relating to the termination of an arbitrator's mandate are to be resolved by the institution rather than by courts. The *travaux préparatoires* made it clear that "the provision was not intended to preclude the parties from varying the grounds which would give rise to the termination of the [arbitrator's] mandate or from entrusting a third person or institution with deciding on such termination."[368]

[366] *Kifayatullah Haji Gulam Rasool et al. v. Smt. Bilkish Ismail Mehsania et al.*, Bombay High Court, India, 26 April 2000, AIR 2000 Bom 424, 2000 (4) BomCR 412, 2000 (4) MhLj 341, available on the Internet at http://www.indiankanoon.org/doc/36136/; *Petro-Canada v. Alberta Gas Ethylene*, Alberta Court of Appeal, Canada, 28 January 1992, [1992] ABCA 9 (CanLII), available on the Internet at http://canlii.ca/t/2dtgl; *N.B.C.C. Ltd. v. J.G. Engineering Pvt. Ltd.*, Supreme Court, India, 5 January 2010, available on the Internet at http://www.indiankanoon.org/doc/1259068/; See also *Ting Kang Chung John v. Teo Hee Lai Building Constructions Pte. Ltd. and Ors.*, High Court, Singapore, [2010] SGHC 20; *Tay Eng Chuan v. United Overseas Insurance Ltd.*, High Court, Singapore, [2009] SGHC 193, [2009] 4 SLR(R).

[367] *Kifayatullah Haji Gulam Rasool et al. v. Smt. Bilkish Ismail Mehsania et al.*, Bombay High Court, India, 26 April 2000, AIR 2000 Bom 424, 2000 (4) BomCR 412, 2000 (4) MhLj 341, available on the Internet at http://www.indiankanoon.org/doc/36136/.

[368] *Official Records of the General Assembly, Fortieth Session, Supplement No. 17* (A/40/17), at para. 136.

Article 15. Appointment of substitute arbitrator

Where the mandate of an arbitrator terminates under article 13 or 14 or because of his withdrawal from office for any other reason or because of the revocation of his mandate by agreement of the parties or in any other case of termination of his mandate, a substitute arbitrator shall be appointed according to the rules that were applicable to the appointment of the arbitrator being replaced.

TRAVAUX PRÉPARATOIRES

The *travaux préparatoires* on article 15 as adopted in 1985 are contained in the following documents:

1. Report of the United Nations Commission on International Trade Law on the work of its eighteenth session (*Official Records of the General Assembly, Fortieth Session, Supplement No. 17* (A/40/17)), paras. 11-333.
2. Reports of the Working Group: A/CN.9/216; A/CN.9/232; A/CN.9/233; A/CN.9/245; A/CN.9/246, annex; A/CN.9/263 and Add.1-2; A/CN.9/264. Relevant working papers are referred to in the reports.
3. Summary records of the 315th and 332nd UNCITRAL meetings.

Article 15 was not amended in 2006.

(available on the Internet at www.uncitral.org).

INTRODUCTION

1. Article 15 deals with two different, though related, questions: the circumstances in which an arbitrator's mandate may end, and the procedure applicable to the appointment of substitute arbitrators.

Scope of application of article 15

2. As article 15 is not among the provisions listed in article 1 (2), it does not apply where the seat of arbitration is either undetermined or located in a foreign jurisdiction. While the possibility of addressing the appointment of substitute arbitrators before the place of arbitration had been determined was discussed, the *travaux préparatoires* clearly indicate that the Model Law should not deal with issues relating to the constitution of the arbitral tribunal that arise prior to the determination of the place of arbitration.[369]

Termination of an arbitrator's mandate

3. Article 15 is one of two provisions of the Model Law dealing with the termination of an arbitrator's mandate. Article 14 addresses situations where an arbitrator becomes *de jure* or *de facto* unable to perform his functions or, for other reasons, fails to act without undue delay. Article 15 firstly confirms what the *travaux préparatoires* characterize as the parties' "unrestricted freedom" to terminate an arbitrator's mandate, a freedom that underscores the significance of the consensual nature of arbitration.[370] Secondly, article 15 confirms that an arbitrator may withdraw from his office for any other reason than those set out in articles 13 (lack of independence or impartiality, failure to meet qualifications required by the parties) and 14 (*de jure* or *de facto* inability to act, failure to act without undue delay). The Model Law does not limit the grounds upon which an arbitrator could withdraw from his or her office, as on a practical view point, an unwilling arbitrator cannot be forced to perform his or her functions.[371] In addition, the *travaux préparatoires* clarify that the Model Law did not seek to regulate the legal responsibility that may be incurred by an arbitrator who withdraws from his or her office for unjustified reasons.[372]

---

[369] *Official Records of the General Assembly, Fortieth Session, Supplement No. 17* (A/40/17), paras. 79-80, 111 and 148.

[370] A/CN.9/264, Analytical commentary on draft text of a model law on international commercial arbitration, under article 15, para. 2, available on the UNCITRAL website at http://www.uncitral.org/uncitral/en/commission/sessions/18th.html.

[371] A/CN.9/264, Analytical commentary on draft text of a model law on international commercial arbitration, under article 15, para. 3, available on the UNCITRAL website at http://www.uncitral.org/uncitral/en/commission/sessions/18th.html.

[372] A/CN.9/264, Analytical commentary on draft text of a model law on international commercial arbitration, under article 15, para. 3, available on the UNCITRAL website at http://www.uncitral.org/uncitral/en/commission/sessions/18th.html.

CASE LAW ON ARTICLE 15

Termination of an arbitrator's mandate

4. In one Australian case, one of the party-appointed arbitrators who could not be available for the scheduled hearing offered his resignation to the party that had appointed him. That party accepted the arbitrator's resignation and appointed a substitute arbitrator. The court found that the arbitrator had withdrawn from his office within the meaning of article 15 and that the party that had appointed him had been entitled to unilaterally appoint a new arbitrator without consulting the other party. According to the court, under the Model Law "an arbitrator nominated by party A might offer to withdraw and make that offer to party A alone and party A, acting alone, might accept that offer to withdraw. It does not seem [...] that the agreement of party B is necessary or that party A is obliged to consult party B about the matter at all."[373]

Appointment of a substitute arbitrator

5. Pursuant to article 15, the appointment of a substitute arbitrator is governed by the rules that were applicable to the appointment of the arbitrator being replaced. Although article 15 is silent as to whether it is subject to any contrary agreement by the parties, the *travaux préparatoires* indicate that "the party autonomy recognized in article 11 for the original appointment of an arbitrator applied with equal force to the procedure of appointing the substitute arbitrator, since article 15 referred to the rules that were applicable to the appointment of the arbitrator being replaced."[374]

6. According to a decision of the Supreme Court of India, the "rules that were applicable to the appointment of the arbitrator being replaced" include any procedure for the initial appointment of arbitrators agreed to by the parties.[375]

---

[373] *Gordian Runoff Ltd. (formerly Gio Insurance Ltd.) v. The Underwriting Members of Lloyd's Syndicates*, Supreme Court of New South Wales (Equity Division), Australia, 19 December 2002 (revised 5 February 2003), [2002] NSWSC 1260, available on the Internet at http://www.austlii.edu.au/au/cases/nsw/NSWSC/2002/1260.html.

[374] *Official Records of the General Assembly, Fortieth Session, Supplement No. 17* (A/40/17), annex I, para. 147.

[375] *Yashwith Construction P. Ltd. v. Simplex Concrete Piles India Ltd.*, Supreme Court, India, 3 July 2006, available on the Internet at http://www.indiankanoon.org/doc/1997730/; *M/S.S.B.P. & Co. v. M/S. Patel Engineering Ltd. & Anr.*, Supreme Court, India, 21 October 2009, available on the Internet at http://www.indiankanoon.org/doc/617127/.

CHAPTER IV. JURISDICTION OF ARBITRAL TRIBUNAL

Article 16. Competence of arbitral tribunal to rule on its jurisdiction

(1) The arbitral tribunal may rule on its own jurisdiction, including any objections with respect to the existence or validity of the arbitration agreement. For that purpose, an arbitration clause which forms part of a contract shall be treated as an agreement independent of the other terms of the contract. A decision by the arbitral tribunal that the contract is null and void shall not entail ipso jure *the invalidity of the arbitration clause.*

(2) A plea that the arbitral tribunal does not have jurisdiction shall be raised not later than the submission of the statement of defence. A party is not precluded from raising such a plea by the fact that he has appointed, or participated in the appointment of, an arbitrator. A plea that the arbitral tribunal is exceeding the scope of its authority shall be raised as soon as the matter alleged to be beyond the scope of its authority is raised during the arbitral proceedings. The arbitral tribunal may, in either case, admit a later plea if it considers the delay justified.

(3) The arbitral tribunal may rule on a plea referred to in paragraph (2) of this article either as a preliminary question or in an award on the merits. If the arbitral tribunal rules as a preliminary question that it has jurisdiction, any party may request, within thirty days after having received notice of that ruling, the court specified in article 6 to decide the matter, which decision shall be subject to no appeal; while such a request is pending, the arbitral tribunal may continue the arbitral proceedings and make an award.

TRAVAUX PRÉPARATOIRES

The *travaux préparatoires* on article 16 as adopted in 1985 are contained in the following documents:

1. Report of the United Nations Commission on International Trade Law on the work of its eighteenth session (*Official Records of the General Assembly, Fortieth Session, Supplement No. 17* (A/40/17)), paras. 11-333.
2. Reports of the Working Group: A/CN.9/216; A/CN.9/232; A/CN.9/245; A/CN.9/246, annex; A/CN.9/263 and Add.1-2; A/CN.9/264. Relevant working papers are referred to in the reports.
3. Summary records of the 315th, 320th and 332nd UNCITRAL meetings.

Article 16 was not amended in 2006.

(Available on the Internet at www.uncitral.org).

INTRODUCTION

1. Article 16 addresses three issues that may arise when the parties disagree as to whether their dispute ought to be resolved in arbitral or judicial proceedings. One is the separability principle, pursuant to which an arbitration clause forming part of a contract is to be treated as an independent, or separate, contract (article 16 (1)). Another issue is the arbitral tribunal's power to make a determination as to its own jurisdiction to deal with the substantive claim in dispute (known as the principle of competence-competence), which is affirmed in article 16 (1) and regulated in articles 16 (2) and 16 (3). Finally, article 16 (3) addresses the courts' power to review jurisdictional decisions rendered by arbitral tribunals in a preliminary phase of the proceedings.

CASE LAW ON ARTICLE 16

Scope of application of article 16

2. As article 16 is not among the provisions listed in article 1 (2), it does not apply if the place of arbitration is either undetermined or located in a foreign jurisdiction.

3. A question that has given rise to divergent case law relates to the impact of the absence in article 1 (2) of any reference to article 16 on the scope of application of the separability and the competence-competence principles.

The question has arisen in cases involving referral applications made under article 8 and based on arbitration agreements providing for a foreign place of arbitration. As was discussed in the section on case law on article 8 (see above, section on article 8, paras. 29-32), courts have adopted different approaches on whether to apply a *prima facie* standard or rather perform a full review of the issue(s) at hand when considering if an action falls within an arbitration agreement that is neither null and void, inoperable or incapable of being performed. Because the *prima facie* approach is based on the theory that the competence-competence principle should be understood as conferring on the arbitral tribunal the power not only to rule on its jurisdiction, but also to do so prior to any court intervention on that matter, some courts have relied on the absence, in article 1 (2), of any reference to article 16 to justify their holding that the *prima facie* approach was inapplicable to the case.[376] However, in several other cases also involving arbitration agreements providing for a foreign place of arbitration, courts have not hesitated to apply the *prima facie* approach.[377]

4. A similar conclusion emerges from the cases dealing with the separability principle. In an Australian case, the court noted that article 16 (1) is, in the strict sense, not applicable where the arbitration agreement provides for a foreign place of arbitration, but nevertheless applied the separability principle to the jurisdictional issue at hand.[378] Several other cases show courts applying the separability principle where the place of arbitration was either undetermined[379] or located in a foreign jurisdiction.[380]

5. Another issue relating to the scope of the separability principle stems from the introductory phrase of the second sentence of article 16 (1) ("For that purpose"). As the preceding sentence refers to the arbitral tribunal's power to rule on its own jurisdiction, the second sentence could be read as limiting the operation of the separability principle to situations where a jurisdictional objection is being examined by the arbitral tribunal, as opposed to a court. However, the cases clearly confirm that the language used in the second sentence does not prevent the application of the separability principle when a jurisdictional question is raised before a court.[381]

The separability of an arbitration clause forming part of a contract

6. Although the separability principle may have other consequences—such as permitting the arbitration clause to be governed by a different law than the law applicable to the contract in which it is contained—, article 16 (1) only deals explicitly with the impact of the principle on jurisdictional issues. It does so in its last sentence, according to which a finding that the contract is null and void will not necessarily entail the invalidity of the arbitration clause contained therein. The arbitral tribunal's jurisdiction will only be affected where the defect causing the invalidity of the main contract necessarily extends, by its very nature, to the arbitration clause.[382]

---

[376] CLOUT case No. 13 (also reproduced under CLOUT case No. 383) [*Deco Automotive Inc. v. G.P.A. Gesellschaft für Pressenautomation mbH*, Ontario District Court, Canada, 27 October 1989]; CLOUT case No. 1011 [*H & H Marine Engine Service Ltd. v. Volvo Penta of the Americas Inc.*, Supreme Court of British Columbia, Canada, 9 October 2009], [2009] BCSC 1389, also available on the Internet at http://canlii.ca/t/262c8.

[377] See for instance: CLOUT case No. 1047 [*Dancap Productions Inc. v. Key Brand Entertainment Inc.*, Ontario Court of Appeal, Ontario, Canada, 13 February 2009], [2009] ONCA 135, also available on the Internet at http://canlii.ca/t/22h4f; CLOUT case No. 509 [*Dalimpex Ltd. v. Janicki*, Ontario Court of Appeal, Ontario, Canada, 30 May 2003], [2003] CanLII 34234 (ON CA), also available on the Internet at http://www.ontariocourts.on.ca/decisions/2003/may/dalimplexC37306.htm; *EDF (Services) Limited v. Appleton & Associates*, Ontario Superior Court of Justice, Canada, 4 September 2007, [2007] CanLII 36078 (ON SC), available on the Internet at http://canlii.ca/t/1sr48; *Pccw Global Ltd. v. Interactive Communications Service Ltd.*, High Court—Court of Appeal, Hong Kong Special Administrative Region of China, 16 November 2006, [2006] HKCA 434, available on the Internet at http://www.hklii.hk/eng/hk/cases/hkca/2006/434.html. Those cases can be viewed as implicitly standing for the proposition that the principle of competence-competence is a general principle of international arbitration law that operates independently from article 16(1).

[378] *Comandate Marine Corp. v. Pan Australia Shipping Pty. Ltd.*, Federal Court, Australia, 20 December 2006, [2006] FCAFC 192 at paras 218ff, available on the Internet at http://www.austlii.edu.au/au/cases/cth/FCAFC/2006/192.html.

[379] CLOUT case No. 19 [*Krutov. v. Vancouver Hockey Club Limited*, Supreme Court of British Columbia, Canada, 22 November 1991], [1991] CanLII 2077 (BC SC), also available on the Internet at http://canlii.ca/t/1cr44.

[380] CLOUT case No. 504 [*D.G. Jewelry Inc. et al. v. Cyberdiam Canada Ltd. et al.*, Ontario Superior Court of Justice, Canada, 17 April 2002]; CLOUT case No. 178 [*Siderurgica Mendes Junior S.A. v. "Icepearl" (The)*, Supreme Court of British Columbia, Canada, 31 January 1996], [1996] CanLII 2746 (BC SC), also available on the Internet at http://canlii.ca/t/1f1n1; CLOUT case No. 349 [*Harper v. Kvaerner Fjellstrand Shipping A.S.*, Supreme Court of British Columbia, Canada, 13 September 1991], [1991] CanLII 1735 (BC SC), available on the Internet at http://canlii.ca/t/1cqvf; *OEMSDF Inc. v. Europe Israel Ltd.*, Ontario Superior Court of Justice, Canada, 22 September 1999, [1999] O.J. No. 3594; *Walter Rau Neusser Oel und Fett A.G. v. Cross Pacific Trading Ltd.*, Australia, 15 August 2005, [2005] FCA 1102, available on the Internet at http://www.austlii.edu.au/au/cases/cth/federal_ct/2005/1102.html; *Blue Limited v. Jaribu Credit Traders Limited*, High Court at Nairobi (Milimani Commercial Courts), Kenya, 25 September 2008, Civil Suit 157 of 2008, available on the Internet at http://kenyalaw.org/.

[381] In addition to the cases cited in the preceding two footnotes, see CLOUT case No. 368 [*Campbell et al. v. Murphy*, Ontario Court of Justice—General Division, Canada, 9 August 1993], [1993] CanLII 5460 (ON SC), also available on the Internet at http://canlii.ca/t/1vskk; CLOUT case No. 32 [*Mind Star Toys Inc. v. Samsung Co. Ltd.*, Ontario Court of Justice—General Division, Canada, 30 April 1992].

[382] A/CN.9/264, Analytical commentary on draft text of a model law on international commercial arbitration, under article 16, para. 2, available on the UNCITRAL website at http://www.uncitral.org/uncitral/en/commission/sessions/18th.html.

7. Several cases illustrate the impact of the separability principle on jurisdictional issues. In some of those cases, the party resisting arbitration unsuccessfully sought to rely on the fact that the main contract was invalid because a condition precedent to the entry into force of that contract had not been fulfilled.[383] In other cases, the separability principle was relied upon by courts to dismiss objections to arbitral jurisdiction asserting that the main contract had been entered into through deceit,[384] or fraud,[385] or that the main contract was void either on grounds of illegality,[386] or because the parties were mistaken as to their respective rights and obligations when they entered into it.[387] A third group of decisions stands for the proposition that the termination of the contract will not necessarily affect the validity of the arbitration clause contained therein.[388] The separability principle was also held to be applicable in cases where it was argued that the main contract was void on grounds of repudiation, fundamental breach or frustration.[389]

The concept of jurisdiction

8. The opening sentence of article 16 (1) makes clear that the existence and validity of the arbitration agreement are jurisdictional issues, a point that is echoed in the cases.[390] Whether the concept of jurisdiction can be extended to other issues than the existence, validity and scope of the arbitral agreement would depend on the interpretation given to the word "including" in the opening sentence of article 16 (1). One case implicitly stands for the proposition that it can, as the court reviewed, pursuant to article 16 (3), a decision of the arbitral tribunal dismissing an argument asserting that it had no power to issue interim measures of protection; however, the court's decision does not directly address the admissibility of application under article 16 (3).[391] In another case that may be viewed as embracing a broader conception of the notion of jurisdiction, the court deemed admissible under article 16 (3) an application seeking the review of a decision of

---

[383] *Cecrop Co. v. Kinetic Sciences Inc.*, Supreme Court of British Columbia, Canada, 9 April 2001, [2001] BCSC 532 (CanLII), available on the Internet at http://canlii.ca/t/4xl1; CLOUT case No. 19 [*Krutov. v. Vancouver Hockey Club Limited*, Supreme Court of British Columbia, Canada, 22 November 1991], [1991] CanLII 2077 (BC SC), also available on the Internet at http://canlii.ca/t/1cr44; *Blue Limited v. Jaribu Credit Traders Limited*, High Court at Nairobi (Milimani Commercial Courts), Kenya, 25 September 2008, Civil Suit 157 of 2008, available on the Internet at http://kenyalaw.org/.

[384] CLOUT case No. 504 [*D.G. Jewelry Inc. et al. v. Cyberdiam Canada Ltd. et al.*, Ontario Superior Court of Justice, Canada, 17 April 2002]; see also *Comandate Marine Corp. v. Pan Australia Shipping Pty. Ltd.*, Federal Court, Australia, 20 December 2006, [2006] FCAFC 192, available on the Internet at http://www.austlii.edu.au/au/cases/cth/FCAFC/2006/192.html, and *Walter Rau Neusser Oel und Fett A.G. v. Cross Pacific Trading Ltd.*, Federal Court, Australia, 15 August 2005, [2005] FCA 1102, available on the Internet at http://www.austlii.edu.au/au/cases/cth/federal_ct/2005/1102.html.

[385] *New World Expedition Yachts LLC v. P.R. Yacht Builders Ltd.*, Supreme Court of British Columbia, Canada, 25 October 2010, [2010] BCSC 1496, available on the Internet at. http://canlii.ca/t/2d2vn.

[386] CLOUT case No. 114 [*Globe Union Industrial Corp. v. G.A.P. Marketing Corp.*, Supreme Court of British Columbia, Canada, 18 November 1994], [1994] CanLII 186 (BC SC), also available on the Internet at http://canlii.ca/t/1dp7k.

[387] *NetSys Technology Group AB v. Open Text Corp.*, Ontario Superior Court of Justice, Canada, 29 July 1999, [1999] CanLII 14937 (ON SC), available on the Internet at http://canlii.ca/t/1w8ss.

[388] *Cecrop Co. v. Kinetic Sciences Inc.*, Supreme Court of British Columbia, Canada, 9 April 2001, [2001] BCSC 532 (CanLII), available on the Internet at http://canlii.ca/t/4xl1; *NetSys Technology Group AB v. Open Text Corp.*, Ontario Superior Court of Justice, Canada, 29 July 1999, [1999] CanLII 14937 (ON SC), available on the Internet at http://canlii.ca/t/1w8ss; CLOUT case No. 178 [*Siderurgica Mendes Júnior S.A. v. "Icepearl" (The)*, Supreme Court of British Columbia, Canada, 31 January 1996], [1996] CanLII 2746 (BC SC), also available on the Internet at http://canlii.ca/t/1f1n1; CLOUT case No. 349 [*Harper v. Kvaerner Fjellstrand Shipping A.S.*, Supreme Court of British Columbia, Canada, 13 September 1991], [1991] CanLII 1735 (BC SC), also available on the Internet at http://canlii.ca/t/1cqvf; CLOUT case No. 114 [*Globe Union Industrial Corp. v. G.A.P. Marketing Corp.*, Supreme Court of British Columbia, Canada, 18 November 1994], [1994] CanLII 186 (BC SC), also available on the Internet at http://canlii.ca/t/1dp7k; *Rampton v. Eyre*, Ontario Court of Appeal, Canada, 2 May 2007, [2007] ONCA 331, available on the Internet at http://canlii.ca/t/1rb0d; *9095-5378 Québec Inc. v. Perform Environnement Inc.*, Superior Court of Quebec, Canada, 18 August 2004, [2004] CanLII 7022 (QC CS), available on the Internet at http://canlii.ca/t/1hnxs.

[389] CLOUT case No. 19 [*Krutov. v. Vancouver Hockey Club Limited*, Supreme Court of British Columbia, Canada, 22 November 1991], [1991] CanLII 2077 (BC SC), also available on the Internet at http://canlii.ca/t/1cr44; *OEMSDF Inc. v. Europe Israel Ltd.*, Ontario Superior Court of Justice, Canada, 22 September 1999, [1999] O.J. No. 3594; CLOUT case No. 20 [*Fung Sang Trading Limited v. Kai Sun Sea Products and Food Company Limited*, High Court—Court of First Instance, Hong Kong, 29 October 1991], [1991] HKCFI 190, also available on the Internet at http://www.hklii.hk/eng/hk/cases/hkcfi/1991/190.html; CLOUT case No. 368 [*Campbell et al. v. Murphy*, Ontario Court of Justice—General Division, Canada, 9 August 1993], [1993] CanLII 5460 (ON SC), also available on the Internet at http://canlii.ca/t/1vskk; CLOUT case No. 32 [*Mind Star Toys Inc. v. Samsung Co. Ltd.*, Ontario Court of Justice—General Division, Ontario, Canada, 30 April 1992].

[390] See for instance: CLOUT case No. 567 [*PT Tugu Pratama Indonesia v. Magma Nusantara Ltd.*, High Court, Singapore, 10 September 2003], also in [2003] SGHC 204, [2003] 4 SLR(R) 257.

[391] CLOUT case No. 626 [*Quintette Coal Ltd. v. Nippon Steel Corp.*, Supreme Court of British Columbia, Canada, 6 July 1988], [1988] CanLII 2923 (BC SC), also available on the Internet at http://canlii.ca/t/20xlg.

the arbitral tribunal that dismissed an objection asserted by the respondent to the effect that the arbitration had to take place in London, England, rather than Calgary, Canada.[392] In a similar case, the Singapore Court of Appeal took for granted that a decision of the arbitral tribunal on the validity of a clause providing for arbitration administered by one institution but governed by the rules of another institution was a jurisdictional decision that could be reviewed under 16 (3).[393] In another case, that same court considered that the fact that the common law doctrine of estoppel prevented the claimant from raising in a second arbitration issues that could have been raised in a first, entailed that the second arbitral tribunal lacked jurisdiction over the case.[394] Furthermore, the Supreme Court of India held that whether the arbitral tribunal has been properly constituted is a jurisdictional issue for the purposes of article 16.[395]

The arbitral tribunal's power to rule on its own jurisdiction

9. The affirmation in article 16 (1) of the power enjoyed by arbitral tribunals to rule on their own jurisdiction echoes provisions found in virtually all modern international arbitration statutes and rules, and reflects what is widely considered to be one of the most basic principles of international commercial arbitration.[396]

The arbitral tribunal's power to examine its jurisdiction on its own motion

10. The inclusion of timeliness requirements in article 16 (2) could be interpreted as implicitly denying arbitral tribunals the power to examine their jurisdiction on their own motion. However, the *travaux préparatoires* reveal that that was not the case. The *travaux préparatoires* indicate that the "words 'including any objections with respect to the existence or validity of the arbitration agreement' [found in article 16 (1)] were not intended to limit the '*Kompetenz-Kompetenz*' of the arbitral tribunal to those cases where a party raised an objection."[397] Furthermore, the *travaux préparatoires* emphasize the arbitral tribunal's power to examine on its own motion issues of public policy bearing on its jurisdiction, including the arbitrability of the dispute.[398]

Applicable law

11. Article 16 (1) is silent on the law that should be applied by the arbitral tribunal while ruling on objections to its jurisdiction. Furthermore, the Model Law does not contain any generally applicable conflict of laws rule concerning the arbitration agreement. However, it does state which law governs issues of capacity, validity and arbitrability in the context of setting-aside applications (article 34) or recognition and enforcement applications (articles 35-36),[399] and the *travaux préparatoires* indicate that the law the arbitral tribunal should apply to jurisdictional objections is "the same as that which the Court specified in article 6 would apply in setting aside proceedings under article 34, since these proceedings constitute the ultimate court control over the arbitral tribunal's decision (article 16 (3))."[400]

Timeliness requirements and consequences of a party's failure to object to the arbitral tribunal's jurisdiction in a timely manner

12. Article 16 (2) is intended to ensure that objections to the arbitral tribunal's jurisdiction will be raised promptly. It also makes clear that a party's participation in the constitution of the arbitral tribunal will not in itself prevent that party from subsequently raising an objection to the tribunal's jurisdiction; in other words, participation in the constitution of a tribunal does not amount to submission to the jurisdiction of that tribunal.

13. One question of practical importance is whether a party's failure to raise a jurisdictional objection in a timely manner precludes it from challenging the validity of the arbitration agreement in subsequent setting aside (article 34) or recognition and enforcement (articles 35 and 36) proceedings. According to the *travaux préparatoires*, this question

[392] *Ace Bermuda Insurance Ltd. v. Allianz Insurance Company of Canada*, Court of Queen's Bench of Alberta, Canada, 21 December 2005, [2005] ABQB 975 (CanLII), available on the Internet at http://canlii.ca/t/1m8vm.

[393] *Insigma Technology Co. Ltd. v. Alstom Technology Ltd.*, Court of Appeal, Singapore, 2 June 2009, [2009] SGCA 24, [2009] 3 SLR(R) 936.

[394] CLOUT case No. 742 [*PT Asuransi Jasa Indonesia (Persero) v. Dexia Bank S.A.*, Court of Appeal, Singapore, 1 December 2006], also in [2006] SGCA 41, [2007] 1 SLR(R) 597.

[395] *M/S. Anuptech Equipments Private v. M/S. Ganpati Co-Op. Housing*, Bombay High Court, India, 30 January 1999, AIR 1999 Bom 219, available on the Internet at http://www.indiankanoon.org/doc/1805967/.

[396] See for instance: CLOUT case No. 20 [*Fung Sang Trading Limited v. Kai Sun Sea Products and Food Company Limited*, High Court—Court of First Instance, Hong Kong, 29 October 1991], [1991] HKCFI 190, also available on the Internet at http://www.hklii.hk/eng/hk/cases/hkcfi/1991/190.html.

[397] *Official Records of the General Assembly, Fortieth Session, Supplement No. 17* (A/40/17), annex I, para. 150.

[398] A/CN.9/264, Analytical commentary on draft text of a model law on international commercial arbitration, under article 16, paras. 3 and 10, available on the UNCITRAL website at http://www.uncitral.org/uncitral/en/commission/sessions/18th.html.

[399] See articles 34 (2) *(a)*(i), 34 (2) *(b)*(i), 36 (1) *(a)*(i) and 36 (1) *(b)*(i).

[400] A/CN.9/264, Analytical commentary on draft text of a model law on international commercial arbitration, under article 16, para. 3, available on the UNCITRAL website at http://www.uncitral.org/uncitral/en/commission/sessions/18th.html.

should be answered in the affirmative,[401] except where the arbitral tribunal's jurisdiction is challenged on public policy grounds, including the inarbitrability of the dispute (articles 34 (2)*(b)* and 36 (1)*(b)*).[402] The preclusionary effect of a party's failure to object in a timely manner to the arbitral tribunal's jurisdiction has been affirmed by courts.[403] However, in one case, a party that had not raised any jurisdictional objection before the arbitral tribunal was later allowed to do so in setting-aside proceedings (article 34), but the circumstances of that case were unusual as that party had never been properly informed of the commencement of the arbitration.[404] (See below, section on article 34, para. 45 and section on article 36, para. 22).

The tribunal's discretion to rule on an objection to its jurisdiction in a preliminary phase or in an award on the merits

14. The first sentence of article 16 (3) grants the arbitral tribunal discretion to rule on a jurisdictional objection raised during the proceedings in a decision rendered before consideration of the merits, or in an award on the merits.[405] A ruling on jurisdiction as a preliminary question was said by one court to be desirable where the case on the merits is difficult and likely to be costly.[406] The arbitral tribunal may also decide to rule on the objection in an award on the merits. This may be a preferable course of action, for example, where the jurisdictional issue is intertwined with a substantive issue,[407] or where the case is fairly simple.[408] (See also below, section on article 34, para. 113).

Judicial review of interim jurisdictional decisions rendered by the arbitral tribunal

15. Article 16 (3) deals with one aspect of the important question of judicial intervention relating to the arbitral process. Derogating from what may be seen as a general principle postponing judicial review of the legality of the arbitration until after the award has been made,[409] it allows a party, under some circumstances, to seek the judicial review of a jurisdictional decision[410] rendered by the arbitral tribunal.

Reviewability of jurisdictional decision not affected by its form

16. A first issue that has arisen in the cases is whether the fact that the arbitral tribunal's preliminary jurisdictional decision takes the form of an interim award entails that it constitutes an award on the merits falling outside the scope of article 16 (3). In a decision, the Hong Kong Court of

[401] A/CN.9/264, Analytical commentary on draft text of a model law on international commercial arbitration, under article 16, paras. 8 and 9, available on the UNCITRAL website at http://www.uncitral.org/uncitral/en/commission/sessions/18th.html.

[402] A/CN.9/264, Analytical commentary on draft text of a model law on international commercial arbitration, under article 16, para. 10, available on the UNCITRAL website at http://www.uncitral.org/uncitral/en/commission/sessions/18th.html.

[403] See for instance: Oberlandesgericht Celle, Germany, 8 Sch 11/02, 4 September 2003, available on the Internet at: http://www.dis-arb.de/en/47/datenbanken/rspr/olg-celle-case-no-8-sch-11-02-date-2003-09-04-id1275; Oberlandesgericht Stuttgart, Germany, 1 Sch 16/01 (1), 20 December 2001, available on the Internet at http://www.dis-arb.de/en/47/datenbanken/rspr/olg-stuttgart-case-no-1-sch-16-01-1-date-2001-12-20-id158; CLOUT case No. 148 [Moscow City Court, Russian Federation, 10 February 1995].

[404] CLOUT case No. 562 [Hanseatisches Oberlandesgericht Hamburg, Germany, 6 Sch 04/01, 8 November 2001], also available on the Internet at http://www.dis-arb.de/en/47/datenbanken/rspr/hanseat-olg-hamburg-case-no-6-sch-04-01-date-2001-11-08-id145.

[405] A/CN.9/264, Analytical commentary on draft text of a model law on international commercial arbitration, under article 16, para. 11, available on the UNCITRAL website at http://www.uncitral.org/uncitral/en/commission/sessions/18th.html.

[406] CLOUT case No. 20 [*Fung Sang Trading Limited v. Kai Sun Sea Products and Food Company Limited*, High Court—Court of First Instance, Hong Kong, 29 October 1991], [1991] HKCFI 190, also available on the Internet at http://www.hklii.hk/eng/hk/cases/hkcfi/1991/190.html.

[407] A/CN.9/264, Analytical commentary on draft text of a model law on international commercial arbitration, under article 16, para. 11, available on the UNCITRAL website at http://www.uncitral.org/uncitral/en/commission/sessions/18th.html.

[408] CLOUT case No. 20 [*Fung Sang Trading Limited v. Kai Sun Sea Products and Food Company Limited*, High Court—Court of First Instance, Hong Kong, 29 October 1991], [1991] HKCFI 190, also available on the Internet at http://www.hklii.hk/eng/hk/cases/hkcfi/1991/190.html.

[409] *Official Records of the General Assembly, Fortieth Session, Supplement No. 17* (A/40/17), annex I, paras 62-63; *Compagnie Nationale Air France v. Mbaye*, Court of Appeal of Quebec, Canada, 31 March 2003, [2003] CanLII 35834 (QC CA), available on the Internet at http://canlii.ca/t/284nd; *GPEC International Ltd. v. Canada (Canadian Commercial Corporation)*, Federal Court—Trial Division, Canada, 2 April 2008, [2008] FC 414 (CanLII), available on the Internet at http://canlii.ca/t/1wgpt; CLOUT case No. 186 [*A. Bianchi S.R.L. v. Bilumen Lighting Ltd.*, Superior Court of Quebec, Canada, 18 May 1990]; CLOUT case No. 182 [*International Civil Aviation Organization (ICAO) v. Tripal Systems Pty. Ltd.*, Superior Court of Quebec, Canada, 9 September 1994].

[410] A decision whereby the tribunal merely refuses to deal with a jurisdictional decision in a preliminary manner is not subject to review under article 16(3): see CLOUT case No. 441 [Oberlandesgericht Köln, Germany, 9 Sch 06/00, 20 July 2000], also available on the Internet at http://www.dis-arb.de/en/47/datenbanken/rspr/olg-k&oumlln-case-no-9-sch-06-00-date-2000-07-20-id228.

Appeal rejected the argument, emphasizing that what mattered to the admissibility of the application was whether the impugned jurisdictional decision had been rendered in a preliminary matter, rather than the form it took.[411] A 2006 decision of the Court of Appeal of Singapore is to the same effect.[412]

Applicable law

17. Article 16 (3) does not specify which law the court should apply while reviewing a jurisdictional decision rendered by the arbitral tribunal. However, it may be noted that the Model Law explicitly mentions which law governs issues of capacity, validity and arbitrability in the context of setting-aside applications (article 34) or recognition and enforcement applications (articles 35-36)[413] and that the *travaux préparatoires* suggest that the conflict-of-laws rules set out in articles 34 and 36 should be followed by arbitral tribunals while ruling on their own jurisdiction (see above in this section, para. 11).

Applicable standard of review

18. Another issue on which article 16 (3) is silent relates to the applicable standard of review: may the court fully review conclusions of fact and law found in the challenged decision, or should it rather adopt a deferential stance and only set it aside if exceptional circumstances are present? This question of practical importance has not been answered consistently by courts. While in several cases courts have taken for granted that interim jurisdictional decisions rendered by arbitral tribunals could be fully reviewed,[414] in the cases where the issue was addressed in greater detail inconsistent conclusions were reached.

19. In one case, an arbitral tribunal had rendered an interim decision dismissing the respondent's contention that the parties were not bound by any arbitration agreement. The respondent subsequently made an application under article 16 (3) to seek a court ruling on the jurisdictional issue and asserted arguments that, according to the claimant, had not been asserted before the arbitral tribunal. The claimant argued that those arguments were inadmissible on the ground that, in the context of an application based on article 16 (3), a court could only determine the jurisdictional issue on the basis of arguments presented to the arbitral tribunal. The High Court of Singapore rejected the argument, noting that a hearing under article 16 (3) is not by way of appeal and that the parties were therefore free to put forward new arguments. Moreover, it added that a court intervening pursuant to article 16 (3) was free to "make [...] an independent determination of the issue of jurisdiction and is not constrained in any way by the findings or the reasoning of the tribunal."[415]

20. In another case, involving a dispute arising out of an insurance contract, the insured commenced arbitration on the basis of a clause providing for an arbitration seated in Calgary, Canada and conducted pursuant to the Alberta statute governing international arbitration. The insurer, the respondent in the arbitration, objected to the arbitral tribunal's jurisdiction on the basis that the parties had agreed that the arbitration would rather be held in London, England. After the arbitral tribunal dismissed the jurisdictional objection, the insurer made an application under article 16 (3) to seek a court ruling thereon. The court proceeded to a detailed analysis of the applicable standard and—relying on the fact that courts "are generally reluctant to interfere with decisions of a commercial arbitral tribunal, particularly in a matter involving an international commercial arbitration," as well as on a line of Canadian cases standing

---

[411] *The Incorporated Owners of Tak Tai Building v. Leung Yau Building Ltd.*, High Court—Court of Appeal, Hong Kong Special Administrative Region of China, 9 March 2005, [2005] HKCA 87, available on the Internet at http://www.hklii.hk/eng/hk/cases/hkca/2005/87.html; see also CLOUT case No. 523 [*Weltime Hong Kong Ltd. & Others v. Ken Forward Engineering Ltd.*, High Court—Court of First Instance, Hong Kong Special Administrative Region of China, 6 March 2001], [2001] HKCFI 831, also available on the Internet at http://www.hklii.hk/eng/hk/cases/hkcfi/2001/831.html; *Brunswick Bowling & Billiards Corporation v. Shanghai Zhonglu Industrial Co. Ltd. and Another*, High Court—Court of First Instance, Hong Kong Special Administrative Region of China, 10 February 2009, [2009] HKCFI 94 at para. 111, available on the Internet at http://www.hklii.hk/eng/hk/cases/hkcfi/2009/94.html, at para. 111.

[412] CLOUT case No. 742 [*PT Asuransi Jasa Indonesia (Persero) v. Dexia Bank S.A.*, Court of Appeal, Singapore, 1 December 2006], also in [2006] SGCA 41, [2007] 1 SLR(R) 597.

[413] See articles 34 (2)*(a)*(i), 34 (2)*(b)*(i), 36 (1)*(a)*(i) and 36 (1)*(b)*(i).

[414] *Assumption Sisters of Nairobi Registered Trustee v. Standard Kebathi & another*, High Court at Nairobi (Nairobi Law Courts), Kenya, 21 November 2008, Civil Case 497 of 2004, available on the Internet at http://kenyalaw.org/; *ERG Petroleos v. Realesser,* Audiencia Provincial de Madrid (sección 8ª), Spain, 13 July 2009, res. 289/2009, 28079370082009100167 (Id cendoj), available on the Internet at http://www.poderjudicial.es/search/indexAN.jsp; *Pemex Exploración v. Corporación Mexicana de Mantenimiento Integral S.A. de C.V.*, Ninth District Court in Civil Matters, Federal District, Mexico, 23 August 2007, Amparo 584/2007-IV; CLOUT case No. 373 [Kammergericht Berlin, Germany, 28 Sch 17/99, 15 October 1999], also available on the Internet at http://www.dis-arb.de/en/47/datenbanken/rspr/kg-berlin-case-no-28-sch-17-99-date-1999-10-15-id35; *Guilde des Musiciens du Québec v. Piché*, Superior Court of Quebec, Canada, 8 June 1998; [1998] JQ No. 4896 *9095-5378 Québec Inc. v. Perform Environnement Inc.*, Superior Court of Quebec, Canada, 18 August 2004, [2004] CanLII 7022 (QC CS), available on the Internet at http://canlii.ca/t/1hnxs; *Canadian Ground Water Association v. Canadian Geoexchange Coalition*, Superior Court of Quebec, Canada, 15 June 2010, [2010] QCCS 2597, available on the Internet at http://canlii.ca/t/2b688; CLOUT case No. 1064 [Hanseatisches Oberlandesgericht Bremen, Germany, 2 Sch 4/01, 10 January 2002], also available on the Internet at http://www.dis-arb.de/en/47/datenbanken/rspr/hanseat-olg-bremen-case-no-2-sch-04-01-date-2002-01-10-id413.

[415] CLOUT case No. 567 [*PT Tugu Pratama Indonesia v. Magma Nusantara Ltd.*, High Court, Singapore, 10 September 2003], [2003] SGHC 204, [2003] 4 SLR(R) 257; see also *Christian Mutual Insurance Company & Central United Life Insurance Company & Connecticut Reassurance Corporation v. Ace Bermuda Insurance Limited*, Court of Appeal, Bermuda, 6 December 2002, [2002] Bda LR 56; *Mexico v. Cargill Inc.*, Ontario Court of Appeal, Canada, 4 October 2011, [2011] ONCA 622 (CanLII), available on the Internet at http://canlii.ca/t/fn9qh.

for the proposition that parties objecting to an arbitral tribunal's jurisdiction must overcome a "powerful presumption" that the tribunal acted within its powers—concluded that the standard of review applicable under article 16 (3) "ought to be [...] one of reasonableness, deference [and] respect."[416]

Impact of article 16 (3) on the reviewability of negative jurisdictional decisions

21. Article 16 (3) only deals explicitly with the reviewability of interim decisions in which the arbitral tribunal rules that it has jurisdiction over the claim; nothing is said in that provision about the reviewability of arbitral decisions denying jurisdiction, also known as negative jurisdictional decisions. However, the *travaux préparatoires* are clear on that matter: while noting that as article 16 (3) does not address the judicial review of negative jurisdictional decisions, article 5 would not preclude resort to a court to obtain a ruling on the arbitral tribunal's jurisdiction, it is nevertheless recognized in the *travaux préparatoires* that "a ruling by the arbitral tribunal that it lacked jurisdiction was final as regards its proceedings since it was inappropriate to compel arbitrators who had made such a ruling to continue the proceedings."[417] That understanding of the effect of article 16 (3) on the reviewability of negative jurisdictional decisions was shared by courts in some jurisdictions, such as Hong Kong,[418] Singapore[419] and Kenya.[420]

22. However, several cases point in the opposite direction. A first group of cases, from Canada, reveal that some courts have applied article 16 (3) to negative jurisdictional rulings, reasoning that if article 16 (3) could only be invoked in relation to preliminary decisions dismissing jurisdictional objections, the claimant would be forced to commence a court action without ever having had the benefit of a judicial ruling on the disputed jurisdictional issue, a situation that was deemed intolerable.[421]

23. A second group of decisions have found negative jurisdictional rulings to be reviewable on the ground that they constitute awards subject to setting-aside proceedings under article 34. Particularly noteworthy is a decision of the German Federal Court of Justice in which the arbitral tribunal had denied jurisdiction on the ground that the respondent had effectively withdrawn from the arbitration agreement. While the court held that the arbitral tribunal's jurisdictional decision was subject to article 34, it also found that none of the grounds exhaustively listed in article 34 allowed the court to set aside the decision on the sole basis that the tribunal had erred in denying jurisdiction. In other words, according to the court, article 34 does not allow courts to review the merits of negative jurisdictional decisions; such decisions can only be set aside in one of the specific circumstances explicitly mentioned in article 34.[422] A negative jurisdictional decision was also reviewed pursuant to article 34, in that instance by a Canadian court. While the court deemed the arbitral tribunal's decision to be reviewable pursuant to article 34, it noted that a review of the merits of that decision was impermissible under article 34 since "an arbitral decision is not invalid because it wrongly decided a point of fact and law." The court also added that the grounds for setting aside awards, which are exhaustively enumerated in article 34, have to be construed narrowly.[423] These two decisions stand in contrast to a decision of the Court of Appeal of Singapore finding that negative jurisdictional rulings do not constitute arbitral awards.[424] (See also below, section on article 34, para. 19).

24. Finally, the Constitutional Court of Croatia agreed to review a negative jurisdictional ruling in a decision

---

[416] *Ace Bermuda Insurance Ltd. v. Allianz Insurance Company of Canada*, Court of Queen's Bench of Alberta, Canada, 21 December 2005, [2005] ABQB 975 (CanLII), available on the Internet at http://canlii.ca/t/1m8vm.

[417] *Official Records of the General Assembly, Fortieth Session, Supplement No. 17* (A/40/17), annex I, para. 163.

[418] *Kenon Engineering Ltd. v. Nippon Kokan Koji Kabushiki Kaisha,* High Court—Court of First Instance, Hong Kong Special Administrative Region of China, 2 July 2003, [2003] HKCFI 568, available on the Internet at http://www.hklii.hk/eng/hk/cases/hkcfi/2003/568.html; CLOUT case No. 20 [*Fung Sang Trading Limited v. Kai Sun Sea Products and Food Company Limited*, High Court—Court of First Instance, Hong Kong, 29 October 1991], [1991] HKCFI 190, also available on the Internet at http://www.hklii.hk/eng/hk/cases/hkcfi/1991/190.html.

[419] CLOUT case No. 742 [*PT Asuransi Jasa Indonesia (Persero) v. Dexia Bank S.A.*, Court of Appeal, Singapore, 1 December 2006], also in [2006] SGCA 41, [2007] 1 SLR(R) 597.

[420] *Sebhan Enterprises Limited v. Westmont Power (Kenya) Limited*, High Court at Nairobi (Milimani Commercial Courts), Kenya, 13 March 2006, Civil Case 239 of 2005, available on the Internet at http://kenyalaw.org/CaseSearch/view_preview1.php?link=15667393821342136509879.

[421] *Re/Max Platine Inc. v. Groupe Sutton-Actuel Inc.*, Court of Appeal of Quebec, 24 July 2008, [2008] QCCA 1405, available on the Internet at http://canlii.ca/t/1zsp5; *Télébec Ltée v. Société Hydro-Québec*, Superior Court of Quebec, Canada, 17 April 1997, [1997] JQ No. 1431; *Micheline Lefebvre et al. v. Les Habitations d'Angoulème*, Superior Court of Quebec, Canada, 13 June 2002, [2000] JQ No. 2733, available on the Internet at http://www.jugements.qc.ca/; *Piché v. Guilde des Musiciens du Québec*, Superior Court of Quebec, Canada, 9 November 1999, [1998] JQ No. 4896.

[422] CLOUT case No. 560 [Bundesgerichtshof, Germany, III ZB 44/01, 6 June 2002], also available on the Internet at http://www.dis-arb.de/en/47/datenbanken/rspr/bgh-case-no-iii-zb-44-01-date-2002-06-06-id185.

[423] CLOUT case No. 1014 [*Bayview Irrigation District #11 v. United Mexican States*, Ontario Superior Court of Justice, Canada, 5 May 2008], [2008] CanLII 22120 (ON SC), available on the Internet at http://canlii.ca/t/1wwtf.

[424] CLOUT case No. 742 [*PT Asuransi Jasa Indonesia (Persero) v. Dexia Bank S.A.*, Court of Appeal, Singapore, 1 December 2006], also in [2006] SGCA 41, [2007] 1 SLR(R) 597.

rendered in connection with an arbitration governed by legislation enacting the Model Law. The applicant did not seek the court's intervention on the basis of any provision of the legislation. It rather invoked provisions of the Croatian constitution setting out remedies available to those who complain of constitutional violations. The court ultimately set aside the tribunal's jurisdictional decision, notably on the ground that it was not adequately reasoned.[425]

Arbitral tribunal's power to continue the proceedings and render an award

25. The last sentence of paragraph (3) provides that the arbitral tribunal may continue the proceedings and even render an award while a court application made pursuant to that same paragraph is pending. However, the Court of Appeal for Bermuda has held that arbitral tribunals should normally wait for a decision by the court before considering the merits, as that approach would save time and costs. However, the court recognized that this approach would only be feasible if an immediate hearing on the court application was available to the parties. In that case, the arbitral tribunal had dismissed an objection to its jurisdiction in a preliminary phase of the proceedings. That decision was challenged pursuant to article 16 (3), but the arbitral tribunal—which chose to continue the proceedings—rendered an award disposing of the merits before a court had had the opportunity to hear the application. As that award was subsequently challenged pursuant to article 34, two court applications challenging the arbitral tribunal's jurisdiction—one based on article 16 (3), the other on article 34—were simultaneously pending. The court decided that the first application ought to be stayed and the jurisdictional objection considered in the context of the setting aside proceedings.[426]

Waiver of article 16 (3)

26. Article 16 (3) does not indicate whether it is a mandatory provision or whether the parties can agree in advance to exclude immediate court intervention in relation to interim jurisdictional rulings. In one case, an appellate court held that article 16 (3) was not mandatory and that the parties had validly excluded immediate court intervention based on that provision by agreeing that the arbitral procedure would be governed by the arbitration rules that did not provide for immediate court intervention in relation to interim jurisdictional rulings.[427]

Consequences of a party's failure to challenge the arbitral tribunal's jurisdictional ruling in a timely manner

27. The Model Law does not indicate whether a party's failure to seek, pursuant to article 16 (3), the judicial review of an interim decision of the arbitral tribunal dismissing an objection to its jurisdiction precludes that party from subsequently raising that same objection either in support of an application to set aside the award (article 34) or to resist an application seeking the recognition and enforcement of the award (articles 35 and 36). In a leading decision, the German Federal Court of Justice answered that question in the affirmative.[428] However, lower courts in other jurisdictions have reached contradictory results: some courts have reached a similar conclusion than the one reached in Germany,[429] while other courts have taken the position that a party who has failed to seek the judicial review of an interim decision of the arbitral tribunal dismissing an objection to its jurisdiction could nevertheless raise the point later in the context of an application to set aside the award on jurisdictional grounds.[430] (See also below, section on article 34, paras. 45-46).

---

[425] Constitutional Court, Croatia, 27 October 2004, U-III/669/2003.

[426] *Christian Mutual Insurance Company & Central United Life Insurance Company & Connecticut Reassurance Corporation v. Ace Bermuda Insurance Limited*, Court of Appeal, Bermuda, 6 December 2002, [2002] Bda LR 56.

[427] *Compagnie Nationale Air France v. Mbaye*, Court of Appeal of Quebec, Canada, 31 March 2003, [2003] CanLII 35834 (QC CA) available on the Internet at http://canlii.ca/t/284nd.

[428] Bundesgerichtshof, Germany, III ZB 83/02, 27 March 2003, available on the Internet at http://www.dis-arb.de/en/47/datenbanken/rspr/bgh-case-no-iii-zb-83-02-date-2003-03-27-id212.

[429] See for instance: *Imprimerie Régionale ARL Ltée v. Ghanotakis,* Superior Court of Quebec, Canada, 13 September 2004, [2004] CanLII 23270 (QC CS), available on the Internet at http://canlii.ca/t/1hspb.

[430] See for instance: *Tan Poh Leng Stanley v. Tang Boon Jek Jeffrey*, High Court, Singapore, 30 November 2000, [2000] SGHC 260, [2000] 3 SLR(R) 847.

Article 17. Power of arbitral tribunal to order interim measures

[As adopted in 1985]

"Unless otherwise agreed by the parties, the arbitral tribunal may, at the request of a party, order any party to take such interim measure of protection as the arbitral tribunal may consider necessary in respect of the subject matter of the dispute. The arbitral tribunal may require any party to provide appropriate security in connection with such measure."

TRAVAUX PRÉPARATOIRES

The *travaux préparatoires* on article 17 as adopted in 1985 are contained in the following documents:

1. Report of the United Nations Commission on International Trade Law on the work of its eighteenth session (*Official Records of the General Assembly, Fortieth Session, Supplement No. 17* (A/40/17)), paras. 11-333.

2. Reports of the Working Group: A/CN.9/246, annex; A/CN.9/263 and Add.1-2; A/CN.9/264. Relevant working papers are referred to in the reports.

3. Summary records of the 332nd UNCITRAL meeting.

(Available on the Internet at www.uncitral.org).

CHAPTER IV A. INTERIM MEASURES AND PRELIMINARY ORDERS

[*As adopted in 2006*]

(*As adopted by the Commission at its thirty-ninth session, in 2006*)

Section 1. Interim measures

Article 17. Power of arbitral tribunal to order interim measures

(1) Unless otherwise agreed by the parties, the arbitral tribunal may, at the request of a party, grant interim measures.

(2) An interim measure is any temporary measure, whether in the form of an award or in another form, by which, at any time prior to the issuance of the award by which the dispute is finally decided, the arbitral tribunal orders a party to:

(a) Maintain or restore the status quo pending determination of the dispute;

(b) Take action that would prevent, or refrain from taking action that is likely to cause, current or imminent harm or prejudice to the arbitral process itself;

(c) Provide a means of preserving assets out of which a subsequent award may be satisfied; or

(d) Preserve evidence that may be relevant and material to the resolution of the dispute.

Article 17 A. Conditions for granting interim measures

(1) The party requesting an interim measure under article 17 (2)(a), (b) and (c) shall satisfy the arbitral tribunal that:

(a) Harm not adequately reparable by an award of damages is likely to result if the measure is not ordered, and such harm substantially outweighs the harm that is likely to result to the party against whom the measure is directed if the measure is granted; and

(b) There is a reasonable possibility that the requesting party will succeed on the merits of the claim. The determination on this possibility shall not affect the discretion of the arbitral tribunal in making any subsequent determination.

(2) With regard to a request for an interim measure under article 17 (2)(d), the requirements in paragraphs (1)(a) and (b) of this article shall apply only to the extent the arbitral tribunal considers appropriate.

TRAVAUX PRÉPARATOIRES

Chapter IV A was adopted in 2006.

The *travaux préparatoires* on section 1 as adopted in 2006 are contained in the following documents:

1. Reports of the United Nations Commission on International Trade Law on the work of its of its thirty-second session (*Official Records of the General Assembly, Fifty-fourth Session, Supplement No. 17* (A/54/17)); thirty-third session (*Official Records of the General Assembly, Fifty-fifth Session, Supplement No. 17* (A/55/17)); thirty-fourth session (*Official Records of the General Assembly, Fifty-sixth Session, Supplement No. 17* (A/56/17)); thirty-fifth session (*Official Records of the General Assembly, Fifty-seventh Session, Supplement No. 17* (A/57/17)); thirty-sixth session (*Official Records of the General Assembly, Fifty-eighth Session, Supplement No. 17* (A/58/17)); thirty-seventh session (*Official Records of the General Assembly, Fifty-ninth Session, Supplement No. 17* (A/59/17)); thirty-eighth session (*Official Records of the General Assembly, Sixtieth Session, Supplement No. 17* (A/60/17)); and thirty-ninth session (*Official Records of the General Assembly, Sixty-first Session, Supplement No. 17* (A/61/17)).

2. Reports of Working Group II (Arbitration) on the work of its thirty-second session (A/CN.9/468); thirty-third session (A/CN.9/485); thirty-fourth session (A/CN.9/487); thirty-sixth session (A/CN.9/508); thirty-seventh session (A/CN.9/523); thirty-eighth session (A/CN.9/524); thirty-ninth session (A/CN.9/545); fortieth session (A/CN.9/547); forty-first session (A/CN.9/569); forty-second session (A/CN.9/573); forty-third session (A/CN.9/589) and forty-fourth session (A/CN.9/592).

3. Relevant working papers, considered by Working Group II (Arbitration), are referred to in the reports of the sessions of the Working Group, including: A/CN.9/WG.II/WP.108 and Add.1; A/CN.9/WG.II/WP.110; A/CN.9/WG.II/WP.111; A/CN.9/WG.II/WP.113 and Add.1; A/CN.9/WG.II/WP.119; A/CN.9/WG.II/WP.121; A/CN.9/WG.II/WP.123; A/CN.9/WG.II/WP.125; A/CN.9/WG.II/WP.127 A/CN.9/WG.II/WP.128. A/CN.9/WG.II/WP.129. A/CN.9/WG.II/WP.131; A/CN.9/WG.II/WP.134; A/CN.9/WG.II/WP.138; A/CN.9/WG.II/WP.141.

(Available on the Internet at www.uncitral.org).

INTRODUCTION

1. Chapter IV A on interim measures and preliminary orders was adopted by UNCITRAL in 2006. It replaces article 17 of the original 1985 version of the Model Law. Section 1 provides a generic definition of interim measures and sets out the conditions for granting such measures. An important innovation of the revision lies in the establishment (in section 4) of a regime for the recognition and enforcement of interim measures, which was modelled, as appropriate, on the regime for the recognition and enforcement of arbitral awards under articles 35 and 36 of the Model Law.

CASE LAW ON ARTICLE 17

Power of the arbitral tribunal to order interim measures—Paragraph (1)

2. Article 17 of the 1985 version of the Model Law provided the arbitral tribunal with the power to "order any party to take such interim measure (...) in respect of the subject matter of the dispute." That provision has been held by courts to be limited to measures that relate directly to the protection of the subject matter of the dispute, and not to confer any power on the arbitral tribunal to enforce its order. [431] Article 17, as amended in 2006, grants a broader mandate to arbitrators, specifically removing the need for interim measures to relate to the "subject matter of the dispute" and providing for a generic definition.[432]

---

[431] CLOUT case No. 565 [Oberlandesgericht Frankfurt a.M., Germany, 24 Sch 01/01, 5 April 2001], also available on the Internet at http://www.dis-arb.de/en/47/datenbanken/rspr/olg-frankfurt-am-case-no-24-sch-01-01-date-2001-04-05-id148.

[432] Explanatory Note by the UNCITRAL Secretariat on the Model Law on International Commercial Arbitration, in UNCITRAL Model Law on International Commercial Arbitration 1985, with amendments as adopted in 2006, United Nations publication, Sales No. E.08.V.4 (available on the Internet at http://www.uncitral.org/pdf/english/texts/arbitration/ml-arb/07-86998_Ebook.pdf), Part Two, at para. 27.

Paragraph (2)*(a)*-*(d)*

3. A New Zealand court has ruled that paragraph (2)*(a)* is aimed at maintaining or restoring a state of affairs pending the determination of a dispute and is not intended to create a restrictive threshold requirement. The term "status quo" has been interpreted to mean "the last peaceable state [of affairs] between the parties."[433]

Relationship between article 9 and article 17 of the 1985 version of the Model Law

4. Prior to the amendment of the Model Law in 2006, a Hong Kong court found that the interim measures referred to in article 9 of the Model Law were intended to be of wider application than an order for preserving "the subject matter of the dispute".[434]

5. An Indian court has held that the existence of an application before an arbitral tribunal for interim measure "does not denude" the court of its powers to make an order for interim measures under article 9. That court took the view that being a superior judicial forum, the court's power has primacy over those of an arbitral tribunal.[435] A Singapore court, however, held that article 9 is merely a permissive provision and creates no power on the court.[436] (See above, section on article 9, paras. 6-10). These inconsistent approaches have now been resolved with article 17 J of the Model Law as amended in 2006, where it is clarified that "a court shall have the *same* power of issuing an interim measure in relation to arbitration proceedings (...)." (See below, section on article 17 J, paras. 1-4).[437]

CASE LAW ON ARTICLE 17 A

1. A New Zealand court declined to go beyond the specific considerations provided in article 17 A when urged to take into account other matters of public interest and to consider the possible impact on third parties and overall justice as conditions for granting interim measures.[438]

Balance of convenience test—paragraph (1)*(a)*

2. It was noted in a case that the issue of whether the harm caused by the defendants is adequately reparable by an award of damages (first part of paragraph 17 (1)*(a)*) and whether that harm substantially outweighs the harm that the defendants are likely to suffer if the interim relief is granted, is essentially an assessment of the balance of convenience.[439]

A prima facie case—"reasonable possibility"-paragraph (1)*(b)*

3. In interpreting the test required under article 17 A (1)*(b)* of "reasonable possibility" of success, a New Zealand court ruled it to be akin to a "serious question to be tried".[440]

---

[433] *Safe Kids in Daily Supervision Limited v. McNeill,* High Court, Auckland, New Zealand, 14 April 2010, [2010] NZHC 605).

[434] CLOUT case No. 39 [*Katran Shipping Co. Ltd. v. Kenven Transportation Ltd.,* High Court—Court of First Instance, Hong Kong, 29 June 1992], [1992] HKCFI 173, also available on the Internet at http://www.hklii.hk/eng/hk/cases/hkcfi/1992/173.html.

[435] *National Highways Authority of India (Nhai) vs China Coal Construction Group Corporation,* Delhi High Court, India, 23 January 2006, AIR 2006 Delhi 134, 2006 (1) ARBLR 265 Delhi, available on the Internet at http://indiankanoon.org/doc/236246/.

[436] *Swift-Fortune Ltd. v. Magnifica Marine SA,* High Court, Singapore, [2006] 2 SLR 323; affirmed in CLOUT case No. 741 [*Swift-Fortune Ltd. v. Magnifica Marine SA*, Court of Appeal, Singapore, 1 December 2006], [2006] SGCA 42.

[437] Emphasis added.

[438] *Safe Kids in Daily Supervision Limited v. McNeill,* High Court, Auckland, New Zealand, 14 April 2010, [2010] NZHC 605).

[439] Ibid.

[440] Ibid.

Section 2. Preliminary orders

Article 17 B. Applications for preliminary orders and conditions for granting preliminary orders

(1) Unless otherwise agreed by the parties, a party may, without notice to any other party, make a request for an interim measure together with an application for a preliminary order directing a party not to frustrate the purpose of the interim measure requested.

(2) The arbitral tribunal may grant a preliminary order provided it considers that prior disclosure of the request for the interim measure to the party against whom it is directed risks frustrating the purpose of the measure.

(3) The conditions defined under article 17 A apply to any preliminary order, provided that the harm to be assessed under article 17 A (1)(a), is the harm likely to result from the order being granted or not.

Article 17 C. Specific regime for preliminary orders

(1) Immediately after the arbitral tribunal has made a determination in respect of an application for a preliminary order, the arbitral tribunal shall give notice to all parties of the request for the interim measure, the application for the preliminary order, the preliminary order, if any, and all other communications, including by indicating the content of any oral communication, between any party and the arbitral tribunal in relation thereto.

(2) At the same time, the arbitral tribunal shall give an opportunity to any party against whom a preliminary order is directed to present its case at the earliest practicable time.

(3) The arbitral tribunal shall decide promptly on any objection to the preliminary order.

(4) A preliminary order shall expire after twenty days from the date on which it was issued by the arbitral tribunal. However, the arbitral tribunal may issue an interim measure adopting or modifying the preliminary order, after the party against whom the preliminary order is directed has been given notice and an opportunity to present its case.

(5) A preliminary order shall be binding on the parties but shall not be subject to enforcement by a court. Such a preliminary order does not constitute an award.

TRAVAUX PRÉPARATOIRES

The *travaux préparatoires* on section 2 as adopted in 2006 are contained in the following documents:

1. Reports of the United Nations Commission on International Trade Law on the work of its of its thirty-second session (*Official Records of the General Assembly, Fifty-fourth Session, Supplement No. 17* (A/54/17)); thirty-third session (*Official Records of the General Assembly, Fifty-fifth Session, Supplement No. 17* (A/55/17)); thirty-fourth session (*Official Records of the General Assembly, Fifty-sixth Session, Supplement No. 17* (A/56/17)); thirty-fifth session (*Official Records of the General Assembly, Fifty-seventh Session, Supplement No. 17* (A/57/17)); thirty-sixth session (*Official Records of the General Assembly, Fifty-eighth Session, Supplement No. 17* (A/58/17)); thirty-seventh session (*Official Records of the General Assembly, Fifty-ninth Session, Supplement No. 17* (A/59/17)); thirty-eighth session (*Official Records of the General Assembly, Sixtieth Session, Supplement No. 17* (A/60/17)); and thirty-ninth session (*Official Records of the General Assembly, Sixty-first Session, Supplement No. 17* (A/61/17)).

2. Reports of Working Group II (Arbitration) on the work of its thirty-second session (A/CN.9/468); thirty-third session (A/CN.9/485); thirty-fourth session (A/CN.9/487); thirty-sixth session (A/CN.9/508); thirty-seventh session (A/CN.9/523); thirty-eighth session (A/CN.9/524); thirty-ninth session (A/CN.9/545); fortieth session (A/CN.9/547); forty-first session (A/CN.9/569); forty-second session (A/CN.9/573); forty-third session (A/CN.9/589) and forty-fourth session (A/CN.9/592).

3. Relevant working papers, considered by Working Group II (Arbitration), are referred to in the reports of the sessions of the Working Group, including: A/CN.9/WG.II/WP.108 and Add.1; A/CN.9/WG.II/WP.110; A/CN.9/WG.II/WP.111; A/CN.9/WG.II/WP.113 and Add.1; A/CN.9/WG.II/WP.119; A/CN.9/WG.II/WP.121; A/CN.9/WG.II/WP.123; A/CN.9/WG.II/WP.125; A/CN.9/WG.II/WP.127 A/CN.9/WG.II/WP.128. A/CN.9/WG.II/WP.129. A/CN.9/WG.II/WP.131; A/CN.9/WG.II/WP.134; A/CN.9/WG.II/WP.138; A/CN.9/WG.II/WP.141.

(Available on the Internet at www.uncitral.org).

INTRODUCTION

1. Section 2 of chapter IV A deals with the application for, and conditions for the granting of, preliminary orders. Preliminary orders provide a means for preserving the status quo until the arbitral tribunal issues an interim measure adopting or modifying the preliminary order. Article 17 B (1) provides that "a party may, without notice to any other party, make a request for an interim measure together with an application for a preliminary order directing a party not to frustrate the purpose of the interim measure requested". Article 17 B (2) permits an arbitral tribunal to grant a preliminary order if "it considers that prior disclosure of the request for the interim measure to the party against whom it is directed risks frustrating the purpose of the measure". Article 17 C contains carefully drafted safeguards for the party against whom the preliminary order is directed, such as prompt notification of the application for the preliminary order and of the preliminary order itself (if any), and an opportunity for that party to present its case "at the earliest practicable time". In any event, a preliminary order has a maximum duration of twenty days and, while binding on the parties, is not subject to court enforcement and does not constitute an award. The term "preliminary order" is used to emphasize its limited nature.

2. There is no case law reported on section 2 of chapter IV A.

Section 3. Provisions applicable to interim measures and preliminary orders

Article 17 D. Modification, suspension, termination

The arbitral tribunal may modify, suspend or terminate an interim measure or a preliminary order it has granted, upon application of any party or, in exceptional circumstances and upon prior notice to the parties, on the arbitral tribunal's own initiative.

Article 17 E. Provision of security

(1) The arbitral tribunal may require the party requesting an interim measure to provide appropriate security in connection with the measure.

(2) The arbitral tribunal shall require the party applying for a preliminary order to provide security in connection with the order unless the arbitral tribunal considers it inappropriate or unnecessary to do so.

Article 17 F. Disclosure

(1) The arbitral tribunal may require any party promptly to disclose any material change in the circumstances on the basis of which the measure was requested or granted.

(2) The party applying for a preliminary order shall disclose to the arbitral tribunal all circumstances that are likely to be relevant to the arbitral tribunal's determination whether to grant or maintain the order, and such obligation shall continue until the party against whom the order has been requested has had an opportunity to present its case. Thereafter, paragraph (1) of this article shall apply.

Article 17 G. Costs and damages

The party requesting an interim measure or applying for a preliminary order shall be liable for any costs and damages caused by the measure or the order to any party if the arbitral tribunal later determines that, in the circumstances, the measure or the order should not have been granted. The arbitral tribunal may award such costs and damages at any point during the proceedings.

TRAVAUX PRÉPARATOIRES

The *travaux préparatoires* on section 3 as adopted in 2006 are contained in the following documents:

1. Reports of the United Nations Commission on International Trade Law on the work of its thirty-second session (*Official Records of the General Assembly, Fifty-fourth Session, Supplement No. 17* (A/54/17)); thirty-third session (*Official Records of the General Assembly, Fifty-fifth Session, Supplement No. 17* (A/55/17)); thirty-fourth session (*Official Records of the General Assembly, Fifty-sixth Session, Supplement No. 17* (A/56/17)); thirty-fifth session (*Official Records of the General Assembly, Fifty-seventh Session, Supplement No. 17* (A/57/17)); thirty-sixth session (*Official Records of the General Assembly, Fifty-eighth Session, Supplement No. 17* (A/58/17)); thirty-seventh session (*Official Records of the General Assembly,*

Fifty-ninth Session, Supplement No. 17 (A/59/17)); thirty-eighth session (*Official Records of the General Assembly, Sixtieth Session, Supplement No. 17* (A/60/17)); and thirty-ninth session (*Official Records of the General Assembly, Sixty-first Session, Supplement No. 17* (A/61/17)).

2. Reports of Working Group II (Arbitration) on the work of its thirty-second session (A/CN.9/468); thirty-third session (A/CN.9/485); thirty-fourth session (A/CN.9/487); thirty-sixth session (A/CN.9/508); thirty-seventh session (A/CN.9/523); thirty-eighth session (A/CN.9/524); thirty-ninth session (A/CN.9/545); fortieth session (A/CN.9/547); forty-first session (A/CN.9/569); forty-second session (A/CN.9/573); forty-third session (A/CN.9/589) and forty-fourth session (A/CN.9/592).

3. Relevant working papers, considered by Working Group II (Arbitration), are referred to in the reports of the sessions of the Working Group, including: A/CN.9/WG.II/WP.108 and Add.1; A/CN.9/WG.II/WP.110; A/CN.9/WG.II/WP.111; A/CN.9/WG.II/WP.113 and Add.1; A/CN.9/WG.II/WP.119; A/CN.9/WG.II/WP.121; A/CN.9/WG.II/WP.123; A/CN.9/WG.II/WP.125; A/CN.9/WG.II/WP.127 A/CN.9/WG.II/WP.128. A/CN.9/WG.II/WP.129. A/CN.9/WG.II/WP.131; A/CN.9/WG.II/WP.134; A/CN.9/WG.II/WP.138; A/CN.9/WG.II/WP.141.

(Available on the Internet at www.uncitral.org).

INTRODUCTION

1. Section 3 sets out rules applicable to both preliminary orders and interim measures.

2. There is no case law reported on section 3 of chapter IV A.

Section 4. Recognition and enforcement of interim measures

Article 17 H. Recognition and enforcement

(1) An interim measure issued by an arbitral tribunal shall be recognized as binding and, unless otherwise provided by the arbitral tribunal, enforced upon application to the competent court, irrespective of the country in which it was issued, subject to the provisions of article 17 I.

(2) The party who is seeking or has obtained recognition or enforcement of an interim measure shall promptly inform the court of any termination, suspension or modification of that interim measure.

(3) The court of the State where recognition or enforcement is sought may, if it considers it proper, order the requesting party to provide appropriate security if the arbitral tribunal has not already made a determination with respect to security or where such a decision is necessary to protect the rights of third parties.

Article 17 I. Grounds for refusing recognition or enforcement

(1) Recognition or enforcement of an interim measure may be refused only:

(a) At the request of the party against whom it is invoked if the court is satisfied that:

(i) Such refusal is warranted on the grounds set forth in article 36 (1)(a)(i), (ii), (iii) or (iv); or

(ii) The arbitral tribunal's decision with respect to the provision of security in connection with the interim measure issued by the arbitral tribunal has not been complied with; or

(iii) The interim measure has been terminated or suspended by the arbitral tribunal or, where so empowered, by the court of the State in which the arbitration takes place or under the law of which that interim measure was granted; or

(b) If the court finds that:

(i) The interim measure is incompatible with the powers conferred upon the court unless the court decides to reformulate the interim measure to the extent necessary to adapt it to its own powers and procedures for the purposes of enforcing that interim measure and without modifying its substance; or

(ii) Any of the grounds set forth in article 36 (1)(b)(i) or (ii), apply to the recognition and enforcement of the interim measure.

(2) Any determination made by the court on any ground in paragraph (1) of this article shall be effective only for the purposes of the application to recognize and enforce the interim measure. The court where recognition or enforcement is sought shall not, in making that determination, undertake a review of the substance of the interim measure.

TRAVAUX PRÉPARATOIRES

The *travaux préparatoires* section 4 as adopted in 2006 are contained in the following documents:

1. Reports of the United Nations Commission on International Trade Law on the work of its of its thirty-second session (*Official Records of the General Assembly, Fifty-fourth Session, Supplement No. 17* (A/54/17)); thirty-third session (*Official Records of the General Assembly, Fifty-fifth Session, Supplement No. 17* (A/55/17)); thirty-fourth session (*Official Records of the General Assembly, Fifty-sixth Session, Supplement No. 17* (A/56/17)); thirty-fifth session (*Official Records of the General Assembly, Fifty-seventh Session, Supplement No. 17* (A/57/17)); thirty-sixth session (*Official Records of the General Assembly, Fifty-eighth Session, Supplement No. 17* (A/58/17)); thirty-seventh session (*Official Records of the General Assembly, Fifty-ninth Session, Supplement No. 17* (A/59/17)); thirty-eighth session (*Official Records of the General Assembly, Sixtieth Session, Supplement No. 17* (A/60/17)); and thirty-ninth session (*Official Records of the General Assembly, Sixty-first Session, Supplement No. 17* (A/61/17))

2. Reports of Working Group II (Arbitration) on the work of its thirty-second session (A/CN.9/468); thirty-third session (A/CN.9/485); thirty-fourth session (A/CN.9/487); thirty-sixth session (A/CN.9/508); thirty-seventh session (A/CN.9/523); thirty-eighth session (A/CN.9/524); thirty-ninth session (A/CN.9/545); fortieth session (A/CN.9/547); forty-first session (A/CN.9/569); forty-second session (A/CN.9/573); forty-third session (A/CN.9/589) and forty-fourth session (A/CN.9/592).

3. Relevant working papers, considered by Working Group II (Arbitration), are referred to in the reports of the sessions of the Working Group, including: A/CN.9/WG.II/WP.108 and Add.1; A/CN.9/WG.II/WP.110; A/CN.9/WG.II/WP.111; A/CN.9/WG.II/WP.113 and Add.1; A/CN.9/WG.II/WP.119; A/CN.9/WG.II/WP.121; A/CN.9/WG.II/WP.123; A/CN.9/WG.II/WP.125; A/CN.9/WG.II/WP.127 A/CN.9/WG.II/WP.128. A/CN.9/WG.II/WP.129. A/CN.9/WG.II/WP.131; A/CN.9/WG.II/WP.134; A/CN.9/WG.II/WP.138; A/CN.9/WG.II/WP.141.

(Available on the Internet at www.uncitral.org).

INTRODUCTION

1. An important innovation under Chapter IV A of the Model Law adopted in 2006 lies in the establishment (in section 4) of a regime for the recognition and enforcement of interim measures, which was modelled, as appropriate, on the regime for the recognition and enforcement of arbitral awards under articles 35 and 36 of the Model Law.

2. There is no case law reported on section 4 of chapter IV A.

Section 5. Court-ordered interim measures

Article 17 J. Court-ordered interim measures

A court shall have the same power of issuing an interim measure in relation to arbitration proceedings, irrespective of whether their place is in the territory of this State, as it has in relation to proceedings in courts. The court shall exercise such power in accordance with its own procedures in consideration of the specific features of international arbitration.

TRAVAUX PRÉPARATOIRES

The *travaux préparatoires* on section 5 as adopted in 2006 are contained in the following documents:

1. Reports of the United Nations Commission on International Trade Law on the work of its of its thirty-second session (*Official Records of the General Assembly, Fifty-fourth Session, Supplement No. 17* (A/54/17)); thirty-third session (*Official Records of the General Assembly, Fifty-fifth Session, Supplement No. 17* (A/55/17)); thirty-fourth session (*Official Records of the General Assembly, Fifty-sixth Session, Supplement No. 17* (A/56/17)); thirty-fifth session (*Official Records of the General Assembly, Fifty-seventh Session, Supplement No. 17* (A/57/17)); thirty-sixth session (*Official Records of the General Assembly, Fifty-eighth Session, Supplement No. 17* (A/58/17)); thirty-seventh session (*Official Records of the General Assembly, Fifty-ninth Session, Supplement No. 17* (A/59/17)); thirty-eighth session (*Official Records of the General Assembly, Sixtieth Session, Supplement No. 17* (A/60/17)); and thirty-ninth session (*Official Records of the General Assembly, Sixty-first Session, Supplement No. 17* (A/61/17)).

2. Reports of Working Group II (Arbitration) on the work of its thirty-second session (A/CN.9/468); thirty-third session (A/CN.9/485); thirty-fourth session (A/CN.9/487); thirty-sixth session (A/CN.9/508); thirty-seventh session (A/CN.9/523); thirty-eighth session (A/CN.9/524); thirty-ninth session (A/CN.9/545); fortieth session (A/CN.9/547); forty-first session (A/CN.9/569); forty-second session (A/CN.9/573); forty-third session (A/CN.9/589) and forty-fourth session (A/CN.9/592).

3. Relevant working papers, considered by Working Group II (Arbitration), are referred to in the reports of the sessions of the Working Group, including: A/CN.9/WG.II/WP.108 and Add.1; A/CN.9/WG.II/WP.110; A/CN.9/WG.II/WP.111; A/CN.9/WG.II/WP.113 and Add.1; A/CN.9/WG.II/WP.119; A/CN.9/WG.II/WP.121; A/CN.9/WG.II/WP.123; A/CN.9/WG.II/WP.125; A/CN.9/WG.II/WP.127 A/CN.9/WG.II/WP.128. A/CN.9/WG.II/WP.129. A/CN.9/WG.II/WP.131; A/CN.9/WG.II/WP.134; A/CN.9/WG.II/WP.138; A/CN.9/WG.II/WP.141.

(Available on the Internet at www.uncitral.org).

INTRODUCTION

1. Article 17 J has been added in 2006 to put it beyond doubt that the existence of an arbitration agreement does not infringe on the powers of the competent court to issue interim measures and that a party to such an arbitration agreement is free to approach the court with a request to order interim measures. That provision gives the court the same power to order interim measures in support of arbitration (as it has in relation to proceedings in court), irrespective of whether the place of arbitration is in the territory of the enacting State.[441] It gives parties the liberty to seek curial assistance from the court if it is expedient to do so (see above, section on article 9, para. 3).

[441] This resolves uncertainty when some courts ruled that article 9 did not sufficiently endow the court with the power to grant interim measures in support of foreign arbitrations: see *Swift-Fortune Ltd. v. Magnifica Marine SA,* Court of Appeal, Singapore, [2007] 1 SLR 629, where the Court considered that a Singapore court had no statutory power under the International Arbitration Act (Cap 143A) to grant interim orders or relief to assist arbitrations conducted abroad, unless it involved a dispute that was justiciable in Singapore. In *Prema Birkdale Horticulture (Macau) Limited v. Venetian Orient Limited and Anor,* Court of First Instance, Hong Kong Special Administrative Region of China, 5 August 2009, [2009] HCMP 905/2009, available on the Internet at http://www.hklii.hk/eng/hk/cases/hkcfi/2009/657.html, the Court stated that in relation to a foreign-seated arbitration, it would be able to exercise such power only if the arbitration proceedings are capable of giving rise to an arbitral award which may be enforced in Hong Kong under the Arbitration Ordinance.

CASE LAW ON ARTICLE 17 J

Relationship between courts and arbitration

2. The powers given in article 17 J are co-extensive with the power given to the arbitral tribunal. A Hong Kong court dealing with provisions of similar nature ruled that such a power should be exercised sparingly and only if there are special reasons to do so.[442] An Indian court also took the view that if a party elects to apply for an interim measure before the arbitral tribunal, it should not seek the same relief from a court on the basis that multiplicity of proceedings ought to be avoided at all causes.[443]

3. A New Zealand court considered that the purpose of court-ordered interim measures is to complement and facilitate the arbitration, not to forestall or to substitute for it.[444]

Application of the court procedure

4. In Ireland, a court had to consider an application for stay of the suit as well as the claimant's application in that case for an interlocutory injunction. Although the court referred the parties to arbitration, it nevertheless proceeded to consider the application for an interlocutory injunction, holding that the same fell to be considered as an application for interim measure under article 17 J.[445]

[442] *Leviathan Shipping Co. v. Sky Sailing Overseas Co.*, Court of First Instance, Hong Kong, 18 August 1998, [1998] 4 HKC 347, available on the Internet at http://www.hklii.hk/eng/hk/cases/hkcfi/1998/549.html.

[443] *Sri Kirshan v. Anad,* Delhi High Court, India, 18 August 2009, OMP No. 597/2008.

[444] *Sensation Yachts Ltd. v. Darby Maritime Ltd.,* Auckland High Court, New Zealand, 16 May 2005, in which a New Zealand court granted interim measures in support of an arbitration in London.

[445] *Osmond Ireland On Farm Business v. Mc Farland*, High Court, Ireland, 30 June 2010, [2010] IEHC 295; in Ireland, the Arbitration Act 2010, incorporating the 2006 Model Law amendments, came into force on 8 June 2010.

CHAPTER V. CONDUCT OF ARBITRAL PROCEEDINGS

Article 18. Equal treatment of parties

The parties shall be treated with equality and each party shall be given a full opportunity of presenting his case.

TRAVAUX PRÉPARATOIRES

The *travaux préparatoires* on article 18 as adopted in 1985 are contained in the following documents:

1. Report of the United Nations Commission on International Trade Law on the work of its eighteenth session (*Official Records of the General Assembly, Fortieth Session, Supplement No. 17* (A/40/17)), paras. 11-333.

2. Reports of the Working Group: A/CN.9/216; A/CN.9/232; A/CN.9/245; A/CN.9/246, annex; A/CN.9/263 and Add.1-2; A/CN.9/264. Relevant working papers are referred to in the reports.

3. Summary records of the 332nd UNCITRAL meeting.

Article 18 was not amended in 2006.

(Available on the Internet at www.uncitral.org).

INTRODUCTION

1. Chapter V provides the legal framework for a fair and effective conduct of the arbitral proceedings.

2. Article 18 embodies the principles that the parties shall be treated with equality and given a full opportunity of presenting their case. A number of provisions illustrate those principles. For example, article 24 (1) provides that, unless the parties have agreed that no oral hearings be held for the presentation of evidence or for oral argument, the arbitral tribunal shall hold such hearings at an appropriate stage of the proceedings, if so requested by a party. It should be noted that article 24 (1) deals only with the general entitlement of a party to oral hearings (as an alternative to proceedings conducted on the basis of documents and other materials) and not with the procedural aspects, such as the length, number or timing of hearings.

3. Another illustration of those principles relates to evidence by an expert appointed by the arbitral tribunal. Article 26 (2) requires the expert, after delivering his or her written or oral report, to participate in a hearing where the parties may put questions to the expert and present expert witnesses to testify on the points at issue, if such a hearing is requested by a party or deemed necessary by the arbitral tribunal. As another provision aimed at ensuring fairness, objectivity and impartiality, article 24 (3) provides that all statements, documents and other information supplied to the arbitral tribunal by one party shall be communicated to the other party, and that any expert report or evidentiary document on which the arbitral tribunal may rely in making its decision shall be communicated to the parties. In order to enable the parties to be present at any hearing and at any meeting of the arbitral tribunal for inspection purposes, they shall be given sufficient notice in advance (article 24 (2)).

CASE LAW ON ARTICLE 18

Equality, full opportunity to present one's case

4. Article 18 of the Model Law lays down the fundamental requirements expected of an arbitral tribunal for procedural justice, namely: 1) equal treatment of the parties; and 2) full opportunity to present one's case. The mandatory nature of these requirements have been consistently upheld by courts as being so foundational that parties may not derogate from them.[446]

Scope of obligation

5. The obligation to treat parties with equality requires the arbitral tribunal to apply similar standards to all parties and their representatives throughout the arbitral process.

[446] CLOUT case No. 743 [*Soh Beng Tee & Co. Pte. Ltd. v. Fairmount Development Pte. Ltd.*, Court of Appeal, Singapore, 9 May 2007], [2007] 3 SLR (4) 86; *Noble China Inc. v. Lei Kat Cheong*, Ontario Court of Justice, Canada, 4 November 1998, [1998] CanLII 14708 (ON SC), published in (1998) 42 O.R. (3d) 69, available on the Internet at http://canlii.ca/t/1vvkr.

6. This principle extends to both evidence and submissions on the facts and on the law. According to a court decision, the principle is complied with where: each party is afforded a reasonable opportunity to fully state its case; each party is given an opportunity to understand, test and rebut its opponent's case; if there are hearings, proper notice is given thereof, and the parties and their advisers have the opportunity to be present throughout the hearings; and each party is given reasonable opportunity to present evidence and argument in support of its own case.[447] In one court decision, the arbitral award in issue has been set aside in part because a document submitted by a party to the arbitral tribunal had been inadvertently omitted from the file given to the applicant.[448] An arbitrator's duty to hold hearings is not discharged by merely allowing a formal presentation by the parties and thereafter disregarding or ignoring it.[449] (See below, section on article 34, para. 65).

7. The principles in article 18 apply to all aspects of arbitral proceedings, and breach of these principles may lead to the challenge of the award or application to set aside the award by an unsuccessful party.[450] The purpose of article 18 is to protect a party from egregious and injudicious conduct by an arbitral tribunal, and is not intended to protect a party from its own failures or strategic choices.[451] Thus, a party which has not attempted to make use of the rights that allegedly have been violated would not be in a position to invoke article 18.[452] Attempts to use this provision by a party who claimed not to be able to understand the language of the proceedings have also not been successful. In one case the court held that the claimant could have sought assistance for interpretation.[453] The Croatian Supreme Court observed that a party was not prevented from presenting its case merely because it was not familiar with the language as such party could have sought for translations.[454] A Spanish provincial court did set aside an award made in the absence of a lawyer who could not attend the hearing, reasoning that the party was deprived of the opportunity to properly present its defence.[455] A New Zealand court has in one case found that an arbitrator, who had unilaterally fixed a hearing date and refused requests for adjournment of the hearing did not afford the party a reasonable opportunity to present its case.[456]

8. According to court decisions, to succeed in an argument that a party has been deprived of the opportunity to present its case, it must be shown that: *(a)* a reasonable litigant in the applicant's position would not have foreseen a reasoning on the part of the arbitral tribunal of the type laid down in the award and *(b)* with adequate notice, it might have been possible to convince the arbitral tribunal to reach a different result.[457] An English court had suggested that an arbitral tribunal has to give the parties an opportunity to present arguments on all of the "essential building blocks" of the tribunal's conclusions. The award was set aside on such failure.[458] The notion of being able reasonably to anticipate the arbitral tribunal's findings is also mirrored in a case before the Swiss Federal Court where it annulled an award on the basis that the arbitral tribunal had based its decision on a legislative provision which the court found was "manifestly non-applicable" to the circumstances of the arbitration and could not therefore have been anticipated by the parties, ruling that the arbitral tribunal in doing so had deprived the claimant of its right to be heard.[459]

9. Not all procedural or technical violations would constitute breaches of this duty. A German court has decided

---

[447] CLOUT case No. 658 [*Trustees of Rotoaira Forest Trust v. Attorney-General,* High Court (Commercial List), Auckland, New Zealand, 30 November 1998], [1999] 2 NZLR 452.

[448] *Attorney-General v. Tozer (No 3),* High Court, Auckland, New Zealand, 2 September 2003, M1528-IM02 CP607/97.

[449] *Front Row Investment Holdings (Singapore) Pte. Ltd. v. Daimler South East Asia Pte. Ltd.,* High Court, Singapore, 15 March 2010, [2010] SGHC 80.

[450] See for instance: *Attorney-General v. Tozer (No 3),* High Court, Auckland, New Zealand, 2 September 2003, M1528-IM02 CP607/97; *Front Row Investment Holdings (Singapore) Pte. Ltd. v. Daimler South East Asia Pte. Ltd.,* High Court, Singapore, 15 March 2010, [2010] SGHC 80.

[451] CLOUT case No. 391 [*Re Corporación Transnacional de Inversiones, S.A. de C.V. et al. v. STET International, S.p.A. et al.*, Ontario Superior Court of Justice, Canada, 22 September 1999], [1999] CanLII 14819 (ON SC), also available on the Internet at http://canlii.ca/t/1vvn5.

[452] CLOUT case No. 391 [*Re Corporación Transnacional de Inversiones, S.A. de C.V. et al. v. STET International, S.p.A. et al.*, Ontario Superior Court of Justice, Canada, 22 September 1999], [1999] CanLII 14819 (ON SC), also available on the Internet at http://canlii.ca/t/1vvn5.

[453] CLOUT case No. 560 [Bundesgerichtshof, Germany, III ZB 44/01, 6 June 2002], also available on the Internet at http://www.dis-arb.de/de/47/datenbanken/rspr/bgh-az-iii-zb-44-01-datum-2002-06-06-id185.

[454] CLOUT case No. 1069 [Supreme Court, Croatia, 5 March 2008, Gž 6/08-2008].

[455] CLOUT case No. 968 [A Coruña Provincial High Court, Spain, Section 6, Case No. 241/2006, 27 June 2006].

[456] *Coromandel Land Trust Ltd. v. Milkt Investment Ltd.,* High Court, Hamilton, New Zealand, 28 May 2009, CIV. 2009-419-232.

[457] CLOUT case No. 658 [*Trustees of Rotoaira Forest Trust v. Attorney-General,* High Court (Commercial List), Auckland, New Zealand, 30 November 1998] [1999] 2 NZLR 452. Another New Zealand case held that the test for procedural fairness in an arbitration was primarily objective: *Acorn Farms Ltd. v. Schnuriger,* High Court, Hamilton, New Zealand, [2003] 3 NZLR 121.

[458] *OAO Northern Shipping Company v. Remolcadores de Marin Sl,* Court of Appeal, Commercial Court, England, 27 July 2007, [2007] 2 Lloyd's Rep 302, [2007] EWHC 1821 (Comm).

[459] Federal Supreme Court, Switzerland, Decision of 9 February 2009, Decision 4A_400/2008, (ASA Bull. 3/2009, p. 495).

that the mere refusal of a request for oral hearing would not amount to violation of the right to be heard. Such a right is sufficiently given if the party has the possibility of filing a defence.[460] A Singapore court had ruled that "only when the alleged breach of natural justice has surpassed the boundaries of legitimate expectation and propriety, resulting in actual prejudice to a party, can or should a remedy be made." The court, in the same case, also noted that courts should seek to support the arbitration process in order to preserve party autonomy and to ensure procedural fairness.[461] A strict approach seems to have been also adopted by a Canadian court, which stated in a case that "the conduct of the Tribunal must be sufficiently serious to offend the court's most basic notions of morality and justice to offend Article 18 or Article 24 of the Model Law".[462] (See below, section on article 24, paras. 3 and 4). An arbitrator who allowed a party to develop a different case to that anticipated and permitted evidence on issues that the other party did not expect to have addressed, was held to have failed to give the other party an opportunity to effectively participate in the hearing.[463]

Exclusion agreement

10. The mandatory nature of article 18 did not, in the view of one Canadian judge, prevent parties from agreeing that neither party would be permitted to bring an application under article 34 to set aside the arbitral award.[464] A contrary view is however expressed by a New Zealand Court of Appeal which held that "[a] contractual provision which purported to exclude a review for breach of natural justice would derogate impermissibly from article[s] 18."[465] (See below, section on article 34, paras. 5-8).

---

[460] CLOUT case No. 659 [Oberlandesgericht Naumburg, Germany, 10 Sch 08/01, 21 February 2002], also available on the Internet at http://www.dis-arb.de/de/47/datenbanken/rspr/olg-naumburg-az-10-sch-08-01-datum-2002-02-21-id166.

[461] CLOUT case No. 743 [*Soh Beng Tee & Co. Pte. Ltd. v. Fairmount Development Pte. Ltd.*, Court of Appeal, Singapore, 9 May 2007], [2007] 3 SLR (4) 86.

[462] *Xerox Corporation Ltd. and Xerox Corporation v. MPI Technologies Inc. and MPI Tech SA*, Ontario Superior Court of Justice, Canada, 30 November 2006, [2006] CanLII 41006 (ON SC), available on the Internet at http://canlii.ca/t/1q4ck.

[463] *A's Co. Ltd. v. Dagger,* High Court, Auckland, New Zealand, 5 June 2003, M1482-SD00.

[464] *Noble China Inc. v. Lei Kat Cheong*, Ontario Court of Justice, Canada, 4 November 1998, [1998] CanLII 14708 (ON SC), published in (1998) 42 O.R. (3d) 69, available on the Internet at http://canlii.ca/t/1vvkr, (excluding recourse to the courts to set aside an award is not contrary to article 18, nor contrary to any other mandatory provision of the Model Law).

[465] *Methanex Motunui Ltd. v. Spellman*, Court of Appeal, Wellington, New Zealand, 17 June 2004, [2004] 3 NZLR 454; in relation to setting aside under article 34, the court stated that "[A] reading of the *travaux préparatoires* associated with the UNCITRAL Model Law suggests that there was no contemplation that parties to arbitral proceedings could seek to limit further the rights of review contemplated by art. 34."

Article 19. Determination of rules of procedure

(1) Subject to the provisions of this Law, the parties are free to agree on the procedure to be followed by the arbitral tribunal in conducting the proceedings.

(2) Failing such agreement, the arbitral tribunal may, subject to the provisions of this Law, conduct the arbitration in such manner, as it considers appropriate. The power conferred upon the arbitral tribunal includes the power to determine the admissibility, relevance, materiality and weight of any evidence.

TRAVAUX PRÉPARATOIRES

The *travaux préparatoires* on article 19 as adopted in 1985 are contained in the following documents:

1. Report of the United Nations Commission on International Trade Law on the work of its eighteenth session (*Official Records of the General Assembly, Fortieth Session, Supplement No. 17* (A/40/17)), paras. 11-333.

2. Reports of the Working Group: A/CN.9/216; A/CN.9/232; A/CN.9/245; A/CN.9/246, annex; A/CN.9/263 and Add.1-2; A/CN.9/264. Relevant working papers are referred to in the reports.

3. Summary records of the 316th, 330th and 332nd UNCITRAL meetings.

Article 19 was not amended in 2006.

(Available on the Internet at www.uncitral.org).

INTRODUCTION

1. Article 19 guarantees the parties' freedom to agree on the procedure to be followed by the arbitral tribunal in conducting the proceedings, subject to a few mandatory provisions on procedure, and empowers the arbitral tribunal, failing agreement by the parties, to conduct the arbitration in such a manner as it considers appropriate. The power conferred upon the arbitral tribunal includes the power to determine the admissibility, relevance, materiality and weight of any evidence.

2. Autonomy of the parties in determining the rules of procedure is of special importance in international cases since it allows the parties to select or tailor the rules according to their specific wishes and needs, unimpeded by traditional and possibly conflicting domestic concepts. The supplementary discretion of the arbitral tribunal is equally important in that it allows the tribunal to tailor the conduct of the proceedings to the specific features of the case without being hindered by non-mandatory domestic rules dealing with the conduct of the proceedings, including any domestic rule on evidence. Moreover, it provides grounds for displaying initiative in solving any procedural question not regulated in the arbitration agreement or the Model Law.

3. In addition to the general provisions of article 19, other provisions in the Model Law recognize party autonomy and, failing agreement, empower the arbitral tribunal to decide on certain matters. Examples of particular practical importance in international cases are article 20 on the place of arbitration, article 22 on the language to be used in the proceedings, and article 28 on the rules applicable to the substance of the dispute.

CASE LAW ON ARTICLE 19

Determination of the procedure by the parties—paragraph (1)

4. The parties' freedom under article 19 (1) is subject to the "mandatory" provisions in the Model Law. A Canadian court had determined that the parties' choice of procedural rules must not conflict with any mandatory provision of the law or with public policy.[466] This maintains the balance between the parties' autonomy over the procedure to be followed and any overriding requirements of the legal regime that governs the arbitration. An arbitration agreement which provides for the arbitration to be dealt with on written submissions only (thus without cross-examination of witnesses) was held to be valid and not contrary to the law or public policy.[467]

---

[466] *Noble China Inc. v. Lei Kat Cheong*, Ontario Court of Justice, Canada, 4 November 1998, [1998] CanLII 14708 (ON SC), published in (1998) 42 O.R. (3d) 69, available on the Internet at http://canlii.ca/t/1vvkr.

[467] *Desputeaux v. Éditions Chouette* (1987) inc., Supreme Court, Canada, 21 March 2003, [2003] 1 S.C.R. 178, 2003 SCC 17, available on the Internet at http://canlii.ca/t/1g2jh.

5. The arbitral tribunal must conduct the arbitration in accordance with the procedure agreed by the parties. Failure by the tribunal to follow the agreed procedure may result in the award being set aside under article 34 (see below, section on article 34, paras. 42 and 108-109) or refused enforcement under article 36 (see below, section on article 36, paras. 39-44).

Relationship between the parties' choice of procedural rules and the Model Law (Difference between the lex arbitri and procedural rules of the arbitration)

6. Parties may adopt institutional rules to regulate the conduct of the arbitration. The role of institutional rules and their interplay with the arbitration law of the seat have sometimes been misunderstood. Two decisions, one by a Court of Appeal in Australia (Queensland)[468] and another by a Singapore court[469] provided that the adoption of rules of arbitral institutions would displace the application of the arbitration law as it would be an "opting out" of the application of the law. Both decisions have been criticized heavily as not recognizing the fundamental juridical difference between arbitral rules and the *lex arbitri* and were not subsequently followed. The Australian (Queensland) decision was described as "wrong" by another court in New South Wales[470] which stated that "the Model Law reserves to the court the power to intervene where an institution fails to perform its procedural function and thus contemplates that the Model Law may have a supervisory or supplementary role over and above the role accorded to other institutions by reason of the parties' contractual choice of rules." The court took the view that article 19 allows parties to adopt procedural rules different from those which would otherwise be applicable under the law of the seat of arbitration and adopting them does not amount to an election to deny the application of the arbitration law. The Queensland Court of Appeal has since also re-visited its earlier decision and confirmed that the adoption of institutional rules is not a derogation to the arbitration law.[471] Similarly, the Singapore legislature has reversed the effect of the court's decision by making clear that the mere adoption of institutional rules is not an election to reject the application of the arbitration law.

Tribunal's procedural discretion in the absence of the parties' agreement—paragraph (2)

Scope of paragraph (2)

7. The power of the arbitral tribunal to determine the appropriate procedure includes the power to determine the applicable, or apply its own, rules of evidence. Such rules may include those relating to the admissibility, relevance, materiality and weight of the evidence and is not impeded by peculiarities of national procedural laws.

8. In a Canadian case, an issue arose as to whether the arbitral tribunal had jurisdiction to order the oral examination of a third party for discovery prior to the substantive hearing. The parties in that case had earlier agreed to adopt the Alberta Rules of Court to govern the discovery process. The Alberta Court of Appeal affirmed the power of the arbitral tribunal to order the examination. The court cited the *travaux préparatoires* on article 19 and accepted that it "speaks of the entitlement of a tribunal to order pre-hearing discovery".[472] The court stated that the parties' adoption of the Alberta Rules of Court which permitted examinations of third parties, read with article 19 of the Model Law, gave wide plenary authority to the arbitral tribunal to give effect to all aspects of the parties' agreement empowering the tribunal to exercise such powers.[473]

9. In exercising its discretion under article 19 (2), the arbitral tribunal should do so within the permitted boundaries of the provisions of the Model Law. In one case, a court suggested that the arbitral tribunal should pre-determine the procedure in particular on admissibility of evidence to avoid subsequent challenges. In that case, the dissatisfied party sought to set aside the award on the premise that the arbitral tribunal in making the award was influenced by the information contained in the documents which had been shown only to the arbitral tribunal and not to the party due to a non-disclosure obligation. The court, however, considered that the arbitral tribunal did not refer to, or make use of, any information disclosed in such documents and the setting aside of the arbitral award was refused.[474]

---

[468] *Eisenwerk Hensel Bayreuth Dipl-Ing Burkhardt Gmbh v. Australian Granites Limited,* Queensland Court of Appeal, Australia, [2001] 1 Qd R 461.

[469] *John Holland Pty. Ltd. v. Toyo Engineering Corp. (Japan)* [2001] SGHC 48—*John Holland Pty. Ltd. v. Toyo Engineering Corp. (Japan),* High Court, Singapore, 14 March 2001, [2001] SGHC 48. This Singapore decision was revised by a legislative amendment (s15A of the International Act, Chapter 143A) which makes clear that adopting institutional rules of arbitration does not amount to election to "opt out" of the Model Law.

[470] *Cargill International SA v. Peabody Australia Mining Ltd.,* Supreme Court of New South Wales, Australia, 11 August 2010, [2010] NSWSC 887, available on the Internet at http://www.austlii.edu.au/au/cases/nsw/NSWSC/2010/887.html.

[471] *Wagners Nouvelle Caledonie Sarl v. Vale Inco Nouvelle Caledonie SAS,* Queensland Court of Appeal, Australia, 20 August 2010, [2010] QCA 219, available on the Internet at http://www.austlii.edu.au/au/cases/qld/QCA/2010/219.html.

[472] The court considered the *travaux préparatoires* contained in A/CN.9/264, Analytical commentary on draft text of a model law on international commercial arbitration, under article 19, available on the UNCITRAL website at http://www.uncitral.org/uncitral/en/commission/sessions/18th.html.

[473] *Jardine Lloyd Thompson Canada Inc. v. SJO Catlin,* Alberta Court of Appeal, Canada, 18 January 2006, [2006] ABCA 18 (CanLII), available on the Internet at http://canlii.ca/t/1mch7.

[474] *Dongwoo Mann+Hummel Co. Ltd. v. Mann+Hummel GmbH,* High Court, Singapore, 8 May 2008, [2008] 3 SLR 871.

Article 20. Place of arbitration

(1) The parties are free to agree on the place of arbitration. Failing such agreement, the place of arbitration shall be determined by the arbitral tribunal having regard to the circumstances of the case, including the convenience of the parties.

(2) Notwithstanding the provisions of paragraph (1) of this article, the arbitral tribunal may, unless otherwise agreed by the parties, meet at any place it considers appropriate for consultation among its members, for hearing witnesses, experts or the parties, or for inspection of goods, other property or documents.

TRAVAUX PRÉPARATOIRES

The *travaux préparatoires* on article 20 as adopted in 1985 are contained the following in documents:

1. Report of the United Nations Commission on International Trade Law on the work of its eighteenth session (*Official Records of the General Assembly, Fortieth Session, Supplement No. 17* (A/40/17)), paras. 11-333.

2. Reports of the Working Group: A/CN.9/216; A/CN.9/232; A/CN.9/245; A/CN.9/246, annex; A/CN.9/263 and Add.1-2; A/CN.9/264. Relevant working papers are referred to in the reports.

3. Summary records of the 321st and 332nd UNCITRAL meetings.

Article 20 was not amended in 2006.

(Available on the Internet at www.uncitral.org).

CASE LAW ON ARTICLE 20

Place of arbitration—paragraph (1)

1. The place of arbitration is a critical connecting factor for the applicability of a given national law. It also determines the place where the award is made.[475] Courts have recognized that arbitration must have a place of arbitration, sometimes referred to as the 'seat' or *locus arbitri*.[476]

Parties may designate the place of arbitration

2. Article 20 (1) provides for the parties' freedom to designate the place of arbitration. Parties may make the choice of a place of arbitration at any time before the arbitration begins; or they may leave it to be made on their behalf by an arbitral institution (if the arbitration is administered in accordance with institutional rules) or by the arbitral tribunal itself.

[475] Article 31 (3) of the Model Law.

[476] See for instance: *Angela Raguz v. Rebecca Sullivan & Ors,* New South Wales Supreme Court, New South Wales Court of Appeal, Australia, 1 September 2000, [2000] NSWCA 240, available on the Internet at http://www.austlii.edu.au/au/cases/nsw/NSWCA/2000/240.html.

3. In one case where the parties had not made any express designation of the place of arbitration in the arbitration agreement, the court nevertheless found that such an agreement could be inferred from the contractual relationship between the parties.[477] Parties' choice of the place of arbitration may be made in the arbitration clause. An arbitration clause which merely read "Arbitration: Hamburg" with no reference to any other place or institution has been held to constitute an agreement on the place of arbitration.[478] Similarly an arbitration clause that provided only for the "venue" to be in London has been held to be a choice of London as the place of the arbitration.[479] Where an arbitration clause provided for both a named place of arbitration as well as purporting to give the parties the liberty to agree to "such other place", the Indian Supreme Court considered that the place named would be the agreed place and that the liberty granted was intended only to allow for an alternative place for hearings for the convenience of the parties.[480]

4. The terms "place of arbitration" and "place or venue of hearing" must not be confused (see below in this section, paras. 8 and 9). Where the parties have agreed to the place of arbitration, the tribunal is bound by the choice of the parties.[481]

Place of arbitration determined by the arbitral tribunal

5. In the absence of any indication as to the place of arbitration, the arbitral tribunal has to decide on the place of arbitration having regard to the circumstances of the case, including the convenience of the parties. In a case, it was held that "an erroneous decision on the question of venue, which ultimately affected the procedure that has been followed in the arbitral proceedings," could open the door to an application under article 34.[482]

6. In exercising its discretion as to the determination of the place of arbitration, the arbitral tribunal must ensure equal treatment of the parties and make a fair decision.[483] One court interpreted the provision in paragraph (1) that the arbitral tribunal shall have "regard to the circumstances of the case" to mean that the tribunal shall have regard to any connections with one or more particular countries that can be identified in relation to (i) the parties; (ii) the dispute which will be the subject of the arbitration; (iii) the proposed procedures in the arbitration, including (if known) the place of hearings; and (iv) the issuance of the award or awards.[484]

[477] CLOUT case No. 439 [Brandenburgisches Oberlandesgericht, Germany, 8 SchH 01/00 (1), 26 June 2000, 8 SchH 01/00], where the court found that the parties had indirectly agreed that the place of arbitration should be in Germany since the contracts were in German, referred to German standard forms, were subject to German law, and the obligations were to be performed in Germany, also available on the Internet at http://www.dis-arb.de/de/47/datenbanken/rspr/brandenburgisches-olg-az-8-schh-01-00-1-datum-2000-06-26-id36.

[478] CLOUT case No. 571 [Hanseatisches Oberlandesgericht Hamburg, Germany, 11 Sch 06/01, 24 January 2003, 11 Sch 06/01], also available on the Internet at http://www.dis-arb.de/de/47/datenbanken/rspr/hanseat-olg-hamburg-az-11-sch-06-01-datum-2003-01-24-id209.

[479] *Shashoua v. Sharma*, High Court, England, 7 May 2009, [2009] EWHC 957 (Comm), available on the Internet at http://www.bailii.org/ew/cases/EWHC/Comm/2009/957.html.

[480] *Dozco India P. Ltd. vs. Doosan Infracore Co. Ltd.*, Supreme Court, India, 8 October 2010. The arbitration clause read : "All disputes arising in connection with this Agreement shall be finally settled by arbitration in Seoul, Korea (or such other place as the parties may agree in writing), pursuant to the rules of agreement then in force of the International Chamber of Commerce." The Claimant argued that the bracketed portion can be interpreted so as to mean that the seat of arbitration could be anywhere else as per the choice of the parties. The Respondent opposed this standing and argued that the bracketed portion was relevant only for the venue of the hearings, as opposed to the seat of the arbitration. The court agreed that the bracketed portion is meant only for the convenience of the arbitral tribunal and/or the parties for conducting the proceedings of the arbitration, but the bracketed portion does not, in any manner, change the seat of arbitration, which is Seoul, Korea.

[481] *Shin Satellite Public Co. Ltd. v. Jain Studios Ltd.*, Supreme Court, India, 31 January 2006, (2006) 2 SSC 628, available on the Internet at http://indiankanoon.org/doc/1601758/; *Jagson Airlines Ltd. v. Bannari Amman Exports (P) Ltd.*, Delhi High Court, India, 28 April 2003, 2003(2) Arb LR 315 (Delhi), available on the Internet at http://indiankanoon.org/doc/1465429/.

[482] *Sanshin Chemicals Industry v. Oriental Carbons and Chemicals Ltd.*, Supreme Court, India, 16 February 2001 AIR 2001 SC 1219, available on the Internet at http://indiankanoon.org/doc/1628722/.

[483] *Sulaikha Clay Mines v. Alpha Clays,* Kerala High Court, India, 9 August 2004, AIR 2005 Ker 3; 2005 Arb LR 237 Kerala, available on the Internet at http://indiankanoon.org/doc/252644/.

[484] *Dubai Islamic Bank PJSC v. Paymentech*, High Court, England, 24 November 2000, [2001] 1 LLR 65 at para. 52.

Failure by the parties and by the arbitral tribunal to determine the place of arbitration

7. Article 20 does not provide for the situation where an arbitral tribunal fails to make such a determination. If the place of arbitration is neither agreed upon by the parties, nor determined by the arbitral tribunal, the courts might have to determine the place of arbitration. In such a case, it was found that the effective place of arbitration, i.e. the place where all relevant actions in the arbitration have taken place or, if this cannot be determined, the place of the last oral hearing, should be the place of arbitration.[485] (See below, section on article 31, para. 11).

Meetings and hearings of the arbitral tribunal—paragraph (2)

8. Paragraph (2) makes clear that the place of arbitration is distinct from the place or venues where hearings may be conducted. Courts have accepted that the term "place of arbitration" as a juridical concept should not be confused with the geographic locale where the hearings may be conducted.[486] In one case, the court ordered the arbitrator to be replaced when he persisted in holding the arbitration outside the agreed place of arbitration.[487]

9. Unless the parties have agreed otherwise, the arbitral tribunal may decide to meet at any place it considers appropriate for consultation among its members, for hearing witnesses, experts or the parties, or for inspection of goods, other property or documents. The distinction between the "place of arbitration" referred to in paragraph (1) and the "venue of hearing" in paragraph (2) was noted in a case before the Singapore Court of Appeal. In that case, the chosen place of arbitration was in Jakarta (Indonesia), but the arbitral tribunal held all hearings in Singapore, and never seated in Jakarta. The arbitration was nevertheless held to have its place in Jakarta. The court considered that the place of arbitration does not change merely because the arbitral tribunal held its hearings at a different place or places; it would only change where the parties so agreed.[488]

---

[485] CLOUT case No. 374 (also reproduced under CLOUT case No. 408) [Oberlandesgericht Düsseldorf, Germany, 6 Sch 02/99, 23 March 2000], also available on the Internet at http://www.dis-arb.de/de/47/datenbanken/rspr/olg-düsseldorf-az-6-sch-02-99-datum-2000-03-23-id46; *Dubai Islamic Bank PJSC v. Paymentech*, High Court, England, 24 November 2000, [2001] 1 LLR 65.

[486] *PT Garuda Indonesia v. Birgen Air*, Court of Appeal, Singapore, 6 March 2002 [2002 1 SLR 393]; *Shashoua v. Sharma*, High Court, London, England, 7 May 2009, [2009] EWHC 957 (Comm), available on the Internet at http://www.bailii.org/ew/cases/EWHC/Comm/2009/957.html; *Dubai Islamic Bank PJSC v. Paymentech*, High Court, England, 24 November 2000, [2001] 1 LLR 65; *Virgilio De Agostini v. Milloil SpA*, Corte di Appello, Italy, 24 March 1998.

[487] *National Highway Authority of India v. Sheladia Associates Inc*, Delhi High Court, India, 21 August 2009, 2009(3) Arb LR 378 (Delhi), available on the Internet at http://indiankanoon.org/doc/396012/.

[488] *PT Garuda Indonesia v. Birgen Air*, Court of Appeal, Singapore, 6 March 2002, [2002 1 SLR 393].

Article 21. Commencement of arbitral proceedings

Unless otherwise agreed by the parties, the arbitral proceedings in respect of a particular dispute commence on the date on which a request for that dispute to be referred to arbitration is received by the respondent.

TRAVAUX PRÉPARATOIRES

The *travaux préparatoires* on article 21 as adopted in 1985 are contained in the following documents:

1. Report of the United Nations Commission on International Trade Law on the work of its eighteenth session (*Official Records of the General Assembly, Fortieth Session, Supplement No. 17* (A/40/17)), paras. 11-333.

2. Reports of the Working Group: A/CN.9/233; A/CN.9/245; A/CN.9/246, annex; A/CN.9/263 and Add.1-2; A/CN.9/264. Relevant working papers are referred to in the reports.

3. Summary records of the 321st and 332nd UNCITRAL meetings.

Article 21 was not amended in 2006.

(Available on the Internet at www.uncitral.org).

INTRODUCTION

1. Article 21 deals with the determination of the point in time at which arbitral proceedings in respect of a particular dispute commences. Unless the parties have agreed on a different point in time, the arbitral proceedings commence on the date on which a request for the particular dispute to be referred to arbitration is received by the respondent.[489] The term "request" to arbitrate is used interchangeably with "notice" to arbitrate.

CASE LAW ON ARTICLE 21

Agreement between the parties

2. Under article 21, parties are entitled to provide for a different point in time or a different factor to ascertain when the arbitration has commenced. Although it is not usual for parties to provide in their agreement a specific point in time for the commencement of arbitration, institutional rules often do so. A reference to certain arbitration rules which provide for the point in time at which arbitral proceedings in respect of a particular dispute commence, would be sufficient to displace the effect of this article.[490] By incorporating institutional rules into the arbitration clause, the parties may agree that the arbitration does not commence until a request for arbitration by one party is actually received by the administering institution as provided in most arbitration rules or when the parties have been notified that all the arbitrators have accepted their appointment.[491] The importance of complying with the agreed method of commencing arbitration is illustrated in a case where the claimant sent the notice of arbitration only to the other party but did not "file" the same with the administering institution. The arbitration clause provided that any "Failure to file a notice of arbitration within twelve (12) months after the occurrences supporting a claim constitutes an irrevocable waiver of that claim". The court held that the arbitration was not commenced until the applicant had "filed" the notice with the institution overseeing the process and distinguished the concept of "filing" with that of "servicing" or "delivering" in that "filing" requires the depositing or placing the notice with the institution overseeing the proceedings.[492]

---

[489] As to written communications, article 3 of the Model Law regulates the fact of receipt as well as the date of receipt of such communications.

[490] *Fuller Austin Insulation Inc. v. Wellington Insurance Co.,* Saskatchewan Queen's Bench, Canada, 15 September 1995, [1995] CanLII 5752 (SK QB), also available on the Internet at http://canlii.ca/t/1nrkb.

[491] International Centre for Settlement of Investment Disputes, ICSID Arbitration Rules, rule 6(1).

[492] *Bell Canada v. The Plan Group,* Court of Appeal for Ontario, Canada, 7 July 2009, [2009] ONCA 548, also available on the Internet at http://canlii.ca/t/24brq.

Notion of "request"

3. According to the *travaux préparatoires*, the request for arbitration must "identify the particular dispute and make clear that arbitration is resorted to and not, for example, indicate merely the intention of later initiating arbitral proceedings." It is irrelevant whether this request is in fact entitled "request" or whether it is called "notice", "application" or "statement of claim".[493] The *travaux préparatoires* make no reference to the question of whether this request has to be made in a written form or whether an oral request is permissible. In most instances, a request for arbitration is given in a written communication from the claimant to the respondent.[494] Although the request need not be in great detail, the recipient of the notice should be in a position to understand what is alleged against him. A letter by the claimant informing the respondent that the claimant had appointed a certain person as arbitrator and inviting the respondent to appoint its arbitrator was considered to constitute a request for the dispute to be referred to arbitration within the meaning of article 21. The arbitral proceedings were considered to have commenced upon receipt of such letter by the respondent.[495] Similarly, a court held that the receipt by the respondent of a request from the claimant to appoint an arbitrator would commence arbitral proceedings, although a mere inquiry into the respondent's position with regard to arbitration would not constitute commencement.[496]

[493] A/CN.9/264, Analytical commentary on draft text of a model law on international commercial arbitration, under article 21, available on the UNCITRAL website at http://www.uncitral.org/uncitral/en/commission/sessions/18th.html.

[494] *Blackpool Borough Council v. F Parkinson Ltd.*, Queen's Bench Division Official Referees' Business, England, 22 October 1991, 58 BLR 85.

[495] CLOUT case No. 20 [*Fung Sang Trading Limited v. Kai Sun Sea Products and Food Company Limited*, High Court—Court of First Instance, Hong Kong, 29 October 1991], also available on the Internet at http://www.hklii.hk/eng/hk/cases/hkcfi/1991/190.html, [1991] HKCFI 190; *Milkfood Ltd. v. M/s GMC Ice Cream (P) Ltd.*, Supreme Court, India, 5 April 2004, [2004] INSC 229.

[496] CLOUT case No. 706 [*Fustar Chemicals Ltd. v. Sinochem Liaoning Hong Kong Ltd.*, High Court—Court of First Instance, Hong Kong, 5 June 1996], [1996] 2 HKC 407.

Article 22. Language

(1) The parties are free to agree on the language or languages to be used in the arbitral proceedings. Failing such agreement, the arbitral tribunal shall determine the language or languages to be used in the proceedings. This agreement or determination, unless otherwise specified therein, shall apply to any written statement by a party, any hearing and any award, decision or other communication by the arbitral tribunal.

(2) The arbitral tribunal may order that any documentary evidence shall be accompanied by a translation into the language or languages agreed upon by the parties or determined by the arbitral tribunal.

TRAVAUX PRÉPARATOIRES

The *travaux préparatoires* on article 22 as adopted in 1985 are contained in the following documents:

1. Report of the United Nations Commission on International Trade Law on the work of its eighteenth session (*Official Records of the General Assembly, Fortieth Session, Supplement No. 17* (A/40/17)), paras. 11-333.
2. Reports of the Working Group: A/CN.9/233; A/CN.9/245; A/CN.9/246, annex; A/CN.9/263 and Add.1-2; A/CN.9/264. Relevant working papers are referred to in the reports.
3. Summary records of the 321st, 322nd and 332nd UNCITRAL meetings.

Article 22 was not amended in 2006.

(Available on the Internet at www.uncitral.org).

INTRODUCTION

1. Article 22 gives primacy to the parties to agree on the language or languages of the arbitral proceedings. It provides as a default provision that the arbitral tribunal shall determine language or languages to be used.

CASE LAW ON ARTICLE 22

Language to be used in the arbitral proceedings

2. Parties' choice of the language may be validly made through the adoption of arbitration rules. In a case before the Croatian Supreme Court, an attempt to resist the enforcement of an award was made on the ground that the language used in the arbitration was not the agreed one, the party was not familiar with the language and had thus been deprived of the ability to present its case. The court held that, as the parties agreed to submit their disputes to an institution, they must be considered as having accepted the language used by the institution, and they could not thereafter complain about it.[497] In a German case, an attempt to resist enforcement of an award was made on the ground that the arbitration was held in Spanish and not in English as agreed in the arbitration clause. The parties, in that case, agreed on English as the language of the proceedings; however, they submitted their disputes to the jurisdiction of an institutional arbitral tribunal and its rules of arbitration, which provided that Spanish should be the language of proceedings. In that respect, the parties subsequently agreed in their pleadings that Spanish would be the language of the proceedings and that English had only an auxiliary function in the relation between the parties. In that context, the court held that "the fact that Spanish was used in the arbitration—rather than English as agreed in the arbitration

[497] CLOUT case No. 1069 [Supreme Court, Croatia, 5 March 2008, Gž 6/08-2]. The award was made by the Arbitration Court attached to the Economic and Agricultural Chamber of the Czech Republic in December 2007, which provided that oral hearings should be held, and decisions made, in Czech (or in Slovak) language. The respondent claimed that, as all the documents and proceedings were not in the English language, it was not able to fully present its case.

clause—did not contravene the agreement of the parties, who agreed to Spanish as the language of the arbitration". The court considered that the use of the Spanish language did not violate the respondent's right to due process, as it failed to prove that it had not been able to present its case or had been otherwise negatively affected.[498] This case illustrates that the default language in institutional rules can co-exist with the parties' explicit agreement on language in the arbitration agreement.

3. Some States have, in enacting the Model Law, provided for a default language in their legislation. Consequently, the language of the arbitration may also be affected by the parties' choice, or the tribunal's determination, of the place of arbitration. In a case where the arbitration clause was silent with respect to the place and the language of arbitration, and given that the parties did not subsequently determine any procedural matters, the arbitral tribunal decided that the place of arbitration was "Cairo, Egypt", which in turn led to the determination that the language of the arbitration was the Arabic language.[499]

4. Issues arising from language used in the arbitration have been raised by parties in setting aside proceedings on the premise of their alleged inability to present their cases properly (or as an argument to resist enforcement). Such defences have yet to find favour with the courts if the language of the arbitral proceedings had explicitly been agreed between the parties or was determined as the result of the application of arbitration rules.[500] In such cases, courts generally saw it as an obligation for the party unable to speak that language to arrange for the necessary translations.[501] It is also considered sufficient that a party is represented by a lawyer who speaks the language.[502] (See below, section on article 34, para. 58, and section on article 36, para. 30).

[498] Oberlandesgericht München, Germany, 34 Sch 26/08, 22 June 2009, available on the Internet at http://www.dis-arb.de/de/47/ldatenbanken/rspr/olg-münchen-az-34-sch-26-08-datum-2009-06-22-id1065.

[499] CLOUT case No. 786 [Cairo Regional Center for International Commercial Arbitration, No.1/1994, Egypt, 31 October 1995].

[500] CLOUT case No. 1069 [Supreme Court, Croatia, 5 March 2008, Gž 6/08-2], where the public policy defence was rejected as the arbitral tribunal was authorized under the applicable Czech arbitration rules to conduct the proceedings in the Czech language.

[501] CLOUT case No. 559 [Oberlandesgericht Celle, Germany, 8 Sch 03/01, 2 October 2001], also available in the Internet at http://www.dis-arb.de/en/47/datenbanken/rspr/olg-celle-case-no-8-sch-03-01-date-2001-10-02-id208; in the case the contract had been drafted in German and Russian languages but the tribunal sent out all its communication in Russian only as it was entitled under the applicable arbitration rules.

[502] Oberlandesgericht München, Germany, 34 Sch 26/08, 22 June 2009, available on the Internet at http://www.dis-arb.de/de/47/datenbanken/rspr/olg-münchen-az-34-sch-26-08-datum-2009-06-22-id1065.

Article 23. Statements of claim and defence

(1) Within the period of time agreed by the parties or determined by the arbitral tribunal, the claimant shall state the facts supporting his claim, the points at issue and the relief or remedy sought, and the respondent shall state his defence in respect of these particulars, unless the parties have otherwise agreed as to the required elements of such statements. The parties may submit with their statements all documents they consider to be relevant or may add a reference to the documents or other evidence they will submit.

(2) Unless otherwise agreed by the parties, either party may amend or supplement his claim or defence during the course of the arbitral proceedings, unless the arbitral tribunal considers it inappropriate to allow such amendment having regard to the delay in making it.

TRAVAUX PRÉPARATOIRES

The *travaux préparatoires* on article 23 as adopted in 1985 are contained in the following documents:

1. Report of the United Nations Commission on International Trade Law on the work of its eighteenth session (*Official Records of the General Assembly, Fortieth Session, Supplement No. 17* (A/40/17)), paras. 11-333.

2. Reports of the Working Group: A/CN.9/233; A/CN.9/245; A/CN.9/246, annex; A/CN.9/263 and Add.1-2; A/CN.9/264. Relevant working papers are referred to in the reports.

3. Summary records of the 322nd, 323rd and 332nd UNCITRAL meetings.

Article 23 was not amended in 2006.

(Available on the Internet at www.uncitral.org).

CASE LAW ON ARTICLE 23

Statements of claim and defence—paragraph (1)

Required elements

1. Article 23 mandates the parties to arbitration to provide statements setting out their claim and defence. The statements referred to in article 23 are to be submitted in addition to the request for arbitration referred to in article 21. A Canadian court observed that the term "statement" is the accepted term used in arbitration proceedings corresponding to the word "pleading" in the litigation process.[503] The statements should identify the facts at issue, the points in dispute and the relief or remedy claimed. These elements have been held by a German court to be essential for defining the dispute on which the arbitral tribunal is to give a decision. That court recognized that the duty to file a statement of claim is therefore an essential and mandatory

[503] CLOUT case No. 118 [*Bab Systems, Inc. v. McLurg,* Ontario Court of Justice, General Division, Canada, 21 December 1994].

obligation.[504] A Canadian court took the view that the pleadings exchanged between the parties pursuant to article 23 (1) constitute one of the sources (other sources include notice of request and contract between the parties) for ascertaining the scope of the submission to arbitration.[505] Courts have held that arbitral tribunals should be bound to decide the dispute in accordance with the parties' pleaded case as set out in the statements of claim and defence. The arbitrator should not be entitled to go beyond the pleaded case and decide on points on which the parties have not given evidence or have not made submissions. If the arbitral tribunal considers that the parties have not framed their cases correctly and that certain points need to be addressed, then the tribunal must indicate its concerns to the parties and allow them to make such amendments to their pleadings and to adduce such additional evidence as may be necessary to deal with those concerns.[506]

2. While the obligation of the parties to furnish the statements is mandatory pursuant to article 23 (1), ("the claimant *shall* state the facts supporting his claim" and "the defendant *shall* state his defence"),[507] the elements comprising these statements may be agreed between the parties ("unless the parties have otherwise agreed as to the required elements of such statement"). According to the *travaux préparatoires,* this formulation is intended to ensure that, although the parties cannot derogate from the principle provided in article 23 (1), they should have the freedom to agree on the specific rules of procedure in respect of the statements of claim and defence.[508]

[504] Bayerisches Oberstes Landesgericht, Germany, 4 Z Sch 02/99, 29 September 1999, available on the Internet at http://www.dis-arb.de/de/47/datenbanken/rspr/bayoblg-az-4-z-sch-02-99-datum-1999-09-29-id18.

[505] CLOUT case No. 16 [*Quintette Coal Ltd. v. Nippon Steel Corp. et.al.,* Court of Appeal for British Columbia, Canada, 24 October 1990], [1990] B.C.J. No. 2241.

[506] *Alenco Inc. v. Niska Gas Storage US,* Alberta Court of Appeal, Canada, LLC [2009] A.W.L.D. 2128; *Ng Chin Siau and Others v. How Kim Chuan,* High Court, Singapore, [2007] 2 SLR 789; [2007] SGHC 31.

[507] Emphasis added.

[508] Report of the United Nations Commission on International Trade Law on the work of its eighteenth session (*Official Records of the General Assembly, Fortieth Session, Supplement No. 17* (A/40/17)), para. 196.

Article 24. Hearings and written proceedings

(1) Subject to any contrary agreement by the parties, the arbitral tribunal shall decide whether to hold oral hearings for the presentation of evidence or for oral argument, or whether the proceedings shall be conducted on the basis of documents and other materials. However, unless the parties have agreed that no hearings shall be held, the arbitral tribunal shall hold such hearings at an appropriate stage of the proceedings, if so requested by a party.

(2) The parties shall be given sufficient advance notice of any hearing and of any meeting of the arbitral tribunal for the purposes of inspection of goods, other property or documents.

(3) All statements, documents or other information supplied to the arbitral tribunal by one party shall be communicated to the other party. Also any expert report or evidentiary document on which the arbitral tribunal may rely in making its decision shall be communicated to the parties.

TRAVAUX PRÉPARATOIRES

The *travaux préparatoires* on article 24 as adopted in 1985 are contained in documents:

1. Report of the United Nations Commission on International Trade Law on the work of its eighteenth session (*Official Records of the General Assembly, Fortieth Session, Supplement No. 17* (A/40/17)), paras. 11-333.

2. Reports of the Working Group: A/CN.9/216; A/CN.9/232; A/CN.9/245; A/CN.9/246, annex; A/CN.9/263 and Add.1-2; A/CN.9/264. Relevant working papers are referred to in the reports.

3. Summary records of the 323rd, 332nd and 324th UNCITRAL meetings.

Article 24 was not amended in 2006.

(Available on the Internet at www.uncitral.org).

CASE LAW ON ARTICLE 24

Oral hearings—paragraph (1)

1. Article 24 (1) of the Model Law allows the tribunal to decide whether there will be oral hearings or whether the decision will be based solely on documents. If, however, a party requests an oral hearing, whether for the presentation of evidence or oral argument, then, in the absence of a prior agreement between the parties to the contrary, the tribunal must comply with the party's request. The Austrian Supreme Court considered the refusal of an arbitral tribunal to hold an oral hearing, despite the request of one party, to be a violation of the right to be heard, as stated in article 24.[509] (See below, section on article 34, para. 60). A failure by the tribunal to hold a hearing despite a request from a party resulted in a German case in the setting aside of the arbitral award under article 34 (2)(*a*)(iv) on the basis that the refusal to hold hearings constituted a violation of article 24 (1) (second sentence) (see below, section on article 34, para. 110).[510]

2. An arbitral tribunal is, however, not bound to hold a hearing unless such a request is made.[511] In a Singapore case, the arbitral tribunal's decision based on the parties' written submissions was later challenged on the basis that no hearings have been held. The court held that neither party requested an oral hearing and therefore no party would be entitled to thereafter complain for lacking the opportunity to orally address the tribunal.[512]

Notice of hearings, documents, and expert reports—paragraphs (2) and (3)

3. The notice of a hearing has a direct connection to a party's right to present its case under article 18 and its purpose is to ensure a minimum standard of procedural

[509] Supreme Court, Austria, 30 June 2010, 7 Ob 111/10i.

[510] CLOUT case No. 659 [Oberlandesgericht Naumburg, Germany, 10 Sch 08/01, 21 February 2002], also available on the Internet at http://www.dis-arb.de/de/47/datenbanken/rspr/olg-naumburg-az-10-sch-08-01-datum-2002-02-21-id166.

[511] *Government of the Republic of the Philippines v. Philippine International Air Terminals Co., Inc.*, High Court, Singapore, 17 November 2006, [2007] 1 SLR (R) 278; [2006] SGHC 206.

[512] CLOUT case No. 742 [*PT Asuransi Jasa Indonesia (Persero) v. Dexia Bank S.A.*, Court of Appeal, Singapore, 1 December 2006], also in [2006] SGCA 41, [2007] 1 SLR(R) 597.

protection. A German court confirmed that the principle of due process requires that parties be notified sufficiently in advance of any hearing and of any meeting of the arbitral tribunal for the purposes of inspection of goods, other property or documents, as provided for under paragraph (2).[513] Failure to comply with this requirement constitutes not only a breach of article 24 but also of article 18 (see above, section on article 18, paras. 3 and 9). According to a New Zealand court, a violation of these provisions could lead to the setting aside of the arbitral award under article 34 of the Model Law or to the refusal to recognize and enforce an arbitral award under article 36 of the Model Law.[514] (See below, section on article 34, paras. 56-57.)

4. The importance of "sufficient advance notice" under article 24 (2) for a hearing is also emphasized in several Indian cases. In one case, an arbitrator did not communicate with the respondent and declared that the proceedings would be held *ex parte* (i.e. without hearing the respondent). The respondent attempted to appear before the arbitrator at a hearing but the hearing had been adjourned. On the written request for a hearing date, the arbitrator replied that the hearing was completed. An award which was subsequently made was set aside and a new arbitrator appointed. The court held that articles 18 and 24 of the Model Law define natural justice as the "essence of fair adjudication, deeply rooted in tradition and conscience, to be ranked as fundamental".[515] An Indian court has also recognized that "a party to the arbitration must not only have notice of the time and place of the meeting, but he should be allowed a reasonable opportunity of presenting his case either by evidence or by arguments or both, and of being fully heard." The court has further stated that the notice must be given sufficiently in advance in order to give the party an opportunity to be heard. If there is no sufficient notice, there cannot be a proper hearing or a valid award, it being a well recognized rule of natural justice that legal rights cannot be determined without giving parties an opportunity to be heard.[516] However, no valid complaint could be made where a party has been duly notified of hearings and of the fact that "no further notice" would be given before the decision is made by the arbitral tribunal.[517]

5. A party's right to be heard includes being given all the statements, documents or other information which have been submitted to the arbitral tribunal. Therefore, paragraph (3) provides that each party shall receive a copy of any communication by the other party to the arbitral tribunal, and of any expert report or other document on which the arbitral tribunal may rely in making its decision.

6. The first sentence of article 24 (3) provides for mandatory disclosure of all information supplied by a party.[518] Paragraph (3), read with article 18 of the Model Law, has been held by a New Zealand court as containing an implied right to present evidence and argument in response to all new material presented to, or relied upon by, the arbitral tribunal to the extent such new material has to be disclosed under paragraph (3).[519] Further, that court took the view that a party should be given notice of: (1) evidence and argument provided by other parties to the arbitration; (2) the report of an independent expert specific to the dispute in question; (3) a document which may be used as proof or which existence or nature represents a new source of information bearing upon the facts in issue in the arbitration or the credibility of a witness. However, the disclosure obligation was not found to extend to internally prepared documents resulting from the reasoning processes of the

[513] CLOUT case No. 402 [Bayerisches Oberstes Landesgericht, Germany, 4 Z Sch 50/99, 16 March 2000], also available on the Internet at http://www.dis-arb.de/en/47/datenbanken/rspr/bayoblg-case-no-4-z-sch-50-99-date-2000-03-16-id13.

[514] *Methanex Motunui Ltd. v. Spellman*, High Court, Auckland, New Zealand, 18 August 2003, [2004] 1 NZLR 99, appealed in *Methanex Motunui Ltd. v. Spellman*, Court of Appeal, Wellington, New Zealand, 17 June 2004, [2004] 3 NZLR 454.

[515] *Impex Corporation And Ors v. Elenjikal Aquamarine Exports Ltd.*, Kerala High Court, India, 9 October 2007, AIR 2008 Ker 199 (Koshy, J), available on the Internet at http://indiankanoon.org/doc/653638/.

[516] *Atul R. Shah v. M/s. V. Vrijlal Lalloobhai And Co.*, Mumbai High Court India, 8 September 1998; AIR 1999 Bom 67, 1998 (4) BomCR 867, 1999 (1) MhLj 629, available on the Internet at http://indiankanoon.org/doc/822561/.

[517] Ibid.

[518] *Redcliff Estates Ltd. v. Enberg*, High Court Christchurch, New Zealand, 22 July 1999 (HC Christchurch, M150/99, Panckhurst J).

[519] *Methanex Motunui Ltd. v. Spellman*, High Court, Auckland, New Zealand, 18 August 2003, [2004] 1 NZLR 99, appealed in *Methanex Motunui Ltd. v. Spellman*, Court of Appeal, Wellington, New Zealand, 17 June 2004, [2004] 3 NZLR 454.

arbitral tribunal, research copies of published works of general application, or documented matters which the arbitral tribunal could properly take judicial notice of, without evidence.[520] A Hong Kong court set aside an award on the basis that a party was given no chance to deal with the expert reports relied upon by the arbitral tribunal which, in effect, prevented the party from presenting its case.[521] A party cannot, however, take advantage of omissions in presenting the required evidence to claim inability to present its case where it had ample opportunity to do so.[522] (See below, section on article 34, para. 66). In a case where an arbitrator obtained a surveyor's report but failed to provide a copy to the parties, the court remitted the case to the arbitrator (instead of setting aside the award) on the ground that the party waived its right to rely on the breach of natural justice as it was aware that a surveyor had been engaged, and instead of demanding a copy of the report, only complained after receipt of the award.[523]

---

[520] *Methanex Motunui Ltd. v. Spellman*, High Court, Auckland, New Zealand, 18 August 2003, [2004] 1 NZLR 99, appealed in *Methanex Motunui Ltd. v. Spellman*, Court of Appeal, Wellington, New Zealand, 17 June 2004, [2004] 3 NZLR 454.

[521] *Paklito Investment Limited v. Klockner East Asia Limited,* High Court—Court of First Instance, Hong Kong, 15 January 1993, [1993] 2 HKLR 39, available on the Internet at http://www.hklii.hk/eng/hk/cases/hkcfi/1993/147.html.

[522] CLOUT case No. 88 [*Nanjing Cereals, Oils and Food Stuffs Import & Export Corp. v. Luckmate Commodities Trading Ltd.*, High Court—Court of First Instance, Hong Kong, 16 December 1994], [1994] HKCFI 140, also available on the Internet at http://www.hklii.hk/eng/hk/cases/hkcfi/1994/140.html. In that case, the applicant claimed that it had no knowledge of the arbitral tribunal's independent investigation into quantum, let alone an opportunity to question it. The court found that despite ample opportunity to do so, the applicant had failed to present any evidence as to quantum to the tribunal during the proceedings. The court exercised its discretion to refuse to set aside the award due to the failure of the defendants to submit their own evidence to the arbitral tribunal.

[523] *Alexander Property Developments v. Clarke,* High Court New Plymouth, New Zealand, 10 June 2004, CIV. 2004-443-89.

Article 25. Default of a party

Unless otherwise agreed by the parties, if, without showing sufficient cause,

(a) the claimant fails to communicate his statement of claim in accordance with article 23 (1), the arbitral tribunal shall terminate the proceedings;

(b) the respondent fails to communicate his statement of defence in accordance with article 23 (1), the arbitral tribunal shall continue the proceedings without treating such failure in itself as an admission of the claimant's allegations;

(c) any party fails to appear at a hearing or to produce documentary evidence, the arbitral tribunal may continue the proceedings and make the award on the evidence before it.

TRAVAUX PRÉPARATOIRES

The *travaux préparatoires* on article 25 as adopted in 1985 are contained in the following documents:

1. Report of the United Nations Commission on International Trade Law on the work of its eighteenth session (*Official Records of the General Assembly, Fortieth Session, Supplement No. 17* (A/40/17)), paras. 11-333.

2. Reports of the Working Group: A/CN.9/216; A/CN.9/232; A/CN.9/245; A/CN.9/246, annex; A/CN.9/263 and Add.1-2; A/CN.9/264. Relevant working papers are referred to in the reports.

3. Summary records of the 325th and 332nd UNCITRAL meetings.

Article 25 was not amended in 2006.

(Available on the Internet at www.uncitral.org).

INTRODUCTION

1. The arbitral proceedings may be continued in the absence of a party, provided that due notice has been given. This applies, in particular, to the failure of the respondent to communicate its statement of defence (article 25 *(b)*). The arbitral tribunal may also continue the proceedings where a party fails to appear at a hearing or to produce documentary evidence without showing sufficient cause for the failure (article 25 *(c)*). However, if the claimant fails to submit its statement of claim, the arbitral tribunal is obliged to terminate the proceedings (article 25 *(a)*). Provisions that empower the arbitral tribunal to carry out its task even if one of the parties does not participate are of considerable practical importance. It is not uncommon for one of the parties to have little interest in cooperating or expediting matters. Such provisions therefore provide international commercial arbitration its necessary effectiveness, within the limits of fundamental requirements of procedural justice.

CASE LAW ON ARTICLE 25

"Sufficient Cause"

2. The power of the arbitral tribunal to continue or terminate the proceedings is a discretionary one and exercisable if the tribunal is satisfied that the defaulting party has not shown "*sufficient cause*" for its failure. This requirement also carries with it the implication that the tribunal should give a reasonable opportunity to the defaulting party to explain its failure to comply. The sufficiency or insufficiency of the reasons is a matter to be determined by the arbitral tribunal and not by the court.[524]

[524] *Indian Oil Corporation Ltd. v. Atv. Projects India Ltd. & Anor WP* (C), Delhi High Court, India, 9 July 2004, 4967/2003, available on the Internet at http://indiankanoon.org/doc/1944087/.

Failure to communicate statement of claim—paragraph *(a)*

3. Where the statement of claim is not filed within such time as mentioned in article 23 of the Model Law, the arbitral tribunal is required to terminate the proceedings. The use of the term "shall" under article 25 *(a)* suggests that the tribunal has no discretion as to whether or not to terminate the proceedings once it is satisfied that the defaulting party has not shown sufficient cause. In a case before a German court, the arbitral tribunal had proceeded to render an award instead of terminating the proceedings when the claimant failed to communicate its statement of claim. The court ruled that the arbitral tribunal was under an obligation to terminate the proceedings in accordance with article 25 *(a)* and the award was thus set aside. However, this does not mean that the arbitral tribunal is obliged to terminate the entire proceedings.[525] In a case before an Indian court, the arbitrator terminated only the proceedings which related to the defaulting party without affecting the rights of the other party. The court found that the claimant's case having been terminated, the other party might still proceed with its counterclaim. An arbitral tribunal in terminating the proceedings must consider the interest of the other parties (co-claimant or respondent) before terminating the entire proceedings. If the arbitral tribunal terminates the proceedings pursuant to article 25 *(a)*, the mandate of the tribunal shall also terminate co-extensively.[526]

Failure to communicate statement of defence—paragraph *(b)*

4. A court set aside a default award issued by an arbitral tribunal which failed to provide a party with an opportunity to remedy its default, thereby failing to act in fairness towards all the parties.[527] The arbitral tribunal, however, is not entirely precluded from drawing inferences from a failure by a party to submit its statement of defence, and certain discretion exists in assessing the cause of the failure to communicate the statement of defence. An Indian Court interpreting article 25 *(b)* observed that, while the arbitral tribunal is required to investigate the merits of the claimant's case, it is nevertheless entitled to draw adverse inference against a party which fails to file its response to the claim and to produce any evidence. In that case, the application by the respondent to set aside the award on the basis that the tribunal drew adverse inference against it for its non-compliance was rejected.[528]

Failure to appear at a hearing or produce documentary evidence—paragraph *(c)*

5. In an action for the setting aside of an arbitral award, a Canadian court, relying on paragraph *(c)*, found that the arbitral tribunal was justified in continuing the proceedings and making an award on the evidence before it, where one of the parties to the arbitration withdrew from participation in the arbitral proceedings.[529] The court found that where the arbitral tribunal had acted in accordance with paragraph *(c)*, the lack of participation by a party did not constitute a ground for setting aside an award.[530] However, it is important to note that the arbitral tribunal must provide the defaulting party a sufficient advance notice so that the parties would then "be able to take part directly or by means of representatives."[531]

6. While paragraph *(c)* permits the arbitral tribunal to proceed in the absence of a party, the tribunal remains bound under article 18 to ensure that the absent party is not deprived of the opportunity to be heard. In one case before a Spanish provincial court, a party's lawyer had informed the arbitral tribunal of his inability to attend as he was required to appear in another criminal trial at the same time. The award made in his absence was subsequently set aside on the ground that the party was deprived of legal representation constituting an inability to present its defence. [532] (See above, section on article 18, para. 7).

---

[525] Bayerisches Oberstes Landesgericht, Germany, 4 Z Sch 02/99, 29 September 1999, available on the Internet at http://www.dis-arb.de/de/47/datenbanken/rspr/bayoblg-az-4-z-sch-02-99-datum-1999-09-29-id18, where the arbitral award was set aside due to procedural errors in violation of the legislation enacting the Model Law, since the arbitral tribunal issued an award instead of terminating the proceedings where the claimant did not submit a statement of claim.

[526] *Indian Oil Corporation Ltd. v. Atv. Projects India Ltd. & Anor WP* (C), Delhi High Court, India, 9 July 2004, 4967/2003, available on the Internet at http://indiankanoon.org/doc/1944087/.

[527] *Rebah Construction CC v. Renkie Building Construction CC,* High Court, South Africa, 11 February 2008, (42794/2007) [2008] ZAGPHC 34; 2008(3) SA 475 (T), available on the Internet at http://www.saflii.org/za/cases/ZAGPHC/2008/34.html. The arbitral tribunal rendered a default award six days after the respondent failed to file its statement of defence and without placing the respondent on terms and/or calling the respondent to file said statement of defence within a certain period. Although that case is not one dealing with a Model Law provision, the court referred to several rules of institutions containing provisions similar to article 26.

[528] *M/s Prime Telesystem Limited v. Sasken Communication Technologies Ltd.& Ors.,* High Court of Delhi India, 18 December 2009, OMP 35/2008 [2009] INDLHTC 5430, available on the Internet at http://indiankanoon.org/doc/820294/.

[529] CLOUT case No. 391 [*Re Corporación Transnacional de Inversiones, S.A. de C.V. et al. v. STET International, S.p.A. et al.*, Ontario Superior Court of Justice, Canada, 22 September 1999], [1999] CanLII 14819 (ON SC), also available on the Internet at http://canlii.ca/t/1vvn5.

[530] Ibid.

[531] CLOUT case No. 968 [A Coruña Provincial High Court, Spain, Section 6, Case No. 241/2006, 27 June 2006].

[532] Ibid.

Article 26. Expert appointed by arbitral tribunal

(1) Unless otherwise agreed by the parties, the arbitral tribunal

(a) may appoint one or more experts to report to it on specific issues to be determined by the arbitral tribunal;

(b) may require a party to give the expert any relevant information or to produce, or to provide access to, any relevant documents, goods or other property for his inspection.

(2) Unless otherwise agreed by the parties, if a party so requests or if the arbitral tribunal considers it necessary, the expert shall, after delivery of his written or oral report, participate in a hearing where the parties have the opportunity to put questions to him and to present expert witnesses in order to testify on the points at issue.

TRAVAUX PRÉPARATOIRES

The *travaux préparatoires* on article 26 as adopted in 1985 are contained in the following documents:

1. Report of the United Nations Commission on International Trade Law on the work of its eighteenth session (*Official Records of the General Assembly, Fortieth Session, Supplement No. 17* (A/40/17)), paras. 11-333.

2. Reports of the Working Group: A/CN.9/216; A/CN.9/232; A/CN.9/245; A/CN.9/246, annex; A/CN.9/263 and Add.1-2; A/CN.9/264. Relevant working papers are referred to in the reports.

3. Summary records of the 325th and 332nd UNCITRAL meetings.

Article 26 was not amended in 2006.

(Available on the Internet at www.uncitral.org).

CASE LAW ON ARTICLE 26

The arbitral tribunal may appoint experts—paragraph (1)*(a)*

1. Parties to arbitration have the primary duty to furnish evidence and introduce experts to assist the arbitral tribunal. Article 26 provides that, apart from party-appointed experts, the arbitral tribunal may also on its own motion initiate the appointment of experts to report to it on specific issues to be determined in the arbitration. This is a power granted to the arbitral tribunal and not an obligation for the arbitral tribunal to appoint an expert in all cases. In one case before the German court, the respondent objected that the arbitral tribunal did not possess the required knowledge of Italian patent law and therefore had a duty to call for a neutral expert opinion. That argument was rejected and the court held that the arbitral tribunal's refusal to appoint an expert did not violate the applicant's right to be heard (article 34 (2)*(a)*(iv) of the Model Law).[533] The court

[533] CLOUT case No. 375 [Bayerisches Oberstes Landesgericht, Germany, 4 Z Sch 23/99, 15 December 1999], also available on the Internet at http://www.dis-arb.de/de/47/datenbanken/rspr/bayoblg-az-4-z-sch-23-99-datum-1999-12-15-id16.

mentioned that, in the absence of any indication to the contrary, it had to be assumed that the arbitral tribunal had complied with its duty to hear all submissions by the parties and that a violation of the right to be heard could only be assumed under special circumstances.[534] Indian courts also underscore the non-mandatory nature of this provision clarifying that it is not an obligation for the arbitral tribunal to call for expert evidence, particularly in cases where the arbitrators themselves are experts in the field.[535]

2. When appointing a tribunal expert, it is advisable that the role and scope of the expert's duty in arbitral proceedings be clearly defined. In a Singapore case, a party attempted to set aside an arbitral award on the ground that the expert's involvement in the case went beyond what had been agreed upon. The applicant submitted that the expert performed tasks, which ought to have been carried out by the arbitral tribunal. The court refused this argument and held that "unless there was strong and unambiguous evidence of irregularity in the manner in which the arbitration was conducted, the integrity of the tribunal should not be questioned". The court emphasized that it would not permit parties to "mount what appeared to be a 'back-door' appeal by attacking the manner in which the tribunal had made use of [the expert] when there was no evidence but only speculation that [the expert] had overstepped his bounds."[536]

Arbitral tribunal expert may be examined at the hearing—paragraph (2)

3. Article 26 (2) of the Model Law makes provision for the possibility of hearing the expert's opinion and to put questions to him during the proceedings. Parties may also present their own expert witnesses. The right to comment on the report of the tribunal-appointed expert had been held to be a basic right by a Hong Kong court.[537]

---

[534] Ibid.

[535] *National Thermal Power Corporation Ltd. v. Wig Brothers Builders and Engineers Ltd.*, High Court of Delhi, India, 17 April 2009 [OMP 16/2003 [2009] INDLHC 1466], available on the Internet at http://indiankanoon.org/doc/1014298/.

[536] *Luzon Hydro Corp. v. Transfield Philippines Inc*, High Court, Singapore, 13 September 2004, [2004] SGHC 204.

[537] *Paklito Investment Limited v. Klockner East Asia Limited,* High Court—Court of First Instance, Hong Kong, 15 January 1993, [1993] 2 HKLR 39, available on the Internet at http://www.hklii.hk/eng/hk/cases/hkcfi/1993/147.html.

Article 27. Court assistance in taking evidence

The arbitral tribunal or a party with the approval of the arbitral tribunal may request from a competent court of this State assistance in taking evidence. The court may execute the request within its competence and according to its rules on taking evidence.

TRAVAUX PRÉPARATOIRES

The *travaux préparatoires* on article 27 as adopted in 1985 are contained in the following documents:

1. Report of the United Nations Commission on International Trade Law on the work of its eighteenth session (*Official Records of the General Assembly, Fortieth Session, Supplement No. 17* (A/40/17)), paras. 11-333.

2. Reports of the Working Group: A/CN.9/216; A/CN.9/233; A/CN.9/245; A/CN.9/246, annex; A/CN.9/263 and Add.1-2; A/CN.9/264. Relevant working papers are referred to in the reports.

3. Summary records of the 325th, 330th and 332nd UNCITRAL meetings.

Article 27 was not amended in 2006.

(Available on the Internet at www.uncitral.org).

INTRODUCTION

1. Because they draw their adjudicative powers from a contract, arbitrators can only issue orders directed at parties to the arbitration, and such orders—unlike orders made by courts—are not self-enforcing. Consequently, the powers enjoyed by arbitral tribunals in relation to the determination of the facts of a case are limited in two ways: first, they are powerless to order non-parties to provide evidence; second, the parties to the arbitral proceedings cannot be compelled by arbitral tribunals to comply with evidentiary orders made against them.[538] In order to ensure that these limitations on arbitral tribunals' powers will not prevent them from considering evidence relevant to the issues in dispute, article 27—like most modern statutes dealing with international commercial arbitration—allows courts to provide assistance in relation to evidentiary matters. Such assistance may be requested either by the arbitral tribunal itself, or by a party with the approval of the arbitral tribunal.

CASE LAW ON ARTICLE 27

Scope of application

2. As article 27 is not among the provisions listed in article 1 (2), it does not confer on local courts the power to provide assistance in evidentiary matters where the place of arbitration is either undetermined or located in a foreign jurisdiction.[539] This results from a clear policy choice to find a compromise between those in favour of international court assistance and those opposed to any provision on court assistance in evidentiary matters.[540] When article 27 was drafted, it was not contemplated that court assistance could be extended to international court assistance (i.e. assistance from a court "in a country other than the one where the arbitration took place"[541]). Article 27 "envisages neither assistance to foreign arbitrations nor requests to foreign courts in arbitral proceedings held under the Model

[538] *Jardine Lloyd Thompson Canada Inc. v. SJO Catlin*, Alberta Court of Appeal, Canada, 18 January 2006, [2006] ABCA 18 (CanLII), available on the Internet at http://canlii.ca/t/1mch7.

[539] *B.F. Jones Logistics Inc. v. Rolko*, Ontario Superior Court of Justice, Canada, 24 August 2004, [2004] CanLII 21276 (ON SC), available on the Internet at http://canlii.ca/t/1hqhz.

[540] A/CN.9/264, Analytical commentary on draft text of a model law on international commercial arbitration, under article 27, para. 4, available on the UNCITRAL website at http://www.uncitral.org/uncitral/en/commission/sessions/18th.html.

[541] A/CN.9/216, para. 61 *(b)*, Report of the Working Group on International Contract Practices on the work of its third session (New York, 16-26 February 1982), available on the UNCITRAL website at http://www.uncitral.org/uncitral/en/commission/sessions/15th.html. According to A/CN.9/245, para. 43, the Report of the Working Group on International Contract Practices on the work of its sixth session, available on the UNCITRAL website at http://www.uncitral.org/uncitral/en/commission/sessions/17th.html, the issue of international court assistance in taking evidence caused some difficulty as "an acceptable system of international court assistance could not be established unilaterally through a model law since the principle of reciprocity and bilaterally or multilaterally accepted procedural rules were essential conditions for the functioning of such a system."

Law."[542] In accordance with the strict wording of article 27, a Canadian court ruled that article 27 only covered requests for court assistance directed to the courts of the enacting State and did not authorize an arbitral tribunal to request court assistance from a court in another jurisdiction.[543] Likewise, article 27 would not apply to requests directed to a court of the enacting State from an arbitral tribunal having its place of arbitration in a different jurisdiction. Such issues of international court assistance are left to the domestic law of the enacting State. Another Canadian provincial court also held that it did not have jurisdiction to enforce a letter of request from a foreign private arbitral tribunal.[544]

3. Courts have begun to adopt a more liberal approach in respect of requests from foreign arbitral tribunals. The Supreme Court of Canada held that "the granting of an order for examination, being discretionary, will depend on the facts and particular circumstances of the individual case". Faced with an application for the enforcement of a letter of request by a foreign arbitral tribunal, the court or judge "must balance the possible infringement of Canadian sovereignty with a natural desire to assist the courts of justice of a foreign land."[545] More importantly, an Ontario court held that reciprocity is no longer a precondition for enforcement of such letters of request for judicial assistance.[546] Furthermore, it could be argued that since the principle according to which, in matters governed by the Model Law, courts shall not intervene except where so provided in the Model Law (article 5) is inapplicable where the place of arbitration is either undetermined or located in a foreign jurisdiction (article 1 (2)), the absence in article 27 of any reference to foreign arbitral tribunals should not be interpreted as preventing courts from providing assistance to such tribunals on the basis of local procedural rules.

Approval of the arbitral tribunal of a request made by a party

4. Article 27 permits court assistance in taking evidence if the arbitral tribunal, or a party with the approval of the arbitral tribunal, applies to the court for assistance in taking evidence. In one Indian case, the application to seek court's assistance in taking evidence failed on the ground that a party did not obtain the approval of the arbitral tribunal.[547] However, where the order of the arbitral tribunal was unclear, a court found, in another case, that approval of the arbitral tribunal under article 27 might be implied or inferred from the circumstances of the case. The court, however, added that where a party wished to seek a subpoena in aid of an arbitration, that party should obtain the express written approval of the arbitrator and thus would be in a position to show the court, if necessary, that such approval, as required by article 27, has been specifically provided.[548]

5. The power of the court to provide judicial assistance could be abused if the party seeking such assistance did so in contravention of the agreed procedure or the directions of the arbitral tribunal. In a Singapore case, a party applied for issuance of a subpoena to compel the person named to disclose documents or answer questions on documents, whereas the arbitral tribunal had earlier rejected such a request. The court application was rejected and the applicant was considered as having abused process.[549] The Singapore Court of Appeal in another case had also noted that "[i]t would be neither appropriate nor consonant for a dissatisfied party to seek the assistance of the court to intervene on the basis that the court is discharging an appellate function, save in the very limited circumstances that have been statutorily condoned."[550] (See also above, section on article 5, para. 6).

---

[542] A/CN. 9/264, Analytical commentary on draft text of a model law on international commercial arbitration, under article 27, para. 4, available on the UNCITRAL website at http://www.uncitral.org/uncitral/en/commission/sessions/18th.html.

[543] CLOUT case No. 391 [*Re Corporación Transnacional de Inversiones, S.A. de C.V. et al. v. STET International, S.p.A. et al.*, Ontario Superior Court of Justice, Canada, 22 September 1999], [1999] CanLII 14819 (ON SC), also available on the Internet at http://canlii.ca/t/1vvn5.

[544] *B.F. Jones Logistics Inc. v. Rolko*, Ontario Superior Court of Justice, Canada, 24 August 2004, [2004] CanLII 21276 (ON SC), also available on the Internet at http://canlii.ca/t/1hqhz.

[545] *Zingre v. The Queen et al.*, Supreme Court, Canada, 1981 CanLII 32 (SCC), [1981] 2 SCR 392, 28 September 1981, available on the Internet at http://canlii.ca/t/1mjlv.

[546] *Republic of France v. De Havilland Aircraft of Canada Ltd. and Byron-Exarcos,* Ontario Court of Appeal, Canada, (1991), 3 O.R. (3d) 705.

[547] *SH. Satinder Narayan Singh v. Indian Labour Cooperative Society Ltd. & Ors.*, High Court of Delhi India, 17 December 2007, OMP 471/2007 [2007] INDLHC 1462, 2008 (1) ARBLR 355 Delhi, available on the Internet at http://www.indiankanoon.org/doc/530842/.

[548] CLOUT case No. 77 [*Vibroflotation A.G. v. Express Builders Co. Ltd.*, High Court—Court of First Instance, Hong Kong, 15 August 1994], [1994] HKCFI 205, also available on the Internet at http://www.hklii.hk/eng/hk/cases/hkcfi/1994/205.html, (the court found evidence of the approval of the arbitral tribunal in the terms of a letter from the arbitral tribunal and in an order of the arbitral tribunal fixing a date for the production of such documents as might be ordered for production by the court).

[549] *ALC v. ALF,* High Court, Singapore, [2010] SGHC 231.

[550] CLOUT case No. 743 [*Soh Beng Tee & Co. Pte. Ltd. v. Fairmount Development Pte. Ltd.*, Court of Appeal, Singapore, 9 May 2007], [2007] 3 SLR (4) 86 at [60]; *Woh Hup Pte. Ltd. v. Lian Teck Construction Pte. Ltd.*, Court of Appeal, Singapore, 10 May 2005, [2005] SGCA 26, where it was noted that "any matter submitted to arbitration should, in general, and certainly wherever possible, be dealt with by the arbitral tribunal".

The court's discretion in deciding whether to execute the request

6. Article 27 is silent with respect to the court's role in determining whether it should exercise its discretion in favour of providing the assistance requested by the applicant. One question of practical importance is whether the court should review the relevance or usefulness of the evidence sought by the applicant. One court has ruled that such an inquiry would be inappropriate, "because the request issues from the arbitral tribunal itself or has the approval of the arbitral tribunal and the role of the court is merely to exercise for the arbitral tribunal the compulsion power which the arbitral tribunal may not have"[551] (see above, section on article 9, para. 9). A Canadian court stated that the purpose of article 27 is to assist the arbitral tribunal in its search for the truth. That court held that courts could assist an arbitral tribunal with obtaining examination for discovery evidence from third parties and that limiting the scope of examinations for discovery in arbitral proceedings cannot be justified on the basis that arbitration is not parallel to the court system.[552]

Article 27 in the context of pre-trial discovery or disclosure

7. Article 27 provides for judicial assistance in "taking evidence." It may be relied upon to seek the court's assistance to compel a person to produce evidence at the arbitral proceedings, during which the merits of the case are to be considered by the tribunal. However, an important question arises in jurisdictions where pre-trial discovery or disclosure is available, i.e., where local rules of procedure applicable in the context of judicial proceedings allow the parties to seek the court's assistance to compel a person, during the pre-trial phase, to provide documents, testimony, or other information that the parties may subsequently choose to produce as evidence at the trial: can such processes be said to relate to "taking evidence" within the meaning of article 27?

8. The question arose in an English case decided in 2003. While England is not considered as a Model Law jurisdiction, its law on arbitration was to a significant extent inspired by the Model Law. For that reason, the party seeking the court's assistance in that case argued that the relevant English provisions ought to be interpreted in light of article 27, which was said to be broad enough to allow courts to intervene in the context of pre-trial discovery or disclosure. However, the court found that the argument's premise was flawed, on the basis that article 27 "is dealing with the taking of evidence and not with the disclosure process" and that "[t]here is nothing in the Model Law which suggests that the Court should assist with the process of disclosure."[553]

9. In another case, a Canadian appellate court explicitly disagreed with that English decision and concluded that article 27 was broad enough to contemplate judicial assistance sought in the context of pre-trial discovery or disclosure. Relying on domestic precedents tending to show that the concept of "evidence" includes both evidence produced at trial and evidence obtained through pre-trial discovery, the court pointed out that article 27 "speaks of assistance in taking evidence," that it would be inappropriate "to add, by implication or otherwise, the words 'at the hearing,'" and that "[i]f the drafters of Article 27 had intended that assistance would only be given for taking evidence at the hearing, they could have expressly said so."[554]

10. Finally, a Hong Kong decision dating from 1994 may also be interpreted as implicitly standing for the proposition that article 27 can be relied upon in the context of pre-trial discovery or disclosure. The applicant, while pursuing discovery in relation to the arbitration, sought the court's assistance under article 27 to obtain potentially-relevant documents from a person who was not a party to the arbitration. While the application was ultimately dismissed, the court did so not because it considered that article 27 did not allow it to intervene in the context of pre-trial discovery or disclosure, but rather because the local rules of civil procedure invoked by the applicant were held not to allow discovery to be obtained against non-parties.[555]

---

[551] CLOUT case No. 68 [*Delphi Petroleum Inc. v. Derin Shipping and Training Ltd.*, Federal Court—Trial Division, Canada, 3 December 1993].

[552] *Jardine Lloyd Thompson Canada Inc. v. Western Oil Sands Inc,* Alberta Court of Appeal, Canada, 21 December 2006, [2006] ABQB 933 (CanLII), available on the Internet at http://canlii.ca/t/1q6bh.

[553] *BNP Paribas and others v. Deloitte and Touche LLP,* Commercial Court, England, 28 November 2003, [2003] EWHC 2874 (Comm).

[554] *Jardine Lloyd Thompson Canada Inc. v. SJO Catlin*, Alberta Court of Appeal, Canada, 18 January 2006, [2006] ABCA 18 (CanLII), available on the Internet at http://canlii.ca/t/1mch7.

[555] CLOUT case No. 77 [High Court—Court of First Instance, Hong Kong, *Vibroflotation A.G. v. Express Builders Co. Ltd.*, 15 August 1994], [1994] HKCFI 205, also available on the Internet at http://www.hklii.hk/eng/hk/cases/hkcfi/1994/205.html.

CHAPTER VI. MAKING OF AWARD AND TERMINATION OF PROCEEDINGS

Article 28. Rules applicable to substance of dispute

(1) The arbitral tribunal shall decide the dispute in accordance with such rules of law as are chosen by the parties as applicable to the substance of the dispute. Any designation of the law or legal system of a given State shall be construed, unless otherwise expressed, as directly referring to the substantive law of that State and not to its conflict of laws rules.

(2) Failing any designation by the parties, the arbitral tribunal shall apply the law determined by the conflict of laws rules which it considers applicable.

(3) The arbitral tribunal shall decide ex aequo et bono *or as amiable compositeur only if the parties have expressly authorized it to do so.*

(4) In all cases, the arbitral tribunal shall decide in accordance with the terms of the contract and shall take into account the usages of the trade applicable to the transaction.

TRAVAUX PRÉPARATOIRES

The *travaux préparatoires* on article 28 as adopted in 1985 are contained in the following documents:

1. Report of the United Nations Commission on International Trade Law on the work of its eighteenth session (*Official Records of the General Assembly, Fortieth Session, Supplement No. 17* (A/40/17)), paras. 11-333.

2. Reports of the Working Group: A/CN.9/216; A/CN.9/232; A/CN.9/245; A/CN.9/246, annex; A/CN.9/263 and Add.1-2; A/CN.9/264. Relevant working papers are referred to in the reports.

3. Summary records of the 326th, 327th and 333rd UNCITRAL meetings.

Article 28 was not amended in 2006.

(Available on the Internet at www.uncitral.org).

INTRODUCTION

1. Article 28 deals with the determination of the rules of law governing the substance of the dispute. Under paragraph (1), the arbitral tribunal decides the dispute in accordance with the rules of law chosen by the parties. This provision is significant in two respects. It grants the parties the freedom to choose the applicable substantive law, which is important where the national law does not clearly or fully recognize that right. In addition, by referring to the choice of "rules of law" instead of "law", the Model Law broadens the range of options available to the parties as regards the designation of the law applicable to the substance of the dispute. For example, parties may agree on rules of law that have been elaborated by an international forum but have not yet been incorporated into any national legal system. Parties could also choose directly an instrument such as the United Nations Convention on Contracts for the International Sale of Goods (Vienna, 1980) as the body of substantive law governing the arbitration, without having to refer to the national law of any State party to that Convention. The power of the arbitral tribunal, on the other hand, follows more traditional lines. When the parties have not chosen the applicable law, the arbitral tribunal shall apply the law (i.e., the national law) determined by the conflict-of-laws rules that it considers applicable.

2. Article 28 (3) recognizes that the parties may authorize the arbitral tribunal to decide the dispute *ex aequo et bono* or as amiable compositeur. This type of arbitration (where the arbitral tribunal may decide the dispute on the basis of principles it believes to be just, without having to refer to any particular body of law) is currently not known or used in all legal systems. The Model Law does not intend to regulate this area. It simply calls the attention of the parties on the need to provide clarification in the arbitration agreement and specifically to empower the arbitral tribunal. However, paragraph (4) makes it clear that in all cases where the

dispute relates to a contract (including arbitration *ex aequo et bono*) the arbitral tribunal must decide in accordance with the terms of the contract and shall take into account the usages of the trade applicable to the transaction.

CASE LAW ON ARTICLE 28

Rules of law chosen by the parties—paragraph (1)

3. A failure of the arbitral tribunal to decide in accordance with the substantive law chosen by the parties may lead to the challenge of the award or application to set aside the award by an unsuccessful party. German courts clarified that article 28 (1) permits a court only to consider if the award was based on the law chosen by the parties, and not whether the arbitral tribunal had misinterpreted or misapplied the law to the substance of the dispute.[556]

Decisions *ex aequo et bono* or as amiable compositeur—paragraph (3)

4. Article 28 (3) requires that parties expressly authorize the arbitral tribunal to decide a case *ex aequo et bono* or as *amiable compositeur*. A Canadian court considered that such express authorization was given if the arbitration agreement in a contract required the contract to be interpreted as an "honourable agreement", i.e. a non-legally binding mutual understanding between the parties, and if the arbitration agreement stated that the arbitral tribunal was to be relieved of all judicial formalities in coming to a decision.[557] Another Canadian court held that the failure to provide reasons for the award did not mean that the case had been decided *ex aequo et bono*.[558]

Arbitral tribunal shall take into account the terms of contract and trade usages—paragraph (4)

5. Paragraph (4) emphasizes that the provision applies "in all cases". This means that the freedom granted to the arbitral tribunal to make an award *ex aequo et bono* or act as *amiable compositeur* in paragraph (3), is subject to the requirement of paragraph (4).[558]

Terms of the contract

6. A Canadian court of appeal ruled that the arbitrator acting as *amiable compositeur* should find a way to reconcile the terms of a contract with good faith in its performance. It may mitigate the strict enforcement of the rights flowing from the contract but not substantially rewrite the contract or strike clauses therefrom.[560] Another court similarly decided that it would go too far to impose arbitration terms found in one contract on three separate, although related, contracts between the parties.[561]

Trade usages

7. The term "trade usages" has been held to include norms contained in published instruments representing best practices and accepted norms of industry or trade. In a case before the Supreme Court of Switzerland, although the parties' choice of law referred to the laws of Switzerland, the arbitral tribunal drew from the practice prevailing under the United Nations Convention on Contracts for the International Sale of Goods (Vienna, 1980) and the 2004 UNIDROIT Principles of International Commercial Contracts. The Supreme Court rejected the challenge against the award, ruling that such references to transnational rules were reasonable especially when the parties have a longstanding international commercial relationship.[562]

8. A Canadian court clarified in one case that the reference to trade usages in paragraph (4) applies only to the arbitral tribunal's decision on the substance of the dispute and could not be used to ascertain whether the arbitration agreement was applicable to the dispute in the first instance.[563]

---

[556] CLOUT case No. 375 [Bayerisches Oberstes Landesgericht, Germany, 4 Z Sch 23/99, 15 December 1999], also available on the Internet at http://www.dis-arb.de/de/47/datenbanken/rspr/bayoblg-az-4-z-sch-23-99-datum-1999-12-15-id16; CLOUT case No. 569 [Hanseatisches Oberlandesgericht Hamburg, Germany, 11 Sch 01/01, 8 June 2001], also available on the Internet at http://www.dis-arb.de/de/47/datenbanken/rspr/hanseat-olg-hamburg-az-11-sch-01-01-datum-2001-06-08-id1274.

[557] CLOUT case No. 507 [*Liberty Reinsurance Canada v. QBE Insurance and Reinsurance (Europe) Ltd.,* Ontario Superior Court of Justice, Canada, 20 September 2002], [2002] CanLII 6636 (ON SC), also available on the Internet at http://canlii.ca/t/1cnp1.

[558] CLOUT case No. 351 [*Food Services of America Inc. (c.o.b. Amerifresh) v. Pan Pacific Specialties Ltd.,* Supreme Court of British Columbia, Canada, 24 March 1997], 32 B.C.L.R. (3d) 225, [1997] CanLII 3604 (BC SC), also available on the Internet at http://canlii.ca/t/1f3zp.

[559] Explanatory Note by the UNCITRAL Secretariat on the Model Law on International Commercial Arbitration, in UNCITRAL Model Law on International Commercial Arbitration 1985, with amendments as adopted in 2006, United Nations publication, Sales No. E.08.V.4 (available on the Internet at http://www.uncitral.org/pdf/english/texts/arbitration/ml-arb/07-86998_Ebook.pdf), Part Two, at para. 36.

[560] *Coderre v. Coderre,* Montreal Court of Appeal, Canada, 13 May 2008, [2008] QCCA 888 (CanLII), available on the Internet at http://canlii.ca/t/1wx0p.

[561] CLOUT case No. 1049 [*Louis Dreyfus, S.A.S. v. Holding Tusculum, B.V.,* Superior Court of Quebec, Canada, 8 December 2008], [2008] QCCS 5903, also available on the Internet at http://canlii.ca/t/21v03.

[562] Federal Supreme Court, Switzerland, 16 December 2009, Decision 4A_240/2009.

[563] CLOUT case No. 507 [*Liberty Reinsurance Canada v. QBE Insurance and Reinsurance (Europe) Ltd.,* Ontario Superior Court of Justice, Canada, 20 September 2002], [2002] CanLII 6636 (ON SC), also available on the Internet at http://canlii.ca/t/1cnp1.

Article 29. Decision-making by panel of arbitrators

In arbitral proceedings with more than one arbitrator, any decision of the arbitral tribunal shall be made, unless otherwise agreed by the parties, by a majority of all its members. However, questions of procedure may be decided by a presiding arbitrator, if so authorized by the parties or all members of the arbitral tribunal.

TRAVAUX PRÉPARATOIRES

The *travaux préparatoires* on article 29 as adopted in 1985 are contained in the following documents:

1. Report of the United Nations Commission on International Trade Law on the work of its eighteenth session (*Official Records of the General Assembly, Fortieth Session, Supplement No. 17* (A/40/17)), paras. 11-333.
2. Reports of the Working Group: A/CN.9/216; A/CN.9/232; A/CN.9/245; A/CN.9/246, annex; A/CN.9/263 and Add.1-2; A/CN.9/264. Relevant working papers are referred to in the reports.
3. Summary records of the 327th and 333rd UNCITRAL meetings.

Article 29 was not amended in 2006.

(Available on the Internet at www.uncitral.org).

CASE LAW ON ARTICLE 29

1. Article 29 provides that all decisions to be made by the arbitral tribunal shall be by a majority vote of its members. The parties may agree that the tribunal adopts a different method of decision-making. It also points to the difference in treatment between matters concerning the substance of the dispute and matters of a procedural nature.

2. There is no case law reported on article 29.

Article 30. Settlement

(1) If, during arbitral proceedings, the parties settle the dispute, the arbitral tribunal shall terminate the proceedings and, if requested by the parties and not objected to by the arbitral tribunal, record the settlement in the form of an arbitral award on agreed terms.

(2) An award on agreed terms shall be made in accordance with the provisions of article 31 and shall state that it is an award. Such an award has the same status and effect as any other award on the merits of the case.

TRAVAUX PRÉPARATOIRES

The *travaux préparatoires* on article 30 as adopted in 1985 are contained in the following documents:

1. Report of the United Nations Commission on International Trade Law on the work of its eighteenth session (*Official Records of the General Assembly, Fortieth Session, Supplement No. 17* (A/40/17)), paras. 11-333.

2. Reports of the Working Group: A/CN.9/216; A/CN.9/232; A/CN.9/245; A/CN.9/246, annex; A/CN.9/263 and Add.1-2; A/CN.9/264. Relevant working papers are referred to in the reports.

3. Summary records of the 328th and 333rd UNCITRAL meetings.

Article 30 was not amended in 2006.

(Available on the Internet at www.uncitral.org).

INTRODUCTION

1. An agreement reached on the issues in dispute in the course of the arbitration may be recorded by the arbitral tribunal as an award on agreed terms. This is often referred to as an award by consent or a "consent award". Article 30 does not empower an arbitral tribunal nor prevent it from initiating or being engaged in any settlement process; such a role will depend on the law or procedure agreed to by the parties.

CASE LAW ON ARTICLE 30

Settlement of dispute during arbitral proceedings—paragraph (1)

2. Article 30 only applies if arbitral proceedings have commenced and the final award has yet to be made. Where a full and final settlement of any claim has been reached *before* arbitral proceedings have commenced, a dispute no longer subsists to be referred to arbitration.[564] It follows that such an agreed settlement may not be made in the form of an award under article 30. However, some States have, in their legislation enacting the Model Law, extended that article to include a settlement agreement reached in the course of conciliation/mediation proceedings to be made in the form of an arbitral award.[565] In contrast, where the parties have commenced the arbitral proceedings and subsequently enter into a settlement agreement (prior to oral hearing), the dispute over the existence of a settlement agreement still falls under the jurisdiction of the arbitral tribunal.[566]

3. In one case, an arbitral tribunal had allowed a request by parties to reopen hearings, even after the hearings had closed, for the purpose of recording the terms of a settlement agreement and to make it in the form of an arbitral award on agreed terms.[567]

Form, content and status of an award on agreed terms—paragraph (2)

4. Courts have strictly upheld the formal requirements for enforcing an award on agreed terms. German courts con-

[564] *Nathani Steels Ltd. v. Associated Construction,* Supreme Court, India, [1995 Supp (3) SCC 324].

[565] See for instance: India, Section 73-74, The Arbitration and Conciliation Act, 1996.

[566] *Doshion Ltd. v. Sembawang Engineers and Constructors Pte. Ltd.,* High Court, Singapore [2011] SGHC 46.

[567] CLOUT case No. 779 [*Ad hoc* arbitration hosted by the Cairo Regional Center for International Commercial Arbitration, Egypt, 17 February 2006].

cluded that only a settlement agreement, which had been recorded in the form of an arbitral award on agreed terms pursuant to the formal requirements of paragraph (2) and which stated that it was an award on its face, could be declared enforceable under article 36 of the Model Law. A mere record of the settlement is insufficient.[568]

Settlement tainted by way of fraud, duress, illegality

5. In one case, certain insurers had offered, and the insured had accepted, a payout "in full and final settlement" of its claim. The commencement of arbitration by the insured was resisted on the ground that the contract of insurance that included the arbitration clause had come to an end upon the settlement. The court held that any question as to whether the parties had reached the settlement willingly or had done so under some coercion or undue influence would have to be decided in separate proceedings and not be treated as part of the subject matter of arbitration.[569] A German court also distinguished between the terms of the underlying settlement agreement and the award made pursuant to such agreement. In that case, the price of the shares to be transferred under the settlement agreement was to be based on an audited balance sheet. The transferee of the shares subsequently alleged that the price paid was based on a falsified balance sheet and sought to nullify the award. The court held that the fact that settlement agreement is void and null would not automatically invalidate the award. The validity of the consent award would be determined in proceedings under article 34 or 36 of the Model Law.[570]

6. It was held in a court decision that not every agreement reached in conciliation or mediation process in the course of arbitral process should be accorded the status of a consent award. The discretion to record such an agreement as an award lies with the arbitral tribunal. An arbitral tribunal should object to doing so if fraud is suspected or if third parties' interests are affected.[571]

---

[568] Oberlandesgericht Frankfurt a.M., Germany, 3 Sch 01/99, 28 June 1999, available on the Internet at http://www.dis-arb.de/en/47/datenbanken/rspr/olg-frankfurt-am-case-no-3-sch-01-99-date-1999-06-28-id49; Oberlandesgericht Frankfurt a.M., Germany, 20 Sch 01/02, 14 March 2003, where the formal requirements applicable to an award on agreed terms were not fulfilled as the settlement did not have the form of an arbitral award, available on the Internet at http://www.dis-arb.de/en/47/datenbanken/rspr/olg-frankfurt-am-case-no-20-sch-01-02-date-2003-03-14-id240.

[569] *Polytron & Fragrance Industries Limited v. National Insurance Co. Limited*, Delhi High Court, India, 27 April 2009, ARB. P. 144/2008, available on the Internet at http://www.indiankanoon.org/doc/1343969/.

[570] CLOUT case No. 407 [Bundesgerichtshof, Germany, III ZB 55/99, 2 November 2000], also available on the Internet at http://www.dis-arb.de/en/47/datenbanken/rspr/bgh-case-no-iii-zb-55-99-date-2000-11-02-id2.

[571] For instance, where a controlling shareholder commenced arbitration against the subsidiary and then influenced the subsidiary to agree not to contest the merits of the claim: See *Kiyue Co. Ltd. v. Aquagen International Pte. Ltd.*, High Court, Singapore, [2003] 3 SLR 130. Although this case was argued on the basis that a minority shareholder of the subsidiary should be given the right to intervene in the arbitration, the scheme to defraud third parties was not lost to the judge when he observed "It is manifestly wrong for a controlling shareholder to sue its subsidiary and then order it not to defend. On this fact alone, equity is against it. And that is not all. It appears that the company had received legal advice to the effect that the claim ought to be resisted."

Article 31. Form and contents of award

(1) The award shall be made in writing and shall be signed by the arbitrator or arbitrators. In arbitral proceedings with more than one arbitrator, the signatures of the majority of all members of the arbitral tribunal shall suffice, provided that the reason for any omitted signature is stated.

(2) The award shall state the reasons upon which it is based, unless the parties have agreed that no reasons are to be given or the award is an award on agreed terms under article 30.

(3) The award shall state its date and the place of arbitration as determined in accordance with article 20 (1). The award shall be deemed to have been made at that place.

(4) After the award is made, a copy signed by the arbitrators in accordance with paragraph (1) of this article shall be delivered to each party.

Travaux préparatoires

The *travaux préparatoires* on article 31 as adopted in 1985 are contained in the following documents:

1. Report of the United Nations Commission on International Trade Law on the work of its eighteenth session (*Official Records of the General Assembly, Fortieth Session, Supplement No. 17* (A/40/17)), paras. 11-333.

2. Reports of the Working Group: A/CN.9/216; A/CN.9/232; A/CN.9/245; A/CN.9/246, annex; A/CN.9/263 and Add.1-2; A/CN.9/264. Relevant working papers are referred to in the reports.

3. Summary records of the 328th, 329th and 333rd UNCITRAL meetings.

Article 31 was not amended in 2006.

(Available on the Internet at www.uncitral.org).

INTRODUCTION

1. Article 31 deals with the form and contents of award. The arbitral award must be in writing and state its date. It must also state the reasons on which it is based, unless the parties have agreed otherwise or the award is "on agreed terms" (i.e., an award that records the terms of an amicable settlement by the parties). It may be added that the Model Law neither requires nor prohibits "dissenting opinions". Article 31 (3) provides that the award shall state the place of arbitration and shall be deemed to have been made at that place. The effect of the deeming provision is to emphasize that the final making of the award constitutes a legal act, which in practice does not necessarily coincide with one factual event. For the same reason that the arbitral proceedings do not need to be carried out at the place designated as the legal "place of arbitration" (see above, section on article 20, paras. 8 and 9), the making of the award may be completed through deliberations held at various places, by telephone or correspondence. In addition, the award does not have to be signed by the arbitrators physically gathering at the same place.

CASE LAW ON ARTICLE 31

Definition of an "award"

2. The term "award" is not defined in the Model Law. Canadian courts have held that the term connotes the decision of an arbitral tribunal that "disposes of part or all of the disputes between the parties".[572] An arbitrator's decision concerning the admissibility of evidence[573] and an order for

[572] *Inforica Inc. v. CGI Information Systems & Management Consultants Inc., Ontario* Court of Appeal, Canada, 11 September 2009, [2009] ONCA 642 (Ont. C.A.), available on the Internet at http://canlii.ca/t/25ls0, citing with approval the decision in *Environmental Export International of Canada Inc. v. Success International Inc.*

[573] *Slocan Forest Products Ltd. v. Skeena Cellulose Inc.*, Supreme Court of British Columbia, Canada, 7 August 2001, [2001] BCSC 1156 (CanLII), available on the Internet at http://canlii.ca/t/4x01.

security for costs[574] were held to be procedural rulings and not awards. However, a decision by an arbitrator declining jurisdiction was held by a court to be an interim award affecting the substantive rights of the parties, even though it may be technically a "procedural" order.[575]

3. The presence of the formal requirements has served as an indication that a decision that could have been construed as an expert determination was actually an arbitral award. A German court had to determine whether a decision made in the form of an "expert opinion-arbitral award" was an award or an expert opinion. The court considered not only the form and title of the document but the nature and effect of the decision. Although presented as an "expert opinion", the decision was final, binding, and enforceable and expressly excluded any review of the merits by the courts. Therefore, the court concluded that the decision was an award and not an expert opinion.[576]

Award in writing, signed by arbitrator(s)—paragraph (1)

4. The requirement for the arbitrators to sign the award has been interpreted by the Netherlands Supreme Court to be a strict one. An award in that case was set aside even though it was signed by two of the three arbitrators. In that case, the third arbitrator was unable to attend the deliberations for medical reasons and was not involved in the making of the award. He gave a dissenting opinion which was attached to the award signed by the two arbitrators. The court held that the signature of all three arbitrators was a mandatory requirement and the dissenting opinion of an arbitrator who did not sign the award did not form part of that award, in particular as the dissenting arbitrator was not involved in the making of the award. The simultaneous transmission of the award and the dissenting opinion was not sufficient to make the dissenting opinion a part of the award.[577]

5. A Canadian court however took a more flexible approach and did not set aside an award despite a signature having been omitted but the court accepted the explanation given to it by the presiding arbitrator.[578]

6. Caution was expressed by a German court when dealing with the situation of an absent or non-participating arbitrator. In that case, the refusal by an arbitrator to participate in the decision-making led the other two arbitrators to notify the parties that they would be proceeding to make the decision without that arbitrator. The award was made by the two arbitrators the next day after that notice was given. The court set aside the award on the ground that the composition of the arbitral tribunal or the arbitration procedure was not in accordance with the agreement of the parties under article 34 (2)*(a)*(iv). The court reasoned that the arbitral tribunal should give the parties adequate notice in advance of its intention to make an award without the involvement of an obstructing arbitrator so as to provide them with the opportunity to attempt to persuade such arbitrator to cooperate or, alternatively, to terminate his or her mandate. In that case, a one day notice was too short.[579]

The arbitral award must state reasons—paragraph (2)

7. Failure by the arbitral tribunal to comply with paragraph (2) and to state reasons for its decision has been used as a ground to set aside the award, or refuse enforcement. A German Court has considered that an award should be set aside only if the arbitral tribunal fails to state the reasons on which the award was based, or the reasoning lacks any substance, and is evidently paradoxical or conflicts with the decision made.[580] (See below, section on article 34, paras. 116-120, and section on article 36, para. 42).

8. In the Netherlands, a court suggested that, in order for lack of reasoning to constitute a ground for setting aside an award, the reasoning must have been so incorrect that it constitutes a failure to explain the award.[581] An Indian court took the view that an award which had stated that the arbitral tribunal had taken into consideration the disputes, claims

---

[574] *Inforica Inc. v. CGI Information Systems & Management Consultants Inc.,* Ontario Court of Appeal, Canada, 11 September 2009, [2009] ONCA 642 (Ont. C.A.), available on the Internet at http://canlii.ca/t/25ls0.

[575] *Premium Brands Operating GP Inc. v. Turner Distribution Systems Ltd.,* Supreme Court of British Columbia, Canada, 1 March 2010, [2010] BCSC 258 (CanLII), available on the Internet at http://canlii.ca/t/28c6m.

[576] CLOUT case No. 664 [Oberlandesgericht Stuttgart, Germany, 1 Sch 21/01, 23 January 2002], also available on the Internet at http://www.dis-arb.de/en/47/datenbanken/rspr/olg-stuttgart-case-no-1-sch-21-01-date-2002-01-23-id171.

[577] *Bursa Büyüksehir Belediyesi v. Güris Insaat VE Mühendislik AS*, Hoge Raad, Netherlands, 5 December 2008, C07/166HR.

[578] CLOUT case No. 12 [*D. Frampton & Co. Ltd. v. Sylvio Thibeault and Navigation Harvey & Frères Inc.,* Federal Court, Trial Division, Canada, 7 April 1988].

[579] CLOUT case No. 662 [Saarländisches Oberlandesgericht, Germany, 4 Sch 02/02, 29 October 2002], also available on the Internet at http://www.dis-arb.de/en/47/datenbanken/rspr/saarländisches-olg-case-no-4-sch-02-02-date-2002-10-29-id200.

[580] CLOUT case No. 569 [Hanseatisches Oberlandesgericht Hamburg, Germany, 11 Sch 01/01, 8 June 2001], also available on the Internet at http://www.dis-arb.de/de/47/datenbanken/rspr/hanseat-olg-hamburg-az-11-sch-01-01-datum-2001-06-08-id1274. The court in that case did not set aside the award as it was satisfied that no such bases existed.

[581] *AZ NV. v. N.N.* (*Nomen Nescio*), Hoge Raad, Netherlands, 8 January 2010, BK 6056, Hoge Raad, 08/02129.

and counterclaims and then simply recorded its findings on each disputed item without any further explanation, had failed to make an award with "reasons".[582]

9. Expressing reasons in commercial terms, as opposed to legal terms, has been held to be adequate. In a case before a Canadian court, the arbitral tribunal had examined the issues raised and specified the facts and contractual provisions upon which its findings were based in the arbitral award. The court observed that it did not matter that the award was expressed in commercial as opposed to legal terms, particularly where the parties chose to select arbitrators with a commercial and not a legal background.[583] An Australian court adopted the view that the standard of reasoning should be the same as for court judgments[584] while another rejected the view that the reasons given must meet the standard applicable to judges.[585]

10. An award which lacked reasons could also be held not to constitute an award at all. The Tunisian Court of Cassation set aside an award because the reasons given were contradictory and therefore were to be considered non-existing.[586]

Award must state its date and place of arbitration—paragraph (3)

11. A court considered that, where it was otherwise possible to establish where the award was made, failure of an arbitral tribunal to state the place of arbitration in the award as required in article 31 (3) would not render the award invalid.[587] Where the place of arbitration was neither agreed upon by the parties nor determined by the arbitral tribunal as required by article 20 (1), a German court concluded that the place of arbitration should be the effective place of arbitration or, if this cannot be determined, the place of the last oral hearing[588] (see above, section on article 20, para. 7).

Signed copy of award to be delivered to each party—paragraph (4)

12. Paragraph (4) requires that the arbitral tribunal completes the making of the award by the delivery of the award to the parties. Most arbitral institutions administering cases will perform this obligation for the arbitrators.[589] For the purposes of determining whether an arbitral award had been properly delivered under this provision, it has been held that the "delivery" and "receipt" of the award were governed by the provision in the law enacting article 3 of the Model Law, and not by other rules of domestic law relating to the service of judicial documents.[590] (See also above, section on article 3, para. 2). Notification should be sent by registered mail with acknowledgement of receipt only after attempt has been made to notify in person or by courier or electronic communications and where, following reasonable enquiry, the addressee's domicile, habitual place of residence or place of business could not be found.

---

[582] *Gora Lal v. Union Of India,* Supreme Court, India 18 December 2003 (2003) 12 SCC 459, available on the Internet at http://www.indiankanoon.org/doc/1255521/.

[583] CLOUT case No. 10 [*Navigation Sonamar Inc. v. Algoma Steamships Limited and others,* Superior Court of Quebec, Canada, 16 April 1987].

[584] *Oil Basins Ltd. v. BHP Billiton Ltd.,* Victoria Court of Appeal, Australia, 16 November 2007, [2007] VSCA 255, available on the Internet at http://www.austlii.edu.au/au/cases/vic/VSCA/2007/255.html.

[585] *Gordian Runoff Ltd. v. Westport Insurance Corporation,* Court of Appeal of New South Wales, Australia, 1 April 2010, [2010] NSWCA 57 at paras. [217-218], available on the Internet at http://www.austlii.edu.au/au/cases/nsw/NSWCA/2010/57.html.

[586] Court of Cassation, Tunisia, 27 November 2008, case No. 20596/2007.

[587] CLOUT case No. 664 [Oberlandesgericht Stuttgart, Germany, 1 Sch 22/01, 4 June 2002], also available on the Internet at http://www.dis-arb.de/ende/47/datenbanken/rspr/olg-stuttgart-case-noaz-1-sch-2122-01-datedatum-2002-01-23-id17106-04-id232.

[588] CLOUT case No. 374 (also reproduced under CLOUT case No. 408) [Oberlandesgericht Düsseldorf, Germany, 6 Sch 02/99, 23 March 2000], also available on the Internet at http://www.dis-arb.de/de/47/datenbanken/rspr/olg-düsseldorf-az-6-sch-02-99-datum-2000-03-23-id46, in an action to set aside an arbitral award under article 34, where the arbitrator had failed to state the place of arbitration in the award, the court found that the place of arbitration was the actual, effective place of the arbitration, and not simply the address on the award.

[589] See for instance: article 34 (1) of the 2012 ICC Arbitration Rules; Rule 28.6 of the Rules of the Singapore International Arbitration Centre (SIAC), 2010; article 26.5 Rules of the London Court of International Arbitration (LCIA), 1998; article 27 (5) of the International Arbitration Rules of the American Arbitration Association (AAA), 2009.

[590] CLOUT case No. 29 [*Kanto Yakin Kogyo Kabushiki-Kaisha v. Can-Eng Manufacturing Ltd.,* Ontario Court of Justice, Canada, 30 January 1992], where the court rejected the argument that the delivery of an arbitral award should be made in accordance with the Hague Convention on the Service Abroad of Judicial and Extrajudicial Documents in Civil or Commercial Matters (1965).

Article 32. Termination of proceedings

(1) The arbitral proceedings are terminated by the final award or by an order of the arbitral tribunal in accordance with paragraph (2) of this article.

(2) The arbitral tribunal shall issue an order for the termination of the arbitral proceedings when:

(a) the claimant withdraws his claim, unless the respondent objects thereto and the arbitral tribunal recognizes a legitimate interest on his part in obtaining a final settlement of the dispute;

(b) the parties agree on the termination of the proceedings;

(c) the arbitral tribunal finds that the continuation of the proceedings has for any other reason become unnecessary or impossible.

(3) The mandate of the arbitral tribunal terminates with the termination of the arbitral proceedings, subject to the provisions of articles 33 and 34 (4).

TRAVAUX PRÉPARATOIRES

The *travaux préparatoires* on article 32 as adopted in 1985 are contained in the following documents:

1. Report of the United Nations Commission on International Trade Law on the work of its eighteenth session (*Official Records of the General Assembly, Fortieth Session, Supplement No. 17* (A/40/17)), paras. 11-333.

2. Reports of the Working Group: A/CN.9/232; A/CN.9/245; A/CN.9/246, annex; A/CN.9/263 and Add.1-2; A/CN.9/264. Relevant working papers are referred to in the reports.

3. Summary records of the 329th and 333rd UNCITRAL meetings.

Article 32 was not amended in 2006.

(Available on the Internet at www.uncitral.org).

INTRODUCTION

1. Article 32 provides that the arbitration terminates either on the issuance of the final award in the arbitration or by an order made by the tribunal in accordance with the conditions set out in paragraph 2. The mandate of the arbitral tribunal terminates with the termination of the arbitration.

CASE LAW ON ARTICLE 32

Termination of the arbitral proceedings by the final award—paragraph (1)

2. Paragraph (1) provides that a final award will terminate the arbitral proceedings. A question is then raised as to what constitutes a "final award". A Singapore court has suggested that a "final award" was one that completes the disposition of "all matters that the arbitral tribunal was expected to decide", including the question of costs.[591] This

[591] *Tang Boon Jek Jeffrey v. Tan Poh Leng Stanley*, Court of Appeal, Singapore, 22 June 2001, [2001] 3 SLR 237, where the court in that case had, in its reasoning, confused between the term "final" (as being chronologically the "last") award in the arbitration and the finality of awards made. The effect of that decision was remedied by legislation: new section 19B(2) was added in 2001 to the Singapore International Arbitration Act to provide that "(2) Except as provided in Articles 33 and 34 (4) of the Model Law, upon an award being made, including an award made in accordance with section 19A, the arbitral tribunal shall not vary, amend, correct, review, add to or revoke the award."

view on what constitutes a "final award" is consistent with that of a Canadian court in a case concerning an issue of pre-judgment interest. In that case, the arbitrator having already delivered the "final" award dealing with income tax matters and costs between the parties was subsequently asked to make a further award on pre-judgment interest. The arbitrator did so as he considered that his mandate had not been terminated. The court upheld the additional award.[592]

Termination of the arbitral proceedings by claimant's withdrawal of claim—paragraph (2)*(a)*

3. The claimant being the party which has commenced the arbitration has the liberty to withdraw its claim against the respondent. The respondent may object to the withdrawal if it has a legitimate interest to see the final resolution of the matters in dispute. A court in Cyprus considered that the courts do not have jurisdiction to review an arbitrator's decision to terminate proceedings on the ground of the claimants' failure to submit their statement of claim within a determined period of time.[593]

Termination of the arbitral proceedings by agreement between the parties—paragraph (2)*(b)*

4. The right of the parties to mutually agree to terminate arbitral proceedings has been expressly recognized by a German court. In that case, the court ruled that a tribunal's order that proceedings had terminated by failure of the parties to pursue the proceedings any further was redundant when the proceedings had already been terminated by an agreement between the parties. Parties may also agree that the arbitral proceedings must be completed within a determined period of time.[594] An Indian court held that the mandate of the arbitral tribunal would be automatically terminated upon the expiry of the agreed period of time for making the award, unless such period would be extended.[595]

Termination of the arbitral proceedings by finding that continuation of proceedings have become unnecessary or impossible—paragraph (2)*(c)*

5. The tribunal has an independent power to terminate the arbitration if it finds that continuation of the proceedings is unnecessary or impossible. An arbitral tribunal invoked that provision and terminated the proceedings when a change in the ownership of the respondent company led it to believe that the respondent was no longer a party to the arbitration. As the respondent company's new owners had not participated in the appointment of the arbitral tribunal, the tribunal considered that the continuation of the arbitration was impossible. Neither party objected to the termination.[596]

Mandate of the arbitral tribunal terminates with the termination of arbitral proceedings—paragraph (3)

6. According to court decisions, upon the termination of the mandate of the arbitral tribunal, the tribunal's jurisdiction over the parties and the arbitration cease. It has no power to reopen the case or make any other award, with a view to recall or revise the earlier award.[597] This limitation is nevertheless subject to the residual power to make corrections, interpretations or an additional award under article 33.

---

[592] *Maruna v. Lopatka,* Supreme Court of British Columbia, Canada, 19 July 2002, [2002] BCSC 1084 (CanLII), available on the Internet at http://canlii.ca/t/582c.

[593] *Dansk Moller Industry A.S. v. Bentex Minerals Co. Ltd. and others*, Cyprus, (2007) 1B C.L.R.692.

[594] CLOUT case No. 667 [Oberlandesgericht Köln, Germany, 9 Sch 19/02, 26 November 2002], also available on the Internet at http://www.dis-arb.de/en/47/datenbanken/rspr/olg-köln-case-no-9-sch-19-02-date-2002-11-26-id336.

[595] *NBCC Ltd. v. JG Engineering Pvt Ltd.,* Supreme Court, India, 5 January 2010, Civil Appeal 8/2010, available on the Internet at http://indiankanoon.org/doc/1259068/; Court of Appeal, Tunisia, 3 December 2002, case No. 134.

[596] CLOUT case No. 782 [Cairo Regional Center for International Commercial Arbitration, Egypt, 11 March 1999]. Note: A change in the shareholding of a company would not normally change the corporate entity of a company. This case should therefore be understood in the light of the fact that the it was made without objections from either parties.

[597] Oberlandesgericht Stuttgart, Germany, 1 Sch 13/01, 20 December 2001 (an arbitral award which revised an earlier final award was set aside), available on the Internet at http://www.dis-arb.de/en/47/datenbanken/rspr/olg-stuttgart-case-no-1-sch-13-01-date-2001-12-20-id160; Oberlandesgericht Dresden, Germany, 11 SchH 01/00, 11 December 2000, available on the Internet at http://www.dis-arb.de/en/47/datenbanken/rspr/olg-dresden-case-no-11-schh-01-00-date-2000-12-11-id66.

Article 33. Correction and interpretation of award; additional award

(1) Within thirty days of receipt of the award, unless another period of time has been agreed upon by the parties:

(a) a party, with notice to the other party, may request the arbitral tribunal to correct in the award any errors in computation, any clerical or typographical errors or any errors of similar nature;

(b) if so agreed by the parties, a party, with notice to the other party, may request the arbitral tribunal to give an interpretation of a specific point or part of the award.

If the arbitral tribunal considers the request to be justified, it shall make the correction or give the interpretation within thirty days of receipt of the request. The interpretation shall form part of the award.

(2) The arbitral tribunal may correct any error of the type referred to in paragraph (1)(a) of this article on its own initiative within thirty days of the date of the award.

(3) Unless otherwise agreed by the parties, a party, with notice to the other party, may request, within thirty days of receipt of the award, the arbitral tribunal to make an additional award as to claims presented in the arbitral proceedings but omitted from the award. If the arbitral tribunal considers the request to be justified, it shall make the additional award within sixty days.

(4) The arbitral tribunal may extend, if necessary, the period of time within which it shall make a correction, interpretation or an additional award under paragraph (1) or (3) of this article.

(5) The provisions of article 31 shall apply to a correction or interpretation of the award or to an additional award.

TRAVAUX PRÉPARATOIRES

The *travaux préparatoires* on article 33 as adopted in 1985 are contained in the following documents:

1. Report of the United Nations Commission on International Trade Law on the work of its eighteenth session (*Official Records of the General Assembly, Fortieth Session, Supplement No. 17* (A/40/17)), paras. 11-333.

2. Reports of the Working Group: A/CN.9/216; A/CN.9/232; A/CN.9/245; A/CN.9/246, annex; A/CN.9/263 and Add.1-2; A/CN.9/264. Relevant working papers are referred to in the reports.

3. Summary records of the 329th and 333rd UNCITRAL meetings.

Article 33 was not amended in 2006.

(Available on the Internet at www.uncitral.org).

CASE LAW ON ARTICLE 33

Computational, clerical, typographic or similar errors may be corrected by the arbitral tribunal—paragraphs (1)*(a)* and (2)

Errors in computation

1. The expression "errors in computation" includes, *inter alia*, miscalculations, the use of incorrect data in calculations, and the omission of data in calculations.[598] An example was a case where the arbitral tribunal had made a factual error in the calculation of the back-pay to which one of the parties was entitled. The court found that the error made by the arbitral tribunal was one of computation within the meaning of article 33.[599]

2. Where an application for correction is pending before the arbitral tribunal, a Canadian court had declined to

[598] CLOUT case No. 208 [Vanol Far East Marketing Pte. Ltd. v. Hin Leong Trading Pte. Ltd., High Court, Singapore, 27 May 1996].

[599] CLOUT case No. 267 [*Zimbabwe Electricity Supply Commission v. Genius Joel Maposa,* Harare High Court, Zimbabwe, 29 March and 9 December 1998].

enforce the award within the 30-day period allowed for in paragraph (1), on the basis that the award had not yet become binding on the parties.[600]

Clerical or typographical errors

3. The expression "clerical or typographical" error includes mistakes made in the course of typing or drafting the arbitral award.[601]

Errors of similar nature

4. A Singapore tribunal has found that the expression errors of "similar nature" could also include certain mistakes made by the parties and reflected in the award. Thus, the provision was considered to be applicable where one of the parties by mistake had forgotten to include certain expenses in its bill of costs upon which the final award on costs was made.[602]

Errors of judgment

5. An arbitral tribunal is not empowered under this article to correct errors of judgment, whether of law or of fact.[603] Similarly, corrections that would recall, reverse or otherwise change the meaning of the arbitral award do not fall within the scope of article 33.[604]

Making an additional award—paragraph (3)

6. A German court held that, even where an application to set aside an award is pending, the arbitral tribunal was not only competent but also required to decide on costs in an additional award. The court ruled that the existence of concurrent setting aside proceedings in court would not affect the enforceability of the additional award made before the setting-aside hearings were concluded. Until the award is set aside, the court must assume its validity and enforce the additional award.[605]

---

[600] CLOUT case No. 625 [*Relais Nordik Inc. v. Secunda Marine Services Limited and Anor,* Federal Court, Canada, 12 April 1990].

[601] Ibid.

[602] CLOUT case No. 208 [Vanol Far East Marketing Pte. Ltd. v. Hin Leong Trading Pte. Ltd., High Court, Singapore, 27 May 1996].

[603] Ibid.

[604] Oberlandesgericht Stuttgart, Germany, 1 Sch 13/01, 20 December 2001 (an arbitral award which revised an earlier final award was set aside), available on the Internet at http://www.dis-arb.de/en/47/datenbanken/rspr/olg-stuttgart-case-no-1-sch-13-01-date-2001-12-20-id160; Oberlandesgericht Dresden, Germany, 11 SchH 01/00, 11 December 2000, available on the Internet at http://www.dis-arb.de/en/47/datenbanken/rspr/olg-dresden-case-no-11-schh-01-00-date-2000-12-11-id66; *Tan Poh Leng Stanley v. Tang Boon Jek Jeffrey*, High Court, Singapore, 30 November 2000, [2000] SGHC 260, [2000] 3 SLR(R) 847, where an arbitral award which revised an earlier final award was set aside. The decision of the High Court was reversed on appeal, see *Tang Boon Jek Jeffrey v. Tan Poh Leng Stanley*, Court of Appeal, Singapore, 22 June 2001, [2001] 3 SLR 237. However, the appeal turned on the definition of when there is a *final award* and did not refute the principal ruling that the arbitral tribunal is not empowered to recall or revise a final award.

[605] CLOUT case No. 663 [Oberlandesgericht Stuttgart, Germany, 1 Sch 22/01, 4 June 2002], also available on the Internet at http://www.dis-arb.de/en/47/datenbanken/rspr/olg-stuttgart-case-no-1-sch-22-01-date-2002-06-04-id232.

CHAPTER VII. RECOURSE AGAINST AWARD

Article 34. Application for setting aside as exclusive recourse against arbitral award

(1) Recourse to a court against an arbitral award may be made only by an application for setting aside in accordance with paragraphs (2) and (3) of this article.

(2) An arbitral award may be set aside by the court specified in article 6 only if:

(a) the party making the application furnishes proof that:

(i) a party to the arbitration agreement referred to in article 7 was under some incapacity; or the said agreement is not valid under the law to which the parties have subjected it or, failing any indication thereon, under the law of this State; or

(ii) the party making the application was not given proper notice of the appointment of an arbitrator or of the arbitral proceedings or was otherwise unable to present his case; or

(iii) the award deals with a dispute not contemplated by or not falling within the terms of the submission to arbitration, or contains decisions on matters beyond the scope of the submission to arbitration, provided that, if the decisions on matters submitted to arbitration can be separated from those not so submitted, only that part of the award which contains decisions on matters not submitted to arbitration may be set aside; or

(iv) the composition of the arbitral tribunal or the arbitral procedure was not in accordance with the agreement of the parties, unless such agreement was in conflict with a provision of this Law from which the parties cannot derogate, or, failing such agreement, was not in accordance with this Law; or

(b) the court finds that:

(i) the subject-matter of the dispute is not capable of settlement by arbitration under the law of this State; or

(ii) the award is in conflict with the public policy of this State.

(3) An application for setting aside may not be made after three months have elapsed from the date on which the party making that application had received the award or, if a request had been made under article 33, from the date on which that request had been disposed of by the arbitral tribunal.

(4) The court, when asked to set aside an award, may, where appropriate and so requested by a party, suspend the setting aside proceedings for a period of time determined by it in order to give the arbitral tribunal an opportunity to resume the arbitral proceedings or to take such other action as in the arbitral tribunal's opinion will eliminate the grounds for setting aside.

TRAVAUX PRÉPARATOIRES

The *travaux préparatoires* on article 34 as adopted in 1985 are contained in the following documents:

1. Report of the United Nations Commission on International Trade Law on the work of its eighteenth session (*Official Records of the General Assembly, Fortieth Session, Supplement No. 17* (A/40/17)), paras. 11-333.

2. Reports of the Working Group: A/CN.9/232; A/CN.9/233; A/CN.9/245; A/CN.9/246, annex; A/CN.9/263 and Add.1-2; A/CN.9/264. Relevant working papers are referred to in the reports.

3. Summary records of the 317th, 318th, 319th, 324th, 330th, 331st and 333rd UNCITRAL meetings.

Article 34 was not amended in 2006.

(Available on the Internet at www.uncitral.org).

INTRODUCTION

1. Article 34 provides uniform grounds upon which (and time periods within which) recourse against an arbitral award may be made. Paragraph (1) provides that the sole recourse against an arbitral award is by application for setting aside, which, pursuant to paragraph (3), must be made within three months of receipt of the award. Article 34 does not preclude a party from seeking court control by way of defence in enforcement proceedings under articles 35 and 36. Article 34 is limited to action before a court (i.e., an organ of the judicial system of a State). The Model Law lists exhaustively the grounds upon which an award may be set aside. This list essentially mirrors that contained in article 36 (1), which is similar to the provisions of article V of the 1958 New York Convention.[606]

2. Although the grounds for setting aside as set out in article 34 (2) are almost identical to those for refusing recognition or enforcement as set out in article 36 (1), a practical difference should be noted. An application for setting aside under article 34 (2) may only be made to a court in the State where the award was rendered whereas an application for enforcement might be made in a court in any State. For that reason, the grounds relating to public policy and non-arbitrability may vary in substance with the law applied by the court (in the State of setting aside or in the State of enforcement).

CASE LAW ON ARTICLE 34

Exclusive recourse against arbitral award— paragraph (1)

Legal nature of setting aside proceedings

3. Courts in numerous jurisdictions have made clear that setting aside proceedings are not appeal proceedings in which evidence is re-evaluated and the correctness of the arbitral tribunal's decision on the merits is examined.[607] The underlying rationale for that approach is that the arbitral tribunal decides in place of the State court and does not

---

[606] Article V of the 1958 New York Convention reads as follows: "1. Recognition and enforcement of the award may be refused, at the request of the party against whom it is invoked, only if that party furnishes to the competent authority where the recognition and enforcement is sought, proof that: *(a)* The parties to the agreement referred to in article II were, under the law applicable to them, under some incapacity, or the said agreement is not valid under the law to which the parties have subjected it or, failing any indication thereon, under the law of the country where the award was made; or *(b)* The party against whom the award is invoked was not given proper notice of the appointment of the arbitrator or of the arbitration proceedings or was otherwise unable to present his case; or *(c)* The award deals with a difference not contemplated by or not falling within the terms of the submission to arbitration, or it contains decisions on matters beyond the scope of the submission to arbitration, provided that, if the decisions on matters submitted to arbitration can be separated from those not so submitted, that part of the award which contains decisions on matters submitted to arbitration may be recognized and enforced; or *(d)* The composition of the arbitral authority or the arbitral procedure was not in accordance with the agreement of the parties, or, failing such agreement, was not in accordance with the law of the country where the arbitration took place; or *(e)* The award has not yet become binding on the parties, or has been set aside or suspended by a competent authority of the country in which, or under the law of which, that award was made.

2. Recognition and enforcement of an arbitral award may also be refused if the competent authority in the country where recognition and enforcement is sought finds that:

(a) The subject matter of the difference is not capable of settlement by arbitration under the law of that country; or *(b)* The recognition or enforcement of the award would be contrary to the public policy of that country."

[607] *Apa Insurance Co. Ltd. v. Chrysanthus Barnabas Okemo*, High Court, Nairobi, Kenya, 24 November 2005, Miscellaneous Application 241 of 2005, available at the Internet at http://www.kenyalaw.org/CaseSearch/case_download.php?go=50003769819788790599459&link=; Simbymanyo; Supreme Court, Spain, 6 April 2004, case No. 301/2007-2771/2005; *Simbymanyo Estates Ltd. v. Seyani Brothers Company (U) Ltd.*, High Court of Kampala, Commercial Division, Uganda, 23 August 2004, Misc. Application No. 555/2002; *Sofía v. Tintorería Paris, Sofía*, Madrid Court of Appeal, Spain, 20 January 2006, case No. 19/2006; *Government of the Republic of the Philippines v. Philippine International Air Terminals Co., Inc.*, High Court, Singapore, 17 November 2006, [2007] 1 SLR (R) 278, [2006] SGHC 206; Cairo Court of Appeal, Egypt, 3 April 2007, case No. 123/119; Cairo Court of Appeal, 7th Economic Circuit, Egypt, 5 February 2008, case No. 71/123; Cairo Court of Appeal, 7th Economic Circuit, Egypt, 3 March 2009, case No. 71/124.

merely constitute a first instance.[608] Consequently, the rules for appeal proceedings in relation to extension of time limits[609] or possible remedies[610] do not apply. In describing the nature of setting aside proceedings, a court held that the "applicable review in annulment proceedings is that of an external trial, (...) in such a way that the competent court examining the case solely decides on the formal guarantees of the proceedings and the arbitral award, but cannot review the merits of the matter."[611] (See also below in this section, paras. 25-29).

4. Moreover, courts have regularly emphasized the exceptional character of the remedy as courts should in principle not interfere with the decision of the arbitral tribunal.[612] The reason given by a court in Singapore for this "minimal curial intervention" which respects the finality of the arbitral process is that it "acknowledges the primacy which ought to be given to the dispute resolution mechanism that the parties have expressly chosen".[613]

Party autonomy

5. In practice, parties occasionally seek to agree on the available recourse against an award, either by excluding or modifying the right to recourse against an award. This raises the question of party autonomy under article 34.

6. Divergent court decisions have been rendered regarding possible exclusions or limitations of the right to apply for the setting aside of an award. A Canadian court held that the parties may agree to exclude any right they would otherwise have to apply to set aside an award under article 34, as long as their agreement does not conflict with any mandatory provision of the legislation enacting the Model Law, and does not confer powers on the arbitral tribunal contrary to public policy.[614] A similar position was adopted, albeit *obiter dicta*, by a court in New Zealand. After expressing certain sympathy for a "contractual stipulation which further limits the grounds upon which review is available, merely supplements article 34, and does not derogate from it", the court held that a right to apply for a review of a violation of the rules of natural justice could not be excluded.[615]

7. A more restricted position has been adopted by the Indian Supreme Court. It held, equally *obiter dicta*, that the exclusion of any recourse against an arbitral award is not valid.[616] In Tunisia, the Court of Cassation differentiated in this respect between arbitrations involving parties that have their headquarters, domiciles, or places of business in Tunisia and those that do not. Only the latter could exclude by agreement the possibility to set aside an award. If both parties have their place of business in Tunisia, such an agreement would be void.[617]

8. Even greater differences exist as to the approaches adopted by courts in relation to the question of whether and to what extent the parties may modify or extend the rules on recourse against an arbitral award or otherwise limit the finality of an award. A court in New Zealand held, albeit *obiter dicta*, that due to the "exclusionary terms" of article 34, the parties could not grant the courts further reaching powers to review an award.[618] On the basis of the same reasoning, the Indian Supreme Court considered void a clause which provided a party which disagreed with a

---

[608] Oberlandesgericht Karlsruhe, Germany, 10 Sch 01/07, 14 September 2007, available on the Internet at http://www.dis-arb.de/de/47/datenbanken/rspr/olg-karlsruhe-az-10-sch-01-07-datum-2007-09-14-id959.

[609] CLOUT case No. 566 [*ABC Co. v. XYZ Ltd.*, High Court, Singapore, 8 May 2003], [2003] 3 SLR 546.

[610] Supreme Court, Spain, 6 April 2004, case No. 301/2007—2771/2005, where appeal to the Supreme Court was not possible as the refusal by the Court of Appeal to set aside an award was not a second instance decision.

[611] *Sofía v. Tintorería Paris*, Madrid Court of Appeal, Spain, 20 January 2006, case No. 19/2006; see also Court of Appeal, Amman, Jordan, 10 June 2008, No. 206/2008.

[612] CLOUT case No. 16 [*Quintette Coal Limited v. Nippon Steel Corp. et al.*, Court of Appeal for British Columbia, Canada, 24 October 1990], [1990] B.C.J. No. 2241.

[613] *CRW Joint Operation v. PT Perusahaan Gas Negara (Persero) TBK*, Court of Appeal, Singapore, 13 July 2011, [2011] SGCA 3, para. 25.

[614] *Noble China Inc. v. Lei Kat Cheong*, Ontario Court of Justice, Canada, 13 November 1998, [1998] CanLII 14708 (ON SC), published in (1998) 42 O.R. (3d) 69, available on the Internet at http://canlii.ca/t/1vvkr, where the application under article 34 was dismissed, since the arbitration agreement excluded recourse under article 34.

[615] *Methanex Motunui Ltd. v. Spellman*, Court of Appeal, Wellington, New Zealand, 17 June 2004, [2004] 3 NZLR 454; CLOUT case No. 375 [Bayerisches Oberstes Landesgericht, Germany, 4 Z Sch 23/99, 15 December 1999], also available on the Internet at http://www.dis-arb.de/de/47/datenbanken/rspr/bayoblg-az-4-z-sch-23-99-datum-1999-12-15-id16, where the court held that a party may not waive the public policy ground in article 34 (2)*(b)*(ii), but may waive the grounds contained in article 34 (2)*(a)*. The court further held that the waiver of legal recourse in the arbitration rules applicable to the arbitral proceedings in that case did not cover setting aside proceedings, but was meant to exclude review of the merits of the case.

[616] *Shin Satellite Public Co. Ltd. v. Jain Studios Ltd.*, Supreme Court, India, 31 January 2006, [2006] 2 SCC 628, available on the Internet at http://www.indiankanoon.org/doc/1601758/.

[617] Court of Cassation, Tunisia, 18 January 2007, case No. 4674.

[618] *Methanex Motunui Ltd. v. Spellman*, Court of Appeal, Wellington, New Zealand, 17 June 2004, [2004] 3 NZLR 454 at para. 105.

first award rendered in proceedings under the auspices of an Indian institution with a right to start new proceedings in London. It considered that the parties could not question the validity of an award in proceedings other than in setting aside proceedings.[619]

Admissibility of setting aside proceedings

General considerations

9. Article 34 deals with the admissibility of actions to set aside an award, as well as the applicable standards therefor. In relation to the admissibility of such actions, there is no guidance in the Model Law on matters such as the required form of applications, their content or the admissible evidence. These issues are regulated in the domestic procedural or arbitration law. Applications which do not comply with such domestic legislation will usually be rejected. A Bulgarian court, for instance, rejected an application to set aside an award as inadmissible as the letter sent to the President of the Bulgarian Supreme Court did not fulfil the requirements for a proper application to set aside an award under Bulgarian Law.[620] Equally, a court rejected certain evidence submitted in the context of such action as the submission did not comply with the relevant legislation.[621]

10. The German Federal Court of Justice held that compliance with the requirements to be met by an application for requesting the setting aside an award had to be examined by the court on its own motion, irrespective of any challenge on that matter by the other party.[622]

Jurisdiction to hear an application under article 34 (Scope of application—territorial element)

11. It is usually considered that, pursuant to article 1 (2), article 6 and article 34 (2) of the Model Law, a court has jurisdiction to hear an application for the setting aside of an arbitral award under article 34 only if the place of arbitration[623] is within the national jurisdiction of such court.[624] Where the parties have agreed that the place of arbitration shall be within a State, only the courts of that State will have jurisdiction to hear an application under article 34[625] even if all hearings of the arbitral tribunal are held in another State.[626] However, if the place of arbitration is neither agreed upon by the parties nor determined by the arbitral tribunal, the courts at the effective place of arbitration, i.e. the place where all relevant actions in the arbitration have taken place or, if this cannot be determined, the place of the last oral hearing, have been considered to have jurisdiction under article 34.[627]

12. By contrast, Indian courts have assumed jurisdiction to set aside awards rendered in arbitral proceedings which had their place of arbitration outside India. One of the arguments was that the Indian enactment of the Model Law in defining its scope of application omitted the explicit statement found in article 1 (2) that its provisions would "only" apply in arbitrations which have their seat in India.[628] In later decisions, courts have adopted a low threshold for assuming that the parties to arbitration proceedings taking place outside India have, at least implicitly, excluded the application of the Indian Arbitration Act.[629] (See also above, section on article 1, para. 10).

---

[619] *M/S. Centrotrade Minerals & Metal. Inc. v. Hindustan Copper Ltd.*, Supreme Court, India, 9 May 2006, [2006] INSC 293.

[620] Supreme Court of Cassation, Bulgaria, Commercial Chamber, case No. 106 of 1 December 2009.

[621] *Baseline Architects Ltd. and others v. National Hospital Insurance Fund Board Management*, High Court, Nairobi, Kenya, 7 May 2008, Miscellaneous Application 1131 of 2007, available on the Internet at http://www.kenyalaw.org/Downloads_FreeCases/Confidential_communications.pdf.

[622] Bundesgerichtshof, Germany, III ZB 53/03, 27 May 2004, available on the Internet at http://www.dis-arb.de/de/47/datenbanken/rspr/bgh-az-iii-zb-53-03-datum-2004-05-27-id281, where the court held that the setting aside proceedings were inadmissible since the decision contrary to the belief of both parties did not constitute an arbitral award.

[623] For the territorial scope of application of the Model Law and the meaning of the concept "*place of arbitration*", see above, section on article 1 (2), paras. 9-11, and article 20.

[624] CLOUT case No. 374 (also reproduced under CLOUT case No. 408) [Oberlandesgericht Düsseldorf, Germany, 6 Sch 02/99, 23 March 2000], also available on the Internet at http://www.dis-arb.de/de/47/datenbanken/rspr/olg-d&uumlsseldorf-az-6-sch-02-99-datum-2000-03-23-id46; *PT Garuda Indonesia v. Birgen Air*, Court of Appeal, Singapore, 6 March 2002, [2002] 1 SLR 393, where the application to set aside the arbitral award was dismissed by the court since the place of arbitration, according to the arbitration agreement, was not within the jurisdiction of such court and a distinction had to be made between the seat of arbitration and the place where the oral hearings took place.

[625] Cairo Court of Appeal, Egypt, 16 January 2008, case No. 92/123; Cairo Court of Appeal, 7th Economic Circuit, Egypt, 2 July 2008, case No. 23/125.

[626] *PT Garuda Indonesia v. Birgen Air*, Court of Appeal, Singapore, 6 March 2002, [2002] 1 SLR 393.

[627] CLOUT case No. 374 (also reproduced under CLOUT case No. 408) [Oberlandesgericht Düsseldorf, Germany, 6 Sch 02/99, 23 March 2000], also available on the Internet at http://www.dis-arb.de/de/47/datenbanken/rspr/olg-d&uumlsseldorf-az-6-sch-02-99-datum-2000-03-23-id46.

[628] *Venture Global Engineering vs. Satyam Computer Services Ltd. & Another*, Supreme Court of India, 10 January 2008, (2008) 4 SCC 190, available on the Internet at http://indiankanoon.org/doc/75785/.

[629] *Yograj Infrastructure Ltd. vs. Ssang Yong Engineering and Construction Co. Ltd.*, Supreme Court, India, 1 September 2011, available on the Internet at http://www.indiankanoon.org/doc/242996/; *Sakuma Exports Ltd. v. Louis Dreyfus Commodities Suisse S.A.*, High Court Bombay, India, 15 November 2011, available on the Internet at http://www.indiankanoon.org/doc/1747056/.

Arbitral award

13. Setting aside proceedings under article 34 are admissible against all types of arbitral awards, irrespective of whether they completely terminate the proceedings or are awards finally determining certain claims only. The mere fact that a party consented to an award on agreed terms pursuant to article 30 does not prohibit it from applying for the setting aside of the award under article 34. Thus, courts considered that where the award on agreed terms was obtained by fraud, it may be set aside.[630] Equally, separate awards on costs may be considered in setting aside proceedings.[631]

14. A controversial issue is whether setting aside proceedings are admissible against an award that merely determines preliminary questions of the claim. There is no uniform terminology for such awards. They are in practice often referred to as "interim awards" or sometimes as "partial awards". A German court considered setting aside proceedings to be inadmissible in a case where a "partial award" determined merely the liability of the respondent for a breach of contract but left the determination of the amount of damages to a second stage. The court considered that the final outcome of the arbitral proceedings was still open. Notwithstanding the determination that the contract had been breached, the claim might still be rejected if no damages could be established.[632]

15. A different approach has been adopted in two decisions of a court in Canada. In the first case, the setting aside proceedings had been initiated against an "interim award" in which the arbitrator had determined that only some claims were justified and would be investigated in the second part of the proceedings. For the court, the relevant question for the admissibility of setting aside proceedings was whether the arbitrator's decision was final on the merits of the case, or was a procedural order or a non-binding decision.[633] In the second case, the action for setting aside had been initiated against a decision by the arbitral tribunal ordering the production of certain documents. The court did not question the admissibility of the application and it rejected the action on the merits, holding that the arbitrator did not exceed his powers in making such decision.[634]

16. Courts have held that setting aside proceedings against procedural orders of arbitral tribunals are inadmissible.[635] According to the decision of a court in Tunisia, an interim award ordering interim measures of protection was not an award in the meaning of article 34, and consequently a motion to set aside such an award was not admissible.[636] In another case, a court also held that no action could be initiated against the preliminary fixing of the arbitrators' fees in the award.[637]

17. A court does not have jurisdiction under article 34 to set aside a decision of an arbitral tribunal or of any other dispute resolution body that does not constitute an arbitral award within the meaning of the Model Law.[638] In one case, it was found that a decision of an arbitral tribunal constituted an arbitral award if it entailed a decision on the merits of the case,[639] while in another case it was stated that a decision of an arbitral tribunal could be considered as an arbitral award if it met the formal requirements of article 31 of the Model Law.[640]

[630] CLOUT case No. 407 [Bundesgerichtshof, Germany, III ZB 55/99, 2 November 2000], also available on the Internet at http://www.dis-arb.de/de/47/datenbanken/rspr/bgh-az-iii-zb-55-99-datum-2000-11-02-id2 where the applicant alleged that forged annual reports had been submitted to induce the party to agree to the settlement which formed the basis of the award on agreed terms.

[631] *VV. and Another v. VW*, High Court, Singapore, 24 January 2008, OS 2160/2006, [2008] SGHC 11.

[632] Oberlandesgericht Frankfurt, Germany, 26 Sch 20/06, 10 May 2007, available on the Internet at http://www.dis-arb.de/de/47/datenbanken/rspr/olg-frankfurt-am-az-26-sch-20-06-datum-2007-05-10-id711.

[633] *The Gazette, Une division de Southam inc v. Rita Blondin et al.,* Quebec Court of Appeal, Canada, 6 August 2003, [2003] R.J.Q. 2090.

[634] *Endorecherche inc. c. Université Laval*, Quebec Court of Appeal, Canada, 9 February 2010, 2010 QCCA 232.

[635] Oberlandesgericht Köln, Germany, 9 Sch 06/03, 3 June 2003, available on the Internet at http://www.dis-arb.de/de/47/datenbanken/rspr/olg-k&oumlln-az-9-sch-06-03-datum-2003-06-03-id351; see also *The Gazette, Une division de Southam inc v. Rita Blondin et al.,* Quebec Court of Appeal, Canada, 6 August 2003, [2003] R.J.Q. 2090.

[636] Court of Appeal, Tunisia, 8 May 2001, case. No. 83.

[637] Court of Appeal, Amman, Jordan, 4 March 2009, No. 218/2008.

[638] CLOUT case No. 441 [Oberlandesgericht Köln, Germany, 9 Sch 06/00, 20 July 2000], also available on the Internet at http://www.dis-arb.de/de/47/datenbanken/rspr/olg-k&oumlln-az-9-sch-06-00-datum-2000-07-20-id228; Oberlandesgericht Frankfurt a. M., Germany, 23 Sch 01/98, 12 May 1999, available on the Internet at http://www.dis-arb.de/de/47/datenbanken/rspr/olg-frankfurt-am-az-23-sch-01-98-datum-1999-05-12-id75; Bundesgerichtshof, Germany, III ZB 53/03, 27 May 2004, available on the Internet at http://www.dis-arb.de/de/47/datenbanken/rspr/bgh-az-iii-zb-53-03-datum-2004-05-27-id281; Oberlandesgericht Naumburg, Germany, 10 Sch 01/05, 20 May 2005, available on the Internet at http://www.dis-arb.de/de/47/datenbanken/rspr/olg-naumburg-az-10-sch-01-05-datum-2005-05-20-id456.

[639] CLOUT case No. 455 [Hanseatisches Oberlandesgericht Hamburg, Germany, 14 Sch 01/98, 4 September 1998], also available on the Internet at http://www.dis-arb.de/de/47/datenbanken/rspr/hanseat-olg-hamburg-az-14-u-111-98-14-sch-01-98-datum-1998-09-04-id33.

[640] CLOUT case No. 441 [Oberlandesgericht Köln, Germany, 9 Sch 06/00, 20 July 2000], also available on the Internet at http://www.dis-arb.de/de/47/datenbanken/rspr/olg-k&oumlln-az-9-sch-06-00-datum-2000-07-20-id228.

18. However, in a number of other decisions, assertions that the award did not meet the requirements of article 31 have not been considered sufficient to render article 34 inapplicable, but have rather been considered to constitute possible grounds for setting aside the arbitral award under paragraph (2).[641]

Award on jurisdiction

19. Diverging court decisions have been rendered on the question whether decisions of arbitral tribunals declining jurisdiction could be subject to the setting aside procedure under article 34. A court in Singapore has considered that such decisions of arbitral tribunals did not constitute an award in the meaning of article 34.[642] By contrast, the German Federal Court of Justice has come to the opposite conclusion, at least if the decision of the arbitral tribunal was rendered in the form of an arbitral award.[643] The issue has been addressed in the national law of some countries.[644] (See above, section on article 16, paras. 21-24; see also below in this section, paras. 43 and 92).

Applications under article 34 by third parties

20. A third party intervener in the arbitration has been allowed to bring an action for the setting aside of an arbitral award where the parties and the arbitral tribunal have, at least tacitly, consented to the intervention and where the intervener has a legal interest in the outcome of the arbitral proceedings.[645]

21. A court in New Zealand, however, held that an application to have an award set aside could only be made by parties to the arbitration agreement. Even third parties which had an interest in the outcome of the arbitral proceedings or would be directly affected by it, lacked legal standing to initiate setting aside proceedings.[646]

Burden of pleading and burden of proof— paragraph (2)

22. Few decisions have dealt explicitly with the burden of pleading and the burden of proof. Concerning the burden

[641] CLOUT case No. 12 [*D. Frampton & Co. Ltd. v. Sylvio Thibeault and Navigation Harvey & Frères Inc.*, Federal Court, Trial Division, Canada, 7 April 1988]; see also CLOUT case No. 569 [Hanseatisches Oberlandesgericht Hamburg, Germany, 11 Sch 01/01, 8 June 2001], also available on the Internet at http://www.dis-arb.de/de/47/datenbanken/rspr/hanseat-olg-hamburg-az-11-sch-01-01-datum-2001-06-08-id1274, where the application to set aside the award raised by the respondent in enforcement proceedings was rejected.

[642] CLOUT case No. 742 [*PT AsuransiJasa Indonesia (Persero) v. Dexia Bank S.A.*, Court of Appeal, Singapore, 1 December 2006], also in [2006] SGCA 41, paras. 62 et seq, relying in its reasoning also on the definition of the term "award" included in the Singapore International Arbitration Act.

[643] CLOUT case No. 560 [Bundesgerichtshof, Germany, III ZB 44/01, 6 June 2002]; CLOUT case No. 570 [Hanseatisches Oberlandesgericht Hamburg, Germany, 11 Sch 02/00, 30 August 2002], also available on the Internet at http://www.dis-arb.de/de/47/datenbanken/rspr/bgh-az-iii-zb-44-01-datum-2002-06-06-id185; Oberlandesgericht Karlsruhe, Germany, 10 Sch 01/07, 14 September 2007, available on the Internet at http://www.dis-arb.de/de/47/datenbanken/rspr/olg-karlsruhe-az-10-sch-01-07-datum-2007-09-14-id959.

[644] Under the Austrian law, the erroneous denial of jurisdiction constitutes an additional ground for setting aside an award. Section 611 (2) No. 1, which corresponds to article 34 (2)*(a)*(i), reads as follows: "An arbitral award shall be set aside if: (1) a valid arbitration agreement does not exists or the arbitral tribunal *has denied its jurisdiction despite the existence of a valid arbitration agreement* (...)" (emphasis added).

[645] Oberlandesgericht Stuttgart, Germany, 1 Sch 08/02, 16 July 2002, available on the Internet at http://www.dis-arb.de/de/47/datenbanken/rspr/olg-stuttgart-az-1-sch-08-02-datum-2002-07-16-id187, where the intervenor was allowed to bring the claim since the parties to the arbitration had accepted its intervention in the arbitration and since the outcome of the arbitration directly or indirectly affected the legal position of the intervenor.

[646] *Methanex Motunui Ltd. v. Spellman*, Court of Appeal, Wellington, New Zealand, 17 June 2004, [2004] 3 NZLR 454.

of pleading, some courts decided that the grounds for setting aside an award listed in paragraph (2)*(b)* were to be considered *ex officio* by the courts[647] and that they could be raised even if the time limit referred to in paragraph (3) had expired.[648] Concerning the burden of proof, a court stated that, under paragraph (2), the applicant has the burden of proving a ground on the basis of which the award should be set aside.[649]

The grounds for setting aside an arbitral award—paragraph (2)[650]

General issues

Construction and application

23. The grounds provided in article 34 (2) are set out in two categories. Grounds which are to be proven by one party are as follows: lack of capacity of the parties to conclude an arbitration agreement; lack of a valid arbitration agreement; lack of notice of appointment of an arbitrator or of the arbitral proceedings or inability of a party to present its case; the award deals with matters not covered by the submission to arbitration; the composition of the arbitral tribunal or the conduct of arbitral proceedings are contrary to the effective agreement of the parties or, failing such agreement, to the Model Law. Grounds that a court may consider of its own initiative are as follows: non-arbitrability of the subject-matter of the dispute or violation of public policy (which is to be understood as serious departures from fundamental notions of procedural justice). Courts construing article 34 have generally held that the list of grounds for setting aside an award in paragraph (2) was exhaustive[651] and should be construed narrowly,[652] and that courts should not extend the grounds listed in paragraph (2) by analogy.[653] Moreover, article 5 was considered to be an unequivocal statement that no residual discretion existed to set aside awards for other reasons.[654]

Standard of review

24. Courts have regularly emphasized that the finality of awards was one of the main purposes of the Model Law and the relevant national legislation based on it, so that

[647] CLOUT case No. 407 [Bundesgerichtshof, Germany, III ZB 55/99, 2 November 2000], also available on the Internet at http://www.dis-arb.de/de/47/datenbanken/rspr/bgh-az-iii-zb-55-99-datum-2000-11-02-id2; Bayerisches Oberstes Landesgericht, Germany, 4 Z Sch 48/99, 10 February 2000, available on the Internet at http://www.dis-arb.de/de/47/datenbanken/rspr/bayoblg-az-4-z-sch-48-99-datum-2000-02-10-id15.

[648] CLOUT case No. 407 [Bundesgerichtshof, Germany, III ZB 55/99, 2 November 2000], also available on the Internet at http://www.dis-arb.de/de/47/datenbanken/rspr/bgh-az-iii-zb-55-99-datum-2000-11-02-id2.

[649] CLOUT case No. 391 [*Re Corporación Transnacional de Inversiones, S.A. de C.V. et al. v. STET International, S.p.A. et al.*, Ontario Superior Court of Justice, Canada, 22 September 1999] [1999] CanLII 14819 (ON SC), also available on the Internet at http://canlii.ca/t/1vvn5.

[650] The grounds for setting aside an award in article 34 (2) are, to a certain extent, similar in substance to the grounds for refusing recognition and enforcement under article 36 (1). Some jurisdictions, when enacting the Model Law, have amended it in order to regulate the relationship between actions for setting aside and actions for enforcement of an award, if the latter concerns an award rendered in that jurisdiction. For instance, in Germany, a request by a party to refuse enforcement of an award rendered in Germany contains at the same time the party's application to have that award set aside in case the defence raised is successful. Thus, proceedings for the enforcement of such an award may, in the end, result in the setting aside of this award. As a consequence, the section on case law on article 34 may also contain references to decisions of such jurisdictions.

[651] CLOUT case No. 10 [*Navigation Sonamar Inc. v. Algoma Steamships Limited and others,* Superior Court of Quebec, Canada, 16 April 1987], 1987 WL 719339 (C.S. Que.), [1987] R.J.Q. 1346, 1987 CarswellQue 1193, J.E. 87-642, EYB 1987-78387; CLOUT case No. 12 [*D. Frampton & Co. Ltd. v. Sylvio Thibeault and Navigation Harvey & Frères Inc.,* Federal Court, Trial Division, Canada, 7 April 1988]; CLOUT case No. 1014 [*Bayview Irrigation District #11 v. United Mexican States*, Ontario Superior Court of Justice, Canada, 5 May 2008], [2008] O.J. No. 185; CLOUT case No. 1049 [*Louis Dreyfus S.A.S. v. Holding Tusculum B.V.*, Superior Court of Quebec, Canada, 8 December 2008], [2008] QCCS 5903 (CanLII), also available on the Internet at http://canlii.ca/t/21v03.

[652] CLOUT case No. 391 [*Re Corporación Transnacional de Inversiones, S.A. de C.V. et al. v. STET International, S.p.A. et al.*, Ontario Superior Court of Justice, Canada, 22 September 1999] [1999] CanLII 14819 (ON SC), also available on the Internet at http://canlii.ca/t/1vvn5.

[653] CLOUT case No. 570 [Hanseatisches Oberlandesgericht Hamburg, Germany, 11 Sch 02/00, 30 August 2002], also available on the Internet at http://www.dis-arb.de/de/47/datenbanken/rspr/hanseat-olg-hamburg-az-11-sch-02-00-datum-2002-08-30-id1273.

[654] CLOUT case No. 1049 [*Louis Dreyfus S.A.S. v. Holding Tusculum B.V.*, Superior Court of Quebec, Canada, 8 December 2008], [2008] QCCS 5903 (CanLII), also available on the Internet at http://canlii.ca/t/21v03; *Newspeed International Ltd. v. Citus Trading Pte. Ltd.*, High Court, Singapore, [2003] 3 SLR(R) 1; CLOUT case No. 76 [*China Nanhai Oil Joint Service Corp Shenzhen Branch v. Gee Tai Holdings Co.*, High Court—Court of First Instance, Hong Kong, 13 July 1994], [1994] 3 HKC 375, [1995] ADRLJ 127, HK HC, where the court enforced the award on the basis that the respondents had participated fully in the arbitral proceedings without objection, notwithstanding that the composition of the arbitral tribunal was irregular.

awards should not be set aside easily.[655] Thus, the appropriate standard of review of arbitral awards under article 34 was considered to be one that sought to preserve the autonomy of the arbitral procedure and to minimize judicial intervention.[656] A Canadian court has highlighted that the underlying arguments for such considerable deference to the awards were "concerns of international community, respect for the capacities of foreign and transnational tribunals and sensitivity to the need of the international commercial system for predictability in the resolution of disputes".[657]

No review of the merits of an arbitral award

25. A great number of cases underline that the Model Law does not permit review of the merits of an arbitral award.[658] This has been found to apply in principle to issues of law[659] as well as to issues of fact[660] and was considered by a court in Singapore to be "trite law".[661]

26. In practice, parties usually tend to argue in their application for setting aside an award that the award is unfair,

[655] *Kenya Shell Ltd. v. Kobil Petroleum Ltd.*, Court of Appeal, Nairobi, Kenya, 10 November 2006, Civil Application 57 of 2006; CLOUT case No. 1014 [*Bayview Irrigation District #11 v. United Mexican States*, Ontario Superior Court of Justice, Canada, 5 May 2008], [2008] O.J. No. 1858.

[656] CLOUT case No. 16 [*Quintette Coal Limited v. Nippon Steel Corp. et al.*, Court of Appeal for British Columbia, Canada, 24 October 1990], [1990] B.C.J. No. 2241; CLOUT case No. 1049 [*Louis Dreyfus S.A.S. v. Holding Tusculum B.V.*, Superior Court of Quebec, Canada, 8 December 2008], [2008] QCCS 5903 (CanLII), also available on the Internet at http://canlii.ca/t/21v03; *CRW Joint Operation v. PT Perusahaan Gas Negara (Persero) TBK,* Court of Appeal, Singapore, 13 July 2011, [2011] SGCA 3.

[657] CLOUT case No. 16 [*Quintette Coal Limited v. Nippon Steel Corp. et al.*, Court of Appeal for British Columbia, Canada, 24 October 1990], [1990] B.C.J. No. 2241; quoting directly from the decision of the US Supreme Court in *Mitsubishi Motors Corp. v. Soler Chrysler-Plymouth, Inc.*, 2 July 1985, No. 83-1569, 473 U.S. 614 (1985); cited also in CLOUT case No. 1014 [*Bayview Irrigation District #11 v. United Mexican States*, Ontario Superior Court of Justice, Canada, 5 May 2008], [2008] O.J. No. 1858.

[658] CLOUT case No. 10 [*Navigation Sonamar Inc. v. Algoma Steamships Limited and others,* Superior Court of Quebec, Canada, 16 April 1987], 1987 WL 719339 (C.S. Que.), [1987] R.J.Q. 1346, 1987 CarswellQue 1193, J.E. 87-642, EYB 1987-78387; CLOUT case No. 148 [Moscow City Court, Russian Federation, 10 February 1995]; CLOUT case No. 375 [Bayerisches Oberstes Landesgericht, Germany, 15 December 1999, 4 Z Sch 23/99], also available on the Internet at http://www.dis-arb.de/de/47/datenbanken/rspr/bayoblg-az-4-z-sch-23-99-datum-1999-12-15-id16; CLOUT case No. 391 [*Re Corporación Transnacional de Inversiones, S.A. de C.V. et al. v. STET International, S.p.A. et al.*, Ontario Superior Court of Justice, Canada, 22 September 1999], [1999] CanLII 14819 (ON SC), also available on the Internet at http://canlii.ca/t/1vvn5, confirmed in *Corporación Transnacional de Inversiones v. Stet International*, Ontario Court of Appeal, Canada, 2000 CanLII 16840 (ON CA), (2000) 49 OR (3d) 414, 15 September 2000; *Tan Poh Leng Stanley v. Tang Boon Jek Jeffrey*, High Court, Singapore, 30 November 2000, [2001] 1 SLR 624; the decision of the High Court was reversed on appeal, see *Tang Boon Jek Jeffrey v. Tan Poh Leng Stanley*, Court of Appeal, Singapore, 22 June 2001, [2001] 3 SLR 237: the High Court stated that the hallmark of the Model Law is that it does not provide for appeals on the merits of an arbitral decision; CLOUT case No. 566 [*ABC Co. v. XYZ Ltd.*, High Court, Singapore, 8 May 2003] [2003] 3 SLR 546; *PT Perusahaan Gas Negara (Persero) TBK v. CRW Joint Operation*, High Court, Singapore, 20 July 2010, [2010] SGHC 202; affirmed in *TBK v. CRW Joint Operation v. PT Perusahaan Gas Negara (Persero),* Court of Appeal, 13 July 2011, [2011] SGCA 3; CLOUT case No. 569 [Hanseatisches Oberlandesgericht Hamburg, Germany, 11 Sch 01/01, 8 June 2001], also available on the Internet at http://www.dis-arb.de/de/47/datenbanken/rspr/hanseat-olg-hamburg-az-11-sch-01-01-datum-2001-06-08-id1274 (the case concerned an alleged non application of the relevant law); Oberlandesgericht Karlsruhe, 10 Sch 04/01, 14 September 2001, available on the Internet at http://www.dis-arb.de/de/47/datenbanken/rspr/olg-karlsruhe-az-10-sch-04-01-datum-2001-09-14-id1268; Oberlandesgericht Stuttgart, Germany, 1 Sch 08/02, 16 July 2002, available on the Internet at http://www.dis-arb.de/de/47/datenbanken/rspr/olg-stuttgart-az-1-sch-08-02-datum-2002-07-16-id187 (where it was stated that there should not be any reassessment of testimonies given during the arbitration), available on the Internet at http://www.dis-arb.de; Cairo Court of Appeal, Egypt, 5 May 2009, case No. 112/124; Amman Court of Appeal, Jordan, 10 June 2008, No. 206/2008.

[659] CLOUT case No. 10 [*Navigation Sonamar Inc. v. Algoma Steamships Limited and others,* Superior Court of Quebec, Canada, 16 April 1987], 1987 WL 719339 (C.S. Que.), [1987] R.J.Q. 1346, 1987 CarswellQue 1193, J.E. 87-642, EYB 1987-78387.

[660] CLOUT case No. 10 [*Navigation Sonamar Inc. v. Algoma Steamships Limited and others,* Superior Court of Quebec, Canada, 16 April 1987], 1987 WL 719339 (C.S. Que.), [1987] R.J.Q. 1346, 1987 CarswellQue 1193, J.E. 87-642, EYB 1987-78387; CLOUT case No. 457 [Hanseatisches Oberlandesgericht Hamburg, Germany, 1 Sch 02/99, 14 May 1999], also available on the Internet at http://www.dis-arb.de/de/47/datenbanken/rspr/hanseat-olg-hamburg-az-1-sch-02-99-datum-1999-05-14-id30.

[661] *PT Perusahaan Gas Negara (Persero) TBK v. CRW Joint Operation*, High Court, Singapore, 20 July 2010, [2010] SGHC 202 (SA), affirmed in *CRW Joint Operation v. PT Perusahaan Gas Negara (Persero) TBK,* Court of Appeal [2011] SGCA 3. See also *Hebei Import and Export Corp v. Polytek Engineering Co. Ltd,* Court of Final Appeal, Hong Kong Special Administrative Region of China, 9 February 1999, [1999] HKCFA 40; CLOUT case No. 391 [*Re Corporación Transnacional de Inversiones, S.A. de C.V. et al. v. STET International, S.p.A. et al.,* Ontario Superior Court of Justice, Canada, 22 September 1999] [1999] CanLII 14819 (ON SC), also available on the Internet at http://canlii.ca/t/1vvn5; *Canada (Attorney General) v. S.D. Myers Inc.*, Federal Court—Trial Division, Canada, 13 January 2004, [2004] 3 FCR 368, available on the Internet at http://canlii.ca/t/1g7jc; CLOUT case No. 1014 [*Bayview Irrigation District #11 v. United Mexican States*, Ontario Superior Court of Justice, Canada, 5 May 2008], [2008] O.J. No. 1858, para. 11: "The Court is not permitted to engage in a hearing de novo on the merits of the Tribunal's decision or to undertake a review such as that conducted by a court in relation to a decision of a domestic tribunal."

does not comply with the terms of the arbitration agreement or is contrary to the law. Therefore, courts have emphasized the exclusion of any review on the merits in relation to allegations of the violation of public policy,[662] the lack of sufficient reasoning,[663] non-compliance of the arbitral tribunal with its mandate,[664] or evident partiality of an arbitrator.[665] In particular, Spanish courts have reiterated regularly that the ultimate purpose of arbitration, i.e. to reach a prompt extrajudicial settlement of disputes, justifies the attribution of *res judicata* effect to awards that were clearly wrong. Consequently, they have limited the review to breaches of the arbitration agreement itself or of the essential procedural guarantees under the Spanish Constitution, excluding any review of breaches of the substantive law applicable to the case.[666]

27. Diverging decisions have been rendered regarding applications to review an arbitral tribunal's decision to reject the evidence offered by a party for reasons relating to substance (see below in this section, paras. 61-64).

28. A German court, while emphasizing that any review on the merits is prohibited, treated the refusal of the arbitrator to hear witnesses presented by parties to be primarily a question of the violation of the right to be heard.[667] Equally, a court in Uganda set aside an award because the arbitrator refused to take evidence relying on non-existing restrictions.[668]

29. The Tunisian Court of Cassation, after emphasizing that a review on the merits would exceed the powers of the court, set aside an award because the reasons given in the arbitral award by the arbitrators for rendering the decision were contradictory and considered non-existing.[669] Equally, a court in Uganda, after first emphasizing the exceptional character of the remedy, has set aside parts of an award which were obviously wrong in its view, deducing from that fact "evident partiality" of the arbitrator.[670]

Judicial discretion

30. In respect of both paragraphs (2)*(a)* and (2)*(b)*, several Canadian decisions provided that even if one of the grounds for setting aside an award were fulfilled, it was still within the discretion of the court to decide whether the award should be upheld or set aside.[671] Such discretion was also assumed by a court in Hong Kong. In determining whether to exercise its discretion, the court looked for guidance in the jurisprudence concerning the 1958 New York Convention. Relying on that jurisprudence, the court came to the conclusion that, since the procedural defect did not affect the outcome of the case, given that the award was based on several conclusions, the court should make use of its discretion in deciding whether to uphold or set aside the award.[672]

Partial setting aside of an award

31. Occasionally, the defects may concern only certain parts of the awards, in particular separate claims. In practice, courts have usually only set aside those parts of the award that were affected by the defect.[673] The unaffected portions of the award still had the *res judicata* effect.[674]

---

[662] *Uniprex S.A. v. Grupo Radio Blanca,* Madrid Court of Appeal, Spain, 22 March 2006, case No. 178/2006-4/2004.

[663] *Sofía v. Tintorería Paris*, Madrid Court of Appeal, Spain, 20 January 2006, case No. 19/2006.

[664] *Simbymanyo Estates Ltd. v. Seyani Brothers Company (U) Ltd.*, Kampala High Court, Uganda, Commercial Division, Uganda, 23 August 2004, Misc. Application No. 555/2002.

[665] Ibid.

[666] *Uniprex S.A. v. Grupo Radio Blanca,* Madrid Court of Appeal, Spain, 22 March 2006, case No. 178/2006-4/2004.

[667] Oberlandesgericht Stuttgart, Germany, 1 Sch 03/10, 30 July 2010, available on the Internet at http://www.dis-arb.de/de/47/datenbanken/rspr/olg-stuttgart-az-1-sch-03-10-datum-2010-07-30-id1077.

[668] *Kilimbe Mines Ltd. v. B.M. Steel Ltd.*, Kampala High Court, Commercial Division, Uganda, 14 July 2005, HCT-00-CC-MC-0002-05.

[669] Court of Cassation, Tunisia, 27 November 2008, case No. 20596/2007.

[670] *R.R.P (U) Ltd. v. ASSIST (U) Ltd.*, Kampala High Court, Commercial Division, Uganda, Misc. Arbitration Cause No. 04 of 2002, 26 September 2002.

[671] CLOUT case No. 502 [*The United Mexican States v. Metalclad Corporation*, British Colombia Supreme Court, Canada, 2 May 2001], also available on the Internet at http://canlii.ca/t/4xfw, where the court argued that the seriousness of the defect in the arbitral procedure should be considered when the court was deciding whether to exercise its discretion to set aside an award under article 34.

[672] *Brunswick Bowling & Billiards Corporation v. Shanghai Zhonglu Industrial Co. Ltd. and Another*, High Court—Court of First Instance, Hong Kong Special Administrative Region of China, 10 February 2009, [2009] HKCFI 94 at para. 111, available on the Internet at http://www.hklii.hk/eng/hk/cases/hkcfi/2009/94.html.

[673] Supreme Court, Egypt, 25 January 2008, case No. 810/71; *Brunswick Bowling & Billiards Corporation v. Shanghai Zhonglu Industrial Co. Ltd. and Another*, High Court—Court of First Instance, Hong Kong Special Administrative Region of China, 10 February 2009, [2009] HKCFI 94 at para. 111, available on the Internet at http://www.hklii.hk/eng/hk/cases/hkcfi/2009/94.html.

[674] Supreme Court, Egypt, 25 January 2008, case No. 810/71.

Incapacity, invalid arbitration agreement— paragraph (2)(*a*)(i)

Incapacity of a party to the arbitration agreement

32. A court in Uganda held that the existence of incapacity of a party to the arbitration agreement must be assessed when the parties entered into the arbitration agreement. Thus, the mere fact that a party entered into liquidation during the arbitral proceedings did not provide a ground for setting aside the award under paragraph (2)(*a*)(i).[675]

The arbitration agreement is invalid

Reviewability of the arbitral tribunal's findings

33. In principle, where an applicant invokes the lack of jurisdiction of the arbitral tribunal in setting aside proceedings, the court may review the existence of an arbitration agreement. Courts in Germany have held that they were not bound by the factual or legal findings of the arbitral tribunal.[676] It has been suggested that the court should limit itself to review the decision of the arbitral tribunal and not engage on a rehearing of the issue unless there were procedural defects in establishing the facts.[677]

34. The arbitration agreement, however, is often contained in a main contract. As a consequence, notwithstanding the doctrine of separability, the inexistence or invalidity of the main contract may be invoked as an argument to show that the arbitration clause is inexistent or invalid. In that light, in a case where the arbitral tribunal had dealt in detail in the arbitral award with the alleged non-existence of the contract containing the arbitration clause, a court held that it should not review the existence of the arbitration clause at the stage of setting aside proceedings.[678]

Doctrine of separability

35. In light of the doctrine of separability, courts have confirmed that the alleged invalidity of the main contract containing the arbitration agreement does not affect, in principle, the validity of the arbitration agreement.[679] (See above, section on article 16, paras. 6 and 7).

Pathological arbitration agreement

36. In practice, the lack of a valid arbitration agreement is often invoked where the arbitration was based on pathological arbitration agreements, i.e. agreements which lack the necessary specificity or clarity or conflict with other dispute resolution clauses contained in the contract. Where contracts contained a clause in favour of the jurisdiction of a court beside the arbitration clause, courts have in most cases found that the clauses had different scopes of application. In general, the forum selection clause was then considered to relate to cases not covered by the arbitration clause or to apply where parties do not invoke the arbitration clause.[680]

37. A pro-arbitration approach is normally also adopted in cases where the arbitration agreement is challenged for its lack of precision. Courts have held that once it is clear that the parties were willing to refer their disputes to arbitration, such agreements are in general to be interpreted widely and, where possible, in favour of the validity of the arbitration agreement (see below, section on article 36,

---

[675] *SDV. Transami Ltd. v. Agrimag Limited et al.*, Kampala High Court, Commercial Division, Uganda, 19 June 2008, HCT-00-CC-AB-0002-2006.

[676] See CLOUT case No. 868 [Bayerisches Oberstes Landesgericht, Germany, 4 Z Sch 23/02, 20 March 2003], also available on the Internet at http://www.dis-arb.de/de/47/datenbanken/rspr/bayoblg-az-4-z-sch-23-02-datum-2003-03-20-id262, confirmed by Bundesgerichtshof, Germany, III ZB 29/03, 23 October 2003, available on the Internet at http://www.dis-arb.de/de/47/datenbanken/rspr/bgh-az-iii-zb-29-03-datum-2003-10-23-id241; Oberlandesgericht Dresden, Germany, 11 Sch 02/06, 7 June 2006, available on the Internet at http://www.dis-arb.de/de/47/datenbanken/rspr/olg-dresden-az-11-sch-02-06-datum-2006-06-07-id1289.

[677] CLOUT case No. 457 [Hanseatisches Oberlandesgericht Hamburg, Germany, 1 Sch 02/99, 14 May 1999], also available on the Internet at http://www.dis-arb.de/de/47/datenbanken/rspr/hanseat-olg-hamburg-az-1-sch-02-99-datum-1999-05-14-id30.

[678] Madrid Court of Appeal, Spain, 30 April 2007, case No. 240/2007-6/2006.

[679] Oberlandesgericht Köln, Germany, 19 Sch 12/08, 21 November 2008.

[680] *Jaral Decoración, S.L v. Peñasco Rodilla, SL*, Madrid Court of Appeal, Spain, 2 February 2007, case No. 94/2007-07/2005; see also in the context of a recourse against a preliminary ruling under article 16 (3), Oberlandesgericht Stuttgart, Germany, 1 SchH 1/09, 10 September 2009, available on the Internet at http://www.dis-arb.de/de/47/datenbanken/rspr/olg-stuttgart-az-1-schh-01-09-datum-2009-09-10-id1032.

para. 21). Where it is, however, not clear whether the parties were indeed willing to refer their disputes to arbitration or any other form of alternative dispute resolution, courts have been more reluctant to adopt an arbitration friendly interpretation. Thus, in a case where one of the apparently conflicting dispute resolution clauses was clearly a mediation clause, contained in the main contract, which conflicted with an arbitration clause concluded separately, a German court set aside the award on the ground that the arbitration agreement was not valid. The court held that the contract provided for mediation.[681]

38. In relation to dispute settlement provisions which give the claimant a choice between arbitral proceedings and State court proceedings, courts have considered such provisions valid.[682]

Awards against non-signatories

39. A court ruled that an arbitration agreement contained in a contract was not automatically binding in relation to a guarantor to the extent the guarantor was not a party to the said agreement and its obligations were independent from the principal agreement.[683]

40. By contrast, arbitration agreements contained in framework agreements were extended to disputes arising out of related contracts. Accordingly, the Hungarian Supreme Court refused to set aside an award dealing with a dispute arising from a contract where the underlying asset management contract contained a broadly worded arbitration clause.[684]

41. Courts have also considered claims based on the ground that a person was not a party to the arbitration agreement under either paragraph (2)*(a)*(i)[685] or paragraph (2)*(a)*(iii).[686]

Expiry of time limit for rendering an award

42. The Model Law does not provide for any time limits for rendering an award. However, the arbitration rules and laws sometimes provide for such time limit. In some cases, courts have held that awards made beyond the expiry of the time agreed by the parties could be set aside.[687] In most cases, the mere fact that the award was rendered after the expiry of such time limits has not resulted in a setting aside of the award. The Jordanian Supreme Court considered that the failure of a party to object to the continuation of the proceedings constituted a waiver of the right to object pursuant to article 4, if not even a consent to an extension of time.[688] (See also below in this section, para. 85).

Erroneous denial of jurisdiction

43. Decisions have found negative jurisdictional rulings to be reviewable on the ground that they constitute awards subject to setting-aside proceedings under article 34. Particularly noteworthy is a decision of the German Federal Court of Justice in which the arbitral tribunal had denied jurisdiction on the ground that the respondent had effectively withdrawn from the arbitration agreement. While the court held that the arbitral tribunal's jurisdictional decision was subject to article 34, it also found that none of the grounds exhaustively listed in article 34 allowed the court to set aside the decision on the sole basis that the tribunal had erred in denying jurisdiction. In other words, according to the court, article 34 does not allow courts to review the merits of negative jurisdictional decisions; such decisions can only be set aside in one of the specific circumstances explicitly mentioned in article 34.[689] A negative jurisdictional decision was also reviewed pursuant to article 34, in that instance by a Canadian court. While the court deemed the arbitral tribunal's decision to be reviewable pursuant to article 34, it noted that a review of the merits of that

[681] Oberlandesgericht Naumburg, Germany, 10 Sch 01/05, 20 May 2005, available on the Internet at http://www.dis-arb.de/de/47/datenbanken/rspr/olg-naumburg-az-10-sch-01-05-datum-2005-05-20-id456.

[682] CLOUT case No. 457 [Hanseatisches Oberlandesgericht Hamburg, Germany, 1 Sch 02/99, 14 May 1999], also available on the Internet at http://www.dis-arb.de/de/47/datenbanken/rspr/hanseat-olg-hamburg-az-1-sch-02-99-datum-1999-05-14-id30.

[683] CLOUT case No. 562 [Hanseatisches Oberlandesgericht Hamburg, Germany, 6 Sch 04/01, 8 November 2001], also available on the Internet at http://www.dis-arb.de/de/47/datenbanken/rspr/hanseat-olg-hamburg-az-6-sch-04-01-datum-2001-11-08-id145.

[684] Supreme Court, Hungary, BH 2007, 193.

[685] CLOUT case No. 562 [Hanseatisches Oberlandesgericht Hamburg, Germany, 6 Sch 04/01, 8 November 2001], also available on the Internet at http://www.dis-arb.de/de/47/datenbanken/rspr/hanseat-olg-hamburg-az-6-sch-04-01-datum-2001-11-08-id145.

[686] CLOUT case No. 12 [*D. Frampton & Co. Ltd. v. SylvioThibeault and Navigation Harvey & Frères Inc.*, Federal Court, Trial Division, Canada, 7 April 1988], where the award was found not to be binding on a person who had signed the arbitration agreement in his professional capacity on behalf of a company and not in his private capacity; the court determined that the arbitral tribunal had gone beyond the scope of the submission to arbitration in that the award affected a third party, who was not a party to the arbitration agreement.

[687] *N.B.C.C. Ltd. v. J.G. Engineering Pvt. Ltd.*, Supreme Court, India, 5 January 2010, available on the Internet at http://www.indiankanoon.org/doc/1259068/; Court of Appeal, Tunisia, 3 December 2002, case No. 134.

[688] Supreme Court, Jordan, 7 November 2007, No. 1242/2007.

[689] CLOUT case No. 560 [Bundesgerichtshof, Germany, III ZB 44/01, 6 June 2002], also available on the Internet at http://www.dis-arb.de/en/47/datenbanken/rspr/bgh-case-no-iii-zb-44-01-date-2002-06-06-id185.

decision was impermissible under article 34 since "an arbitral decision is not invalid because it wrongly decided a point of fact and law." The court also added that the grounds for setting aside awards, which are exhaustively enumerated in article 34, have to be construed narrowly.[690] These two decisions stand in contrast to a decision of the Court of Appeal of Singapore finding that negative jurisdictional rulings do not constitute arbitral awards.[691] (See above, section on article 16, paras. 21-24)

Waiver

44. Decisions have provided that if a party did not raise objections to the existence of an arbitration agreement at the latest in the submission of the statement of defence (article 16 (2)), such party was precluded from raising that objection in an application under article 34.[692] However, where the respondent failed to submit a statement of defence due to the arbitral tribunal's failure to request the respondent to submit such a statement of defence, it was found that the party would then not be precluded from raising such objection under article 34.[693]

45. Diverging court decisions have been rendered on whether the failure of a party to apply for court review of the arbitral tribunal's decision on jurisdiction under article 16 (3) would imply a waiver of such party's objection to jurisdiction. German courts have considered that a failure to challenge a preliminary ruling of the arbitral tribunal assuming jurisdiction in proceedings under article 16 (3) precludes a party to raise the lack of jurisdiction of the arbitral tribunal in setting aside proceedings or as a defence against enforcement.[694] (See also above, section on article 16, paras. 13 and 27 and section on article 36, para. 22). Courts in Singapore and Hungary have come to the opposite conclusion. The High Court in Singapore considered an application under article 16 (3) to be optional so that the failure to make use of that option could not preclude reliance on an alleged lack of jurisdiction in setting aside proceedings.[695] The Hungarian Supreme Court also considered that there was no provision explicitly providing for such preclusionary effects. Moreover, the court stated that a participation of the defendant in the arbitral proceedings could not be interpreted as a waiver of rights under article 4. According to that court decision, as article 16 does not explicitly mention the parties' right to derogate from it, article 4 does not apply.[696]

46. In one case dealing with a similar issue in substance, but in the context of enforcement proceedings, the High Court in Hong Kong excluded reliance on that defence on the basis of the "doctrine of estoppel". The party opposing enforcement had invoked the arbitration agreement to contest the jurisdiction of the court in the originally initiated court proceedings and had then, after an unsuccessful challenge to the jurisdiction of the arbitral tribunal, participated in the arbitral proceedings. In that light, the court rejected the evidence submitted by the party to prove that the arbitration agreement was allegedly invalid under the law of the country where the arbitration took place (see below, section on article 36, para. 22).[697]

---

[690] CLOUT case No. 1014 [*Bayview Irrigation District #11 v. United Mexican States*, Ontario Superior Court of Justice, Canada, 5 May 2008], [2008] CanLII 22120 (ON SC), available on the Internet at http://canlii.ca/t/1wwtf.

[691] CLOUT case No. 742 [*PT Asuransi Jasa Indonesia (Persero) v. Dexia Bank S.A.*, Court of Appeal, Singapore, 1 December 2006], also in [2006] SGCA 41, [2007] 1 SLR(R) 597.

[692] CLOUT case No. 148 [Moscow City Court, Russian Federation, 10 February 1995]; Oberlandesgericht Köln, Germany, 19 Sch 12/08 , 21 November 2008; Oberlandesgericht Stuttgart, Germany, 1 Sch 13/01, 20 December 2001, available on the Internet at http://www.dis-arb.de/de/47/datenbanken/rspr/olg-stuttgart-az-1-sch-13-01-datum-2001-12-20-id160.

[693] CLOUT case No. 562 [Hanseatisches Oberlandesgericht Hamburg, Germany, 6 Sch 04/01, 8 November 2001], also available on the Internet at http://www.dis-arb.de/de/47/datenbanken/rspr/hanseat-olg-hamburg-az-6-sch-04-01-datum-2001-11-08-id145.

[694] Bundesgerichtshof, Germany, III ZB 83/02, 27 March 2003, available on the Internet at http://www.dis-arb.de/de/47/datenbanken/rspr/bgh-az-iii-zb-83-02-datum-2003-03-27-id212, rejecting the complaint on a point of law only against the decision of Oberlandesgericht Oldenburg, Germany, 9 SchH 09/02, 15 November 2002, both available on the Internet at http://www.dis-arb.de/de/47/datenbanken/rspr/olg-oldenburg-az-9-schh-09-02-datum-2002-11-15-id235.

[695] *Tan Poh Leng Stanley v. Tang Boon Jek Jeffrey*, High Court, Singapore, 30 November 2000, [2001] 1 SLR 624, where an arbitral award which revised an earlier final award was set aside; the decision of the High Court was reversed on appeal, see Court of Appeal, Singapore, *Tang Boon Jek Jeffrey v. Tan Poh Leng Stanley*, 22 June 2001, [2001] 3 SLR 237.

[696] Supreme Court, Hungary, BH 2007, 193.

[697] *Jiangxi Provincial Metal & Mineral Import & Export Corp. v. Sulanser Co. Ltd.*, High Court—Court of First Instance, Hong Kong, 6 April 1995, [1995] HKCF 1449, available on the Internet at http://www.hklii.hk/eng/hk/cases/hkcfi/1995/449.html.

The party was unable to present its case—paragraph (2)(*a*)(ii)

Relationship to other grounds

47. In practice, alleged violations of the ability to present one's case, regularly also referred to as the violation of the right to be heard or of due process or of "natural justice",[698] are among the most frequently grounds referred to in application for setting aside arbitral awards. Courts have also dealt with such allegations under the heading of violations of procedural public policy (article 34 (2)(*b*)(ii))[699] or non-compliance with the applicable procedural rules (article 34 (2)(*a*)(iv)).[700] The case law does not reveal any generally accepted delimitation between the different grounds but it seems that the submissions of the parties are the primary criteria in determining under which ground or defence the alleged violation of the right to be heard is discussed.[701] In none of the decisions available has the rejection of an application for setting aside an award been based on a presumably wrong classification of the alleged defect. To the contrary, some decisions explicitly state that the right to be heard can be invoked under different grounds.[702]

Standard of review

48. In some jurisdictions, courts have defined what constitutes a violation of a party's right to present its case before dealing with the alleged violation in the case at hand. In particular, German courts have regularly adopted such an approach in light of the fact that the right to be heard is also guaranteed and protected by the German constitution. They have assumed that, in connection with arbitral proceedings, it entails two separate basic obligations. The first obligation is that a party may give its view in respect of the subject matter of the dispute, both in relation to facts and law, and be informed about the view of the other side. It obliges the arbitral tribunal not only to allow submissions of the parties but *inter alia* also prevents it from basing its decision on evidence or materials not known to the parties.[703] The second obligation is that the arbitral tribunal takes note of the arguments and takes them into account for its decision in so far as relevant.[704]

49. According to the Hungarian Supreme Court, the notion of the ability to present one's case includes the ability to make written and oral presentations of a party's position and to present the evidence before the arbitral tribunal, as well as the other party's possibility to be informed of the evidence presented.[705]

50. Courts in New Zealand have generally emphasized that the right to present one's case includes also the possibility to respond to evidence and arguments as may emanate from the other parties in the course of the arbitral proceedings, including at hearings.[706]

51. In addition, some courts have added qualitative requirements as to the gravity of the breach or its effect on the award. To justify the setting aside of an arbitral award for a violation of due process (article 18 of the Model Law), courts have held that the conduct of the arbi-

---

[698] *Government of the Republic of the Philippines v. Philippine International Air Terminals Co., Inc.*, High Court, Singapore, 17 November 2006, [2007] 1 SLR (R) 278, [2006] SGHC 206; see also *Attorney General v. Lyall Tozer*, High Court, New Zealand, 2 September 2003, M1528-IM02 CP607/97, stating that "natural justice" is covered by article 34 (2)(*a*)(ii) as well as by the public policy defence.

[699] CLOUT case No. 391 [*Re Corporación Transnacional de Inversiones, S.A. de C.V. et al. v. STET International, S.p.A. et al.*, Ontario Superior Court of Justice, Canada, 22 September 1999], [1999] CanLII 14819 (ON SC), also available on the Internet at http://canlii.ca/t/1vvn5, confirmed in *Corporación Transnacional de Inversiones v. Stet International*, Ontario Court of Appeal, Canada, 2000 CanLII 16840 (ON CA), (2000) 49 OR (3d) 414, 15 September 2000; Amman Court of Appeal, Jordan, 10 June 2008, No. 206/2008; Oberlandesgericht Köln, Germany, 19 Sch 12/08, 21 November 2008.

[700] CLOUT case No. 375 [Bayerisches Oberstes Landesgericht, Germany, 4 Z Sch 23/99, 15 December 1999], also available on the Internet at http://www.dis-arb.de/de/47/datenbanken/rspr/bayoblg-az-4-z-sch-23-99-datum-1999-12-15-id16; Oberlandesgericht Oldenburg, Germany, 9 SchH 03/05, 30 May 2006, available on the Internet at available on the Internet at http://www.dis-arb.de/de/47/datenbanken/rspr/olg-oldenburg-az-9-schh-03-05-datum-2006-05-30-id752.

[701] CLOUT case No. 391 [*Re Corporación Transnacional de Inversiones, S.A. de C.V. et al. v. STET International, S.p.A. et al.*, Ontario Superior Court of Justice, Canada, 22 September 1999], [1999] CanLII 14819 (ON SC), also available on the Internet at http://canlii.ca/t/1vvn5, confirmed in *Corporación Transnacional de Inversiones v. Stet International*, Ontario Court of Appeal, Canada, 2000 CanLII 16840 (ON CA), (2000) 49 OR (3d) 414, 15 September 2000, where the court held that "concepts of fairness and natural justice enunciated in article 18 significantly overlap the issues of inability to present one's case and conflict with public policy set out in article 34 (2)(*a*)(ii) and (*b*)(ii)."

[702] Oberlandesgericht München, Germany, 34 Sch 12/09, 5 October 2009.

[703] Ibid.

[704] CLOUT case No. 375 [Bayerisches Oberstes Landesgericht, Germany, 4 Z Sch 23/99, 15 December 1999], also available on the Internet at http://www.dis-arb.de/de/47/datenbanken/rspr/bayoblg-az-4-z-sch-23-99-datum-1999-12-15-id16; Oberlandesgericht München, Germany, 34 Sch 12/09, 5 October 2009.

[705] Supreme Court, Hungary, BH 2003, 127 at 1.

[706] *Methanex Motunui Ltd. v. Spellman*, Court of Appeal, Wellington, New Zealand, 17 June 2004, [2004] 3 NZLR 454; *Attorney General v. Lyall Tozer*, High Court of New Zealand, 2 September 2003, M1528-IM02 CP607/97; CLOUT case No. 658 [*Trustees of Rotoaira Forest Trust v. Attorney-General*, High Court (Commercial List) Auckland, New Zealand, 30 November 1998], [1999] 2 NZLR 452.

tral tribunal must be sufficiently serious to offend most basic notions of morality and justice.[707] This would for example be the case if an arbitral tribunal deliberately conceals documents from a party, or if it obtains its own evidence on which it later relies, but fails to disclose the evidence to at least one party.[708]

52. Courts in Germany have required that the alleged violation of the ability to present one's case have an effect on the content of the award to constitute a valid ground for setting aside an arbitral award.[709] In a case where presentation of a witness was rejected during the arbitral proceedings, the court required that the applicant set out what the rejected witness would have said and how that would have affected the outcome of the case.[710]

Lack of participation or representation

53. A party's inability to present its case may result from a variety of facts. Courts have made clear that a party cannot invoke a lack of proper participation or proper representation in the arbitral proceedings as a ground to set aside an award (or to resist enforcement, see below, section on article 36, para. 25) if that is not due to circumstances attributable to the arbitral tribunal or extraneous events beyond the parties' control.[711] Equally, the mere non-participation in the proceedings or certain parts of it, even if based on the erroneous assumption that the arbitral tribunal lacks jurisdiction, does not qualify as a violation of the right to be heard.[712] The latter only entails that the party be given the opportunity to participate in the proceedings.

54. A number of decisions on that question have been rendered in the context of enforcement proceedings, and provide information on how the lack of participation or representation and its impact on due process has been interpreted by State courts (see below, section on article 36, paras. 23-31).[713]

Information about the arbitration and the constitution of the arbitral tribunal

55. In a German decision, an award was set aside since the party challenging the award had not been informed that the presiding arbitrator was confirmed and that, consequently, the tribunal was constituted.[714]

---

[707] CLOUT case No. 391 [*Re Corporación Transnacional de Inversiones, S.A. de C.V. et al. v. STET International, S.p.A. et al.*, Ontario Superior Court of Justice, Canada, 22 September 1999], [1999] CanLII 14819 (ON SC), also available on the Internet at http://canlii.ca/t/1vvn5, confirmed in Ontario Court of Appeal, Canada, *Corporación Transnacional de Inversiones v. Stet International*, 2000 CanLII 16840 (ON CA), (2000) 49 OR (3d) 414, 15 September 2000.

[708] Ibid.

[709] CLOUT case No. 569 [Hanseatisches Oberlandesgericht Hamburg, Germany, 11 Sch 01/01, 8 June 2001], also available on the Internet at http://www.dis-arb.de/de/47/datenbanken/rspr/hanseat-olg-hamburg-az-11-sch-01-01-datum-2001-06-08-id1274 where the setting aside of the award was requested in an action for the enforcement of the award.

[710] Oberlandesgericht Oldenburg, Germany, 9 SchH 3/05, 30 May 2006, available on the Internet at http://www.dis-arb.de/de/47/datenbanken/rspr/olg-oldenburg-az-9-schh-03-05-datum-2006-05-30-id752.

[711] As an illustration, in a decision rendered in the context of enforcement proceedings on the same substantive issue, see *Structural Construction Co. Ltd. v. International Islamic Relief*, High Court, Nairobi, Kenya, 6 October 2006, Miscellaneous Case 596 of 2005, available at the Internet at http://www.kenyalaw.org/CaseSearch/view_preview1.php?link=15047352840327161414879.

[712] CLOUT case No. 391 [*Re Corporación Transnacional de Inversiones, S.A. de C.V. et al. v. STET International, S.p.A. et al.*, Ontario Superior Court of Justice, Canada, 22 September 1999], [1999] CanLII 14819 (ON SC), also available on the Internet at http://canlii.ca/t/1vvn5, pointing to the possibility of default proceedings explicitly provided for in article 25.

[713] Cairo Court of Appeal, Egypt, 5 May 2009, case No. 112/124, where the Court has found an award not to violate the right to due process where a party was unable to attend the hearing, allegedly since it was not granted a visa for the country where the hearing took place; while the court found that the party had failed to furnish sufficient proof that it was refused a visa, the court further underlined that, in any case, the party had been notified of the arbitral proceedings; CLOUT case No. 501 [*Grow Biz International, Inc. v. D.L.T. Holdings Inc.*, Prince Edward Island Supreme Court—Trial Division, Canada, 23 March 2001], [2001] PESCTD 27, also available on the Internet at http://canlii.ca/t/4tjr, where allegations by a Canadian franchisee that it lacked sufficient funds to participate in an arbitration hearing and that therefore its rights of defence were infringed were rejected by the Court; see also, Oberlandesgericht Stuttgart, Germany, 1 Sch 12/01, 6 December 2001, available on the Internet at http://www.dis-arb.de/en/47/datenbanken/rspr/olg-stuttgart-case-no-1-sch-12-01-date-2001-12-06-id159; Ontario Court of Appeal, Canada, *Znamensky Selekcionno-Gibridny Center LLC v. Donaldson International Livestock Ltd.*, 29 April 2010, [2010] ONCA 303: a party is, however, unable to present its case if the lack of participation is due to the fact that it or its witnesses received death threats and the hearing was not transferred to a safe place.

[714] CLOUT case No. 562 [Hanseatisches Oberlandesgericht Hamburg, Germany, 6 Sch 04/01, 8 November 2001], also available on the Internet at http://www.dis-arb.de/de/47/datenbanken/rspr/hanseat-olg-hamburg-az-6-sch-04-01-datum-2001-11-08-id145.

Proper service of documents

56. Different approaches exist as to the assumption of a violation of the right to be heard in cases where service of the documents at the last known address of the defendant was not successful and one had to rely on rules of substituted service. Some courts have insisted on a strict compliance with all formalities under the rules of substitute service. The Bulgarian Supreme Court, for example, did not consider it sufficient that the initiating document delivered to the defendant's registered office was returned with the notice "not delivered" where a second attempt to serve the document on the defendant, as required under the law, had not been made.[715]

57. A Higher Regional Court in Germany, by contrast, deduced from the arbitration agreement an obligation for a party to inform the other party(ies) about changes in the address. Thus, the court considered it sufficient that the arbitral tribunal served the relevant document to the respondent's last known address, without making further enquiries as to the actual address of the respondent's general manager.[716]

Language

58. In several cases, respondents sought to base their alleged inability to present their cases properly on their inability to understand the language of the proceedings. As shown in cases dealing with that issue, but in the context of enforcement proceedings, such defences have not been successful if the language of the arbitral proceedings had been explicitly agreed upon between the parties or was determined according to the applicable arbitration rules (see below, section on article 36, para. 30; see also above, section on article 22, paras. 2 and 4).[717]

Reasonable time to respond

59. A German court held that due process normally requires the arbitral tribunal to give the parties reasonable time to respond to a submission by the other party. However, the court decided that due process was not violated where a party was given only a short time-period to respond to an application for the issuance of an award on agreed terms, if the terms of the settlement were not in dispute and the opposing party had sufficient time to consult with its lawyers before agreeing to the settlement.[718]

Refusal to hold oral hearings

60. The Austrian Supreme Court considered the refusal of an arbitral tribunal to hold an oral hearing, despite the request of one party, to be a violation of the right to be heard, as stated in article 24.[719] The High Court in Singapore held in a case where none of the parties had requested an oral hearing that a proper presentation of one's case does not necessarily entail an oral hearing but could also take place through other means.[720]

Rejection of evidence offered or presented

61. In practice, courts are regularly faced with applications for setting aside arbitral awards where the parties base the alleged inability to present their case on the tribunal's refusal to admit certain evidence offered. Several courts have determined that the notion of "otherwise unable to present its case" covers violations of a party's right to use the relevant means of evidence for its case.[721] A court in Spain set aside an award rendered in proceedings where the arbitrator had been refused access by the other party to premises, the construction of which was the subject mat-

[715] Supreme Court of Cassation, Bulgaria, 31 October 2008, case No. 728.

[716] CLOUT case No. 870 [Oberlandesgericht Dresden, Germany, 11 Sch 19/05, 15 March 2005], available on the Internet at http://www.dis-arb.de/de/47/datenbanken/rspr/olg-dresden-az-11-sch-19-05-datum-2005-03-15-id531.

[717] CLOUT case No. 1069 [Supreme Court, Croatia, 5 March 2008, Case No. Gž 6/08-2], where the public policy defence was rejected as the arbitral tribunal was authorized under the applicable Czech arbitration rules to conduct the proceedings in the Czech language; CLOUT case No. 559 [Oberlandesgericht Celle, Germany, 8 Sch 03/01, 2 October 2001], also available on the Internet at http://www.dis-arb.de/de/47/datenbanken/rspr/olg-celle-az-8-sch-03-01-datum-2001-10-02-id208, confirmed by Bundesgerichtshof, III ZB 06/02, 30 January 2003, available on the Internet at http://www.dis-arb.de/de/47/datenbanken/rspr/bgh-az-iii-zb-06-02-datum-2003-01-30-id197 where the contract had been drafted in German and Russian, but the arbitral tribunal made all its communications in Russian as it was entitled under the applicable arbitration rules; the Court generally considered that the party which is unable to understand the language should arrange for the necessary translations if the language of the arbitral proceedings had explicitly been agreed upon between the parties or was determined according to the applicable arbitration rules. Moreover, it has been generally considered sufficient that a party is represented by a lawyer who speaks the language, see Oberlandesgericht München, Germany, 34 Sch 26/08, 22 June 2009, available on the Internet at http://www.dis-arb.de/de/47/datenbanken/rspr/olg-m&uumlnchen-az-34-sch-26-08-datum-2009-06-22-id1065.

[718] Oberlandesgericht Dresden, Germany, 11 Sch 02/00, 25 October 2000, available on the Internet at http://www.dis-arb.de/de/47/datenbanken/rspr/olg-dresden-az-11-sch-02-00-datum-2000-10-25-id1262.

[719] Supreme Court, Austria, 30 June 2010, 7 Ob 111/10i.

[720] *Government of the Republic of the Philippines v. Philippine International Air Terminals Co., Inc.*, High Court, Singapore, 17 November 2006, [2007] 1 SLR (R) 278, [2006] SGHC 206.

[721] CLOUT case No. 371 [Hanseatisches Oberlandesgericht Bremen, Germany, 2 Sch 04/99, 30 September 1999], also available on the Internet at http://www.dis-arb.de/de/47/datenbanken/rspr/hanseat-olg-bremen-az-2-sch-04-99-datum-1999-09-30-id28, where the notion of "otherwise unable to present its case" was discussed in the context of an enforcement procedure; in the end, no violation was found to exist as it was not possible to determine whether the evidence rejected could have caused the case to be decided differently.

ter of the dispute. Instead of making use of court assistance to physically inspect the premises, the arbitrator finally relied on witness evidence.[722]

62. However, whenever the refusal to take evidence offered could be justified by procedural or substantive reasons, courts have not considered such refusal as a violation of the right to be heard. For example, no violation of due process was found to exist in a case where the arbitral tribunal decided that it would not be necessary in the circumstances of the case to consider additional evidence or to hear again certain witnesses.[723] The same applies in cases where the arbitral tribunal considered the evidence and weighed it differently than as presented by the parties.[724] Furthermore, it has been stated that the arbitral tribunal was not required to give reasons for such a decision.[725]

63. German courts have regularly held that arbitral tribunals are the ones to decide whether evidence is relevant and should be admitted. Decisions on that matter by arbitral tribunals could not be reviewed unless they were arbitrary.[726]

64. A court in Canada considered that a tribunal cannot draw adverse inferences from a party's failure to present evidence if that party is prohibited by law from doing so. In the case at hand, however, the court denied that that was the case.[727]

Inability to comment on relevant evidence

65. Closely connected to the right to present one's own evidence is the right to comment on other relevant evidence either submitted by another party or taken by the arbitral tribunal on its own motion.[728] It has been held by a court that a party should have the opportunity to comment on all facts and factual issues which may be relevant for the arbitral award.[729] Also, other taking of evidence, such as the examination of property, without informing one party properly, has been considered to constitute a violation of the right to present one's case.[730] Equally, reliance by the arbitral tribunal on a document which had inadvertently been included into the file for the arbitral tribunal but not into that of the other party resulted in a setting aside of the award.[731] (See above, section on article 18, para. 6).

Independent investigations by the arbitral tribunal

66. Independent investigations by the arbitral tribunal, without informing the parties, may constitute a violation of the right to be heard. In a case where the arbitral tribunal had expressly stated that its decision as to the amount of the claim was based on independent investigation, the respondents claimed that they had not been able to present their case as to quantum since they were not aware of the evidence which the arbitral tribunal had collected on its

---

[722] *Egson Construcciones S.A. (Ecosa) v. Canteras y Construcciones S.A,* Court of Appeal, Madrid, Spain, 25 January 2008.

[723] Oberlandesgericht Frankfurt a.M., Germany, 26 Sch 01/03, 10 July 2003, available on the Internet at http://www.dis-arb.de/de/47/datenbanken/rspr/olg-frankfurt-am-az-26-sch-01-03-datum-2003-07-10-id226.

[724] *FINDESCO S.L.U v. Ms. Letitia et al.*, Barcelona Court of Appeal, Spain, 18 January 2008, case No. 13/2008—261/2007, where the expert report and the documents were considered by the tribunal but were given little probative value.

[725] CLOUT case No. 375 [Bayerisches Oberstes Landesgericht, Germany, 4 Z Sch 23/99, 15 December 1999], also available on the Internet at http://www.dis-arb.de/de/47/datenbanken/rspr/bayoblg-az-4-z-sch-23-99-datum-1999-12-15-id16; Oberlandesgericht Oldenburg, Germany, 9 SchH 03/05, 30 May 2005, available on the Internet at http://www.dis-arb.de/de/47/datenbanken/rspr/olg-oldenburg-az-9-schh-03-05-datum-2006-05-30-id752.

[726] Oberlandesgericht München, Germany, 34 Sch 15/09, 29 October 2009, available on the Internet at http://www.dis-arb.de/de/47/datenbanken/rspr/olg-m&uumlnchen-az-34-sch-15-09-datum-2009-10-29-id1029; Oberlandesgericht Köln, Germany, 19 Sch 12/08, 21 November 2008; Oberlandesgericht Karlsruhe, Germany, 10 Sch 8/08, 27 March 2009.

[727] *United Mexican States v. Marvin Roy Feldman Karpa*, Ontario Court of Appeal, Canada, 11 January 2005, [2005] Can LII 249 (ON C.A.).

[728] *Methanex Motunui Ltd. v. Spellman*, Court of Appeal, Wellington, New Zealand, 17 June 2004, [2004] 3 NZLR 454.

[729] Oberlandesgericht Köln, Germany, 19 Sch 12/08, 21 November 2008. See also, for instance, in a case on enforcement dealing with a similar issue, the High Court in Hong Kong refused enforcement of an award which was largely based on the report of an expert appointed by the arbitral tribunal against the objection of the defendant and where the defendant was refused the opportunity to comment on the report: *Paklito Investments Ltd. v. Klockner East Asia Ltd.*, High Court—Court of First Instance, Hong Kong, 15 January 1993.

[730] Logroño Court of Appeal, Spain, 7 February 2007, case No. 26/2007 (case involving consumer), where the arbitral tribunal decided after a hearing to examine the property of one party (in the presence of that party) without informing the other party about it.

[731] High Court of New Zealand, *Attorney General v. Lyall Tozer*, 2 September 2003, M1528-IM02 CP607/97.

own motion. The court found that, since it must have been clear to the respondents that the quantum was going to be an issue for the arbitral tribunal and the respondents had ample opportunity to present their arguments and evidence to the arbitral tribunal but failed to do so, there were not sufficient grounds to set aside the award.[732] (See above, section on article 24, para. 6).

67. In a similar case, the court considered the investigations in principle authorized by the applicable arbitration rules to constitute a violation of the right to be heard if a party could not comment on their result.[733]

68. It has been held that decisions which came as a surprise to both parties as they were based on considerations or legal doctrines which had not been raised or pleaded by the parties, may constitute a violation of the right to be heard (see below in this section, para. 73). Those matters have been dealt with by courts in the context of enforcement proceedings (see below, section on article 36, para. 28).[734]

Reliance on own expertise

69. A Court of Appeal in New Zealand rejected a challenge of an award based on an alleged violation of the right to be heard. In that case, the party argued that the arbitrator relied solely on his own expertise in rendering the award, as he determined a price for the delivery of natural gas based on a model he prepared, without discussing it with the parties. The Court held that the model prepared by the arbitrator was not an "expert report", nor an "evidentiary document" in the sense of article 24 (3), which had to be communicated to the parties. As the arbitrator had been chosen for his expert knowledge and the arbitration agreement expressly provided for the use of such knowledge, the court considered the refusal to discuss the model with the parties not to constitute a violation of the rules of natural justice.[735] A court in Jordan rendered a similar decision, stating that arbitrators may rely on their personal knowledge and not on expert opinions to assess damages without the threat of having the award set aside.[736] Along the same lines, the High Court in Hong Kong considered it generally permissible that the arbitral tribunal, chosen for its expertise, draws inferences from the primary facts presented to it which depart from the positions of the parties. In the case at hand, the court held, however, that the arbitral tribunal should have conveyed to the parties its interpretation of the applicable law, given that it deviated from the interpretation submitted by one of them and not contested by the other.[737]

Award on issues not indicated to the parties before rendering the award

70. A court considered that an arbitral tribunal violated the parties' right to be heard because the award was based on a legal doctrine that had not been discussed with the parties, which were unable to make any arguments or submit evidence in that regard.[738]

71. In a case dealing with the question of a violation of natural justice, a court in Singapore stated that the extent to which the disputed issue was pleaded and/or raised in the arbitration, and the impact on the award of an alleged failure to plead and argue the disputed issue, were elements to be considered.[739]

72. The High Court in New Zealand required from a party alleging a violation of the right to be heard that it show first, that a reasonable litigant in the claimant's position would not have foreseen a reasoning on the part of the arbitral tribunal of the type laid down in the award and, second, that with adequate notice it might have been possible to convince the arbitral tribunal to reach a different result.[740] Courts stated that an arbitral tribunal should normally be precluded from taking into account evidence or arguments extraneous to the hearing or the pleading without giving the parties further notice and an opportunity to respond. Courts made clear that arbitrators are not bound to adopt the position of either party, and are free to make

---

[732] CLOUT case No. 88 [*Nanjing Cereals, Oils and Foodstuffs Import & Export Corporation v. Luckmate Commodities Trading Ltd.*, High Court—Court of First Instance, Hong Kong, 16 December 1994], also available on the Internet at http://www.hklii.hk/eng/hk/cases/hkcfi/1994/140.html, where the court also found that, even if the respondents had shown sufficient grounds under article 34, the court would have exercised its discretion to refuse to set aside an award, due to the failure of the respondents to present their case properly by submitting their own evidence to the arbitral tribunal.

[733] *APEX Tech Investment Ltd. v. Chuang's Development (China) Ltd.*, High Court—Court of First Instance, Hong Kong, 8 September 1995, CACV000231/1995.

[734] Oberlandesgericht Stuttgart, Germany, 1 Sch 12/01, 6 December 2001, available on the Internet at http://www.dis-arb.de/en/47/datenbanken/rspr/olg-stuttgart-case-no-1-sch-12-01-date-2001-12-06-id159; Oberlandesgericht München, Germany, 34 Sch 12/09, 5 October 2009.

[735] *Methanex Motunui Ltd. v. Spellman*, Court of Appeal, Wellington, New Zealand, 17 June 2004, [2004] 3 NZLR 454.

[736] Amman Court of Appeal, Jordan, 10 June 2008, No. 206/2008.

[737] *Brunswick Bowling & Billiards Corporation v. Shanghai Zhonglu Industrial Co. Ltd. and Another*, High Court—Court of First Instance, Hong Kong Special Administrative Region of China, 10 February 2009, [2009] HKCFI 94 at para. 111, available on the Internet at http://www.hklii.hk/eng/hk/cases/hkcfi/2009/94.html, at paras. 26 et ff., where the court used its discretion to uphold the award.

[738] CLOUT case No. 1049 [*Louis Dreyfus S.A.S. v. Holding Tusculum B.V.*, Superior Court of Quebec, Canada, 8 December 2008], [2008] QCCS 5903 (CanLII), also available on the Internet at http://canlii.ca/t/21v03.

[739] CLOUT case No. 743 [*Soh Beng Tee & Co. Pte. Ltd. v. Fairmont Development Pte. Ltd.*, Court of Appeal, Singapore, 9 May 2007], [2007] 3 SLR (R) 86.

[740] CLOUT case No. 658 [*Trustees of Rotoaira Forest Trust v. Attorney-General*, High Court (Commercial List) Auckland, New Zealand, 30 November 1998], [1999] 2 NZLR 452.

their own assessment of evidence and value judgment between the positions presented by the parties. In that context, courts held that it could not come as a surprise to the parties that the arbitral tribunal did not adopt the valuation method of either party but adopted its own position.[741]

73. German courts have on several occasions dealt with allegations that the right to be heard had been infringed by the arbitral tribunal as the latter did not comply with allegedly existing information duties so that its decision came as a surprise to the parties. The courts have made clear that the arbitral tribunal is under no obligation to discuss with the parties the case or its preliminary legal view on the facts. Only where the arbitral tribunal intends to deviate from a legal position previously communicated to the parties or where its decision would, for other reasons, come as a surprise to the parties should the arbitral tribunal inform the parties accordingly.[742] The mere request for documents relied upon by one party, however, is not sufficient to justify the conclusion that the arbitral tribunal will follow the interpretation of that party, and that the arbitral tribunal should be required to inform the parties if it intends to base its award on a different interpretation. Equally, suggestions made in the context of a settlement proposal by the arbitral tribunal were usually not found to be covered by that obligation. For instance, an arbitral tribunal which had suggested in its settlement proposal to write off goods over seven years did not infringe a party's right to be heard by rendering an award based on a writing-off period of four years only. It should have been clear to the parties that the seven-year period was mentioned only for the purpose of a settlement, but not an expression of the arbitral tribunal's preliminary view on the issue.[743] (See also below, section on article 36, para. 28).

Consideration of the arguments of the parties

74. Pursuant to the consistent jurisprudence of German courts, it is not sufficient that the arbitral tribunal merely heard the arguments presented by the parties and took note of the evidence offered by them. It must also take them into account in the arbitral award.[744] Although, in principle, there might be a violation of due process where the arbitral tribunal had failed to consider a claim or defence presented by one of the parties in the arbitration, a court considered due process not to be violated where the arbitral tribunal had in fact determined that the counterclaim presented by the respondent was factually unfounded.[745]

75. Courts have considered that arbitral tribunals have no obligation to address all details of the arguments raised and the evidence presented by the parties in the reasoning of their decisions.[746]

"Effects on the award"—requirement

76. Some courts have required proof from the party relying on violation of the right to be heard that the award was based on such violation. The status accorded to this requirement differs. Courts have considered it to be an integral part of the ground for setting aside (or resisting enforcement)[747] and to be a crucial factor in exercising discretion to uphold an award (or enforce it), despite the existence of a ground for setting aside (or refusing enforcement).[748] In that context, the refusal to hold a hearing was not considered to constitute a violation of the right to be heard as the party did not prove that presentation of arguments at such hearing would have led to a different decision.[749]

[741] *Soh Beng Tee & Co. Pte. Ltd. v. Fairmont Development Pte. Ltd.*, 9 May 2007, [2007] 3 SLR (R) 86 which emphasized that the parties often select arbitrators for their experience; see also *VV. and Another v. VW*, High Court, Singapore, 24 January 2008, OS 2160/2006, [2008] SGHC 11; Oberlandesgericht München, Germany, 34 Sch 12/09, 5 October 2009.

[742] Oberlandesgericht Stuttgart, Germany, 1 Sch 03/10, 30 July 2010, available on the Internet at http://www.dis-arb.de/de/47/datenbanken/rspr/olg-stuttgart-az-1-sch-03-10-datum-2010-07-30-id1077.

[743] Oberlandesgericht München, Germany, 34 Sch 12/09, 5 October 2009.

[744] CLOUT case No. 375 [Bayerisches Oberstes Landesgericht, Germany, 4 Z Sch 23/99, 15 December 1999], also available on the Internet at http://www.dis-arb.de/de/47/datenbanken/rspr/bayoblg-az-4-z-sch-23-99-datum-1999-12-15-id16; Oberlandesgericht München, Germany, 34 Sch 12/09, 5 October 2009.

[745] CLOUT case No. 456 [Hanseatisches Oberlandesgericht Hamburg, Germany, 6 Sch 11/98, 4 November 1998], also available on the Internet at http://www.dis-arb.de/de/47/datenbanken/rspr/hanseat-olg-hamburg-az-6-sch-11-98-datum-1998-11-04-id32.

[746] CLOUT case No. 375 [Bayerisches Oberstes Landesgericht, Germany, 4 Z Sch 23/99, 15 December 1999], also available on the Internet at http://www.dis-arb.de/de/47/datenbanken/rspr/bayoblg-az-4-z-sch-23-99-datum-1999-12-15-id16; Oberlandesgericht Frankfurt a.M., Germany, 26 Sch 01/03, 10 July 2003, available on the Internet at http://www.dis-arb.de/de/47/datenbanken/rspr/olg-frankfurt-am-az-26-sch-01-03-datum-2003-07-10-id226; Oberlandesgericht Frankfurt, Germany, 26 SchH 03/09, 27 August 2009, in that latter case rendered in the context of enforcement proceedings, it was stated that the mere silence of the award on certain points raised by the defendant does not mean that the arbitral tribunal has not considered the argument, unless the specific circumstances of the case show the contrary, as for instance, when the argument is of crucial relevance for the legal outcome. Also in the context of enforcement proceedings, a court in Canada stated that the absence of reasons in the award does not mean that a party's right to be heard during the arbitration was violated: CLOUT case No. 30 [Ontario Court, General Division, Canada, *Robert E. Schreter v. Gasmac Inc.*, 13 February 1992], [1992] O.J. No. 257.

[747] CLOUT case No. 371 [Hanseatisches Oberlandesgericht Bremen, Germany, (2) Sch 04/99, 30 September 1999], also available on the Internet at http://www.dis-arb.de/de/47/datenbanken/rspr/hanseat-olg-bremen-az-2-sch-04-99-datum-1999-09-30-id28, rendered in the context of enforcement proceedings.

[748] *Brunswick Bowling & Billiards Corporation v. Shanghai Zhonglu Industrial Co. Ltd. and Another*, High Court—Court of First Instance, Hong Kong Special Administrative Region of China, 10 February 2009, [2009] HKCFI 94 at para. 111, available on the Internet at http://www.hklii.hk/eng/hk/cases/hkcfi/2009/94.html, paras. 36; *APEX Tech Investment Ltd. v. Chuang's Development (China) Ltd.*, High Court—Court of First Instance, Hong Kong, 8 September 1995, CACV000231/1995, rendered in the context of enforcement proceedings.

[749] Oberlandesgericht Karlsruhe, Germany, 10 Sch 8/08, 27 March 2009.

Waiver

77. Parties that refuse to participate in the arbitration proceedings have been considered by courts to have deliberately forfeited the opportunity to be heard.[750]

Scope of submission—paragraph 2*(a)*(iii)

Meaning of scope of submission

78. The question of the delimitation of the scope of submission to arbitration in the meaning of article 34 (2)*(a)*(iii) and, in particular, its delimitation with regard to the question of the validity of an arbitration agreement under article 34 (2)*(a)*(i) has been raised in case law in a variety of different situations.

79. Parties relied on an alleged excess of the scope of submission to arbitration in a variety of situations where already the existence of an arbitration agreement between the parties was an issue which might have fallen within the ambit of paragraph (2)*(a)*(i) in setting aside proceedings. For example, the Supreme Court in Hungary discussed the scope of submission to arbitration under paragraph (2)*(a)*(iii) in a situation where already the existence of an arbitration agreement between the parties was challenged, because the person signing the agreement allegedly had no power to do so or the defendant in the arbitration was not the legal successor of the party who had signed the arbitration clause.[751] Equally, cases of awards against non-signatories or on the basis of allegedly terminated or assigned arbitration agreements have sometimes been treated in the context of paragraph (2)*(a)*(iii).[752]

80. By contrast, the courts in Singapore have usually excluded from the ambit of paragraph (2)*(a)*(iii) cases where the arbitral tribunal lacked jurisdiction to deal with disputes between the parties.[753] Accordingly, paragraph (2)*(a)*(iii) only covers situations in which an arbitral tribunal, which has jurisdiction to hear disputes between the parties, exceeded (or failed to exercise) the authority that was granted to it. That involves cases where the tribunal exceeds its power by deciding matters not referred to it. Equally covered are disputes referred to arbitration which were not within the parties' arbitration agreement or went beyond the scope of that agreement.[754] The failure to deal with every issue referred to the tribunal would justify setting aside the award only if it led to actual prejudice to either party to the dispute.[755] By contrast, mere errors of law or fact leading to an erroneous exercise of existing powers have not been considered sufficient to justify the setting aside of an award.[756]

Delimitation of the scope of the submission to arbitration

81. The scope of submission to arbitration, also referred to as the scope of the mandate of the arbitral tribunal, is primarily determined by the parties. In principle, they have an unfettered discretion as to the disputes submitted to arbitration, subject to the very few restrictions imposed by statute, in particular, the non-arbitrability of certain disputes.[757] Occasionally, the terms of a court order referring the parties to arbitration may become relevant to the determination of the mandate of the arbitral tribunal.[758]

82. Several courts have stated that, in determining the "terms of the submission" to arbitration and "scope of the submission" in paragraph (2)*(a)*(iii), the arbitration agreement and other relevant contractual provisions, the notice of request for arbitration, and the pleadings exchanged between the parties are to be taken into account.[759] In general, courts have adopted a broad interpretation of the

---

[750] CLOUT case No. 391 [*Re Corporación Transnacional de Inversiones, S.A. de C.V. et al. v. STET International, S.p.A. et al.*, Ontario Superior Court of Justice, Canada, 22 September 1999], [1999] CanLII 14819 (ON SC), also available on the Internet at http://canlii.ca/t/1vvn5, confirmed in *Corporación Transnacional de Inversiones v. Stet International*, Ontario Court of Appeal, Canada, 15 September 2000, [2000] CanLII 16840 (ON CA), (2000) 49 OR (3d) 414; Cairo Court of Appeal, Egypt, 9 June 2009, case No. 102/123.

[751] Supreme Court, Hungary, BH 2007, 193.

[752] CLOUT case No. 1014 [*Bayview Irrigation District #11 v. United Mexican States*, Ontario Superior Court of Justice, Canada, 5 May 2008], O.J. No. 1858.

[753] *CRW Joint Operation v. PT Perusahaan Gas Negara (Persero) TBK*, Court of Appeal, Singapore, 13 July 2011, [2011] SGCA 3 para 31; affirming the decision of the High Court in the matter *PT Perusahaan Gas Negara (Persero) TBK v. CRW Joint Operation*, 20 July 2010, [2010] SGHC 202; see also CLOUT case No. 740 [*Aloe Vera of America, Inc. v. Asianic Food (S) Pte. Ltd.* and another, High Court, Singapore, 10 May 2006], [2006] 3 SLR 174 (206), where, in that case rendered in the context of enforcement procedures, the court rejected the argument that the arbitral tribunal had exceeded its mandate by rendering an award against a person who had signed the arbitration agreement only in his capacity as general manager of the company and not in his personal capacity.

[754] *PT Perusahaan Gas Negara (Persero) TBK v. CRW Joint Operation,* High Court, Singapore, 20 July 2010, [2010] SGHC 202, para. 26; affirmed in *CRW Joint Operation v. PT Perusahaan Gas Negara (Persero) TBK*, Court of Appeal, Singapore, 13 July 2011, [2011] SGCA 3.

[755] *CRW Joint Operation v. PT Perusahaan Gas Negara (Persero) TBK*, Court of Appeal, Singapore, 13 July 2011, [2011] SGCA 3, para. 32.

[756] *CRW Joint Operation v. PT Perusahaan Gas Negara (Persero) TBK*, Court of Appeal, Singapore, 13 July 2011, [2011] SGCA 3.

[757] For the question of what law governs the determination of the tribunal's mandate, see section on article 36, paras. 32-34.

[758] *Desputeaux v. Éditions Chouette* (1987) inc., Supreme Court, Canada, 21 March 2003, [2003] 1 S.C.R. 178, 2003 SCC 17, available on the Internet at http://canlii.ca/t/1g2jh.

[759] CLOUT case No. 16 [*Quintette Coal Limited v. Nippon Steel Corp. et al.*, Court of Appeal for British Columbia, Canada, 24 October 1990], [1990] B.C.J. No. 2241; CLOUT case No. 1049 [*Louis Dreyfus S.A.S. v. Holding Tusculum B.V.*, Superior Court of Quebec, Canada, 8 December 2008], [2008] QCCS 5903 (CanLII), also available on the Internet at http://canlii.ca/t/21v03.

mandate of the arbitral tribunal. For instance, the Canadian Supreme Court stated that the mandate should not be interpreted restrictively as being limited to what is expressly set out in the arbitration agreement but should cover also "everything that is closely connected with that agreement".[760] Along the same lines, a court found that the arbitral tribunal did not exceed its powers since the interpretation of the main contract made by the arbitral tribunal was not unreasonable.[761]

83. The High Court in Singapore rejected the argument that an arbitral tribunal exceeded its mandate in the first part of the arbitral proceedings devoted to the determination of the law applicable to the arbitration agreement in holding, *inter alia,* that the doctrine of severability applied to the case.[762]

Arbitral awards on matters not claimed

84. Arbitral awards that go beyond the relief claimed may be considered as decisions beyond the scope of the mandate of the arbitral tribunal.[763] That was, for example, assumed in a case where interests on sums in arrears were awarded though they had not been claimed.[764]

Expiry of time limit for rendering the award

85. The applicable arbitration rules or laws or the agreement of the parties sometimes provide that the award has to be rendered within a particular time. The expiration of such time limit or unjustified prolongation by the arbitral tribunal or the arbitral institution are regularly raised as grounds for setting aside. A court in Tunisia granted such an application in a case where the arbitration agreement in a rent contract provided for the rendering of the award within one month. The arbitral tribunal had extended the time twice by three months to which the applicant had objected. The court held that, while the applicable arbitration law entitled the arbitral tribunal to extend that period twice, such extensions should, in light of the parties' agreement, not have been longer than one month. As a consequence the court considered that the tribunal exceeded its powers by rendering the award outside the agreed upon time limit.[765] In a similar case, where the arbitrator had exceeded the time limit of ninety days by approximately forty days, the Bahraini Court of Cassation held that the arbitrator "must abide by such an agreement unless the parties explicitly or implicitly agree, in writing, on an extension"[766] and that once "the time limit elapses, the arbitrator's jurisdiction (...) terminates (...) and the award issued thereafter is null". Thus, the court ordered the setting aside of the award.[767] (See also above in this section, para. 42.)

Certain claims not covered

86. In a majority of cases, parties argued that certain claims raised were not covered by the arbitration agreement because they either arose from related contracts or were tort claims. In relation to tort claims, a Canadian court held that such claims were within the arbitrator's mandate, provided that they arose out of a commercial relationship, which was within the scope of the arbitration clause.[768]

87. Where the arbitration agreement was contained in a treaty and provided that alleged breaches of only certain provisions of such treaty should be settled by arbitration, the arbitral tribunal was found to be dealing with an issue not falling within the terms of the submission to arbitration if it based its award on other provisions of the treaty. However, the court also held that the award would not be set aside if the decision was also based on other grounds that were within the scope of submission to arbitration.[769]

---

[760] *Desputeaux v. Éditions Chouette* (1987) inc., Supreme Court, Canada, 21 March 2003, [2003] 1 S.C.R. 178, 2003 SCC 17, para. 35, available on the Internet at http://canlii.ca/t/1g2jh.

[761] CLOUT case No. 16 [*Quintette Coal Limited v. Nippon Steel Corp. et al.,* Court of Appeal for British Columbia, Canada, 24 October 1990], [1990] B.C.J. No. 2241.

[762] *Government of the Republic of the Philippines v. Philippine International Air Terminals Co. Inc.*, High Court, Singapore, 17 November 2006, [2007] 1 SLR (R) 278, [2006] SGHC 206.

[763] For a discussion of the issue under the heading of "incorrect procedure" see, Oberlandesgericht München, Germany, 34 Sch 12/09, 5 October 2009.

[764] *Jaral Decoración, S.L v. Peñasco Rodilla, SL,* Madrid Court of Appeal, Spain, 2 February 2007, case No. 94/2007—7/2005.

[765] Court of Appeal, Tunisia, 3 December 2002, case No. 134; see also, *N.B.C.C. Ltd. v. JG Engineering Pvt. Ltd.*, Supreme Court, India, 5 January 2010.

[766] Court of Cassation, Bahrain, 17 November 2003, action No. 433/2003.

[767] Ibid.

[768] CLOUT case No. 584 [*Dunhill Personnel System v. Dunhill Temps Edmonton,* Alberta Queen's Bench, Canada, 30 September 1993] 13 Alta L. R. (2d) 240.

[769] CLOUT case No. 502 [*The United Mexican States v. Metalclad Corporation,* British Colombia Supreme Court, Canada, 2 May 2001], also available on the Internet at http://canlii.ca/t/4xfw.

Disregard of the contract or the law

88. In practice, parties frequently base their applications to set aside an award on the ground that the arbitral tribunal exceeded its mandate, by rendering a decision without taking due account of the contract or the applicable law. The underlying rationale of this argument is the obligation for the arbitral tribunal under article 28, paragraphs (1) and (4) to decide in accordance with the applicable law and the terms of the contract. For instance, a court in Egypt set aside an award where the arbitrator decided *ex aequo et bono* without being expressly authorized by the parties to do so.[770] A court in Oman set aside an award because the arbitrator did not apply the contract concluded between the parties.[771] It may be noted that courts have frequently considered such applications as an effort to review the tribunal's decision on the merits or to re-evaluate the evidence presented and have rejected them.[772]

89. A court in Egypt emphasized the importance of distinguishing between "the non-application of the applicable law by the arbitrator, which is considered a non-respect of the parties' will, and the faults resulting from such application." The court therefore merely ascertained itself that the arbitral tribunal "deduced the solutions it reached from (the agreed-upon) Egyptian legal sources and not from other foreign sources."[773]

Reclassification of issues

90. A Court of Appeal in Spain held that an arbitrator does not exceed his mandate if he reclassifies claims by the parties within the scope of the *iura novit curia* principle.[774] By contrast, where an arbitral tribunal awarded interests on sums in arrears notwithstanding that no such interests were claimed, the arbitral tribunal was considered to have exceeded its mandate. However, the same court adopted a different view in relation to an award on the costs of the proceedings. It held that like in court proceedings, the arbitral tribunal could award such costs of its own motion, without exceeding its mandate.[775]

The arbitral tribunal has no power to revise or recall the final award

91. Decisions have provided that, if the arbitral tribunal, after issuing the final award, reopened the case by issuing another award, the effect of which was to recall or revise the earlier award, the latter award should be set aside since the mandate of the arbitral tribunal was terminated upon issuance of the final award.[776] The only powers of the arbitral tribunal after the final award is issued are those under article 33 of the Model Law, and article 33 does not empower the arbitral tribunal to recall or reverse a final award.[777]

Erroneous denial or acceptance of jurisdiction

92. It has been held by courts that an arbitral tribunal which erroneously declines jurisdiction does not exceed its mandate in the meaning of paragraph (2)*(a)*(iii). Pursuant to article 16 (1) of the Model Law, the arbitral tribunal has the power to decide on its jurisdiction. The mere fact that the decision is wrong does not justify its setting aside under paragraph (2)*(a)*(iii).[778] According to a court in Singapore, that is the case even where the erroneous decision may be based on findings which are inconsistent with that of an earlier award by a different tribunal.[779]

93. More frequent in practice is the allegation that the arbitral tribunal exceeded its mandate by erroneously assuming jurisdiction though the arbitration agreement was not valid, had been terminated or the applicant was not a party to the arbitration agreement. The High Court in Singapore held in a case where the award had been

[770] Cairo Court of Appeal, Egypt, 8 January 2002, case No. 72/117; Oberlandesgericht München, Germany, 34 Sch 10/05, 22 June 2005, available on the Internet at http://www.dis-arb.de/de/47/datenbanken/rspr/olg-m&uumlnchen-az-34-sch-10-05-datum-2005-06-22-id403.

[771] First Instance Court, Oman, 19 October 1998, case No. 2/98.

[772] *Simbymanyo Estates Ltd. v. Seyani Brothers Company (U) Ltd.*, Kampala High Court, Commercial Division, Uganda, 23 August 2004, Misc. Application No. 555/2002; *SDV. Transami Ltd. v. Agrimag Limited et al.*, Kampala High Court, Commercial Division, Uganda, 19 June 2008, HCT-00-CC-AB-0002-2006; *Chevron Kenya Ltd. & Chevron Uganda Ltd. v. Daqare Transporters Ltd.*, Kampala High Court, Commercial Division, Uganda, 3 March 2009, Misc. Application No. 490/2008; Cairo Court of Appeal, Egypt, 5 May 2009, case No. 112/124.

[773] Cairo Court of Appeal, Egypt, 5 May 2009, case No. 112/124.

[774] *Urbaser v. Babcock,* Madrid Court of Appeal, Spain, 27 October 2008, case No. 542/2008—2/2008; in favour of an arbitrator's power to reframe issues, see also *SDV. Transami Ltd. v. Agrimag Limited et al.*, Kampala High Court, Commercial Division, Uganda, 19 June 2008, HCT-00-CC-AB-0002-2006.

[775] *Jaral Decoración, S.L v. Peñasco Rodilla, SL,* Madrid Court of Appeal, Spain, 2 February 2007, case No. 94/2007—7/2005.

[776] Oberlandesgericht Stuttgart, Germany, 1 Sch 13/01, 20 December 2001, available on the Internet at http://www.dis-arb.de/de/47/datenbanken/rspr/olg-stuttgart-az-1-sch-13-01-datum-2001-12-20-id160; *Tan Poh Leng Stanley v. Tang Boon Jek Jeffrey*, High Court, Singapore, 30 November 2000 [2001] 1 SLR 624, where an arbitral award which revised an earlier final award was set aside; the decision of the High Court was reversed on appeal, see *Tang Boon Jek Jeffrey v. Tan Poh Leng Stanley*, Court of Appeal, Singapore, 22 June 2001, [2001] 3 SLR 237.

[777] *Tan Poh Leng Stanley v. Tang Boon Jek Jeffrey*, High Court, Singapore, 30 November 2000, [2001] 1 SLR 624.

[778] CLOUT case No. 560 [Bundesgerichtshof, Germany, III ZB 44/01, 6 June 2002], also available on the Internet at http://www.dis-arb.de/de/47/datenbanken/rspr/bgh-az-iii-zb-44-01-datum-2002-06-06-id185; CLOUT case No. 742 [*PT AsuransiJasa Indonesia (Persero) v. Dexia Bank S.A.*, Court of Appeal, Singapore, 1 December 2006], [2006] SGCA 41.

[779] CLOUT case No. 742 [*PT AsuransiJasa Indonesia (Persero) v. Dexia Bank S.A.*, Court of Appeal, Singapore, 1 December 2006], [2006] SGCA 41 at para. 46.

rendered not only against the company but also against its general manager who had signed the contract on behalf of the company that the arbitral tribunal's decision on its jurisdiction does not constitute an excess of the tribunal's mandate even if it erroneously included a third party into the arbitration.[780] Arbitral tribunals are empowered to decide on their own jurisdiction which, if contested, may be raised in the context of a different defence.[781]

Claims based on clause in terminated or assigned agreements

94. Usually, where a contract had allegedly been assigned to a different party and had in the meantime been terminated, claims based on that contract would still fall within the scope of submission to arbitration, in particular where the claims were based on pre-termination facts (see below, section on article 36, para. 37).[782]

Scrutiny in case of awards without reasons

95. To determine whether an arbitral tribunal exceeded its mandate, parties have in general to rely on the reasoning of the award. Thus, the failure of the arbitral tribunal to give any reasons seriously hampers a party's ability to determine if the award dealt with a dispute beyond the terms of submission. Court decisions differ as to whether the failure to provide reasons constitutes or not, on its own, a ground for setting aside (or refusing to enforce) an award. A Court of Appeal in Egypt set aside awards which, absent a party agreement to that effect, contained no grounds supporting the tribunal's findings.[783]

The court should only set aside arbitral awards that are outside the scope of the submission to arbitration

96. It was stated by a court that where the conclusion of the arbitral tribunal was based on two or several independent grounds, the award should be set aside only in relation to those grounds which are beyond the scope of the submission to arbitration.[784] An award was partially set aside in a case where the arbitral tribunal awarded interests on the sums in arrears without being asked to do so. Thus, only the part of the award relating to the interests claimed was set aside.[785]

"Incorrect" composition of the arbitral tribunal—paragraph 2(*a*)(iv)

The arbitral tribunal was not composed according to the agreement of the parties

97. Of primary relevance for assessing the proper composition of the arbitral tribunal is the arbitration agreement.[786]

98. A court considered that, irrespective of the fact that the arbitration agreement merely provided for a sole arbitrator, the participation of an administrative secretary in the proceedings in addition to the sole arbitrator did not lead to an improperly constituted tribunal, provided his/her tasks were limited to administrative matters including the recording of the taking of evidence.[787]

---

[780] CLOUT case No. 740 [*Aloe Vera of America, Inc. v. Asianic Food (S) Pte. Ltd. and another*, High Court, Singapore, 10 May 2006], [2006] 3 SLR 174 (206), where, in that case rendered in the context of enforcement procedures, the court rejected the argument that the arbitral tribunal had exceeded its mandate by rendering an award against a person who had signed the arbitration agreement only in his capacity as general manager of the company and not in his personal capacity.

[781] Oberlandesgericht Karlsruhe, Germany, 10 Sch 01/07, 14 September 2007, available on the Internet at http://www.dis-arb.de/de/47/datenbanken/rspr/olg-karlsruhe-az-10-sch-01-07-datum-2007-09-14-id959.

[782] Oberlandesgericht Stuttgart, Germany, 1 Sch 12/01, 6 December 2001, available on the Internet at http://www.dis-arb.de/en/47/datenbanken/rspr/olg-stuttgart-case-no-1-sch-12-01-date-2001-12-06-id159, rendered in the context of enforcement proceedings; but, see for a void contract invalidating the arbitration clause contained therein, Court of Cassation, Bahrain, 17 November 2003, action No. 433/2003.

[783] Cairo Court of Appeal, Egypt, 2 December 2008, case No. 114/124.

[784] CLOUT case No. 502 [*The United Mexican States v. Metalclad Corporation*, British Colombia Supreme Court, 2 May 2001] also available on the Internet at http://canlii.ca/t/4xfw, where the arbitral award was not set aside in its entirety, since the arbitral tribunal had identified breaches to the North American Free Trade Agreement (NAFTA), one of them being within the scope of the mandate of the arbitral tribunal.

[785] *Jaral Decoración, S.L v. Peñasco Rodilla, SL*, Madrid Court of Appeal, Spain, 2 February 2007, case No. 94/2007—7/2005.

[786] CLOUT case No. 440 [Oberlandesgericht Köln, Germany, 9 Sch 15/99, 22 December 1999], also available on the Internet at http://www.dis-arb.de/de/47/datenbanken/rspr/olg-k&oumlln-az-9-sch-15-99-datum-1999-12-22-id130.

[787] *Clement C. Ebokan v. Ekwenibe & Sons Trading Company*, Lagos Court of Appeal, Nigeria, 22 January 2001, [2001] 2 NWLR 32.

Non-compliance with applicable rules for the constitution of arbitral tribunal

99. In a case where the applicable arbitration rules authorized the arbitral tribunal to rule on the challenge of arbitrators and to appoint substitute arbitrators, the arbitral award was set aside because the arbitral tribunal had refused to accept an arbitrator who was not part of a list of arbitrators.[788]

Conflict of constitution process with mandatory provisions of the Model Law

100. Appointment by a default mechanism provided for either in the arbitration agreement or the chosen arbitration rules does not lead to an incorrectly composed arbitral tribunal. In particular, where the sanction for a party's non-compliance with its appointment obligations is the appointment through a preselected appointing authority, courts have considered such procedures to be in line with the principles of the Model Law.[789] Even in one case where the arbitration agreement provided as a sanction for the non-compliance with an appointment obligation that the right to appoint would be transferred to the other party, an award issued by two arbitrators appointed accordingly by only one party was not set aside. The court concluded in that case that the existing agreement between the parties was not contrary to the Model Law. The other party was considered to be sufficiently protected through the availability of challenge procedures.[790]

101. An arbitral award issued by an appeal board rejecting an appeal against an earlier arbitral award due to late payment of fees was not set aside since such rejection was in accordance with the arbitration rules agreed to between the parties, and the arbitration rules did not conflict with mandatory provisions of the Model Law.[791]

Lack of arbitrator's independence and impartiality

102. The Danish Supreme Court held that a party which had not challenged an arbitrator for lack of independence during the arbitral proceedings even though it knew that the arbitrator had acted as counsel in a related matter could not later apply for setting aside the award for that reason, irrespective of whether the connections had been sufficiently close to justify a challenge of the arbitrator.[792]

103. Equally, the failure to further refer a challenge, initially rejected by the arbitral tribunal or the relevant institution, to the courts has been held to exclude any later right to apply for the setting aside of the award for lack of impartiality.[793]

"Incorrect" procedure–paragraph 2*(a)*(iv)

Relevant standards

104. Irrespective of the fact that the Model Law explicitly allows for majority decisions, an award rendered by a majority of the members of the arbitral tribunal was set aside in a case where the arbitration clause in a shareholders' agreement provided for unanimity. The court considered that the procedure to render the award was contrary to the agreed upon procedure.[794] A court in Hong Kong held, however, that where the agreed upon procedure would conflict with mandatory provisions of the Model Law, deviations by the arbitral tribunal from the agreed upon procedure do not justify the setting aside of the award.[795]

105. The chosen arbitration rules prevail over the non-mandatory provisions of the law at the place of arbitration. Thus, the representation of a party by a foreign lawyer in

[788] CLOUT case No. 436 [Bayerisches Oberstes Landesgericht, Germany, 4 Z Sch 17/98, 24 February 1999], also available on the Internet at http://www.dis-arb.de/de/47/datenbanken/rspr/bayoblg-az-4-z-sch-17-98-datum-1999-02-24-id22, where the court made also clear that the final decision in regard to the challenge of an arbitrator has to be made by a State court, in line with the legislation enacting article 13 (3) of the Model Law.

[789] Oberlandesgericht Köln, Germany, 9 Sch 23/00, 16 October 2000, available on the Internet at http://www.dis-arb.de/de/47/datenbanken/rspr/olg-k&oumlln-az-9-sch-23-00-datum-2000-10-16-id155 (that decision was rendered in the context of enforcement procedures).

[790] CLOUT case No. 440 [Oberlandesgericht Köln, Germany, 9 Sch 15/99, 22 December 1999], also available on the Internet at http://www.dis-arb.de/de/47/datenbanken/rspr/olg-k&oumlln-az-9-sch-15-99-datum-1999-12-22-id130.

[791] CLOUT case No. 455 [Hanseatisches Oberlandesgericht Hamburg, Germany, 14 Sch 01/98, 4 September 1998], also available on the Internet at http://www.dis-arb.de/de/47/datenbanken/rspr/hanseat-olg-hamburg-az-14-u-111-98-14-sch-01-98-datum-1998-09-04-id33.

[792] *JKM Transport ApS v. Danish Crown*, Supreme Court, Denmark, 16 December 2009, Case 337/2007.

[793] Federal District Court, Mexico, 12 June 2001

[794] Murcia Court of Appeal, Spain, 8 October 2009, case No. 448/2009—161/2008.

[795] *Brunswick Bowling & Billiards Corporation v. Shanghai Zhonglu Industrial Co. Ltd. and Another*, High Court—Court of First Instance, Hong Kong Special Administrative Region of China, 10 February 2009, [2009] HKCFI 94 at para. 111, available on the Internet at http://www.hklii.hk/eng/hk/cases/hkcfi/2009/94.html.

an arbitration in Egypt did not result in the setting aside of an award, notwithstanding that the Egyptian law required representation by an Egyptian lawyer. A court in Egypt held that the chosen arbitration rules did not contain any restrictions as to legal representation in the proceedings and superseded, on that matter, the more stringent requirements of Egyptian law.[796]

106. In the absence of an agreement of the parties on specific rules, the relevant standard is the arbitration law at the place of arbitration. A court stated that the general provisions of the code of procedure (by opposition to specific provisions of the law on arbitration) do not apply, unless explicitly provided for in the arbitration law.[797] A court decided that the failure to be represented by a lawyer does not constitute a ground for setting aside an award as that obligation was not included in the arbitration law itself.[798]

107. As to claims that the arbitral procedure was not in accordance with the Model Law, some decisions seem to require procedural errors of a certain degree of seriousness in order for the award to be set aside, for instance violations of important procedural rules[799] or violations of mandatory provisions.[800] Several recent Canadian decisions have come to the same conclusion, deducing from the wording of paragraph (2)*(a)*(iv) and its use of the word "may" (in the chapeau of paragraph (2)) a residual discretion of the court to enforce awards despite violation of procedural rules.[801] The rationale given for the approach was "to avoid the trivialization of judicial review in cases of minor violation of the procedure".[802] In determining whether to exercise discretion, courts should take into account the nature of the breach in question and "determine whether the breach is of such a nature to undermine the integrity of the process, and assess the extent to which the breach had any bearing on the award itself".[803]

Failure to adhere to parties' agreement

108. Equally, the application of a set of arbitration rules different from the one chosen by the parties has been considered to justify the setting aside of an award.[804]

109. In contrast, in a case on a similar issue, the defendant argued that the arbitral tribunal should have applied an institution's former rules, not the amended ones, and that therefore, for procedural reasons, the award should not be enforced, the court decided to exercise its discretion and did not set aside the award.[805]

Procedural problems

110. A court concluded that when a party (in that case, the claimant) requests that a hearing be held, the arbitral tribunal is obliged to hold such hearing at an appropriate stage of the proceedings (article 24 (1) of the Model Law). The court added that the principle of oral proceedings in arbitration had a different meaning than in court proceedings in that hearings in arbitral proceedings were to be held if so requested by a party but only to the extent the parties had not agreed otherwise.[806] (See also above in this section, para. 60 and in the section on article 24, para. 1).

---

[796] Cairo Court of Appeal, Egypt, 7 May 2008, case No. 76/123.

[797] Supreme Court, Hungary, BH 1999, 128.

[798] Amman Court of Appeal, Jordan, 10 June 2008, No. 206/2008, where the issue was treated in the context of public policy.

[799] CLOUT case No. 436 [Bayerisches Oberstes Landesgericht, Germany, 4 Z Sch 17/98, 24 February 1999], also available on the Internet at http://www.dis-arb.de/de/47/datenbanken/rspr/bayoblg-az-4-z-sch-17-98-datum-1999-02-24-id22; CLOUT case No. 455 [Hanseatisches Oberlandesgericht Hamburg, Germany, 14 Sch 01/98, 4 September 1998], also available on the Internet at http://www.dis-arb.de/de/47/datenbanken/rspr/hanseat-olg-hamburg-az-14-u-111-98-14-sch-01-98-datum-1998-09-04-id33, where the court found that there would be a violation of important procedural rules if the arbitral tribunal did not adhere to the procedure agreed to between the parties; CLOUT case No. 519 [*Wuzhou Port Foreign Trade Development Corp v. New Chemic Ltd.*, High Court—Court of First Instance, Hong Kong Special Administrative Region of China, 8 December 2000], [2001] 3 HKC 395, also available on the Internet at http://www.hklii.hk/eng/hk/cases/hkcfi/2000/1143.html, where the defendant submitted that the award should be set aside on the ground that the arbitral procedure was not in accordance with the agreement of the parties, based on articles 34 (2)*(a)*(iv); the defendant argued that the arbitral tribunal should have applied its former rules, not the amended ones; the court decided to exercise its discretion in favour of the claimant; CLOUT case No. 527 [*Chongqi Machinery Import & Export Co. Ltd. v. Yiu Hoi & Others Trading as Tin Lee Ship Builders & Trading Co.*, Court of First Instance, Hong Kong Special Administrative Region of China, 11 October 2001]; CLOUT case No. 528 [*Shenzhen City Tong Yin Foreign Trade Corp. Ltd. v. Alps Co. Ltd.*, Court of First Instance, Hong Kong, 15 October 2001].

[800] Bayerisches Oberstes Landesgericht, Germany, 4 Z Sch 02/99, 29 September 1999, available on the Internet at http://www.dis-arb.de/de/47/datenbanken/rspr/bayoblg-az-4-z-sch-02-99-datum-1999-09-29-id18.

[801] *Michel Rhéaume v. Société d'investissements l'Excellence Inc.*, Quebec Court of Appeal, Canada, 10 December 2010, 2010 QCCA 2269, available on the Internet at http://canlii.ca/t/2dvpr.

[802] CLOUT case No. 1049 [*Louis Dreyfus S.A.S. v. Holding Tusculum B.V.*, Superior Court of Quebec, Canada, 8 December 2008], [2008] QCCS 5903 (CanLII), also available on the Internet at http://canlii.ca/t/21v03.

[803] *Michel Rhéaume v. Société d'investissements l'Excellence Inc.*, Quebec Court of Appeal, Canada, 10 December 2010, 2010 QCCA 2269, available on the Internet at http://canlii.ca/t/2dvpr.

[804] *Siginon Maritime Ltd. v. Gitutho Associates and Others,* High Court, Mombasa, Kenya, 28 July 2005, Miscellaneous Civil Application 719 of 2004, available on the Internet at http://www.kenyalaw.org/CaseSearch/case_download.php?go=29136052918379844525034&link=.

[805] CLOUT case No. 519 [*Wuzhou Port Foreign Trade Development Corp v. New Chemic Ltd.*, High Court—Court of First Instance, Hong Kong Special Administrative Region of China, 8 December 2000], [2001] 3 HKC 395.

[806] CLOUT case No. 659 [Oberlandesgericht Naumburg, Germany, 10 Sch 08/01, 21 February 2002], available on the Internet at http://www.dis-arb.de/de/47/datenbanken/rspr/olg-naumburg-az-10-sch-08-01-datum-2002-02-21-id166.

111. In a Canadian case, the application to set aside the award was inter alia based on an alleged violation of the principle that, once the award was rendered, the arbitral tribunal became *functus officio,* i.e., it lost its decision-making power in relation to the issues covered by the award. In a dispute concerning the dissolution of a joint venture, the arbitrators had rendered a first award ordering a remedy which, due to the subsequent insolvency of the company in question, became moot. The applicant considered the re-opening of the proceedings in that matter to be a violation of the procedural rule that with the award on a certain issue the arbitral tribunal becomes *functus officio*. The Canadian court rejected the application denying the violation of a procedural rule.[807]

112. A court in Egypt rejected the allegation that the arbitral tribunal's refusal to join other parties to the proceedings constituted a violation of procedural rules.[808]

Failure to render preliminary ruling on jurisdiction

113. Some jurisdictions have adopted article 16 of the Model Law in a slightly amended form stating that the tribunal shall or at least should deal with objections against its jurisdiction in a preliminary ruling on jurisdiction.[809] A violation of this rule, i.e. the inclusion of the tribunal's decision on its jurisdiction in the final award on the merits, was not considered to constitute a ground for setting aside such an award.[810] (See above, section on article 16, para. 14).

Failure to apply the law applicable to the substance of the dispute

114. Courts have decided that arbitral awards could be set aside if the arbitral tribunal applied a law to the substance of the dispute different from the one agreed to by the parties (article 28 (1) of the Model Law, see also above in this section, para. 88).[811] However, it was stressed that the court could review only whether the arbitral tribunal based its decision on the law chosen by the parties and not whether it applied or interpreted it correctly.[812]

115. A German court set aside an award in which the arbitrators decided *ex aequo et bono* without being explicitly authorized to do so. In arbitral proceedings concerning the validity and termination of a lease agreement, the arbitral tribunal had considerably adapted the contract and ordered its continuation in an amended form. The court held that an authorization to decide *ex aequo et bono* could not be deduced from the parties' settlement negotiations but had to be made expressly.[813]

Failure to give sufficient reasons

116. The alleged failure of the arbitral tribunal to give sufficient reasons in the award has been raised by applicants under different headings as a ground for setting aside or refusing enforcement of awards. While some have argued that allegedly insufficient or non-existing reasoning

---

[807] CLOUT case No. 1049 [*Louis Dreyfus S.A.S. v. Holding Tusculum B.V.*, Superior Court of Quebec, Canada, 8 December 2008], [2008] QCCS 5903 (CanLII), also available on the Internet at http://canlii.ca/t/21v03.

[808] Cairo Court of Appeal, Egypt, 7 May 2008, case No. 76/123.

[809] For instance, Germany where Section 1040 (3) of the German Code of Civil Procedure ("ZPO") provides that the tribunal should rule on a plea that it lacks jurisdiction "in general by means of a preliminary ruling".

[810] Tallin District Court, Estonia, 2-06-9525, 28 February 2007.

[811] *Brunswick Bowling & Billiards Corporation v. Shanghai Zhonglu Industrial Co. Ltd. and Another*, High Court—Court of First Instance, Hong Kong Special Administrative Region of China, 10 February 2009, [2009] HKCFI 94 at para. 111, available on the Internet at http://www.hklii.hk/eng/hk/cases/hkcfi/2009/94.html, according to which the question of applying a choice of law clause is not matter of procedure.

[812] CLOUT case No. 375 [Bayerisches Oberstes Landesgericht, Germany, 4 Z Sch 23/99, 15 December 1999], also available on the Internet at http://www.dis-arb.de/de/47/datenbanken/rspr/bayoblg-az-4-z-sch-23-99-datum-1999-12-15-id16; CLOUT case No. 569 [Hanseatisches Oberlandesgericht Hamburg, Germany, 11 Sch 01/01, 8 June 2001], also available on the Internet at http://www.dis-arb.de/de/47/datenbanken/rspr/hanseat-olg-hamburg-az-11-sch-01-01-datum-2001-06-08-id1274 where the application to set aside the award was made in an action to have the award declared enforceable; Cairo Court of Appeal, 5 May 2009—Case No. 112/124.

[813] Oberlandesgericht München, Germany, 34 Sch 10/05, 22 June 2005.

constitutes a violation of natural justice[814] or of procedural public policy,[815] others have classified it as an incorrect procedure breaching the provisions of article 31 (2).[816]

117. Different views exist as to the relevant standards for reasoning. (See also above, section on article 31, paras. 7-10). One Australian court adopted the view that the standard of reasoning should be the same as for court judgments.[817] However, in general, courts have adopted a lower threshold, rejecting the view that the reasons given in an award must meet the standard applicable to court decisions.[818] Accordingly, the arbitral tribunal should state the facts and explain succinctly why, on the basis of such facts, the decision was rendered. A court in Spain held that the relevant reasoning should attain two objectives, first to convince the parties to the proceedings that the judicial decision was just and correct and, second, to allow the implementation of the award.[819] A court in Egypt held that the reasoning must not be contradictory and that it must "allow whoever reviews the award to determine the logic followed by the arbitrator in fact or at law."[820] The reason given by a court for a lower threshold in comparison to court judgment was that arbitration aims at settling disputes expeditiously.[821]

118. In evaluating the sufficiency of the reasons expressed, a court considered that the fact that an arbitral award did not expressly disclose any legal reasoning did not make the reasoning insufficient where the arbitrators were commercial persons.[822] Along the same lines, German courts have required that the reasons given should allow deducing the underlying rationale and should address the main arguments.[823]

119. Concerning the consistency of the reasoning, it has been held that there must be a consistency between the claims and defences raised and the reasoning in the award in so far as the arbitrator's adjustment may not result in an alteration of the cause of action.[824] The Tunisian Court of Cassation set aside an award because the reasons given were contradictory and therefore considered as non-existing.[825]

120. The requirement that there should be reasoning in the award was also addressed in a number of decisions relating to enforcement proceedings (see case law on article 36, para. 42).

Non-compliance with the formal requirements for an award

121. In addition to the lack of sufficient reasoning, parties have regularly sought to rely on the non-compliance with other formalities concerning the award or its notification, in order to have awards set aside. The success of such efforts has been dependent on the relevant court's approach to such formalities.

122. The fact that an award was signed by only two arbitrators was not considered by a Canadian court to constitute a ground for setting aside the award, even though the reason for the omitted signature was not stated in the award as provided by article 31, because the reason for the omitted signature was formally given to the court in the setting aside proceedings by the president of the arbitral tribunal.[826]

---

[814] CLOUT case No. 30 [*Robert E. Schreter v. Gasmac Inc.*, Ontario Court, General Division, Canada, 13 February 1992], [1992] O.J. No. 257, dealing with that matter in the context of enforcement procedure.

[815] *Uniprex S.A. v. Grupo Radio Blanca,* Madrid Court of Appeal, Spain, 22 March 2006, case No. 178/2006—4/2004; see also *Smart Systems Technology Inc. v. Domotique Secant Inc.*, Quebec Court of Appeal, Canada, 11 March 2008, [2008] Q.J. No. 1782.

[816] Oberlandesgericht Rostock, Germany, 1 Sch 04/06, 18 September 2007, available on the Internet at http://www.dis-arb.de/de/47/datenbanken/rspr/olg-rostock-az-1-sch-04-06-datum-2007-09-18-id729; Oberlandesgericht Oldenburg, Germany, 9 SchH 03/05, 30 May 2006, available on the Internet at http://www.dis-arb.de/de/47/datenbanken/rspr/olg-oldenburg-az-9-schh-03-05-datum-2006-05-30-id752.

[817] *Oil Basins Ltd. v. BHP Billiton Ltd.*, Victoria Court of Appeal, Australia, 16 November 2007, [2007] VSCA 255, available on the Internet at http://www.austlii.edu.au/au/cases/vic/VSCA/2007/255.html.

[818] *Gordian Runoff Limited v. Westport Insurance Corporation,* Court of Appeal of New South Wales, Australia, 1 April 2012, [2010] NSWCA 57, available on the Internet at http://www.austlii.edu.au/au/cases/nsw/NSWCA/2010/57.html.

[819] *Uniprex S.A. v. Grupo Radio Blanca,* Madrid Court of Appeal, Spain, 22 March 2006, case No. 178/2006—4/2004.

[820] Cairo Court of Appeal, Egypt, 5 May 2009, case No. 112/124.

[821] Cairo Court of Appeal, Egypt, 3 April 2007, case No. 123/119.

[822] CLOUT case No. 10 [*Navigation Sonamar Inc. v. Algoma Steamships Limited and others,* Superior Court of Quebec, Canada, 16 April 1987], 1987 WL 719339 (C.S. Que.), [1987] R.J.Q. 1346, 1987 CarswellQue 1193, J.E. 87-642, EYB 1987-78387.

[823] Oberlandesgericht Rostock, Germany, 1 Sch 04/06, 18 September 2007, available on the Internet at http://www.dis-arb.de/de/47/datenbanken/rspr/olg-rostock-az-1-sch-04-06-datum-2007-09-18-id729.

[824] *Uniprex S.A. v. Grupo Radio Blanca,* Madrid Court of Appeal, Spain, 22 March 2006, case No. 178/2006—4/2004.

[825] Court of Cassation, Tunisia, 27 November 2008, case No. 20596/2007.

[826] CLOUT case No. 12 [*D. Frampton &Co. Ltd. v. Sylvio Thibeault and Navigation Harvey & Frères Inc.,* Federal Court, Trial Division, Canada, 7 April 1988].

123. Parties have sought, on several occasions before Spanish courts, to justify the setting aside of awards based on deficiencies in the service of the award on the parties. While they have been successful in several consumer related cases, a court rejected such an application in a commercial case. In its view, the arbitral proceedings terminate with the rendering of an award so that deviations from the agreed upon procedure for notifying the award are not covered by paragraph (2)*(a)*(iv).[827]

124. Other issues raised in setting aside proceedings which were not successful because of the inability to establish the necessary facts concern, inter alia, the allegedly improper use of an expert, and going beyond the terms of reference agreed with the parties.[828]

Waiver

125. In several decisions, courts held that the failure to object to the composition of the arbitral tribunal during the proceedings precluded a party from attacking an award on the ground that the arbitral tribunal was incorrectly composed. The cases include decisions relating to an alleged lack of independence of members of the arbitral tribunal where the relevant facts were already known during the arbitral proceedings. The failure to make use of the possibility to challenge an arbitrator in court under article 13 (3) of the Model Law was considered by a Jordanian court to prevent a party from raising the issue in an application to set aside the arbitral award.[829] However, this reasoning would not apply where the arbitral tribunal failed to decide on a challenge.[830]

126. The lack of objection to procedures is frequently considered to constitute a waiver of the right to raise such objection at the post award stage. Consequently, a party was held to be prevented from invoking non-compliance with an alleged multi-stage dispute resolution process where such non-compliance had not already been raised in the arbitral proceedings.[831] Equally, the failure to complain about the lack of hearing as provided for in the arbitration agreement was considered to have resulted in a loss of the right to rely on it at the post award stage.[832]

127. In addition, a court considered that a party which had not objected to the admission of evidence—the case concerned the admission of offers made without prejudice in settlement negotiations—was considered to have waived its rights in this regard.[833] However, it is required that the party be aware of the derogation from the agreed upon procedure. In a Kenyan case, the fact that, contrary to the parties' agreement, no written record of the proceedings existed became apparent after the award had been rendered. A party needed to refer to the record to prove that the claimant had renounced certain claims during the proceedings. The court held that the party had not waived the right to raise the lack of the agreed written recording of the proceedings by further participating in the proceedings, because the party was not aware of the defect.[834]

Non-arbitrability—paragraph 2*(b)*(i)

128. Dealing with the question of jurisdiction in the Canadian Copyright Act, a court held that the mere fact that the arbitral tribunal had to apply rules forming part of public order did not make the dispute non-arbitrable. Equally, the fact that the decision might also have a bearing on third parties, in so far the arbitral tribunal can determine the existence of a copyright, was not considered sufficient to make the dispute non arbitrable.[835]

Public policy—paragraph 2*(b)*(ii)

129. Most decisions that had to address the concept of public policy under paragraph (2)*(b)*(ii) have confirmed the narrow scope of the provision and that it should be applied only in instances of most serious procedural or substantive

---

[827] *FINDESCO S.L.U v. Ms. Letitia et al.*, Barcelona Court of Appeal, Spain, 18 January 2008, case No. 13/2008—261/2007, where the fact that the award had been registered in front of a notary showed that it had been rendered within the time prescribed by the law.

[828] *Luzon Hydro Corp. v. Transfield Philippines Inc.*, High Court, Singapore, 13 September 2004 [2004] SGHC 204.

[829] Supreme Court, Jordan, 7 November 2007, No. 1242/2007.

[830] Oberlandesgericht Stuttgart, Germany, 1 Sch 08/02, 16 July 2002, available on the Internet at http://www.dis-arb.de/de/47/datenbanken/rspr/olg-stuttgart-az-1-sch-08-02-datum-2002-07-16-id187.

[831] *Uniprex S.A. v. Grupo Radio Blanca,* Madrid Court of Appeal, Spain, 22 March 2006, case No. 178/2006—4/2004.

[832] Oberlandesgericht München, Germany, 34 Sch 12/09, 5 October 2009.

[833] *Apa Insurance Co. Ltd. v. Chrysanthus Barnabas Okemo*, High Court, Nairobi, Kenya, 24 November 2005, Miscellaneous Application 241 of 2005, available on the Internet at http://www.kenyalaw.org/CaseSearch/case_download.php?go=50003769819788790599459&link=.

[834] *Siginon Maritime Ltd. v. Gitutho Associates and Others,* High Court, Mombasa, Kenya, 28 July 2005, Miscellaneous Civil Application 719 of 2004, available on the Internet at http://www.kenyalaw.org/CaseSearch/case_download.php?go=29136052918379844525034&link=.

[835] *Desputeaux v. Éditions Chouette (1987) inc.*, Supreme Court, Canada, 21 March 2003, [2003] 1 S.C.R. 178, 2003 SCC 17.

injustice. It has been found that the provision should be given a restrictive interpretation[836] and should be applied only in exceptional cases.[837]

130. Public policy has been found to include both substantive and procedural aspects.[838] In a number of jurisdictions, a distinction is made between national public policy and international public policy which is considered to be a narrower concept. In India, for example, the Supreme Court held in an action to set aside an award that, unlike for the proceedings to enforce foreign awards, in setting aside proceedings it is not necessary to adopt a narrow interpretation of the concept.[839] As has been stated by a German court, the difference between the two concepts is one of degree and not of category.[840]

131. Pursuant to a court in Singapore, the concepts of public policy for setting aside a "domestic" award under article 34 and for the enforcement of a foreign award are identical. The court saw no need to distinguish between the two regimes as all awards falling within the ambit of the legislation on international arbitration are considered to have an "international focus".[841] The courts in Singapore have requested that a party must state precisely which part of public policy is affected and by which part of the award.[842]

Standard of review

132. In defining the appropriate standard of review under paragraph (2)*(b)*(ii), courts found that the public policy defence should be applied only if: (1) a fundamental principle of the law or morality or justice was violated,[843] (2) the award fundamentally offended the most basic and explicit principles of justice and fairness or showed intolerable ignorance or corruption on part of the arbitral tribunal,[844] or (3) the award was in conflict with a principle concerned with the very foundations of public and economic life.[845] For example, the public policy defence would be applicable in case of corruption, bribery, fraud and serious procedural irregularities.[846]

---

[836] CLOUT case No. 323 [*Zimbabwe Electricity Supply Authority v. Genius Joel Maposa,* Supreme Court, Zimbabwe, 21 October and 21 December 1999]; CLOUT case No. 520 [*Shanghai City Foundation Works Corp. v. Sunlink Ltd.,* High Court—Court of First Instance, Hong Kong Special Administrative Region of China, 2 February 2001, [2001] 3 HKC 521]; Oberlandesgericht Karlsruhe, 10 Sch 04/01, 14 September 2001, available on the Internet at http://www.dis-arb.de/de/47/datenbanken/rspr/olg-karlsruhe-az-10-sch-04-01-datum-2001-09-14-id1268; Madrid Court of Appeal, Spain 16 October 2006, case No. 470/2006—9/2004; *PT AsuransiJasa Indonesia (Persero) v. Dexia Bank S.A.*, Court of Appeal, Singapore, 1 December 2006, SGCA 41[2006], at para. 59; *Desputeaux v. Éditions Chouette (1987) inc.*, Supreme Court, Canada, 21 March 2003, [2003] 1 S.C.R. 178, 2003 SCC 17.

[837] CLOUT case No. 10 [Superior Court of Quebec, Canada, *Navigation Sonamar Inc. v. Algoma Steamships Limited and others,* 16 April 1987], 1987 WL 719339 (C.S. Que.), [1987] R.J.Q. 1346, 1987 CarswellQue 1193, J.E. 87-642, EYB 1987-78387]; Oberlandesgericht Stuttgart, Germany, 1 Sch 08/02, 16 July 2002, available on the Internet at http://www.dis-arb.de/de/47/datenbanken/rspr/olg-stuttgart-az-1-sch-08-02-datum-2002-07-16-id187, where the court determined that public policy should only be applied in exceptional cases and that public policy does not constitute an appeal on the merits of the arbitral award.

[838] CLOUT case No. 391 [*Re Corporación Transnacional de Inversiones, S.A. de C.V. et al. v. STET International, S.p.A. et al.*, Ontario Superior Court of Justice, Canada, 22 September 1999], [1999] CanLII 14819 (ON SC), also available on the Internet at http://canlii.ca/t/1vvn5, confirmed in *Corporación Transnacional de Inversiones v. Stet International*, Ontario Court of Appeal, Canada, 2000 CanLII 16840 (ON CA), (2000) 49 OR (3d) 414, 15 September 2000, available on the Internet at http://canlii.ca/t/1cvn9.

[839] *Oil & Natural Gas Corporation Ltd. v. Saw Pipes Ltd.,* Supreme Court, India, 17 April 2003, [2003] INSC 236; the broad concept was also extended to the recognition of foreign awards in *Phulchand Exports Ltd. v. OOO Patriot*, Supreme Court, India,12 October 2011, [2011] INSC 1038.

[840] Bundesgerichtshof, Germany, III ZB 17/08, 30 October 2008, available on the Internet at http://www.dis-arb.de/de/47/datenbanken/rspr/bgh-az-iii-zb-17-08-datum-2008-10-30-id875 .

[841] *AJT v. AJU,* Court of Appeal, Singapore, 22 August 2011, [2011] SGCA 41, para. 37; see also *Phulchand Exports Ltd. v. OOO Patriot,* Supreme Court, India 12 October 2011, [2011] INSC 1038, in the context of enforcement proceedings.

[842] *VV. and Another v. VW*, High Court, Singapore, 24 January 2008, OS 2160/2006, [2008] SGHC 11.

[843] CLOUT case No. 323 [*Zimbabwe Electricity Supply Authority v. Genius Joel Maposa,* Supreme Court, Zimbabwe, 21 October and 21 December 1999].

[844] CLOUT case No. 391 [*Re Corporación Transnacional de Inversiones, S.A. de C.V. et al. v. STET International, S.p.A. et al.*, Ontario Superior Court of Justice, Canada, 22 September 1999], [1999] CanLII 14819 (ON SC), also available on the Internet at http://canlii.ca/t/1vvn5, confirmed in *Corporación Transnacional de Inversiones v. Stet International*, Ontario Court of Appeal, Canada, 2000 CanLII 16840 (ON CA), (2000) 49 OR (3d) 414, 15 September 2000, available on the Internet at http://canlii.ca/t/1cvn9; *United Mexican States v. Marvin Roy Feldman Karpa*, Ontario Court of Appeal, Canada, 11 January 2005, 2005 Can LII 249 (ON C.A.).

[845] Oberlandesgericht Karlsruhe, 10 Sch 04/01, 14 September 2001, dealing with the relationship between public policy and constitutional rights, available on the Internet at http://www.dis-arb.de/de/47/datenbanken/rspr/olg-karlsruhe-az-10-sch-04-01-datum-2001-09-14-id1268; CLOUT case No. 570 [Hanseatisches Oberlandesgericht Hamburg, Germany, 11 Sch 02/00, 30 August 2002], also available on the Internet at http://www.dis-arb.de/de/47/datenbanken/rspr/hanseat-olg-hamburg-az-11-sch-02-00-datum-2002-08-30-id1273.

[846] CLOUT case No. 391 [*Re Corporación Transnacional de Inversiones, S.A. de C.V. et al. v. STET International, S.p.A. et al.*, Ontario Superior Court of Justice, Canada, 22 September 1999], [1999] CanLII 14819 (ON SC), also available on the Internet at http://canlii.ca/t/1vvn5, confirmed in *Corporación Transnacional de Inversiones v. Stet International*, Ontario Court of Appeal, Canada, 2000 CanLII 16840 (ON CA), (2000) 49 OR (3d) 414, 15 September 2000, available on the Internet at http://canlii.ca/t/1cvn9; CLOUT case No. 1014 [*Bayview Irrigation District #11 v. United Mexican States*, Ontario Superior Court of Justice, Canada, 5 May 2008], [2008] O.J. No. 1858; CLOUT case No. 323 [*Zimbabwe Electricity Supply Authority v. Genius Joel Maposa,* Supreme Court, Zimbabwe, 21 October and 21 December 1999].

Procedural public policy

133. Procedural laws have been considered part of public policy only when they set forth the basic principles upon which the procedural system is based[847] or express fundamental procedural principles.[848] Decisions have found that a violation of a party's right to be heard could constitute a violation of procedural public policy, but only if there was a causal link between such violation of the right to be heard and the content of the award.[849] For instance, there was no violation of the right to be heard if the arbitral tribunal considered the claim or defence, but found it immaterial.[850] Where the legal argument of a party had been the subject of oral hearing, and the arbitral tribunal addressed the argument in its decision, the party's right to be heard has not been considered violated,[851] nor has public policy been found to require that the arbitral award expressly deals with each and every argument presented by the parties.[852]

134. The complete absence of any reasoning was considered to constitute a violation of public policy at least in cases where the award had to give reasons under the applicable rules, and without such reasoning it could not be determined whether the arbitral tribunal exceeded its mandate.[853]

135. In practice, parties regularly allege that the enforcement of the arbitral award against them would violate public policy as they never submitted to arbitration. The High Court in Singapore rejected such a defence in a case where it was based on the alleged prohibited piercing of the corporate veil as the arbitral tribunal had invoked the alter ego doctrine. The court made clear that, irrespective of whether the court may have come to a different conclusion on the basis of the facts before it, the alter ego doctrine applied by the arbitral tribunal is in itself not offensive to the law of Singapore.[854]

Substantive public policy

136. It was generally acknowledged in court decisions dealing with substantive public policy that article 34 (2)*(b)* (ii) does not permit a review of the merits of a case. Thus, awards should not be set aside in order to correct a possible breach of equity or a wrong decision, except where the decision was incompatible with a fundamental aspect of justice.[855] The same would apply to incorrect interpretations of contractual clauses,[856] erroneous qualifications of legal relationships, weighing of evidence or rejections of requests for examining evidence.[857] A court in Spain has described public policy in that regard as a guarantee that notwithstanding that

[847] CLOUT case No. 10 [*Navigation Sonamar Inc. v. Algoma Steamships Limited and others,* Superior Court of Quebec, Canada, 16 April 1987], [1987] WL 719339 (C.S. Que.), [1987] R.J.Q. 1346, 1987 CarswellQue 1193, J.E. 87-642, EYB 1987-78387; CLOUT case No. 146 [Moscow City Court, Russian Federation, 10 November 1994].

[848] CLOUT case No. 457 [Hanseatisches Oberlandesgericht, Germany, 1 Sch 02/99, 14 May 1999], also available on the Internet at http://www.dis-arb.de/de/47/datenbanken/rspr/hanseat-olg-hamburg-az-1-sch-02-99-datum-1999-05-14-id30.

[849] CLOUT case No. 375 [Bayerisches Oberstes Landesgericht, Germany, 4Z Sch 23/99, 15 December 1999], also available on the Internet at http://www.dis-arb.de/de/47/datenbanken/rspr/bayoblg-az-4-z-sch-23-99-datum-1999-12-15-id16; CLOUT case No. 457 [Hanseatisches Oberlandesgericht, Germany, 1 Sch 02/99, 14 May 1999]; CLOUT case No. 569 [Hanseatisches Oberlandesgericht Hamburg, Germany, 11 Sch 01/01, 8 June 2001], also available on the Internet at http://www.dis-arb.de/de/47/datenbanken/rspr/hanseat-olg-hamburg-az-11-sch-01-01-datum-2001-06-08-id1274, where the application to set aside the award was made in an action to have the award declared enforceable.

[850] CLOUT case No. 569 [Hanseatisches Oberlandesgericht Hamburg, Germany, 11 Sch 01/01, 8 June 2001], also available on the Internet at http://www.dis-arb.de/de/47/datenbanken/rspr/hanseat-olg-hamburg-az-11-sch-01-01-datum-2001-06-08-id1274.

[851] Hanseatisches Oberlandesgericht Hamburg, 6 Sch 07/01, 17 January 2002, available on the Internet at http://www.dis-arb.de/de/47/datenbanken/rspr/hanseat-olg-hamburg-az-6-sch-07-01-datum-2002-01-17-id191, rendered in the context of enforcement procedures.

[852] CLOUT case No. 569 [Hanseatisches Oberlandesgericht Hamburg, Germany, 11 Sch 01/01, 8 June 2001], also available on the Internet at http://www.dis-arb.de/de/47/datenbanken/rspr/hanseat-olg-hamburg-az-11-sch-01-01-datum-2001-06-08-id1274.

[853] *Smart Systems Technology Inc. v. Domotique Secant Inc.,* Quebec Court of Appeal, Canada, 11 March 2008, [2008] Q.J. No. 1782, rendered in the context of enforcement procedures.

[854] CLOUT case No. 740 [*Aloe Vera of America, Inc. v. Asianic Food (S) Pte. Ltd. and another*, High Court, Singapore, 10 May 2006], [2006] 3 SLR 174 (206), a case rendered in the context of enforcement proceedings.

[855] Oberlandesgericht Karlsruhe, 14 September 2001, 10 Sch 04/01, available on the Internet at http://www.dis-arb.de/de/47/datenbanken/rspr/olg-karlsruhe-az-10-sch-04-01-datum-2001-09-14-id1268de (relationship between public policy and constitutional rights); *Mahican Investment Ltd. & 3 others v. Giovanni Gaida & 80 others*, Nairobi High Court, Kenya, 11 October 2005, Miscellaneous Civil Application 792 of 2004, available on the Internet at http://www.kenyalaw.org/CaseSearch/case_download.php?go=2257490761928453047371 9&link= .

[856] Oberlandesgericht Köln, Germany, 19 Sch 12/08, 21 November 2008.

[857] Supreme Court, Hungary, BH 2007, 193.

an award suffer from substantive breaches of the law, at least from the "perspective of substantive constitutional law, that award will be correct".[858]

137. There are different approaches to the definition of public policy. According to the narrow interpretation of public policy, adopted for example by the courts in Singapore, an award, even if wrong, should only be set aside if it would "shock the conscience",[859] or is "clearly injurious to the public good or (…) wholly offensive to the ordinary reasonable and fully informed member of the public, or where it violates the forum's most basic notion of morality and justice".[860] In this context, German courts have made clear that it is not sufficient that the award infringes mandatory provisions, but only such mandatory provisions which are essential for the society as a whole and are part of public policy, whether national or international.[861] Equally, the Croatian Supreme Court has determined explicitly that even in an action to enforce a domestic award, not every violation of mandatory law amounts to a violation of public policy.[862]

138. Some courts have adopted a different approach to public policy, in particular of national public policy. A court in Spain held that public policy, defined as the "public, private, political, moral and economic legal principles that are absolutely mandatory for the preservation of a societal model for a nation and at a given time", covers "arbitrary, patently unreasonable or unreasonable decisions" that would infringe the right to effective judicial protection.[863] According to the Indian Supreme Court, an award is also contrary to public policy if it is "patently illegal".[864]

139. Equally, courts in Kenya have held that the notion of Kenyan public policy covers awards which are either "*(a)* inconsistent with the constitution or other laws of Kenya, whether written or unwritten or *(b)* inimical to the national interest of Kenya or *(c)* contrary to justice or morality."[865] Defining the second category further in a decision rendered in the context of enforcement proceedings, the courts held that that included "the interests of national defence and security, good diplomatic relations with friendly nations and the economic prosperity of Kenya."[866]

140. The Hungarian Supreme Court stated that public policy involves a value judgment of the law in general and therefore, "changes in content both in time and space, always depending on the respective social order and political-moral sentiment."[867] As a consequence, the court held that unacceptably high fees of lawyers resulting from an extremely high amount in dispute, though they did not violate a particular law, were contrary to public policy. The underlying rationale was that such high fees could restrict the parties' right to access to justice as it would put the losing party in an intolerable financial situation.[868]

141. The Supreme Court of Canada held that the court must examine the award as a whole and determine whether the decision itself, in its disposition of the case, violated matters of public policy.[869] The court furthermore made it clear that not every violation of a mandatory provision amounts to a violation of public policy.[870]

142. However, public policy has been found to be violated if the arbitral award has been obtained by fraudulent

[858] *Uniprex S.A. v. Grupo Radio Blanca,* Madrid Court of Appeal, Spain, 22 March 2006, case No. 178/2006—4/2004.

[859] *PT AsuransiJasa Indonesia (Persero) v. Dexia Bank S.A.*, Court of Appeal, Singapore, 1 December 2006, [2006] SGCA 41 para. 59.

[860] *PT AsuransiJasa Indonesia (Persero) v. Dexia Bank S.A.*, Court of Appeal, Singapore, 1 December 2006, [2006] SGCA 41 para. 59; see also Oberlandesgericht Dresden, Germany, 11 Sch 01/05, 20 April 2005, available on the Internet at http://www.dis-arb.de/de/47/datenbanken/rspr/olg-dresden-az-11-sch-01-05-datum-2005-04-20-id307.

[861] Bundesgerichtshof, Germany, III ZB 17/08, 30 October 2008, available on the Internet at http://www.dis-arb.de/de/47/datenbanken/rspr/bgh-az-iii-zb-17-08-datum-2008-10-30-id875; Oberlandesgericht Karlsruhe, 10 Sch 04/01, 14 September 2001, available on the Internet at available on the Internet at http://www.dis-arb.de/de/47/datenbanken/rspr/olg-karlsruhe-az-10-sch-04-01-datum-2001-09-14-id1268.

[862] CLOUT case No. 1068 [Supreme Court, Croatia, 30 May 2008, Gž 2/08-2], in a decision rendered in the context of enforcement proceedings.

[863] *Uniprex S.A. v. Grupo Radio Blanca,* Madrid Court of Appeal, Spain, 22 March 2006, case No. 178/2006—4/2004.

[864] *Oil & Natural Gas Corporation Ltd. v. Saw Pipes Ltd.*, Supreme Court, India, 17 April 2003, [2003] INSC 236; cited with approval also in *M/S. Centrotrade Minerals & Metal. Inc. v. Hindustan Copper Ltd*, Supreme Court, India, 9 May 2006, [2006] INSC 293.

[865] *Christ for all Nations v. Apollo Insurance Co. Ltd.*, High Court, Kenya, Civil Case 477 of 1999, [1999] L.L.R. 1635; *Apa Insurance Co. Ltd. v. Chrysanthus Barnabas Okemo*, Nairobi High Court, Kenya, 24 November 2005, Miscellaneous Application 241 of 2005, available at the Internet at http://www.kenyalaw.org/CaseSearch/case_search_one.php?casParties=&casSubject=&casNumber=Misc+Appli+241+of+2005&casCourt=&casJudges=&casType=&casAdvocates=&casCitation=&casYear=&check_submit=1&submitter=SEARCH+%BB.

[866] *Christ for all Nations v. Apollo Insurance Co. Ltd.*, High Court, Kenya, Civil Case 477 of 1999, [1999] L.L.R. 1635.

[867] Supreme Court, Hungary, BH 2003, 127 at 5c.

[868] Ibid.

[869] *Desputeaux v. Éditions Chouette (1987) inc.*, Supreme Court, Canada, 31 March 2003, [2003] 1 S.C.R. 178.

[870] *Desputeaux v. Éditions Chouette (1987) inc.*, Supreme Court, Canada, 31 March 2003, [2003] 1 S.C.R. 178 ; see also *Smart Systems Technology Inc. v. Domotique Secant Inc.*, Quebec Court of Appeal, Canada, 11 March 2008, [2008] Q.J. No. 1782; that decision was rendered in the context of enforcement proceedings.

means.[871] Public policy was also found to be violated if the arbitral award would allow a party to take advantage of a position that it had deliberately engineered.[872]

143. According to German courts, awards which infringe human rights are contrary to public policy.[873] In practice, however, allegations that the award violates the constitutional guarantee of property or of equal treatment have not been successful.

144. Courts have made clear on several occasions that, in principle, they should not review the evaluation of the facts by the arbitral tribunal unless the defendant claims that the taking of evidence by the arbitral tribunal was already contrary to fundamental principles.[874] According to the Singapore Court of Appeal, the public policy exception should in general be limited to the tribunal's findings of law and not include its findings of fact, unless there is "fraud, breach of natural justice or some other recognized vitiating factor."[875]

Illegal contracts

145. Awards enforcing contracts which are illegal under the applicable law, or otherwise leading to illegal actions, may be contrary to public policy. According to a court in Singapore, a party trying to rely on such an illegality, where the latter has been rejected by the arbitral tribunal, has to furnish the proofs that the underlying contract was illegal, and that the "error was of such a nature that enforcement of the award" would be "clearly injurious to the public good" or would contravene "fundamental notions and principles of justice".[876]

146. The High Court in Singapore set aside an award based on an agreement by which—according to the court's interpretation—a Thai party agreed to withdraw its criminal charges against the applicant, which under Thai law was illegal as it concerned non-compoundable offences.[877] On appeal, however, the judgment was overruled. The Court of Appeal held that in principle the court was not bound by the arbitral tribunal's findings as to the facts and the law and that it was for the court to decide whether the underlying contract was contrary to the laws of Singapore. However, a court should also, in relation to the public policy defence, only reopen the arbitral tribunal's findings concerning facts and law in exceptional circumstances.[878]

147. However, where a party has allegedly sought to deceive the arbitral tribunal by a fraudulent claim of expenses, no violation of public policy has been found where such deception was not relied upon by the arbitral tribunal.[879]

148. Furthermore, it has been found that, while a bribe was intrinsically immoral for both parties, a payment that was in the nature of a ransom, i.e. an amount that the payer had no other choice than to pay, only involved immorality on the part of the blackmailer. The court therefore found that an award that provided for reimbursement of an amount paid as ransom did not violate public policy.[880]

Alleged infringements of competition law

149. Awards which endorse contracts or behaviour infringing competition law have been considered by courts in several jurisdictions to be contrary to public policy. For example, a court in Germany held that the main prohibitions of competition law are part of public policy as they express a country's decision for a free market and compliance with them is of fundamental importance for the State.[881]

---

[871] CLOUT case No. 407 [Bundesgerichtshof, Germany, 2 November 2000, III ZB 55/99], also available on the Internet at http://www.dis-arb.de/de/47/datenbanken/rspr/bgh-az-iii-zb-55-99-datum-2000-11-02-id2.

[872] CLOUT case No. 323 [*Zimbabwe Electricity Supply Authority v. Genius Joel Maposa,* Supreme Court, Zimbabwe, 21 October and 21 December 1999].

[873] Oberlandesgericht Karlsruhe, 10 Sch 04/01, 14 September 2001, available on the Internet at http://www.dis-arb.de/de/47/datenbanken/rspr/olg-karlsruhe-az-10-sch-04-01-datum-2001-09-14-id1268; Oberlandesgericht Dresden, Germany, 11 Sch 01/05, 20 April 2005, available on the Internet at http://www.dis-arb.de/de/47/datenbanken/rspr/olg-dresden-az-11-sch-01-05-datum-2005-04-20-id307.

[874] CLOUT case No. 868 [Bayerisches Oberstes Landesgericht, Germany, 4 Z Sch 23/02, 20 March 2003], also available on the Internet at http://www.dis-arb.de/de/47/datenbanken/rspr/bayoblg-az-4-z-sch-23-02-datum-2003-03-20-id262, confirmed by Bundesgerichtshof, Germany, III ZB 29/03, 23 October 2003, available on the Internet at http://www.dis-arb.de/de/47/datenbanken/rspr/bgh-az-iii-zb-29-03-datum-2003-10-23-id241.

[875] *AJT v. AJU,* Court of Appeal, Singapore, 22 August 2011, [2011] SGCA 41, paras. 69 and 65.

[876] *AJT v. AJU,* High Court, Singapore, [2010] SGHC 201, 16 July 2010.

[877] *AJT v. AJU,* High Court, Singapore, 16 July 2010, [2010] SGHC 201.

[878] *AJT v. AJU,* Court of Appeal, Singapore, 22 August 2011, [2011] SGCA 41.

[879] CLOUT case No. 502 [*The United Mexican States v. Metalclad Corporation,* British Colombia Supreme Court, Canada, 2 May 2001], also available on the Internet at http://canlii.ca/t/4xfw.

[880] CLOUT case No. 185 [*Transport de cargaison (Cargo Carriers) v. Industrial Bulk Carriers,* Court of Appeal of Quebec, Canada, 15 June 1990].

[881] Oberlandesgericht Dresden, Germany, 11 Sch 01/05, 20 April 2005, available on the Internet at http://www.dis-arb.de/de/47/datenbanken/rspr/olg-dresden-az-11-sch-01-05-datum-2005-04-20-id307.

Alleged infringements of insolvency law

150. Insolvency law includes, in many countries, mandatory provisions the infringement of which may constitute a violation of public policy. Such a violation was, for example, assumed by the German Federal Court of Justice in a case where the arbitrator dealt in the award *inter alia* with claims which had not been registered with the insolvency representative. The obligation to register claims with the insolvency representative was considered to be such a crucial element in an orderly distribution of the assets of the debtor that it is part of public policy. By contrast, other mandatory provisions of the insolvency law such as the treatment of still executory contracts were considered by German courts not to be part of public policy.[882]

Principle of proportionality

151. The principle of proportionality as a part of public policy has been invoked by parties in various instances where they disagreed with the amount awarded either in relation to the performance of a contract, its breach, or in relation to costs. For example, in a case before the High Court of Singapore, a party applied for the setting aside of an award on costs alleging that, since the amount was nearly three times as high as its claim, the award violated the principle of proportionality which it considered to be part of public policy. The High Court rejected that application holding that the principle did not form part of the narrow concept of public policy in Singapore.[883]

Further examples from practice

152. Public policy was not found to be violated where the award ordered the defendant in the arbitral proceedings to pay an amount in a currency other than the currency of the country where the arbitration took place.[884]

153. Different views exist as to whether the principle of *res judicata* forms part of public policy. That has been assumed by a decision in Singapore according to which awards which are contrary to the *res judicata* effect of an earlier award or decision in the jurisdiction infringe public policy.[885] By contrast, a Canadian court has come to the opposite conclusion.[886]

Time limit—paragraph (3)

154. The time limit for starting setting aside proceedings was considered by a Spanish court to be a procedural time limit with the effect that it must be observed by the courts *ex officio* and does not require that the other party raises it.[887] Moreover, the High Court of Singapore considered that it lacked the power to extent the time limit.[888]

155. Courts have confirmed on several occasions that the time limit only starts to run when the award has been received by the party seeking the setting aside of the award, either by conveying the award or a copy of it to that party or by reading it to the party.[889] The dates given in the award itself or the date of notification of the award to a party in the arbitration were not considered relevant. If more than one party was involved in the arbitration, then the time period started separately for each party.[890]

156. A German court dealt with the question of whether the time limit started to run in a case where the award was first served by e-mail and then in paper form. Notwithstanding that the parties had in principle agreed on communications by e-mail, the court held that, following the requirement that the award be signed by the arbitrators in article 31 (4), only the service of the signed original of the award set the time period in motion. In its view, the signature requirement could not be replaced even by a digital signature.[891]

---

[882] Bundesgerichtshof, Germany, III ZB 17/08, 30 October 2008, available on the Internet at http://www.dis-arb.de/de/47/datenbanken/rspr/bgh-az-iii-zb-17-08-datum-2008-10-30-id875.

[883] *VV. and Another v. VW*, High Court, Singapore, 24 January 2008, OS 2160/2006, [2008] SGHC 11; for a different view that public policy was violated by too high fees, see Supreme Court of Hungary, BH 2003, 127 at 5c.

[884] CLOUT case No. 149 [Moscow City Court, Russian Federation, 18 September 1995].

[885] *PT Asuransi Jasa Indonesia (Persero) v. Dexia Bank S.A.*, Court of Appeal, Singapore, 1 December 2006, [2006] SGCA 4.

[886] CLOUT case No. 1049 [*Louis Dreyfus S.A.S. v. Holding Tusculum B.V.*, Superior Court of Quebec, Canada, 8 December 2008], [2008] QCCS 5903 (CanLII), also available on the Internet at http://canlii.ca/t/21v03.

[887] La Coruña Court of Appeal, Spain, 28 April 2006, case No. 133/2006—1/2006.

[888] CLOUT case No. 566 [*ABC Co. v. XYZ Ltd.*, High Court, Singapore, 8 May 2003] [2003] 3 SLR 546.

[889] *Siginon Maritime Ltd. v. Gitutho Associates and Others,* High Court, Mombasa, Kenya, 28 July 2005, Miscellaneous Civil Application 719 of 2004 (award dated 4 February 2004—delivered only on 30 June 2004 to the applicant in the setting aside proceedings), available on the Internet at http://www.kenyalaw.org/CaseSearch/case_download.php?go=29136052918379844525034&link; Cairo Court of Appeal, Egypt, 6 May 2008, case No. 140/124; see also *Moohan v. S. & R. Motors [Donegal] Ltd.*, High Court, Ireland, 31 July 2009, [2009] IEHC 391.

[890] Cairo Court of Appeal, Egypt, 10 January 2008, case No. 23/124.

[891] Oberlandesgericht Oldenburg, Germany, 9 SchH 03/05, 30 May 2006, available on the Internet at http://www.dis-arb.de/de/47/datenbanken/rspr/olg-oldenburg-az-9-schh-03-05-datum-2006-05-30-id752.

157. A court in India held that in large organizations, like the Indian railway in the case at hand, the reference to the "party" which must take notice of the award is to be construed to mean the person directly connected with and controlling the proceedings. Consequently, the court considered that the relevant point in time was not the service on the General Manager but the service on the Chief Engineer responsible for the arbitration.[892]

158. According to a Kenyan court, it is sufficient for receipt in the sense of paragraph (3) that the party has been informed that the award is ready for collection. It is not necessary that the party has actually collected the award, to avoid making the commencement of the limitation period dependent on the party's discretion.[893]

159. In case of partial awards, the time limit was considered to run separately for each award.[894] In case of interlocutory (interim) awards, the position depends on the view adopted on the admissibility of setting aside proceedings. If one considers them inadmissible, the time limits for the interlocutory awards also commence running with receipt of the final award.[895]

160. The time limit also prevents subsequent amendments of a timely application for setting aside an award if these amendments are based on different factual allegations.[896] Timely applications to courts which lacked jurisdictions did not suspend the running of time.[897]

Remission—paragraph (4)

161. In a case where an arbitrator obtained a surveyor's report but failed to provide a copy to the parties, the court remitted the case to the arbitrator (instead of setting aside the award) on the ground that the party waived its right to rely on the breach of natural justice as it was aware that a surveyor had been engaged, and instead of demanding a copy of the report, only complained after receipt of the award.[898]

162. Where the arbitral tribunal has issued a final award, courts did not find it appropriate to remit the case to the arbitral tribunal for the purpose of enabling the arbitral tribunal to recall or revise its decision on the merits of the case or to take fresh evidence on the merits of the case.[899]

---

[892] *Union of India v. Tecco Trichy Engineers & Contractors,* Supreme Court, India, 16 March 2005, [2005] INSC 180.

[893] *Mahican Investment Ltd. & 3 others v. Giovanni Gaida & 80 others,* High Court, Nairobi, Kenya, 11 October 2005, Miscellaneous Civil Application 792 of 2004, available at the Internet at http://www.kenyalaw.org/CaseSearch/case_download.php?go=22574907619284530473719&link=.

[894] Oberlandesgericht Oldenburg, Germany, 9 SchH 3/05, 30 May 2006, available on the Internet at http://www.dis-arb.de/de/47/datenbanken/rspr/olg-oldenburg-az-9-schh-03-05-datum-2006-05-30-id752.

[895] Oberlandesgericht Frankfurt, Germany, 26 Sch 20/06, 10 May 2007, available on the Internet at http://www.dis-arb.de/de/47/datenbanken/rspr/olg-frankfurt-am-az-26-sch-20-06-datum-2007-05-10-id711.

[896] CLOUT case No. 566 [*ABC Co. v. XYZ Ltd.*, High Court, Singapore, 8 May 2003] [2003] 3 SLR 546]; Tokyo District Court, Japan, 28 July 2009.

[897] La Coruña Court of Appeal, Spain, 28 April 2006, case No. 133/2006—1/2006.

[898] *Alexander Property Developments v. Clarke,* High Court New Plymouth, New Zealand, 10 June 2004, CIV. 2004-443-89.

[899] CLOUT case No. 12 [*D. Frampton & Co. Ltd. V. SylvioThibeault and Navigation Harvey & Frères Inc.*, Federal Court, Trial Division, Canada, 7 April 1988]; CLOUT case No. 391 [*Re Corporación Transnacional de Inversiones, S.A. de C.V. et al. v. STET International, S.p.A. et al.*, Ontario Superior Court of Justice, Canada, 22 September 1999], [1999] CanLII 14819 (ON SC), also available on the Internet at http://canlii.ca/t/1vvn5, confirmed in *Corporación Transnacional de Inversiones v. Stet International*, Ontario Court of Appeal, Canada, 15 September 2000, 2000 CanLII 16840 (ON CA), (2000) 49 OR (3d) 414, available on the Internet at http://canlii.ca/t/1cvn9; *Tan Poh Leng Stanley v. Tang Boon Jek Jeffrey*, High Court, Singapore, [2001] 1 SLR 624, 30 November 2000, the decision of the High Court was reversed on appeal, see *Tang Boon Jek Jeffrey v. Tan Poh Leng Stanley*, Court of Appeal, Singapore, 22 June 2001, [2001] 3 SLR 237.

CHAPTER VIII. RECOGNITION AND ENFORCEMENT OF AWARDS

Article 35. Recognition and enforcement

(1) An arbitral award, irrespective of the country in which it was made, shall be recognized as binding and, upon application in writing to the competent court, shall be enforced subject to the provisions of this article and of article 36.

[As adopted in 1985]

*(2) The party relying on an award or applying for its enforcement shall supply the duly authenticated original award or a duly certified copy thereof, and the original arbitration agreement referred to in article 7 or a duly certified copy thereof. If the award or agreement is not made in an official language of this State, the party shall supply a duly certified translation thereof into such language.****

[As amended in 2006]

*(2) The party relying on an award or applying for its enforcement shall supply the original award or a copy thereof. If the award is not made in an official language of this State, the court may request the party to supply a translation thereof into such language.****

****The conditions set forth in this paragraph are intended to set maximum standards. It would, thus, not be contrary to the harmonization to be achieved by the model law if a State retained even less onerous conditions.*

TRAVAUX PRÉPARATOIRES

The *travaux préparatoires* on article 35 as adopted in 1985 are contained in the following documents:

1. Report of the United Nations Commission on International Trade Law on the work of its eighteenth session (*Official Records of the General Assembly, Fortieth Session, Supplement No. 17* (A/40/17)), paras. 11-333.

2. Reports of the Working Group: A/CN.9/216; A/CN.9/232; A/CN.9/233; A/CN.9/246, annex; A/CN.9/263 and Add.1-2; A/CN.9/264. Relevant working papers are referred to in the reports.

3. Summary records of the 329th, 320th and 333rd UNCITRAL meetings.

(Available on the Internet at www.uncitral.org).

The *travaux préparatoires* on article 35 (2) as amended in 2006 are contained in the following documents:

1. *Official Records of the General Assembly, Sixty-First session, Supplement No. 17* (A/61/17), paras. 87-181 and annex 1.

2. Relevant working papers, considered by Working Group II (Arbitration), are referred to in the reports of the sessions of the Working Group.

INTRODUCTION

1. By treating awards rendered in international commercial arbitration in a uniform manner irrespective of where they were made, the Model Law distinguishes between "international" and "non international" awards instead of relying on the traditional distinction between "foreign" and "domestic" awards. This new line is based on substantive grounds rather than territorial borders. The place of arbitration is often chosen for reasons of convenience of the parties and the dispute may have little or no connection with the State where the arbitration legally takes place. Consequently, the recognition and enforcement of "international" awards, whether "foreign" or "domestic", should be governed by the same provisions.

2. By modelling the recognition and enforcement rules on the relevant provisions of the 1958 New York Convention, the Model Law supplements, without conflicting with, the regime of recognition and enforcement created by that successful Convention.

3. Under article 35 (1) any arbitral award, irrespective of the country in which it was made, shall be recognized as binding and enforceable, subject to the provisions of article 35 (2) and of article 36 (the latter of which sets forth the grounds on which recognition or enforcement may be refused). Based on the desire of overcoming territorial restrictions, reciprocity is not included as a condition for recognition and enforcement.

4. The Model Law does not lay down procedural details of recognition and enforcement, which are left to national procedural laws and practices. The Model Law merely sets certain conditions for obtaining enforcement under article 35 (2). It was amended in 2006 to liberalize formal requirements and reflect the amendment made to article 7 on the form of the arbitration agreement (see above, in the section on article 7, para. 2). Presentation of a copy of the arbitration agreement is no longer required under article 35 (2).

CASE LAW ON ARTICLE 35

Recognition and enforcement of arbitral awards—paragraph (1)

Mandatory character of recognition and enforcement of arbitral awards

5. A court held that the word "shall" in article 35 (1) makes it clear that both recognition and enforcement are mandatory, subject only to the specific exceptions listed in article 36.[900] The existence of a residual jurisdiction to refuse enforcement for other reasons is generally denied.[901] However, in a country where the legislation enacting the Model Law had omitted the word "only" contained in the chapeau of article 36 (1), a court held that it had general discretion to refuse enforcement on grounds other than those defined in article 36.[902]

6. Discretion is assumed in the opposite case, i.e. when in principle a ground to refuse enforcement exists. A Canadian court, for example, held that even if one of the circumstances set out in article 36 (1) existed, enforcement could still be ordered in the exercise of judicial discretion.[903] Equally, courts in Hong Kong have declared awards enforceable irrespective of the fact that the arbitral tribunal had been appointed by the wrong subdivision of the chosen arbitral institution[904] or made its own investigations without giving the parties an opportunity to comment thereon.[905] The assumption of such discretion is normally based on the use of the word "may" in the chapeau of article 36 (1).

Applicable procedure

7. Proceedings for the recognition and enforcement of awards under article 35 are court proceedings, and the procedural rules of the country where recognition and enforcement is sought apply to such proceedings.

8. It was determined by a Canadian court that only the formal requirements of article 35 applied to an application for recognition and enforcement of arbitral awards under the legislation enacting the Model Law, to the exclusion of any other requirements in the domestic procedural law of the country where enforcement was sought.[906] The law applicable to the merits is irrelevant.[907]

9. The law of the State where recognition and enforcement is sought is also relevant for the determination of time limits

---

[900] CLOUT case No. 366 [*Europcar Italia S.p.A. v. Alba Tours International Inc.,* Ontario Court of Justice, Canada, General Division, 21 January 1997].

[901] CLOUT case No. 740 [*Aloe Vera of America, Inc. v. Asianic Food (S) Pte. Ltd. and another*, High Court, Singapore, 10 May 2006], [2006] 3 SLR 174 (206).

[902] *Resort Condominium v. Bolwell*, Supreme Court of Queensland, Australia, 29 October 1993.

[903] CLOUT case No. 366 [*Europcar Italia S.p.A. v. Alba Tours International Inc.,* Ontario Court of Justice, Canada, General Division, 21 January 1997], [1997] O.J. No. 133, 23 O.T.C. 376 (Gen. Div.); see also CLOUT case No. 30 [*Robert E. Schreter v. Gasmac Inc.,* Ontario Court, General Division, Canada, 13 February 1992], [1992] O.J. No. 257, para. 29.

[904] CLOUT case No. 76 [*China Nanhai Oil Joint Service Corporation, Shenzhen Branch v. Gee Tai Holdings Co. Ltd.,* High Court—Court of First Instance, Hong Kong, 13 July 1994], [1994] 3 HKC 375, [1995] ADRLJ 127, HK HC, where recognition and enforcement of the arbitral award was granted although the arbitral award was issued by the Shenzhen Sub-commission of the China International Economic and Trade Arbitration Commission (CIETAC) and not, as provided in the arbitration agreement, CIETAC Beijing.

[905] *APEX Tech Investment Ltd. v. Chuang's Development (China) Ltd.*, High Court—Court of First Instance, Hong Kong, 8 September 1995, CACV000231/1995.

[906] CLOUT case No. 584 [*Dunhill Personnel System v. Dunhill Temps Edmonton*, Alberta Queen's Bench, Canada, 30 September 1993], 13 Alta L.R.(2d) 240.

[907] Oberlandesgericht München, Germany, 34 Sch 14/09, 1 September 2009, available on the Internet at http://www.dis-arb.de/de/47/datenbanken/rspr/olg-m&uumlnchen-az-34-sch-14-09-datum-2009-09-01-id1013.

within which a party must apply for the relevant action. It has been held by a Canadian court that a declaration of enforceability of an award may be time-barred if also a domestic arbitral award cannot be enforced any longer. In the case at hand, the court did not apply the ten-year time limit for judgments, but the shorter two-year period for other decisions.[908] According to the court, the starting point for the limitation period was the time when the award could no longer be set aside in the country of origin.

Jurisdiction to hear an application under article 35

10. It follows from the above mentioned nature of the proceedings that the court where an application is lodged must have jurisdiction to hear the case. A Canadian court concluded that article 35 of the Model Law granted the competent courts in the country where recognition and enforcement were sought the jurisdiction to hear an application for enforcement of an arbitral award notwithstanding the fact that such courts would not have had jurisdiction to hear contractual disputes between the parties.[909] By contrast, a German court refused to assume jurisdiction over a defendant which was domiciled in a foreign country and had no assets in Germany.[910]

11. The court's power under article 35 is limited to decide whether the award will be recognized and enforced in its own jurisdiction, and cannot extend to the setting aside of an award.[911] Setting aside falls within the competence of the courts at the seat of arbitration.[912]

Arbitral award

12. Whether a decision by an arbitral tribunal constitutes an arbitral award is determined primarily on the basis of the law of the State where recognition and enforcement is sought, according to several court decisions.[913] The fact that an arbitral award has been confirmed by a judgment in the jurisdiction where the award was made, does not exclude the enforcement of the award. A Canadian court decision confirmed that such an award should not be considered as having been merged with the judgment and should therefore be enforced as an arbitral award and not as a foreign judgment. The argument given by the court was that otherwise the purpose of the enforcement provisions of the Model Law would be defeated.[914]

13. Courts have decided that proceedings pursuant to article 35 are admissible only against awards, not against decisions of other dispute resolution bodies.[915] In case of international awards rendered in the State where enforcement is sought, the arbitration law determines what constitutes an award, in particular the formal requirements.[916] Certain courts considered that the absence of signatures on the award does not prevent the issuance of a declaration of enforceability if reasons are given.[917] Notwithstanding the fact that in principle an award has to be signed by all arbitrators, a court considered that an arbitral tribunal's decision which was intended to be binding was an award even if no reasons were given for the absence of signature by one of the arbitrators.[918]

[908] CLOUT case No. 1009 [*Yugraneft Corp. v. Rexx. Management Corp.,* Supreme Court, Canada, 20 May 2010], [2010] SCC 19, [2010] 1 S.C.R. 649, where the court held that time limits under the applicable statute of limitation constituted authorized "rules of procedure" under article III of the 1958 New York Convention.

[909] CLOUT case No. 351 [*Food Services of America Inc. (c.o.b. Amerifresh) v. Pan Pacific Specialties Ltd.,* Supreme Court of British Columbia, Canada, 24 March 1997], [1997] B.C.J. No. 1921; (1997) 32 B.C.L.R. (3d) 225.

[910] Kammergericht Berlin, Germany, 20 Sch 07/04, 10 August 2006, available on the Internet at http://www.dis-arb.de/de/47/datenbanken/rspr/kg-berlin-az-20-sch-07-04-datum-2006-08-10-id596, where the parties settled the case before the German Federal Court of Justice could decide the controversial issue.

[911] Cairo Court of Appeal, 7th Economic Circuit, Egypt, 2 July 2008, case No. 23/125.

[912] Cairo Court of Appeal, Circuit 91 Commercial, Egypt, 16 January 2008, case No. 92/124.

[913] Oberlandesgericht Düsseldorf, Germany, I-26 Sch 05/03, 19 January 2005, available on the Internet at http://www.dis-arb.de/de/47/datenbanken/rspr/olg-d&uumlsseldorf-az-i-26-sch-05-03-datum-2005-01-19-id308; see also CLOUT case No. 30 [*Robert E. Schreter v. Gasmac Inc.,* Ontario Court, General Division, Canada, 13 February 1992], at paras. 31 et seq., where the court held that the law at the place where recognition and enforcement are requested determines whether the award is merged into a judgment rendered at the place of arbitration.

[914] CLOUT case No. 30 [*Robert E. Schreter v. Gasmac Inc.,* Ontario Court, General Division, Canada, 13 February 1992].

[915] Bayerisches Oberstes Landesgericht, 4 Z Sch 35/02, 13 May 2003, available on the Internet at http://www.dis-arb.de/de/47/datenbanken/rspr/bayoblg-az-4-z-sch-35-02-datum-2003-05-13-id225; Oberlandesgericht Naumburg, 10 Sch 01/00 (1), 17 April 2000, available on the Internet at http://www.dis-arb.de/de/47/datenbanken/rspr/olg-naumburg-az-10-sch-01-00-1-datum-2000-04-17-id57; Oberlandesgericht Frankfurt, 26 Sch 29/05, 20 December 2005, available on the Internet at http://www.dis-arb.de/de/47/datenbanken/rspr/olg-frankfurt-am-az-26-sch-29-05-datum-2005-12-20-id525, in regard to the classification of the decision overruled by the Bundesgerichtshof, 1 March 2007, III ZB 07/06, available on the Internet at http://www.dis-arb.de/de/47/datenbanken/rspr/bgh-az-iii-zb-07-06-datum-2007-03-01-id665.

[916] Bayerisches Oberstes Landesgericht, Germany, 4 Z Sch 12/03, 10 July 2003, available at http://www.dis-arb.de/de/47/datenbanken/rspr/bayoblg-az-4-z-sch-12-03-datum-2003-07-10-id234.

[917] Oberlandesgericht Köln, Germany, 24 April 2006.

[918] Oberlandesgericht München, Germany, 34 Sch 26/08, 22 June 2009, available on the Internet at http://www.dis-arb.de/de/47/datenbanken/rspr/olg-m&uumlnchen-az-34-sch-26-08-datum-2009-06-22-id1065.

14. Awards on agreed terms have been recognized and enforced on the same terms as any other arbitral awards.[919] Equally, preliminary rulings in the sense of article 16 (3) in which the arbitral tribunal confirms its jurisdiction have been declared enforceable, at least where they contain a final decision on costs.[920]

15. In enforcement proceedings where the respondent claimed that the lack of specificity in the arbitral award would make execution impossible, the court found that the form and scope of the award did not hinder a declaration of enforceability, since the possibility of ordering actual enforcement measures was not a prerequisite for such a declaration of enforceability under article 35.[921]

Content of decision

16. On several occasions, courts have dealt with applications either by the applicant or the party resisting enforcement to alter the operative part of the award. The prevailing view is that such alterations are in general not possible. Thus, one court refused to make deductions from the amount awarded as that would de facto have resulted in reevaluating the merits.[922]

17. Alterations of the dispositive part have been allowed by courts where they merely corrected obvious spelling or calculation mistakes, for example where the dates given from which interest should accrue were obviously wrong.[923] Equally, references to statutory interest rates have been supplemented by actual figures, or interests awarded for a certain period were calculated.[924]

Confidentiality

18. In accordance with the *travaux préparatoires,* one aspect of the recognition of an arbitral award as binding under paragraph (1) is the right to rely on such an award in other proceedings.[925] For instance, the Bermuda Privy Council found that a party was entitled to invoke in different proceedings an arbitral award, despite the fact that the confidentiality agreement contained in the arbitration agreement governing the first arbitration proceedings expressly provided that the award should not be disclosed at any time to any individual or entity which was not a party to the arbitration.[926]

19. Concerns as to a breach of the confidentiality of the arbitral proceedings have also been raised in enforcement proceedings before courts. A court in Singapore ruled that confidentiality should not be used in an effort to thwart or hinder effective enforcement of an otherwise valid award.[927] Equally, a Canadian court has determined that reliance on the arbitral award in enforcement proceedings does not constitute a breach of a confidentiality duty under an arbitration agreement. The court also rejected an application for an order to keep the enforcement proceedings confidential as no special circumstances existed which could justify such an order.[928]

---

[919] CLOUT case No. 407 [Bundesgerichtshof, Germany, III ZB 55/99, 2 November 2000], also available on the Internet at http://www.dis-arb.de/de/47/datenbanken/rspr/bgh-az-iii-zb-55-99-datum-2000-11-02-id2.

[920] Bundesgerichtshof, Germany, III ZB 35/06, 18 January 2007, available on the Internet at http://www.dis-arb.de/de/47/datenbanken/rspr/bgh-az-iii-zb-35-06-datum-2007-01-18-id649.

[921] CLOUT case No. 452 [Bayerisches Oberstes Landesgericht, Germany, 4 Z Sch 31/99, 27 June 1999], also available on the Internet at http://www.dis-arb.de/de/47/datenbanken/rspr/bayoblg-az-4-z-sch-31-99-datum-1999-07-27-id20.

[922] *Apa Insurance Co. Ltd. v. Chrysanthus Barnabas Okemo*, High Court, Nairobi, Kenya, 24 November 2005, Miscellaneous Application 241 of 2005.

[923] Oberlandesgericht München, Germany, 34 Sch 15/09, 29 October 2009, where the decision provided that interest should accrue from 27.12.2008 instead of 27.12.2007, available on the Internet at http://www.dis-arb.de/de/47/datenbanken/rspr/olg-m&uumlnchen-az-34-sch-15-09-datum-2009-10-29-id1029,

[924] Oberlandesgericht Hamm, Germany, 29 Sch 2/03, 02 December 2003, available on the Internet at http://www.dis-arb.de/de/47/datenbanken/rspr/olg-hamm-az-29-sch-02-03-datum-2003-12-02-id517; *Ras Pal Gazi Construction Company Ltd. v. Federal Capital Development Authority*, Supreme Court, Nigeria, SC 45/96, 18 May 2001, [2001] 10 NWLR 559.

[925] A/CN.9/264, Analytical commentary on draft text of a model law on international commercial arbitration, under article 35, para. 4, which provides that recognition not only constitutes a necessary condition for enforcement but also may be standing alone, for instance where an award is relied on in other proceedings, available on the UNCITRAL website at http://www.uncitral.org/uncitral/en/commission/sessions/18th.html.

[926] *Associated Electric & Gas Insurance Services Ltd. v. European Reinsurance Company of Zurich*, Privy Council, Bermuda, 29 January 2003, Appeal No. 93 of 2001, [2003] UKPC 11.

[927] *International Coal Pte. Ltd. v. Kristle Trading Ltd.*, High Court, Singapore, [2008] SGHC 182.

[928] *Gea Group AG v. Ventra Group Co. & Timothy Graham*, Ontario Superior Court of Justice, Canada, 9 January 2009, CV-08-7635-00CL.

Formal requirements—paragraph (2) (as adopted in 1985)

Time for compliance

20. Courts have held that enforcement of an arbitral award should not be refused where formal deficiencies in the original application for enforcement were corrected either by the applicant or the arbitral tribunal which registered the award with the court.[929]

Legal nature of requirements

21. The legal nature of the requirements in paragraph (2) and the role of the courts in particular in relation to the scrutiny of the arbitration agreement have been an issue in a number of decisions.

22. Certain courts have consistently qualified those requirements as mere rules of evidence but not as requirements for the admissibility of an application to have foreign awards declared enforceable.[930] Consequently, non-compliance with them only becomes an issue if the other party challenges the existence or authenticity of the award or the arbitration agreement.

23. Along the same lines, a Spanish court held that the obligation to submit with the application the arbitration agreement does not entitle a court to examine the validity of the arbitration agreement on its own motion.[931]

24. Divergent court decisions have been rendered regarding the extent and the nature of the court's obligation to examine compliance with article 35 (2) (or its equivalent in article IV of the 1958 New York Convention),[932] in particular if the existence of a valid arbitration agreement is challenged. The High Court of Singapore held that the enforcement process is a mechanistic one. Consequently, the obligation for the applicant to submit the arbitration agreement does not require a judicial investigation by the court into the existence of the arbitration agreement. It is for the party opposing enforcement to prove that one of the grounds for resisting enforcement exists, i.e. that the tribunal lacked jurisdiction.[933] By contrast, other courts have made a distinction between the conclusion of an arbitration agreement to be proven by the applicant, if contested, and its validity.[934]

Submission of arbitration agreement

25. Concerning the arbitration agreement to be submitted, certain courts held that the submission of a facsimile or any other record of the agreement is sufficient.[935]

---

[929] CLOUT case No. 459 [*Medison Co. Ltd. v. Victor (Far East) Ltd.*, High Court—Court of First Instance, Hong Kong Special Administrative Region, Court of First Instance, 8 April 2000], [2000] 2 HKC 502 available on the Internet at http://www.hklii.hk/eng/hk/cases/hkcfi/2000/684.html; *Clement C. Ebokan v. Ekwenibe & Sons Trading Company,* Lagos Court of Appeal, Nigeria, 22 January 2001, [2001] 2 NWLR 32.

[930] Oberlandesgericht München, Germany, 34 Sch 19/08, 27 February 2009, available on the Internet at http://www.dis-arb.de/de/47/datenbanken/rspr/olg-m&uumlnchen-az-34-sch-19-08-datum-2009-02-27-id974.

[931] Madrid Court of Appeal, Spain, 4 March 2005, case No. 86/2005—52/2005; Valencia Court of Appeal, Spain, 11 October 2005, case No. 603/05.

[932] Article IV of the1958 New York Convention reads as follows: "1. To obtain the recognition and enforcement mentioned in the preceding article, the party applying for recognition and enforcement shall, at the time of the application, supply: *(a)* The duly authenticated original award or a duly certified copy thereof; *(b)* The original agreement referred to in article II or a duly certified copy thereof. 2. If the said award or agreement is not made in an official language of the country in which the award is relied upon, the party applying for recognition and enforcement of the award shall produce a translation of these documents into such language. The translation shall be certified by an official or sworn translator or by a diplomatic or consular agent."

[933] CLOUT case No. 740 [*Aloe Vera of America, Inc. v. Asianic Food (S) Pte. Ltd. and another*, High Court, Singapore, 10 May 2006], [2006] 3 SLR 174 (206); *Denmark Skibstekniske Konsulenter A/S I Likvidation (formerly known as Knud E Hansen A/S) v. Ultrapolis 3000 Investments Ltd. (formerly known as Ultrapolis 3000 Theme Park Investments Ltd)*, High Court, Singapore, 9 April 2010, [2010] SGHC 108, at para. 22.

[934] Oberlandesgericht München, Germany, 34 Sch 04/08, 19 January 2009, available on the Internet at http://www.dis-arb.de/de/47/datenbanken/rspr/olg-m&uumlnchen-az-34-sch-04-08-datum-2009-01-19-id1062; Oberlandesgericht München, Germany, 34 Sch 20/08, 12 October 2009, available on the Internet at http://www.dis-arb.de/de/47/datenbanken/rspr/olg-m&uumlnchen-az-34-sch-20-08-datum-2009-10-12-id1023.

[935] *Denmark Skibstekniske Konsulenter A/S I Likvidation (formerly known as Knud E Hansen A/S) v. Ultrapolis 3000 Investments Ltd. (formerly known as Ultrapolis 3000 Theme Park Investments Ltd)*, High Court, Singapore, 9 April 2010, [2010] SGHC 108, at para. 22 (copy of standard conditions containing the arbitration agreement).

Article 36. Grounds for refusing recognition or enforcement

(1) Recognition or enforcement of an arbitral award, irrespective of the country in which it was made, may be refused only:

(a) at the request of the party against whom it is invoked, if that party furnishes to the competent court where recognition or enforcement is sought proof that:

(i) a party to the arbitration agreement referred to in article 7 was under some incapacity; or the said agreement is not valid under the law to which the parties have subjected it or, failing any indication thereon, under the law of the country where the award was made; or

(ii) the party against whom the award is invoked was not given proper notice of the appointment of an arbitrator or of the arbitral proceedings or was otherwise unable to present his case; or

(iii) the award deals with a dispute not contemplated by or not falling within the terms of the submission to arbitration, or it contains decisions on matters beyond the scope of the submission to arbitration, provided that, if the decisions on matters submitted to arbitration can be separated from those not so submitted, that part of the award which contains decisions on matters submitted to arbitration may be recognized and enforced; or

(iv) the composition of the arbitral tribunal or the arbitral procedure was not in accordance with the agreement of the parties or, failing such agreement, was not in accordance with the law of the country where the arbitration took place; or

(v) the award has not yet become binding on the parties or has been set aside or suspended by a court of the country in which, or under the law of which, that award was made; or

(b) if the court finds that:

(i) the subject-matter of the dispute is not capable of settlement by arbitration under the law of this State; or

(ii) the recognition or enforcement of the award would be contrary to the public policy of this State.

(2) If an application for setting aside or suspension of an award has been made to a court referred to in paragraph (1)(a)(v) of this article, the court where recognition or enforcement is sought may, if it considers it proper, adjourn its decision and may also, on the application of the party claiming recognition or enforcement of the award, order the other party to provide appropriate security.

TRAVAUX PRÉPARATOIRES

The *travaux préparatoires* on article 36 as adopted in 1985 are contained in the following documents :

1. Report of the United Nations Commission on International Trade Law on the work of its eighteenth session (*Official Records of the General Assembly, Fortieth Session, Supplement No. 17* (A/40/17)), paras. 11-333.

2. Reports of the Working Group: A/CN.9/216; A/CN.9/232; A/CN.9/233; A/CN.9/245; A/CN.9/246, annex; A/CN.9/263 and Add.1-2; A/CN.9/264. Relevant working papers are referred to in the reports.

3. Summary records of the 329th, 331st, 320th, 330th and 333rd UNCITRAL meetings.

Article 36 was not amended in 2006.

(Available on the Internet at www.uncitral.org).

INTRODUCTION

1. Although the grounds on which recognition or enforcement may be refused under the Model Law are identical to those listed in article V of the 1958 New York Convention,[936] the grounds listed in the Model Law are relevant not only to foreign awards but to all awards rendered in the sphere of application of the piece of legislation enacting the Model Law. Generally, it was deemed desirable to adopt, for the sake of harmony, the same approach and wording as this important Convention. However, the first ground on the list as contained in the 1958 New York Convention (which provides that recognition and enforcement may be refused if "the parties to the arbitration agreement were, under the law applicable to them, under some incapacity") was modified since it was viewed as containing an incomplete and potentially misleading conflict-of-laws rule.

CASE LAW ON ARTICLE 36

The grounds for refusing enforcement—paragraph (1) Construction and application

General principles

2. Courts construing article 36 found that the list of grounds for refusing recognition and enforcement of an arbitral award in paragraph (1) was exclusive[937] and should be construed narrowly.[938]

3. Notwithstanding the principle of narrow interpretation, the various grounds to resist enforcement listed in article 36 have been relied upon by the parties in an indiscriminate way. That has applied, in particular, to alleged violations of the right to be heard or other due process requirements and challenges to the jurisdiction of the arbitral tribunal. Consequently, courts have also considered such alleged violations of the right to be heard under different grounds, including under the grounds referred to in paragraphs 1*(a)*(ii), 1*(a)*(iv) and 1*(b)*(ii).[939] The same applies to jurisdictional complaint, where the grounds contained in paragraphs 1*(a)*(i) and 1*(a)*(iii) are often used interchangeably.

---

[936] Article V of the 1958 New York Convention reads as follows: "1. Recognition and enforcement of the award may be refused, at the request of the party against whom it is invoked, only if that party furnishes to the competent authority where the recognition and enforcement is sought, proof that: *(a)* The parties to the agreement referred to in article II were, under the law applicable to them, under some incapacity, or the said agreement is not valid under the law to which the parties have subjected it or, failing any indication thereon, under the law of the country where the award was made; or *(b)* The party against whom the award is invoked was not given proper notice of the appointment of the arbitrator or of the arbitration proceedings or was otherwise unable to present his case; or *(c)* The award deals with a difference not contemplated by or not falling within the terms of the submission to arbitration, or it contains decisions on matters beyond the scope of the submission to arbitration, provided that, if the decisions on matters submitted to arbitration can be separated from those not so submitted, that part of the award which contains decisions on matters submitted to arbitration may be recognized and enforced; or *(d)* The composition of the arbitral authority or the arbitral procedure was not in accordance with the agreement of the parties, or, failing such agreement, was not in accordance with the law of the country where the arbitration took place; or *(e)* The award has not yet become binding on the parties, or has been set aside or suspended by a competent authority of the country in which, or under the law of which, that award was made. 2. Recognition and enforcement of an arbitral award may also be refused if the competent authority in the country where recognition and enforcement is sought finds that: *(a)* The subject matter of the difference is not capable of settlement by arbitration under the law of that country; or *(b)* The recognition or enforcement of the award would be contrary to the public policy of that country."

[937] CLOUT case No. 453 [Bayerisches Oberstes Landesgericht, Germany, 4 Z Sch 02/00, 12 April 2000], also available on the Internet at http://www.dis-arb.de/en/47/datenbanken/rspr/bayoblg-case-no-4-z-sch-02-00-date-2000-04-12-id12; Appellate Commercial Court, Serbia, 25 March 2010, 175/2010(1).

[938] CLOUT case No. 391 [*Re Corporación Transnacional de Inversiones, S.A. de C.V. et al. v. STET International, S.p.A. et al.*, Ontario Superior Court of Justice, Canada, 22 September 1999], [1999] CanLII 14819 (ON SC), also available on the Internet at http://canlii.ca/t/1vvn5.

[939] Oberlandesgericht Frankfurt, Germany, 26 SchH 03/09, 27 August 2009, available on the Internet at http://www.dis-arb.de/de/47/datenbanken/rspr/olg-frankfurt-am-az-26-schh-03-09-datum-2009-08-27-id1012; Oberlandesgericht Stuttgart, Germany, 1 Sch 12/01, 6 December 2001, http://www.dis-arb.de/en/47/datenbanken/rspr/olg-stuttgart-case-no-1-sch-12-01-date-2001-12-06-id159.

Exclusive character of list of grounds

Residual discretion to refuse enforcement for other reasons?

4. It was expressly stated in a decision that the court lacked any residual discretion to refuse enforcement for reasons other than those contained in article 36 (1).[940] In general, the exclusion of any discretion of the court to refuse recognition and enforcement of an award is either apparent from the legislative materials or clearly underlies the relevant decisions. However, there are jurisdictions where such a residual discretion was either alleged or could not be excluded. This usually originates from the manner in which the Model Law has been enacted, or the 1958 New York Convention has been implemented in the State concerned.[941]

Substantive defences against underlying claim

5. A Canadian court made clear that grounds for resisting enforcement based on the merits of the dispute should have been raised before the arbitral tribunal, and not before the enforcement court.[942] However, different views exist as to whether such defences are also excluded if they either arose after the award had been rendered or could for other reasons not be raised during the arbitral proceedings. This applies in particular to the question of set-off defences. Some courts have considered such additional defences generally to be inadmissible in enforcement proceedings under articles 35 and 36.[943] However, the German Federal Court of Justice held that, under considerations of procedural economy, such defences can be raised in proceedings for a declaration of enforceability.[944]

Parallel recognition and enforcement proceedings

6. Occasionally parties initiate proceedings for the recognition and enforcement of arbitral awards in several countries at the same time. The question is whether the existence of other exequatur proceedings in different countries constitutes an obstacle for a court assuming jurisdiction.

7. A Spanish court held that there is no threat of contradictory decisions, as any decision rendered in exequatur proceedings has a limited territorial scope dealing with the recognition (and enforcement) in that particular jurisdiction. Thus, the refusal of recognition and enforcement in one jurisdiction does not contradict a decision providing for recognition and enforcement in another country.[945]

Narrow interpretation and enforcement despite the existence of grounds

8. The narrow interpretation of the various grounds for refusing recognition and enforcement of an arbitral award is regularly justified with the same arguments which are also raised in connection with the construction of the grounds to set aside awards: the courts should exercise a large degree of deference to the arbitral tribunal in making use of their discretion to refuse recognition and enforcement of an arbitral award, and they should seek to minimize judicial intervention when reviewing international commercial arbitral awards.[946]

9. In relation to the grounds for refusing recognition and enforcement, courts have held that it was within the discretion of the enforcing court to recognize and enforce an arbitral award despite the existence of a ground to resist recognition and enforcement, even where the award had not become binding or had been set aside by a court in the jurisdiction where the award was made.[947] In this respect, a court found that even if the defendant had not waived its right to object on the ground of lack of jurisdiction, the court would still declare the award enforceable since it was satisfied that the defendant obtained what it had agreed to, provided the court was convinced that the defendant's rights were not violated in any material way.[948] In another decision, the High Court in Hong Kong held that one factor which

---

[940] CLOUT case No. 740 [*Aloe Vera of America, Inc. v. Asianic Food (S) Pte. Ltd. and another*, High Court, Singapore, 10 May 2006], [2006] 3 SLR 174 (206).

[941] *Resort Condominium v. Bolwell*, Supreme Court of Queensland, Australia, 29 October 1993.

[942] *Phesco Inc. v. Canac. Inc.*, Quebec Superior Court, Canada, 14 November 2000, J.E. 2000-2268, AZ-50080781.

[943] CLOUT case No. 453 [Bayerisches Oberstes Landesgericht, Germany, 4 Z Sch 02/00, 12 April 2000], also available on the Internet at http://www.dis-arb.de/en/47/datenbanken/rspr/bayoblg-case-no-4-z-sch-02-00-date-2000-04-12-id12.

[944] Bundesgerichtshof, Germany, III ZB 57/10, 30 September 2010, available on the Internet at http://www.dis-arb.de/de/47/datenbanken/rspr/bgh-az-iii-zb-57-10-datum-2010-09-30-id1079; Bundesgerichtshof, Germany, III ZB 11/07, 17 January 2008, available on the Internet at http://www.dis-arb.de/de/47/datenbanken/rspr/bgh-az-iii-zb-11-07-datum-2008-01-17-id777.

[945] *Pavan S.R.L. v. Leng D'Or,* Court of First Instance, Spain, *S.A.*, 11 June 2007.

[946] CLOUT case No. 351 [*Food Services of America Inc. (c.o.b. Amerifresh) v. Pan Pacific Specialties Ltd.*, Supreme Court of British Columbia, Canada, 24 March 1997], 32 B.C.L.R. (3d) 225.

[947] CLOUT case No. 30 [*Robert E. Schreter v. Gasmac Inc.*, Ontario Court, General Division, Canada, 13 February 1992], [1992] O.J. No. 257; CLOUT case No. 358 [*Canadian National Railway Co. v. Southern Railway of British Columbia Ltd.*, Supreme Court of British Columbia, Canada, 11 May 1998], [1998] B.C.J. No. 1097]; CLOUT case No. 366 [*Europcar Italia S.p.A. v. Alba Tours International Inc.*, Ontario Court of Justice, General Division, Canada, 21 January 1997], [1997] O.J. No. 133, 23 O.T.C. 376 (Gen. Div.).

[948] CLOUT case No. 76 [*China Nanhai Oil Joint Service Corporation, Shenzhen Branch v. Gee Tai Holdings Co. Ltd.*, High Court—Court of First Instance, Hong Kong, 13 July 1994], [1994] 3 HKC 375, [1995] ADRLJ 127, HK HC, where recognition and enforcement of the arbitral award was granted although the arbitral award was issued by the Shenzhen Sub-commission of the China International Economic and Trade Arbitration Commission (CIETAC) and not, as provided in the arbitration agreement, CIETAC Beijing.

could justify making use of the court's pro-enforcement discretion was the fact that the violation of the relevant rule did not affect the outcome of the case, i.e. that the additional material to be submitted in the arbitral proceedings would not have changed the arbitral tribunal's view.[949]

Burden of proof

10. Courts have regularly held that the burden of proof regarding the grounds listed in paragraph 1*(a)* is upon the party resisting enforcement.[950] Courts have also considered that they should not examine on their own motion the validity of an arbitration agreement, if that matter was not raised by the party against which the award is to be enforced.[951] Concerning the grounds listed in paragraph 1*(b)*, several courts have held that the burden of proof for a violation of public policy remains with the party that sought to resist enforcement.[952] However, at least one court decided that there was no onus of proof on the respondent.[953]

Exclusion agreement

11. The question whether parties to arbitration may waive their right to resist enforcement is usually provided for in the legislation. A court considered that the parties to an arbitration agreement might validly agree to waive their right to invoke grounds to resist enforcement under article 36.[954]

Preclusion

12. The extent to which a party's failure to make use of existing remedies at the place of arbitration has a bearing on its ability to raise the same defects in exequatur proceedings has given rise to diverging court decisions.[955]

13. A Canadian Court rejected the proposal that a party's failure to raise alleged defects as defences in proceedings to have the award homologized (declared enforceable) at the place of arbitration should preclude it from raising such defects in the Canadian exequatur proceedings.[956] Equally, courts in Hong Kong and Singapore came to the same conclusion in relation to a party's failure to make use of remedies available at the place of arbitration.[957] The underlying rationale is that a party faced with an award against it is free to decide whether to apply for the setting aside of the award in the country of origin or to wait until the other party applies for enforcement and raise objections as a defence in such proceedings.

14. By contrast, some German courts have considered that a party would be precluded to raise defences in exequatur proceedings in Germany where it had not made use of the remedies available for such defects at the place of arbitration within the time limit provided for such remedies.[958] In other German decisions, such preclusionary effects were denied in cases where a party already contested the conclusion of a valid arbitration agreement.[959]

---

[949] *Paklito Investments Ltd. v. Klockner East Asia Ltd.*, High Court—Court of First Instance, Hong Kong, 15 January 1993, [1993] (Vol. 2) Hong Kong Law Reports 40.

[950] High Commercial Court, Serbia, 29 December 2008, 807/2008(3); CLOUT case No. 740 [*Aloe Vera of America, Inc. v. Asianic Food (S) Pte. Ltd. and another*, High Court, Singapore, 10 May 2006], [2006] 3 SLR 174 (206); *Paklito Investments Ltd. v. Klockner East Asia Ltd.*, High Court—Court of First Instance, Hong Kong, 15 January 1993, 1993 (Vol. 2) Hong Kong Law Reports 40.

[951] Madrid Court of Appeal, Spain, 4 March 2005, case No. 86/2005—52/2005; the approach was later amended in relation to arbitrations involving consumers in Madrid Court of Appeal, Spain, 13 February 2008, case No. 73/2008.

[952] Oberlandesgericht München, Germany, 34 Sch 18/06, 22 January 2007, available on the Internet at http://www.dis-arb.de/de/47/datenbanken/rspr/olg-m&uumlnchen-az-34-sch-18-06-datum-2007-01-22-id652.

[953] CLOUT case No. 30 [*Robert E. Schreter v. Gasmac Inc.,* Ontario Court, General Division, Canada, 13 February 1992], [1992] O.J. No. 257.

[954] CLOUT case No. 351 [*Food Services of America Inc. (c.o.b. Amerifresh) v. Pan Pacific Specialties Ltd.,* Supreme Court of British Columbia, Canada 24 March 1997], 32 B.C.L.R. (3d) 225.

[955] See e.g. the discussion in CLOUT case No. 740 [*Aloe Vera of America, Inc. v. Asianic Food (S) Pte. Ltd. and another*, High Court, Singapore, 10 May 2006], [2006] 3 SLR 174 (206) paras. 53 et seq.

[956] *Smart Systems Technologies Inc. v. Domotique Secant Inc.*, Court of Appeal of Quebec, 11 March 2008, 2008 QCCA 444.

[957] *Paklito Investments Ltd. v. Klockner East Asia Ltd.*, High Court—Court of First Instance, Hong Kong, 15 January 1993, [1993] (Vol. 2) Hong Kong Law Reports 40; CLOUT case No. 740 [*Aloe Vera of America, Inc. v. Asianic Food (S) Pte. Ltd. and another*, High Court, Singapore, 10 May 2006], [2006] 3 SLR 174 (206).

[958] Oberlandesgericht Karlsruhe, Germany, 9 Sch 02/05, 27 March 2006, available on the Internet at http://www.dis-arb.de/de/47/datenbanken/rspr/olg-karlsruhe-az-9-sch-02-05-datum-2006-03-27-id561; Oberlandesgericht Karlsruhe, Germany, 9 Sch 01/06, 3 July 2006, available on the Internet at http://www.dis-arb.de/de/47/datenbanken/rspr/olg-karlsruhe-az-9-sch-01-06-datum-2006-07-03-id560; Oberlandesgericht Karlsruhe, Germany, 9 Sch 02/07, 14 September 2007, available on the Internet at http://www.dis-arb.de/de/47/datenbanken/rspr/olg-karlsruhe-az-9-sch-02-07-datum-2007-09-14-id706; Kammergericht Berlin, 20 Sch 02/08, 17 April 2008, available on the Internet at http://www.dis-arb.de/de/47/datenbanken/rspr/kg-berlin-az-20-sch-02-08-datum-2008-04-17-id871; those decisions must be considered against the background that the German legislator, when adopting the Model Law extended the time limit for setting aside proceedings also to defences in exequatur proceedings for domestic awards.

[959] Bundesgerichtshof, Germany, III ZB 100/09, 16 December 2010, available on the Internet at http://www.dis-arb.de/de/47/datenbanken/rspr/bgh-az-iii-zb-100-09-datum-2010-12-16-id1192; Oberlandesgericht München, Germany, 34 Sch 04/08, 19 January 2009, available on the Internet at http://www.dis-arb.de/de/47/datenbanken/rspr/olg-m&uumlnchen-az-34-sch-04-08-datum-2009-01-19-id1062; Oberlandesgericht München, Germany, 34 Sch 20/08, 12 October 2009, available on the Internet at http://www.dis-arb.de/de/47/datenbanken/rspr/olg-m&uumlnchen-az-34-sch-20-08-datum-2009-10-12-id1023.

Valid arbitration agreement—Paragraph (1)*(a)*(i)

Existence—validity of the arbitration agreement

15. Different views exist as to whether paragraph (1)*(a)*(i) merely covers the "validity" of the arbitration agreement in a narrow sense or generally all questions pertaining to the existence, including the formation, of an arbitration agreement upon which an arbitral tribunal could base its jurisdiction.

16. Courts have distinguished between the conclusion of the arbitration agreement on the one hand and its validity on the other hand. The invalidity of the arbitration agreement constitutes a ground for resisting recognition and enforcement under paragraph (1)*(a)*(i), which has to be proven by the defendant. By contrast, the conclusion of an arbitration agreement, i.e. its existence, is considered as a precondition for any actions to have an award declared enforceable. Consequently, courts have considered that it has to be proven by the applicant.[960]

17. A different approach has been adopted by other courts.[961] For instance, the High Court in Singapore considered that the question whether a person is a party to the arbitration agreement comes within the scope of paragraph (1)*(a)*(i). Consequently, a party seeking to resist enforcement has to prove that it did not become a party to the arbitration agreement.[962]

Scope of review and applicable law

18. A German court held that the enforcement court is in principle not entitled to review the factual finding of the arbitral tribunal concerning the conclusion of the arbitration agreement. The prohibition of any review of the merits also extends to the arbitral tribunal's evaluation of the evidence offered concerning the formation of the arbitration agreement.[963] Along the same lines, the High Court of Singapore stated that an enforcement court should be reluctant to second guess the decision of the arbitral tribunal on its jurisdiction, in particular if the law upon which the decision was based is a foreign law.[964]

19. Often courts, however, do not address the issue of a potentially limited review of the arbitral tribunal's findings as to its jurisdiction but merely state that they are not bound by the factual or legal determination of the arbitral tribunal in this respect. Thus, another German court did not even address the problem when it reviewed the classification of two dispute resolution clauses as arbitration clauses by the arbitral tribunal and came to the conclusion that the clauses were mediation, not arbitration, clauses.[965]

20. Few cases discuss the law governing the arbitration agreement in greater detail. Where the main contract contains a choice of law clause, it is usually extended to the arbitration agreement without any further discussion.[966]

Non-signatories and pathological arbitration agreements

21. Awards rendered against non-signatories, which cannot be considered to be parties to the arbitration agreement, have in general not been declared enforceable.[967] By contrast, defences based on an alleged lack of precision have rarely been successful. Once it had been established that the parties wanted to arbitrate their disputes, courts have undertaken considerable efforts to prevent such clauses from being frustrated. Clauses such as "Rules/Arbitration: International Cotton Association rules and Arbitration" were considered to be sufficiently precise.[968] Equally, refer-

---

[960] Oberlandesgericht München, Germany, 34 Sch 04/08, 19 January 2009, available on the Internet at http://www.dis-arb.de/de/47/datenbanken/rspr/olg-m&uumlnchen-az-34-sch-04-08-datum-2009-01-19-id1062; Oberlandesgericht München, Germany, 34 Sch 20/08, 12 October 2009, available on the Internet at http://www.dis-arb.de/de/47/datenbanken/rspr/olg-m&uumlnchen-az-34-sch-20-08-datum-2009-10-12-id1023; Supreme Court of Cassation, Bulgaria, 31 October 2008, case No. 728.

[961] CLOUT case No. 740 [*Aloe Vera of America, Inc. v. Asianic Food (S) Pte. Ltd. and another*, High Court, Singapore, 10 May 2006], [2006] 3 SLR 174 (206) where the court relied on the decision by the English Court of Appeal in *Dardana Ltd. v. Yukos Oil Co.*, [2002] 2 Lloyd's Rep 326; to the same effect, *Dallah Real Estate and Tourism Holding Company v. Ministry of Religious Affairs, Government of Pakistan*, English Supreme Court, [2010] UKSC 46.

[962] CLOUT case No. 740 [*Aloe Vera of America, Inc. v. Asianic Food (S) Pte. Ltd. and another*, High Court, Singapore, 10 May 2006], [2006] 3 SLR 174 (206); see also, *Altain Khuder LLC v. IMC Mining Inc. & Anor,* Victoria Supreme Court, Australia, [2011] VSC 1 and [2011] VSC 12 (Croft J) but was later reversed by the Court of Appeal in [2011] VSCA 248.

[963] CLOUT case No. 457 [Hanseatisches Oberlandesgericht Hamburg, Germany, 1 Sch 02/99, 14 May 1999], also available on the Internet at http://www.dis-arb.de/de/47/datenbanken/rspr/hanseat-olg-hamburg-az-1-sch-02-99-datum-1999-05-14-id30 where the defendant alleged that the arbitral tribunal had wrongly assumed that it had received the confirmation letter containing the arbitration agreement.

[964] CLOUT case No. 740 [*Aloe Vera of America, Inc. v. Asianic Food (S) Pte. Ltd. and another*, High Court, Singapore, 10 May 2006], [2006] 3 SLR 174 (206), paras. 61 et seq.

[965] Oberlandesgericht Naumburg, Germany, 10 Sch 01/05, 20 May 2005, available on the Internet at http://www.dis-arb.de/de/47/datenbanken/rspr/olg-naumburg-az-10-sch-01-05-datum-2005-05-20-id456; Oberlandesgericht Frankfurt, Germany, 26 SchH 03/09, 27 August 2009, available on the Internet at http://www.dis-arb.de/de/47/datenbanken/rspr/olg-frankfurt-am-az-26-schh-03-09-datum-2009-08-27-id1012.

[966] See for instance: CLOUT case No. 740 [*Aloe Vera of America, Inc. v. Asianic Food (S) Pte. Ltd. and another*, High Court, Singapore, 10 May 2006], [2006] 3 SLR 174 (206), para. 61.

[967] *Structural Construction Co. Ltd. v. International Islamic Relief*, High Court, Nairobi, Kenya, 6 October 2006, Miscellaneous Case 596 of 2005, available at the Internet at http://www.kenyalaw.org/CaseSearch/view_preview1.php?link=15047352840327161414879.

[968] Oberlandesgericht Frankfurt, Germany, 26 SchH 03/09, 27 August 2009, available on the Internet at http://www.dis-arb.de/de/47/datenbanken/rspr/olg-frankfurt-am-az-26-schh-03-09-datum-2009-08-27-id1012.

ence to non-existing arbitral institutions were, whenever possible, interpreted in an arbitration friendly way to provide for arbitration under the rules of an existing institution.[969] (See also above, section on article 8, para. 22). However, a court denied the existence of a valid arbitration agreement in case of a conflict between the clause in the main contract providing for mediation which could be followed by court proceedings and a separately concluded arbitration agreement.[970] By contrast, the mere fact that the arbitration agreement gave one party the choice between arbitration and court proceedings was not considered to render that agreement invalid.[971] (See above, section on article 34, paras. 36-38).

Waiver

22. In one decision, a court found that the defendant had waived its right to raise the jurisdictional objection because it participated in the arbitral proceedings without expressly reserving its right to later object to the award on the ground that the arbitral tribunal lacked jurisdiction.[972] Furthermore, certain courts have held that a failure to challenge an interim award on jurisdiction pursuant to article 16 (3) also prevents a party from relying on the alleged lack of a valid arbitration agreement in subsequent enforcement proceedings.[973] In a case, the party opposing enforcement had invoked the arbitration agreement to contest the jurisdiction of the court in the originally initiated court proceedings and had then, after an unsuccessful challenge of the arbitral tribunal's jurisdiction, participated in the arbitral proceedings. In that light, the court rejected all evidence submitted by the party to prove that the arbitration agreement was allegedly invalid under Chinese law as the law of the country where the arbitration took place.[974]

Due Process—Paragraph (1)*(a)*(ii)

The concept of "unable to present his case"

23. The alleged violation of the right to be heard in the sense of paragraph (1)*(a)*(ii), also referred to as violation of "natural justice"[975] or of "due process", belongs to the most frequently raised ground to resist recognition and enforcement in practice.

24. It is sometimes suggested that paragraph (1)*(a)*(ii) only covers general violations of the right to present one's case and not issues pertaining to evidence which would be dealt with under paragraph (1)*(a)*(iv).[976] However, certain courts have dealt with rejections by arbitral tribunals of evidence in the context of defences under paragraph (1)*(a)* (ii). A court, while emphasizing that any review on the merits is prohibited, treated the refusal of the arbitrator to

[969] CLOUT case No. 373 [Kammergericht Berlin, Germany, 28 Sch 17/99, 15 October 1999], also available on the Internet at http://www.dis-arb.de/de/47/datenbanken/rspr/kg-berlin-az-28-sch-17-99-datum-1999-10-15-id35, where a clause providing for arbitration under the "Arbitration Rules of the German Central Chamber of Commerce" was considered to provide for arbitration under the Rules of the German Institution of Arbitration; CLOUT case No. 559 [Oberlandesgericht Celle, Germany, 8 Sch 03/01, 2 October 2001], also available on the Internet at http://www.dis-arb.de/de/47/datenbanken/rspr/olg-celle-az-8-sch-03-01-datum-2001-10-02-id208, confirmed by Bundesgerichtshof, III ZB 06/02, 30 January 2003, available on the Internet at http://www.dis-arb.de/de/47/datenbanken/rspr/bgh-az-iii-zb-06-02-datum-2003-01-30-id197.

[970] Oberlandesgericht Naumburg, Germany, 10 Sch 01/05, 20 May 2005, available on the Internet at http://www.dis-arb.de/de/47/datenbanken/rspr/olg-naumburg-az-10-sch-01-05-datum-2005-05-20-id456.

[971] CLOUT case No. 457 [Hanseatisches Oberlandesgericht Hamburg, Germany, 1 Sch 02/99, 14 May 1999], also available on the Internet at http://www.dis-arb.de/de/47/datenbanken/rspr/hanseat-olg-hamburg-az-1-sch-02-99-datum-1999-05-14-id30, where the court held that the clause neither lacked the required certainty nor constituted an undue burden for the other party which would have rendered it invalid under the German law on general conditions; CLOUT case No. 559 [Oberlandesgericht Celle, Germany, 8 Sch 03/01, 2 October 2001], also available on the Internet at http://www.dis-arb.de/de/47/datenbanken/rspr/olg-celle-az-8-sch-03-01-datum-2001-10-02-id208, confirmed by Bundesgerichtshof, III ZB 06/02, 30 January 2003, available on the Internet at http://www.dis-arb.de/de/47/datenbanken/rspr/bgh-az-iii-zb-06-02-datum-2003-01-30-id197.

[972] CLOUT case No. 76 [*China Nanhai Oil Joint Service Corporation, Shenzhen Branch v. Gee Tai Holdings Co. Ltd.,* High Court—Court of First Instance, Hong Kong, 13 July 1994], [1994] 3 HKC 375, [1995] ADRLJ 127, HK HC; see also Oberlandesgericht Stuttgart, Germany, 1 Sch 13/01, 20 December 2001, available on the Internet at http://www.dis-arb.de/de/47/datenbanken/rspr/olg-stuttgart-az-1-sch-13-01-datum-2001-12-20-id160, where the participation in the arbitration was additionally considered to result in a new arbitration agreement.

[973] Bundesgerichtshof, Germany, III ZB 83/02, 27 March 2003, available on the Internet at http://www.dis-arb.de/de/47/datenbanken/rspr/bgh-az-iii-zb-83-02-datum-2003-03-27-id212, rejecting the complaint on a point of law only against the decision of Oberlandesgericht Oldenburg, Germany, 9 SchH 09/02, 15 November 2002, available on the Internet at http://www.dis-arb.de/de/47/datenbanken/rspr/olg-oldenburg-az-9-schh-09-02-datum-2002-11-15-id235; see also the discussion in the section on article 16, para. 27.

[974] *Jiangxi Provincial Metal & Mineral Import & Export Corp. v. Sulanser Co. Ltd.*, High Court, Hong Kong, 6 April 1995, [1995] HKCFI 449, available on the Internet at http://www.hklii.hk/eng/hk/cases/hkcfi/1995/449.html.

[975] CLOUT case No. 30 [*Robert E. Schreter v. Gasmac Inc.,* Ontario Court, General Division, Canada, 13 February 1992], [1992] O.J. No. 257]; see also *Government of the Republic of the Philippines v. Philippine International Air Terminals Co. Inc.*, High Court, Singapore, 17 November 2006, [2007] 1 SLR (R) 278; [2006] SGHC 206.

[976] CLOUT case No. 457 [Hanseatisches Oberlandesgericht Hamburg, Germany, 1 Sch 02/99, 14 May 1999], also available on the Internet at http://www.dis-arb.de/de/47/datenbanken/rspr/hanseat-olg-hamburg-az-1-sch-02-99-datum-1999-05-14-id30; see also CLOUT case No. 371 [Hanseatisches Oberlandesgericht Bremen, Germany, 2 Sch 04/99, 30 September 1999], also available on the Internet at http://www.dis-arb.de/de/47/datenbanken/rspr/hanseat-olg-bremen-az-2-sch-04-99-datum-1999-09-30-id28.

hear witnesses to be primarily a question of the violation of the right to be heard under paragraph (1)*(a)*(ii).[977] Issues raised in practice in conjunction with violation of due process include refusals to take evidence,[978] absence of consideration by the arbitral tribunal of evidence presented, as well as the language of the proceedings.[979] (See also above, section on article 34, paras. 47-77).

25. Courts in various jurisdictions have made clear that a party cannot invoke a lack of proper participation or proper representation in the arbitral proceedings as a ground to resist enforcement if that is not due to circumstances attributable to the arbitral tribunal or extraneous events beyond the parties' control. Consequently, a court considered that a lack of participation by the legal representatives which is due to unclear instructions by the parties is not sufficient to constitute violation of due process.[980] In line therewith, a court in Egypt held that an award did not violate the right to due process where one party was unable to attend the hearing, allegedly since it was not granted a visa for the country where the hearing took place. While the court found that the party had failed to furnish sufficient proof that it was refused a visa, the court further underlined that, in any case, the party had been notified of the arbitral proceedings. In that case, the party had the opportunity to participate in the proceedings.[981]

26. Equally, the lack of participation due to insufficient funding[982] or because the hearing was not held at the place of arbitration[983] were not considered sufficient to justify an assumption of a violation of the right to be heard. However, according to a Canadian court, a party is unable to present its case if the lack of participation is due to the fact that it or its witnesses received death threats and the hearing has not been transferred to a safe place.[984]

27. A party can only present its case properly if the relevant documents are served upon it. In this context, a court considered it sufficient that the arbitral tribunal served the relevant document to the respondent's last known address. The court denied any obligation of the arbitral tribunal to make further enquiries as to the current address of the respondent's general manager. It deduced from the arbitration agreement an obligation for the parties to inform the other party about changes in the address.[985]

28. Certain courts have on several occasions dealt with allegations that the right to be heard had been violated by the arbitral tribunal which allegedly had infringed information duties so that its decision came as a surprise to the parties. Courts have made clear that the arbitral tribunal is under no obligation to discuss with the parties the case or its preliminary legal view on the facts. The arbitral tribunal should inform the parties in instances where it would decide to deviate from a legal position previously communicated to the parties or where its decision would for other reasons come as a surprise to the parties.[986] (See also above, section on article 34, paras. 68 and 73.)

29. Courts have considered that arbitral tribunals are not under an obligation to address all details of the arguments raised and the evidence offered by the parties in the reasoning of their decisions.[987] In particular, arguments or evidence which are irrelevant to the arbitral tribunal's decision do not

[977] Oberlandesgericht Stuttgart, Germany, 1 Sch 03/10, 30 July 2010, available on the Internet at http://www.dis-arb.de/de/47/datenbanken/rspr/olg-stuttgart-az-1-sch-03-10-datum-2010-07-30-id1077; see also Oberlandesgericht Frankfurt, Germany, 26 SchH 03/09, 27 August 2009, available on the Internet at http://www.dis-arb.de/de/47/datenbanken/rspr/olg-frankfurt-am-az-26-schh-03-09-datum-2009-08-27-id1012; Oberlandesgericht München, Germany, 34 Sch 12/09, 5 October 2009.

[978] Oberlandesgericht Stuttgart, Germany, 1 Sch 03/10, 30 July 2010, available on the Internet at http://www.dis-arb.de/de/47/datenbanken/rspr/olg-stuttgart-az-1-sch-03-10-datum-2010-07-30-id1077.

[979] CLOUT case No. 559 [Oberlandesgericht Celle, Germany, 8 Sch 03/01, 2 October 2001], also available on the Internet at http://www.dis-arb.de/de/47/datenbanken/rspr/olg-celle-az-8-sch-03-01-datum-2001-10-02-id208, confirmed by Bundesgerichtshof, III ZB 06/02, 30 January 2003, available on the Internet at http://www.dis-arb.de/de/47/datenbanken/rspr/bgh-az-iii-zb-06-02-datum-2003-01-30-id197; in that case, the contract had been drafted in German and Russian but the arbitral tribunal sent all its communication in Russian only as it was entitled under the applicable arbitration rules; Oberlandesgericht München, Germany, 34 Sch 26/08, 22 June 2009, available on the Internet at http://www.dis-arb.de/de/47/datenbanken/rspr/olg-m&uumlnchen-az-34-sch-26-08-datum-2009-06-22-id1065; CLOUT case No. 1069 [Supreme Court, Croatia, 5 March 2008, 5 March 2008, Case No. Gž 6/08-2].

[980] *Structural Construction Co. Ltd. v. International Islamic Relief*, High Court, Nairobi, Kenya, 6 October 2006, Miscellaneous Case 596 of 2005, available at the Internet at http://www.kenyalaw.org/CaseSearch/view_preview1.php?link=15047352840327161414879.

[981] Cairo Court of Appeal, Egypt, 5 May 2009, case No. 29/125.

[982] CLOUT case No. 501 [*Grow Biz International Inc. v. D.L.T Holdings Inc.*, Supreme Court of Prince Edward Island, Canada, 23 March 2001], [2001] PESCTD 27, also available on the Internet at http://canlii.ca/t/4tjr.

[983] Oberlandesgericht Stuttgart, Germany, 1 Sch 12/01, 6 December 2001, http://www.dis-arb.de/en/47/datenbanken/rspr/olg-stuttgart-case-no-1-sch-12-01-date-2001-12-06-id159.

[984] *Znamensky Selekcionno-Gibridny Center LLC v. Donaldson International Livestock Ltd.*, Ontario Court of Appeal, Canada, 29 April 2010, 2010 ONCA 303.

[985] Oberlandesgericht Dresden, Germany, 11 Sch 19/05, 15 March 2005, available on the Internet at http://www.dis-arb.de/de/47/datenbanken/rspr/olg-dresden-az-11-sch-19-05-datum-2005-03-15-id531.

[986] Oberlandesgericht Stuttgart, Germany, 1 Sch 03/10, 30 July 2010, available on the Internet at http://www.dis-arb.de/de/47/datenbanken/rspr/olg-stuttgart-az-1-sch-03-10-datum-2010-07-30-id1077; Oberlandesgericht Karlsruhe, Germany, 10 Sch 8/08, 27 March 2009.

[987] Oberlandesgericht Stuttgart, Germany, 1 Sch 12/01, 6 December 2001, available on the Internet at http://www.dis-arb.de/en/47/datenbanken/rspr/olg-stuttgart-case-no-1-sch-12-01-date-2001-12-06-id159; Oberlandesgericht Frankfurt, Germany, 26 SchH 03/09, 27 August 2009, available on the Internet at http://www.dis-arb.de/de/47/datenbanken/rspr/olg-frankfurt-am-az-26-schh-03-09-datum-2009-08-27-id1012; Oberlandesgericht Frankfurt a.M., Germany, 26 Sch 01/03, 10 July 2003, available on the Internet at http://www.dis-arb.de/de/47/datenbanken/rspr/olg-frankfurt-am-az-26-sch-01-03-datum-2003-07-10-id226.

have to be mentioned. In the absence of indications to the contrary, some courts have considered that there is a presumption that the tribunal has complied with its obligation to take the parties' submissions into account. Thus, the mere silence of the award on certain points raised by the defendant does not mean that the arbitral tribunal has not considered the argument, unless specific circumstances of the case evidence the contrary as, for example, when the argument is of crucial relevance for the legal outcome.[988] A court in Canada stated that the absence of reasons in the award does not mean that a party's right to be heard during the arbitration was violated.[989]

30. In several cases, respondents sought to base their alleged inability to present their cases properly on their inability to understand the language of the proceedings. Such defences have not been successful if the language of the arbitral proceedings had explicitly been agreed upon between the parties or was determined in line with the chosen arbitration rules.[990] In such cases, courts generally considered that the party which is unable to understand the language should arrange for the necessary translations.[991] Moreover, it has been generally considered sufficient that a party is represented by a lawyer who speaks the language.[992] (See also above, section on article 22, paras. 2 and 4).

31. The party seeking to resist enforcement has to prove that it was not given an opportunity to properly present its case, in particular where there is a different account of the events.[993] Moreover, some courts have required proof from the party resisting enforcement that the arbitral award was based on the violation of the right to be heard.[994]

Scope of Mandate—paragraph 1(*a*)(iii)

32. The alleged excess of scope of submission to arbitration has been invoked by the parties in a large variety of situations. They range from allegations that certain claims were not covered by the arbitration agreement[995] over general complaints about the arbitral tribunal's decision on its jurisdiction[996] to allegations that a party never became a party to the arbitration agreement[997] or the latter has been terminated.[998]

[988] Oberlandesgericht Frankfurt, Germany, 26 SchH 03/09, 27 August 2009, available on the Internet at http://www.dis-arb.de/de/47/datenbanken/rspr/olg-frankfurt-am-az-26-schh-03-09-datum-2009-08-27-id1012.

[989] CLOUT case No. 30 [*Robert E. Schreter v. Gasmac Inc.,* Ontario Court, General Division, Canada, 13 February 1992], [1992] O.J. No. 257.

[990] CLOUT case No. 1069 [Supreme Court, Croatia, 5 March 2008, Case No. Gž 6/08-2], where the public policy defence was rejected as the arbitral tribunal was authorized under the applicable Czech arbitration rules to conduct the proceedings in the Czech language.

[991] CLOUT case No. 559 [Oberlandesgericht Celle, Germany, 8 Sch 03/01, 2 October 2001], also available on the Internet at http://www.dis-arb.de/de/47/datenbanken/rspr/olg-celle-az-8-sch-03-01-datum-2001-10-02-id208, confirmed by Bundesgerichtshof, III ZB 06/02, 30 January 2003, available on the Internet at http://www.dis-arb.de/de/47/datenbanken/rspr/bgh-az-iii-zb-06-02-datum-2003-01-30-id197; in that case, the contract had been drafted in German and Russian, but the tribunal sent out all its communication in Russian only as it was entitled under the applicable arbitration rules.

[992] Oberlandesgericht München, Germany, 34 Sch 26/08, 22 June 2009, available on the Internet at http://www.dis-arb.de/de/47/datenbanken/rspr/olg-m&uumlnchen-az-34-sch-26-08-datum-2009-06-22-id1065.

[993] *Paklito Investments Ltd. v. Klockner East Asia Ltd.*, High Court—Court of First Instance, Hong Kong, 15 January 1993 [1993] (Vol. 2), Hong Kong Law Reports 40.

[994] CLOUT case No. 371 [Hanseatisches Oberlandesgericht Bremen, Germany, (2) Sch 04/99, 30 September 1999], also available on the Internet at http://www.dis-arb.de/de/47/datenbanken/rspr/hanseat-olg-bremen-az-2-sch-04-99-datum-1999-09-30-id28.

[995] CLOUT case No. 584 [*Dunhill Personnel System v. Dunhill Temps Edmonton*, Alberta Queen's Bench, Canada, 30 September 1993], 13 Alta L. R. (2d) 240; CLOUT case No. 67 [*AAMCO Transmissions Inc. v. Kunz*, Saskatchewan Court of Appeal, Canada, 17 September 1991], 97 Saskatchewan Reports, 5; CLOUT case No. 371 [Hanseatisches Oberlandesgericht Bremen, Germany, 2 Sch 04/99, 30 September 1999], also available on the Internet at http://www.dis-arb.de/de/47/datenbanken/rspr/hanseat-olg-bremen-az-2-sch-04-99-datum-1999-09-30-id28.

[996] CLOUT case No. 740 [*Aloe Vera of America, Inc. v. Asianic Food (S) Pte. Ltd. and another*, High Court, Singapore, 10 May 2006], [2006] 3 SLR 174 (206).

[997] CLOUT case No. 740 [*Aloe Vera of America, Inc. v. Asianic Food (S) Pte. Ltd. and another*, High Court, Singapore, 10 May 2006], [2006] 3 SLR 174 (206) paras. 64 et seq.

[998] Oberlandesgericht Stuttgart, Germany, 1 Sch 12/01, 6 December 2001, available on the Internet at http://www.dis-arb.de/en/47/datenbanken/rspr/olg-stuttgart-case-no-1-sch-12-01-date-2001-12-06-id159; CLOUT case No. 559 [Oberlandesgericht Celle, Germany, 8 Sch 03/01, 2 October 2001], also available on the Internet at http://www.dis-arb.de/de/47/datenbanken/rspr/olg-celle-az-8-sch-03-01-datum-2001-10-02-id208, confirmed by Bundesgerichtshof, III ZB 06/02, 30 January 2003, available on the Internet at http://www.dis-arb.de/de/47/datenbanken/rspr/bgh-az-iii-zb-06-02-datum-2003-01-30-id197.

33. According to the High Court in Singapore, allegations that the arbitral tribunal rendered an award against a party not bound by the arbitration agreement are not covered by the ground to resist enforcement under paragraph 1*(a)*(iii). They relate to the question of the jurisdiction of the arbitral tribunal and not to the scope of its mandate.[999] Equally, allegations that a party has assigned the claims and could therefore no longer actively pursue them were considered to relate to the merits of a claim and not to fall under the defence in paragraph 1*(a)*(iii).[1000]

34. By contrast, allegations that an arbitral tribunal awarded more than requested by the claimant are often treated as falling within the ambit of paragraph 1*(a)*(iii). However, in determining what has been claimed by a party, a court considered that the arbitral tribunal may go beyond the mere wording of the request and interpret the request in light of the other documents submitted to it.[1001]

The question of the jurisdiction of the arbitral tribunal has already been determined by the courts at the place of arbitration

35. With reference to the rights of a party under paragraph (1)*(a)*(iii) to raise objections as to the jurisdiction of the arbitral tribunal at the enforcement stage, a court considered that the enforcement court had the right to make a final determination on the jurisdiction of the arbitral tribunal even if the same issue had been subject to determination in setting aside proceedings at the place of arbitration.[1002] However, another court decided that that question should be determined in accordance with the domestic procedural law of the enforcement court concerning the recognition of foreign judgment. Therefore, the court did not hear an objection as to the jurisdiction of the arbitral tribunal at the enforcement stage, since such issue had already been determined by the courts at the place of arbitration.[1003]

36. In the context of enforcement of foreign arbitral awards, the question of the determination of the law governing the scope of submission to arbitration has been raised. A court in Canada has found that the question whether an arbitral award contained decisions on matters beyond the scope of the submission to arbitration should be determined under the law applicable to the arbitration agreement.[1004] In another Canadian decision, however, enforcement has been refused as the court came to the conclusion that the arbitral award was based both on matters that were covered by the arbitration clause and matters expressly excluded therefrom. The court stated that the case turned solely on the interpretation of the arbitration agreement and the principles of common law relating to interpreting such an agreement. That decision did not contain any reference to the law applicable to the arbitration agreement.[1005]

37. A court considered that where a contract had allegedly been assigned to a different party and had in the meantime been terminated, claims based on that contract would still fall within the arbitrator's mandate, in particular where the claims were based on pre-termination facts (see above, section on article 34, para. 94).[1006]

---

[999] CLOUT case No. 740 [*Aloe Vera of America, Inc. v. Asianic Food (S) Pte. Ltd. and another*, High Court, Singapore, 10 May 2006], [2006] 3 SLR 174 (206) paras. 64 et seq, where the allegation concerned a general manager of a company who had signed the contract in his professional capacity.

[1000] Oberlandesgericht Stuttgart, Germany, 1 Sch 12/01, 6 December 2001, available on the Internet at http://www.dis-arb.de/en/47/datenbanken/rspr/olg-stuttgart-case-no-1-sch-12-01-date-2001-12-06-id159.

[1001] Ibid.

[1002] CLOUT case No. 509 [*Canada, Dalimpex Ltd. v. Janicki*, Court of Appeal for Ontario, 30 May 2003], [2003] 64 Ontario Reports (3d) 737; 228 Dominion Law Reports (4th) 179, where the court adjourned the enforcement proceedings awaiting the judgment in the setting-aside proceedings. The court also stated that if the application for setting aside would be denied, the merits of the jurisdictional objection would be determined by the enforcement court.

[1003] CLOUT case No. 371 [Hanseatisches Oberlandesgericht Bremen, Germany, (2) Sch 4/99, 30 September 1999], also available on the Internet at http://www.dis-arb.de/de/47/datenbanken/rspr/hanseat-olg-bremen-az-2-sch-04-99-datum-1999-09-30-id28.

[1004] CLOUT case No. 30 [*Robert E. Schreter v. Gasmac Inc.*, Ontario Court, General Division, Canada, 13 February 1992], [1992] O.J. No. 257, where the court granted recognition and enforcement since the respondent had not provided proof that under the law applicable to the arbitration agreement, the arbitral tribunal made decisions on matters outside the terms of the submission to arbitration.

[1005] CLOUT case No. 67 [*AAMCO Transmissions Inc. v. Kunz*, Saskatchewan Court of Appeal, Canada, 17 September 1991], 97 Saskatchewan Reports 5.

[1006] Oberlandesgericht Stuttgart, Germany, 1 Sch 12/01, 6 December 2001, available on the Internet at http://www.dis-arb.de/en/47/datenbanken/rspr/olg-stuttgart-case-no-1-sch-12-01-date-2001-12-06-id159; see for a void contract invalidating the arbitration clause contained therein, Court of Cassation, Bahrain, 17 November 2003, action No. 433/2003; CLOUT case No. 559 [Oberlandesgericht Celle, Germany, 8 Sch 03/01, 2 October 2001], also available on the Internet at http://www.dis-arb.de/de/47/datenbanken/rspr/olg-celle-az-8-sch-03-01-datum-2001-10-02-id208, confirmed by Bundesgerichtshof, III ZB 06/02, 30 January 2003, available on the Internet at http://www.dis-arb.de/de/47/datenbanken/rspr/bgh-az-iii-zb-06-02-datum-2003-01-30-id197.

Composition of the arbitral tribunal, procedural errors—paragraph 1*(a)*(iv)

The arbitral tribunal was not composed according to the agreement of the parties

38. In practice, the defence of an incorrectly composed arbitral tribunal is primarily used to challenge non-compliance with agreed standards or rules as well as the alleged lack of independence or impartiality of one of the arbitrators (see above, section on article 34, paras. 97 and 98). Of primary relevance for assessing the proper composition of the arbitral tribunal is the arbitration agreement. In determining whether the composition of the arbitral tribunal was in accordance with the agreement of the parties, one court took into consideration the manner in which the agreement would have been applied in the State where the arbitration took place.[1007] Notwithstanding the importance of the right to appoint one's own arbitrator, the obligation to select the arbitrator from a list of potential arbitrators does not lead to an incorrectly composed tribunal if the chosen rules provide for such a list procedure.[1008]

The arbitral tribunal did not follow procedures agreed upon by the parties

39. Procedural issues raised in court proceedings on enforcement concern all types of procedural requirements. They range from the general requirement to preserve the parties' right to be heard[1009] and more specifically the obligation to hold an oral hearing,[1010] to the use of the correct language[1011] and the application of the proper rules and laws to reasoning or signature requirements of the award.[1012]

40. The procedural rules agreed upon by the parties, in particular the arbitration rules chosen by them are relevant to the determination of compliance by the arbitral tribunal with the procedure agreed upon by the parties. Thus, the refusal to hold a hearing does not prevent the enforcement of an award, where the applicable arbitration rules give the tribunal discretion to do so.[1013] Arbitral proceedings in a language different from the one agreed upon may give rise to a defence under paragraph 1*(a)*(iv). In this context, courts have not only considered the language requirement of the arbitration agreement but also to subsequent communications which, in practice, resulted in a modification to the language requirements.[1014]

41. The procedural rules to be observed by the arbitral tribunal also encompass the rules relating to the determination of the law applicable to the merits. Enforcement of an award can, however, not be refused on the ground of an application of the "wrong" law, if an award applies the proper law but in its reasoning also refers to another law.[1015]

42. Regarding the requirement that reasons be given by the arbitral tribunal in the award, Canadian courts have emphasized that the existence of at least some reasoning is crucial for any review of whether the award is contrary to public policy or the arbitral tribunal has exceeded the scope of its mandate. In one case dealing with that issue, the complete absence of any reasoning led to a refusal to recognize the award as that would be contrary to public policy in cases where the parties had agreed that reasons should be given.[1016] A crucial factor for the court in that case was also that, in the absence of any reasoning, it was impossible to deduce whether the arbitral tribunal had exceeded its mandate or violated procedural rules. The court emphasized that the orders rendered by the arbitral tribunal raised doubts as to the compliance of the arbitral tribunal with its mandate. Those factors were absent in another Canadian decision, where the court enforced an award which contained no reasoning, as there were no indications that the arbitral tribunal exceeded its power.[1017]

[1007] CLOUT case No. 76 [*China Nanhai Oil Joint Service Corporation, Shenzhen Branch v. Gee Tai Holdings Co. Ltd.,* High Court—Court of First Instance, Hong Kong, 13 July 1994], [1994] 3 HKC 375, [1995] ADRLJ 127, HK HC.

[1008] Oberlandesgericht Frankfurt, 26 SchH 03/09, Germany, 27 August 2009, available on the Internet at http://www.dis-arb.de/de/47/datenbanken/rspr/olg-frankfurt-am-az-26-schh-03-09-datum-2009-08-27-id1012.

[1009] CLOUT case No. 457 [Hanseatisches Oberlandesgericht Hamburg, Germany, 1 Sch 02/99, 14 May 1999], also available on the Internet at http://www.dis-arb.de/de/47/datenbanken/rspr/hanseat-olg-hamburg-az-1-sch-02-99-datum-1999-05-14-id30.

[1010] CLOUT case No. 371 [Hanseatisches Oberlandesgericht Bremen, Germany, (2) Sch 4/99, 30 September 1999], also available on the Internet at http://www.dis-arb.de/de/47/datenbanken/rspr/hanseat-olg-bremen-az-2-sch-04-99-datum-1999-09-30-id28.

[1011] Oberlandesgericht München, Germany, 34 Sch 26/08, 22 June 2009, available on the Internet at http://www.dis-arb.de/de/47/datenbanken/rspr/olg-m&uumlnchen-az-34-sch-26-08-datum-2009-06-22-id1065.

[1012] Ibid.

[1013] CLOUT case No. 371 [Hanseatisches Oberlandesgericht Bremen, (2) Sch 4/99, Germany, 30 September 1999], also available on the Internet at http://www.dis-arb.de/de/47/datenbanken/rspr/hanseat-olg-bremen-az-2-sch-04-99-datum-1999-09-30-id28.

[1014] Oberlandesgericht München, Germany, 34 Sch 26/08, 22 June 2009, available on the Internet at http://www.dis-arb.de/de/47/datenbanken/rspr/olg-m&uumlnchen-az-34-sch-26-08-datum-2009-06-22-id1065.

[1015] CLOUT case No. 569 [Hanseatisches Oberlandesgericht Hamburg, Germany, 11 Sch 01/01, 8 June 2001], also available on the Internet at http://www.dis-arb.de/de/47/datenbanken/rspr/hanseat-olg-hamburg-az-11-sch-01-01-datum-2001-06-08-id1274.

[1016] *Smart Systems Technology Inc. v. Domotique Secant Inc.,* Court of Appeal of Quebec, Canada, 11 March 2008, [2008] Q.J. No. 1782.

[1017] CLOUT case No. 30 [*Robert E. Schreter v. Gasmac Inc.,* Ontario Court, General Division, Canada, 13 February 1992], [1992] O.J. No. 257.

43. A different justification for upholding an award, despite non-compliance with the obligation to include reasons as provided for under the applicable arbitration rules, was given in a Canadian decision. In that case, the court adopted a narrow interpretation of the notion of "incorrect procedure". It held that the lack of any reasoning did not in itself bring into question the fairness of the hearing or the decision-making process but only occurred after the termination of the actual proceedings. Therefore, it was in itself not sufficiently serious to constitute a violation of the parties' agreement to apply the arbitration rules to the arbitral proceedings.[1018] In the same decision, the court also had to address the allegation that the lack of reasoning evidenced that the arbitral tribunal did not decide the case on the basis of the applicable law but acted *ex aequo et bono*. The court held that, in the absence of any evidence that the arbitral tribunal had not decided the case on the basis of the applicable law, the fact that the arbitral tribunal had not given reasons in the award did not in itself support the allegation of the respondent that the arbitral tribunal had decided the dispute *ex aequo et bono*.[1019]

44. Some courts have required that such violation to rules of procedure must have affected the outcome of the proceedings to justify a refusal to enforcement.[1020]

The arbitral award has not become binding, has been set aside or suspended—paragraph (1)*(a)*(v)

The arbitral award has not yet become binding upon the parties

45. In the absence of a definition of when an award becomes binding, courts in several jurisdictions had to address that matter. A Canadian court found that an arbitral award was binding and could be enforced irrespective of any confirmation of the arbitral award by a court in the jurisdiction where the award was made.[1021] Other courts held that an award was binding under the law of the country in which it was made if there was no statutory remedy against the award providing for a review of its merits.[1022]

The arbitral award has been set aside or suspended

46. After an arbitral award is made, the claimant may seek enforcement of the award either before the courts in the State where the award was made or before the courts in another State (where, for instance, the debtor has assets). Where, however, the award is set aside (or "annulled" or "vacated") by the competent court in the State of origin, the enforcement of the award in the State of origin would not be possible. The party seeking enforcement may then try to have the award enforced by a court in another State. The issue that faces the court in the State of enforcement is whether there are any circumstances that allow the court to enforce the award, disregarding the fact that the award has been set aside in the State of origin.[1023]

47. In one decision, it was found that if the arbitral award had been set aside at the place of arbitration, the award was no longer binding and the enforcement court therefore had no power to recognize or enforce such arbitral award. According to the same decision, this would be the case even though there was a possibility that the decision setting aside the award would be revised in further proceedings which were pending at the place of arbitration.[1024]

48. Canadian courts have confirmed at least *obiter dicta* that they have discretion to enforce awards which have been set aside in their countries of origin.[1025]

49. A court held that the suspension of the arbitral award by court order at the place of arbitration had no bearing on the court's discretion to refuse enforcement. It further considered that a suspension of the arbitral award by operation of law, i.e. elapse of time for applying to enforcement at place of arbitration, could not be equated to a court-ordered suspension under paragraph (1)*(a)*(v).[1026]

[1018] CLOUT case No. 351 [*Food Services of America Inc. (c.o.b. Amerifresh) v. Pan Pacific Specialties Ltd.*, Supreme Court of British Columbia, Canada, 24 March 1997], 32 B.C.L.R. (3d) 225.

[1019] Ibid.

[1020] Oberlandesgericht München, Germany, 34 Sch 26/08, 22 June 2009, available on the Internet at http://www.dis-arb.de/de/47/datenbanken/rspr/olg-m&uumlnchen-az-34-sch-26-08-datum-2009-06-22-id1065.

[1021] CLOUT case No. 385 [Ontario Court of Justice, Canada, *Murmansk Trawl Fleet v. Bimman Realty Inc.* 19 December 1994], [1994] O.J. No. 3018 where the Court pointed out that a confirmation of an award necessary in another State only relates to that State.

[1022] CLOUT case No. 372 [Oberlandesgericht Rostock, Germany, 1 Sch 03/99, 28 October 1999], also available on the Internet at http://www.dis-arb.de/de/47/datenbanken/rspr/olg-rostock-az-1-sch-03-99-datum-1999-10-28-id60; CLOUT case No. 509 [Court of Appeal for Ontario, Canada, *Dalimpex Ltd. v. Janicki*, 30 May 2003], [2003] 64 Ontario Reports (3d) 737; 228 Dominion Law Reports (4th) 179; CLOUT case No. 530 [*Société Nationale d'Opérations Pétrolièrers de la Côte d'Ivoire Holding v. Keen Lloyd Resources Ltd,* High Court—Court of First Instance, Hong Kong Special Administrative Region of China, 20 December 2001], also available on the Internet at http://www.hklii.hk/eng/hk/cases/hkcfi/2001/173.html.

[1023] For a discussion on that matter, see A/CN.9/460, paras. 128-144, available on the Internet at http://www.uncitral.org.

[1024] CLOUT case No. 372 [Oberlandesgericht Rostock, Germany, 1 Sch 03/99, 28 October 1999], also available on the Internet at http://www.dis-arb.de/de/47/datenbanken/rspr/olg-rostock-az-1-sch-03-99-datum-1999-10-28-id60.

[1025] CLOUT case No. 30 [*Robert E. Schreter v. Gasmac Inc.,* Ontario Court, General Division, Canada, 13 February 1992], [1992] O.J. No. 257, para. 29.

[1026] CLOUT case No. 366 [*Europcar Italia S.p.A. v. Alba Tours International Inc.,* Ontario Court of Justice, General Division, Canada, 21 January 1997], [1997] O.J. No. 133, 23 O.T.C. 376 (Gen. Div.).

The subject-matter of the dispute is not capable of settlement by arbitration under the law of this State—paragraph (1)*(b)*(i)

50. In line with the provision of paragraph (1)*(b)*(i), a Canadian court has stated that the law of the State where recognition and enforcement is sought is relevant for determining whether a dispute is arbitrable.[1027]

51. A court, applying the exception of paragraph (1)*(b)* (i), held that an award for costs cannot be enforced against a person who was not party to an arbitration agreement but was found by an arbitrator to be a party to the arbitral proceeding. The court considered the provisions of the 1958 New York Convention and the Model Law, and concluded that only a party named in the arbitration agreement could be subjected to enforcement proceedings under the relevant international instruments.[1028]

Public policy—paragraph (1)*(b)*(ii)

Standard of review

52. Courts which had to define the appropriate standard of review under paragraph (1)*(b)*(ii) supported a restrictive interpretation of the defence. The public policy defence should be applied only if the arbitral award fundamentally offended the most basic and explicit principles of justice and fairness in the enforcement State, or evidences intolerable ignorance or corruption on part of the arbitral tribunal.[1029] Courts have also stated that to refuse to enforce an award on the ground that it violates public policy, the award must either be contrary to the essential morality of the State in question[1030] or disclose errors that affect the basic principles of public and economic life.[1031] Not every infringement of mandatory law amounts to a violation of public policy.[1030] Occasionally it was also required that the violation of public policy must be obvious.[1033] Public policy was defined in a jurisdiction so as to cover cases where the arbitral award is "patently in violation of statutory provisions".[1034]

Procedural public policy

53. It was found that procedural public policy was violated only if the award was the result of a procedure which differed from the fundamental principles of procedural law of the enforcement State,[1035] or, if it could not be considered the result of a fair and constitutional procedure, because it contained substantial errors touching upon the very foundations of public and economic life.[1036] According to a German court, such fundamental principles are the right to be heard and the right to actively participate in the proceedings.[1035]

54. A court determined that the right to be duly informed about the arbitral procedure and duly notified of the hearings formed part of procedural public policy. In the same decision, the court held that, despite the fact that under the law applicable to the arbitration the mere dispatch of the

---

[1027] CLOUT case No. 30 [*Robert E. Schreter v. Gasmac Inc.*, Ontario Court, General Division, Canada, 13 February 1992], [1992] O.J. No. 257, para. 29; CLOUT case No. 740 [*Aloe Vera of America, Inc. v. Asianic Food (S) Pte. Ltd. and another*, High Court, Singapore, 10 May 2006], [2006] 3 SLR 174 (206).

[1028] CLOUT case No. 510 [*Javor v. Francoeur*, Supreme Court of British Columbia, Canada, 6 March 2003] [2003], 13 British Columbia Law Reports (4th) 195.

[1029] CLOUT case No. 30 [*Robert E. Schreter v. Gasmac Inc.*, Ontario Court, General Division, Canada, 13 February 1992], [1992] O.J. No. 257; CLOUT case No. 37 [*Arcata Graphics Buffalo Ltd. v. Movie (Magazine) Corp.*, Ontario Court, General Division, Canada, 12 March 1993]; CLOUT case No. 391 [*Re Corporación Transnacional de Inversiones, S.A. de C.V. et al. v. STET International, S.p.A. et al.*, Superior Court of Justice, Canada, 22 September 1999], [1999] CanLII 14819 (ON SC), also available on the Internet at http://canlii.ca/t/1vvn5; CLOUT case No. 511 [*Desputeraux v. Les Editions Chouettes (1987) Inc.*, Supreme Court of Canada, 21 March 2003], [2003] 1 Supreme Court Reports 178.

[1030] CLOUT case No. 37 [*Arcata Graphics Buffalo Ltd. v. Movie (Magazine) Corp.*, Ontario Court, General Division, Canada, 12 March 1993]; CLOUT case No. 520 [*Shanghai City Foundation Works Corp. v. Sunlink Ltd*, High Court—Court of First Instance, Hong Kong Special Administrative Region of China, 2 February 2001], [2001] 3 HKC 521.

[1031] CLOUT case No. 456 [Hanseatisches Oberlandesgericht Hamburg, Germany, 6 Sch 11/98, 4 November 1998], also available on the Internet at http://www.dis-arb.de/de/47/datenbanken/rspr/hanseat-olg-hamburg-az-6-sch-11-98-datum-1998-11-04-id32.

[1032] CLOUT case No. 1068 [Supreme Court, Croatia, 30 May 2008, Gž 2/08-2].

[1033] Oberlandesgericht München, Germany, 34 Sch 18/06, 22 January 2007, available on the Internet at http://www.dis-arb.de/de/47/datenbanken/rspr/olg-m&uumlnchen-az-34-sch-18-06-datum-2007-01-22-id652.

[1034] *Phulchand Exports Ltd. v. OOO Patriot*, Supreme Court, India, 12 October 2011, [2011] INSC 1038.

[1035] Oberlandesgericht München, Germany, 34 Sch 26/08, 22 June 2009, holding that mere deviations from procedural requirements under the national law are not sufficient, available on the Internet at http://www.dis-arb.de/de/47/datenbanken/rspr/olg-m&uumlnchen-az-34-sch-26-08-datum-2009-06-22-id1065.

[1036] CLOUT case No. 371 [Hanseatisches Oberlandesgericht Bremen, (2) Sch 4/99, Germany, 30 September 1999], also available on the Internet at http://www.dis-arb.de/de/47/datenbanken/rspr/hanseat-olg-bremen-az-2-sch-04-99-datum-1999-09-30-id28.

[1037] Oberlandesgericht München, Germany, 34 Sch 26/08, 22 June 2009, available on the Internet at http://www.dis-arb.de/de/47/datenbanken/rspr/olg-m&uumlnchen-az-34-sch-26-08-datum-2009-06-22-id1065.

notice of arbitration, without any proof of receipt, was acceptable, such legal fiction of receipt could not be considered sufficient for a valid notice under the law of the country where enforcement was sought.[1038] Where the alleged violation of public policy consisted of a violation of the right to be heard, certain courts have required that the party prove that the pleading or evidence rejected would have had an impact on the outcome of the case.[1039]

55. The complete absence of any reasoning was considered to constitute a violation of public policy at least in cases where the award had to give reasons under the applicable rules, and without such reasoning it could not be determined whether the tribunal exceeded its mandate, which in light of the particular facts of the case could not be excluded.[1040]

56. The finality of awards and the principle of *res judicata* are considered to form part of public policy. It was held that where the parties have agreed to re-arbitrate a dispute in order to involve a third party in the proceedings, it would not violate public policy and the principle of finality in arbitration to enforce the arbitral award issued in the second proceedings, since the party who won the first arbitration had waived any rights derived from the first award by submitting the dispute to a second arbitration.[1041]

Substantive public policy

57. Substantive public policy concerns primarily the content of the award. Consequently, courts in several jurisdictions have repeatedly stated that ensuring conformity with substantive public policy did not permit a review of the merits of the case.[1042]

58. The principle of proportionality as a part of public policy has been invoked by parties in various instances where they disagreed with the amount awarded regarding either performance or breach of a contract, or costs. Certain courts have held that only extreme violations of the principle of proportionality can constitute a violation of public policy.[1043]

59. Furthermore, it was held that the mere fact that the arbitral award violated certain laws or regulations of the enforcement State was not sufficient to constitute a violation of public policy.[1044] In practice, courts have considered that there was no violation of public policy in cases where awarded liquidated damages[1045] or payments for breach of contract[1046] would not have been in conformity with the law of the enforcement State, or where a decision on costs[1047] was incorrect.

[1038] CLOUT case No. 402 [Highest Regional Court of Bavaria, Germany, Germany, 4 Z Sch 50/99, 16 March 2000], also available on the Internet at http://www.dis-arb.de/de/47/datenbanken/rspr/bayoblg-az-4-z-sch-50-99-datum-2000-03-16-id13.

[1039] CLOUT case No. 371 [Hanseatisches Oberlandesgericht Bremen, Germany, (2) Sch 4/99, 30 September 1999], also available on the Internet at http://www.dis-arb.de/de/47/datenbanken/rspr/hanseat-olg-bremen-az-2-sch-04-99-datum-1999-09-30-id28; Oberlandesgericht Karlsruhe, Germany, 10 Sch 8/08, 27 March 2009.

[1040] *Smart Systems Technology Inc. v. Domotique Secant Inc.*, Court of Appeal of Quebec, Canada, 11 March 2008, [2008] Q.J. No. 1782.

[1041] CLOUT case No. 233 [*Durco (Pvt.) Ltd. v. Dajen (Pvt.) Ltd.*, Harare High Court, Zimbabwe, 10 July and 20 August 1997]; confirmed by CLOUT case No. 234 [*Dajen (Pvt) Ltd. v. Durco (Pvt) Ltd.*, Supreme Court of Zimbabwe, 22 June and 7 September 1998, case No. SC 141/98].

[1042] CLOUT case No. 30 [*Robert E. Schreter v. Gasmac Inc.*, Ontario Court, General Division, Canada, 13 February 1992], [1992] O.J. No. 257; CLOUT case No. 740 [*Aloe Vera of America, Inc. v. Asianic Food (S) Pte. Ltd. and another*, High Court, Singapore, 10 May 2006], [2006] 3 SLR 174 (206).

[1043] Oberlandesgericht Dresden, Germany, 11 Sch 01/05, 20 April 2005, available on the Internet at http://www.dis-arb.de/de/47/datenbanken/rspr/olg-dresden-az-11-sch-01-05-datum-2005-04-20-id307; Oberlandesgericht Celle, Germany, 8 Sch 06/05, 6 October 2005, available on the Internet at http://www.dis-arb.de/de/47/datenbanken/rspr/olg-celle-az-8-sch-06-05-datum-2005-10-06-id192; Kammergericht Berlin, Germany, 23 Sch 06/02, 27 May 2002, available on the Internet at http://www.dis-arb.de/de/47/datenbanken/rspr/kg-berlin-az-23-sch-06-02-datum-2002-05-27-id264.

[1044] CLOUT case No. 443 [Oberlandesgericht Dresden, Germany, 11 Sch 06/98, 13 January 1999], also available on the Internet at http://www.dis-arb.de/de/47/datenbanken/rspr/olg-dresden-az-11-sch-06-98-datum-1999-01-13-id43.

[1045] Ibid.

[1046] CLOUT case No. 30 [*Robert E. Schreter v. Gasmac Inc.*, Ontario Court, General Division, Canada, 13 February 1992], [1992] O.J. No. 257.

[1047] CLOUT case No. 444 [Oberlandesgericht Dresden, Germany, 11 Sch 08/01, 8 May 2001], also available on the Internet at http://www.dis-arb.de/de/47/datenbanken/rspr/olg-dresden-az-11-sch-08-01-datum-2001-05-08-id106.

60. Furthermore, it was also determined that an award including interest rate expressed on a monthly basis (instead of an annual basis) was not contrary to public policy even though the legal system of the enforcement State contained statutory limitations on interest rates that are not expressed on an annual basis.[1048] In another case where the interest according to the award would exceed the principal of the claim and contravene the so-called *in duplum* rule, the court found that the award could be interpreted as impliedly subject to the *in duplum* rule and that it would be recognized and enforced accordingly.[1049]

61. In several cases the potential availability of remedies at the place of arbitration were considered by the courts to be factors which played a role in rejecting allegations that the enforcement of an award would be contrary to public policy as the award violated basic notions of natural justice[1050] or the party had no right to defend itself properly.[1051]

62. Substantive public policy may be violated where the award is based on a contract tainted in one way or another by bribery or corruption. Thus the Supreme Court of Thailand refused to enforce an award which was based on a construction contract which had been obtained by bribery.[1052]

Adjourn the decision on recognition and enforcement—paragraph (2)

63. A court found that it was a matter of judicial discretion whether to adjourn the decision on recognition and enforcement and, if that would be the case, whether to order the respondent to provide security. In exercising such discretion, the court determined that the main test was that of the balance of convenience to the parties, and that special weight should be given to the fact that the adjudication on the merits has already taken place.[1053] In another decision, it was found that the decision on recognition and enforcement should be adjourned as the court was satisfied that the application for setting aside the arbitral award at the place of arbitration had some merit.[1054]

[1048] CLOUT case No. 37 [*Arcata Graphics Buffalo Ltd. v. Movie (Magazine) Corp.,* Ontario Court, General Division, Canada, 12 March 1993].

[1049] CLOUT case No. 342 [Harare High Court, Zimbabwe, *Conforce (Pvt.) Limited v. The City of Harare,* 1 March and 5 April 2000].

[1050] CLOUT case No. 740 [*Aloe Vera of America, Inc. v. Asianic Food (S) Pte. Ltd. and another*, High Court, Singapore, 10 May 2006], [2006] 3 SLR 174 (206).

[1051] Bundesgerichtshof, Germany, III ZR 332/99, 1 February 2001, available on the Internet at http://www.dis-arb.de/de/47/datenbanken/rspr/bgh-az-iii-zr-332-99-datum-2001-02-01-id1259.

[1052] Supreme Court, Thailand, case No. 7277/2549, available on the Internet at http://www.supremecourt.or.th.

[1053] CLOUT case No. 366 [*Europcar Italia S.p.A. v. Alba Tours International Inc.,* Ontario Court of Justice, General Division, Canada, 21 January 1997], [1997] O.J. No. 133, 23 O.T.C. 376 (Gen. Div.), where the court of the country where enforcement was sought found that justice to both parties could best be achieved by an adjournment of the court's decision, conditional upon the respondent furnishing security, pending a determination of the application for setting aside by the courts in the country where the arbitral award was made.

[1054] CLOUT case No. 514 [*Powerex Corp. v. Alcan Inc.,* British Colombia Supreme Court, Canada, 10 July 2003], [2003] British Columbia Judgments No. 1674.

Part two

LIST OF CASES

LIST OF CASES BY COUNTRY/ARTICLE

Australia

Article 1

Electra Air Conditioning B.V. Appellant v. Seeley International Pty. Ltd., Federal Court, Australia, 8 October 2008, [2008] FCAFC 169

Article 3

Uganda Telecom Limited v. Hi-Tech Telecom Pty. Ltd., Federal Court, Australia, 22 February 2011, [2011] FCA 131

Article 7

Lief Investments Pty. Limited v. Conagra International Fertiliser Company, Supreme Court of New South Wales – Court of Appeal, Australia, 16 July 1998, [1998] NSWSC 481

Article 8

Francis Travel Marketing Pty. Limited v. Virgin Atlantic Airways Limited, Supreme Court of New South Wales – Court of Appeal, Australia, 7 May 1996, [1996] NSWSC 104

Shipowners' Mutual Protection and Indemnity Assoc (Luxembourg) v. Hodgetts & Anor, Supreme Court of Queensland – Court of Appeal, Australia, 6 May 1998, [1998] QCA 88

Hi-Fert Pty. Ltd. & Anor v. Kiukiang Maritime Carriers Inc. & Anor, Federal Court, Australia, 24 November 1998, [1998] FCA 1485

Comandate Marine Corp. v. Pan Australia Shipping Pty. Ltd., Federal Court, Australia, 20 December 2006, [2006] FCAFC

APC Logistics Pty. Ltd. v. C.J. Nutracon Pty. Ltd., Federal Court, Australia, 16 February 2007, [2007] FCA 136

Timoney Technology Limited & Anor. v. ADI Limited, Supreme Court of Victoria, Australia, 17 October 2007, [2007] VSC 402

Paharpur Cooling Towers Ltd. v. Paramount (Wa) Ltd., Supreme Court of Western Australia – Court of Appeal, Australia, 13 May 2008, [2008] WASCA 110

Wes Trac Pty. Ltd. v. Eastcoast OTR Tyres Pty. Ltd., Supreme Court of New South Wales, Australia, 29 August 2008, [2008] NSWSC 894

Electra Air Conditioning B.V. v. Seeley International Pty. Ltd., Federal Court, Australia, 8 October 2008, [2008] FCAFC 169

Gilgandra Marketing Co-Operative Limited v. Australian Commodities & Marketing Pty. Ltd. & Anor, Supreme Court of New South Wales, Australia, 22 October 2010, [2010] NSWSC 1209

Article 10

Gordian Runoff Ltd. (formerly Gio Insurance Ltd.) v. The Underwriting Members of Lloyd's Syndicates, Supreme Court of New South Wales, Australia, 19 December 2002 (revised 5 February 2003), [2002] NSWSC 1260

Electra Air Conditioning B.V. v. Seeley International Pty. Ltd., Federal Court, Australia, 8 October 2008, [2008] FCAFC 169

Article 14

Gordian Runoff Ltd. (formerly Gio Insurance Ltd.) v. The Underwriting Members of Lloyd's Syndicates, Supreme Court of New South Wales, Australia, 19 December 2002 (revised 5 February 2003), [2002] NSWSC 1260

Article 15

Gordian Runoff Ltd. (formerly Gio Insurance Ltd.) v. The Underwriting Members of Lloyd's Syndicates, Supreme Court of New South Wales, Australia, 19 December 2002 (revised 5 February 2003), [2002] NSWSC 1260

Article 16

Walter Rau Neusser Oel und Fett A.G. v. Cross Pacific Trading Ltd., Federal Court, Australia, 15 August 2005, [2005] FCA 1102

Comandate Marine Corp. v. Pan Australia Shipping Pty. Ltd., Federal Court, Australia, 20 December 2006, [2006] FCAFC 192

Article 19

Eisenwerk Hensel Bayreuth Dipl-Ing Burkhardt Gmbh v. Australian Granites Limited, Queensland Court of Appeal, Australia, [2001] 1 Qd R 461

Cargill International SA v. Peabody Australia Mining Ltd., Supreme Court of New South Wales, Australia, 11 August 2011, [2010] NSWSC 887

Wagners Nouvelle Caledonie Sarl v. Vale Inco Nouvelle Caledonie SAS, Queensland Court of Appeal, Australia, 20 August 2010, [2010] QCA 219

Article 20

Angela Raguz v. Rebecca Sullivan & Ors, New South Wales Supreme Court, New South Wales Court of Appeal, Australia, 1 September 2000, [2000] NSWCA 240

Article 31

Oil Basins Ltd. v. BHP Billiton Ltd., Victoria Court of Appeal, Australia, 16 November 2007, [2007] VSCA 255

Gordian Runoff Ltd. v. Westport Insurance Corporation, New South Wales Court of Appeal, Australia, 1 April 2010, [2010] NSWCA 57

Article 34

Oil Basins Ltd. v. BHP Billiton Ltd., Victoria Court of Appeal, Australia, 16 November 2007, [2007] VSCA 255

Gordian Runoff Limited v. Westport Insurance Corporation, New South Wales Court of Appeal, Australia, 1 April 2012, [2010] NSWCA 57

Article 35

Resort Condominium v. Bolwell, Supreme Court of Queensland, Australia, 29 October 1993

Article 36

Resort Condominium v. Bolwell, Supreme Court of Queensland, Australia, 29 October 1993

Austria

Article 1

CLOUT case No. 106 [Supreme Court, Austria, 2 Ob 547/93, 10 November 1994]

Article 34

Supreme Court, Austria, 30 June 2010, 7 Ob 111/10i

Bahrain

Article 34

Court of Cassation, Bahrain, 17 November 2003, action No. 433/2003

Article 36

Court of Cassation, Bahrain, 17 November 2003, action No. 433/2003

Bulgaria

Article 34

Supreme Court of Cassation, Bulgaria, 31 October 2008, case No. 728

Supreme Court of Cassation, Bulgaria, 1 December 2009, case No. 106

Article 36

Supreme Court of Cassation, Bulgaria, 31 October 2008, case No. 728

Bermuda

Article 7

CLOUT case No. 127 [*Skandia International Insurance Company and Mercantile & General Reinsurance Company and various others*, Supreme Court, Bermuda, 21 January 1994]

Article 11

Montpelier Reinsurance Ltd. v. Manufacturers Property & Casualty Limited, Supreme Court, Bermuda, 24 April 2008, [2008] Bda LR 24

Article 16

Christian Mutual Insurance Company & Central United Life Insurance Company & Connecticut Reassurance Corporation v. Ace Bermuda Insurance Limited, Court of Appeal, Bermuda, 6 December 2002, [2002] Bda LR 56

Article 35

Associated Electric & Gas Insurance Services Ltd. v. European Reinsurance Company of Zurich, Privy Council, Bermuda, 29 January 2003, Appeal No. 93 of 2001, [2003] UKPC 11

Canada

Article 1

CLOUT case No. 13 (also reproduced under CLOUT case No. 383) [*Deco Automotive Inc. v. G.P.A. Gesellschaft für Pressenautomation mbH*, Ontario District Court, Canada, 27 October 1989]

CLOUT case No. 586 [*Kaverit Steel and Crane Ltd. v. Kone Corp.*, Alberta Court of Appeal, Canada, 16 January 1992]

CLOUT case No. 28 [*BWV Investments Ltd. v. Saskferco Products Inc., UHDE-GmbH, et al.,* Saskatchewan Court of Queen's Bench, Canada, 19 March 1993]

CLOUT case No. 111 [*Borowski v. Heinrich Fiedler Perforiertechnik GmbH,* Alberta Court of Queen's Bench, Canada, 12 August 1994]

CLOUT case No. 116 [*BWV Investments Ltd. v. Saskferco Products Inc. et. al. and UHDE GmbH,* Saskatchewan Court of Appeal, Canada, 25 November 1994] (this case revised CLOUT case No. 28 [*BWV Investments Ltd. v. Saskferco Products Inc., UHDE-GmbH, et al.,* Saskatchewan Court of Queen´s Bench, Canada, 19 March 1993]

CLOUT case No. 390 [*Re Carter et al. and McLaughlin et al.,* Ontario Court, Canada, 1 February 1996]

CLOUT case No. 502 [*The United Mexican States v. Metalclad Corp.*, British Columbia Supreme Court, Canada, 2 May 2001]

CLOUT case No. 505 [*Ross v. Christian and Timbers, Inc.*, Ontario Superior Court of Justice, Canada, 30 April 2002]

Desputeaux v. Éditions Chouette (1987) inc., Supreme Court, Canada, 21 March 2003, [2003] 1 S.C.R. 178, 2003 SCC 17

CLOUT case No. 1048 [*Patel v. Kanbay International Inc.,* Ontario Court of Appeal, Canada, 23 December 2008]

Article 2

CLOUT case No. 627 [*Sport Maska Inc. v. Zittrer and others*, Supreme Court, Canada, 24 March 1988]

Noble China Inc. v. Lei Kat Cheong, Ontario Court of Justice, Canada, 4 November 1998, [1998] CanLII 14708 (ON SC), in (1998) 42 O.R. (3d) 69

Article 3

CLOUT case No. 384 [*Skorimpex Foreign Trade Co. v. Lelovic Co.*, Ontario Court of Justice, Canada, 26 April 1991]

CLOUT case No. 29 [*Kanto Yakin Kogyo Kabushiki-Kaisha v. Can-Eng Manufacturing Ltd.,* Ontario Court of Justice, Canada, 30 January 1992]

Bell Canada v. The Plan Group, Ontario Court of Appeal, Canada, 7 July 2009, [2009] ONCA 548

Article 5

CLOUT case No. 383 [*Deco Automotive Inc. v. G.P.A. Gesellschaft für Pressenautomation mbH,* Ontario District Court, Canada, 27 October 1989]

CLOUT case No. 16 [*Quintette Coal Limited v. Nippon Steel Corp. et al.,* Court of Appeal for British Columbia, Canada, 24 October 1990]

CLOUT case No. 18 [*Rio Algom Limited v. Sammi Steel Co.,* Ontario Court of Justice, Canada, 1 March 1991]

CLOUT case No. 182 [*International Civil Aviation Organization (ICAO) v. Tripal Systems Pty. Ltd.*, Superior Court of Quebec, Canada, 9 September 1994]

CLOUT case No. 116 [*BWV Investments Ltd. v. Saskferco Products Inc. et. al. and UHDE GmbH,* Saskatchewan Court of Appeal, Canada, 25 November 1994]

Noble China Inc. v. Lei Kat Cheong, Ontario Court of Justice, Canada, 4 November 1998, [1998] CanLII 14708 (ON SC), in (1998) 42 O.R. (3d) 69

CLOUT case No. 391 [*Re Corporación Transnacional de Inversiones, S.A. de C.V. et al. v. STET International, S.p.A. et al.,* Superior Court of Justice, Canada, 22 September 1999]

CLOUT case No. 392 [*Compagnie Nationale Air France v. Libyan Arab Airlines,* Superior Court of Quebec, Canada, 15 February 2000]

CLOUT case No. 516 [*Microtec Sécuri-T Inc. v. Centre d'Arbitrage Commercial National et International du Québec (CACNIQ),* Superior Court of Quebec, Canada, 14 March and 2 June 2003]

Compagnie Nationale Air France v. Mbaye, Court of Appeal of Quebec, Canada, 31 March 2003 [2003] CanLII 35834 (QC CA)

CLOUT case No. 513 [*Western Oil Sands Inc. v. Allianz Insurance Co. et al.,* Alberta Court of Queen's Bench, Canada, 2 February 2004]

CLOUT case No. 1009 [*Yugraneft Corp. v. Rexx Management Corp.*, Supreme Court, Canada, 20 May 2010]

Article 7

Importations Cimel Ltée v. Pier Augé Produits de Beauté, Court of Appeal of Quebec, Canada, 27 October 1987, 1987 CanLII 1165 (QC CA)

C.C.I.C. Consultech International v. Silverman, Court of Appeal of Quebec, Canada, 24 May 1991, 1991 CanLII 2868 (QC CA)

Empressa de Turismo Nacional & Internacional v. Vacances sans frontière ltée, Court of Appeal of Quebec, Canada, 9 October 1992, 1992 CanLII 3546 (QC CA)

CLOUT case No. 34 [*Miramichi Pulp and Paper Inc. v. Canadian Pacific Bulk Ship Services Ltd.,* Federal Court – Trial Division, Canada, 9 October 1992]

CLOUT case No. 368 [*Campbell et al. v. Murphy,* Ontario Court – General Division, Canada, 9 August 1993]

CLOUT case No. 70 [*Nanisivik Mines Ltd. and Zinc Corporation of America v. Canarctic Shipping Co. Ltd.,* Federal Court – Court of Appeal, Canada, 10 February 1994]

CLOUT case No. 178 [*Siderurgica Mendes Junior S.A. v. "Icepearl" (The),* Supreme Court of British Columbia, Canada, 31 January 1996]

CLOUT case No. 365 [*Schiff Food Products Inc. v. Naber Seed & Grain Co. Ltd.,* Saskatchewan Court of Queen's Bench, Canada, 1 October 1996]

Ferguson Bros. of St. Thomas v. Manyan Inc., Ontario Court of Justice, Canada, 27 May 1999, [1999] OJ No. 1887

CLOUT case No. 389 [*Canadian National Railway Company v. Lovat Tunnel Equipment Inc.,* Ontario Court of Appeal, Canada, 8 July 1999]

CLOUT case No. 391 [*Re Corporación Transnacional de Inversiones, S.A. de C.V. et al. v. STET International, S.p.A. et al.,* Superior Court of Justice, Canada, 22 September 1999], confirmed in *Corporación Transnacional de Inversiones v. Stet International,* Ontario Court of Appeal, Canada, 15 September 2000

Thyssen Canada Ltd. v. Mariana (The), Federal Court – Court of Appeal, Canada, 22 March 2000, [2000] CanLII 17113 (FCA), [2000] 3 FC 398

2961-8667 *Québec Inc. v. Fafard,* Court of Appeal of Quebec, Canada, 31 March 2004, [2004] QJ No. 4085, REJB 2004-60643

Dongnam Oil & Fats Co. v. Chemex Ltd., Federal Court – Trial Division, Canada, 10 December 2004, [2004] FC 1732 (CanLII)

Achilles (USA) v. Plastics Dura Plastics (1977) ltée/Ltd., Court of Appeal of Quebec, Canada, 23 November 2006, [2006] QCCA 1523

Rampton v. Eyre, Ontario Court of Appeal, Canada, 2 May 2007, [2007] ONCA 331

Dell Computer Corp. v. Union des Consommateurs, Supreme Court, Canada, 13 July 2007, [2007] SCC 34, [2007] 2 SCR 801

Librati v. Barka Co. Ltd., Superior Court of Quebec, Canada, 5 December 2007, [2007] QCCS 5724

Investissement Charlevoix Inc. v. Gestion Pierre Gingras Inc., Court of Appeal of Quebec, Canada, 21 June 2010, [2010] QCCA 1229 (CanLII)

Article 8

CLOUT case No. 9 [*Coopers and Lybrand Limited (Trustee) for BC Navigation S.A. (Bankrupt),* Federal Court – Trial Divison, Canada, 2 November 1987]

CLOUT case No. 65 [*ODC Exhibit Systems Ltd. v. Lee, Expand International et al.,* Supreme Court of British Columbia, Canada, 28 November 1988]

CLOUT case No. 619 [*Boart Sweden Ab and others v. NYA Strommes AB and others,* Ontario Supreme Court, Canada, 21 December 1988]

CLOUT case No. 15 [*Navionics Inc. v. Flota Maritima Mexicana S.A. et al.,* Federal Court – Trial Division, Canada, 17 January 1989]

CLOUT case No. 14 [*Iberfreight S.A. et al. v. Ocean Star Container Line AG and J.W. Lunstedt KG,* Federal Court – Court of Appeal, Canada, 2 June 1989]

CLOUT case No. 13 (also reproduced under CLOUT case No. 383) [*Deco Automotive Inc. v. G.P.A. Gesellschaft für Pressenautomation mbH,* Ontario District Court, Canada, 27 October 1989]

CLOUT case No. 17 [*Stancroft Trust Limited, Berry and Klausner v. Can-Asia* Capital Company, Limited, Mandarin Capital Corporation and Asiamerica Capital Limited, Court of Appeal for British Columbia, Canada, 26 February 1990]

Desbois v. Industries A.C. Davie Inc., Court of Appeal of Quebec, Canada, 26 April 1990, [1990] CanLII 3619 (QC CA)

CLOUT case No. 19 [*Krutov v. Vancouver Hockey Club Limited,* Supreme Court of British Columbia, Canada, 22 November 1991]

CLOUT case No. 586 [*Kaverit Steel and Crane Ltd. v. Kone Corp.,* Alberta Court of Appeal, Canada, 16 January 1992]

CLOUT case No. 31 [*Gulf Canada Resources Ltd. v. Arochem International Ltd.,* Court of Appeal for British Columbia, Canada, 10 March 1992]

CLOUT case No. 33 [*Ruhrkohle Handel Inter GMBH and National Steel Corp. et al. v. Fednav Ltd. and Federal Pacific,* Federal Court – Court of Appeal, Canada, 29 May 1992]

CLOUT case No. 35 [*Canada Packers Inc. et al. v. Terra Nova Tankers Inc. et al.,* Ontario Court of Justice – General Division, Canada, 1 October 1992]

CLOUT case No. 34 [*Miramichi Pulp and Paper Inc. v. Canadian Pacific Bulk Ship Services Ltd.,* Federal Court – Trial Division, Canada, 9 October 1992]

CLOUT case No. 70 [*Nanisivik Mines Ltd. and Zinc Corporation of America v. Canarctic Shipping Co. Ltd.,* Federal Court – Court of Appeal, Canada, 10 February 1994], [1994] 2 FC 662

CLOUT case No. 72 [*Continental Resources Inc. v. East Asiatic Co. (Canada) et al.,* Federal Court – Trial Division, Canada, 22 March 1994]

CLOUT case No. 183 [*Automatic Systems Inc. v. Bracknell Corp.,* Ontario Court of Appeal, Canada, 25 April 1994]

CLOUT case No. 74 [*Automatic Systems Inc. v. E.S. Fox Ltd. and Chrysler Canada Ltd.,* Ontario Court of Appeal, Canada, 25 April 1994]

CLOUT case No. 112 [*Kvaerner Enviropower Inc. v. Tanar Industries Ltd.,* Court of Queen's Bench of Alberta, Canada, 13 July 1994], confirmed in *Tanar Industries Ltd. v. Kvaerner Enviropower Inc.,* Alberta Court of Appeal, Canada, 25 October 1994, [1994] ABCA 346

CLOUT case No. 113 [*T1T2 Limited Partnership v. Canada,* Ontario Court of Justice – General Division, Canada, 10 November 1994]

CLOUT case No. 116 [*BWV Investments Ltd. v. Saskferco Products Inc. et. al. and IHDE GmbH,* Saskatchewan Court of Appeal, Canada, 25 November 1994]

CLOUT case No. 119 [*ABN Amro Bank Canada v. Krupp Mak Maschinenbau GmbH,* Ontario Court of Justice – General Division, Canada, 23 December 1994]

Arbella S.A. v. Aghia Markella (The), Federal Court – Trial Division, Canada, 28 April 1995, [1995] FCJ No. 723

Bab Systems Inc. v. McLurg, Ontario Court of Appeal, Canada, 11 May 1995, [1995] CanLII 1099 (ON CA)

ABN Amro Bank Canada v. Krupp MaK Maschinenbau GmbH, Ontario Court of Justice – General Division, Canada, 7 June 1995, [1995] CanLII 7081 (ON SC)

CLOUT case No. 386 [*ATM Compute GmbH v. DY 4 Systems, Inc.,* Ontario Court of Justice, Canada, 8 June 1995]

CLOUT case No. 179 [*The City of Prince George v. A.L. Sims & Sons Ltd.,* Court of Appeal for British Columbia, Canada, 4 July 1995]

Fuller Austin Insulation Inc. v. Wellington Insurance Co., Saskatchewan Court of Queen's Bench, Canada, 15 September 1995, [1995] CanLII 5752 (SK QB)

CLOUT case No. 178 [*Siderurgica Mendes Junior S.A. v. "Icepearl" (The),* Supreme Court of British Columbia, Canada, 31 January 1996]

Décarel Inc. et al. v. Concordia Project Management Ltd., Court of Appeal of Quebec, Canada, 30 July 1996, 500-09-000596-957

Burlington Northern Railroad Co. v. Canadian National Railway Co., Supreme Court, Canada, 21 January 1997, [1997] 1 SCR 5, 1997 CanLII 395 (SCC); *Burlington Northern Railroad Co. v. Canadian National Railway Co.,* Court of Appeal for British Columbia, Canada, 18 May 1995, [1995] CanLII 1802 (BC CA

Ocean Fisheries Ltd. v. Pacific Coast Fishermen's Mutual Marine Insurance Co. (C.A.), Federal Court – Court of Appeal, Canada, 30 October 1997, [1998] 1 FC 586

CLOUT case No. 382 [*Methanex New Zealand Ltd. v. Fontaine Navigation S.A., Tokyo Marine Co. Ltd., The Owners and all Others,* Federal Court – Trial Division, Canada, 9 January 1998]

Simmonds Capital Limited v. Eurocom International Limited, Federal Court – Trial Division, Canada, 15 January 1998, [1998] CanLII 7229 (FC)

CLOUT case No. 352 [*Nutrasweet Kelco Co. v. Royal-Sweet International Technologies Ltd. Partnership,* Court of Appeal for British Columbia, Canada, 23 February 1998]

CLOUT case No. 388 [*Temiskaming Hospital v. Integrated Medical Networks, Inc.,* Ontario Court of Justice – General Division, Canada, 31 March 1998]

Coldmatic Refrigeration of Canada Ltd. v. P.U.M.A. s.r., Ontario Court of Justice – General Division, Canada, 24 April 1998, [1998] OJ No. 1697

Abitibi-Price Sales Corp. v. C.V. Scheepv.Ondernemineg "Sambeek", Federal Court – Trial Division, Canada, 12 November 1998, [1998] CanLII 8706 (FC)

CLOUT case No. 355 [*Restore International Corp. v. K.I.P. Kuester International Products Corp.,* Supreme Court of British Columbia, Canada, 15 January 1999]

Ferguson Bros. of St. Thomas v. Manyan Inc., Ontario Superior Court of Justice, Canada, 27 May 1999, [1999] OJ No. 1887

CLOUT case No. 356 [*Seine River Resources Inc. v. Pensa Inc.,* Supreme Court of British Columbia, Canada, 15 June 1999]

CLOUT case No. 391 [*Re Corporación Transnacional de Inversiones, S.A. de C.V. et al. v. STET International, S.p.A. et al.,* Superior Court of Justice, Canada, 22 September 1999]

OEMSDF Inc. v. Europe Israel Ltd., Ontario Superior Court of Justice, Canada, 22 September 1999, [1999] O.J. No. 3594

Turnbridge v. Cansel Survey Equipment (Canada) Ltd., Supreme Court of British Columbia, Canada, 17 February 2000, [2000] BCSC 287

Thyssen Canada Ltd. v. Mariana (The), Federal Court – Court of Appeal, Canada, 22 March 2000, [2000] 3 FC 398

CLOUT case No. 381 [*Fibreco Pulp Inc. v. Star Shipping A/S,* Federal Court – Court of Appeal, Canada, 24 May 2000]

Laurentienne-vie, Cie d'assurances Inc. v. Empire, Cie d'assurance-vie, Court of Appeal of Quebec, Canada, 12 June 2000, [2000] CanLII 9001 (QC CA)

Cangene Corp. v. Octapharma AG, Court of Queen's Bench of Manitoba, Canada, 30 June 2000, [2000] MBQB 111 (CanLII)

Zeldin v. Goldis, Ontario Superior Court of Justice, Canada, 9 August 2000, [2000] O.J. No. 3001

Corporación Transnacional de Inversiones v. Stet International, Ontario Court of Appeal, Canada, 15 September 2000, confirming CLOUT case No. 391 [Re *Corporación Transnacional de Inversiones, S.A. de C.V. et al. v. STET International, S.p.A. et al.,* Superior Court of Justice, Canada, 22 September 1999]

CLOUT case No. 501 [*Grow Biz International, Inc. v. D.L.T. Holdings Inc.,* Prince Edward Island Supreme Court – Trial Division, Canada, 23 March 2001]

Cecrop Co. v. Kinetic Sciences Inc., Supreme Court of British Columbia, Canada, 9 April 2001, [2001] BCSC 532

CLOUT case No. 504 [*D.G. Jewelry Inc. et al. v. Cyberdiam Canada Ltd. et al.,* Ontario Superior Court of Justice, Canada, 17 April 2002]

Mariana Maritime S.A. v. Stella Jones Inc., Federal Court – Court of Appeal, Canada, 24 May 2002, [2002] FCA 215

Canada (Attorney General) v. Marineserve.MG Inc., Supreme Court of Nova Scotia, Canada, 24 May 2002, [2002] NSSC 147

CLOUT case No. 508 [*United Laboratories, Inc. v. Abraham,* Ontario Superior Court of Justice, Canada, 8 October 2002]

CLOUT case No. 509 [*Dalimpex Ltd. v. Janicki,* Ontario Court of Appeal, Canada, 30 May 2003]

Pacific Erosion v. Western Quality Seeds, Supreme Court of British Columbia, Canada, 9 September 2003, [2003] BCSC 1743

Mitsui et al. v. Egon Oldendorff et al., Supreme Court of British Columbia, Canada, 30 September 2003, [2003] BCSC 1478

Canada (Attorney General) v. S.D. Myers Inc., Federal Court – Trial Division, Canada, 13 January 2004, [2004] 3 FCR 368

CLOUT case No. 512 [*Instrumenttitehdas Kytola Oy v. Esko Industries Ltd.*, Court of Appeal for British Columbia, Canada, 15 January 2004]

Acier Leroux Inc. v. Tremblay, Court of Appeal of Quebec, Canada, 11 March 2004, [2004] CanLII 28564 (QC CA)

Société Asbestos Limitée v. Charles Lacroix et al., Court of Appeal of Quebec, Canada, 7 September 2004, [2004] CanLII 21635 (QC CA)

Dongnam Oil & Fats Co. v. Chemex Ltd., Federal Court – Trial Division, Canada, 10 December 2004, [2004] FC 1732 (CanLII)

Société de Cogénération de St-Félicien, Société en Commandite/St-Felicien Cogeneration Limited Partnership v. Industries Falmec Inc., Court of Appeal of Quebec, Canada, 25 April 2005, [2005] QCCA 441 (CanLII)

Agrawest & AWI v. BMA, Prince Edward Island Supreme Court – Trial Division, Canada, 23 June 2005, [2005] PESCTD 36

GreCon Dimter Inc. v. J. R. Normand Inc., Supreme Court, Canada, 22 July 2005, [2005], SCC 46

Ace Bermuda Insurance Ltd. v. Allianz Insurance Company of Canada, Court of Queen's Bench of Alberta, Canada, 21 December 2005, [2005] ABQB 975

Achilles (USA) v. Plastics Dura Plastics (1977) ltée/Ltd., Court of Appeal of Quebec, Canada, 23 November 2006, [2006] QCCA 1523

Pandora Select Partners, LP v. Strategy Real Estate Investments Ltd., Ontario Superior Court of Justice, Canada, 20 March 2007, [2007] CanLII 8026 (ON SC)

Cogismaq International Inc. v. Lafontaine, Superior Court of Quebec, Canada, 20 March 2007, 2007 QCSC 1214

Rampton v. Eyre, Ontario Court of Appeal, Canada, 2 May 2007, [2007] ONCA 331

Dell Computer Corp. v. Union des Consommateurs, Supreme Court, Canada, 13 July 2007, [2007] SCC 34, [2007] 2 SCR 801

EDF (Services) Limited v. Appleton & Associates, Ontario Superior Court of Justice, Canada, 4 September 2007, [2007] CanLII 36078 (ON SC)

Canada (Attorney General) v. Reliance Insurance Company, Ontario Superior Court of Justice, Canada, 5 October 2007, [2007] CanLII 41899 (ON SC)

9110-9595 *Québec inc. v. Bergeron*, Court of Appeal of Quebec, Canada, 12 October 2007, [2007] QCCA 1393

Sumitomo Canada v. Saga Forest Carriers et al., Provincial Court of British Columbia, Canada, 22 November 2007, [2007] BCPC 373

Resin Systems Inc. v. Industrial Service & Machine Inc., Alberta Court of Appeal, Canada, 13 March 2008, [2008] ABCA 104

GPEC International Ltd. v. Canada (Canadian Commercial Corporation), Federal Court – Trial Division, Canada, 2 April 2008, [2008] FC 414

CLOUT case No. 1014 [*Bayview Irrigation District #11 v. United Mexican States*, Ontario Superior Court of Justice, Canada, 5 May 2008]

CLOUT case No. 1015 [*Sport Hawk USA Inc. v. New York Islanders Hockey Club*, Ontario Superior Court of Justice, Canada, 5 May 2008]

CLOUT case No. 1016 [*Dens Tech-Dens, k.g. v. Netdent-Technologies Inc.*, Court of Appeal of Quebec, Canada, 26 June 2008]

CLOUT case No. 1049 [*Louis Dreyfus S.A.S. v. Holding Tusculum B.V.*, Superior Court of Quebec, Canada, 8 December 2008]

CLOUT case No. 1048 [*Patel v. Kanbay International Inc.*, Ontario Court of Appeal, Canada, 23 December 2008]

CLOUT case No. 1047 [*Dancap Productions Inc. v. Key Brand Entertainment Inc.*, Ontario Court of Appeal, Canada, 13 February 2009]

CLOUT case No. 1046 [*PS Here, L.L.C. v. Fortalis Anstalt*, Court of Appeal of Quebec, Canada, 19 March 2009]

CLOUT case No. 1044 [*Jean Estate v. Wires Jolley LLP*, Ontario Court of Appeal, Canada, 29 April 2009]

Popack v. Lipszyc, Ontario Court of Appeal, Canada, 30 April 2009, [2009] ONCA 365, confirming *Popack v. Lipszyc*, Ontario Superior Court of Justice, 2 September 2008

CLOUT case No. 1042 [*Bombardier Transportation v. SMC Pneumatics (UK) Ltd.,* Court of Appeal of Quebec, Canada, 4 May 2009]

CLOUT case No. 1011 [*H & H Marine Engine Service Ltd. v. Volvo Penta of the Americas Inc.,* Supreme Court of British Columbia, Canada, 9 October 2009]

Location Imafa, s.e.c. c. Fedex Ground Package System Ltd., Superior Court of Quebec, Canada, 8 June 2010, [2010] QCCS 2829 (CanLII)

Investissement Charlevoix Inc. v. Gestion Pierre Gingras Inc., Court of Appeal of Quebec, Canada, 21 June 2010, [2010] QCCA 1229

Société du Port Ferroviaire de Baie-Comeau-Hauterive v. Jean Fournier Inc., Court of Appeal of Quebec, Canada, 26 November 2010, [2010] QCCA 2161

El Nino Ventures Inc. v. GCP Group Ltd., Supreme Court of British Columbia, Canada 24 December 2010, [2010] BCSC 1859

Article 9

CLOUT case No. 11 [*Relais Nordik v. Secunda Marine Services Limited,* Federal Court – Trial Division, Canada, 19 February 1988]

CLOUT case No. 68 [*Delphi Petroleum Inc. v. Derin Shipping and Training Ltd.,* Federal Court – Trial Division, Canada, 3 December 1993]

CLOUT case No. 71 [*Trade Fortune Inc. v. Amalgamated Mill Supplies Ltd.,* Supreme Court of British Columbia, Canada, 25 February 1994]

Navi-Mont Inc. v. Rigel Shipping Canada Inc., Federal Court – Trial Division, Canada, 28 May 1997, [1997], CanLII 5130 (FC)

Amican Navigation Inc. v. Densan Shipping Co., Federal Court – Trial Division, Canada, 21 October 1997, [1997] CanLII 6263 (CF)

CLOUT case No. 353 [*TLC Multimedia Inc. v. Core Curriculum Technologies Inc.,* Supreme Court of British Columbia, Canada, 6 July 1998]

Ordina Shipmanagement Ltd. v. Unispeed Group Inc., Federal Court – Trial Division, Canada, 20 November 1998, [1998] CanLII 8785 (FC)

CLOUT case No. 354 [*Silver Standard Resources Inc. v. Joint Stock Company Geolog, Cominco Ltd. and Open Type Stock Company Dukat GOK,* Court of Appeal for British Columbia, Canada, 11 December 1998]

CLOUT case No. 393 [*Frontier International Shipping Corp. v. Tavros (The), Federal Court* – Trial Division, Canada, 23 December 1999]

Article 10

Thésaurus Inc. v. Xpub Média Inc., Court of Quebec, Canada, 20 August 2007, [2007] QCCQ 10436

Article 11

Quintette Coal Ltd. v. Nippon Steel Corp., Supreme Court of British Columbia, Canada, 24 March 1988, [1988] BCJ No. 492

Canadian Reinsurance Co. v. Lloyd's Syndicate PUM 91, Ontario Court of Justice – General Division, Canada, 27 January 1995, 1995 CarswellOnt 2356, 17 CCLI (3d) 165, 6 BLR (3d) 102

Banque Nationale du Canada v. Premdev. Inc., Court of Appeal of Quebec, Canada, 10 March 1997, [1997] CanLII 10830 (QC CA)

Voynaud v. Éditions La Pensée Inc., Court of Quebec, Canada, 2 April 1998

Lavergne v. Pure Tech International Inc., Superior Court of Quebec, Canada, 9 July 1998, [1998] QJ No. 2308 (SC)

Lamothe v. Lamothe, Superior Court of Quebec, Canada, 2 April 2001

Robitaille v. Centre Rail-Control Inc., Superior Court of Quebec, Canada, 17 May 2001, J.E., 2001-1153

CLOUT case No. 506 [*Masterfile Corp. v. Graphic Images Ltd.,* Ontario Superior Court of Justice, Ontario, Canada, 26 June 2002]

I-D Foods Corporation v. Hain-Celestial Group Inc., Superior Court of Quebec, Canada, 6 July 2006, [2006] QCCS 3889

Gestion Christian Veilleux v. Chabot, Superior Court of Quebec, Canada, 7 September 2006, [2006] QCCS 6071

Rampton v. Eyre, Ontario Court of Appeal, Canada, 2 May 2007, [2007] ONCA 331

Villeneuve v. Pelletier, Superior Court of Quebec, Canada, 27 January 2010, [2010] QCCS 320 St-Jean v. Poirier, Court of Quebec, Canada, 2 September 2010, [2010] QCCQ 7681

Article 12

Desbois v. Industries A.C. Davie Inc., Court of Appeal of Quebec, Canada, 26 April 1990, [1990] CanLII 3619 (QC CA)

Article 13

Groupe de Charles Lacroix v. Syndicat des Travailleurs Horaires de l'Amiante C.S.N. Inc., Superior Court of Quebec, Canada, 27 September 2002, [2002] CanLII 30068 (QC CS)

Habitations d'Angoulème Inc. v. Létourneau, Court of Quebec, Canada, 22 April 2005, [2005] CanLII 12888 (QC CQ)

Nikiforos v. Petropoulos, Superior Court of Quebec, Canada, 21 June 2007, [2007] QCCS 3144

Monkland 5765 Plus v. 9101-8309 Québec Inc., Superior Court of Quebec, Canada, 30 January 2008, [2008] QCCS 253

Oiknine v. Rosenberg-Solny, Superior Court of Quebec, Canada, 29 October 2009, [2009] QCCS 5106

Article 14

Petro-Canada v. Alberta Gas Ethylene, Alberta Court of Appeal, Canada, 28 January 1992, [1992] ABCA 9

Article 16

CLOUT case No. 626 [*Quintette Coal Ltd. v. Nippon Steel Corp.,* Supreme Court of British Columbia, Canada, 6 July 1988]

CLOUT case No. 13 (also reproduced under CLOUT case No. 383) [*Deco Automotive Inc. v. G.P.A. Gesellschaft für Pressenautomation mbH,* Ontario District Court, Canada, 27 October 1989]

CLOUT case No. 186 [*A. Bianchi S.R.L. v. Bilumen Lighting Ltd.,* Superior Court of Quebec, Canada, 18 May 1990]

CLOUT case No. 349 [*Harper v. Kvaerner Fjellstrand Shipping A.S.,* Supreme Court of British Columbia, Canada, 13 September 1991]

CLOUT case No. 19 [*Krutov. v. Vancouver Hockey Club Limited,* Supreme Court of British Columbia, Canada, 22 November 1991]

CLOUT case No. 32 [*Mind Star Toys Inc. v. Samsung Co. Ltd.,* Ontario Court of Justice – General Division, Canada, 30 April 1992]

CLOUT case No. 368 [*Campbell et al. v. Murphy,* Ontario Court of Justice – General Division, Canada, 9 August 1993]

CLOUT case No. 182 [*International Civil Aviation Organization (ICAO) v. Tripal Systems Pty. Ltd.,* Superior Court of Quebec, Canada, 9 September 1994]

CLOUT case No. 114 [*Globe Union Industrial Corp. v. G.A.P. Marketing Corp.,* Supreme Court of British Columbia, Canada, 18 November 1994]

CLOUT case No. 178 [*Siderurgica Mendes Junior S.A. v. "Icepearl" (The),* Supreme Court of British Columbia, Canada, 31 January 1996]

Télébec Ltée v. Société Hydro-Québec, Superior Court of Quebec, Canada, 17 April 1997, [1997] JQ No. 1431

Guilde des Musiciens du Québec v. Piché, Superior Court of Quebec, Canada, 8 June 1998, [1998] JQ No. 4896

NetSys Technology Group AB v. Open Text Corp., Ontario Superior Court of Justice, Canada, 29 July 1999, [1999] CanLII 14937 (ON SC)

OEMSDF Inc. v. Europe Israel Ltd., Ontario Superior Court of Justice, Canada, 22 September 1999, [1999] O.J. No. 3594

Piché v. Guilde des Musiciens du Québec, Superior Court of Quebec, Canada, 9 November 1999

Cecrop Co. v. Kinetic Sciences Inc., Supreme Court of British Columbia, Canada, 9 April 2001 [2001] BCSC 532

CLOUT case No. 504 [*D.G. Jewelry Inc. et al. v. Cyberdiam Canada Ltd. et al.,* Ontario Superior Court of Justice, Canada, 17 April 2002]

Micheline Lefebvre et al. v. Les Habitations d'Angoulème, Superior Court of Quebec, Canada, 13 June 2002, [2000] JQ No. 2733

Compagnie Nationale Air France v. Mbaye, Court of Appeal of Quebec, Canada, 31 March 2003, [2003] CanLII 35834 (QC CA)

CLOUT case No. 509 [*Dalimpex Ltd. v. Janicki,* Ontario Court of Appeal, Ontario, Canada, 30 May 2003]

9095-5378 *Québec Inc. v. Perform Environnement Inc.,* Superior Court of Quebec, Canada, 18 August 2004, [2004] CanLII 7022 (QC CS)

Imprimerie Régionale ARL Ltée v. Ghanotakis, Superior Court of Quebec, Canada, 13 September 2004, [2004] CanLII 23270 (QC CS)

Ace Bermuda Insurance Ltd. v. Allianz Insurance Company of Canada, Court of Queen's Bench of Alberta, Canada, 21 December 2005, [2005] ABQB 975

Rampton v. Eyre, Ontario Court of Appeal, Canada, 2 May 2007, [2007] ONCA 331

EDF (Services) Limited v. Appleton & Associates, Ontario Superior Court of Justice, Canada, 4 September 2007, [2007] CanLII 36078 (ON SC),

GPEC International Ltd. v. Canada (Canadian Commercial Corporation), Federal Court – Trial Division, Canada, 2 April 2008, [2008] FC 414

CLOUT case No. 1014 [*Bayview Irrigation District #11 v. United Mexican States,* Ontario Superior Court of Justice, Canada, 5 May 2008]

Re/Max Platine Inc. v. Groupe Sutton-Actuel Inc., Court of Appeal of Quebec, 24 July 2008, [2008] QCCA 1405

CLOUT case No. 1047 [*Dancap Productions Inc. v. Key Brand Entertainment Inc.,* Ontario Court of Appeal, Canada, 13 February 2009]

CLOUT case No. 1011 [*H & H Marine Engine Service Ltd. v. Volvo Penta of the Americas Inc.,* Supreme Court of British Columbia, Canada, 9 October 2009]

Canadian Ground Water Association v. Canadian Geoexchange Coalition, Superior Court of Quebec, Canada, 15 June 2010, [2010] QCCS 2597

New World Expedition Yachts LLC v. P.R. Yacht Builders Ltd., Supreme Court of British Columbia, Canada, 25 October 2010, [2010] BCSC 1496

Mexico v. Cargill Inc., Ontario Court of Appeal, Canada, 4 October 2011, [2011] ONCA 622

Article 18

Noble China Inc. v. Lei Kat Cheong, Ontario Court of Justice, Canada, 4 November 1998, [1998] CanLII 14708 (ON SC), in (1998) 42 O.R. (3d) 69

CLOUT case No. 391 [*Re Corporación Transnacional de Inversiones, S.A. de C.V. et al. v. STET International, S.p.A. et al.,* Superior Court of Justice, Canada, 22 September 1999]

Xerox Corporation Ltd. and Xerox Corporation v. MPI Technologies Inc. and MPI Tech SA, Ontario Superior Court of Justice, Canada, 30 November 2006, [2006] CanLII 41006 (ON SC),

Article 19

Noble China Inc. v. Lei Kat Cheong, Ontario Court of Justice, Canada, 4 November 1998, [1998] CanLII 14708 (ON SC), in (1998) 42 O.R. (3d) 69

Desputeaux v. Éditions Chouette (1987) inc., Supreme Court, Canada, 21 March 2003, [2003] 1 S.C.R. 178, 2003 SCC 17

Jardine Lloyd Thompson Canada Inc. v. SJO Catlin, Alberta Court of Appeal, Canada, 18 January 2006, [2006] ABCA 18

Article 21

Fuller Austin Insulation Inc. v. Wellington Insurance Co., Saskatchewan Queen's Bench, Canada, 15 September 1995, [1995] CanLII 5752 (SK QB)

Bell Canada v. The Plan Group, Court of Appeal for Ontario, Canada, 7 July 2009, [2009] ONCA 548

Article 23

CLOUT case No. 16 [*Quintette Coal Ltd. v. Nippon Steel Corp. et.al.,* Court of Appeal for British Columbia, Canada, 24 October 1990]

CLOUT case No. 118 [*Bab Systems, Inc. v. McLurg,* Ontario Court of Justice, General Division, Canada, 21 December 1994]

Alenco Inc. v. Niska Gas Storage US, Alberta Court of Appeal, Canada, LLC [2009] A.W.L.D. 2128

Article 25

CLOUT case No. 391 [*Re Corporación Transnacional de Inversiones, S.A. de C.V. et al. v. STET International, S.p.A. et al.*, Superior Court of Justice, Canada, 22 September 1999]

Article 27

Zingre v. The Queen et al., Supreme Court, Canada, 1981 CanLII 32 (SCC), [1981] 2 SCR 392, 28 September 1981

Republic of France v. De Havilland Aircraft of Canada Ltd. and Byron-Exarcos, Ontario Court of Appeal, Canada, (1991), 3 O.R. (3d) 705

CLOUT case No. 68 [*Delphi Petroleum Inc. v. Derin Shipping and Training Ltd.,* Federal Court – Trial Division, Canada, 3 December 1993]

CLOUT case No. 391 [*Re Corporación Transnacional de Inversiones, S.A. de C.V. et al. v. STET International, S.p.A. et al.*, Superior Court of Justice, Canada, 22 September 1999]

B.F. Jones Logistics Inc. v. Rolko, Ontario Superior Court of Justice, Canada, 24 August 2004, [2004] CanLII 21276 (ON SC)

Jardine Lloyd Thompson Canada Inc. v. SJO Catlin, Alberta Court of Appeal, Canada, 18 January 2006, [2006] ABCA 18

Jardine Lloyd Thompson Canada Inc. v. Western Oil Sands Inc., Alberta Court of Appeal, Canada, 21 December 2006, [2006] ABQB 933

Article 28

CLOUT case No. 351 [*Food Services of America Inc. (c.o.b. Amerifresh) v. Pan Pacific Specialties Ltd.,* Supreme Court of British Columbia, Canada, 24 March 1997]

CLOUT case No. 507 [*Liberty Reinsurance Canada v. QBE Insurance and Reinsurance (Europe) Ltd.,* Ontario Superior Court of Justice, Canada, 20 September 2002]

Coderre v. Coderre, Montreal Court of Appeal, Canada, 13 May 2008, [2008] QCCA 888

CLOUT case No. 1049 [*Louis Dreyfus S.A.S. v. Holding Tusculum B.V.*, Superior Court of Quebec, Canada, 8 December 2008]

Article 31

CLOUT case No. 10 [*Navigation Sonamar Inc. v. Algoma Steamships Limited and others,* Superior Court of Quebec, Canada, 16 April 1987]

CLOUT case No. 29 [*Kanto Yakin Kogyo Kabushiki-Kaisha v. Can-Eng Manufacturing Ltd.,* Ontario Court, General division, Canada, 30 January 1992]

Slocan Forest Products Ltd. v. Skeena Cellulose Inc., Supreme Court of British Columbia, Canada, 7 August 2001, [2001] BCSC 1156

Inforica Inc. v. CGI Information Systems & Management Consultants Inc., Ontario Court of Appeal, Canada, 11 September 2009, [2009] ONCA 642 (Ont. C.A.)

Premium Brands Operating GP Inc. v. Turner Distribution Systems Ltd., Supreme Court British Columbia, Canada, 1 March 2010, [2010] BCSC 258

Article 32

Maruna v. Lopatka, Supreme Court of British Columbia, Canada, 19 July 2002, [2002) BCSC 1084

Article 33

CLOUT case No. 625 [*Relais Nordik Inc. v. Secunda Marine Services Limited and Anor,* Federal Court, Canada, 12 April 1990]

Article 34

CLOUT case No. 10 [*Navigation Sonamar Inc. v. Algoma Steamships Limited and others,* Superior Court of Quebec, Canada, 16 April 1987]

CLOUT case No. 12 [*D. Frampton & Co. Ltd. v. Sylvio Thibeault and Navigation Harvey & Frères Inc.,* Federal Court, Trial Division, Canada, 7 April 1988]

CLOUT case No. 185 [*Transport de cargaison (Cargo Carriers) v. Industrial Bulk Carriers,* Quebec Court of Appeal, Canada, 15 June 1990]

CLOUT case No. 16 [*Quintette Coal Limited v. Nippon Steel Corp. et al.,* Court of Appeal for British Columbia, Canada, 24 October 1990]

CLOUT case No. 30 [Ontario Court, General Division, Canada, *Robert E. Schreter v. Gasmac Inc.,* 13 February 1992]

CLOUT case No. 584 [*Dunhill Personnel System v. Dunhill Temps Edmonton,* Alberta Queen's Bench, Canada, 30 September 1993]

Noble China Inc. v. Lei Kat Cheong, Ontario Court of Justice, Canada, 13 November 1998, in (1998) 42 O.R. (3d) 69

CLOUT case No. 391 [*Re Corporación Transnacional de Inversiones, S.A. de C.V. et al. and STET International, S.p.A. et al.,* Superior Court of Justice, Ontario, Canada, 22 September 1999]

CLOUT case No. 501 [*Grow Biz International, Inc. v. D.L.T. Holdings Inc.,* Prince Edward Island Supreme Court – Trial Division, Canada, 23 March 2001]

CLOUT case No. 502 [*The United Mexican States v. Metalclad Corp.,* British Columbia Supreme Court, Canada, 2 May 2001]

Desputeaux v. Éditions Chouette (1987) inc., 21 March 2003, [2003] 1 S.C.R. 178, 2003 SCC 17

The Gazette, Une division de Southam inc v. Rita Blondin et al., Quebec Court of Appeal, Canada, 6 August 2003, [2003] R.J.Q. 2090

Canada (Attorney General) v. S.D. Myers Inc., Federal Court – Trial Division, Canada, 13 January 2004, [2004] 3 FCR 368

United Mexican States v. Marvin Roy Feldman Karpa, Ontario Court of Appeal, Canada, 11 January 2005, [2005] Can LII 249 (ON C.A.)

Smart Systems Technology Inc. v. Domotique Secant Inc., Quebec Court of Appeal, Canada, 11 March 2008, [2008] Q.J. No. 1782

CLOUT case No. 1014 [*Bayview Irrigation District #11 v. United Mexican States,* Ontario Superior Court of Justice, Canada, 5 May 2008]

CLOUT case No. 1049 [*Louis Dreyfus S.A.S. v. Holding Tusculum B.V.,* Superior Court of Quebec, Canada, 8 December 2008]

Endorecherche Inc. v. Université Laval, Quebec Court of Appeal, Canada, 9 February 2010, 2010 QCCA 232

Znamensky Selekcionno-Gibridny Center LLC v. Donaldson International Livestock Ltd., Ontario Court of Appeal, Canada, 29 April 2010, [2010] ONCA 303

Michel Rhéaume v. Société d'investissements l'Excellence Inc., Quebec Court of Appeal, Canada, 10 December 2010, [2010] QCCA 2269

Article 35

CLOUT case No. 30 [*Robert E. Schreter v. Gasmac Inc.,* Ontario Court, General Division, Canada, 13 February 1992]

CLOUT case No. 584 [*Dunhill Personnel System v. Dunhill Temps Edmonton,* Alberta Queen's Bench, Canada, 30 September 1993]

CLOUT case No. 366 [*Europcar Italia S.p.A. v. Alba Tours International Inc.,* Ontario Court of Justice, Canada, General Division, 21 January 1997]

CLOUT case No. 351 [*Food Services of America Inc. (c.o.b. Amerifresh) v. Pan Pacific Specialties Ltd.,* Supreme Court of British Columbia, Canada, 24 March 1997]

Gea Group AG v. Ventra Group Co. & Timothy Graham, Ontario Superior Court of Justice, Canada, 9 January 2009, CV-08-7635-00CL

CLOUT case No. 1009 [*Yugraneft Corp. v. Rexx. Management Corp.,* Supreme Court, Canada, 20 May 2010]

Article 36

CLOUT case No. 67 [*AAMCO Transmissions Inc. v. Kunz,* Saskatchewan Court of Appeal, Canada, 17 September 1991]

CLOUT case No. 30 [*Robert E. Schreter v. Gasmac Inc.,* Ontario Court, General Division, Canada, 13 February 1992]

CLOUT case No. 37 [*Arcata Graphics Buffalo Ltd. v. Movie (Magazine) Corp.,* Ontario Court, General Division, Canada, 12 March 1993]

CLOUT case No. 584 [*Dunhill Personnel System v. Dunhill Temps Edmonton,* Alberta Queen's Bench, Canada, 30 September 1993]

CLOUT case No. 385 [Ontario Court of Justice, Canada, *Murmansk Trawl Fleet v. Bimman Realty Inc.,* 19 December 1994]

CLOUT case No. 366 [*Europcar Italia S.p.A. v. Alba Tours International Inc.,* Ontario Court of Justice, General Division, Canada, 21 January 1997]

CLOUT case No. 351 [*Food Services of America Inc. (c.o.b. Amerifresh) v. Pan Pacific Specialties Ltd.,* Supreme Court of British Columbia, Canada, 24 March 1997]

CLOUT case No. 358 [*Canadian National Railway Co. v. Southern Railway of British Columbia Ltd.,* Supreme Court of British Columbia, Canada, 11 May 1998]

CLOUT case No. 391 [*Re Corporación Transnacional de Inversiones, S.A. de C.V. et al. v. STET International, S.p.A. et al.,* Superior Court of Justice, Canada, 22 September 1999]

Phesco Inc. v. Canac. Inc., Quebec Superior Court, Canada, 14 November 2000, J.E. 2000-2268, AZ-50080781

CLOUT case No. 501 [Prince Edward Island Supreme Court, Canada, *D.L.T Holdings Inc. v. Grow Biz International Inc.,* Prince Edward Island Supreme Court, Trial Division, Canada, 23 March 2001]

CLOUT case No. 511 [*Desputeraux v. Les Editions Chouettes (1987) Inc.,* Supreme Court, 21 March 2003]

CLOUT case No. 509 [*Canada, Dalimpex Ltd. v. Janicki,* Court of Appeal for Ontario, 30 May 2003]

CLOUT case No. 514 [*Powerex Corp. v. Alcan Inc.,* British Colombia Supreme Court, Canada, 10 July 2003]

Smart Systems Technologies Inc. v. Domotique Secant Inc., Court of Appeal of Quebec, 11 March 2008, 2008 QCCA 444

Znamensky Selekcionno-Gibridny Center LLC v. Donaldson International Livestock Ltd., Ontario Court of Appeal, Canada, 29 April 2010, 2010 ONCA 303

Croatia

Article 8

CLOUT case No. 1072 [High Commercial Court, Croatia, 29 April 2001]

CLOUT case No. 1071 [*Hrvatsko Mirovinsko Osiguranje d.o.o. v. EDIS d.o.o.,* High Commercial Court, Croatia, 17 April 2007]

CLOUT case No. 1070 [*Berica v. Grupa Gava,* High Commercial Court, Croatia, 21 May 2007]

Article 16

Constitutional Court, Croatia, 27 October 2004, U-III/669/2003

Article 18

CLOUT case No. 1069 [Supreme Court, Croatia, 5 March 2008, Gž 6/08-2008]

Article 22

CLOUT case No. 1069 [Supreme Court, Croatia, 5 March 2008, Gž 6/08-2008]

Article 34

CLOUT case No. 1069 [Supreme Court, Croatia, 5 March 2008, Gž 6/08-2008]

CLOUT case No. 1068 [Supreme Court, Croatia, 30 May 2008, Gž 2/08-2]

Article 36

CLOUT case No. 1069 [Supreme Court, Croatia, 5 March 2008, 5 March 2008, Gž 6/08-2008]

Cyprus

Article 32

Dansk Moller Industry A.S. v. Bentex Minerals Co. Ltd. and others, Cyprus, (2007) 1B C.L.R.692

Denmark

Article 34

JKM Transport ApS v. Danish Crown, Supreme Court, Denmark, 16 December 2009, case 337/2007

Egypt

Article 1

CLOUT case No. 786 [Cairo Regional Center for International Commercial Arbitration No. 1/1994, Egypt, 31 October 1995]

Article 4

CLOUT case No. 780 [Cairo Regional Center for International Commercial Arbitration, No. 312/2002, Egypt, 28 November 2004]

Article 22

CLOUT case No. 786 [Cairo Regional Center for International Commercial Arbitration No. 1/1994, Egypt, 31 October 1995]

Article 30

CLOUT case No. 779 [Ad hoc arbitration hosted by the Cairo Regional Center for International Commercial Arbitration, Egypt, 17 February 2006]

Article 32

CLOUT case No. 782 [Cairo Regional Center for International Commercial Arbitration, Egypt, 11 March 1999]

Article 34

Cairo Court of Appeal, Egypt, 8 January 2002, case No. 72/117

Cairo Court of Appeal, Egypt, 3 April 2007, case No. 123/119

Cairo Court of Appeal, Egypt, 10 January 2008, case No. 23/124

Cairo Court of Appeal, Egypt, 16 January 2008, case No. 92/123

Supreme Court, Egypt, 25 January 2008, case No. 810/71

Cairo Court of Appeal, 7th Economic Circuit, Egypt, 5 February 2008, case No. 71/123

Cairo Court of Appeal, Egypt, 6 May 2008, case No. 140/124

Cairo Court of Appeal, Egypt, 7 May 2008, case No. 76/123

Cairo Court of Appeal, 7th Economic Circuit, Egypt, 2 July 2008, case No. 23/125

Cairo Court of Appeal, Egypt, 2 December 2008, case No. 114/124

Cairo Court of Appeal, 7th Economic Circuit, Egypt, 3 March 2009, case No. 71/124

Cairo Court of Appeal, Egypt, 5 May 2009, case No. 112/124

Cairo Court of Appeal, Egypt, 9 June 2009, case No. 102/123

Article 35

Cairo Court of Appeal, Circuit 91 Commercial, Egypt, 16 January 2008, case No. 92/124

Cairo Court of Appeal, 7th Economic Circuit, Egypt, 2 July 2008, case No. 23/125

Article 36

Cairo Court of Appeal, Egypt, 5 May 2009, case No. 29/125

Estonia

Article 34

Tallin District Court, Estonia, 2-06-9525, 28 February 2007

Germany

Article 2

Oberlandesgericht Naumburg, Germany, 10 Sch 01/00, 17 April 2000

Bundesgerichtshof, Germany, III ZB 53/03, 27 May 2004

Article 3

CLOUT case No. 402 [Bayerisches Oberstes Landesgericht, Germany, 4 Z Sch 50/99, 16 March 2000]

CLOUT case No. 870 [Oberlandesgericht Dresden, Germany, 11 Sch 19/05, 15 March 2005]

Article 4

CLOUT case No. 659 [Oberlandesgericht Naumburg, Germany, 10 Sch 08/01, 21 February 2002]

Oberlandesgericht Stuttgart, Germany, 1 Sch 08/02, 16 July 2002

Article 7

Bundesgerichtshof, Germany, III ZR 214/05, 12 January 2006

Bundesgerichtshof, Germany, VII ZR 105/06, 25 January 2007

Article 8

CLOUT case No. 557 [Bayerisches Oberstes Landesgericht, Germany, 4 Z SchH 13/99, 28 February 2000]

CLOUT case No. 406 [Bundesgerichtshof, Germany, II ZR 373/98, 3 April 2000]

CLOUT case No. 561 [Bundesgerichtshof, Germany, XII ZR 42/98, 3 May 2000]

CLOUT case No. 404 [Bundesgerichtshof, Germany, III ZR 33/00, 14 September 2000]

Bundesgerichtshof, Germany, III ZR 281/00, 4 October 2001

Bundesgerichtshof, Germany, II ZR 65/03, 19 July 2004

Bundesgerichtshof, Germany, III ZR 265/03, 13 January 2005

Bundesgerichtshof, Germany, III ZR 214/05, 12 January 2006

Bundesgerichtshof, Germany, VII ZR 105/06, 25 January 2007

Bundesgerichtshof, Germany, III ZR 164/06, 1 March 2007

Bundesgerichtshof, Germany, III ZR 22/06, 31 May 2007

Bundesgerichtshof, Germany, XI ZR 66/08, 13 January 2009

Article 11

Hanseatisches Oberlandesgericht Hamburg, Germany, 14 Sch 02/98, 22 July 1998

Bayerisches Oberstes Landesgericht, Germany, 4 Z SchH 02/98, 16 September 1998

CLOUT case No. 438 [Bayerisches Oberstes Landesgericht, Germany, 4 Z SchH 01/99, 4 June 1999]

Bayerisches Oberstes Landesgericht, Germany, 4 Z SchH 12/99, 20 June 2000

CLOUT case No. 439 [Brandenburgisches Oberlandesgericht, Germany, 8 SchH 01/00 (1), 26 June 2000]

Bayerisches Oberstes Landesgericht, Germany, 4 Z SchH 01/01, 23 February 2001

Oberlandesgericht Dresden, Germany, 11 Sch 01/01, 28 February 2001

Kammergericht Berlin, Germany, 23/29 Sch 16/01, 26 June 2002

Bayerisches Oberstes Landesgericht, 4 Z SchH 09/01, Germany, 16 January 2002

Bayerisches Oberstes Landesgericht, 4 Z SchH 04/02, Germany, 13 May 2002

Oberlandesgericht Koblenz, Germany, 2 Sch 04/03 (2), 19 February 2004

Oberlandesgericht München, Germany, 34 SchH 11/09, 29 January 2010

Article 12

Kammergericht Berlin, Germany, 28 Sch 24/99, 22 March 2000

CLOUT case No. 665 [Oberlandesgericht Naumburg, Germany, 10 SchH 03/01, 19 December 2001]

CLOUT case No. 902 [Landgericht München II, Germany, 2 OH 1728/01, 27 June 2002]

Oberlandesgericht Hamm, Germany, 17 SchH 13/01, 22 July 2002

Hanseatisches Oberlandesgericht Hamburg, Germany, 6 SchH 03/02, 11 March 2003

CLOUT case No. 1062 [Oberlandesgericht Köln, Germany, 9 Sch (H) 22/03, 2 April 2004]

Hanseatisches Oberlandesgericht Hamburg, Germany, 11 SchH 01/04, 28 June 2004

Hanseatisches Oberlandesgericht Hamburg, Germany, 9 SchH 01/05, 12 July 2005

Oberlandesgericht Karlsruhe, 10 Sch 02/06, Germany, 4 July 2006

Oberlandesgericht München, Germany, 34 SchH 05/06, 5 July 2006

Article 13

Kammergericht Berlin, Germany, 28 Sch 24/99, 22 March 2000

CLOUT case No. 442 [Oberlandesgericht Köln, Germany, 9 SchH 30/00, 14 September 2000]

Oberlandesgericht Dresden, Germany, 11 Sch 01/01, 28 February 2001

Hanseatisches Oberlandesgericht Hamburg, Germany, 9 SchH 01/05, 12 July 2005

Oberlandesgericht München, Germany, 34 SchH 10/05, 6 February 2006

Article 14

Oberlandesgericht Köln, Germany, 9 SchH 27/02, 11 April 2003

Oberlandesgericht Hamm, Germany, 17 SchH 07/03, 18 September 2003

Article 16

CLOUT case No. 373 [Kammergericht Berlin, Germany, 28 Sch 17/99, 15 October 1999]

CLOUT case No. 441 [Oberlandesgericht Köln, Germany, 9 Sch 06/00, 20 July 2000]

CLOUT case No. 562 [Hanseatisches Oberlandesgericht Hamburg, Germany, 6 Sch 04/01, 8 November 2001]

Oberlandesgericht Stuttgart, Germany, 1 Sch 16/01 (1), 20 December 2001

CLOUT case No. 1064 [Hanseatisches Oberlandesgericht Bremen, Germany, 2 Sch 4/01, 10 January 2002]

CLOUT case No. 560 [Bundesgerichtshof, Germany, III ZB 44/01, 6 June 2002]

Bundesgerichtshof, Germany, III ZB 83/02, 27 March 2003

Oberlandesgericht Celle, Germany, 8 Sch 11/02, 4 September 2003

Article 17 [as adopted in 1985]

CLOUT case No. 565 [Oberlandesgericht Frankfurt a.M., Germany, 24 Sch 01/01, 5 April 2001]

Article 18

CLOUT case No. 659 [Oberlandesgericht Naumburg, Germany, 10 Sch 08/01, 21 February 2002]

CLOUT case No. 560 [Bundesgerichtshof, Germany, III ZB 44/01, 6 June 2002]

Article 20

CLOUT case No. 374 (also reproduced under CLOUT case No. 408) [Oberlandesgericht Düsseldorf, Germany, 6 Sch 02/99, 23 March 2000]

CLOUT case No. 439 [Brandenburgisches Oberlandesgericht, Germany, 8 SchH 01/00 (1), 26 June 2000]

CLOUT case No. 571 [Hanseatisches Oberlandesgericht Hamburg, Germany, 11 Sch 06/01, 24 January 2003]

Article 22

CLOUT case No. 559 [Oberlandesgericht Celle, Germany, 8 Sch 03/01, 2 October 2001]

Oberlandesgericht München, Germany, 34 Sch 26/08, 22 June 2009

Article 23

Bayerisches Oberstes Landesgericht, Germany, 4 Z Sch 02/99, 29 September 1999

Article 24

CLOUT case No. 402 [Bayerisches Oberstes Landesgericht, Germany, 4 Z Sch 50/99, 16 March 2000]

CLOUT case No. 659 [Oberlandesgericht Naumburg, Germany, 10 Sch 08/01, 21 February 2002]

Article 25

Bayerisches Oberstes Landesgericht, Germany, 4 Z Sch 02/99, 29 September 1999

Article 26

CLOUT case No. 375 [Bayerisches Oberstes Landesgericht, Germany, 4 Z Sch 23/99, 15 December 1999]

Article 28

CLOUT case No. 375 [Bayerisches Oberstes Landesgericht, Germany, 4 Z Sch 23/99, 15 December 1999]

CLOUT case No. 569 [Hanseatisches Oberlandesgericht Hamburg, Germany, 11 Sch 01/01, 8 June 2001]

Article 30

Oberlandesgericht Frankfurt a.M., Germany, 3 Sch 01/99, 28 June 1999

CLOUT case No. 407 [Bundesgerichtshof, Germany, III ZB 55/99, 2 November 2000]

Oberlandesgericht Frankfurt a.M., Germany, 20 Sch 01/02, 14 March 2003

Article 31

CLOUT case No. 374 (also reproduced under CLOUT case No. 408) [Oberlandesgericht Düsseldorf, Germany, 6 Sch 02/99, 23 March 2000]

CLOUT case No. 569 [Hanseatisches Oberlandesgericht Hamburg, Germany, 11 Sch 01/01, 8 June 2001]

CLOUT case No. 664 [Oberlandesgericht Stuttgart, Germany, 1 Sch 21/01, 23 January 2002]

CLOUT case No. 662 [Saarländisches Oberlandesgericht, Germany, 4 Sch 02/02, 29 October 2002]

Article 32

Oberlandesgericht Dresden, Germany, 11 SchH 01/00, 11 December 2000

Oberlandesgericht Stuttgart, Germany, 1 Sch 13/01, 20 December 2001

CLOUT case No. 667 [Oberlandesgericht Köln, Germany, 9 Sch 19/02, 29 October 2002]

Article 33

Oberlandesgericht Dresden, Germany, 11 SchH 01/00, 11 December 2000

Oberlandesgericht Stuttgart, Germany, 1 Sch 13/01, 20 December 2001

CLOUT case No. 663 [Oberlandesgericht Stuttgart, Germany, 1 Sch 22/01, 4 June 2002]

Article 34

CLOUT case No. 455 [Hanseatisches Oberlandesgericht Hamburg, Germany, 14 Sch 01/98, 4 September 1998]

CLOUT case No. 456 [Hanseatisches Oberlandesgericht Hamburg, Germany, 6 Sch 11/98, 4 November 1998]

CLOUT case No. 436 [Bayerisches Oberstes Landesgericht, Germany, 4 Z Sch 17/98, 24 February 1999]

Oberlandesgericht Frankfurt a. M., Germany, 23 Sch 01/98, 12 May 1999

CLOUT case No. 457 [Hanseatisches Oberlandesgericht Hamburg, Germany, 1 Sch 02/99, 14 May 1999]

Bayerisches Oberstes Landesgericht, Germany, 4 Z Sch 02/99, 29 September 1999

CLOUT case No. 371 [Hanseatisches Oberlandesgericht Bremen, Germany, (2) Sch 4/99, 30 September 1999]

CLOUT Case No. 375 [Bayerisches Oberstes Landesgericht, Germany, 4 Z Sch 23/99, 15 December 1999]

CLOUT case No. 440 [Oberlandesgericht Köln, Germany, 9 Sch 15/99, 22 December 1999]

Bayerisches Oberstes Landesgericht, Germany, 4 Z Sch 48/99, 10 February 2000

CLOUT case No. 374 (also reproduced under CLOUT case No. 408) [Oberlandesgericht Düsseldorf, Germany, 6 Sch 02/99, 23 March 2000]

CLOUT case No. 441 [Oberlandesgericht Köln, Germany, 9 Sch 06/00, 20 July 2000]

Oberlandesgericht Köln, Germany, 9 Sch 23/00, 16 October 2000

Oberlandesgericht Dresden, Germany, 11 Sch 02/00, 25 October 2000

CLOUT case No. 407 [Bundesgerichtshof, Germany, III ZB 55/99, 2 November 2000]

CLOUT case No. 569 [Hanseatisches Oberlandesgericht Hamburg, Germany, 11 Sch 01/01, 8 June 2001]

Oberlandesgericht Karlsruhe, 10 Sch 04/01, 14 September 2001

CLOUT case No. 559 [Oberlandesgericht Celle, Germany, 8 Sch 03/01, 2 October 2001]

CLOUT case No. 562 [Hanseatisches Oberlandesgericht Hamburg, Germany, 6 Sch 04/01, 8 November 2001]

Oberlandesgericht Stuttgart, Germany, 1 Sch 12/01, 6 December 2001

Oberlandesgericht Stuttgart, Germany, 1 Sch 13/01, 20 December 2001

Hanseatisches Oberlandesgericht Hamburg, Germany, 6 Sch 07/01, 17 January 2002

CLOUT case No. 659 [Oberlandesgericht Naumburg, Germany, 10 Sch 08/01, 21 February 2002]

CLOUT case No. 560 [Bundesgerichtshof, Germany, III ZB 44/01, 6 June 2002]

Oberlandesgericht Stuttgart, Germany, 1 Sch 08/02, 16 July 2002

CLOUT case No. 570 [Hanseatisches Oberlandesgericht Hamburg, Germany, 11 Sch 02/00, 30 August 2002]

Oberlandesgericht Oldenburg, Germany, 9 SchH 09/02, 15 November 2002

Bundesgerichtshof, Germany, III ZB 83/02, 27 March 2003

CLOUT case No. 868 [Bayerisches Oberstes Landesgericht, Germany, 4 Z Sch 23/02, 20 March 2003], confirmed by Bundesgerichtshof, Germany, III ZB 29/03, 23 October 2003

Oberlandesgericht Köln, Germany, 9 Sch 06/03, 3 June 2003

Oberlandesgericht Frankfurt a.M., Germany, 26 Sch 01/03, 10 July 2003

Bundesgerichtshof, Germany, III ZB 53/03, 27 May 2004

CLOUT case No. 870 [Oberlandesgericht Dresden, Germany, 11 Sch 19/05, 15 March 2005]

Oberlandesgericht Dresden, Germany, 11 Sch 01/05, 20 April 2005

Oberlandesgericht Naumburg, Germany, 10 Sch 01/05, 20 May 2005

Oberlandesgericht München, Germany, 34 Sch 10/05, 22 June 2005,

Oberlandesgericht Oldenburg, Germany, 9 SchH 03/05, 30 May 2006

Oberlandesgericht Dresden, Germany, 11 Sch 02/06, 7 June 2006

Oberlandesgericht Frankfurt, Germany, 26 Sch 20/06, 10 May 2007

Oberlandesgericht Karlsruhe, Germany, 10 Sch 01/07, 14 September 2007

Oberlandesgericht Rostock, Germany, 1 Sch 04/06, 18 September 2007

Bundesgerichtshof, Germany, III ZB 17/08, 30 October 2008

Oberlandesgericht Köln, Germany, 19 Sch 12/08, 21 November 2008

Oberlandesgericht Karlsruhe, Germany, 10 Sch 8/08, 27 March 2009

Oberlandesgericht München, Germany, 34 Sch 26/08, 22 June 2009

Oberlandesgericht Frankfurt, Germany, 26 SchH 03/09, 27 August 2009

Oberlandesgericht Stuttgart, Germany, 1 SchH 01/09, 10 September 2009

Oberlandesgericht München, Germany, 34 Sch 12/09, 5 October 2009

Oberlandesgericht München, Germany, 34 Sch 15/09, 29 October 2009

Oberlandesgericht Stuttgart, Germany, 1 Sch 03/10, 30 July 2010

Article 35

CLOUT case No. 452 [Bayerisches Oberstes Landesgericht, Germany, 4Z Sch 31/99, 27 June 1999]

Oberlandesgericht Naumburg, Germany, 10 Sch 01/00 (01), 17 April 2000

CLOUT case No. 407 [Bundesgerichtshof, Germany, III ZB 55/99, 2 November 2000]

Bayerisches Oberstes Landesgericht, Germany, 4 Z Sch 35/02, 13 May 2003

Bayerisches Oberstes Landesgericht, Germany, 4 Z Sch 12/03, 10 July 2003

Oberlandesgericht Hamm, Germany, 29 Sch 2/03, 02 December 2003

Oberlandesgericht Düsseldorf, Germany I-26 Sch 05/03, 19 January 2005

Oberlandesgericht Frankfurt, Germany, 26 Sch 29/05, 20 December 2005

Kammergericht Berlin, Germany, 20 Sch 07/04, 10 August 2006

Bundesgerichtshof, Germany, III ZB 35/06, 18 January 2007

Oberlandesgericht München, Germany, 34 Sch 04/08, 19 January 2009

Oberlandesgericht München, Germany, 34 Sch 19/08, 27 February 2009

Bundesgerichtshof, Germany, III ZB 07/06, 1 March 2007

Oberlandesgericht München, Germany, 34 Sch 26/08, 22 June 2009

Oberlandesgericht München, Germany, 34 Sch 14/09, 1 September 2009

Oberlandesgericht München Germany, 34 Sch 20/08, 12 October 2009

Oberlandesgericht München, Germany, 34 Sch 15/09, 29 October 2009

Article 36

CLOUT case No. 443 [Oberlandesgericht Dresden, Germany, 11 Sch 06/98, 13 January 1999]

CLOUT case No. 457 [Hanseatisches Oberlandesgericht Hamburg, Germany, 1 Sch 02/99, 14 May 1999]

CLOUT case No. 371 [Hanseatisches Oberlandesgericht Bremen, Germany, (2) Sch 4/99, 30 September 1999]

CLOUT case No. 373 [Kammergericht Berlin, Germany, 28 Sch 17/99, Germany, 15 October 1999]

CLOUT case No. 372 [Oberlandesgericht Rostock, Germany, 1 Sch 03/99, 28 October 1999]

CLOUT case No. 402 [Highest Regional Court of Bavaria, Germany, 16 March 2000]

CLOUT case No. 453 [Bayerisches Oberstes Landesgericht, Germany, 4 Z Sch 02/00, 12 April 2000]

Bundesgerichtshof, Germany, III ZR 332/99, 1 February 2001

CLOUT case No. 444 [Oberlandesgericht Dresden, Germany, 11 Sch 08/01, 8 May 2001]

CLOUT case No. 569 [Hanseatisches Oberlandesgericht Hamburg, Germany, 11 Sch 01/01, 8 June 2001]

CLOUT case No. 559 [Oberlandesgericht Celle, Germany, 8 Sch 03/01, 2 October 2001]

Oberlandesgericht Stuttgart, Germany, 1 Sch 12/01, 6 December 2001

Oberlandesgericht Stuttgart, Germany, 1 Sch 13/01, 20 December 2001

Kammergericht Berlin, Germany, 23 Sch 06/02, 27 May 2002

Oberlandesgericht Oldenburg, Germany, 9 SchH 09/02, 15 November 2002

Bundesgerichtshof, Germany, III ZB 83/02, 27 March 2003

Oberlandesgericht Frankfurt a.M., Germany, 26 Sch 01/03, 10 July 2003

Oberlandesgericht Dresden, Germany, 11 Sch 01/05, 20 April 2005

Oberlandesgericht Naumburg, Germany, 10 Sch 01/05, 20 May 2005

Oberlandesgericht Celle, Germany, 8 Sch 06/05, 6 October 2005

CLOUT case No. 870 [Oberlandesgericht Dresden, Germany, 11 Sch 19/05, 15 March 2005]

Oberlandesgericht Karlsruhe, Germany, 9 Sch 02/05, 27 March 2006

Oberlandesgericht Karlsruhe, Germany, 9 Sch 01/06, 3 July 2006

Oberlandesgericht München, Germany, 34 Sch 18/06, 22 January 2007

Oberlandesgericht Karlsruhe, Germany, 9 Sch 02/07, 14 September 2007

Bundesgerichtshof, Germany, III ZB 11/07, 17 January 2008

Kammergericht Berlin, Germany, 20 Sch 02/08, 17 April 2008

Oberlandesgericht München, Germany, 34 Sch 04/08, 19 January 2009

Oberlandesgericht Karlsruhe, Germany, 10 Sch 8/08, 27 March 2009

Oberlandesgericht München, Germany, 34 Sch 26/08, 22 June 2009

Oberlandesgericht Frankfurt, Germany, 26 SchH 03/09, 27 August 2009

Oberlandesgericht München, Germany, 34 Sch 12/09, 5 October 2009

Oberlandesgericht München, Germany, 34 Sch 20/08, 12 October 2009

Oberlandesgericht Stuttgart, Germany, 1 Sch 03/10, 30 July 2010

Bundesgerichtshof, Germany, III ZB 57/10, 30 September 2010

Bundesgerichtshof, Germany, III ZB 100/09, 16 December 2010

Hong Kong

Article 1

CLOUT case No. 20 [*Fung Sang Trading Limited v. Kai Sun Sea Products and Food Company Limited,* High Court – Court of First Instance, Hong Kong, 29 October 1991]

CLOUT case No. 39 [*Katran Shipping Co. Ltd. v. Kenven Transportation Ltd.,* High Court – Court of First Instance, Hong Kong, 29 June 1992]

CLOUT case No. 58 [*Ananda Non-Ferrous Metals Ltd. v. China Resources Metal and Minerals Co. Ltd.,* High Court – Court of First Instance, Hong Kong, 12 July 1993]

CLOUT case No. 75 [*China Resources Metal and Minerals Co. Ltd. v. Ananda Non-Ferrous Metals Ltd.,* High Court – Court of First Instance, Hong Kong, 7 July 1994]

CLOUT case No. 77 [*Vibroflotation A.G. v. Express Builders Co. Ltd.,* High Court – Court of First Instance, Hong Kong, 15 August 1994]

CLOUT case No. 101 [*Private Company "Triple V" Inc. Ltd. v. Star (Universal) Co. Ltd. and Sky Jade Enterprises Group Ltd.,* High Court – Court of First Instance, Hong Kong, 27 January 1995]

CLOUT case No. 108 [*D. Heung & Associates, Architects & Engineers v. Pacific Enterprises (Holdings) Company Limited,* High Court – Court of First Instance, Hong Kong, 4 May 1995]

CLOUT Case No. 707 [*In the Matter of Mech-Power Hong Kong – China Limited,* High Court – Court of First Instance, Hong Kong, 4 June 1996]

CLOUT Case No. 706 [*Fustar Chemicals Ltd. v. Sinochem Liaoning Hong Kong Ltd.,* High Court – Court of First Instance, Hong Kong, 5 June 1996]

CLOUT Case No. 601 [*China Ocean Shipping Co., Owners of the M/V. Fu Ning Hai v. Whistler International Ltd., Charters of the M/V. Fu Ning Hai,* High Court – Court of First Instance, Hong Kong Special Administrative Region of China, 24 May 1999]

CLOUT case No. 526 [*Union Charm Development Ltd. v. B+B Construction Co, Ltd.,* High Court – Court of First Instance, Hong Kong Special Administrative Region of China, 12 June 2001]

Article 2

CLOUT case No. 690 [*Mayers v. Dlugash,* High Court – Court of First Instance, Hong Kong, 10 June 1994]

Westco Airconditioning Ltd. v. Sui Chong Construction & Engineering Co. Ltd., High Court – Court of First Instance, Hong Kong, 3 February 1998, [1998] HKCFI 946

Article 2 A

CLOUT case No. 78 *Astel-Peiniger Joint Venture v. Argos Engineering & Heavy Industries Co. Ltd.,* High Court – Court of First Instance, Hong Kong, 18 August 1994],

Article 3

CLOUT case No. 20 [*Fung Sang Trading Limited v. Kai Sun Sea Products and Food Company Limited,* High Court – Court of First Instance, Hong Kong, 29 October 1991]

Article 4

CLOUT case No. 676 [*Attorney-General v. Vianini Lavori Spa,* High Court – Court of First Instance, Hong Kong, 11 February 1991]

Article 5

CLOUT case No. 77 [*Vibroflotation A.G. v. Express Builders Co. Ltd.*, High Court – Court of First Instance, Hong Kong, 15 August 1994]

CLOUT Case No. 601 [*China Ocean Shipping Co., Owners of the M/V. Fu Ning Hai v. Whistler International Ltd., Charters of the M/V. Fu Ning Hai*, High Court – Court of First Instance, Hong Kong Special Administrative Region of China, 24 May 1999]

Article 7

CLOUT case No. 673 [*Trans-medica Pharma-Handelsgesellschaft mbH v. Ananda Pharmaceuticals & Chemicals Ltd.*, Court of Appeal, Hong Kong, 22 June 1990]

CLOUT case No. 38 [*China State Construction Engineering Corporation, Guangdong Branch v. Madiford Limited,* High Court - Court of First Instance, Hong Kong, 2 March 1992]

CLOUT case No. 43 [*Hissan Trading Co. Ltd. v. Orkin Shipping Corporation,* High Court – Court of First Instance, Hong Kong, 8 September 1992]

CLOUT case No. 44 [*William Company v. Chu Kong Agency Co. Ltd. and Guangzhou Ocean Shipping Company,* High Court – Court of First Instance, Hong Kong, 17 February 1993]

CLOUT case No. 688 [*China National Electronic Import & Export Shenzhen Company v. Choi Chuk Ming (trading as ERWO Enterprises Company),* High Court – Court of First Instance, Hong Kong, 9 March 1993]

CLOUT case No. 813 [*Tianjin Medicine & Health Products Import & Export Corporation v. J. A. Moeller (Hong Kong) Limited, High Court* – Court of First Instance, Hong Kong, 27 January 1994]

CLOUT case No. 62 [*Oonc Lines Limited v. Sino–American Trade Advancement Co. Ltd.*, High Court – Court of First Instance, Hong Kong, 2 February 1994]

CLOUT case No. 64 [*H. Small Limited v. Goldroyce Garment Limited,* High Court – Court of First Instance, Hong Kong, 13 May 1994]

CLOUT case No. 78 [*Astel–Peiniger Joint Venture v. Argos Engineering & Heavy Industries Co. Ltd.*, High Court – Court of First Instance, Hong Kong, 18 August 1994]

P.T. Wearwel International v. Vf Asia Ltd., High Court – Court of First Instance, Hong Kong, 19 August 1994, [1994] 3 HKC 344

CLOUT case No. 87 [*Gay Constructions Pty. Ltd. and Spaceframe Buildings (North Asia) Ltd. v. Caledonian Techmore (Building) Limited & Hanison Construction Co. Ltd. (as a third party),* High Court – Court of First Instance, Hong Kong, 17 November 1994]

Jiangxi Provincial Metal and Minerals Import and Export Corporation v. Sulanser Co. Ltd., High Court, Hong Kong, 6 April 1995, [1995] HKCFI 449

Westco Airconditioning Ltd. v. Sui Chong Construction & Engineering Co. Ltd., High Court – Court of First Instance, Hong Kong, 3 February 1998, [1998] HKCFI 946

Arta Properties Limited v. Li Fu Yat Tso et al., High Court – Court of First Instance, Hong Kong, 2 June 1998, [1998] HKCU 721

CLOUT case No. 460 [*Hercules Data Comm Co. Ltd. v. Koywa Communications Ltd.*, High Court – Court of First Instance, Hong Kong Special Administrative Region of China, 23 October 2000]

CLOUT case No. 449 [China Merchant Heavy Industry Co. Ltd. v. JGC Corp., High Court – Court of Appeal, Hong Kong Special Administrative Region of China, 4 July 2001]

Tommy C.P. Sze. & Co. v. Li & Fung (trading) Ltd. & Others, High Court – Court of First Instance, Hong Kong Special Administrative Region of China, 28 October 2002, [2002] HKCFI 682

Tsang Yuk Ching t/a Tsang Ching Kee Eng. Co. v. Fu Shing Rush Door Joint Venture Co. Ltd., High Court – Court of First Instance, Hong Kong Special Administrative Region of China, 5 September 2003, [2003] HKCFI 680

Kenon Engineering Ltd. v. Nippon Kokan Koji Kabushiki Kaisha, High Court – Court of Appeal, Hong Kong Special Administrative Region of China, 7 May 2004, [2004] HKCA 101

Kolinker Industrial Equipment Ltd. v. Longhill Industries Ltd. & Another, District Court, Hong Kong Special Administrative Region of China, 3 June 2004, [2004] HKDC 65

Tai–Ao Aluminium (Taishan) Co. Ltd. v. Maze Aluminium Engineering Co. Ltd. & Another, High Court – Court of First Instance, Hong Kong Special Administrative Region of China, 17 February 2006, [2006] HKCFI 220

Grandeur Electrical Co. Ltd. v. Cheung Kee Fung Cheung Construction Co. Ltd., High Court – Court of Appeal, Hong Kong Special Administrative Region of China, 25 July 2006, [2006] HKCA 305

Pccw Global Ltd. v. Interactive Communications Service Ltd., High Court – Court of Appeal, Hong Kong Special Administrative Region of China, 16 November 2006, [2006] HKCA 434

Newmark Capital Corporation Ltd. and Others v. Coffee Partners Ltd. and Another, High Court – Court of First Instance, Hong Kong Special Administrative Region of China, 8 February 2007, [2007] HKCFI 113

Ho Fat Sing t/a Famous Design Engineering Co. v. Hop Tai Construction Co. Ltd., District Court, Hong Kong Special Administrative Region of China, 23 December 2008, [2008] HKDC 339

Fai Tak Engineering Co. Ltd. v. Sui Chong Construction & Engineering Co. Ltd., District Court, Hong Kong Special Administrative Region of China, 22 June 2009, [2009] HKDC 141

Article 8

CLOUT case No. 671 [*Landale Development Limited v. Zhum Heng Development Limited,* District Court, Hong Kong, 12 January 1990]

CLOUT case No. 44 [*William Company v. Chu Kong Agency Co. Ltd. and Guangzhou Ocean Shipping Company,* High Court – Court of First Instance, Hong Kong, 17 February 1993]

CLOUT case No. 688 [*China National Electronic Import & Export Shenzhen Company v. Choi Chuk Ming (trading as ERWO Enterprises Company),* High Court – Court of First Instance, Hong Kong, 9 March 1993]

CLOUT case No. 57 [*Lucky–Goldstar International (H.K.) Limited v. Ng Moo Kee Engineering Limited,* High Court – Court of First Instance, Hong Kong, 5 May 1993]

CLOUT case No. 78 [*Astel–Peiniger Joint Venture v. Argos Engineering & Heavy Industries Co. Ltd.,* High Court – Court of First Instance, Hong Kong, 18 August 1994]

P.T. Wearwel International v. Vf Asia Ltd., High Court – Court of First Instance, Hong Kong, 19 August 1994, [1994] 3 HKC 344

CLOUT case No. 89 [*York Airconditioning & Refrigeration Inc. v. Lam Kwai Hung Trading as North Sea A/C Elect. Eng. Co.,* High Court – Court of First Instance, Hong Kong, 16 December 1994]

CLOUT case No. 128 [*Tai Hing Cotton Mill Limited v. Glencore Grain Rotterdam B. V. and another,* Court of Appeal, Hong Kong, 24 November 1995]

Nahai West Shipping Co. v. Hong Kong United Dockyards Ltd., High Court – Court of First Instance, Hong Kong, 5 February 1996, [1996] 2 HKC 639

Nassetti Ettore Spa v. Lawton Development Limited, High Court – Court of First Instance, Hong Kong, 19 April 1996, [1996] HKCU 290

CLOUT Case No. 706 [*Fustar Chemicals Ltd. v. Sinochem Liaoning Hong Kong Ltd.,* High Court – Court of First Instance, Hong Kong, 5 June 1996]

CLOUT case No. 710 [*Louis Dreyfus Trading Ltd. v. Bonarich International (Group) Ltd.,* High Court – Court of First Instance, Hong Kong, 24 March 1997]

Orienmet Minerals Co. Ltd. v. Winner Desire Ltd., High Court – Court of First Instance, Hong Kong, 7 April 1997, [1997] HKCFI 299

Westco Airconditioning Ltd. v. Sui Chong Construction & Engineering Co. Ltd., High Court – Court of First Instance, Hong Kong, 3 February 1998, [1998] HKCFI 946

CLOUT case No. 604 [*Glencore International A.G. v. Bright China International Ltd. & Others,* High Court – Court of First Instance, Hong Kong, 24 April 1998]

Arta Properties Limited v. Li Fu Yat Tso et al., High Court – Court of First Instance, Hong Kong, 2 June 1998, [1998] HKCU 721

Hanjin Shipping Co. Ltd. v. Grand King Shipping Ltd., High Court – Court of First Instance, Hong Kong Special Administrative Region of China, 20 November 1998, [1999] HKCFI 403

Shell Hong Kong Ltd. v. Esa Consulting Engineers Ltd. and Another, High Court – Court of First Instance, Hong Kong Special Administrative Region of China, 25 November 1998, [1998] HKCFI 1003

Comtec Components Ltd. v. Interquip Ltd., High Court – Court of First Instance, Hong Kong Special Administrative Region of China, 3 December 1998, [1998] HKCFI 803

Sun Fook Kong (Civil) Ltd. v. Wellead Construction & Engineering Co. Ltd. and another, High Court – Court of First Instance, Hong Kong Special Administrative Region of China, 7 May 1999, [1999] HKCFI 233

Mitsui Oil (Asia) Pte. Ltd. v. Chun Yeung Industrial (HK) Ltd., High Court – Court of First Instance, Hong Kong Special Administrative Region of China, 24 September 1999, [1999] HKCFI 846

Chung Siu Hong Celment and Others v. Primequine Corporation Ltd. And Others, High Court – Court of First Instance, Hong Kong Special Administrative Region of China, 28 September 1999, [1999] HKCFI 1472

P & O Nedlloyd Limited v. Wah Hing Seafreight (China) Co. Ltd., High Court – Court of First Instance, Hong Kong Special Administrative Region of China, 25 November 1999, [1999] HKCU 1412

CLOUT case No. 460 [*Hercules Data Comm Co. Ltd. v. Koywa Communications Ltd.,* High Court – Court of First Instance, Hong Kong Special Administrative Region of China, 23 October 2000]

CLOUT case No. 521 [*F & D Building Services Engineering Co. Ltd. v. Chevalier (E & M Contracting),* High Court – Court of First Instance, Hong Kong Special Administrative Region of China, 23 February 2001]

CLOUT case No. 522 [*Paladin Agricultural Ltd. & Others v. Excelsior Hotel (Hong Kong) Ltd.,* High Court – Court of First Instance, Hong Kong Special Administrative Region of China, 6 March 2001]

Leung Kwok Tim t/a Tim Yip Engineering Co. v. Builders Federal (Hong Kong) Ltd., High Court – Court of First Instance, Hong Kong Special Administrative Region of China, 17 March 2001, [2001] HKCFI 823

CLOUT case No. 449 [*China Merchant Heavy Industry Co. Ltd. v. JGC Corp.,* High Court – Court of Appeal, Hong Kong Special Administrative Region of China, 4 July 2001]

Liu Man Wai and Another v. Chevalier (Hong Kong) Ltd., High Court – Court of First Instance, Hong Kong Special Administrative Region of China, 29 January 2002, [2002] HKCFI 399

Cathay Pacific Airways Ltd. v. Hong Kong Air Cargo Terminals Ltd., High Court – Court of First Instance, Hong Kong Special Administrative Region of China, 7 March 2002, [2002] HKCFI 9

Liu Man Wai and Another v. Chevalier (Hong Kong) Ltd., High Court – Court of Appeal, Hong Kong Special Administrative Region of China, 26 June 2002, [2002] HKCA 280

Getwick Engineers Ltd. v. Pilecon Engineering Ltd., High Court – Court of First Instance, Hong Kong Special Administrative Region of China, 28 August 2002, [2002] HKCFI 189

Dah Chong Hong (Engineering) Ltd. v. Boldwin Construction Co. Ltd., High Court – Court of First Instance, Hong Kong Special Administrative Region of China, 4 October 2002, [2002] HKCU 1180

Tommy C.P. Sze. & Co. v. Li & Fung (trading) Ltd. & Others, High Court – Court of First Instance, Hong Kong Special Administrative Region of China, 28 October 2002, [2002] HKCFI 682

Good Year Professional Service Co. v. Penta–Ocean Construction Co. Ltd., High Court – Court of First Instance, Hong Kong Special Administrative Region of China, 5 November 2002, [2002] HKCFI 786

Pacific Crown Engineering Ltd. v. Hyundai Engineering & Construction Co. Ltd., High Court – Court of First Instance, Hong Kong Special Administrative Region of China, 23 April 2003, [2003] HKCFI 924

Hoo Cheong Building Construction Co. Ltd. V. Jade Union Investment Ltd., High Court – Court of First Instance, Hong Kong Special Administrative Region of China, 5 March 2004, [2004] HKCFI 21

Thorn Security (Hong Kong) Ltd. v. Cheung Kee Fung Cheung Construction Co. Ltd., High Court – Court of Appeal, Hong Kong Special Administrative Region of China, 30 July 2004, [2004] HKCA 217

New Sound Industries Ltd. v. Meliga (HK) Ltd., High Court – Court of Appeal, Hong Kong Special Administrative Region of China, 11 January 2005, [2005] HKCU 66

The Incorporated Owners of Sincere House v. Sincere Co. Ltd., Lands Tribunal, Hong Kong Special Administrative Region of China, 18 May 2005, [2005] HKCU 625

Tai–Ao Aluminium (Taishan) Co. Ltd. v. Maze Aluminium Engineering Co. Ltd. & Another, High Court – Court of First Instance, Hong Kong Special Administrative Region of China, 17 February 2006, [2006] HKCFI 220

Grandeur Electrical Co. Ltd. v. Cheung Kee Fung Cheung Construction Co. Ltd., High Court – Court of Appeal, Hong Kong Special Administrative Region of China, 25 July 2006, [2006] HKCA 305

Pccw Global Ltd. v. Interactive Communications Service Ltd., High Court – Court of Appeal, Hong Kong Special Administrative Region of China, 16 November 2006, [2006] HKCA 434

Newmark Capital Corporation Ltd. and Others v. Coffee Partners Ltd. and Another, High Court – Court of First Instance, Hong Kong Special Administrative Region of China, 8 February 2007, [2007] HKCFI 113

Wong King Chuen and Another v. The Hong Kong Football Association Ltd., High Court – Court of First Instance, Hong Kong Special Administrative Region of China, 15 August 2007, [2007] HKCFI 854

Ocean Park Corporation v. Proud Sky Co. Ltd., High Court – Court of First Instance, Hong Kong Special Administrative Region of China, 28 November 2007, [2007] HKCFI 1221

Re Southern Materials Holding (H.K.) Co. Ltd., High Court – Court of First Instance, Hong Kong Special Administrative Region of China, 13 February 2008, [2008] HKCFI 98

Paquito Lima Buton v. Rainbow Joy Shipping Ltd. Inc., Court of Final Appeal, Hong Kong Special Administrative Region of China, 28 April 2008, [2008] HKCFA 30

Ho Fat Sing t/a Famous Design Engineering Co. v. Hop Tai Construction Co. Ltd., District Court, Hong Kong Special Administrative Region of China, 23 December 2008, [2008] HKDC 339

Fai Tak Engineering Co. Ltd. v. Sui Chong Construction & Engineering Co. Ltd., District Court, Hong Kong Special Administrative Region of China, 22 June 2009, [2009] HKDC 141

Aggressive Construction Company Limited v. Data–Form Engineering Limited, High Court – Court of First Instance, Hong Kong Special Administrative Region of China, 13 October 2009, [2009] HKCU 1533

Rondabosh International Ltd. v. China Ping an Insurance (Hong Kong) Co. Ltd., High Court – Court of First Instance, Hong Kong Special Administrative Region of China, 29 December 2009, [2009] HKCFI 1198

Chok Yick Interior Design & Engineering Co. Ltd. v. Fortune World Enterprises Ltd. and another, High Court – Court of First Instance, Hong Kong Special Administrative Region of China, 29 January 2010, [2010] HKCFI 84

Article 9

CLOUT case No. 39 [*Katran Shipping Co. Ltd. v. Kenven Transportation Ltd.*, High Court – Court of First Instance, Hong Kong, 29 June 1992]

CLOUT case No. 77 [*Vibroflotation A.G. v. Express Builders Co. Ltd.*, High Court – Court of First Instance, Hong Kong, 1994] HKCFI 205, 15 August 1994]

CLOUT case No. 692 [*The Owners of the Ship or vessel "Lady Muriel v. Transorient Shipping Limited"*, Court of Appeal, Hong Kong, 3 May 1995]

Taxfield Shipping Ltd. v. Asiana Marine Inc. and others, High Court – Court of First Instance (Construction and Arbitration Proceedings), Hong Kong Special Administrative Region of China, 7 March 2006, [2006] HKCFI 271

Article 11

CLOUT case No. 20 [*Fung Sang Trading Limited v. Kai Sun Sea Products and Food Company Limited,* High Court – Court of First Instance, Hong Kong, 29 October 1991]

CLOUT case No. 40 [*Pacific International Lines (PTE) Ltd. & Another v. Tsinlien Metals and Minerals Co. Ltd.,* High Court – Court of First Instance, Hong Kong, 30 July 1992]

CLOUT case No. 62 [*Oonc Lines Limited v. Sino-American Trade Advancement Co. Ltd.,* High Court – Court of First Instance, Hong Kong, 2 February 1994]

CLOUT case No. 109 [*Private Company "Triple V" Inc. v. Star (Universal) Co. Ltd. and Sky Jade Enterprises Group Ltd.,* Court of Appeal, Hong Kong, 7 July 1995]

Article 12

Pacific China Holdings Ltd. v. Grand Pacific Holdings Ltd., High Court – Court of First Instance, Hong Kong Special Administrative Region of China, 18 July 2007, [2007] HKCFI 715

Jung Science Information Technology Co. Ltd. v. Zte. Corporation, High Court – Court of First Instance, Hong Kong Special Administrative Region of China, 22 July 2008, [2008] HKCFI 606

Article 13

Pacific China Holdings Ltd. v. Grand Pacific Holdings Ltd., High Court – Court of First Instance, Hong Kong Special Administrative Region of China, 18 July 2007, [2007] HKCFI 715

Article 14

Noble Resources Pte. Ltd. v. China Sea Grains and Oils Industry Co. Ltd., High Court – Court of First Instance, Hong Kong Special Administrative Region of China, 29 March 2006, [2006] HKCFI 334

Article 16

CLOUT case No. 20 [*Fung Sang Trading Limited v. Kai Sun Sea Products and Food Company Limited,* High Court – Court of First Instance, Hong Kong, 29 October 1991]

CLOUT case No. 523 [*Weltime Hong Kong Ltd. & Others v. Ken Forward Engineering Ltd.,* High Court – Court of First Instance, Hong Kong Special Administrative Region of China, 6 March 2001]

Kenon Engineering Ltd. v. Nippon Kokan Koji Kabushiki Kaisha, High Court – Court of First Instance, Hong Kong Special Administrative Region of China, 2 July 2003, [2003] HKCFI 568

The Incorporated Owners of Tak Tai Building v. Leung Yau Building Ltd., High Court – Court of Appeal, Hong Kong Special Administrative Region of China, 9 March 2005, [2005] HKCA 87

Pccw Global Ltd. v. Interactive Communications Service Ltd., High Court – Court of Appeal, Hong Kong Special Administrative Region of China, 16 November 2006, [2006] HKCA 434

Brunswick Bowling & Billiards Corporation v. Shanghai Zhonglu Industrial Co. Ltd. and Another, High Court – Court of First Instance, Hong Kong Special Administrative Region of China, 10 February 2009, [2009] HKCFI 94

Article 17 [as adopted in 1985]

CLOUT case No. 39 [*Katran Shipping Co. Ltd. v. Kenven Transportation Ltd.,* High Court – Court of First Instance, Hong Kong, 29 June 1992]

Article 17 J

Leviathan Shipping Co. v. Sky Sailing Overseas Co., Court of First Instance, Hong Kong Special Administrative Region of China, 18 August 1998, [1998] 4 HKC 347

Prema Birkdale Horticulture (Macau) Limited v. Venetian Orient Limited and Anor, Court of First Instance, Hong Kong, 5 August 2009, Special Administrative Region of China, [2009] HCMP 905/2009

Article 21

CLOUT case No. 20 [*Fung Sang Trading Limited v. Kai Sun Sea Products and Food Company Limited,* High Court – Court of First Instance, Hong Kong, 29 October 1991]

CLOUT Case No. 706 [*Fustar Chemicals Ltd. v. Sinochem Liaoning Hong Kong Ltd.,* High Court – Court of First Instance, Hong Kong, 5 June 1996]

Article 24

Paklito Investment Limited v. Klockner East Asia Limited, High Court – Court of First Instance, Hong Kong, 15 January 1993, [1993] 2 HKLR 39

CLOUT case No. 88 [*Nanjing Cereals, Oils and Food Stuffs Import & Export Corp. v. Luckmate Commodities Trading Ltd.,* High Court – Court of First Instance, Hong Kong, 16 December 1994]

Article 26

Paklito Investment Limited v. Klockner East Asia Limited, High Court – Court of First Instance, Hong Kong, 15 January 1993, [1993] 2 HKLR 39

Article 27

CLOUT case No. 77 [*Vibroflotation A.G. v. Express Builders Co. Ltd.,* High Court – Court of First Instance, Hong Kong, 15 August 1994]

Article 34

CLOUT case No. 76 [*China Nanhai Oil Joint Service Corporation, Shenzhen Branch v. Gee Tai Holdings Co. Ltd.,* High Court – Court of First Instance, Hong Kong, 13 July 1994]

CLOUT case No. 88 [*Nanjing Cereals, Oils and Foodstuffs Import & Export Corporation v. Luckmate Commodities Trading Ltd.,* High Court – Court of First Instance, Hong Kong, 16 December 1994]

Jiangxi Provincial Metal & Mineral Import & Export Corp. v. Sulanser Co. Ltd., High Court, Hong Kong, 6 April 1995, [1995] HKCFI 449

APEX Tech Investment Ltd. v. Chuang's Development (China) Ltd., High Court – Court of First Instance, Hong Kong, 8 September 1995, CACV000231/1995

Hebei Import and Export Corp v. Polytek Engineering Co. Ltd., Court of Final Appeal, Hong Kong Special Administrative Region of China, 9 February 1999 [1999] HKCFA 40

CLOUT case No. 519 [*Wuzhou Port Foreign Trade Development Corp v. New Chemic Ltd.,* High Court – Court of First Instance, Hong Kong Special Administrative Region of China, 8 December 2000]

CLOUT case No. 520 [*Shanghai City Foundation Works Corp. v. Sunlink Ltd.,* High Court – Court of First Instance, Hong Kong Special Administrative Region of China, 2 February 2001]

CLOUT case No. 527 [*Chongqi Machinery Import & Export Co. Ltd. v. Yiu Hoi & Others Trading as Tin Lee Ship Builders & Trading Co.,* High Court – Court of First Instance, Hong Kong Special Administrative Region of China, 11 October 2001]

CLOUT case No. 528 [*Shenzhen City Tong Yin Foreign Trade Corp. Ltd. v. Alps Co. Ltd.,* High Court – Court of First Instance, Hong Kong Special Administrative Region of China, 15 October 2001]

Brunswick Bowling & Billiards Corporation v. Shanghai Zhonglu Industrial Co. Ltd. and ors., High Court – Court of First Instance, Hong Kong Special Administrative Region of China, 10 February 2009

Article 35

CLOUT case No. 76 [*China Nanhai Oil Joint Service Corporation, Shenzhen Branch v. Gee Tai Holdings Co. Ltd.,* High Court – Court of First Instance, Hong Kong, 13 July 1994]

APEX Tech Investment Ltd. v. Chuang's Development (China) Ltd., High Court – Court of First Instance, Hong Kong, 8 September 1995, CACV000231/1995

CLOUT case No. 459 [*Medison Co. Ltd. v. Victor (Far East) Ltd.,* High Court – Court of First Instance, Hong Kong Special Administrative Region of China, 8 April 2000]

Article 36

Paklito Investment Limited v. Klockner East Asia Limited, High Court – Court of First Instance, Hong Kong, 15 January 1993, [1993] 2 HKLR 39

CLOUT case No. 76 [*China Nanhai Oil Joint Service Corporation, Shenzhen Branch v. Gee Tai Holdings Co. Ltd.,* High Court – Court of First Instance, Hong Kong, 13 July 1994]

Jiangxi Provincial Metal & Mineral Import & Export Corp. v. Sulanser Co. Ltd., High Court, Hong Kong, 6 April 1995, [1995] HKCFI 449

CLOUT case No. 520 [*Shanghai City Foundation Works Corp. v. Sunlink Ltd.,* High Court – Court of First Instance, Hong Kong Special Administrative Region of China, 2 February 2001]

CLOUT case No. 530 [*Société Nationale d'Opérations Pétrolièrers de la Côte d'Ivoire Holding v. Keen Lloyd Resources Ltd.,* High Court – Court of First Instance, Hong Kong Special Administrative Region of China, 20 December 2001]

Hungary

Article 34

Supreme Court, Hungary, BH 1999, 128

Supreme Court, Hungary, BH 2003, 127 at 5c

Supreme Court, Hungary, BH 2007, 193

India

Article 1

R.M. Investment and Trading Co. v. Boeing Co, Supreme Court, India, 10 February 1994, [A.I.R. 1994 S.C. 1136]

Bhatia International v. Bulk Trading, Supreme Court, India, [(2002) 4 SCC 105]

Shreejee Traco (I) Pvt. Ltd. v. Paper Line International, Supreme Court, India, [(2003) 9 SCC 79]

Venture Global Engineering v. Satyam Computer Services Ltd., Supreme Court, India, 10 January 2008, [(2008) 4 SCC 190; A.I.R. 2008 SC 1061]

Comed Chemicals Limited v. C N Ramchand, Supreme Court, India, 6 November 2008, [A.I.R. 2009 S.C. 494]

Article 5

Indian Oil Corporation Ltd. v. Atv. Projects India Ltd. & Anor WP (C), Delhi High Court, India, 9 July 2004, 4967/2003

Article 7

CLOUT case No. 177 [*M.M.T.C. Limited v. Sterlite Industries (India) Ltd.,* Supreme Court, India, 18 November 1996]

Jagdish Chander v. Ramesh Chander & Ors, Supreme Court, India, 26 April 2007

Great Offshore Ltd. v. Iranian Offshore Engineering & Construction Company, Supreme Court, India, 25 August 2008

Indowind Energy Ltd. v. Wescare (I) Ltd. & Anr., Supreme Court, India, 27 April 2010

Article 8

Shin–Etsu Chemical Co. Ltd. v. M/S. Aksh Optifibre Ltd. & Anr, Supreme Court, India, 12 August 2005

Article 9

Max India Limited v. General Binding Corporation, Delhi High Court, India, 16 July 2009

Article 10

CLOUT case No. 177 [*M.M.T.C. Limited v. Sterlite Industries (India) Ltd.*, Supreme Court, India, 18 November 1996]

Article 11

M/S S.B.P. & Co. v. M/S Patel Engineering Ltd. & Anr., Supreme Court, India, 26 October 2005, (2005) 8 SCC 618

Ministry Of Railway, New Delhi v. Patel Engineering Company Ltd., Supreme Court, India, 18 August 2008

National Insurance Co. Ltd. v. Boghara Polyfab (P) Ltd., Supreme Court, India, 18 September 2008, (2009) 1 SCC 267

M/S. Everest Holding Ltd. v. Shyam Kumar Shrivastava & Ors., Supreme Court, India, 24 October 2008

Visa International Ltd. v. Continental Resources (Usa) Ltd., Supreme Court, India, 2 December 2008

Union Of India v. M/S. Singh Builders Syndicate, Supreme Court, India, 26 February 2009

Indian Oil Corp. Ltd. & Ors. v. M/S Raja Transport(P) Ltd., Supreme Court, India, 24 August 2009

Denel (Proprietary Limited) v. Bharat Electronics Ltd. & Amp., Supreme Court, India, 10 May 2010

Alva Aluminium *Ltd. Bangkok v. Gabriel India Limited*, Supreme Court, India, 16 November 2010

Article 12

Indian Oil Corp. Ltd. & Ors. v. M/S Raja Transport(P) Ltd., Supreme Court, India, 24 August 2009

Article 14

Mr. Hasmukhlal H. Doshi & Another v. Mr. Justice M.L. Pendse & Others, Bombay High Court, India, 17 April 2000, [2000 (3) BomCR 672, (2000) 2 BOMLR 684, 2000 (3) MhLj 690]

Kifayatullah Haji Gulam Rasool et al. v. Smt. Bilkish Ismail Mehsania et al., Bombay High Court, India, 26 April 2000, [AIR 2000 Bom 424, 2000 (4) BomCR 412, 2000 (4) MhLj 341]

Shri Pinaki Das Gupta v. Publicis (India) Communications, Delhi High Court, India, 7 October 2004, 115 (2004) DLT 345, (2005) 139 PLR 26

Ahluwalia Contracts (India) Ltd. v. Housing And Urban Development, Delhi High Court, India, 30 November 2007

N.B.C.C. Ltd. v. J.G.Engineering Pvt. Ltd., Supreme Court, India, 5 January 2010, [Civil Appeal 8/2010]

Article 15

Yashwith Construction P. Ltd. v. Simplex Concrete Piles India Ltd., Supreme Court, India, 3 July 2006

M/S.S.B.P. & Co. v. M/S. Patel Engineering Ltd. & Anr., Supreme Court, India, 21 October 2009

Article 16

M/S. Anuptech Equipments Private v. M/S. Ganpati Co–Op. Housing, Bombay High Court, India, 30 January 1999, [AIR 1999 Bom 219]

Article 17 [as adopted in 1985]

National Highways Authority of India (Nhai) vs China Coal Construction Group Corpn., Delhi High Court, India, 23 January 2006, [AIR 2006 Delhi 134, 2006 (1) ARBLR 265 Delhi]

Article 17 J

Sri Kirshan v. Anad, Delhi High Court, India, 18 August 2009, [OMP No. 597/2008]

Article 20

Jagson Airlines Ltd. v. Bannari Amman Exports (P) Ltd., Delhi High Court, India, 28 April 2003, [2003(2) Arb LR 315 (Delhi)]

Sulaikha Clay Mines v. Alpha Clays, Kerala High Court, India, 9 August 2004, [AIR 2005 Ker 3, 2005 Arb LR 237 Kerala]

Shin Satellite Public Co. Ltd. v. Jain Studios Ltd., Supreme Court, India, 31 January 2006, [(2006) 2 SCC 628]

National Highway Authority of India v. Sheladia Associates Inc, Delhi High Court, India, 21 August 2009, [2009(3) Arb LR 378 (Delhi)]

Dozco India P. Ltd. v. Doosan Infracore Co. Ltd., Supreme Court, India, 8 October 2010

Article 21

Milkfood Ltd. v. M/s GMC Ice Cream (P) Ltd., Supreme Court, India, 5 April 2004, [2004] INSC 229

Article 24

Atul R. Shah v. M/s. V. Vrijlal Lalloobhai And Co., Bombay High Court, India, 8 September 1998; [AIR 1999 Bom 67, 1998 (4) BomCR 867, 1999 (1) MhLj 629]

Impex Corporation And Ors v. Elenjikal Aquamarine Exports Ltd., Kerala High Court, India, 9 October 2007, [AIR 2008 Ker 199]

Article 25

Indian Oil Corporation Ltd. v. Atv. Projects India Ltd. & Anor WP (C), Delhi High Court, India, 9 July 2004, [4967/2003]

M/s Prime Telesystem Limited v. Sasken Communication Technologies Ltd. & Ors., High Court of Delhi India, 18 December 2009, [OMP 35/2008 [2009] INDLHTC 5430]

Article 26

National Thermal Power Corporation Ltd. v. Wig Brothers Builders and Engineers Ltd., High Court of Delhi, India, 17 April 2009 [OMP 16/2003 [2009] INDLHC 1466]

Article 27

SH. Satinder Narayan Singh v. Indian Labour Cooperative Society Ltd. & Ors., High Court of Delhi India, 17 December 2007, [OMP 471/2007 [2007] INDLHC 1462, 2008 (1) ARBLR 355 Delhi]

Article 30

Nathani Steels Ltd. v. Associated Construction, Supreme Court, India, [1995 Supp (3) SCC 324]

Polytron & Fragrance Industries Limited v. National Insurance Co. Limited, Delhi High Court, India, 27 April 2009, [ARB. P. 144/2008]

Article 31

Gora Lal v. Union Of India, Supreme Court, India, 18 December 2003, [2003] 12 SCC 459

Article 32

N.B.C.C. Ltd. v. JG Engineering Pvt. Ltd., Supreme Court, India, 5 January 2010, [Civil Appeal 8/2010]

Article 34

Oil & Natural Gas Corporation Ltd. v. Saw Pipes Ltd., Supreme Court, India, 17 April 2003, [2003] INSC 236

Union of India v. Tecco Trichy Engineers & Contractors, Supreme Court, India, 16 March 2005, [2005] INSC 180

Shin Satellite Public Co. Ltd. v. Jain Studios Ltd., Supreme Court, India, 31 January 2006, [2006] 2 SCC 628

M/S. Centrotrade Minerals & Metal. Inc. v. Hindustan Copper Ltd., Supreme Court, India, 9 May 2006, [2006] INSC 293

Venture Global Engineering vs. Satyam Computer Services Ltd. & Another, Supreme Court of India, 10 January 2008, [2008] 4 SCC 190

N.B.C.C. Ltd. v. JG Engineering Pvt. Ltd., Supreme Court, India, 5 January 2010, [Civil Appeal 8/2010]

Yograj Infrastructure Ltd. vs. Ssang Yong Engineering and Construction Co. Ltd., Supreme Court, India, 1 September 2011

Phulchand Exports Ltd. v. OOO Patriot, Supreme Court, India, 12 October 2011, [2011] INSC 1038

Sakuma Exports Ltd. v. Louis Dreyfus Commodities Suisse S.A., Bombay High Court, India, 15 November 2011

Article 36

Phulchand Exports Ltd. v. OOO Patriot, Supreme Court India, 12 October 2011, [2011] INSC 1038

Ireland

Article 8

Barnmore Demolition and Civil Engineering Ltd. v. Alandale Logistics Ltd., Pynest Ltd., Dublin Airport Authority Plc and Barry Donohue (as liquidator of Pynest), High Court (Commercial), Ireland, 11 November 2010, [2010] No. 5910P

Article 9

Osmond Ireland On Farm Business v. Mc Farland, High Court, Ireland, 30 June 2010, [2010] IEHC 295

Article 17 J

Osmond Ireland On Farm Business v. Mc Farland, High Court, Ireland, 30 June 2010, [2010] IEHC 295

Article 34

Moohan v. S. & R. Motors [Donegal] Ltd., High Court, Ireland, 31 July 2009, [2009] IEHC 391

Italy

Article 20

Virgilio De Agostini v. Milloil SpA, Corte di Appello, Italy, 24 March 1998

Jordan

Article 11

Supreme Court, Jordan, 10 December 2003, No. 2003/3094

Supreme Court, Jordan, 9 March 2005, No. 2004/3820

Supreme Court, Jordan, 29 June 2006, No. 2005/4449

Supreme Court, Jordan, 21 November 2006, No. 2006/1682

Supreme Court, Jordan, 18 December 2006, No. 2006/2598

Article 34

Supreme Court, Jordan, 7 November 2007, No. 1242/2007

Court of Appeal, Amman, Jordan, 10 June 2008, No. 206/2008

Court of Appeal, Amman, Jordan, 4 March 2009, No. 218/2008

Kenya

Article 8

Seca Africa Ltd. v. Kirloskar Kenya Ltd. & 3 others, High Court, Nairobi, Kenya, 28 January 2005, Civil Suit 307 of 1999

Stephen Okero Oyugi v. Law Society of Kenya & Another, High Court, Nairobi (Nairobi Law Courts), Kenya, 15 April 2005, Civil Suit 482 of 2004

Megdev Construction Limited v. Pioneer General Assurance Society Limited, High Court, Nairobi, Kenya, 14 June 2005, Civil Suit 291 of 2001

Mugoya Construction & Engineering Ltd. v. National Social Security Fund Board of Trustees & another, High Court, Nairobi (Commercial Division Milimani Courts), Kenya, 27 July 2005, Civil Suit 59 of 2005

Mehta Electrical Limited & 4 others v. N. K. Brothers Limited & another, High Court, Nairobi (Milimani Commercial Division), Kenya, 16 August 2005, Civil Suit 37 of 2005

Velji Shamji Constructions Ltd. v. Westmall Supermarket Ltd., High Court, Mombasa, Kenya, 8 September 2005, Civil Suit 254 of 2004

Charles Njogu Lofty v. Bedouin Enterprises Ltd., Court of Appeal, Nairobi, Kenya, 16 September 2005, Civil Appeal 253 of 2003

Don-Woods Company Ltd. v. Kenya Pipeline Company Ltd., High Court, Nairobi, Kenya, 7 October 2005, Civil Suit 1041 of 2004

Virginia E. Wambui O Tieno-Mbugua v. Africa Air Rescue Health Services (K) Ltd., High Court, Nairobi (Nairobi Law Courts), Kenya, 12 September 2006, Civil Case 563 of 2006

M. M. Galgalo & 3 others v. Musikali Kombo & another, High Court, Nairobi (Nairobi Law Courts), Kenya, 29 September 2006, Civil Case 382 of 2006

Livingstone Kamadi Obuga v. Uhuru Kenyatta & 3 others, High Court, Nairobi (Nairobi Law Courts), Kenya, 18 December 2006, Civil Suit 1159 of 2006

Very Rev. Peter Karanja & another v. Alice Wahito Ndegwa, High Court, Nairobi (Nairobi Law Courts), Kenya, 8 March 2007, Civil Case 908 of 2006

Alfred Wekesa Sambu & 4 others v. Mohammed Hatimy & 12 others, High Court, Nairobi, Kenya, 16 May 2007, Civil Suit 1281 of 2006

Pamela Akora Imenje v. Akora ITC International Ltd. & another, High Court, Nairobi (Milimani Commercial Courts), Kenya, 17 August 2007, Civil Case 368 of 2005

Governors Balloon Sararis Ltd. v. Skyship Company Ltd. County Council of Trans, High Court, Nairobi (Milimani Commercial Courts), Kenya, 11 September 2008, Civil Case 461 of 2008

Article 9

Communications Carrier Ltd. & Another v. Telkom Kenya Limited, High Court, Nairobi (Milimani Commercial Courts), Kenya, 14 November 2005, Civil Case 249 of 2007

Santack Enterprises Limited v. Kenya Building Society Limited, High Court, Nairobi (Nairobi Law Courts), Kenya, 5 March 2008, Civil Suit 298 of 2007

Wellness Health & Fitness Centre Ltd. v. Shamsher Kenya Ltd., High Court, Nairobi (Milimani Commercial Courts), Kenya, 8 April 2008, Civil Suit 30 of 2008

Blue Limited v. Jaribu Credit Traders Limited, High Court, Nairobi (Milimani Commercial Courts), Kenya, 25 September 2008, Civil Suit 157 of 2008

Article 11

M-Link Communications Company Ltd. v. Communication Commission of Kenya & another, High Court, Nairobi (Milimani Commercial Courts), Kenya, 23 November 2005, Civil Suit 2071 of 2000

William Oluande v. American Life Insurance Company (K) Limited, High Court, Nairobi (Nairobi Law Courts), Kenya, 10 February 2006, Miscellaneous Application 721 of 2004

Pan African Builders & Contractors Ltd. v. National Social Security Fund Board of Trustees, High Court, Nairobi (Milimani Commercial Courts), Kenya, 27 March 2006, Civil Case 701 of 2005

Henry Muriithi Mvungu & another v. Bruno Rosiello, High Court, Nairobi (Milimani Commercial Courts), Kenya, 18 July 2006, Miscellaneous Civil Application 264 of 2006

Article 16

Sebhan Enterprises Limited v. Westmont Power (Kenya) Limited, High Court, Nairobi (Milimani Commercial Courts), Kenya, 13 March 2006, Civil Case 239 of 2005

Blue Limited v. Jaribu Credit Traders Limited, High Court, Nairobi (Milimani Commercial Courts), Kenya, 25 September 2008, Civil Suit 157 of 2008

Assumption Sisters of Nairobi Registered Trustee v. Standard Kebathi & another, High Court , Nairobi (Nairobi Law Courts), Kenya, 21 November 2008, Civil Case 497 of 2004

Article 34

Christ for all Nations v. Apollo Insurance Co. Ltd., High Court, Kenya, Civil Case 477 of 1999, [1999] L.L.R. 1635

Siginon Maritime Ltd. v. Gitutho Associates and Others, High Court, Mombasa, Kenya, 28 July 2005, Miscellaneous Civil Application 719 of 2004

Mahican Investment Ltd. & 3 others v. Giovanni Gaida & 80 others, High Court, Nairobi, Kenya, 11 October 2005, Miscellaneous Civil Application 792 of 2004

Apa Insurance Co. Ltd. v. Chrysanthus Barnabas Okemo, High Court, Nairobi, Kenya, 24 November 2005, Miscellaneous Application 241 of 2005

Structural Construction Co. Ltd. v. International Islamic Relief, High Court, Nairobi, Kenya, 6 October 2006, Miscellaneous Case 596 of 2005

Kenya Shell Ltd. v. Kobil Petroleum Ltd., Court of Appeal, Nairobi, Kenya, 10 November 2006, Civil Application 57 of 2006

Baseline Architects Ltd. and others v. National Hospital Insurance Fund Board Management, High Court, Nairobi, Kenya, 7 May 2008, Miscellaneous Application 1131 of 2007

Article 35

Apa Insurance Co. Ltd. v. Chrysanthus Barnabas Okemo, High Court, Nairobi, Kenya, 24 November 2005, Miscellaneous Application 241 of 2005

Article 36

Structural Construction Co. Ltd. v. International Islamic Relief, High Court, Nairobi, Kenya, 6 October 2006, Miscellaneous Case 596 of 2005

Malaysia

Article 5

Sunway Damansara Sdn Bhd v. Malaysia National Insurance Bhd & Anor, Court of Appeal, Malaysia, [2008] 3 MLJ 872

Sundra Rajoo v. Mohamed Abd Majed, High Court, Malaysia, 23 March 2011, [D24–NCC(ARB) 13-2010]

Mexico

Article 8

Constructora Aboumrad Amodio Berho, S.A. de C.V. v. Cinemex Universidad, S.A. de C.V., Tercer Tribunal Colegiado en Materia Civil, Primer Circuito, Mexico, 8 March 2001, D.C. 1303/2001

Desarrollos Empresariales S.A. de C.V. et al. V. Grupo Radio Centro S.A. de C.V., Décimo Segundo Tribunal Colegiado en Materia Civil, Primer Circuito, Mexico, 1 July 2004, R.C. 222/2004

Servicios Administrativos de Emergencia S.A. de C.V. v. A.D.T. Security Services S.A. de C.V., Tercer Tribunal Colegiado en Materia Civil, Primer Circuito, Mexico, 19 May 2005, R.C. 14/2005

Suprema Corte de Justicia de la Nación (Primera Sala), Mexico, 11 January 2006

Article 16

Pemex Exploración v. Corporación Mexicana de Mantenimiento Integral S.A. de C.V., Juzgado Noveno de Distrito en Materia Civil en el Distrito Federal, (Ninth District Court in Civil Matters, Federal District) Mexico, 23 August 2007, Amparo 584/2007-IV

Article 34

Federal District Court, Mexico, 12 June 2001

Netherlands

Article 31

Bursa Büyüksehir Belediyesi v. Güris Insaat VE Mühendislik AS, Hoge Raad, Netherlands, 5 December 2008, C07/166HR

AZ NV. v. N.N. (Nomen Nescio), Hoge Raad, Netherlands, 8 January 2010, BK 6056, 08/02129

New Zealand

Article 2

Pathak v. Tourism Transport Ltd., High Court, Auckland, New Zealand, 20 August 2002, [2002] 3 NZLR 681

Methanex Motunui Ltd. v. Spellman, Court of Appeal, Wellington, New Zealand, 17 June 2004, [2004] 3 NZLR 454

Article 8

The Property People Ltd. v. Housing NZ Ltd., High Court, Auckland, New Zealand, 7 December 1999, [1999] 14 PRNZ 66

Article 9

Pathak v. Tourism Transport Ltd., High Court, Auckland, New Zealand, 20 August 2002, [2002] 3 NZLR 681

Article 17 [as adopted in 2006]

R&M Wright Ltd. v. Ellerslie Gateway Models Ltd., High Court, New Zealand, 11 July 1990, HC AK CP188/90

Safe Kids in Daily Supervision Limited v. McNeill, High Court, Auckland, New Zealand, 14 April 2010, [2010] NZHC 605

Article 17 A

Safe Kids in Daily Supervision Limited v. McNeill, High Court, Auckland, New Zealand, 14 April 2010, [2010] NZHC 605

Article 17 J

Sensation Yachts Ltd. v. Darby Maritime Ltd., High Court, Auckland, New Zealand, 16 May 2005

Article 18

CLOUT case No. 658 [*Trustees of Rotoaira Forest Trust v. Attorney–General,* High Court, Auckland, New Zealand, 30 November 1998]

Acorn Farms Ltd. v. Schnuriger, High Court, Hamilton, New Zealand, 20 February and 22 May 2003, [2003] 3 NZLR 121

A's Co. Ltd. v. Dagger, High Court, Auckland, New Zealand, 5 June 2003, M1482-SD00

Attorney-General v. Tozer (No 3), High Court, Auckland, New Zealand, 2 September 2003, M1528-IM02 CP607/97

Methanex Motunui Ltd. v. Spellman, Court of Appeal, Wellington, New Zealand, 17 June 2004, [2004] 3 NZLR 454

Coromandel Land Trust Ltd. v. Milkt Investment Ltd., High Court, Hamilton, New Zealand, 28 May 2009, CIV. 2009-419-232

Article 24

Redcliff Estates Ltd. v. Enberg, High Court, Christchurch, New Zealand, 22 July 1999 [HC Christchurch, M150/99]

Methanex Motunui Ltd. v. Spellman, High Court, Auckland, New Zealand, 18 August 2003, [2004] 1 NZLR 99, appealed in *Methanex Motunui Ltd. v. Spellman,* Court of Appeal, Wellington, New Zealand, 17 June 2004, [2004] 3 NZLR 454

Alexander Property Developments v. Clarke, High Court, New Plymouth, New Zealand, 10 June 2004, CIV. 2004-443-89

Article 34

CLOUT case No. 658 [*Trustees of Rotoaira Forest Trust v. Attorney-General,* High Court, Auckland, New Zealand, 30 November 1998]

Attorney General v. Lyall Tozer, High Court, New Zealand, 2 September 2003, M1528-IM02 CP607/97

Methanex Motunui Ltd. v. Spellman, Court of Appeal, Wellington, New Zealand, 17 June 2004, [2004] 3 NZLR 454

Nigeria

Article 11

Bendex Eng. v. Efficient Pet. (Nig.), Court of Appeal – Enugu Division, Nigeria, 13 December 2000, [2001] 8 NWLR (Part 715) 333

Ogunwale v. Syrian Arab Republic, Court of Appeal – Lagos Division, Nigeria, 6 December 2001, [2002] 9 NWLR (Part 771) 127

Article 34

Clement C. Ebokan v. Ekwenibe & Sons Trading Company, Court of Appeal – Lagos Division, Nigeria, 22 January 2001, [2001] 2 NWLR 32

Article 35

Clement C. Ebokan v. Ekwenibe & Sons Trading Company, Court of Appeal – Lagos Division, Nigeria, 22 January 2001, [2001] 2 NWLR 32

Ras Pal Gazi Construction Company Ltd. v. Federal Capital Development Authority, Supreme Court, Nigeria, SC 45/96, 18 May 2001, [2001] 10 NWLR 559

Oman

Article 34

First Instance Court, Oman, 19 October 1998, case No. 2/98

Russian Federation

Article 4

CLOUT case No. 637 [Presidium of the Supreme Court, Russian Federation, 24 November 1999]

Article 16

CLOUT case No. 148 [Moscow City Court, Russian Federation, 10 February 1995]

Article 34

CLOUT case No. 146 [Moscow City Court, Russian Federation, 10 November 1994]

CLOUT case No. 148 [Moscow City Court, Russian Federation, 10 February 1995]

CLOUT case No. 149 [Moscow City Court, Russian Federation, 18 September 1995]

Serbia

Article 36

High Commercial Court, Serbia, 29 December 2008, 807/2008(3)

Appellate Commercial Court, Serbia, 25 March 2010, 175/2010(1)

Singapore

Article 1

Re Sanpete Builders (S) Pte. Ltd., High Court, Singapore, [1989] SLR 164

CLOUT case No. 208 [*Vanol Far East Marketing Pte. Ltd. v. Hin Leong Trading Pte. Ltd.,* High Court, Singapore, 27 May 1996]

Mitsui Engineering and Shipbuilding Co. Ltd. v. PSA Corp., Keppel Engineering Pte. Ltd., High Court, Singapore, [2003] 1 SLR 446

Metalform Asia Pte. Ltd. v. Holland Leedon Pte. Ltd., Court of Appeal, Singapore, [2007] 2 SLR 268

Article 2

Black & Veatch Singapore Pte. Ltd. v. Jurong Engineering Ltd., Court of Appeal, Singapore, [2004] 4 SLR(R) 19

Evergreat Construction Co. Pte. Ltd. v. Presscrete Engineering Pte. Ltd., Court of Appeal, Singapore, [2006] 1 SLR 634.

Metalform Asia Pte. Ltd. v. Holland Leedon Pte. Ltd., Court of Appeal, Singapore, [2007] 2 SLR 268

Insigma Technology Co. Ltd. v. Alstom Technology Ltd., Singapore Court of Appeal, Singapore, 2 June 2009, [2009] SGCA 24, [2009] 3 SLR(R) 936

Navigator Investment Services Ltd. v. Acclaim Insurance Brokers Pte. Ltd., Court of Appeal, Singapore, [2010] 1 SLR 25

Car & Cars Pte. Ltd. v. Volkswagen AG, High Court, Singapore, [2010] 1 SLR 625

Article 5

Mitsui Engineering & Shipbuilding Co. Ltd. v. Easton Graham Rush and another, Supreme Court, Singapore, 16 February 2004, [2004] SGHC 26, [2004] 2 SLR(R) 14

NCC International AB v. Alliance Concrete Singapore Pte. Ltd., Court of Appeal, Singapore, 26 February 2008, [2008] SGCA 5, [2008] 2 SLR(R) 565

ALC v. ALF, High Court, Singapore, [2010] SGHC 231

Article 7

Concordia Agritrading Pte. Ltd. v. Cornelder Hoogewerff, High Court, Singapore, 13 October 1999, [1999] SGHC 269, [1999] 3 SLR(R) 618

WSG Nimbus Pte. Ltd. v. Board of Control for Cricket in Sri Lanka, High Court, Singapore, 13 May 2002, [2002] SGHC 104

P. T. Tri-M.G. Intra Asia Airlines v. Norse Air Charter Limited, High Court, Singapore, 12 January 2009, [2009] SGHC 13

Article 9

WSG Nimbus Pte. Ltd. v. Board of Control for Cricket in Sri Lanka, High Court, Singapore, 13 May 2002, [2002] SGHC 104

Econ Corp. International Ltd. v. Ballast-Nedam International B.V., High Court, Singapore, 10 December 2002, [2002] SGHC 293, [2003] 2 SLR(R) 15

Front Carriers Ltd. v. Atlantic & Orient Shipping Corp., High Court, Singapore, 19 July 2006, [2006] SGHC 127, [2006] 3 SLR(R) 854

CLOUT case No. 741 [Swift-Fortune Ltd. v. Magnifica Marine SA, Court of Appeal, Singapore, 1 December 2006]

NCC International AB v. Alliance Concrete Singapore Pte. Ltd., Court of Appeal, Singapore, 26 February 2008, [2008] SGCA 5, [2008] 2 SLR(R) 565

Article 14

Tay Eng Chuan v. United Overseas Insurance Ltd., High Court, Singapore, [2009] SGHC 193, [2009] 4 SLR(R)

Ting Kang Chung John v. Teo Hee Lai Building Constructions Pte. Ltd. and Ors., High Court, Singapore, [2010] SGHC 20

Article 16

Tan Poh Leng Stanley v. Tang Boon Jek Jeffrey, High Court, Singapore, 30 November 2000, [2000] SGHC 260, [2000] 3 SLR(R) 847

CLOUT case No. 567 [*PT Tugu Pratama Indonesia v. Magma Nusantara Ltd.,* High Court, Singapore, 10 September 2003]

CLOUT case No. 742 [*PT Asuransi Jasa Indonesia (Persero) v. Dexia Bank S.A.,* Court of Appeal, Singapore, 1 December 2006]

Insigma Technology Co. Ltd. v. Alstom Technology Ltd., Court of Appeal, Singapore, 2 June 2009, [2009] SGCA 24, [2009] 3 SLR(R) 936

Article 17 [as adopted in 1985]

Swift–Fortune Ltd. v. Magnifica Marine SA, High Court, Singapore, [2006] 2 SLR 323; affirmed in CLOUT case No. 741 [*Swift-Fortune Ltd. v. Magnifica Marine SA,* Court of Appeal, Singapore, 1 December 2006]

Article 17 J

CLOUT case No. 741 [*Swift–Fortune Ltd. v. Magnifica Marine SA,* Court of Appeal, Singapore, 1 December 2006]

Article 18

CLOUT case No. 743 [*Soh Beng Tee & Co. Pte. Ltd. v. Fairmount Development Pte. Ltd.*, Court of Appeal, Singapore, 9 May 2007]

Front Row Investment Holdings (Singapore) Pte. Ltd. v. Daimler South East Asia Pte. Ltd., High Court, Singapore, 15 March 2010, [2010] SGHC 80

Article 19

John Holland Pty. Ltd. v. Toyo Engineering Corp. (Japan), High Court, Singapore, 14 March 2001, [2001] SGHC 48

Dongwoo Mann+Hummel Co. Ltd. v. Mann+Hummel GmbH, High Court, Singapore, 8 May 2008, [2008] 3 SLR 871

Article 20

PT Garuda Indonesia v. Birgen Air, Court of Appeal, Singapore, 6 March 2002, [2002 1 SLR 393]

Article 23

Ng Chin Siau and Others v. How Kim Chuan, High Court, Singapore, [2007] 2 SLR 789; [2007] SGHC 31

Article 24

Government of the Republic of the Philippines v. Philippine International Air Terminals Co, Inc., High Court, Singapore, 17 November 2006, [2007] 1 SLR (R) 278; [2006] SGHC 206

CLOUT case No. 742 [*PT Asuransi Jasa Indonesia (Persero) v. Dexia Bank S.A.*, Court of Appeal, Singapore, 1 December 2006]

Article 26

Luzon Hydro Corp. v. Transfield Philippines Inc., High Court, Singapore, 13 September 2004, [2004] SGHC 204

Article 27

Woh Hup Pte. Ltd. v. Lian Teck Construction Pte. Ltd., Court of Appeal, Singapore, 10 May 2005, [2005] SGCA 26

CLOUT case No. 743 [*Soh Beng Tee & Co. Pte. Ltd. v. Fairmount Development Pte. Ltd.*, Court of Appeal, Singapore, 9 May 2007]

ALC v. ALF, High Court, Singapore, [2010] SGHC 231

Article 30

Kiyue Co. Ltd. v. Aquagen International Pte. Ltd., High Court, Singapore, [2003] 3 SLR 130

Doshion Ltd. v. Sembawang Engineers and Constructors Pte. Ltd., High Court, Singapore [2011] SGHC 46

Article 32

Tang Boon Jek Jeffrey v. Tan Poh Leng Stanley, Court of Appeal, Singapore, 22 June 2001, [2001] 3 SLR 237

Article 34

CLOUT case No. 208 [*Vanol Far East Marketing Pte. Ltd. v. Hin Leong Trading Pte. Ltd.*, High Court, Singapore, 27 May 1996*]*

Tan Poh Leng Stanley v. Tang Boon Jek Jeffrey, High Court, Singapore, 30 November 2000, [2001] 1 SLR 624; Tang Boon Jek Jeffrey v. Tan Poh Leng Stanley, Court of Appeal, Singapore, 22 June 2001, [2001] 3 SLR 237

PT Garuda Indonesia v. Birgen Air, Court of Appeal, Singapore, 6 March 2002, [2002] 1 SLR 393

CLOUT case No. 566 [*ABC Co. v. XYZ Ltd.,* High Court, Singapore, 8 May 2003]

Newspeed International Ltd. v. Citus Trading Pte. Ltd., High Court, Singapore, [2003] 3 SLR(R) 1

Luzon Hydro Corp. v. Transfield Philippines Inc., High Court, Singapore, 13 September 2004 [2004] SGHC 204

CLOUT case No. 740 [*Aloe Vera of America, Inc. v. Asianic Food (S) Pte. Ltd. and another,* High Court, Singapore, 10 May 2006]

Government of the Republic of the Philippines v. Philippine International Air Terminals Co. Inc., High Court, Singapore, 17 November 2006, [2007] 1 SLR (R) 278; [2006] SGHC 206

CLOUT case No. 742 [*PT AsuransiJasa Indonesia (Persero) v. Dexia Bank S.A.,* Court of Appeal, Singapore, 1 December 2006]

CLOUT case No. 743 [*Soh Beng Tee & Co. Pte. Ltd. v. Fairmont Development Pte. Ltd,* Singapore Court of Appeal, 9 May 2007]

VV. and Another v. VW, High Court, Singapore, 24 January 2008, OS 2160/2006, [2008] SGHC 11

PT Perusahaan Gas Negara (Persero) TBK v. CRW Joint Operation, High Court, Singapore, 20 July 2010, [2010] SGHC 202, affirmed in *CRW Joint Operation v. PT Perusahaan Gas Negara (Persero) TBK,* Court of Appeal, Singapore, 13 July 2011, [2011] SGCA 3

AJT v. AJU, Court of Appeal, Singapore, 22 August 2011, [2011] SGCA 41

Article 35

CLOUT case No. 740 *[Aloe Vera of America, Inc. v. Asianic Food (S) Pte. Ltd. and another,* High Court, Singapore, 10 May 2006]

International Coal Pte. Ltd. v. Kristle Trading Ltd, High Court, Singapore [2008] SGHC 182

Denmark Skibstekniske Konsulenter A/S I Likvidation (formerly known as Knud E Hansen A/S) v. Ultrapolis 3000 Investments Ltd. (formerly known as Ultrapolis 3000 Theme Park Investments Ltd), High Court, Singapore, 9 April 2010, [2010] SGHC 108

Article 36

CLOUT case No. 740 [*Aloe Vera of America, Inc. v. Asianic Food (S) Pte. Ltd. and another,* High Court, Singapore, 10 May 2006]

Government of the Republic of the Philippines v. Philippine International Air Terminals Co. Inc., High Court, Singapore, 17 November 2006, [2007] 1 SLR (R) 278; [2006] SGHC 206

South Africa

Article 25

Rebah Construction CC v. Renkie Building Construction CC, High Court, South Africa, 11 February 2008, 42794/2007 [2008] ZAGPHC 34

Spain

Article 3

CLOUT case No. 971 [Constitutional Court, Spain, Case No. 2771/2005, 5 July 2005]

CLOUT case No. 969 [Madrid Provincial High Court, Spain, Section 21, Case No. 208/2006, 18 April 2006]

CLOUT case No. 967 [Madrid Provincial High Court, Spain, Section 19, Case No. 225/2006, 12 September 2006]

Article 7

Pueblo Film Distribution Hungary K.F.T. (Hungary) v. Laurenfilm S.A., Tribunal Supremo, Spain, 31 May 2005, rec. 743/2003

D. Andrés v. Díez Carrillo S.L., Audiencia Provincial de Palma de Mallorca (sección 5ª), Spain, 5 October 2006, rec. apel. 399/2006

Article 8

Clínica Columbia S.A. v. RMN San Antonio S.L., Juzgado de Primera Instancia, Bilbao, Spain, 2 November 2005

D. Andrés v. Díez Carrillo S.L., Audiencia Provincial de Palma de Mallorca (sección 5ª), Spain, 5 October 2006, rec. apel. 399/2006

Article 11

Sogecable S.A. v. Auna Telecomunicaciones S.A., Audiencia Provincial de Madrid (sección 14ª), Spain, 29 July 2005, res. 585/2005

Ms. Cristina-Victoria Utrilla Utrilla (Spain) v. Explotaciones Mineras Justiniano Muñoz S.L., Juzgado de lo Mercantil número 1 de Madrid, Spain, 5 July 2006

A. A.H. Turistica Pensinsular S.L. v. DIRECCIONooo C.B., Audiencia Provincial de Zaragoza (sección 2ª), Spain, 6 February 2007, res. 52/07

Article 16

ERG Petroleos v. Realesser, Audiencia Provincial de Madrid (sección 8ª), Spain, 13 July 2009, res. 289/2009

Article 18

CLOUT case No. 968 [A Coruña Provincial High Court, Spain, Section 6, Case No. 241/2006, 27 June 2006]

Article 25

CLOUT case No. 968 [A Coruña Provincial High Court, Spain, Section 6, Case No. 241/2006, 27 June 2006]

Article 34

Supreme Court, Spain, 6 April 2004, case No. 301/2007 – 2771/2005

Sofía v. Tintorería Paris, Madrid Court of Appeal, Spain, 20 January 2006, case No. 19/2006

Uniprex S.A. v. Grupo Radio Blanca, Madrid Court of Appeal, Spain, 22 March 2006, case No. 178/2006 – 4/2004

La Coruña Court of Appeal, Spain, 28 April 2006, case No. 133/2006 – 1/2006

Madrid Court of Appeal, Spain, 16 October 2006, case No. 470/2006 – 9/2004

Jaral Decoración, S.L v. Peñasco Rodilla, SL, Madrid Court of Appeal, Spain, 2 February 2007, case No. 94/2007 – 7/2005

Logroño Court of Appeal, Spain, 7 February 2007, case No. 26/2007

Madrid Court of Appeal, Spain, 30 April 2007, case No. 240/2007 – 6/2006

FINDESCO S.L.U v. Ms. Letitia et al., Barcelona Court of Appeal, Spain, 18 January 2008, case No. 13/2008 – 261/2007

Egson Construcciones S.A. (Ecosa) v. Canteras y Construcciones S.A, Madrid Court of Appeal, Spain, 25 January 2008

Urbaser v. Babcock, Madrid Court of Appeal, Spain, 27 October 2008, case No. 542/2008 – 2/2008

Murcia Court of Appeal, Spain, 8 October 2009, case No. 448/2009 – 161/2008.

Article 35

Madrid Court of Appeal, Spain, 4 March 2005, case No. 86/2005 – 52/2005

Valencia Court of Appeal, Spain, 11 October 2005, case No. 603/05

Article 36

Madrid Court of Appeal, Spain, 4 March 2005, case No. 86/2005 – 52/2005

Pavan S.R.L. v. Leng D'Or, Court of First Instance, Spain, S.A., 11 June 2007

Madrid Court of Appeal, Spain, 13 February 2008, case No. 73/2008

Switzerland

Article 18

Federal Supreme Court, Switzerland, 9 February 2009, Decision 4A_400/2008

Article 28

Federal Supreme Court, Switzerland, 16 December 2009, Decision 4A_240/2009

Thailand

Article 36

Supreme Court, Thailand, case No. 7277/2549

Tunisia

Article 31

Court of Cassation, Tunisia, 27 November 2008, case No. 20596/2007

Article 32

Court of Appeal, Tunisia, 3 December 2002, case No. 134

Article 33

Court of Cassation, Tunisia, 27 November 2008, case No. 20596/2007

Article 34

Court of Appeal, Tunisia, 8 May 2001, case No. 83

Court of Appeal, Tunisia, 3 December 2002, case No. 134

Court of Cassation, Tunisia, 18 January 2007, case No. 4674

Court of Cassation, Tunisia, 27 November 2008, case No. 20596/2007

Uganda

Article 8

East African Development Bank v. Ziwa Horticultural Exporters Limited, High Court at Kampala, Uganda, 20 October 2000, [2000] UGCommC 8

Fulgensius Mungereza v. Africa Central, Supreme Court at Mengo, Uganda, 16 January 2004, [2004] UGSC 9

Eastern and Southern African Trade & Anor. v. Hassan Basajjabalaba & Anor., High Court at Kampala, Uganda, 13 April 2007, [2007] UGCommC 30

Article 9

Roko Construction Ltd. v. Aya Bakery (U) Ltd., High Court at Kampala (Civil Division), Uganda, 3 October 2007, [2007] UGHC 31

Pan Afric Impex (U) Ltd. v. Bank PLC and Another, High Court at Kampala (Commercial Court Division), Uganda, 13 February 2008, [2008] UGCommC 18

Article 11

CLOUT case No. 900 [Centre for Arbitration and Dispute Resolution, Uganda, 15 July 2004], cause No. 10/04

CLOUT case No. 899 [Centre for Arbitration and Dispute Resolution, Uganda, 26 November 2004], cause No. 09/04

CLOUT case No. 897 [Centre for Arbitration and Dispute Resolution, Uganda, 30 September 2005], cause No. 03/05

CLOUT case No. 896 [Centre for Arbitration and Dispute Resolution, Uganda, 30 January 2006], cause No. 07/05

CLOUT case No. 895 [Centre for Arbitration and Dispute Resolution, Uganda, 17 March 2006], cause No. 01/06

Uganda Post Ltd. v. R.4 International Ltd., Centre for Arbitration and Dispute Resolution, Uganda, 1 September 2009, [2009] UGCADER 5

Article 12

CLOUT case No. 900 [Centre for Arbitration and Dispute Resolution, Uganda, 15 July 2004], cause No. 10/04

Article 14

Roko Construction Ltd. v. Aya Bakery (U) Ltd., Center for Arbitration and Dispute Resolution, Uganda, 22 August 2008, [2008] UGCADER 1

Article 34

R.R.P (U) Ltd. v. ASSIST (U) Ltd., Kampala High Court, Commercial Division, Uganda, Misc. Arbitration Cause No. 04 of 2002, 26 September 2002

Simbymanyo Estates Ltd. v. Seyani Brothers Company (U) Ltd., High Court of Kampala, Commercial Division, Uganda, 23 August 2004, Misc. Application No. 555/2002

Kilimbe Mines Ltd. v. B.M. Steel Ltd., Kampala High Court, Commercial Division, Uganda, 14 July 2005

SDV. Transami Ltd. v. Agrimag Limited et al., Kampala High Court, Commercial Division, Uganda, 19 June 2008

Chevron Kenya Ltd. & Chevron Uganda Ltd. v. Daqare Transporters Ltd., Kampala High Court, Commercial Division, Uganda, 3 March 2009, Misc. Application No. 490/2008

United Kingdom

Article 18

OAO Northern Shipping Company v. Remolcadores de Marin SL, Court of Appeal, Commercial Court, England, 27 July 2007, [2007] 2 Lloyd's Rep 302, [2007] EWHC 1821 (Comm)

Article 20

Dubai Islamic Bank PJSC v. Paymentech, High Court, England, 24 November 2000, [2001] 1 LLR 65

Shashoua v. Sharma, High Court, England, 7 May 2009, [2009] EWHC 957 (Comm)

Article 21

Blackpool Borough Council v. F Parkinson Ltd., Queen's Bench Division Official Referees' Business, England, 22 October 1991, 58 BLR 85

Article 27

BNP Paribas and others v. Deloitte and Touche LLP, Commercial Court, England, 28 November 2003, [2003] EWHC 2874 (Comm)

United States of America

Article 1

McDowell Valley Vineyards, Inc. v. Sabaté USA Inc., District Court, California, United States of America, 2 November 2005, [2005] WL 2893848 (N.D. Cal. 2005)

Article 8

Marconi Communications Inc. v. Vidar-SMS Co. Ltd., United States District Court, Northern District of Texas, United States of America, 22 August 2001, Civil No. CV-1293-L (2001)

Article 12

HSMV. Corp. v. ADI Ltd., Central District Court for California, United States of America, 8 November 1999, 72 F. Supp. 2d 1122 (C.D. Cal. 1999)

Zimbabwe

Article 33

CLOUT case No. 267 [*Zimbabwe Electricity Supply Commission v. Genius Joel Maposa,* Harare High Court, Zimbabwe, 29 March and 9 December 1998]

Article 34

CLOUT case No. 323 [*Zimbabwe Electricity Supply Authority v. Genius Joel Maposa,* Supreme Court, Zimbabwe, 21 October and 21 December 1999]

Article 36

CLOUT case No. 233 [*Durco (Pvt.) Ltd. v. Dajen (Pvt.) Ltd.,* Harare High Court, Zimbabwe, 10 July and 20 August 1997]; confirmed by CLOUT case No. 234 [*Dajen (Pvt) Ltd. v. Durco (Pvt.) Ltd.,* Supreme Court of Zimbabwe, 22 June and 7 September 1998]

CLOUT case No. 342 [Harare High Court, Zimbabwe, *Conforce (Pvt.) Limited v. The City of Harare,* 1 March and 5 April 2000]